Real World
Photoshop 3

Real World Photoshop 3
Industrial Strength Production Techniques

David Blatner
Bruce Fraser

Edited by Stephen F. Roth

Peachpit Press

Open House

David

For Fay, Harry, Ann, Abe, Katie, and Rita,
who laid the foundation in my family.

Bruce

For Ella Thompson, my grandmother,
who taught me the value of hard work.

Real World Photoshop 3

David Blatner and Bruce Fraser

Copyright ©1996 by David Blatner and Bruce Fraser

Peachpit Press
2414 Sixth Street
Berkeley, CA 94710
510/548-4393
Fax: 510/548-5991

Find us on the World Wide Web at: http://www.peachpit.com
Peachpit Press is a division of Addison-Wesley Publishing Company

Interior design and production by Stephen F. Roth/Open House
Cover illustration by Robert Dietz
Image credits and permissions, page 558

ISBN 1–56609–169–1

9 8 7 6 5 4 3 2 1

Printed on recycled paper

Printed and bound in the United States of America

Overview

The Big Picture

Contents

What's Inside

Preface

Photoshop in the Real World

If you're reading this book because you want to produce embossed type, fractalized tree branches, or spherized images in Photoshop, you're in the wrong place. If you're after tips and tricks on how to get the coolest special effects in your images, look elsewhere. There are (at least) half a dozen good books on those subjects.

But if you're looking to move images through Photoshop—getting good scans in, working your will on them, and putting out world-class, camera-ready film—this is the book for you. Its *raison d'être* is to answer the questions that people in production environments ask every single day (and not without some frustration).

▶ What settings should I use in the Separation Setup dialog box?

▶ How do I bring out shadow details in my images without blowing away the highlights?

▶ What methods are available to neutralize color casts?

▶ How do I calibrate my monitor? (And should I?)

▶ What problems will I run into with the Dust and Scratches filter? Are there better alternatives?

▶ What screen angles should I use for duotones?

> ▶ How do I put a drop shadow on top of a process-color tint in Quark-XPress or PageMaker?

> ▶ What's the best way to silhouette an image for catalog work?

These questions, and dozens of others, face Photoshop users all the time. And unfortunately, the books we've seen on Photoshop—much less Photoshop's own manuals—simply don't address these crucial, run-of-the-mill, day-in-and-day-out production issues.

This book does.

Ask Your Printer

We wrote this book for a lot of reasons, but the biggest one was probably our frustration with the knee-jerk advice we kept hearing about desktop prepress: "Ask your printer."

Go ahead. Ask your printer what values you should enter in the Monitor Setup, Printing Inks Setup, and Separation Setup dialog boxes. In our experience, with nine out of ten printers you'll be lucky if you get anything better than wild guesses. You can just forget about black generation curves or anything similarly esoteric.

In this new age of desktop prepress, there's simply no one you can ask (whether you're a designer, a prepress shop . . . or a printer). *You're* in the pilot's seat, with your hand on the stick (and the trigger). Where do you turn when the bogies are incoming?

We're hoping that you'll turn to this book.

Developing Your "Spidey Sense"

Flipping through several hundred pages isn't exactly practical, though, when you've got a missile on your tail. So we try to do more with this book than tell you which key to press, or what value to enter where. We're trying to help you develop what our friend and colleague Greg Vander Houwen calls your "spidey sense" (those who didn't grow up on Spiderman comics may not relate completely, but you get the idea).

When you're in the crunch, you've gotta have an intuitive, almost instinctive feel for what's going on in Photoshop, so you can finesse it to your needs. Canned techniques just don't cut it. So you'll find a fair amount of conceptual discussion here, describing how Photoshop "thinks" about images, and suggesting how you might think about them as well.

The Step-by-Step Stuff

Along with those concepts, we've included just about every step-by-step production technique we know of. From scanning to silhouettes and drop shadows, to tonal correction, sharpening, and color separation, we've tried to explain how to get images into Photoshop—and back out again—with the least pain and the best quality.

And yes, in the course of explaining those techniques, we *will* tell you which key to press, and what values to enter in what dialog boxes.

History is Important

We hear some of you mumbling under your breath, "We've been doing prepress for thirty years, and we don't need to learn a new way of doing it." We don't want to be too confrontational, but we can only reply, "Okay, put down this book, ignore the new tools and techniques, and go out of business like almost every other typesetter and color house that hasn't yet entered the '90s."

The key to succeeding in today's prepress market is understanding both the digital and the traditional realms. Our goal in this book is to help you with both. If you're new to prepress, we try to give you the background you need. If you're an old pro, we try to provide an entry into the heart of digital imaging—the world of zeros and ones.

Our goal is not to detract from the way you've been doing things. It's to show you how those approaches can be incorporated with the new tools, improved, and pushed to new limits.

Whither Photography?

This book isn't just about prepress. It's also about photography and about images. We believe that photographers understand tone and color as well as any other skilled group of professionals, and one of our aims has been to help photographers translate their own understanding of images into Photoshop's digital world.

Digital imaging will undoubtedly change the practice of photography, but images still come from an intentional act on the part of the image maker, and that isn't going to change—no matter whether the photons are captured by goo smeared on celluloid or by photoelectric sensors. We believe that digital imaging offers the photographer as many opportunities as it creates pitfalls. To all the photographers out there who are nervous about the digital revolution, we say, "Come on in, the water's fine." And more to the point, we can't *do* this stuff without you.

The Depth of Understanding

We were crazy to take on this book. If we weren't, we wouldn't have tried to unravel such an insanely complex subject. Writing this book has been a humbling experience—we thought we knew how Photoshop worked when we started, but as the book grew, we realized how much we still had (and have) to learn. The process of acquiring knowledge is largely a matter of remapping the boundaries of our ignorance.

We don't claim to have the ultimate answers, but the answers we do have are tried, tested, and effective. The methods we discuss in this book may not be the only way to get good results from Photoshop, but they're the product of many long days and nights of research and testing, of badgering anyone we thought might have an answer with endless questions, and of even more long nights of experiments, more testing, and trying to present these insights in some coherent form. (Bruce vaguely remembers wondering, while making coffee at 4 AM, why one of his kitchen faucets was labeled "cyan". . . .)

While our grasp on reality may have occasionally been tenuous during the production of this book, the techniques we present are firmly grounded in the real world—hence the title.

How the Book is Organized

The biggest problem we've faced in writing about Photoshop is not just that it's the "deepest" program we've ever used, but that almost every technique and feature relies on every other technique and feature. In that way, Photoshop is impossible to talk about without circular reasoning. Nevertheless, we've tried to impose some order by breaking our topics down into five general sections.

The world of Photoshop. In the first five chapters, we attempt to lay the groundwork for the rest of the book. We put all this information first because we feel that it's patently impossible to be effective in Photoshop without it.

▶ Building a Photoshop System.

▶ Essential Photoshop Tips and Tricks.

▶ Image Essentials.

▶ Color Essentials.

▶ Color Preferences.

Global corrections. Now that we've laid the groundwork, we jump into really working with images. In these chapters, we explore techniques you'll want to employ with almost every image you work with in Photoshop.

▶ Tonal Correction.

▶ Color Correction.

▶ Sharpening.

Images. The origin and type of the images you work with determine what you can or need to do with them.

▶ Scanners.

▶ Capturing Images.

▶ Duotones.

▶ Line Art.

Local corrections. In the next two chapters, we really get down to the nitty-gritty of manipulating images—selecting pixels, and pushing them into place.

▶ Selections.

▶ Essential Image Techniques.

Great results with new tools. Digital imaging is changing all the time, so the ways we do our work must change, too.

▶   The Digital Darkroom.

▶   Color Management Systems.

After Photoshop. Sometimes it's hard to remember that there is life outside of Photoshop. In the last two chapters of the book, we show how to get those images out of Photoshop into the real world.

▶   Storing Images.

▶   Output Methods.

Thank You!

We'd like to give special thanks to a few of the many people who helped evolve a shadow of an idea into what you hold in your hands. Our first vote of thanks goes to our editor, Steve Roth and our managing editor, Jeff "Doom" Carlson, both of Open House. Steve continually challenged us to make the book better and clearer, and forced us to learn things we only thought we knew. Jeff handled the gargantuan task of bringing all the elements together in time meet our deadlines.

Cindy Bell of Design Language and Kim Carlson made sure we didn't sound like complete fools, and Scott Sandeman-Allen of Roderick Scott Corporation gave the manuscript a thorough and sometimes challenging technical read.

We particularly appreciate Mark Hamburg, Photoshop's chief architect, for providing patient and clear answers to a constant string of arcane e-mail questions. Thanks also go to Russell Brown, Luanne Cohen, John Cornicello, George Jardine, Bryan Lamkin, John Leddy, John Peck, and LaVon Peck at Adobe, who all helped and inspired us in their diverse ways, as did Matt Brown, wherever he happened to be working.

Other vendors were generous in providing equipment, support and encouragement. Special thanks go to Bruce Berkoff, Richard Falk and Tony Bojorquez of Radius, Barry Weiss and Jerry De Avila of Adaptive Solutions,

Paul McAfee, Joe Runde, John Metzger, Cliff Wilson, Hapet Berberian and Jay Kelbley at Kodak, Jan deClippeleer and Robin O'Leary at Agfa, Joshua Weisberg at Apple, Gary Daily and Chris Cooksey at Daystar, Mark Radogna at NewGen Systems, Bruce Bradshaw and Jim Dunn at Leaf Systems, and John Harcourt at Nikon.

Many third-party software vendors provided invaluable help too, including Herb Paynter at ImageXPress, Rita Amladi at Cybertopia, Matthew Klipstein at Digital Stock, Tom Hughes at Photo Disc, Andrei Herasimchuk at Specular International, Tami Stodgehill at Strata, and Stephen Herron of Isis Imaging.

Sam Merrell and Steve Pollock read early drafts of several crucial chapters: we thank them for their reality checks and good humor. Thanks also go to Stephen Johnson for his generosity of spirit, his constant encouragement, and for the many hours he spent with us in deep discussions that ranged from the technical to the philosophical.

If we see any further than others, it's because we stand on the shoulders of true Photoshop giants, including Greg Vander Houwen, Glenn Mitsui, Diane Fenster, Peter Fink, Jeff McCord, Bob Schaffel, Chuck Weger, Doug Peltonen, Bart Nagel, David Biedny, Eric Reinfield, Deke McClelland, and Bill Niffenegger, pixelmeisters all.

Thanks also to the many people who helped us along the way, including Eric Shropshire of R.R. Donnelly, Jay Nelson of *Design Tools Monthly*, Steve Abrahamson of Trumatch, Randy Anderson, and Greg Swann of *Photoshop Techniques*.

And thank you to the regulars on CompuServe's DTP Forum, Adobe Forum, and Photo Forum, for questions as well as answers.

The folks at Seattle Imagesetting—Neil Kvern (yes, he's Ole's brother), Jim Rademaker, and Chuck and Dolores Cantellay, among others—as always provided great service and great quality. Thanks go to Kevin Thorson, Paul Yovino, and the rest at Consolidated for putting it all on paper for us.

We also want to thank all our friends at Peachpit Press—Ted, Keasley, Gregor, Roslyn, Cary, Trish, Hannah, Bernhard, and at least a dozen others. And, finally, thanks to everyone at "Peachpit North"—Marci Eversole, Toby Malina, Michele Dionne and Steve Broback of Thunder Lizard Productions, Glenn Fleishman of Point of Presence, Don Sellers, and Olav Martin Kvern.

Bruce. "To Pamela, the woman of my dreams, for her patience and understanding, and for the occasional well-timed whack upside o' the head; Squompy the cat for a sense of perspective; various musicians who helped keep me semisane while I worked on this book."

David. "My deepest appreciation to Debbie Carlson, my friend and partner, and to my family and friends—including Don, Snookie, and Suzanne Carlson—who have had to put up with 'the book is almost done' for way too long."

Building a Photoshop System

Putting It All Together

Photoshop is about as rich a program as you'll ever encounter, and much of this book focuses on ways to make you more efficient in your use of it. But no quantity of tips, tricks, and workarounds can compensate for hardware that's inadequate to the task, or a poorly configured system. So in this chapter we look at building an environment for Photoshop.

We'll first look at the hardware resources Photoshop needs, and then at some software add-ons that we find really useful.

Hardware

Photoshop takes full advantage of fast Macs—the faster the better—but the speed of the Mac is only one part of the equation. Even the fastest Mac available will seem sluggish if you don't have enough RAM, and Photoshop refuses to work at all if you don't have enough hard disk space. How much is enough? It depends entirely on the size of the files you're working with.

The Macintosh

Many Photoshop operations involve huge quantities of number crunching, so the speed of your Mac's processor makes a big difference. But more than just about any other application we know, Photoshop exploits the power of the Power Macs. The slowest Power Mac, the 60 MHz Power Macintosh 6100, runs Photoshop about twice as fast, across the board, as the fastest 68040-based Mac.

You can still assemble a very productive system around a 68040-based Mac, but the writing is on the wall for these machines. If your current Photoshop machine isn't a Power Mac, your next one certainly should be.

RAM

You can never be too thin, too rich, or have too much RAM. Just how much RAM you need depends on your file size—remember that additional layers and channels increase the size of the file—but we don't recommend even trying to run Photoshop on a system with less than 16 MB of RAM. It's possible—we've done it—but you have to kill all your INITs and other RAM-gobblers, and it generally becomes an exercise in frustration. A 16 MB Mac is the bare minimum for Photoshop.

For optimum performance, you should allocate to Photoshop an amount of RAM equal to three times the size of your file, plus about five megabytes for the program itself (see Figure 1-1). The file size adds up quickly, particularly if you use a lot of layers or channels, but the biggest single factor affecting Photoshop performance is the availability of enough RAM. Copying pixels takes RAM; taking a snapshot takes RAM; in fact, doing anything takes RAM because Photoshop always saves a version of your image in a memory buffer so that you can quickly undo.

Figure 1-1

Allocating RAM to Photoshop

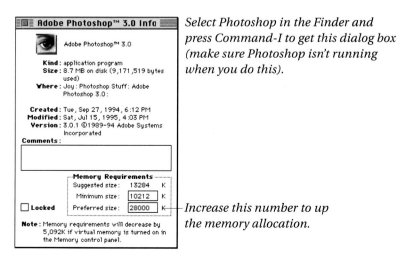

Select Photoshop in the Finder and press Command-I to get this dialog box (make sure Photoshop isn't running when you do this).

Increase this number to up the memory allocation.

If you're working with 2 MB images, you should have at least 11 or 12 MB allocated to Photoshop. If you're working with 18 MB Photo CD images, you better have at least 64 MB in your machine. For larger images you need even more.

Note that a few Photoshop filters (Lens Flare, for instance) require that you have enough physical RAM to load the entire image into memory. Even though Photoshop has a virtual-memory scheme (see below), if you don't have the RAM, these effects just won't work.

Virtual memory. Since Apple instituted a virtual-memory scheme in System 7, there's been an ongoing debate over whether or not to use it while running Photoshop. Virtual memory lets you run more applications at one time because it sets aside hard disk space as "temporary RAM." (On Power Macs, virtual memory has the side effect of reducing the amount of memory that you need to allocate to programs.) However, hard disks are nowhere near as fast as RAM, so you get a significant slowdown.

Photoshop has its own virtual-memory scheme that comes into play anytime it needs more RAM than you have allocated to it (see "Scratch Disk Space," below).

Nonetheless, you can use virtual memory (either the Mac's—invoked through the Memory control panel—or Connectix's RAM Doubler) in conjunction with Photoshop, but only in a limited, specific way. Do not use virtual memory to allocate more RAM to Photoshop than you physically have. Your performance will suffer horribly, because Apple's (or RAM Doubler's) virtual memory will work at cross-purposes with Photoshop's own very efficient virtual-memory scheme. And do not use Apple's virtual memory *unless* you're working on a Power Mac, because Apple's virtual memory on 680x0 chips doesn't use the Modern Memory Manager (RAM Doubler is okay, though).

Ultimately, the only time we turn on virtual memory is when we are working on a Power Mac with too little RAM (like 16 MB). In this case, turning it on reduces the amount of RAM the actual program takes up, so there's a little more room for your images, and you can run additional programs. One other drawback to Apple's virtual memory is that the system "freezes" temporarily whenever it's reading from the disk; if you're painting at that moment, your work might be interrupted.

Tip: Disk Cache Settings. The Disk Cache setting in the Memory control panel is crucial: too large a cache will slow Photoshop to a crawl. The absolute maximum value you should use is 96 K—anything larger results in severe performance degradation. We recommend setting it at 32 K and leaving it there.

Scratch Disk Space

Photoshop 3 uses scratch disk space—the space available for its virtual-memory—differently from earlier versions. It requires scratch disk space equal to the amount of RAM you've allocated to Photoshop. That means if you've given Photoshop 120 MB of RAM, you must have 120 MB of free disk space, even if you're only trying to open a tiny file.

The other big difference between Photoshop 3 and earlier versions is that the new version is constantly optimizing the scratch space. For those of you who have learned to regard disk access as a warning signal that things are about to get very slow, this can be a source of anxiety; let us assure you that it's a necessary and normal part of Photoshop 3's functioning. People are often especially concerned when they see disk access immediately after opening a file. This, too, is normal; Photoshop is simply setting itself up to be more efficient down the line.

Tip: Use the Efficiency Indicator. Unless you've got way too much RAM, or you work on files that are mighty small, there's a good chance that Photoshop is going to start using its built-in virtual memory technique. That means that Photoshop is going to be reading and writing to your scratch disk (whatever hard drive you've specified in the Scratch Disk preferences under the File menu). Here's one way you can check to see if Photoshop is writing to your scratch disk (another method is covered in the next tip).

In the lower-left corner of the document window, there's a popup menu that shows document size, scratch size, or "efficiency" (see Figure 1-2). If you set this to Scratch Size, the first number shows the amount of RAM being used by all open documents, and the second number shows the amount of RAM that's allocated to Photoshop. If the first number is bigger than the second, Photoshop is using your hard drive as virtual memory. When the indicator is set to Efficiency, a reading of less than 100 percent indicates that virtual memory is coming into play.

Figure 1-2
Scratch size

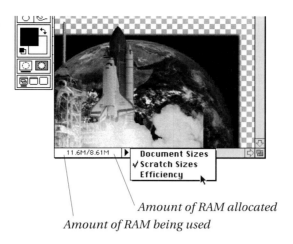

Amount of RAM allocated
Amount of RAM being used

Tip: Watching Your Scratch Disk. The second method we use to watch our scratch disk is to open a window (typically an empty folder) on the desktop, and place it where we can see it while in Photoshop (see Figure 1-3). This way, we can watch how much space is left. Of course, the folder has to be on the scratch disk, and "Show disk info in header" must be turned on in the Views control panel (in your System folder).

Figure 1-3
Disk size window

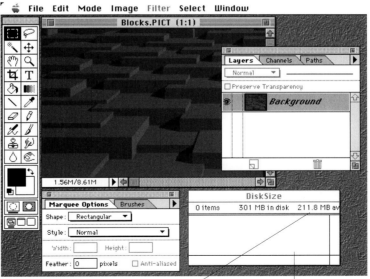

If this number starts getting smaller,
Photoshop is writing to disk.

This window is on the
Finder's Desktop
(not in Photoshop)

Tip: Contiguous Scratch Disk Space. Photoshop runs faster and more smoothly when the scratch disk space is contiguous and unfragmented. If you can, dedicate a partition or an entire hard disk to Photoshop's scratch space.

Tip: Clearing Your RAM. You know that Photoshop gets sluggish when you run out of RAM. And you know that whenever you take a snapshot or copy a large chunk of your document to the clipboard, Photoshop guzzles down two or three times your document size in RAM. If you don't have two to three times the document size of RAM in your machine, life slows down significantly. You can clear up the amount of RAM that Photoshop is using by "emptying" the snapshot, clipboard, and Undo buffers.

1. Select a tiny area of your document—we usually try to grab just a handful of pixels.

2. Take a snapshot (select Snapshot from the Edit menu). If you've not taken a snapshot before, you can leave out this step.

3. Copy (Command-C).

4. Deselect (Command-D, or choose None from the Select menu).

The final step, deselecting the pixels, clears out the Undo buffer so you get the maximum amount of RAM left over to do other work.

RAID arrays. A striped RAID hard disk array can be a worthwhile investment, if you're dealing with images too large for your available RAM on a regular basis. It won't give you the performance you get from having enough RAM, but it's cheaper, and Photoshop's virtual memory performance is much more tolerable than that from a single fixed disk.

However, given sufficient RAM, relatively few Photoshop tasks are dependent on disk speed—with the notable exceptions of opening and saving files. If you have a choice between buying RAM and buying a fast hard drive, you should invest in RAM first.

Application-Specific Accelerators

Application-specific accelerators based on DSP (Digital Signal Processor) chips can make a huge difference to the speed of some Photoshop tasks, particularly Gaussian Blur, Feather, and Unsharp Mask. A tenfold speed increase is common when adding an accelerator to a 68040-based machine, while on a Power Mac the gain is more modest—a speed increase between 200 and 400 percent. To see these speed increases, you need the optimum amount of RAM—slightly over three times the file's size—so (like hard drives), an investment in RAM is a better bet than a DSP accelerator.

Each of the DSP-based accelerators on the market accelerates slightly different suites of Photoshop functions, and each does different things on different Macs. For example, all of them accelerate the Unsharp Mask and Gaussian Blur filters; most accelerate RGB-to-CMYK conversions on 680x0-based Macs, but few (if any) do so on Power Macs—they can't do it any faster than the Mac itself.

Note that the results of DSP-accelerated filters may not be absolutely identical to those you get from the native Photoshop ones. Adobe-certified DSP accelerators—ones that bear the Adobe Charged logo—are certified to produce results that are "visually identical" to the Adobe filters.

We haven't found this to be a problem in any of our imaging work, but it could conceivably create difficulties in some scientific applications. In general, we've found that we get slightly better quality from DSP accelerators such as Adaptive Solutions' PowerShop, and the Radius (or the older SuperMac) Thunder series—particularly when using the Gaussian Blur and Unsharp Mask filters—than we do from the unaccelerated Photoshop filters; but the differences are so slight that you can only detect them by comparing the images mathematically using Calculations.

DSP acceleration is a transitional technology that will almost certainly go away in the future as the computers themselves get faster, but they can make a huge difference to the performance of older machines. If you've heavily invested in RAM on an older machine, a DSP accelerator can help you get another year or two of use out of it.

Video Acceleration

There's a widespread belief that accelerated video boards speed up Photoshop. Unfortunately, it's ill-informed. The bottleneck in redrawing Photoshop images on the screen isn't in the video system—it's in getting the image data out of RAM (or even worse, from disk) to the video system.

There are still reasons to add an accelerated video board to your system, however. For editing in Photoshop, you really need a 24-bit color display—16-bit color is fine for looking at images, but it has serious shortcomings for visual editing. The built-in video on older Macs only supports 24-bit color at relatively low (832 x 624) resolutions; so if you're using a large monitor (which we highly recommend), you'll need an add-on video board, and any add-on video board needs acceleration to provide decent redraw speed in 24-bit color mode.

If you're relying on the built-in video on a Power Mac, though, the only reason to add a third-party video board is to obtain higher resolutions than the built-in video offers.

Third-Party Software

Photoshop has also spawned a whole industry of software add-ons. We find that most of these are more useful as creative tools than they are for production, but we have a few favorites we can't live without.

Color management. Getting great color is emphasized throughout this book, and one way to do that is to use a color management system, such as Kodak's Color Management System (KCMS), Agfa's FotoTune, or Apple's ColorSync. We discuss these in Chapter 16, *Color Management Systems.*

While it's not a color management system, we also sometimes use PixelCraft's ColorAccess software for separating RGB images into CMYK.

ScanPrep Pro. ScanPrep Pro from ImageXPress is one of the few examples of artificial intelligence (or applied ignorance, if you're cynical) in image processing we've seen that actually works. ScanPrep Pro automates the whole process of scanning, correcting, sharpening, and separating images (see Figure 1-4). Of course, you still have to start with good originals. It also offers a CopyDot feature that does the best job we've seen on scanning line art and previously screened material. If you're in a production setting where you need to scan and process many images every day, ScanPrep Pro might be just the thing for you.

Epilog. Total Integration's Epilog is a full-blown Adobe PostScript Level 2 RIP (raster image processor) implemented as a Photoshop Acquire plug-in. It lets us bring any PostScript file into Photoshop—at any resolution, in grayscale, RGB, or CMYK—and it does so with a minimum of fuss. You

Figure 1-4
ScanPrep Pro

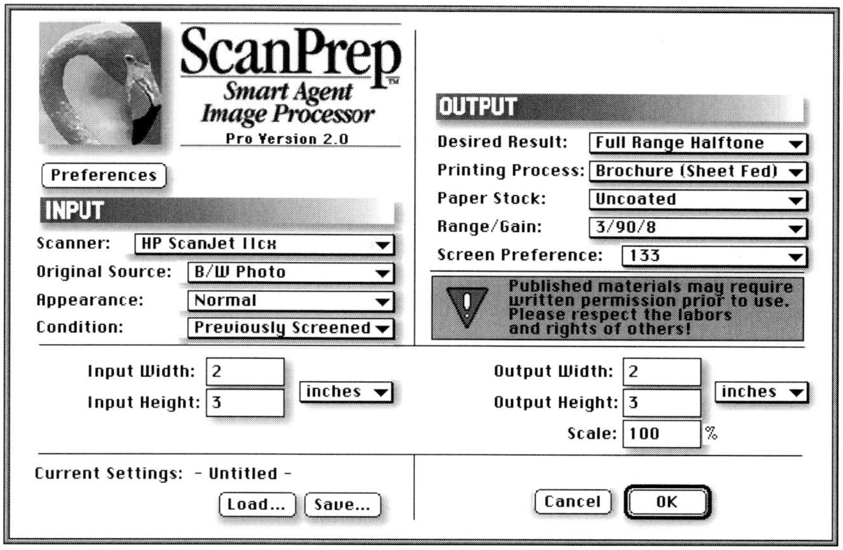

can even import PostScript that some other program wrote to disk. We use Epilog to import EPS files from PageMaker, QuarkXPress, FreeHand, and many other programs.

Version 1.0 was a little flaky (as version 1.0 of anything often is), but in our experience, version 2.0 has been pretty bulletproof. If you need to rasterize a lot of vector art into Photoshop, Epilog is the way to go.

Live Picture. Live Picture is the ultimate companion to Photoshop. It's hands down the best compositing tool we've seen on the Mac, letting us sling around multiple 100-plus MB files in near real-time. It also has very sophisticated automatic masking features that let you silhouette objects by defining inside and outside colors, then simply dragging the brush over the areas that you want inside and outside the mask. With version 2.0, you can convert the mask to a clipping path, and export the image and clipping path as an EPS file.

Although we discuss silhouetting in Chapter 14, *Essential Image Techniques*, we actually use Live Picture for most of our silhouetting work on very large images.

QuicKeys. The Macintosh computer shouldn't even be sold without a copy of CE Software's QuicKeys on the hard disk. Unfortunately, you have to buy your own. QuicKeys lets you create keyboard shortcuts for any menu item, or any action, in just about any program on the Mac. Even better, you can assign a keystroke to a sequence of actions. It's a great way to customize Photoshop to the way you want it to work.

For example, David has QuicKey shortcuts set up to select menu items such as Unsharp Mask, Image Size, and Save As. While you could use the Commands palette to add keystrokes to these menu items (see "Palettes" in Chapter 2, *Essential Photoshop Tips and Tricks*), that only lets you use function keys (like F4 or Shift-F4); QuicKeys lets you use any keystroke you want (the more intuitive the keystroke, the easier it is to remember).

Even better, David has keystrokes that stop him from accidentally saving over an image (see "Tip: Save QuicKey" in Chapter 17, *Storing Images*), for switching to a different image when more than one image is open, and for batch processing multiple files (running the same filters and manipulations on each one).

Photomatic. DayStar Digital's Photomatic 2.0 lets you automate Photoshop in a way similar to QuicKeys, but it's significantly more versatile because you can actually script Photoshop to automatically perform a number of processes on your images. For instance, you might create a script that would set up the Image Size dialog box a certain way, then adjust curves and apply sharpening. While the script doesn't incorporate any intelligence (like ScanPrep Pro does), if you have a number of images that require the same settings, Photomatic could make your life significantly happier.

At the time of this writing, it was unclear as to how DayStar Digital would be marketing Photomatic 2.0. Currently, the software is free to anyone who can download it from an Internet site (www.daystar.com), but that may change in the future.

DeBabelizer. DeBabelizer, from Equilibrium, is possibly the most powerful image-conversion utility on the planet. It's not an image editor like Photoshop, but when it comes to changing bit depth, adjusting indexed color palettes, or converting a whole series of files to a different file type, nothing beats this program.

Ultimately, it's designed to ease the problems inherent in working with multiple file formats—often with differing color palettes. While its interface is pretty clunky, if you're doing multimedia or have to deal with images from a number of different sources, it's worth muddling through.

Specular Collage. While Live Picture is great at compositing, Specular Collage is significantly less expensive, and has some very nice tools for doing image layout. We say "image layout" rather than "compositing" because it's not designed to create masks or manipulate pixels. It's more like a page-layout program, in that you put together all the images and masks elsewhere (like Photoshop) and then piece them together in Collage.

Because Collage works with low-resolution proxies of the elements, you can move, rotate, crop, and scale them quickly. When you're finished with the image, you can export a final high-resolution image as either a flattened file or a Photoshop document with separate layers.

ICEfields. Printing color with stochastic screening is all the rage these days, and for good reason. You can get excellent results with this technique, increasing visible detail and removing concerns of moiré patterning (see "Hybrid Color Screening" in Chapter 18, *Output Methods*). We think newspapers, catalogs, and pieces produced with screen printing or flexography stand to gain the most from stochastic screening.

Isis Imaging's ICEfields is a utility that reads CMYK TIFF images and processes them into stochastically screened DCS files (we talk about file types in Chapter 17, *Storing Images*). Performing the conversion to a stochastic screen on the Mac means you can print the image on any image-setter, not just one that has been outfitted with stochastic screening software (like Agfa's CrystalRaster or Linotype-Hell's Diamond Screening). The newest version even lets you set up your images with clipping paths, so that parts of the image can print with stochastic screens and the rest can print with a traditional halftone.

There are other software-based stochastic screening programs, such as Second Glance Software's LaserSeps, but we've had little reason to switch to them.

The Power of Photoshop

Photoshop is not a island, complete unto itself. Rather, it's surrounded by hardware and software that supports or hinders it. If you focus on any piece of the whole and ignore the rest, you'll undoubtedly run into trouble (or at the very least, you'll be less efficient than you might have been).

We're going to focus on Photoshop for the rest of the book, but while you read, keep in mind these other factors: memory considerations, hardware, and third-party software. That way, you'll really be prepared to harness the power of Photoshop.

2 Essential Photoshop Tips and Tricks

Making Photoshop Fly

Photoshop is deep. Really deep. It's like those National Geographic movies that talk about the world below the surface of the ocean: on the surface it's smooth and straightforward, but down below you'll find things that'll knock your socks off.

In this chapter, we dive down deep and map out some of the canyons along the sea bed. You can dog-paddle around Photoshop without these tips, but you'll never really swim with the sharks until you've explored these territories.

Don't forget your flippers!

Windows

Screen space is at almost as great a premium as memory these days—every little bit helps. We like to work in full-screen mode with Photoshop (see Figure 2-1) instead of wasting space on title bars, scroll bars, and the like. You can switch to either of two full-screen modes in the Tool palette, or by pressing F. The first time you press F (or when you click on the middle icon in the palette), the image window takes over the screen (up to the menu bar) and the background becomes 50-percent gray. The second time, the menu bar disappears, too, and the background becomes black.

Figure 2-1
Full-screen mode

Click here or press F. . .

. . . to switch to full-screen mode.

(See "Make the Palettes Go Away," later in this chapter, for an important related tip.)

David rarely uses the menuless full-screen mode unless he's showing an image to a client, or really needs every bit of screen real estate. The 50-percent gray is a more neutral background than black, and he finds the menus helpful while working. Bruce spends more time in the menuless mode, especially when he's working on high-resolution images, though he sometimes wishes he could toggle the menu bar on and off.

Tip: Rotating Through Your Windows. We often find ourselves in Photoshop with five or more windows open at a time—a frustrating situation when we need to move through them all quickly. The list of open documents in the Windows menu is a small blessing, but a keystroke would be even better. Of course, Photoshop offers no such keystroke.

QuicKeys to the rescue! We rely on the Select Rear Window shortcut (under QuicKeys's Specials submenu; see Figure 2-2). When you press the appropriate keystroke (David has it set to Command-Shift-Tab), the back window pops to the front. This way, you can rotate through the windows without taking your hands off the keyboard, even if you're in full-screen mode with no menus.

Figure 2-2

Defining a QuicKey shortcut to toggle through windows

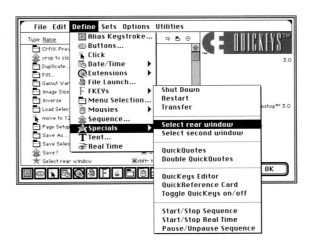

Tip: Use New Window. You often want to see your image at 1:1 (screen pixels to image pixels), but work at some other magnification. Instead of jumping back and forth between magnification views, try opening a second window by selecting New Window from the View menu. You can leave one window set to 1:1, and change the other window to whatever view you want to work at. Whenever you change something in one window, Photoshop updates the other window almost immediately. You can also use this tip to display an image in RGB and CMYK Preview modes simultaneously.

Navigation

In this section we first explore some of the fastest ways to move around your image, including zooming in and out. Then we move on to moving pixels around within your document, and from one document to another.

Magnification

Images got pixels. Computer screens got pixels. But how does one type of pixel relate to the other type of pixel? When you display an image on your screen, Photoshop has to match image pixels to screen pixels (see Figure 2-3).

Figure 2-3

Matching pixels

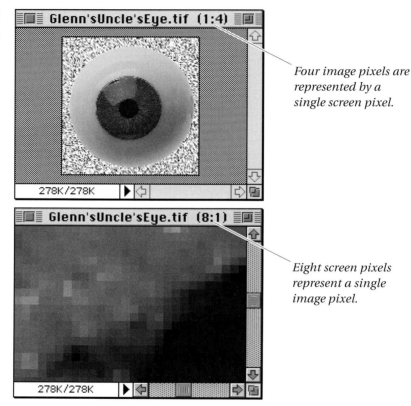

Four image pixels are represented by a single screen pixel.

Eight screen pixels represent a single image pixel.

The ratio in the title bar of the document window tells you how Photoshop is matching those pixels up. The first number is always the number of screen pixels (Bruce likes to remember this by thinking, "I see the screen before I see the image"). In a 4:1 view, four screen pixels represent a single image pixel, so you're zoomed close in. In 1:2 view, a single screen pixel represents two image pixels, so you're zoomed farther out.

Tip: Don't Select the Zoom Tool. We never select the Zoom tool from the Tool palette. You can always get the Zoom tool temporarily by holding down Command-spacebar (to zoom in) or Command-Option-spacebar (to zoom out). You can click to zoom in or out by doubling or halving the present value (from 1:2 to 1:4 to 1:8, and so on), or drag around an area to zoom in. The pixels within the marquee are magnified to fill the screen.

Tip: Zoom with Keystrokes. If you just want to change the overall magnification of an image, press Command-plus (+) or Command-minus (-) to zoom in or out. We find this especially handy because it resizes the window at the same time if necessary (unless the Never Resize Screen checkbox is turned on in the Zoom Tool Options palette; we typically leave it off).

Tip: Keystroke Problem in System 7. For many people, zooming out with Command-Option-spacebar stopped working when they switched to or reinstalled System 7. They use the shortcut, and it just doesn't work. And then they notice that their keyboards don't work right!

The reason? Apple graciously sneaked in a "feature": when you press this keystroke, the system switches keyboard layouts. If you've performed a full install of System 7.5, you probably have upwards of 15 different keyboard layouts in your System file (one for each language supported). The keystroke switches among them, never giving you the chance to zoom in (and in the meantime, screwing up your typing).

The solution is either to remove all the keyboard layouts (double-click on the System file in the System folder and drag all the keyboard layout files to the Trash) or to press the spacebar *first*, then the modifier keys. In System 7.5.1 or later—that's System 7.5 with the System upgrade—you can disable this "feature" by unchecking "Use Command-Option-spacebar to rotate through keyboard layouts" in the Keyboard control panel.

Tip: Jump to One Extreme. If you're at 1:2 view (zoomed a little out) and you want to go to 14:1 view (zoomed way in), you could click a bunch of times with Command-spacebar, or repeatedly press Command-plus. Or you could save yourself some trouble: press Command-Option-plus (+). This zooms all the way to 16:1. Then press Command-minus (-) twice, and you're there.

Command-Option-minus (-) does just the opposite: it jumps all the way to 1:16.

Tip: Get to 1:1 Quickly. You can jump to 1:1 view quickly by double-click-ing on the Zoom tool in the Tool palette. This is just the same as clicking the 1:1 button in the Zoom Tool Options palette.

Tip: Fit Window in Screen. Double-clicking on the Hand tool, on the other hand (no pun left unturned), is the same as pressing Zoom to Screen in the Zoom Tool Options palette—it makes the image and the document window as large as it can, without going out of the screen's boundaries.

Tip: Zoom Factor. Adobe sneaked a feature into the Window menu: the Zoom Factor. When you select this, Photoshop lets you type a magnifica-tion level numerically. For instance, if you want to zoom to 1:6, you can type the number 6, then select Reduction in the dialog box (see Figure 2-4). To jump to 6:1, select Magnification instead. Bonus tip: we've made a QuicKey to select the Zoom Factor by pressing Control-V (this is the same keystroke as in QuarkXPress).

Figure 2-4
Zoom Factor

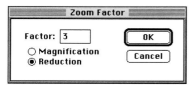

Moving

If you're like most Photoshop users, you find yourself moving around the image a lot. Do a little here . . . do a little there . . . and so on. But when you're doing this kind of navigation, you should rarely use the scroll bars. There are much better ways.

Tip: Use the Grabber Hand. The best way to make a small move around your image is with the Grabber Hand. Don't choose it from the Tool pal-ette. Instead, hold down the spacebar to get the Grabber Hand. Then just click and drag to where you want to go.

Tip: End Up Down Home. We like the extended keyboard—the kind with function keys and the built-in keypad. Most people ignore the very help-ful Page Up, Page Down, Home, and End keys in Photoshop, but we find them invaluable for perusing an image for dust or scratches.

When you press Page Up or Page Down, Photoshop scrolls the image by almost an entire page's worth of pixels up or down. It leaves a small band of overlap, just in case. Unfortunately, there's no Page Left or Page Right button, so we're forced to use the horizontal scroll bar or the Grabber Hand.

Also note that pressing the Home button jumps you to the upper-left corner, and the End button jumps you to the lower-right corner of the document. David often uses this technique when using the Cropping tool. He lazily sets the cropping rectangle approximately where he wants it, then zooms in to the upper-left corner to precisely adjust that corner point. Then, with one hit of the End key, he's transported to the lower-right, where he can adjust that corner.

Tip: Moving Among the Layers. The Grabber Hand and scroll bars only let you move around your image on a two-dimensional plane. What about moving into the third dimension—the layer dimension?

You can move among layers (without ever touching the Layers palette) by using keystrokes: Command-[or Command-] (the square brackets) move to the previous or next visible layer. If you add the Option key to that, Photoshop jumps to the bottom or top layer (helpful if you've got a mess o' layers).

One cool added feature here is that if only one layer is visible when you press these keystrokes, it hides that layer and shows the next layer. This is great for cycling through a number of layers.

Tip: Click on Your Layer. Here's another way to select a different layer without clicking on it in the Layers palette: Command-click with the Move tool. If you click on pixels that "belong" to a different layer than the one you're on, Photoshop jumps to that layer. For instance, if you've got a picture of your mom on Layer 3, and you're currently on the Background layer, you can Command-click on your mom with the Move tool to jump to Layer 3.

This typically only works when you click on a pixel that has an opacity greater than 50 percent. (We say "typically" because it sometimes *does* work if the total visible opacity is less than 50 percent —see "Info Palette," later in this chapter.) If your mom has a feathered halo around her, you may not be able to get this to work if you click on the feathered part.

Moving Pixels

The obvious way to move pixels is to select them and move them with one of the selection tools (the Marquee tool, the Lasso, or the Wand). But a less obvious and sometimes more flexible alternative, the Move tool, is only a keystroke away (press V).

With the Move tool, you can move an entire layer around without selecting anything. When you do have something selected, you don't have to worry about positioning the cursor before you click and drag. This is a great speedup, especially when working with heavily feathered selections. (Also, check out "Duplicating Pixels," later in this chapter.)

Tip: Arrow Keys Move, Too. When moving pixels around, don't forget the arrow keys. Each press of the key moves your selection by one pixel. If you add the Shift key, the selection moves ten pixels. Modifier keys work, too: hold down the Option key when you first press an arrow key, and the selection is duplicated, floated, and moved one pixel (don't keep holding down the Option key after that, unless you want a *lot* of duplicates).

Holding down the Command and Option keys while pressing the arrow keys moves the selection without moving the pixels underneath it. This is an essential technique for precision placement of a selection.

If you've got the Move tool selected (press V), and nothing is selected when you press the arrow keys, the entire layer moves by one or ten pixels.

Tip: Moving Multiple Layers. One of the problems with layers is that you often can't do the same thing to more than one layer at a time. But remember: there are always workarounds!

If you want to move more than one layer at a time with the Move tool, you can link the layers by clicking in the second column of the Layers palette (see Figure 2-5). Whichever layer tile you click on (other than the one that's already active) is linked with the current layer. Now when you use the Move tool (with no selections), both layers move.

Tip: Drag with Preview. It pays to have a little patience (David—otherwise known as Mr. Type A—isn't convinced). When moving either a selection or a whole layer, if you click and immediately drag, all you see is a gray outline of the moving pixels. But if you click, wait for about half a

Figure 2-5
Linking layers
for moving

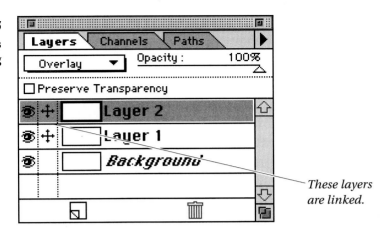

*These layers
are linked.*

second, and *then* start dragging, you can actually watch the selected pixels move. For precision placement, there's nothing like it.

Note that this doesn't work with linked layers. We don't know why—linking layers has nothing to do with this feature—but that's the way it is.

Tip: Drag and Drop Selections and Layers. Those of us who were properly indoctrinated on the Macintosh can't envision a world without Cut and Paste. However, there are times to use the clipboard and times not to. In Photoshop, you often want to avoid the clipboard because you're dealing with large amounts of data. Every time you move something to or from the clipboard, you eat up more RAM, or hard drive space, which can slow you down.

If you want to move a selection of pixels from one document to another, you can do so by dragging it from one window into the other. Photoshop moves the pixels "behind the scenes," so as to avoid unnecessary memory requirements. To move the selection, you can do one of three things.

▶ Drag the selection with one of the Selection tools.

▶ Drag anywhere in the image window with the Move tool.

▶ If the selection is floating, drag the Floating Selection tile from the Layers palette into the other document's window.

Note that you can move whole layers from one document to another in the same way (but here you have to use the click and drag from the Layers palette technique).

Tip: Placing Your Drag-and-Drop Selection. In the last tip we talked about how to drag and drop a selection from one image into another. In that tip, and in this one, we're assuming that the pixel dimensions of the two images are different.

When you let go of the mouse button, the selection is placed into the image right where you dropped it. You have two other options, though.

▶ To place the selection in the center of the image, hold down the Shift key when you lift the mouse button.

▶ To place the selection where it was in the original image, hold down the Option key. Photoshop uses pixel coordinates for this placement. It matches the coordinate of the upper-left corner of the selection to the same coordinate in the new image.

For instance, if the original selection includes the upper-left corner of the image (coordinate 0,0), when you Option-drop the selection into a new image, Photoshop puts the selection in the upper-left corner of the other image (see Figure 2-6). If the upper-left corner of the selection is at coordinate 120,300 (you can see the coordinates in the Info palette), then the same pixel appears at the same coordinates after you Option-drop the selection, even if the two images have different resolutions.

Tip: Pin-Registering Duplicates. As we noted earlier, the previous tip only applies when the two images have different pixel dimensions. If they have the *same* pixel dimensions, however, Photoshop pin-registers the duplication for you, so you don't need to hold down any modifier keys.

Tip: Moving Pixels to a Specific Coordinate. In multimedia (and more rarely in prepress work), you often want to move the same bunch of pixels to the same place in a number of images (for example, to make a button appear at the same place on a number of different screens you're building in Photoshop). Here's one way we've found to do it with QuicKeys.

1. Copy the area you want pasted into the other images.

2. Make sure you're viewing the new document (the one you're pasting into) at a 1:1 view ratio. You also want the image to completely fill the

Figure 2-6

Pixel placement of
dropped selections

If we just drag the selection into another document, it's dropped in the upper-left corner.

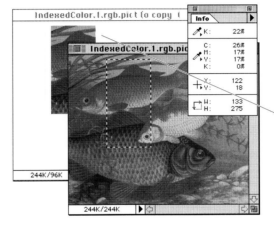

If we hold down the Option key, the pixels are dropped in exactly the same place in the second document.

document window (double-click on either the Grabber Hand or the Zoom tool).

3. Make a tiny selection in the upper-left corner of the document (it has to be smaller than the selection you're pasting), and paste.

4. While you're sure you have the Marquee or the Move tool selected, run a QuicKey Click shortcut that drags from pixel 0,0 to the pixel coordinate where you want the selection to appear.

The trick is that if you have a tiny selection in the upper-left corner of the screen when you paste, the pasted object gets inserted at coordinate 0,0. It's only then that you can use the QuicKey Click shortcut accurately. This doesn't necessarily work if your image is bigger than your screen, or if you're at a view ratio of anything other than 1:1.

Dialog Boxes

Dialog boxes seem like simple things, but since you probably spend a good chunk of your time in Photoshop looking at them, wouldn't it be great to be more efficient while you're there? Here are a bunch of tips that will let you fly through those pesky beasts.

Tip: Scroll 'n' Zoom. The most important lesson to learn about dialog boxes in Photoshop is that just because one is open, it doesn't mean that you can't do anything else. For instance, in many dialog boxes—such as the Levels and Curves dialog boxes—you can still scroll around any open documents (not just the active one) by holding down the spacebar and dragging. You can even zoom in and out of the active window using the Command-spacebar and Command-Option-spacebar techniques.

Note that some dialog boxes, most notoriously the Distort filters, don't let you scroll or zoom at all. Pity.

Tip: Turning on Checkboxes. You don't have to painstakingly aim your cursor at the middle of a checkbox to turn it on or off. Instead, just click anywhere on the box, or even on the word(s) to the right of it. This is true in almost all Macintosh applications.

Tip: Save Your Settings. Many dialog boxes in Photoshop have Save and Load buttons that let you save to disk all the settings that you've made in a dialog box. They're particularly useful when you're going through the iterative process of editing an image.

For instance, let's say you're adjusting the tone of an image with Curves. You increase this and decrease that, and add some points here and there . . . . Finally, when you're finished, you press OK and find—much to your dismay—that you need to make one additional change. If you jump right back into Curves, you degrade your image a second time—not good (see Chapter 6, *Tonal Correction*). If you undo first, you lose the changes you made the first time.

But if you've saved the curve to disk before leaving the dialog box, you can undo, go back to the dialog box, and load in the settings you had saved. Then you can add that one last move to the curve, without introducing a second round of image-degrading corrections.

Just for reference, here's a list of the dialog boxes in Photoshop that have Load and Save buttons.

▶ Levels

▶ Curves

▶ Hue/Saturation

▶ Replace Color

▶ Selective Color

▶ Variations

▶ Halftone Screen
(in Mode: Bitmap)

▶ Screen (in Page Setup)

▶ Transfer Function
(in Page Setup)

▶ Monitor Setup

▶ Printing Inks Setup

▶ Separation Setup

▶ Separation Tables

▶ Color Range

Tip: Instant Replay. There's one other way to undo and still save any tonal-adjustment settings you've made. If you hold down the Option key while selecting *any* feature from the Adjust submenu (under the Image menu), Photoshop opens the dialog box with the last-used settings.

Keystrokes

We love keystrokes. They make everything go much faster, or at least they make it *feel* like we're working faster. Here are a few keystrokes that we use all the time while in dialog boxes.

Option. Holding down the Option key while in a dialog box almost always changes the Cancel button into a Reset button, letting you reset the dialog box to its original state (the way it was when you first opened it). If you want to go keystrokes the whole way, type Command-Option-period to do the same thing.

Command-Z. You already know Command-Z (what Seattle's Mac user group calls "Just Undo It"), because it's gotten you out of more jams than you care to think about. Well, Command-Z performs an undo within dialog boxes, too. It undoes the last change you made. We use this all the time when we mistype.

Arrow keys. Many dialog boxes in Photoshop have text fields where you enter or change numbers (see Figure 2-7). You can change those numbers using the Up and Down arrow keys. Press once, and the number increases or decreases by one. If you hold down the Shift key while pressing the arrow key, it changes by ten. (Note that some dialog boxes change by a tenth or even a hundredth; when you hold down Shift, they change by ten times as much.)

Figure 2-7
Numerical fields
in dialog boxes

Pressing the Up or Down arrow key changes this number.

Add Shift to change in increments of 10.

A few dialog boxes use the arrow keys in a different way, or don't use them at all. In the Lens Flare filter, for instance, the arrow keys move the position of the effect, and arrow keys don't do anything in the Distort filters.

Tab key. As in most Macintosh applications, the Tab key selects the next text field in dialog boxes with multiple text fields. You can use this in conjunction with the previous tip in dialog boxes such as the Unsharp Mask filter, or you can simply tab to the next field and type in a number if you already know the value you want.

Previewing

Most of Photoshop's tonal- and color-correction features and many of its filters offer a Preview checkbox in their dialog boxes. Plus, all the filters that have a dialog box have a proxy window that shows the effect applied to a small section of the image (some dialog boxes have both). It often takes Photoshop a significant amount of time to actually apply an effect to the whole image, particularly if it's a large, high-resolution one, so using the previewing features efficiently can save you lots of time.

Preview checkbox. When you turn on the Preview checkbox, the effect is applied to the current selection, or if nothing is selected, to the entire image. If you leave the Preview option unchecked, nothing happens to the image as you move the sliders or type in new values (see Figure 2-8).

Figure 2-8
Previews

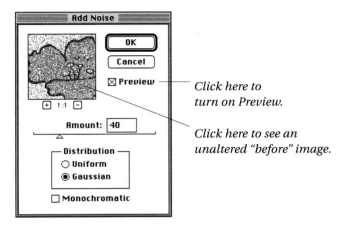

Click here to
turn on Preview.

Click here to see an
unaltered "before" image.

The Preview options in the first four Image Adjust commands—Levels, Curves, Brightness and Contrast, and Color Balance—behave a little differently. When Preview is turned on, the preview works exactly the same as it does anywhere else. But when it's turned off, Video LUT Animation kicks in (if it's turned on—see Figure 2-9).

Figure 2-9
Turning on
Video LUT Animation

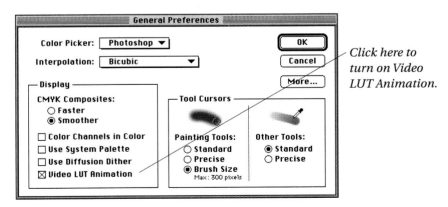

Click here to
turn on Video
LUT Animation.

If Video LUT Animation is turned off, the previews in the four Image Adjust commands behave exactly the same as all other previews—they apply the effect to the image when they're turned on, and they do nothing when they're turned off.

Video LUT Animation. Video LUT stands for "video lookup table." The circuitry that drives your monitor, whether it's an add-on card or built-in video, uses a lookup table to convert digital RGB values to the analog voltages that actually drive your monitor. Monitor calibrators work by manipulating the values in this table to produce the requested gamma and white point. But Photoshop also uses it to perform another nifty trick.

When you change an image using one of the Image Adjust features with Preview turned on, Photoshop has to recalculate every pixel being displayed to show you a preview (see Figure 2-10). This can take some time, particularly with a large screen on a slower Macintosh.

When you use the Video LUT Animation feature instead, Photoshop simply changes the lookup table. It can do this in real time (or, as we used to say when we were lads, instantly) so you get constant feedback as you move the controls. The catch is that the *entire screen* changes, not just the image.

When you have Video LUT Animation turned on, the Preview checkbox acts as a manual override: when you check Preview, you get the real, honest-to-goodness calculated pixels, and when you turn it off, you get the simulation created by manipulating the lookup table.

There are three major benefits to turning on Video LUT Animation.

▶ You can see tonal adjustments as you make them in Levels, Curves, Hue/Saturation, and so on.

▶ Video LUT Animation is much faster than the preview you get while the Preview checkbox is turned on.

▶ It allows you to use the indispensable black-point and white-point clipping display in Levels (see Figure 6-17 on page 153).

We turn Video LUT Animation on and leave it on. However, there are three good reasons *not* to use it, so we often turn on the Preview option to override it.

▶ First, although it's faster than the real preview, it's less accurate. Sometimes, particularly in Duotone or CMYK modes, it can be *very* inaccurate indeed—the results vary with different video cards—but even in RGB or grayscale, you'll see subtle differences between the Video LUT Animation preview and the real thing.

Figure 2-10

Preview and
Video LUT
Animation

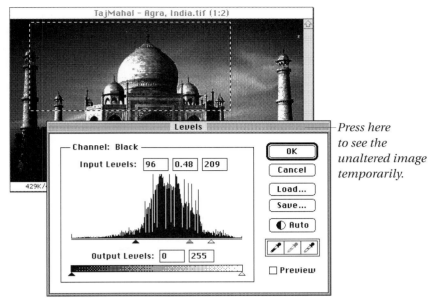

*Press here
to see the
unaltered image
temporarily.*

When Preview is turned off, the entire screen appears to change.

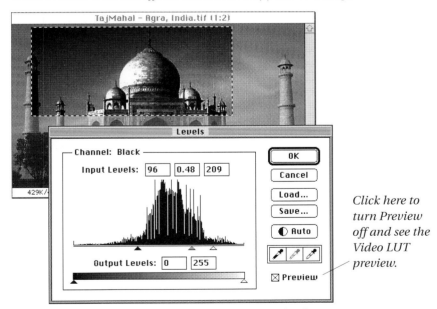

*Click here to
turn Preview
off and see the
Video LUT
preview.*

When Preview is turned on, the screen reflects the final image.

► Second, it applies the effect to the entire screen, not just to the selection or the image. As a result, you lose the context in which you view the image. If you're trying to set a neutral balance and your neutral desktop turns green or blue, it plays havoc with your color perception.

► Finally, it sometimes (though rarely) results in really bizarre effects (or even system crashes) with some monitors and video cards. If weirdness ensues, turn it off.

On the other hand, when we're working on a selection or when we're working in CMYK, we turn the Preview checkbox on. We *always* check the real preview before we press OK to apply the changes to the file.

Tip: Seeing Before-and-Afters. You can always toggle between a preview of the effect and the unaltered image, but the method for doing so is different with Video LUT Animation on and with it off.

With Preview turned off, you can toggle between the corrected and uncorrected versions of the image by clicking on the dialog box's title bar. This temporarily turns off Video LUT Animation (see Figure 2-10).

With Video LUT Animation off in General Preferences, when you turn off the Preview checkbox you see the unaltered image ("before"). Turn Preview on again to see the effect of the changes ("after").

Proxies. The proxy in dialog boxes shows only a small part of the image, but it updates almost instantly. Previewing time-consuming filters such as Unsharp Mask or Motion Blur on a large file can take a long time, and some very time-consuming filters such as the Distort filters don't offer a preview at all, so we rely on the proxy a lot.

Tip: Before and After in Proxies. You can always see a before-and-after comparison by clicking in the proxy. As long as you hold down the mouse button, you can see the unaltered version.

Tip: Changing the Proxy View. To see a different part of the image, click and drag in the proxy (no modifier keys are necessary). Alternatively, you can click in the document itself. The cursor changes to a small rectangle—wherever you click shows up in the Preview window.

Similarly, you can zoom the proxy in and out. The *slow* way is to click on the little (+) and (-) buttons. Much faster is to click the proxy with either the Command or Option keys held down—the former zooms in, the latter zooms out.

Note that proxies only show the layer you're working on at any one time. This makes sense, really; only that layer is going to be affected.

New Dialog Box

Before we move on to essential tips about tools, we need to take a quick look at the New dialog box, which has a few very helpful hidden features.

Tip: Clairvoyant Image Size. The New dialog box tries to read your mind. If you have something copied to the clipboard when you create a new document, Photoshop plugs the pixel dimensions, resolution, and color model of that copied piece into the proper places of the dialog box for you.

If you'd rather use the values from the last new image you created, hold down the Option key while selecting New from the File menu (or press Command-Option-N).

Tip: Copying Sizes from Other Documents. Russell Brown, that king of Photoshop tips and tricks, reminded us to keep our eyes open. Why, for instance, is the Window menu not grayed out when you have the New dialog box open? Because you can select items from it!

If you want your new document to have the same pixel dimensions, resolution, and color mode as a document you already have open, you can select that document from the bottom of the Window menu. Voilà! The statistics are copied.

Tools

After you're finished moving around in your image, zooming in and out, and moving pixels hither and yon, it's time to get down to work with Photoshop's tools. Photoshop's tools have all sorts of hidden properties that can make life easier and—more important—more efficient. Let's look at a number of tips and techniques for getting the most out of these instruments of creation.

Tip: Tool Keystrokes. The most important productivity tip we've found in Photoshop to date has been the ability to select each and every tool with a keystroke. Unlike most programs, the keystrokes for Photoshop's tools do not use any modifier keys. You press the key without Command, Option, or Shift. Figure 2-11 shows the keystroke for each tool.

Figure 2-11

Keystrokes for tools

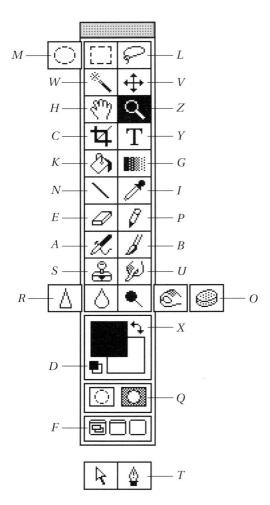

Some tools in the Tool palette have multiple modes. For instance, the Dodge tool also "contains" the Burn and the Sponge tools. For these tools, you can press their keystrokes again to toggle among the choices. Press M once, and you jump to the Marquee tool; press it again, and it switches to the Elliptical Marquee tool; press once more, and it switches back to the Rectangular Marquee tool. And so on.

Note that there are speedy routes to the Options and Brushes palettes, too. We'll cover those in "Palettes," later in this chapter.

Eyedropper

Matching colors by eye can be difficult. Instead, use the tool designed for the job: the Eyedropper.

Tip: Eyedropper Keystroke. You can always grab the eyedropper from the Tool palette (or press I), but if you already have a painting tool selected, it's faster just to use the Option key to toggle between the Eyedropper tool and the painting tool.

Tip: How Many Pixels Are You Looking At? Almost every image has noise in it—pixels that are just plain wrong. If you're clicking around with the Eyedropper tool, there's a reasonable chance that you'll click right on one of those noise pixels, resulting in a color you don't expect (or want). The key is to change what the Eyedropper is looking at.

We usually change the Sample Size popup menu in the Eyedropper Options palette to 3 by 3 Average. This way, the eyedropper looks at nine pixels (the pixel you click on, plus the eight surrounding it) and averages them. If you're working on a very high-resolution image, however, you should switch to 5 by 5 Average.

Tip: Don't Limit Your Eyedropping. Don't forget that when you're working with the Eyedropper tool, you can click on *any* open document, or even the Picker, Swatches, or Scratch palettes. This usually even works when a dialog box is open.

Type Tool

Photoshop is not renowned for its typographic prowess. In fact, it's often downright painful to get good-looking type out of it. However, here are a few tips that may help in the process. (Note that there are also some Type tool tips in Chapter 14, *Essential Image Techniques*.)

Tip: Layers Have Type Memory. This isn't a tip as much as an interesting feature. Did you know that each layer in a document remembers what font you last used? If you use Palatino on Layer 1, then switch to Layer 2 and use Helvetica, when you move back to Layer 1 and click with the Type tool, the Type dialog box remembers that you were using Palatino there. Well, it's nice that it's one less thing to remember.

Tip: Rebuilding the Font List. If you use more than ten or fifteen fonts, you should certainly be using a font-management utility such as Master-Juggler or Suitcase. If you add or remove a font using one of these utilities while Photoshop is open, Photoshop won't update its internal font list properly (so the font won't appear or disappear from the Font popup menu in the Type dialog box).

You can force Photoshop to rebuild the font list by Option-clicking on the image with the Type tool. Well, actually it's more complicated than that. When you hold down the Option key before clicking, you get the Eyedropper tool. So you need to sort of click and hold down the Option key at the same time, which is really difficult. Sometimes it works better if you press the Option key immediately after clicking. It takes a little practice; just work on it until you get it right. (Wouldn't an "Update" button be easier? Are you listening, Adobe?)

Gradient Tool

One of the complaints Adobe heard most in times gone by was that blends in Photoshop resulted in banding. The answer they always gave was to "add noise" to the blend. It's true; noise reduces banding significantly. And fortunately, when Photoshop 3 came out, the program started adding the noise for us. You can stop it, if you want, by turning off the Dither checkbox in the Gradient Options palette. But there's almost no reason to do this.

Tip: Adding More Noise. If you're still getting banding even with Dither turned on, you may want to add even more noise to a blend. However, note that you don't always need to apply the Add Noise filter to the entire gradient; use the filter selectively.

Instead, you might find it better to add noise to only one or two channels. View each channel separately (see Chapter 13, *Selections*) to see where the banding is more prevalent. Then add some noise just to the blend area in that channel.

Tip: Blends in CMYK. Eric Reinfeld pounded it into our heads one day: if you're going to make blends in Photoshop images that will end up in CMYK mode, create them in CMYK mode. Sometimes changing modes from RGB to CMYK can give you significant color shifts in blends.

Tip: Gradients on Layers. Some people make hard work of creating a blend that fades away into transparency. They go through endless convolutions of Layer Masks and Channel Options and so on. They're making it difficult for themselves by not opening their eyes. In the Gradient Options palette there is a Style popup menu which gives you the options of blending from Foreground to Transparent, or from Transparent to Foreground. Seek and ye shall find . . . .

Paint Brushes

We can't tell you how to make great art using Photoshop's painting tools, but we can give you some hints about how to use them more efficiently. One of the key speedups in painting is to alternate brush sizes with keystrokes (we talk about that in "Palettes," later in this chapter). Here are some other quickie tips that might help, too.

Tip: Touching Up Line Art. We talk about scanning and converting to line art in Chapter 10, *Line Art*, but since we're on the topic of tools, we should discuss the Pencil tool for just a moment. One of the best techniques for retouching line art (black-and-white) images is the Auto Erase feature in the Pencil Options palette.

When Auto Erase is turned on, the Pencil tool works like this: if you click on any color other than the foreground color, that pixel—and all others you touch before lifting the mouse button—is changed to the foreground color (this is the way it works, even with Auto Erase turned off). If you click on the foreground color, however, that pixel—and all others you encounter—is changed to the background color.

This effectively means you don't have to keep switching the foreground and background colors while you work.

Tip: Partial Pixel Brushes. It was David Biedny who first posted this tip on America Online: if you want to draw a line that appears to be less than one pixel thick, use a one-pixel brush (the smallest you can) but draw with tints of the color you're working in. If you want a half-pixel black line, try drawing a one-pixel, 50-percent gray line. Try it!

Tip: Sample Merged. If you're working on a multilayer image, you may find yourself frustrated with the Smudge, Blur, Sharpen, Magic Wand, or

Clone tools. That's because sometimes you want these tools to "see" the layers below the one you're working on, and sometimes you do not. Fortunately, Photoshop gives you a choice for each of these tools with the Sample Merged checkbox in the Options palette.

When Sample Merged is turned off, each tool acts as though the other layers weren't even there. But if you turn it on, look out! Photoshop sees the other layers (both above and below it) and acts as though they were merged together (see Figure 2-12).

The benefit of this is great, but people often don't see the downfall. Let's say your background contains a blue box, and Layer 1 has an overlapping yellow box. When you paint or smudge or blur or whatever with Sample Merged turned on, Photoshop "sucks up" the blue and paints it into Layer 1. If you think about it, that's what it should and has to do. But it can really throw you for a loop if you're not prepared.

Cropping Tool

We almost always scan a little bigger than we need, just in case. So we end up using the Cropping tool a lot. The nice thing about the Cropping tool (as opposed to the Crop feature in the Edit menu) is that you can make fine adjustments before agreeing to go through with the paring. Just drag

Figure 2-12
Sample Merged

Using the Rubber Stamp to copy from here . . .

. . . to here

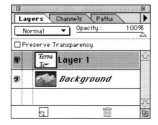

Sample Merged turned on: the clouds in the layer below get picked up with the rubber stamp.

Sample Merged turned off: the clouds don't get picked up.

one of the corner handles. Here are a couple more ways you can fine-tune the crop.

Tip: Rotating While Cropping. If cropping an image down is the most common postscan step, what is the second most common? Rotating, of course. You can crop and rotate at the same time with the Cropping tool: after dragging out the cropping rectangle with the Cropping tool, hold down the Option key and drag on one of the corner handles. The rectangle rotates. When you click in the center area, Photoshop crops and rotates the image to straighten the rectangle. It can be tricky to get exactly the right angle by eye—keep an eye on the Info palette.

Tip: Resampling While Cropping. The Options Palette for the Cropping tool lets you specify output size and resolution. If you set height and width, the aspect ratio of the crop is constrained. If you set resolution, when you hammer down the gavel to perform the crop, Photoshop resamples the image to that resolution. This is handy when you want to resample down, but be careful that you don't ask for more resolution than you really have; resampling up is best avoided. You don't have to specify all three values. If you leave Height or Width blank, the aspect ratio isn't constrained. If you leave Resolution blank, no resampling occurs.

Tip: Moving the Cropping Rectangle. If the cropping rectangle isn't in the right place, you can always move it. However, most people move the whole rectangle by moving one corner and then the other. You can move the whole thing in one fell swoop by Command-dragging one of the corner handles.

Eraser

The Eraser tool has gotten a bad rap. "Never use it," people say. But that's just holdover resentment for the pathetic pre-3.0 Eraser. Now that we're in the latter half of the '90s, we can not only accept the Eraser and take it into our fold of useful tools, we've even built a set of techniques around it (see "Digital Dodging and Burning" in Chapter 15, *The Digital Darkroom*).

The primary advancement in the Eraser is that you can erase using any brush—soft or hard. Plus, you can make the Eraser tool work like the Airbrush, Pencil, Brush, or Block (the original, MacPaint-like eraser). And what's more, you can control the opacity of the Eraser. This makes the eraser fully usable, in our opinion.

Tip: Switching Eraser Mode. You know that you can press E to get the Eraser tool. But wouldn't it be great if there were a keystroke to jump to a different *type* of eraser? Fortunately, there is. Press E again, and you move through the list of eraser types: Airbrush, Paintbrush, Pencil, and Block. Then if you want to change opacity, you can press a number key from 1 to 0 (1 is ten percent, 2 is twenty percent, and so on).

Tip: Erase to Saved. If you've never used Erase to Saved, you just haven't lived. Erase to Saved is a feature of the Eraser tool that lets you replace pixels in your image with pixels from the image that is saved on disk. For instance, you can open a file, mess with it until it's a mess, then revert *parts of it* to the original using the Eraser tool with Erase to Saved turned on (see "When Things Go Worng," later in this chapter).

Many people use the Rubber Stamp tool to go back to the saved version (it works exactly the same way), but we reserve it for cloning from a Snapshot, which the Eraser cannot do (see "Snapshots" in Chapter 14, *Essential Image Techniques*).

Palettes

Bruce has a second monitor set up on his computer just so he can open all of Photoshop's palettes on it and free up his primary monitor's precious space. There's little doubt that palettes are both incredibly important and yet incredibly annoying at times. Fortunately, Photoshop has some built-in but hidden features that make working with palettes a much happier experience. For instance, palettes are "sticky"—if you move them near the side of the monitor or near another palette, they'll snap-to align to that side or palette. This (if nothing else) helps you keep a neat and tidy screen on which to work.

Tip: Make the Palettes Go Away. If you only have one monitor on which to store both your image and Photoshop's plethora of palettes, remember two keyboard shortcuts. First, pressing Tab makes the palettes disappear (or reappear, if they're already hidden). We find this absolutely invaluable, and use it daily.

Second, pressing Option-Tab makes only the Tool palette disappear (or reappear). This is a less common keystroke for us; we find it most helpful when we're working with only the Paths palette and the Tool palette. The strange (and unfortunate) thing about the Tab keystroke is that it hides any paths you're working on, along with the palettes. Option-Tab, however, doesn't do that because it leaves the Paths palette alone.

Tip: Making Palettes Smaller. Another way to maximize your screen real estate is by collapsing one or more of your open palettes. If you double-click in the white area just under a palette's title bar, the palette collapses to just the title bar and name (see Figure 2-13). Or if you click in the zoom box of a palette (the checkbox in the upper-right corner of the palette), the palette reduces in size to only a few key elements. For instance, if you click in the zoom box of the Layers palette, you can still use the Opacity sliders and Mode popup menu (but the Layer tiles and icons get hidden).

Figure 2-13

Collapsing palettes

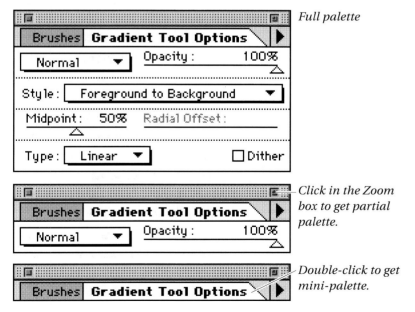

Full palette

Click in the Zoom box to get partial palette.

Double-click to get mini-palette.

Tip: Mix and Match Palettes. There's one more way to save space on your computer screen: mix and match your palettes. Palettes in Photoshop have a curious attribute: you can drag one on top of another and they become one. Then if you want, you can drag them apart again by clicking and dragging the palette's tab heading.

For instance, David always keeps his Layers, Channels, and Paths palettes together in one palette (see Figure 2-14). When he wants to work with one of these, he can click on that palette's tab heading. Or better yet, he uses a keystroke assigned in the Commands palette (see "Commands Palette," below) to bring it forward.

Figure 2-14

Mixing and matching palettes

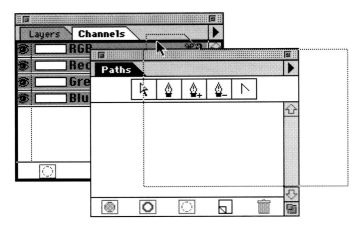

While you could, in theory, put all the palettes into one, he finds it much more useful to have several palette bunches: Layers/Channels/Paths, Colors/Color Picker/Scratch Pad, and Brushes/Options.

Bruce, on the other hand, always keeps the Layers and Channels palettes and the Brushes and Options palettes separate, even when he's working on a single-monitor system. Neither of us ever mixes the Info palette with another palette, because we want it open all the time.

Commands Palette

If you're like us, you try to avoid the menus whenever possible. One way to do this is to use the Commands palette, which lets you make a button out of any Photoshop menu item. It also lets you assign a keystroke to that button, using Edit Commands in the palette's popout menu (see Figure 2-15).

Also, note that if you have a whole mess of commands in the Commands palette, you should break them into multiple columns (you can have up to nine, depending on the size of your monitor). But if it's getting that big, wouldn't it be easier just to use the menus?

Figure 2-15
Edit Commands

Tip: Colorize the Commands. The Commands palette is a great tool if you like setting up keystrokes for Photoshop's features (we do). But if you can't remember the keystrokes, you have to leave the palette open so you can click the appropriate button instead. If you leave this palette open a lot, try color-coding the buttons in groups. Perhaps the commands you use the most would be red; the buttons having to do with file management (Save, Open, and so on) would be blue.

You can assign colors to buttons in the Commands Preferences dialog box, or by selecting Edit Commands from the popout menu in the Commands palette and pressing the Change button.

Tip: Editing Shortcuts. You can also edit the Commands palette with key-click shortcuts. Command-click on a button to delete it. Control- or Shift-click on a button to edit a command. Note, however, that these key combinations only allow you to change the attributes of single buttons. You still need to select Edit Commands from the popout menu to add a command or change the number of columns.

Options Palette

The tools in the Tool palette only go so far. You often need to modify their default settings in the Options palette. Try this: select the tool, then press Return. The Options palette, even if hidden, appears at this command. Plus, if there is a number-input field in the palette, Photoshop selects it for you. For instance, when you press Return with the Lasso or Marquee tools selected, the Lasso Options or Marquee Options palette appears and the Feather field is highlighted in the palette.

If there is more than one number-input field in the palette, you can press Tab to jump from one to the next. Finally, when you're finished with your changes, press Return again to exit from the palette and resume work.

Tip: Resetting the Tools. Photoshop power users are forever changing the settings in palettes, especially the Tool Options palette. But every now and again, it's nice to level the playing field. In this case, you can reset the tool options for either a single tool or for all the tools in the Options palette's popout menu (see Figure 2-16).

Figure 2-16
Options palette

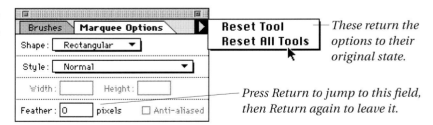

These return the options to their original state.

Press Return to jump to this field, then Return again to leave it.

Brushes Palette

If there's one thing that makes us crazy in Photoshop, it's forever moving the cursor around the screen to change options, to change tools, or (especially) to change brush sizes. We can't tell you how happy we were to discover this next little tip.

Tip: Brush Keystrokes. Did you know that the [and] keys (the square brackets) move left and right through the Brushes palette? We now keep one hand on the keyboard and one on our mouse (or tablet pen); when we want to change tools, we press the key for that tool. When we want to change brush size, we cycle through the brushes with the [and] keys until we find the size we like.

If you want to go for extremes, you can also type Shift-[and Shift-]. These jump to the first and last brushes in the palette.

Tip: Opacity by the Numbers. In between changing brush sizes, we're forever changing brush opacity while painting or retouching. If you're still moving the sliders around in the Brush Options palette (or the Options palette for any other painting/editing tool), don't; instead, just type a number from 0 to 9. Zero gives you 100-percent opacity, 1 gives you 10 percent, 2 gives you 20 percent, and so on.

Layers Palette

The most obvious new feature in Photoshop 3 was the ability to create multiple layers in an image; almost every layer control is to be found in the Layers palette. With such a crucial palette, there have to be at least a few good tips around here. No?

Tip: Quick New Layers. We constantly find ourselves wanting a newly pasted selection to sit on a new layer. The fastest way we've found to do this is to paste the pixels in, then—while the selection is still floating— Option-click on the New Layer icon in the Layers palette. A slightly slower method is to double-click on the Floating Selection tile in the Layers palette; that way, Photoshop lets you name the layer and set its mode.

Tip: Displaying Multiple Layers. Every click takes another moment or two, and many people click in the display column of the Layers palette (the one with the little eyeballs in it) once for each layer they want to see. Cut out the clicker-chatter, and just click and drag through the column for all the layers you want to see.

Tip: Click to Turn Off Layers. Another way to make multiple layers appear or disappear is by Option-clicking in the display column of the

Layers palette. When you Option-click on an eyeball, Photoshop hides all the layers except the one you clicked on. Then, if you Option-click again, it redisplays them all again. Even though this trick doesn't save you a lot of time, it sure feels like it does (which is often just as cool).

Tip: Turn Off Layer Previews. Even on the fastest machines, Photoshop can be dragged down by performing extra tasks in the background. For example, if you have the Channels or Layers palettes open, every time you do anything to your image, Photoshop has to update those little preview thumbnails (see Figure 2-17). But if you don't use the thumbnails, why not speed up the process and turn the previews off (by choosing Palette Options from the popout menu on the palettes)? Large previews don't seem to take any longer to calculate than small previews, but they occupy a great deal more screen real estate. We keep the previews turned off unless we're working on an image that has so many layers or channels that we can't remember which is which. Needless to say, we try to avoid that situation whenever possible.

Figure 2-17
Layer previews

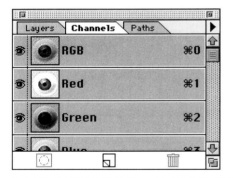

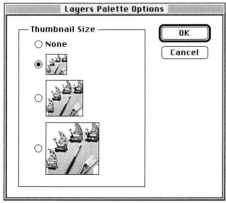

Info Palette

In a battle of the palettes, we don't know which Photoshop palette would win the "most important" prize, but we do know which would win in the "most telling" category: the Info palette. We never close this palette. It just provides us with too much critical information.

At its most basic task, as a densitometer, it tells us the gray values and RGB or CMYK values in our image. But there's much more. When you're working in RGB, the Info palette shows you how pixels will translate into CMYK or Grayscale. When working in Levels or Curves, it displays before-and-after values (see Chapter 6, *Tonal Correction*).

But wait, there's more! When you rotate a selection with Free Rotation or with the Cropping tool, the Info palette displays what angle you're at. And when you scale, it shows percentages. If you've selected a color that is out of the CMYK gamut (depending on your setup; see Chapter 5, *Color Preferences*), a gamut alarm appears in the Info palette.

One more feature often goes unnoticed: when you have transparency showing (*e.g.*, on layers that have transparency when no background is showing), the Info palette even gives you an opacity ("Op") reading (see Figure 2-18).

Figure 2-18
The Info palette

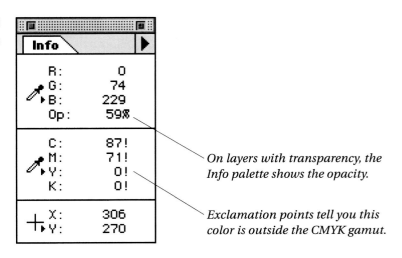

On layers with transparency, the Info palette shows the opacity.

Exclamation points tell you this color is outside the CMYK gamut.

Tip: Measuring Distances. "Why don't you have a measurement tool?" This is a common question asked of Adobe's development team. Their answer: "We do! It's the Line tool." The trick? Select the Line tool in the Tool palette (press N), press Return (to jump to the Options palette), then type 0 (zero) and Return again (to get out of the Options palette). Now when you drag out a line on your image, Photoshop doesn't draw anything (it's a zero-width line).

Where's the measurement? In the Info palette, of course. The palette displays horizontal and vertical distances, along with the total distance in whatever measurement system you've set up in Units Preferences.

Tip: Measuring Angles. We know you always make sure your images are placed squarely on the scanner before you scan them, but you may occasionally have to level someone else's crooked scan. Again, the Info palette and a zero-width line can help immensely (see Figure 2-19).

1. Find the horizon line, or an edge that you know should be horizontal, and draw a line along it using the Line tool.

2. Read the angle from the Info palette, then plug that same number into the Rotate Arbitrary command under the Image menu.

Positive angles are counterclockwise, negative ones are clockwise.

Figure 2-19
Measuring angles

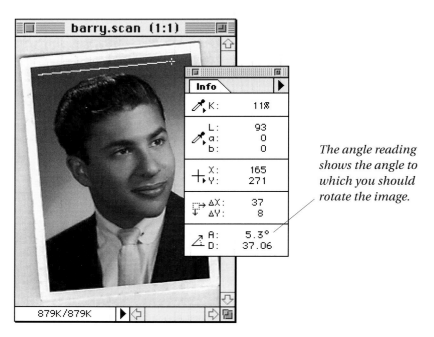

The angle reading shows the angle to which you should rotate the image.

Tip: Switch Units. While we typically work in pixel measurements, we do on occasion need to see "real world" physical measurements such as inches or centimeters. Instead of traversing the menus to open the Units dialog box (in the Preferences submenu under the File menu), we find it's usually faster to select from the Info palette's popout menus. Just click on the tiny triangle (see Figure 2-20).

Figure 2-20

Changing units

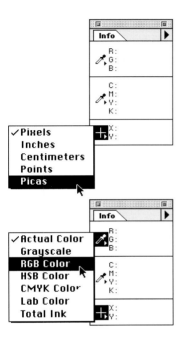

Color Palettes

The Scratch Pad, the Color Picker, and the Color palette all fit into one category, so we almost always group them together into one palette on our screen and switch among them as necessary.

Most novice Photoshop users select a foreground or background color by clicking once on the icons in the Tool palette and choosing from the Color dialog box. Many pros, however, have abandoned this technique, and focus instead on these color palettes (the one time you need to use the dialog box is when you're specifying colors by numerical values). Here are a few tips to make this technique more . . . ah . . . palettable.

Tip: Switching Color Bars. The Color Bar is not just another place to meet people. It's the rectangular area at the bottom of the Color Picker palette. While the spectrum of colors that appear here usually covers the RGB gamut, you can switch to a different spectrum by Shift-clicking on the area. Click once, and you switch to CMYK; again, and you get a gradient in grayscale; a third time, and you see a gradient from your foreground color to your background color. Shift-clicking again takes you back to RGB.

Tip: Using the Scratch Pad. If you're like us, you took one look at the Scratch Pad palette, figured you'd never use it, and closed it up. But now it's time to bring it forth from its hiding place. The palette is useful for more than just doodling or mixing colors. For instance, you can clone (using the Rubber Stamp tool) from the image into the palette, or back out again. This is great for testing out various painterly effects in a safe, removed area before taking the plunge with your real image.

You can even skip the cloning altogether. Just select an area from your image, and drag it right into the Scratch palette. When you're done fiddling, you can drag what's in the scratch area back into your document (we've never come up with a good use for this, but you might).

Tip: Editing the Color Swatches. You've probably ignored all those swatches in the Swatches palette because they never seem to include colors that have anything to do with your images. Don't ignore . . . explore! You can add, delete, and edit those little color swatches in the Swatches palette. Table 2-1 shows you how.

Table 2-1	To do this . . .	Do this . . .
Editing the	Add foreground color	Click any empty swatch
Swatches palette	Delete a color	Command-click
	Replace a color with foreground color	Shift-click
	Insert foreground color between two others	Shift-Option-click

You can't actually edit a color that's already there. Instead, you can click on the swatch (to make it the current foreground color), edit the foreground color, then Shift-click back on the swatch (which replaces it with the current foreground color).

Preferences

There's a scene in Monty Python's *Life of Brian* where Brian is trying to persuade his followers to think for themselves. He shouts, "Every one of you is different! You're all individuals!" One person raises his hand and replies, "I'm not."

This is the situation we often find with Photoshop users. Even though each person uses the program differently, they think they need to use it just like everyone else. Not true. You can customize Photoshop in a number of ways, through its Preferences submenu (under the File menu). We're not going to discuss every preference. Instead, we'll take a look at some of the key items we think you should be aware of under the Preferences submenu. First we'll cover the General Preferences dialog box (press Command-K); then we'll look at some other preferences. (We explore Photoshop's color preferences more in Chapter 5, *Color Preferences.*)

Note that we don't differentiate between items in the General Preferences dialog box and those in the More Preferences dialog box, which you get by clicking the More button. If you don't see what we're talking about in one box, try the other.

Tip: Propagating Your Preferences. Any time you make a change to one of the Preferences dialog boxes, Photoshop remembers your alteration, and when you quit, saves it in the "Adobe Photoshop 3.0 Prefs" file in the Preferences folder of the System Folder. If anything happens to that file, all your changes are gone. Because of this, we recommend keeping a backup of that file someplace (people often back up their images without realizing they should back up this sort of data file, too).

Certain kinds of crashes (mostly caused by software other than Photoshop) can corrupt Photoshop's Preferences file. If Photoshop starts acting strange on us, our first step is always to replace the Preferences file with a clean copy.

Note that if you administer a number of different Macintoshes that are running Photoshop, you may want to standardize the same preferences on all machines. The answer: copy the Photoshop Prefs file to each computer's Preferences folder.

Short Pantone Names. The previous version of Photoshop named its Pantone colors with a suffix: CVC. Unfortunately, other programs (notably QuarkXPress) used "CV". To ensure compatibility (especially at color-separation time), you now have the choice in Photoshop to use the shorter suffix. While it hardly matters whether this is on or off (XPress now recognizes both spellings), we suggest you turn this checkbox on.

Video LUT Animation. We talked about Video LUT Animation back in the Previewing section of "Dialog Boxes," earlier in this chapter. Quick recap: turn it on and leave it on.

Export Clipboard. When the Export Clipboard checkbox is on, Photoshop converts whatever is on the clipboard into a PICT format when you leave Photoshop. This is helpful—indeed, necessary—if you want to paste a selection into some other program. But if you've got a megabyte or two or ten megabytes on the clipboard, that conversion is going to take some time. In situations when you're running low on RAM, it can even crash your Mac, though this is rarer than it used to be.

We recommend leaving Export Clipboard off until you really need it.

Brush Sizes. When you painted or edited pixels in pre-3.0 versions of Photoshop, the program would display the cursor only as a Brush icon (or Rubber Stamp icon, or whatever you were using). Because it was sometimes difficult to tell which pixel the tool would affect, Photoshop implemented the crosshairs feature—when Caps Lock is down, the cursor switches to a crosshair icon displaying precisely which pixel Photoshop is "looking at."

But most brushes affect more than one pixel at a time, so in version 3.0, when you set Tool Cursors to Brush Size (in the General Preferences dialog box), Photoshop shows you exactly how large the brush is while you're painting or editing (see Figure 2-21). After working with this for awhile, you'll wonder how you could ever go back.

Figure 2-21
Brush Size

You can still get the crosshairs with the Caps Lock key. Note that Photoshop can't show Brush Size cursors for brushes over 300 pixels in diameter, and it reverts back to the regular tool icon.

Save Metric Color Tags. The Save Metric Color Tags option is only useful if you use EfiColor to create Photoshop separation tables, if you create separations using those tables, if you import the separated images into QuarkXPress 3.3 or later, *and* if you then want to use EfiColor to correct the color for a different output device than the one to which it's targeted. We discuss our reservations about EfiColor in Chapter 16, *Color Management Systems*. If all of the above apply to you, you can save yourself a couple of seconds by turning this option on; otherwise, leave it off.

CMYK Composites. Remember that your monitor is displaying colors in RGB. If you're working with a CMYK image, Photoshop has to convert all those CMYK values to RGB values on the fly. The CMYK Composites preference defaults to Faster, which results in a reasonably good approximation of the CMYK value. However, we prefer quality over quantity, so we typically change this to Smoother. It's a little slower, but on a fast machine it's hardly noticeable. The difference is particularly obvious on CMYK gradients—you'll see obvious banding when the option is set to Faster. This option only affects screen display; it has no effect on your data.

Diffusion Dither. If, for some bizarre reason, you work in 8-bit color (we hardly ever work with Photoshop in less than "Thousands" of colors), Photoshop has to do even more work at displaying its plethora of colors on your screen. This is usually done with dithering of some sort. You can choose the method: when Use Diffusion Dither is turned on in the General Preferences dialog box, Photoshop generates colors using a "random" pixel placement. Otherwise, it uses a standard pattern. Neither of these methods is particularly attractive, but we prefer the standard pattern, so we leave the checkbox turned off. However, Diffusion Dither often produces a nicer look when zoomed in closer than 1:1.

Image Previews. When you save a document in Photoshop, the program can save little thumbnails of your image as file icons. These thumbnails can be helpful, or they can simply be a drag to your productivity. We always set Image Previews to Ask When Saving, so we get a choice for each file (see "Preview Options" in Chapter 17, *Storing Images*).

Dynamic Sliders in Picker. This one is very subtle. When Dynamic Sliders in Picker is turned on, the bars for the sliders in the Picker palette change color as you drag. The target color changes as you drag, whether it's turned on or not—it just affects the sliders themselves. On a slower machine you may want to turn it off, as it can exact a slight performance penalty, but we've never noticed it.

2.5 Format Compatibility. There are still those in the world who continue to battle with Photoshop 2.5.1 every day, instead of upgrading to a newer version. Perhaps they don't have enough RAM or hard drive space to work with the newer version. Perhaps they simply prefer to work with outdated technology. But whatever the reason, there they are. And sometimes we have to deal with them.

If you have to work with such a person, turn on 2.5 Format Compatibility in the More Preferences dialog box. The benefit: when you save a file in native Photoshop format, you (or someone else) can open that document in Photoshop 2.5. But the downsides are hefty.

▶ All layer information is lost once you open the file in the earlier version (the file is flattened). If you save the document and open it in 3.0 again, the layers are gone, gone, gone.

▶ Your image file size is as much as 50 percent larger when this is turned on. Photoshop has to store tons of extra info.

▶ If you're a channeling kind of guy or gal, beware: you can't open more than 16 channels in earlier versions of Photoshop. Additional channels are lost for all time.

Our preference is clear: turn this off, and leave it off unless you really need it.

More Preferences

Let's take a look at a few more ways to customize Photoshop. These are each found on the Preferences submenu under the File menu.

Gamut Warning. Bruce thinks the Gamut Warning is basically useless—he'd rather just see what's happening to the out-of-gamut colors when they're converted—but for the record, when you turn on Gamut Warning from the Mode menu, it displays all the out-of-gamut pixels in the color you choose here (for more on Photoshop's out-of-gamut display features, see "Gamut Alarm" in Chapter 7, *Color Correction*).

If you do want to use this feature (David likes it), we recommend you choose a really ugly color that doesn't appear anywhere in your image, such as a bright lime green. This way, when you switch on Gamut Warning, the out-of-gamut areas are quite obvious.

Transparency. Transparency is not a color, it's a state of mind. Therefore, when you see it on a layer, what should it look like? Typically, Photoshop displays transparency as a grid of white and gray boxes in a checkerboard pattern. The Transparency Preferences dialog box lets you change the colors of the checkerboard and set the size of the squares, though we've never found a reason to do so (see Figure 2-22).

Figure 2-22
Transparency
preferences

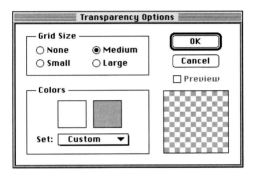

When Things Go Worng

It's 11 PM on the night before your big presentation. You've been working on this image for thirteen hours, and you're beginning to experience "pixel vision." After making a selection, you run a filter, look carefully, and decide that you don't like the effect. But before you can reach Undo, you accidentally click on the document window, deselecting the area.

That's not so bad, is it? Not until you realize that undoing will only undo the deselection, not the filter . . . and that you haven't saved for half an hour. The mistake remains, and there's no way to get rid of it without losing the last 30 minutes of brain-draining work. Or is there? In this section of the chapter, we take a look at the various ways you can save yourself when something goes terribly wrong.

The first few techniques are pretty obvious. But as you get into the later techniques, you'll find some great ways to dig yourself out of some pretty deep holes.

Undo. The first defense against any offensive mistake is, of course, Undo. You can find this under the Edit menu, but we suggest keeping one hand conveniently on the Command and Z keys, ready and waiting for the blunder that is sure to come sooner or later. Note that Photoshop is smart enough not to count some things as "undoable." Taking a snapshot, for instance, doesn't count; so you can take a snapshot and then undo whatever you did just before the snapshot. Similarly, you can open the Histogram, hide edges, change foreground or background colors, zoom, scroll, or even duplicate the file, and Photoshop still lets you go back and undo the previous action.

Revert to Saved. This command is pretty easy to interpret. If you've really messed up something in your image, often the best option is simply to revert the entire file back to the last saved version by selecting Revert to Saved from the File menu. It's the same as closing the file without saving changes, then reopening it. Any changes you've made since then are lost, however, so proceed with caution.

Magic Erase. Sometimes you make just a little boo-boo, and you only want to revert a small portion of your image to the last saved version. One way to do this is with the Magic Eraser tool (turn on the Erase to Saved checkbox in the Eraser Options palette). The Magic Eraser works just like the Eraser tool—so you can set brush type, size, and opacity—but instead of erasing, it reverts pixels to how they were last saved.

When you first use the Magic Eraser tool, Photoshop has to load the entire saved version of the image into memory. This takes time, especially with a large image. If we're going to play with this tool, we usually click once just to tell Photoshop to go ahead and load the original. While it's shuffling away, we can get up and stretch our eyeballs.

Tip: Magic Eraser Keystroke. Note that you don't have to actually turn on Erase to Saved in the Eraser Options palette; you can hold down the Option key while working with the Eraser tool to erase to saved. (When Erase to Saved is turned on, the Option key turns it off.)

Rubber Stamp From Snapshot or Saved. Another way to paint with an earlier version of the image is to use the Rubber Stamp tool (press S) with the Option popup menu in the Rubber Stamp Options palette set to From Snapshot or From Saved. There are two great benefits of using the Rubber Stamp tool rather than the Magic Eraser tool.

▶ The Rubber Stamp tool can revert back to either the last saved version *or* the last snapshot you took. If you take a lot of snapshots (Bruce does; David always forgets to), this is really helpful.

▶ You can set calculation modes in the Rubber Stamp Options palette. That means you can paint from the saved version using Multiply (perhaps to build up density), Screen (to recover from underexposure), or any other mode.

Fill with Saved or Snapshot. The last technique that can help in case of a catastrophic "oops" is the Fill command in the Edit menu (or pressing Shift-Delete). This lets you fill any selection (or the entire image, if nothing is selected) with the pixels from the last-saved or last-snapshot image. We usually use this in preference to the Rubber Stamp or Magic Eraser tools, especially when the area to be reverted is easily selectable. Sometimes when we paint with those tools, we overlook some pixels (it's hard to use a brush to paint *every* pixel in an area at 100 percent). This is never a problem when you use the Fill command.

Easter Eggs

It's a tradition in Macintosh software to include Easter Eggs—those wacky little undocumented, nonutilitarian features that serve only to amuse the programmer and (they hope) the user. Note that if your friends think you have no sense of humor, you might want to skip this section; it might just annoy you.

There are (at least) four Easter Eggs in Photoshop: three hidden screens and one quote list.

Knoll Software. At the heart of Photoshop lie Tom and John Knoll, the folks who first brought this program to the world. Their company, Knoll Software, is celebrated with its very own splash screen, which you get by holding down the Option key while selecting About Photoshop from the Apple menu.

Tiger Mountain. A tradition even older than Easter Eggs is code names. Almost all software has a code name that the developers use before the product is christened with a real shipping name. Photoshop 3 was code-named Tiger Mountain (it's a Brian Eno reference, if you care), and the original Tiger Mountain splash screen somehow stuck around in the shipping version. To see it, hold down the Command key while selecting About Photoshop from the Apple menu.

Quotes. If you watch either the standard About Photoshop screen or the Tiger Mountain splash screen, you'll notice that the credits at the bottom of the screen start to scroll by, thanking everyone and their dog for participating in the development process. Don't get impatient—the last person on the list is someone special. (Actually, if you *are* the impatient type, try holding down the Option key once the credits start rolling; that speeds them up.)

At any time before or during the rolling credits, try clicking once on either the Adobe logo in the upper-left corner of the box, or between the word "Adobe" and the picture. If the screen disappears, you've clicked in the wrong place. If nothing happens, you've done it right. Now just wait until the scrolling credits are finished, and you'll be treated to some very funny quotations.

Merlin Lives! Finally (at least, this is the last one we know about), there's a little hidden dialog box nestled away. When you hold down the Option key while selecting Palette Options from the popout menus in either the Paths, Layers, or Channels palette, Merlin happily jumps out. Don't forget to try clicking on Merlin for that extra kick.

The World of Photoshop

If our publisher weren't screaming bloody murder to get this book to the printer, we'd still be writing tips. But instead of waiting until the next edition of the book, try finding them for yourself. The more you *play* with Photoshop, the more you'll be rewarded with treasures from the deep.

3 Image Essentials

It's All Zeros and Ones

Let's get one thing perfectly clear: this book is not about pictures or work flow or even computers. This book is about zeros and ones. As Laurie Anderson so plainly pointed out, no one wants to be a zero and everyone (at least in America) wants to be "number one." The digital age is built entirely on the interplay between the two.

To be sure, the digital world (in which zeros and ones, offs and ons, and whites and blacks frolic together in cooperation, not competition) is not as confusing as some people make it out to be. And, as it turns out, you can't really be efficient with digital imaging without knowing a little bit about that dark underworld. In this chapter we're going to break it all down for you. To some of you, most of this chapter is going to sound pretty basic, but we urge you to peruse it anyhow. You might be surprised at how many "power users" find themselves stumped by something as small as a misunderstanding of how—and why—bitmapped images work.

Bitmapped versus Object-Oriented Graphics

In all the grand canon of computer imaging, there are really only two kinds of graphics: bitmapped and object-oriented.

Bitmapped images. Bitmapped images are simply collections of dots (we call them *pixels* or *sample points*) laid out in a big grid. The pixels can be different colors, and the number of dots can vary. No matter what the picture is—whether it's a modernist painting of a giraffe or a photograph of your mother—it's always described using lots of dots. This is the only way to represent the fine detail and subtle gradations of photorealistic images.

Almost every bitmapped image comes from one of three sources: capture devices (such as scanners, video cameras, or digital cameras), painting and image-editing programs (such as Photoshop), and screen-capture programs (like Exposure Pro, the System itself, and a host of others). If you create a graphic with any of these tools, it's a bitmapped image.

Object-oriented graphics. Object-oriented graphics are both more complex and simpler than bitmapped images. On the one hand, instead of describing a rectangle with thousands (or millions) of dots, object-oriented graphics just say, "Draw a rectangle this big and put it here." Clearly, this is a much more efficient and space-saving method for describing some images. However, object-oriented graphics can include many different types of objects—lines, boxes, circles, curves, polygons, and text blocks, and all those items can have a variety of attributes—line weight, type formatting, fill color, graduated fills, and so on.

To use an analogy, object-oriented graphics are like directions saying, "Go three blocks down the street, turn left at the 7-11, and go another five blocks," while bitmapped images are more like saying, "Take a step. Now take another step. And another...." When you work in Photoshop, you're working with bitmapped images (though you can import some object-oriented graphics, converting them to bitmaps, and you can use object-oriented techniques to create selections and masks).

Most object-oriented graphics come from two primary sources: drawing programs (FreeHand, Canvas, Illustrator, and so on), and computer-aided design (CAD) programs. You might also get object-oriented graphics from other programs, such as a program that makes graphs.

Bitmaps as objects. It turns out that the distinction between bitmapped and object-oriented graphics is slightly fuzzy, because object-oriented graphics can include bitmaps as objects in their own right. For instance, you can put a scanned image into an Adobe Illustrator illustration. The scan actually acts like an object on the page, much like a rectangle or oval. If you include a bitmap as an object in an illustration, you can rotate it and scale it, but you can't go into the image and change the pixels.

Words, Words, Words

While terminology might not keep you up at night, we in the writin' business have to worry about such things. In fact, one of our first controversies in writing this book concerned the term *bitmap*.

Bruce maintains that, strictly speaking, bitmaps are only black-and-white images. This is how Photoshop uses the term. He prefers to describe images made up of colored dots as *raster* images (the word "raster" refers to a group of lines—in this case, lines of pixels—that collectively make up an image). David thinks that only people who wear pocket protectors (some of his best friends do) would use the word "raster." With the first controversy comes the first compromise: we'll call these creatures we're working with in Photoshop "bitmapped images"—whether

they're black and white, gray-scale, or color.

Another problem we've encountered is what to call all those little dots in a bitmapped image. As we mentioned earlier, when we talk about points in a bitmapped image, we like to call them *pixels, samples,* or *sample points.*

The phrase "sample points" comes from what a scanner does: it samples an image—checking what color or gray value it finds—every 300th of an inch, every 100th of an inch, or whatever. However, not all bitmapped images are scanned. "Pixel" is a more generic term because it specifies the smallest "picture element" in an image. Occasionally, you'll run into someone who refers to pixels as "pels." They may not wear pocket protectors, but they've almost certainly had an unnaturally close relationship with an

IBM mainframe computer somewhere in their past.

When we talk about scanning an image in, or printing an image out, we talk about samples or pixels per inch (Bruce prefers the latter, or *ppi;* David likes the former, or *spi*); and when we talk about the resolution of a bitmapped image saved on disk, we just talk about the total number of pixels. Note that many people use "dots per inch" (*dpi*) for any and all kinds of resolution. We prefer to reserve the term "dots per inch" (dpi) for use when speaking of printers and image-setters, which actually create dots on paper or film.

We use the term "pixels" for one other thing: screen resolution. However, to be clear, we always try to specify "screen pixels" versus "image pixels."

Note that an object-oriented graphic file might include a bitmap as its *only* object. In this situation, the file is a bitmapped image that you can open for editing in a painting or image-processing application. Photoshop's EPS (Encapsulated PostScript) files are good examples of this. While EPS is typically an object-oriented file format, you can create a bitmap-only EPS in Photoshop.

Objects in bitmapped graphics. Just to round out the confusion, we should mention that Photoshop lets you include an object called called a *clipping path* in bitmapped images. A clipping path in an image is invisible; it simply acts as a cookie cutter, allowing you to produce irregularly shaped images such as the silhouetted product shots you often see in ads (see "Clipping Paths" in Chapter 17, *Storing Images*).

Bitmapped Images

Photoshop lets you open, create, edit, and save bitmapped images. Bitmapped images are its *sine qua non*, its *raison d'être*, its "precious bodily fluid." So to get the most out of Photoshop, you've got to understand bitmapped images inside and out.

Every bitmapped graphic has three basic characteristics: dimension, bit depth, and color model (which Photoshop refers to as *image mode*).

Dimension

Bitmapped images are always big rectangular grids. Like checkerboards or chessboards or parquet floors in your kitchen, these big grids are made of little squares (see Figure 3-1). The *dimensions* of the bitmap grid refer to the number of pixels wide and tall it is. A chessboard is always eight squares by eight squares. The grid of pixels that makes up your computer screen might be 640 by 480.

Figure 3-1

Bitmaps as grids of squares

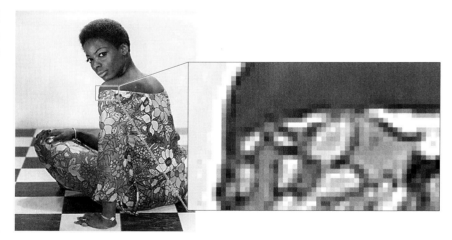

A bitmapped image can be any dimension you like, limited only by the capabilities of your capture device, the amount of storage space you have available, and your patience—the more pixels in the image, the more space it takes up, and the longer it takes to do anything with it.

Note that *dimension has nothing to do with physical size* in inches or picas. Bitmapped images in their pure digital state have no physical size; they're just data. They exist as Platonic ideals, waiting to be realized by reproduction in some physical form. No matter how you stretch or shrink a bitmapped image, it still contains the same number of pixels.

When you print a bitmapped image, you print it at a specific size, and the relationship between that size and the number of pixels the image contains is called the *resolution* of the image. But it's very important to understand that resolution isn't innate to the digital image; it's a rubber measurement that changes depending on the physical size at which you reproduce the image. We'll discuss resolution and why it's important in more detail later in this chapter.

Bit Depth

Each pixel in a bitmapped image is represented by a particular number of zeros and ones, otherwise known as *bit depth* (one bit can be either a zero or a one). That number dictates the range of possible values for each pixel, and hence the total number of colors (or shades of gray) that the image can contain.

A 1-bit image (one in which each pixel is represented by one bit) can only contain blacks and whites. If you have two bits of information describing a pixel, there are four possible combinations (00, 01, 10, and 11), hence four possible values, and four possible colors or gray levels (see Figure 3-2). Eight bits of information give you 256 possible values; 24 bits of information result in over 16 million possible colors. (With 24-bit RGB images, each sample actually has three 8-bit values—one each for red, green, and blue; see Color Plate 1 on page 123.)

Figure 3-2
Bit depth

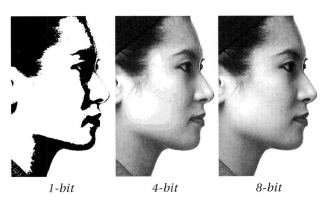

1-bit   *4-bit*   *8-bit*

We call 1-bit images *flat* or *bilevel* bitmaps. A *deep* bitmap is any image that has more than one bit describing each pixel (see Figure 3-3).

Bit depth has an important relationship to the quality of an image, which we'll cover more fully later in this chapter.

Figure 3-3
A "deep" bitmap

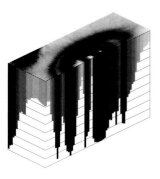

Image Mode

The problem with bit depth is that it doesn't really tell us (or Photoshop) what each color (numerical value) means. A 1-bit image is easy: each pixel can only be on or off. It doesn't have to be black or white, though; if you were twisted enough, you could make this orange or blue.

But as we've seen, each pixel in an 8-bit image can be described using one of 256 values. Are those 256 levels of gray? Or 256 colors? Or something else? We'll let you in on a sad, sordid little secret here. Everyone who works with color on computers discovers it eventually anyway: computers don't understand color at all—they just understand numbers: zeros and ones.

The color model—otherwise known as image mode—is the missing piece of the puzzle, the magic decoder ring that tells how to translate each pixel's numerical value into a color or a shade of gray. Actually, image mode and color model aren't exactly the same thing, but they're so closely related that it makes sense to discuss them as aspects of the same thing.

If the image mode is set to Grayscale under the Mode menu, the value of each pixel is a grayscale value: 0 is black, 255 is white. If image mode is Indexed, then each value is tagged to a specific, arbitrarily chosen color. (An indexed color image can only have 256 different colors in it; see "Indexed Color," later in this chapter.)

However, if the image mode is set to RGB, Lab, or CMYK, then the color of the pixel is actually made up of multiple 8-bit values. For instance, in an RGB image, each pixel is described using three 8-bit values, each of which specifies a level of brightness for the red, green, and blue channels (see Color Plate 1 on page 123). In a CMYK image, Photoshop looks at and composites four 8-bit images.

You can look at the individual channels and view each one as a grayscale image. The color image is made by colorizing each channel with the appropriate color and stacking them one atop the other.

Note that unless you're working with esoteric scientific or medical imaging equipment, you won't have to tell Photoshop which image mode to use: virtually every file format that Photoshop recognizes has the secret decoder ring built in. But you need to understand image modes and their related color models if you want to do much useful work with Photoshop. (For a fuller discussion of color models, see Chapter 4, *Color Essentials*.)

We'll look at each mode that Photoshop uses, and why you'd want to use one or another, later in this chapter.

Resolution

Resolution is one of the most overused and under-understood words in desktop publishing. People use it when talking about scanners and printers, images and screens, halftones, and just about anything else they can get their hands on. Then they wonder why they're confused. Don't worry; resolution is easy.

As we noted earlier, a bitmapped image in its pure digital state has no physical size—it's just a bunch of pixels. But you can't see a pure digital image unless you can decipher zeros and ones in your head. So whenever you give an image tangible expression, whether it's as an ephemeral representation on the screen or as a permanent printed form, you confer upon it the property of physical size. And with size comes resolution.

The resolution of a bitmapped image is the number of pixels in each unit of measurement. If we're talking in inches, then we talk about the number of pixels per inch (ppi), which is what most people mean when they say "dots per inch" (dpi).

If your bitmapped image has 72 pixels per inch, and it's 72 pixels long on each side, then it's an inch long on each side. If you print it at half the size, you'll still have the same number of pixels, but they'll be crammed into half the space, so each inch will contain 144 of them. If we take the same bitmapped image and change it to 36 pixels per inch (changing its resolution), suddenly the image is two inches on each side (same number of pixels, but each one is twice as big as the original; see Figure 3-4).

You can also look at bitmap resolution in another way: if you know the size of an image and its resolution, you can figure out its dimensions. When you scan a picture that is three inches on each side at 100 pixels per inch, you know that the bitmapped image has 300 pixels on each side

Figure 3-4
Scaling and
resolution

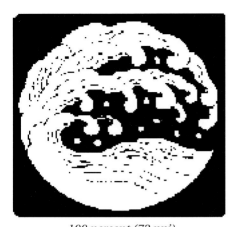

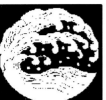

*25 percent
(288 ppi)*

*50 percent
(144 ppi)*

100 percent (72 ppi)

*50 percent
(144 ppi)*

100 percent (72 ppi)

300 percent (24 ppi)

(100 per inch). If you scan it at 300 pixels per inch, the dimensions shoot up to 900 pixels on each side.

The key to making resolution work for you (rather than against you) is in knowing how many pixels you need for the intended purpose to which you'll put the image. We discuss how much data you need for different purposes later in this chapter.

How Much Is Enough?

If bigger were better, we'd be out of business (you'd be hard pressed to call us statuesque). And when it comes to resolution of bitmapped images, bigger is not only worse, but costly, too. The higher the resolution of an image, the longer it takes to open, edit, save, or print. Plus, while the cost of hard drives has come down in recent years, you're still paying between 50 cents and a dollar per megabyte of storage. That means you'll save $100 just by reducing ten 8-by-10-inch images from 300 ppi to 225 ppi (see "Bitmaps and File Size," later in this chapter).

Of course, smaller isn't necessarily better, either. If your image resolution is too low, your image will look pixelated (see Figure 3-5); you'll start to see the pixels themselves, or adverse effects due to excessively large pixels. Loss of detail and mottling are the two worst offenders in this category.

Figure 3-5
Pixelation in too-low-resolution images

100 percent
200 ppi

300 percent
66 ppi

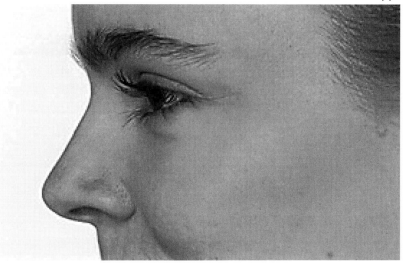

Maybe you thought you could save even more money by reducing those eight-by-tens down to 150 ppi. However, when the client rejects the job because the image is too pixelated, that savings will be more than wiped out when you have to redo the job. So if bigger isn't better, and too small is even worse, then how much is enough? How much image data do you need? The first consideration is image mode: the requirements are very different for line art than they are for grayscale and color.

Terms of Resolution

Not everyone talks about resolution in terms of ppi. Depending on the circumstance, your personality, and the time of day, you might discuss a file's resolution in a number of ways, but they're all different ways of talking about the same essential concept: *how much information* the file contains. Here's a quick rundown of your options.

Image size. The first way to discuss resolution is the way we've done it up until now (and the way we do it in most places in this book): spec both the physical size and number of pixels per inch. For example, you might say a file is 4 by 5 inches at 225 ppi. This makes the most sense to someone doing page layout, because they're typically concerned with how the image is going to look on the printed page. Note, however, that you have to specify both the size and the resolution; otherwise you're only telling half the story.

Dimensions. You can sidestep the question of resolution by simply specifying the dimensions of the bitmapped image; that is, the number of pixels on each side of the bitmap grid. This doesn't tell you what physical size it is, but if you understand how much resolution you need for different output methods, it's useful shorthand for expressing how big the image *could be*, depending on what you wanted to do with it. It tells you how much information there is in the file. Hard-core Photoshop users like to talk in dimensions because they don't necessarily know (or care) how large the final output will be.

For instance, you could say a scan from a 35 mm original is a 2,048-by-3,076 image. What does that tell you? With experience, you'd know that your file size is 18 MB, and at 225 ppi you could print a full-bleed letter-sized page. Later on we'll discuss how you can figure all this out for yourself.

File size. The third way to discuss resolution is by the file's size on disk. You can quickly get a sense of the difference in information content of two files when we tell you that the first is 900 K and the second is 12 MB. In fact, a lot of digital imaging gurus *only* think in file size. If you ask them, "What's the resolution of that file?" they look at you like you're an idiot.

Once you become accustomed to working with a number of different sizes, you'll recognize that the 900 K RGB file is about the size of a 640-by-480 RGB image. At 72 ppi (screen resolution) that's pretty big, but at 300 ppi (typical

Line art

For bilevel (black-and-white, 1-bit) images, the resolution never needs to be higher than that of the printer you're using. If you're printing to a 300-dpi desktop laser printer, there's no reason to have more than 300 pixels per inch in your image (the printer can only image 300 dots per inch, so any extras just get thrown away). However, when you print to a 1,200-dpi imagesetter, that 300-ppi image appears jaggy.

If you're printing to an imagesetter, you should plan on using an image resolution of *at least* 800 ppi—preferably 1,000 ppi or more (see Figure 3-6). Line art with an image resolution of less than 800 shows jaggies and broken lines. Of course, if you're then going to print that artwork resolution for a high-quality print job), the image is only about two inches wide.

The resolution of Photo CD images is often specced by file size. The highest-resolution Photo CD image is 18 MB; the highest resolution of Pro Photo CD is 64 MB.

Single-side dimension. People who work with continuous-tone film recorders, such as the Solitaire or the FIRE1000, frequently talk about a file's resolution in terms of the dimension of one side—typically the width—of the image. For instance, they might ask for "a 4 K file." That means the image should be exactly 4,096 pixels across.

"K" usually means file size (kilobytes). However, in this case it's 1,024 pixels (see Table 3-1).

The height of the image is relatively unimportant in this case, though if you're imaging to film, it's usually assumed that you know the other dimension of the image because it's dictated by the

Table 3-1 Resolution in K

K	Number of pixels across
1	1,024
2	2,048
3	3,072*
4	4,096
5	5,120*
6	6,144*
7	7,168*
8	8,192

* rarely used

aspect ratio of the film you're using. High-quality film recorders usually write out to 4-by-5-inch chromes (positive transparencies), so if you want to fill the image area, it's usually assumed that the short side of your 8 K image will contain somewhere around 6,550 pixels.

Res. One other method of discussing resolution uses the term *res*. "Res" is simply the number of pixels per millimeter, and if we had anything to say about the matter, it'd be stricken from common us-

Table 3-2 Resolution in res

Res	Pixels per inch
1	25.4
2	50.8
3	76.2
4	101.6
5	127
6	152.4
7	177.8
8	203.2
9	228.6
10	254
11	279.4
12	304.8
20	508
40	1,016
60	1,524
80	2,032

age. People usually talk about res when they're discussing scanning resolution. For example, a file scanned at res 12 is scanned at 12 sample points (pixels) per millimeter—which is 120 sample points per centimeter, or—in common usage—304.8 sample points per inch (see Table 3-2).

onto newsprint or porous paper, you can often get away with a lower resolution such as 400 or 600 ppi, because the jaggies will disappear with the spreading ink.

See Chapter 10, *Line Art*, for techniques to increase the resolution and appearance of line art images at lower resolutions.

Grayscale and Color Halftones

There's a relatively simple formula for figuring out the proper resolution for printing grayscale and color ("deep") bitmapped images to halftoning devices like laser printers and imagesetters: image resolution should be two times the screen frequency *at most*. For instance, if you're printing a

Figure 3-6

Resolution of
line art

144 ppi   *300 ppi*

800 ppi   *1,200 ppi*

halftone image at 133 lpi, the image resolution should be no larger
than 266 ppi (see Figure 3-7, and Color Plate 2 on page 124). Any higher
resolution is almost certainly wasted information.

We've heard from people who claim to see a difference between 2 times
the screen frequency and 2.5 times the screen frequency, but no one has
ever shown us a print sample that supported this contention. It's absolutely certain that anything higher than 2.5 times the screen frequency is
wasted if you're printing to a PostScript output device.

If you go to print an image whose resolution exceeds that multiplier,
Photoshop warns you, and PostScript just discards the extra information
when it gets to the printer. You can print the image, but it takes longer to
print, and you don't get any better results than you would with a lower-
resolution version.

In fact, we rarely use even twice the line screen. With a good 80 percent of
images, you can use 1.5 times the screen frequency, and you can often get
away with less, sometimes even as low as 1.2 times the screen frequency.

Figure 3-7 Resolution of grayscale images

266 ppi (2:1)   *200 ppi (1.5:1)*

166 ppi (1.25:1)   *133 ppi (1:1)*

That means the resolution of the image that you're printing at 133 lpi *could* be as low as 160 ppi (but if you want to play it safe, you might use 200 ppi).

So which multiplier should you use? It depends on your quality requirements, the quality of your reproduction method, the kind of images you're reproducing, and your system. If you're working with a less-powerful computer, less RAM, or a smaller hard drive, think lower resolution.

Quality requirements. The only reliable way we've found to answer the question of what's "good enough" is whether the person paying for the job smiles when they sign the check. There's no absolute index of quality, and clients have widely differing expectations. The best course of action is to prepare Match Prints or other high-quality laminated film proofs of a few different images, using different multipliers to see where the trade-off works for you.

Reproduction method. Images destined for uncoated stock and newsprint can generally withstand a lower multiplier than those printed on coated stock at a high screen frequency, because the more porous stock causes greater dot gain: the halftone dots grow larger because the ink bleeds into the paper. If you're producing a rag or a newspaper and you're still using the two-times-frequency rule, you're wasting someone's time and money—we hope it's not yours.

Image detail. The need for higher resolution also depends on the content of the image itself. Reducing the multiplier reduces the clarity of small details, so higher resolution is most important with images that have small (and important) details.

Most pictures of people work fine at 1.25 times the screen frequency, but trees with fine branches and leaves might do best with 1.5 times screen frequency. And if the image has a lot of fine diagonal or curved lines (such as rigging on a sailboat, or small text), you may want to use a resolution of 2 times the frequency, particularly if you're paying through the teeth for a 200-lpi print job on high-quality coated stock. Of course, in those cases it's probably worth spending a little extra on Match Prints or other high-quality laminated proofs to test some of the more difficult images at different resolutions.

Many Photoshop neophytes assume that if they have a 300-ppi scanner, they should scan at 300 ppi even if the image is going to be reproduced at actual size with a 133-lpi screen. If you use a 2x multiplier or 266 ppi instead, that's a savings of one megabyte for a little 4-by-5-inch image. A 1.5x multiplier saves you almost three megabytes, and 1.25x brings your original 5 MB image down to only 1.58 MB. That could mean quite a large difference in printing time or costs. (See Chapter 12, *Capturing Images*, for more information on scanning resolution, and Chapter 18, *Output Methods,* for a fuller discussion of halftone output issues.)

If a lot of this halftone talk is going over your head, we recommend a book that David coauthored with Steve Roth called *Real World Scanning and Halftones.*

Grayscale and Color Continuous-Tone Output

If you're printing to a continuous-tone output device such as a dye-sublimation printer or a film recorder, you can forget all that fancy math. In an ideal world, you simply want the resolution of your file to match the resolution of the output device. If you're printing to a 300-dpi dye-sublimation printer, you want 300-ppi resolution—about 18 MB for a letter-sized page. If you're printing to an 8 K film recorder, you really do want 8,096 pixels on the short side of the image. That's a lot of data: about 240 MB for a 4-by-5-inch piece of film!

Sometimes, though, this simply isn't practical; you may not be able to make a scan that large. More important, the original may not contain enough useful information in the first place. It's possible to scan a 35 mm slide to a 75 MB file, but you'll see a lot of film grain, and the scan may not contain any more *useful* information than one that's half that size.

Some high-end continuous-tone output devices such as the FIRE1000 film recorder and the Iris ink-jet printer have very sophisticated resampling algorithms, better than anything Photoshop provides. You may be able to produce a very acceptable 4-by-5 digital chrome (positive transparency) or a 16-by-20 Iris print from a 75 MB file, even though its resolution is only about half that of the output device. Again, it's worth making some tests using different resolutions.

Resampling

One of the most important issues in working with bitmapped images— and, unfortunately, one which few people seem to understand—is how the resolution can change relative to (or independently of) the size of your image.

There are two ways that you can change resolution: scaling and resampling. You can scale or resample an image or part of an image in several ways, but you get the most control through the Image Size dialog box (see "Tip: Faster File Figuring," later in this chapter).

In Photoshop, you can scale a bitmap without altering its resolution. Or you can change the resolution of a bitmapped image without changing its size. These processes are called *resampling*, because you're changing the number of pixels in the image. You're adding or removing pixels.

If you take a 2-by-2-inch, 100-ppi image and change the size to 1 inch square without changing the resolution, Photoshop has to throw away a bunch of pixels; that's called *downsampling*. If you double the size by *upsampling*, it has to add more pixels by *interpolating* between other pixels in the image (see Figure 3-8).

Figure 3-8
Resampling

Original image

Downsampled

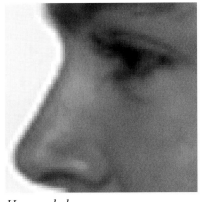

While downsampling is a normal and necessary procedure, there's almost never any reason to upsample. It simply adds data, not information, so your image is blurry instead of pixelated.

Upsampled

Upsampling versus Downsampling

The rule to remember with upsampling is, "Just don't do it if you can avoid it; and if you *can't* avoid it, use bicubic interpolation." Adding pixels to a file can reduce aliasing (a.k.a. the jaggies) and mottling in some situations (and exaggerate them in others), but it can't add details that weren't there in the first place: you don't get something for nothing, and there's no such thing as a free lunch. (The one place that upsampling is really useful is in creating line art; see Chapter 10, *Line Art*.)

Downsampling is much less problematic, because it's simply throwing away data in a more or less intelligent manner. In fact, it's a common and necessary practice: we often scan at a higher resolution than is strictly necessary, to allow for cropping and for unanticipated changes in output size or method. We downsample to the required resolution before printing to save time and storage space.

Resampling methods. Photoshop can downsample and interpolate using three methods: Nearest Neighbor, Bilinear, and Bicubic. You choose which you want in the General Preferences dialog box (see Figure 3-9).

Figure 3-9

Photoshop's resampling
(interpolation) methods

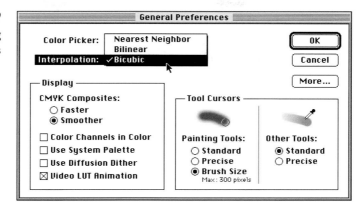

▶ **Nearest Neighbor** is the most basic, and it's very fast: to create a new pixel, Photoshop simply looks at the pixel next to it and copies its value. Unfortunately, the results are usually lousy unless the image is made of colored lines or shapes (like an image from Illustrator or FreeHand).

▶ **Bilinear** is slightly more complex, and produces somewhat better quality: the program sets the color or gray value of each pixel according to the pixels surrounding it. The effect is similar to averaging the neighboring pixels, but Photoshop is actually using a more sophisticated algorithm. The result is that some pictures can be upsampled pretty well with bilinear interpolation. However, we really have never found a good reason to use it; instead, we use bicubic.

▶ **Bicubic** interpolation creates the best effects, but takes the longest. Like bilinear, it looks at surrounding pixels, but the equation it uses is much more complex and calculation intensive (see Figure 3-10), producing smoother tonal gradations.

Image Mode

As we said earlier, pixel depth can tell you that pixel number 45 has a value of 165, but that doesn't mean anything until you know what image mode the bitmapped image is saved in. That 45 could represent a level of gray, or a particular color, or that might only be one value in a set of three or four other 8-bit values. Fortunately, Photoshop makes it easy to see what image mode a bitmapped image is in, as well as to convert it to a different mode, if you want.

Figure 3-10   Results of different interpolation methods

Original   *Nearest neighbor*   *Bicubic*

Ultimately, an image mode is simply a method of organizing the bits to describe a color. In a perfect world, you could say to a printer, "I'd like this box to be navy blue," and they'd know exactly what you were talking about. However, even Bruce and David can't agree on what "navy blue" looks like, much less you and your printer. So color scientists created a whole mess of ways for us to describe colors with some precision—to each other and to a computer.

Photoshop only reads and writes a handful of the many different modes they came up with. Fortunately, they're the most important of the bunch, at least for those in the world of graphic arts. Each of the following image modes appears on Photoshop's Mode menu. Note that what mode your image is in determines the file formats you can save in. For instance, you cannot save as PICT if the file is in CMYK mode. We'll talk more about this in Chapter 17, *Storing Images*.

Bitmap

David really wishes that Adobe had picked a different word for this image mode. All images in Photoshop are *bitmapped*, but only "flat" black-and-white images, in which each pixel is defined using one bit of data (a zero or a one), are *bitmaps*. Perhaps "B&W" would have been more user-friendly to those of us who think that "rasters" have something to do with reggae.

One-bit pictures have a particular difference when it comes to PostScript printing: the white areas throughout the image can appear transparent, showing through to whatever the image is printing over. Ordinarily, images are opaque, except for the occasional white silhouetted background (see "Silhouettes" in Chapter 14, *Essential Image Techniques*).

There's one other major difference between the other image modes and Bitmap mode: you're much more limited in the sorts of image editing you can do. For instance, you can't use any filters, and because there's no such thing as anti-aliasing in 1-bit images, you can't use tools that require this, such as the Smudge tool, the Blur tool, or the Magic Wand.

Bilevel bitmaps are the most generic of images, so you can save them in almost any file format (though there are some transparency weirdnesses; see "Drop Shadows" in Chapter 14, *Essential Image Techniques*).

Grayscale

Although you can spec grayscale images with various numbers of bits per pixel in other programs, grayscale files in Photoshop are always either 8- or 16-bit images: anything less than 8-bit gets converted to 8-bit, anything more than 8-bit gets converted to 16-bit. Eight-bit is by far the more common, although an increasing number of scanners allow you to bring more than eight bits into Photoshop.

With 8-bit grayscale, each pixel has a value from 0 (black) to 255 (white), so there are a maximum of 256 levels of gray possible. With 16-bit grayscale, each pixel has a value from 0 (black) to 65,535 (white), for a theoretical maximum of 65,536 possible gray shades.

However, in practice, few scanners can actually deliver all those gray shades, so 16-bit files usually have loads of redundancy. Also, Photoshop's support for them is limited to making global adjustments using the Levels and Curves commands. You can't even make a selection. Nevertheless, with some difficult images, it's worthwhile bringing the high-bit data into Photoshop.

Eight-bit grayscale images are also pretty generic, so you can save them in almost any format this side of MacPaint. If you want to save 16-bit grayscale images, your choices are limited to Photoshop format and TIFF.

Duotone

When you print a grayscale image on a printing press, those 256 levels of gray often get reduced to 100 or so because of the limitations of the printing press. You can counter this flattening effect considerably—increasing the tonal range of the printed image—by printing the image with more than one color of ink. This is called printing a *duotone* (for two inks), a *tritone* (for three inks), or a *quadtone* (for four).

The key is that the extra colors aren't typically used to simulate colors in the image; rather, they're used to enhance the underlying grayscale image. Those expensive Ansel Adams books on your coffee table were very likely printed using three or four (or even five or six) *different* black and gray inks.

Duotones also allow you to exploit the presence of a spot color in a two-color job. However, you have to take some care in matching the spot color to the subject in a duotone: duotones of people generally look ghastly if the second color is a green shade.

Photoshop has a special image mode for duotones, tritones, and quadtones, and even though the file may appear to be in color, each pixel is still saved using only eight bits of information. The trick is that Photoshop saves the 8-bit grayscale image along with a set of contrast curves for each ink.

Creating a good duotone is an art as much as a science. We'll discuss it in some detail in Chapter 9, *Duotones*. Note that if you want to place duotone images in a page-layout application for spot-color separation, you have to save the file in EPS format, the only non-native format that Photoshop supports for duotone-mode images.

Indexed Color

As we said, each pixel in a grayscale image is defined with eight bits of information, so the file can contain up to 256 different pixel values. But each of those values, from 1 to 256, doesn't have to be a level of gray. The Indexed Color image mode is a method for producing 8-bit, 256-color files. Indexed-color bitmaps use a table of 256 colors, chosen from the full 24-bit palette. A given pixel's color is defined by reference to the table: "This pixel is color number 123, this pixel is color number 81," and so on.

While indexed color can save disk space (it only requires eight bits per sample point, rather than the full 24 in RGB—see below), it only gives you 256 different colors. That's not a lot of colors, when you compare it to the 16.7 million different colors you can get in RGB mode. However, because many computer screens only display in 8-bit mode, indexed-color images are perfect for multimedia or screen presentation applications.

There are also a few (severe) limitations with Indexed Color mode. First, you can't use any filters or tools that require anti-aliasing (such as the Smudge tool or the Dodge/Burn tool) because Photoshop can't anti-alias in this mode. Therefore, you should always do your image editing in RGB mode and then convert to Indexed Color mode as a last step.

Another problem with indexed color stems from a problem with the color lookup tables. If the table changes when you move the picture from one program to another, then all the colors in the image change (see Color Plate 3 on page 125). Pixel number 123 might still have a value of 81, but that "color number 81" may have changed from red to blue in the process.

Lastly, note that you can't separate indexed-color images into CMYK values using a program such as QuarkXPress or Adobe PageMaker. If you're printing these images to paper, you might consider converting them to RGB or CMYK while still in Photoshop. However, you won't improve the image any in the process—you're still only getting 256 colors.

You can save indexed-color images in Photoshop, CompuServe GIF, PICT, Amiga IFF, or BMP formats (see "Reasonable Niche File Formats" in Chapter 17, *Storing Images*).

RGB

Every color computer monitor and television in the world displays color using the RGB image mode, in which every color is produced with varying amounts of red, green, and blue light. (These colors are called *additive primaries* because the more red, green, or blue light you add, the closer to white you get.) In Photoshop, files saved in the RGB mode typically use a set of three 8-bit grayscale files, so we say that RGB files are "24-bit" files.

These files can include up to approximately 16 million colors—more than enough to qualify as photographic quality. This is the mode in which we prefer to work when editing color images. Also, most scanners save images in RGB format. The exception is high-end drum scanners; these usually include "color computers" that automatically convert files to CMYK mode (see below) as they're scanned.

If you're outputting your files to a film recorder—to 35 mm or 4-by-5 film, for instance—you should always save your files in RGB mode (see Chapter 18, *Output Methods*).

Tip: To RGB or to CMYK. A great philosophical debate rages on whether it's better to work in RGB or in CMYK. As with most burning philosophical questions, there's no easy answer to this one, but that doesn't deter us from supplying one anyway. If you get CMYK scans from a drum scanner, work in CMYK. In all other cases, we recommend staying in RGB for as long as possible. We discuss this question in much more detail in Chapter 7, *Color Correction*.

You can save 24-bit RGB files in Photoshop, EPS, TIFF, PICT, Amiga IFF, BMP, JPEG, PCX, Pixar, Raw, Scitex CT, or Targa formats, but unless you have compelling reasons to do otherwise, we suggest you stick with Photoshop, TIFF, or EPS.

Photoshop also lets you work (in a limited way) with 48-bit RGB files, which contain three 16-bit channels instead of three 8-bit ones. The limitations are the same as for 16-bit grayscale images as mentioned above. Despite these limitations, we occasionally find bringing high-bit data into Photoshop worthwhile for challenging images (see "Working with a High-Bit Scan" in Chapter 7, *Color Correction*).

CMYK

Traditional full-color printing presses can only print four colors in a run: cyan, magenta, yellow, and black. Every other color in the spectrum is simulated using various combinations of those colors. When you open a file saved in the CMYK mode, Photoshop has to convert the CMYK values to RGB values on the fly, in order to display it on your computer screen. It's important to remember that when you look at the screen, you're looking at an RGB version of the data.

If you buy high-end drum scans, they'll almost certainly be CMYK files. Otherwise, to print your images on press or on many desktop color printers, you'll have to convert your RGB images to CMYK. We discuss Photoshop's tools for doing so in Chapter 5, *Color Preferences*.

You can save CMYK files in Photoshop, TIFF, EPS, JPEG, Scitex CT, and Raw formats, but the first three are by far the most common.

Lab

The problem with RGB and CMYK modes is that a given RGB or CMYK specification doesn't really describe a *color*. Rather, it's a set of instructions that a specific output device uses to produce a color. The problem is that different devices produce different colors from the same RGB or CMYK specifications. If you've ever seen a wall full of television screens at a department store, you know what we're talking about: the same image—with the same RGB values—looks different on each screen.

And if you've ever sat through a printing press run, you'll know that the 50th impression probably isn't exactly the same color as the 5,000th or the 50,000th. So, while a pixel in a scanned image may have a particular RGB or CMYK value, you can't tell what that color really *looks like*. RGB and CMYK are both *device-specific* color modes.

However, a class of *device-independent* or *perceptually based* modes has been developed over the years. All of them are based, more or less, on a color space defined by the Commission Internationale de l'Éclairage (CIE) in 1931. The Lab mode in Photoshop is one such derivative.

Lab doesn't describe a color by the components that make it up (RGB or CMYK, for instance). Instead, it describes *what a color looks like*. Device-independent color spaces are at the heart of the various color management systems now available that improve color correspondence between your screen, color printouts, and final printed output (see Chapter 16, *Color Management Systems*).

A file saved in the Lab mode describes what a color looks like under rigidly specified conditions; it's up to you (or Photoshop, or your color management software) to decide what RGB or CMYK values are needed to create that color on your chosen output device.

Photoshop uses the Lab mode as a reference when switching between CMYK and RGB modes, taking the values in your Monitor Setup, Separation Setup, and Printing Inks Setup dialog boxes into account (see Chapter 5, *Color Preferences*, for more information on this conversion). You can save Lab images in Photoshop, EPS, TIFF, or Raw formats.

Tip: L Is for Luminosity. One useful property of the Lab mode is that it stores the luminance information (the "L" channel) separately from the color information (the "A" and "B" channels). This can be handy if you want to adjust the tonal values in the image without affecting the hues. It's also useful for some sharpening tricks.

Multichannel

The last image mode that Photoshop offers is the Multichannel mode. This mode is the generic mode: like RGB or CMYK, multichannel mode has more than one 8-bit channel; however, you can set the color and name of each channel to anything you like.

This flexibility can be a blessing or a curse. Back in the days when color scanners cost a fortune, we used to scan in color on grayscale scanners by scanning the image three times through red, green, and blue acetate, then combining the three images into a single multichannel document that we then turned into RGB. Fortunately we don't have to do that anymore.

These days, many scientific and astronomical images are made in "false color"—the channels may be a combination of radar, infrared, and ultraviolet, in addition to various colors of visible light. Some of our gonzo digital photographer friends are using Multichannel mode to combine infrared and visible-spectrum photographs into composite images of surreal beauty.

However, we mostly use Multichannel mode as an intermediary step. For instance, you can use it to store extra channels for transparency masks or selections in other images. Your only options for saving multichannel images are the Photoshop and Raw formats.

Bitmaps and File Size

As we said at the beginning of this chapter, bitmapped images are rectangles with hundreds, or thousands, or hundreds of thousands of pixels. Each of those pixels has to be saved on disk. If each pixel is defined using eight bits of color information, then the file is eight times bigger than a flat bitmap. Similarly, a 24-bit file is a full three times bigger than that, and a 48-bit file is twice the size of a 24-bit one.

Big files take a long time to open, edit, print, or save. Many people who complain about how slow editing is in Photoshop are simply working with files much bigger than they need. Instead, you can save yourself the complaining and reduce your file size when you can. Here's a quick run-down of how each attribute of a bitmapped image affects file size.

Dimensions and resolution. When you increase the number of pixels in a bitmap, you increase the file's size by the square of the value. That means if you double the resolution, you quadruple the file size (2×2); triple the resolution, and your file is nine times as large (3×3). There can easily be a multimegabyte difference between a 300-ppi and a 225-ppi image.

Bit depth. Increasing bit depth increases file size by a simple multiplier. Therefore, a 24-bit image is three times as large as an 8-bit image, and 24 times as large as a 1-bit image.

Image mode. Image mode doesn't necessarily increase file size, but going from RGB (24-bit) to CMYK (32-bit) mode does because it alters bit depth.

Figuring File Size

Now that you know the factors that affect the size of bitmaps, it's a simple matter to calculate file size using the following formula.

$\text{Resolution}^2 \times \text{Width} \times \text{Height} \times \text{Bits per sample} \div 8{,}192$

For example, if you have a 4-by-5-inch, 1-bit image at 300 ppi, you know that the file size is 220K—$300^2 \times 4 \times 5 \times 1 \div 8192$. A 24-bit image of the same size would be 5,273 K (just about five megabytes). In case you were wondering, this formula works because 8,192 is the number of bits in a kilobyte.

Tip: Faster File Figuring. There's an even easier way to calculate file sizes than doing the math yourself—let the computer do it for you. Photoshop's Image Size dialog box is a very handy calculator for figuring dimensions, resolution, and file size. Simply type in the values you want, and Photoshop shows you how big the file would be (see Figure 3-11).

Billions and Billions of Bits

Would you hire a carpenter who didn't know anything about wood? Bit-mapped graphics are the wood of Photoshop; they're the material you

Figure 3-11

The Image Size
dialog box

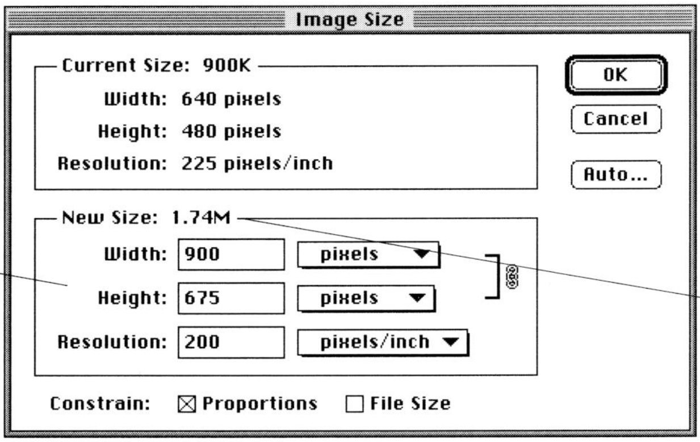

As you change values in
these fields . . .

```
╔════════════════════ Image Size ═════════════════════╗
║ ┌─ Current Size: 900K ──────────────┐  ┌──────────┐ ║
║ │    Width:  640 pixels             │  │    OK    │ ║
║ │    Height: 480 pixels             │  └──────────┘ ║
║ │    Resolution: 225 pixels/inch    │  ┌ Cancel ──┐ ║
║ └───────────────────────────────────┘  └──────────┘ ║
║                                         ┌ Auto... ──┐║
║ ┌─ New Size: 1.74M ──────────────────┐  └──────────┘ ║
║ │    Width:  [900  ]  [ pixels    ▼] │               ║
║ │    Height: [675  ]  [ pixels    ▼] │               ║
║ │    Resolution: [200] [pixels/inch ▼]│              ║
║ └─────────────────────────────────────┘              ║
║  Constrain:  ⊠ Proportions  □ File Size              ║
╚══════════════════════════════════════════════════════╝
```

. . . Photoshop
shows you the file
size that will result.

use to construct your images. Without a firm understanding of the strengths as well as the weaknesses of your material, you won't get very far with this power tool of a program.

In the next chapter, we move away from the wood, and start looking at the hammer-and-nails aspects of Photoshop: the essential tools you need to get your work done efficiently.

Color Essentials

What Makes a Color

You may have been taught back in kindergarten that the primary colors are red, yellow, and blue, and that all other colors can be made from them. Bruce still vividly recalls the day when his first-grade teacher, Mrs. Anderson, told him that he could make gray by using equal amounts of red, yellow, and blue. After looking at the lurid, weird, multicolored mess that was supposed to be a gray cat, he quite sensibly started over using a 2B pencil, and concluded that Mrs. Anderson was either color-blind or clueless. He traces his sometimes-inconvenient tendency to question authority to that day.

The details of Mrs. Anderson's lesson were certainly fallacious, but they contained an important kernel of truth—the notion that we can create all colors by combining three primary constituents. People have many different ways of thinking about, talking about, and working with color, but the notion of three ingredients that make up a color occurs again and again. Art directors may feel comfortable specifying color changes with the terms *hue*, *lightness*, and *saturation*. Those who came to color through the computer may be more at home with levels of RGB. Scientists think about color in all sorts of strange ways, including CIE Lab, HSB, or LCH. And dyed-in-the-wool prepress folks think in CMYK dot percentages.

Although Photoshop tries to accommodate all these ways of thinking about color—and it does a pretty good job—many Photoshop users find themselves locked into seeing color in only one way. This is natural and understandable—we all have one way of thinking about color that seems to make more sense than the others—but it can make life with Photoshop more difficult than it needs to be. If you understand that all the different ways of looking at color are based on the same notion—combining three ingredients—you can learn to translate among the ways Photoshop lets you work with them, and choose the right one for the task at hand.

"Wait a minute," you say. "CMYK has four constituents, not three!" You question authority too, when that authority doesn't make sense. Well, in our role as temporary authority figures, we'll do what authority figures often do when asked hard questions: we ask you to trust us. Set this issue aside for the moment. We promise we'll deal with it later.

In this chapter, we take a hard look at some fundamental color relationships and how Photoshop presents them. This stuff might seem a little theoretical at times, but we urge you to slog through it; it's essential for our later discussions about tonal and color correction.

Primary Colors

The concept of *primary* colors is at the heart of much of the color work we do on computers. When we work with primary colors, we're talking about three colors that we can combine to make all the other colors. We can define colors by specifying varying proportions of primary colors, and we can color-correct images by adjusting the relationship of the primary colors. Ignoring for the moment which specific colors constitute the primaries, there are two fundamental principles of primary colors.

▶   They are the irreducible components of color.

▶   The primary colors, combined in varying proportions, can produce an entire spectrum of color.

The *secondary* colors, by the way, are produced by combining two primary colors and excluding the third. But we don't much care about that.

Additive and Subtractive Color

Before becoming preoccupied with the behavior of spherical objects like apples, billiard balls, and planets, Sir Isaac Newton performed some experiments with light and prisms. He found that he could break white light down into red, green, and blue components, a fairly trivial phenomenon that had been known for centuries. His breakthrough was the discovery that he could *reconstitute* white light by recombining those red, green, and blue components. Red, green, and blue—the primary colors of light—are known as the *additive primary* colors because as you add color, the result becomes more white (the absence of colored light is black; see Figure 4-1). This is how computer monitors and televisions produce color.

But color on the printed page works differently. Unlike a television, the page doesn't emit light; it just reflects whatever light hits it. To produce color images in print, we don't work with the light directly. Instead, we use pigments (like ink, dye, toner, or wax) that *absorb* some colors of light and reflect others.

The primary colors of pigments are cyan, yellow, and magenta. We call these the *subtractive primary* colors because as you add pigments to a white page, they subtract (absorb) more light, and the reflected color becomes darker. (We sometimes find it easier to remember: you *add* additive colors to get white, and you *subtract* subtractive colors to get white.) Cyan absorbs all the red light, magenta absorbs all the green light, and yellow absorbs all the blue light. If we add the maximum intensities of cyan, magenta, and yellow, we get black—in theory (see Figure 4-1).

Mrs. Anderson had the right idea about primary colors; she just picked the wrong ones. No matter how hard you try, you'll never be able to create cyan using red, yellow, and blue crayons.

An Imperfect World

A little while ago, we asked you to trust us on the subject of CMYK. Well, we just told you that combining cyan, magenta, and yellow would, *in theory,* produce black. In practice, however, it produces a muddy brown mess. Why? In the words of our friend and colleague Bob Schaffel, "God made RGB . . . man made CMYK." To that we add: "Who do you trust more?"

Imperfect pigments. If we had perfect CMY pigments, we wouldn't have to add black (K) as a fourth color. But despite our best efforts, our cyan pigments always contain a little red, our magentas always contain a little green, and our yellows always contain a trace of blue. So when we print in color, we add black to help with the reproduction of dark colors. Plus, by adding black, we can reduce the total amount of ink needed to create dark areas, which not only saves money but solves some . . . uh . . . *sticky* printing problems. See Chapter 5, *Color Preferences*, for more on this.

Imperfect conversions. If we only had to deal with CMY, life would be a lot simpler. However, a large part of the problem of reproducing color images in print is that scanners—since they deal with light—see color in RGB, and we have to translate those values into CMYK to print them. Unfortunately, this conversion is a thorny one (see "How the Color Preferences Interact" in Chapter 5, *Color Preferences*, for more on this subject).

The Color Wheel

Before moving on to weightier matters such as gravity, calculus, and his impending thirtieth birthday, Sir Isaac Newton provided the world of color with one more key concept: if we take the colors of the spectrum and arrange them around the circumference of a wheel, the relationships among primaries become much clearer (see Figure 4-2).

The important thing to notice about this color wheel is that the additive and subtractive primary colors are opposite each other, equidistant around the wheel. These relationships are key to understanding how color works. For instance, cyan sits opposite to red on the color wheel because it is, in fact, the opposite of red: cyan pigments appear cyan because they absorb red light and reflect blue and green. Cyan is, in short, the absence of red.

Colors that lie directly opposite each other on the wheel are known as *complementary* colors.

Figuring Saturation and Brightness

So far, we've talked about color in terms of three primary colors. But there are other ways of specifying color in terms of three ingredients. The most familiar one describes color in terms of hue (the property we refer to when we talk about "red" or "orange"), saturation (the "purity" of the color), and brightness.

Newton's basic two-dimensional color wheel lets us see the relationships between different hues, but to describe colors more fully, we need a more complex, three-dimensional model. We can find one of these in the Apple Color Picker (see Figure 4-3).

Figure 4-1
Additive and
subtractive primaries

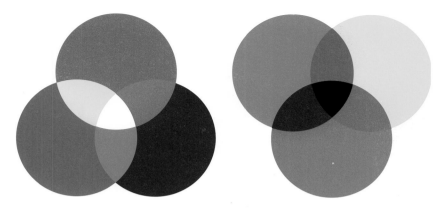

Figure 4-1
Additive and
subtractive primaries

In the Apple Color Picker, we can see the hues are arranged around the edge of the wheel, and colors become progressively more "pastel" as we move into the center—the farther in you go, the less saturated or "pure" the color is. Beside the wheel, we have a slider that makes the color lighter or darker. The Color Picker is a graphical representation of the HSB (hue, saturation, and brightness) color model.

Tristimulus Models and Color Spaces

Ignoring the inconvenience of CMYK, all the ways we've talked about of specifying and thinking about color involve three primary ingredients. Color scientists call these *tristimulus* models. (A *color* model is simply a way of thinking about color and representing it numerically: a tristimulus model represents colors by using three numbers.) If you go deep into the physiology of color, you'll find that our perceptual systems are actually wired in terms of three different responses to light that go together to produce the sensation of color. So the tristimulus approach is more

Figure 4-2
The color wheel

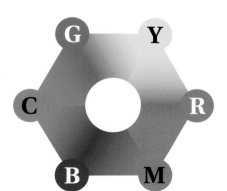

Emitted and reflected (additive and subtractive) colors are complementary to one another. Red is complementary to cyan, green to magenta, and blue to yellow.

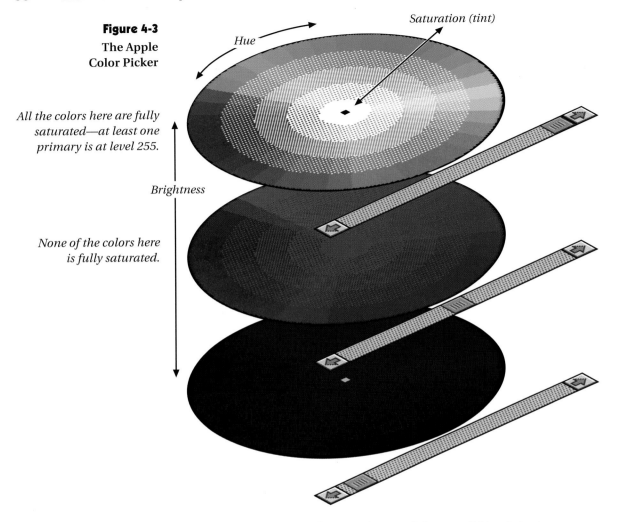

Figure 4-3
The Apple
Color Picker

Hue

Saturation (tint)

All the colors here are fully saturated—at least one primary is at level 255.

Brightness

None of the colors here is fully saturated.

than just a mathematical convenience—it has a solid basis in the way our nervous systems work.

But tristimulus models have another useful property. Because they specify everything in terms of three ingredients, we can (with very little effort) view them as three-dimensional objects with X, Y, and Z axes. Each color has a location in this three-dimensional object, specified by the three values. These three-dimensional models are called *color spaces*, a term that gets thrown around a great deal in the world of color.

We like to think of the HSB color space as a giant cylinder; the brightness slider in the Apple Color Picker determines which "slice" of the cylinder we're looking at. But, like any metaphor, there's a good side and a bad side to looking at color this way.

Color Relationships at a Glance

It's worth spending however long it takes to understand the color relationships we're discussing in this chapter. We all have a favorite color space, but if you can learn to view color in more than one way—understanding how to achieve the same results by manipulating CMY, RGB, and HSB—you'll find the world of color correction much less alien, and you'll be much more able to select the right tool for the job.

We suggest memorizing these fundamentals.

▶ 100% cyan = 0 red

▶ 100% magenta = 0 green

▶ 100% yellow = 0 blue

▶ Increasing RGB values corresponds exactly to reducing CMY values, and vice versa.

▶ Reducing saturation (making something more "gray") means introducing the complementary color; to desaturate red, for example, we add cyan.

▶ The complement of a primary color is produced by combining equal amounts of the other two primary colors.

▶ Lightening or darkening a saturated color desaturates that color.

▶ Changing the hue of a color often changes lightness as well.

▶ Saturation changes can cause hue changes.

Saturated Primaries—CMY versus RGB

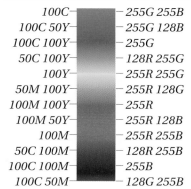

100C	255G 255B
100C 50Y	255G 128B
100C 100Y	255G
50C 100Y	128R 255G
100Y	255R 255G
50M 100Y	255R 128G
100M 100Y	255R
100M 50Y	255R 128B
100M	255R 255B
50C 100M	128R 255B
100C 100M	255B
100C 50M	128G 255B

The colors at left are fully saturated—each contains 100 percent of one or two primaries. The additive and subtractive primaries have an inverse relationship.

Desaturating Saturated Colors

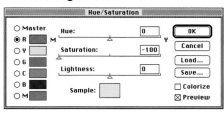

Desaturating the reds removes red and adds other primaries to the red areas. Adding a third primary "pollutes" the saturated color, causing it to go gray. It may or may not affect lightness.

255R 255G
64R 128G 192B
128R 128G 128B
64R 192G 128B
255R 255B

Lightness and Saturation

Lightening or darkening a saturated color (here, +50 and -50) desaturates it; either it pulls the primaries back from 100 percent, or it pollutes them with a third primary, or both. Also note the hue shift in the darkened version.

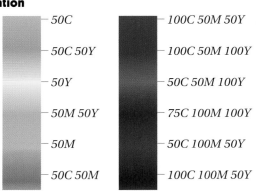

50C	100C 50M 50Y
50C 50Y	100C 50M 100Y
50Y	50C 50M 100Y
50M 50Y	75C 100M 100Y
50M	50C 100M 50Y
50C 50M	100C 100M 50Y

Figure 4-4 Device-dependent color and color gamuts

Since this figure is printed with process inks on paper, it can only simulate the results of sending the same RGB or CMYK values to various devices. It depicts relative appearances, not actual results. Likewise, the color wheel just represents the gamuts of different devices, rather than actually showing those gamuts. See also Figure 7-4 on page 199, and Figure 16-1 on page 460.

Screen display

Dye-sublimation printer

Process inks, coated stock

Process inks, newsprint

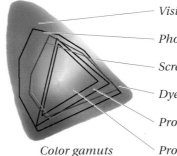

Color gamuts

Visible light
Photographic film
Screen display (red)
Dye-sub printer (blue)
Process inks, coated stock
Process inks, newsprint

▶ **The good side.** The Apple Color Picker is a great way to start learning about color, and how changing a single primary changes your colors.

▶ **The bad side.** The simple HSB model can't really describe how we *see* colors. For instance, we know that cyan appears much lighter than blue; but in our HSB cylinder, they both have the same brightness and saturation values.

Therefore, while the color picker is a step in the right direction, we have to go further to understand how to work with color.

How Colors Affect Each Other

There are a lot of times in Photoshop when we find ourselves working with one color space, but thinking about the changes in terms of another.

As you'll see in Chapter 7, *Color Correction*, for instance, we generally recommend that you use curves to adjust RGB values, but base your changes on the resulting CMYK percentages as displayed in the Info palette. So it can speed up your work a lot to take some time and figure out how color spaces interact—what happens in one space when you work in another.

Here are some ways to think about RGB, CMY, and HSB colors, and how they relate to each other.

Tone. One of the least understood—yet most important—effects of adding colors together is that adding or removing primaries not only affects hue and saturation; it also affects tone. When you increase any RGB component to change the hue—adding light—the color gets lighter. The reverse is true with CMY because you're adding ink, and hence making the color darker.

Hue. Every color, except for the primaries, contains opposing primary colors. In RGB mode, red is "pure," but orange contains red alongside a good dose of green (and possibly some blue, too). In CMYK, magenta is pure, and red is not—it contains some amount of yellow in addition to magenta. So to change a color's hue, you add or subtract primary colors.

In the process, you will probably affect the color's tone—adding or removing light (or ink) so the color gets lighter or darker.

Saturation. A saturated RGB color is made up of only one or two primaries; the third primary is always zero. When you add a trace of the third color—in order to change the hue slightly, for instance—you desaturate the color.

Likewise, if you increase the saturation of a color using the Hue/Saturation dialog box (or any other), you're removing one of the primaries. If you get out to the edge, where one of the primaries is maxed out and the other two are still changing, you're going to change the hue and the tone.

There's another important consideration pertaining to saturated colors. When you saturate a color in an RGB image, you wind up with detail in only one of the three channels. One of the others is always solid white, and the other is always solid black. It's this—not just the difficulty of reproducing them—that makes saturated colors in images difficult to handle, because all the detail is being carried by only one channel.

Neutrals. A color made up of equal values of red, green, and blue is always a neutral gray (though we may have to do quite a bit of work to make it come out that way on screen or—once we've converted it to CMYK—on press). The "darkness" of the gray depends on how much red, green, and blue there is—more light makes for a lighter gray. This is important for a number of reasons, including monitor adjustments and correcting color casts.

For a quick summary of relationships among the color spaces, see the sidebar "Color Relationships at a Glance," earlier in the chapter.

Device-Independent Color

Basically, the problem with HSB, RGB, and CMY (and even CMYK) is that they don't describe how a color looks; they only describe the color's ingredients. If you've ever walked into a television store, you know what we're talking about. There are about a hundred televisions on the wall, each of them showing the same image (they're receiving the same color information), but *none* of them displays the colors in the same way.

In fact, if we send the same RGB values to ten different monitors, or the same CMYK values to ten different presses, we'll end up with ten different colors (see Figure 4-4 on page 90). We call RGB and CMYK *device dependent*, because the color we get varies from device to device.

So, Photoshop has a problem in trying to display colors properly on your monitor: it doesn't know what the colors should *look like* to you. It doesn't know what those RGB or CMYK values really mean.

Plus, the program has to take all the little quirks of human vision into account. For instance, our eyes are more sensitive to some colors and brightness levels than to others, and we're more sensitive to small changes in bright colors than we are to small changes in dark ones (if you've had trouble teasing all the subtle shadow details out of your scanned images, this is one reason why). RGB and CMYK don't give Photoshop the information it needs to know what color is actually being described.

Lab Color

Fortunately, there's CIE Lab, which appears on the Mode menu simply as Lab. Lab is designed to describe what colors *look like*, regardless of the device they're displayed on, so we call it *device independent*.

Whereas in HSB the hues are represented as lying around a wheel, Lab color uses a more accurate but significantly less intuitive arrangement. In Lab, the third axis (which lies perpendicular to the page and is roughly equivalent to brightness in HSB) is the luminance axis—it represents how bright the color appears to the human eye. But unlike brightness in HSB, it takes into account the fact that we see green as brighter than blue.

Whole books have been written on Lab color (we've even read some of them), and while they may be of interest to color scientists, they're unlikely to help you get great-looking images on a deadline. For now, there are really only three things you need to know about Lab color.

▶ While HSB, HSL, and LCH are based on the way we think about color, and RGB and CMYK are based on the ways devices such as monitors and printers produce color, Lab is based on the way humans actually *see* color. A Lab specification actually describes the color that most people will see when they look at an object under specified lighting conditions.

▶ Photoshop thinks in Lab when it does mode changes. For instance, when you switch from RGB mode to CMYK mode, Photoshop uses Lab to decide what *color* is being specified by each device-dependent RGB value, then comes up with the right device-dependent CMYK equivalent. We'll see why this is so important in the next chapter, *Color Preferences*.

▶ Finally, you shouldn't feel dumb if you find it hard to get your head around Lab color. It *is* difficult to visualize, because it's an abstract mathematical construct—it isn't based on amounts of things we can understand readily, like RGB or HSB. It uses amounts of three primaries to specify colors, but those primaries don't correspond to anything we can actually experience.

Working with Colors

When you work with Photoshop, it lets you view and adjust your colors in all sorts of different ways. It's difficult to adjust saturation in an image, for example, by manipulating RGB or CMYK values directly, so Photoshop provides tools that let you apply changes in hue, saturation, and brightness to the underlying RGB or CMYK data. Likewise, if you have an RGB image but you plan to print it in CMYK, you can use Photoshop's Info palette to keep track of what's happening to the CMYK values you'll eventually get when you do the mode change from RGB to CMYK.

We do face two fairly large problems, however. The first is that every time we do a mode change, we lose some image information, because our images only have 256 shades of each color, and as we convert from one color space to another, some of these get lost due to rounding errors. Photoshop lets us work around this by providing information about what we'll get after we've done the color-space conversion, without our actually having to do so until we've perfected our images. We discuss this in much more detail in Chapter 7, *Color Correction.*

The second problem is that the color spaces in which most of our images are stored, RGB and CMYK, are device dependent—the color we'll get varies depending on the device we send it to. Worse, each device has a range of colors it can reproduce—called the *color gamut*—and some devices have a much wider gamut than others (see Figure 4-4 on page 90). For example, color film can record a wider range of colors than a color monitor can display, and the monitor displays a wider range of colors than we can reproduce with ink on paper; so no matter what we do, some of the colors captured on film simply can't be reproduced in print.

Fortunately, Photoshop has tools that let us remove some (if not all) of the variability from our RGB and CMYK color definitions, and it lets us specify the gamut of our monitor and our CMYK output devices. The next chapter, *Color Preferences,* is devoted to explaining what those tools are, how they work, and how to use them.

5 Color Preferences
Configuring Photoshop's Color Engine

In the last chapter, we broke the sad news that RGB and CMYK are very ambiguous ways of specifying color, since the actual color you get will vary from device to device. In this chapter, we'll look at the tools Photoshop gives you to try to keep your color consistent, and to make what you see on the screen at least resemble, if not actually match, what you get in your printed output.

Even if you know that you're never going to go near print—that all your output will be to an RGB device such as a film recorder or the computer screen—you should still read the sections in this chapter that deal with setting up your monitor, because it's your primary window on your digital images. If you plan to print your images on anything from a lowly desktop ink-jet printer to a modern state-of-the-art press, the information in this chapter is essential.

Unless you're working with a traditional drum scanner that produces CMYK files, preparing your images for print will involve converting them from RGB to CMYK. When you make that conversion, you want to preserve the colors you see on the monitor and/or in the original image. This brings you face to face with two sticky problems. The first, as we explained in Chapter 4, *Color Essentials*, is that RGB and CMYK values don't have specific color meanings. The second is that reproducing what you see in a photograph or on the screen is basically impossible with four-color printing. Film can capture a wider range of color than the monitor can display, and the monitor in turn displays a wider range of colors than ink on paper can reproduce.

But even if you can't reproduce your original images exactly, you can get close. How close you get depends on many different factors, not the least being how you set up the conversion in Photoshop. But it also depends on controlling all the variables in the printing process as closely as possible.

Photoshop does not and cannot know anything about what happens to an image once you press the Print button, other than what you tell it. If you want to produce good color, you have to give Photoshop accurate information about your printing conditions, and you have to ride herd on the printing process to make sure that information continues to be accurate.

Photoshop's Color Preferences

It seems a little odd to devote an entire chapter to three dialog boxes, but the Preferences settings that deal with color—Monitor Setup, Printing Inks Setup, and Separation Setup—are so important that it's well worth spending the time learning what they do and how they do it. If you want to get consistent, reliable results from Photoshop, you need to bite the bullet and conquer them—they affect almost everything you do with tone and color in Photoshop, sometimes in ways that we find distinctly nonobvious.

What do these dialog boxes do? They let you tell Photoshop *what colors you're talking about* when you feed it a set of RGB or CMYK values. You've probably figured out that Printing Inks Setup and Separation Setup control the way Photoshop generates CMYK color separations. And you may have an inkling that Monitor Setup has something to do with calibration. But the real story is a bit more complicated.

Part of the confusion stems from the names. Monitor Setup doesn't really do anything to your monitor, and Printing Inks Setup doesn't do anything to your printing inks. How could it, after all? Ink is ink, and making selections in a dialog box isn't going to change the nature of what's in the can.

So what *do* these things do? The short answer is that they define the RGB and CMYK color spaces that Photoshop uses. But like many short answers, that one probably isn't very helpful. The long answer is a bit more complex, but we'll try to keep it as jargon-free as possible.

Photoshop's Internal Color Management

Photoshop has a limited but quite flexible color management system (CMS) at its core. (For more on CMSes, see Chapter 16, *Color Management Systems.*) When you work in color in Photoshop, it tries to keep the color consistent across different color spaces, and to represent that color consistently on your screen. As we explained in Chapter 4, *Color Essentials,* this is not a trivial undertaking, so it isn't surprising that it often fails.

As long as you're working in RGB on a monitor (which is also RGB), Photoshop doesn't need to know what colors your RGB or CMYK values mean—it just cheerfully juggles zeros and ones as requested. But when you want to switch from one color space to another, or view a CMYK image on your RGB screen, Photoshop has to make some assumptions about the actual colors represented by those values so it can correctly translate the colors.

Photoshop uses CIE Lab as a yardstick with which to measure device-dependent color specifications. It uses the information you provide in Monitor Setup, Printing Inks Setup, and Separation Setup to determine what color in the Lab space is represented by your RGB or CMYK values.

We've told you that the actual colors you get from RGB or CMYK values depend on the device to which you send them. Monitor Setup, Printing Inks Setup, and Separation Setup are the mechanisms that let you specify how your monitor and your printing process behave; they answer the question, "What colors do you mean by these RGB or CMYK values?" This has several implications—some obvious, and some less so.

How the Color Preferences Interact

Let's look at how these preferences are wired together. They affect each other in subtle ways; getting a handle on how each affects the other is important if you want to produce predictable results, and get your screen to match your output.

Monitor Setup. Monitor Setup is the most far-reaching of the color prefs. Here's the part that seems counterintuitive: it affects the way Photoshop displays everything *except* RGB (and in some cases, grayscale) files. What it attempts to do is to tell Photoshop what color you see on the screen when the monitor receives a given set of RGB values. Photoshop uses this information in two ways.

▶ When you convert RGB to CMYK or Lab, Photoshop uses Monitor Setup to determine what colors you want to reproduce in the new color space.

▶ When you display a CMYK or Lab file, Photoshop has to convert these values to RGB to drive the monitor, so it uses Monitor Setup to determine the proper RGB values to reproduce the image's colors on your screen.

Let's say you convert an RGB file to CMYK, then change the Monitor Setup, open the same RGB file, and convert it to CMYK once more. What you see on screen when you look at the RGB file doesn't change a lick. But you *do* get different CMYK data the second time, because Photoshop interprets the RGB values differently based on the changes in Monitor Setup. The two CMYK files look different on the screen and print differently, because you've redefined the color meaning of the RGB values in the original file, and Photoshop tries to reproduce the color faithfully in each case.

Similarly, if you open a CMYK or Lab file, then change Monitor Setup, the screen display changes. You haven't done anything to the image data, and it still prints the same, but Photoshop thinks you've changed your monitor; so it calculates new RGB values that it thinks will faithfully represent the colors in the file on your "new" monitor.

Monitor Setup also affects the display of grayscale images if you turn on Use Dot Gain for Grayscale Images in Printing Inks Setup. We'll discuss why and how, later in this chapter.

To summarize, Monitor Setup can affect both what you see on the screen, and what you get in print when viewing Lab, CMYK, or (when Use Dot Gain for Grayscale Images is turned on in Printing Inks Setup) grayscale images. Plus, it affects what you get when you convert an image from RGB to any other color mode, including Grayscale.

Printing Inks Setup. Printing Inks Setup is a little simpler. In Printing Inks Setup, you're telling Photoshop what color your inks are. As you might expect, this affects the CMYK values you get when you convert RGB to CMYK (again, because Photoshop is trying to reproduce the image's color by mixing together varying amounts of those inks).

A little less obvious is that it also affects the way CMYK images display on the monitor. When you display a CMYK image, Photoshop has to first

Photoshop and Lab

Much has been written about Photoshop's use of Lab as its internal color space. Most of it is misleading. There's a fairly common belief that when you work in RGB or CMYK, Photoshop converts these values into Lab, does its calculations in Lab, then converts the results back into the color space you were using. This isn't true, and we should be glad it isn't true, for two reasons.

First, color-space conversion is time-consuming, so such an approach would be very slow—look at how long Photoshop takes to do a mode change from one color space to another. Second, color-space conversions lose about half a bit of information due to rounding errors. When you only have eight bits per color to start with, multiple color-space conversions

degrade your image more quickly than you can say "Jack Robinson."

A single mode change turns your 256 shades of each primary color into somewhere around 210 shades. If Photoshop had to convert between color spaces every time you adjusted the contrast, the hue, or the saturation, you'd quickly end up with an image that contained very few colors indeed. Unless you actually convert your image to Lab by choosing it from the Mode menu, Photoshop does all its calculations in the native color space of the document.

A more sophisticated but also incorrect view holds that Photoshop uses Lab to do color-space conversions by converting from the source color space (usually RGB) to Lab, then converting Lab

to the target color space (usually CMYK). This would make for two time-consuming, image-degrading color-space conversions.

Fortunately, the program is a bit smarter than that. When you change your Monitor, Printing Inks, or Separation Setups, Photoshop uses Lab color as a reference to determine what the RGB and CMYK values *mean*, and builds a lookup table. Then when you change modes, Photoshop uses that lookup table to convert the colors.

If you're as insanely curious and distrustful of authority as we are, you may have noticed that you get different results when you convert an RGB image to CMYK, and when you convert the same image first to Lab, then to CMYK. Now you know why.

figure out what colors the CMYK values represent, based on the settings in Printing Inks Setup (if it knows what the ink colors are, it can figure out what the image's CMYK values mean). Then it uses the settings in Monitor Setup to convert those colors to the correct RGB values.

Separation Setup. Like Printing Inks Setup, Separation Setup affects the results you get when you convert an RGB file to CMYK. However, it doesn't affect the way CMYK files display on your screen. While Printing Inks Setup tells Photoshop the color of your inks, Separation Setup simply tells Photoshop how you want to use those inks to create your colors.

The key to Separation Setup is that most RGB colors can be reproduced by many different, equally valid CMYK equivalents. By varying the proportion of the black ink and the CMY inks, you can achieve the same

Color Prefs at a Glance

Monitor Setup defines the RGB color space you're using. Printing Inks Setup defines the color of the inks on your chosen paper. Separation Setup tells Photoshop how you want to use the inks to reproduce color—how much total ink, and how much black ink in relation to cyan, magenta, and yellow. Here's how the preferences affect different kinds of images.

► When you display a grayscale file, Photoshop uses Monitor Setup to convert it to RGB for display. If Use Dot Gain for Grayscale Images is turned on, Photoshop *also* takes into account the dot gain setting in Printing Inks Setup when it converts the grayscale to RGB for display.

► When you display an RGB file, none of the preferences has any effect.

► When you display a CMYK file, Photoshop uses Printing Inks Setup to interpret the colors, and Monitor Setup to convert them to RGB for display.

► When you display a Lab file, Photoshop uses Monitor Setup to convert the colors to RGB for display.

► When you convert an RGB file to Lab, Photoshop uses Monitor Setup to interpret the RGB colors.

► When you convert an RGB file to CMYK, Photoshop uses Monitor Setup to interpret the RGB colors, and Printing Inks Setup and Separation Setup to arrive at the CMYK equivalents.

color. In theory, 45C 30M 70Y and 35C 20M 60Y 10K will give you the same color, though in practice your mileage may vary. The problem is that different combinations are appropriate for different situations (press type, paper stock, image, and so on).

Separation Setup lets you control the total amount of ink that's laid down, and lets you specify how much black is used.

Photoshop uses the information in Separation Setup only when you generate color separations by converting RGB or Lab images to CMYK.

Putting them all together. Why do we place such emphasis on understanding how the Preferences settings interact? Because it's temptingly easy to view a CMYK file that you've printed, and make your screen match the printed output by adjusting the Monitor Setup information. The trouble with this approach is that it doesn't work! While the screen display may match your printed piece, the next time you go to make separations, you'll get different results, and things won't match anymore. It's like trying to lift yourself off the ground by pulling on your shoelaces. You have to know what to tweak, and when. Given the way the three preferences interact, your strategy should be as follows.

1. Set your Monitor Setup preferences, then leave them alone.

2. Adjust the monitor to match the settings in Monitor Setup.

3. Set the Printing Inks Setup and Separation Setup preferences according to the job at hand. (Unless you always print to the same press on the same paper, you'll need different settings for different output conditions.)

Calibrating the System

The color preferences give us a way to tell Photoshop how our devices behave, so that Photoshop can do its best to make the monitor match the printed output, and vice versa. Unfortunately, Photoshop is no help at all in *telling* us how our devices behave. It doesn't know, and has no way of finding out. It simply believes whatever we tell it, like the trusting six-year-old it is.

This is where *calibration* comes in: you have to adjust the devices to make sure that the information you gave Photoshop is true. But before you even touch Photoshop, there are a few other things you need to do if you want to create a calibrated environment.

Input devices and monitors. Calibration is simply the process of bringing a device to a known state. The settings in Monitor Setup and Printing Inks Setup are like the tune-up specs for your car. Just knowing them isn't going to make your car run better—you have to actually do the tune-up to bring the car up to those specs.

Monitors vary a lot over the course of time. They're subject to both short-term variation (they change as they're warming up) and long-term variation (they wear out and get dim). If you want to use the monitor as any kind of reliable guide as to what you'll see in your final output, you need to calibrate it to make sure that the information in Monitor Setup still holds true.

Tip: If You Just Want to Go by the Numbers . . . It's quite possible to do good work with Photoshop using an uncalibrated monitor. We suspect that most Photoshop users have less-than-optimum calibrations, at best.

If you want to simply go by the numbers—reading the RGB levels and the CMYK dot percentages—you can use the Info palette to check your color, and simply ignore what you see on the monitor. Even with a calibrated monitor, you should *always* check those numbers anyway.

If you aren't concerned with the monitor appearance, you can simply set the Monitor Setup values to the aim points suggested below under "Monitor Calibration," and forget about them henceforth.

Output devices. Calibration is also necessary for output devices. Photoshop's digital data exists in an ideal state—it isn't subject to change by outside forces. But what results when that digital data hits the distinctly imperfect analog world of printing is subject to a host of variables—if you've ever seen a newspaper being printed, you know that reproducing color images by smooshing colored grease into a fast-moving roll of tree bark is an inherently variable process.

The imagesetter must be calibrated and the film chemistry controlled to ensure that a 50-percent dot in the digital data actually results in a 50-percent dot on the film. The platemaking exposure must be tightly controlled to make sure that the 50-percent dot on the film doesn't grow to a 75-percent dot on the plate. The press itself is subject to a whole host of variables that are outside the scope of this book.

If you're relying on a service bureau to produce your film, and a commercial printer to print your pages, they're responsible for taking care of their own calibration. We've found that the majority do so, and do so well. But if you've been getting inconsistent results on your print jobs, you may want to ask your service bureau how often they calibrate their imagesetter. If the answer you get doesn't make sense, it may be time to look for a new service bureau.

Creating a Consistent Environment

Three factors combine to produce the sensation we describe as color: the object, the light source that illuminates the object, and the observer. You are the observer, and your color vision is subject to subtle changes brought on by things as disparate as age, diet, mood, and how much sleep you've had. There isn't a lot you can do about those, and their effects are relatively minor, but it's good to bear them in mind because they make the phenomenon of color very subjective. The other factors that affect your color vision are, fortunately, easier to control.

Lighting. Consistent lighting is vital if you want to create a calibrated system. In the United States, color transparencies and print proofs are almost always evaluated using light with a controlled color temperature of 5,000 Kelvins (K). In Europe and Asia, 6,500 K is the standard—it's a little more blue. (Strictly speaking, the relevant standards—D50 and D65—are daylight curves that aren't absolutely identical to the black-body radiation described by the Kelvin scale, but for all practical purposes they're interchangeable.)

You need to provide a consistent lighting environment for viewing your printed output, otherwise the thing you're trying to match—the original image or the final output—will be constantly changing. You can go whole hog and install D50 lighting everywhere, bricking up any offending windows in the process, but for most of us that's impractical. You can, however, situate your monitor so that it's shielded from direct window light, turn off room lights for color-critical evaluations, and put a D50 bulb in a ten-dollar desk lamp for evaluating photographs and printed material. Bruce has one that sits beside his monitor, so he can easily compare printed samples with the screen display.

A hood to shield the monitor from stray reflections is also worthwhile— a cardboard box spray-painted matte black may not be elegant, but it's every bit as effective as more expensive solutions, and doesn't distort the color the way most antiglare shields do.

Context. Your color perception is dramatically affected by surrounding colors. Again, you can go to extremes and paint all your walls neutral gray. (Bruce wound up doing this because his office was painted pale pink when he first moved in, and he found that it was introducing a color cast into almost everything—including his dreams.)

It's easier and more important, however, to make your desktop pattern neutral. Pink-marble, green-plaid, or family-snapshot desktop patterns may seem fun and harmless, but they'll seriously interfere with your color judgment. We also recommend not wearing Hawaiian shirts when you're making critical color judgments. Designer black, you'll be happy to know, is just great.

Tip: Neutral-Gray Desktops. Pattern number 4 in System 7.5's Desktop Patterns control panel is a solid 50-percent gray, and provides a nondistracting background. But if you want to compare the desktop with the standard 18-percent reflectance gray card sold by almost every photography store in the land, set the desktop color to around 190R 190G 190B. The easiest way to do this is to copy a single pixel of that color in Photoshop and paste it into Desktop Patterns. If you're running an older version of the system, you can change the desktop colors directly through the General Controls control panel.

Once you've stabilized your environment, you can start setting up Photoshop to give you consistent color.

Monitor Setup and Calibration

The first step in calibrating your Photoshop system is to set up your monitor to match the settings in Monitor Setup (see Figure 5-1). This allows Photoshop to give you the best representation it's capable of when it's displaying Lab and CMYK images. The numbers you plug into Monitor Setup provide the information Photoshop needs to match printed CMYK output to screen colors, and to display CMYK and Lab images, but changing those numbers has no effect on the way RGB images are displayed.

Figure 5-1
Monitor Setup

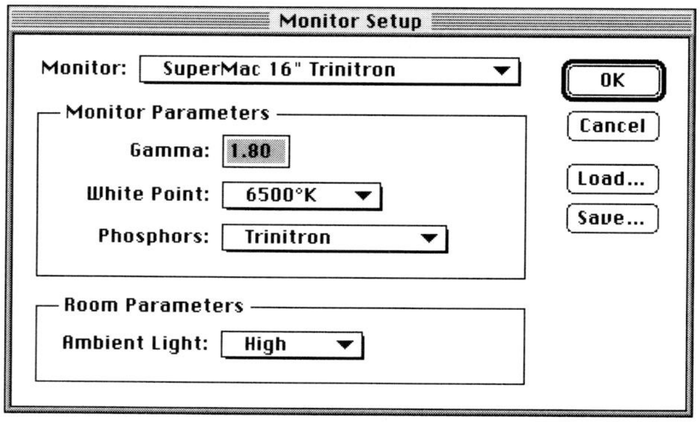

The calibration process, however, changes the on-screen appearance of all your images—RGB, CMYK, and Lab. The goal is to make the monitor actually behave the way you've told Photoshop it behaves. To do so, you need to take five steps.

1. Evaluate your monitor.

2. Choose a target gamma to match your output process.

3. Choose a target white point to match your lighting.

4. If your monitor isn't one of the types Photoshop lists, get the phosphor chromaticities from the vendor.

5. Calibrate the monitor to the settings you've chosen.

Monitor Setup Settings

First, you need to decide how you want to set the gamma settings and a white point for your monitor. All monitors have a native gamma and white point that the vendor will be quite happy to quote you. Unfortunately, what they'll quote you are the specs for a brand-new monitor with the brightness and contrast settings at factory defaults, which almost certainly won't apply to your particular monitor. In any case, those specs are irrelevant—whatever calibration method you use will override them. Instead, pick sensible aim points, then calibrate the monitor to match them.

Before doing so, however, look at the sidebar "Evaluating Your Monitor." At some point in its life, every monitor reaches a state where it can no longer be brought into a useful state of calibration—it wears out. You can still use it, but you won't be able to rely on it for judgments about tone and color. If you're forced to work with a worn-out monitor, it doesn't much matter what settings you plug into Monitor Setup, but it *is* important that, once you've decided on the settings, you leave them alone if you want to get consistent color separations. Now let's look at the individual settings in Monitor Setup.

Monitor. The names in the Monitor popup menu are just that: names. If your monitor is on the list, choose it; it simply loads some canned values into the other settings. If your monitor isn't on the list, but you know that it's similar to one that's on the list, choose that one. Otherwise, choose "Other". Monitors vary so much that canned settings aren't terribly useful, and you're going to override most of them anyway. Once you've decided on all your settings, you can save them under a new Monitor name using the Save button, and then load them again as needed using the Load button.

Gamma. The Gamma setting describes your monitor's contrast. This is something of an oversimplification; we could get derailed into long technical discussions about gamma, but they're available elsewhere and they aren't strictly germane to the task at hand. As a starting point, we recommend choosing a gamma setting of 1.8 for print and 2.2 for video and multimedia.

Under normal viewing conditions, a monitor with a gamma of 1.8 comes fairly close to representing the contrast range you can achieve with ink on coated paper. A gamma setting of 2.2 has a little more contrast, and displays a wider contrast range than you're likely to be able to reproduce in print, but it works well for multimedia and video.

Some color management systems, notably Agfa's FotoTune, recommend a linear (1.0) monitor gamma setting, presumably to match scanners—which typically do have a linear gamma response. We think this is seriously brain-dead. If you set your monitor to linear gamma, your images will appear hopelessly washed-out on screen, even if you crank the contrast knob all the way up. Besides, it's much easier to apply a gamma correction during the scan, particularly if you have a high-bit scanner, than it is to get a monitor to behave at all reasonably at linear gamma. If you're using FotoTune, edit your monitor profiles to change the gamma to 1.8, then calibrate your monitor to a gamma of 1.8.

White Point. The White Point setting describes the color your monitor displays when it displays white. It may seem odd to think of white as having a color, but if you look at a sheet of white paper under an incandescent light bulb, then look at the same sheet of paper under a cool fluorescent, you'll find that it looks slightly more red under the incandescent light.

If you're using controlled lighting to view your printed proofs, set the white point to the same color temperature as your lighting. If you don't have controlled lighting, but you do have a hardware monitor calibrator and you're planning on printing your image, set the white point to match the controlled lighting used by the people who will eventually print your job—5,000 K in the USA, 6,500 K in the rest of the world. If you have neither controlled lighting nor a hardware monitor calibrator, you can adjust the monitor to match a sheet of white paper, but you'll be guessing as to the actual color temperature. In that case, 5,000 K is probably as good a guess as any.

Phosphors. This setting tells Photoshop the color of the monitor's pure, saturated red, green, and blue. If you're dealing with a monitor that's on Photoshop's list, you can simply leave this setting alone. If not, you can either take your best guess based on the kind of tube your monitor uses, or you can ask the manufacturer for the *xy chromaticity* values for red, green, and blue for your monitor. The response should be three pairs of numbers, all between zero and one, with at least four digits after the decimal point. Choose Custom for your Phosphors setting, and plug those numbers into the Phosphors dialog box.

Some hardware calibrators will report the actual measured phosphor chromaticities. If you have one of those calibrators, choose Custom, and plug in the measured values (see Figure 5-2).

Figure 5-2
Phosphors

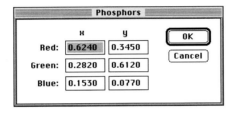

Ambient Light. This little popup menu is designed to compensate for the effect of ambient light on your monitor's screen, but it's caused us endless hours of grief trying to figure out *exactly* what it does. Eventually, Photoshop product manager John Leddy tracked down the information and was kind enough to share it with us.

The High setting does nothing, so this is the one you should choose if you're using some kind of hardware monitor calibration (keep Photoshop out of the way, and let the calibration software do its work). The other two settings, Medium and Low, apply small gamma tweaks to the Lightness channel of Photoshop's internal Lab values, darkening the screen image slightly. They also affect RGB-to-Lab and RGB-to-CMYK conversion, however (a setting of Low will make printed output come out lighter), so use them to compensate for changing room lighting at your peril. We set this option at High, and leave it alone.

For the record, the Medium setting applies a 1.07 gamma tweak to the Lightness channel; the Low setting applies a 1.15 gamma tweak. The effect that these settings have on RGB-to-CMYK conversions is considerable: using the default separation and inks settings, a 50-percent gray that translates to 51C 38M 37Y 18K with the Ambient Light setting at High will translate to 48C 35M 35Y 13K with the Ambient Light setting at Low—quite a difference. (You may get slightly different numbers, because your Monitor Setup probably isn't the same as ours, but the difference between the two sets of values will be similar.)

Monitor Calibration

Once you've entered your monitor settings, you have to calibrate the monitor to match those settings. You can either do this by eyeball, using the Gamma control panel that comes with Photoshop, or you can use a hardware monitor-calibration utility such as DayStar's (or Kodak's) Colorimeter24, Radius's (formerly SuperMac's) SuperMatch or SuperMatch Pro, LightSource's Colortron, or X-Rite's Monitor Optimizer. All these instruments do the same basic task, although the details of the implementation and the measuring methods they use vary considerably.

Eyeballs versus suction cups. Hardware calibration is much more accurate (and much easier) than using our eyeballs, which are very good at comparing colors but not at all good at measuring them. If you want your monitor to be as accurate as possible, a hardware calibrator is a worthwhile investment—but only if your monitor warrants it (see the sidebar "Evaluating Your Monitor").

If you opt for hardware calibration, don't use the Gamma control panel. All the calibration utilities work by downloading a lookup table to the video

Evaluating Your Monitor

Monitors lose brightness over time, and eventually they simply wear out. Long before the menu bar is burned into the screen, the monitor has lost so much of its brightness range that it probably can't be accurately calibrated to our suggested settings.

Calibration utilities work by selectively *reducing* the brightness of the red, green, and blue channels (making them dimmer). So when you calibrate your monitor, the first thing you'll notice is that it isn't as bright as it was in its uncalibrated state. If the monitor's not very bright to begin with, it's a problem.

Here's our simple rule of thumb. Turn the brightness and contrast controls all the way up. If the monitor is brighter at those settings than you like, it's a worthwhile candidate for hardware calibration. If it isn't as bright as you'd like, it's a candidate for replacement—it's only going to get dimmer over time, and you'll find it very difficult to bring it into a usable state of calibration.

driver, and there's only room for one, so whichever one you last used is the one that's in effect.

Tip: Ignore the Gamma Choices. We've talked to many users who have stumbled onto the special gamma options buried deep within Apple's Monitors control panel. (If you open Monitors and Option-click on the Options button, you're offered a choice of different gamma settings. The actual settings will vary, depending on which video card or built-in video you're using.) Ignore them. All they do is download a different lookup table to the same slot in the video driver. The calibration you perform with the Gamma control panel or a hardware calibrator will overwrite any gamma selections you make in Monitors.

Calibrating using the Gamma control panel. The Gamma control panel that comes with Photoshop is something of a blunt instrument, and its use involves a lot of trial and error, particularly when you first calibrate the monitor (see Figure 5-3). But it's free, and it's a lot better than nothing.

Figure 5-3

Gamma
control panel

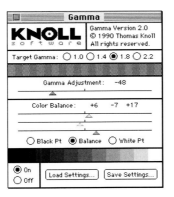

Here's our recommended procedure for calibrating with Gamma. Be warned that it's quite rigorous; but we spent many hours calibrating many different monitors using Gamma before we discovered the joys of hardware monitor calibration, and we're convinced that it's worth taking the extra effort if you want to get the best results that Gamma can provide.

1. Make sure that your monitor has warmed up—it needs to be on for at least half an hour before it's stable enough to calibrate.

2. Set the desktop pattern to a neutral gray—we use 127R 127G 127B.

Avoid using patterns on the desktop—just make all the screen pixels the same color.

3. Open an image or two in Photoshop to help you determine reasonable Brightness and Contrast settings—the Fruit and Portrait images in the Tutorial folder on the Photoshop CD are good for this purpose.

4. Turn your monitor's brightness and contrast controls all the way up. This should be uncomfortably bright (see the sidebar "Evaluating Your Monitor").

5. Open the Gamma control panel, select your target gamma from the radio buttons at the top, and click the On button at the lower left. You should see an immediate decrease in your monitor's brightness.

6. Drag the Gamma Adjustment slider until the gray swatches above it appear to be the same shade. It helps if you defocus your eyes slightly while you're looking at the swatches—that way, you see the color rather than the individual pixels.

This is where trial and error starts. If the monitor still looks too bright (based on the way it displays the images you chose in step 3 above), you'll have to back off the monitor's brightness and/or contrast controls, drag the Gamma Adjustment slider, then go through the iterative process of setting white and black point (described below).

When you're aiming for a gamma of 1.8, leave the brightness knob alone and just bring down the contrast. Most monitors have a native gamma of around 2.2–2.4, which results in quite a bit more contrast than you're trying to achieve; reducing the contrast has the effect of reducing the gamma. Only adjust the brightness if reducing the contrast makes your reference image look much too flat.

Once the brightness, contrast, and gamma adjustments are roughly in balance, you can start working on the white point. You set the white point by comparing the appearance of a piece of white paper to the appearance of white on the monitor. This works best when you have a controlled lighting setup for viewing printed material (see "Creating a Consistent Environment," earlier in this chapter).

1. Adjust the White Point sliders for red, green, and blue until the monitor white appears the same hue as the paper. Usually you'll need to back off the blue quite a bit, and possibly the green as well.

2. Adjust the Balance sliders for red, green, and blue to eliminate color casts that appear in the gray swatches at the bottom of the Gamma control panel. You may find it useful to use a printed reference such as the Kodak 18-percent gray card.

3. If necessary, adjust the Black Point sliders for red, green, and blue to eliminate color casts at the shadow end of the gray swatches.

Now it's time for some more trial and error. You may have noticed that the White Point, Balance, and Black Point adjustments all affect each other. They also throw the Gamma Adjustment setting out of whack. We wish this weren't the case, because it makes doing a good job of calibration with the Gamma control panel a lot of work.

1. If the monitor now appears too dim and you turned the contrast down in an earlier step, turn the contrast back up until the monitor appearance is acceptable, then readjust the gamma slider.

2. Once you've done this, put pieces of sticky tape over both the contrast and brightness controls on the monitor. If they get moved, you'll have undone all the work you've done so far, and you'll have to go back to square one.

3. If necessary, readjust the white point, balance, and black point once more, but make very small moves, and only do so if you feel that you're improving the situation. Readjust the Gamma setting once more.

5. *Save your settings!*

You've calibrated the monitor. The Gamma setting you entered in Monitor Setup should be pretty accurate. If you used controlled lighting to view the piece of paper when you set the white point of the monitor, the White Point setting in Monitor Setup should also be pretty accurate.

If you don't have controlled lighting, you're guessing anyway. At least try to keep the lighting consistent—the eye is very adaptable when it comes to changing white points, and your monitor will give a reasonable approximation of how your printed material will look under the controlled lighting your service bureau and printer will almost certainly use.

Hardware calibration. Compared to using Gamma, using any of the hardware monitor calibrators is a walk in the park. They're generally pretty self-explanatory. Nevertheless, we've come up with a few pointers on a couple of specific products. If they don't apply to you, you can skip ahead.

Tip: DayStar Colorimeter24. DayStar's (or Kodak's) Colorimeter24 lets you calibrate your monitor to a given gamma and white point (the settings you entered in the Monitor Setup dialog box). It also comes with canned settings for a variety of popular monitors.

When you use the Colorimeter24 to calibrate your monitor, *don't* choose the monitor type that corresponds to your monitor—these are intended for use with the ColorSet Calibration software as a visual calibrator, without the hardware. Instead, choose one of the generic profiles for your tube type and intended white point setting—Sony P22 if your monitor uses a Trinitron tube, and Hitachi EBU if it doesn't.

Tip: SuperMatch Pro. The SuperMatch Pro calibrator is also easy to use, but unlike DayStar's Colorimeter24, it doesn't give you much help in setting your monitor's analog controls—it just tells you to set the brightness so that on-screen black appears black, and to set the contrast so that it's "pleasing."

We've found that the SuperMatch calibrator is quite sensitive to ambient light. You'll get better results calibrating the monitor in a dark room (that doesn't mean you are then condemned to *using* it only in a dark room). Failing that, try to shield the monitor from ambient light—a cardboard hood spray-painted matte black works very well.

When you use the SuperMatch Pro application to calibrate your monitor, the first two steps direct you to adjust the brightness and contrast controls. The dialog box displays two vertical scales, one marked Black Level, the other marked Intensity. In the first step, if you can't get the Black Level to read less than 5 with the brightness turned all the way up, and you've shielded the calibrator from ambient light, turn the brightness down. If the Black Level reading goes down when you shield the calibrator, ambient light is affecting the calibration. Aim for a Black Level of 5 or less.

In the second step, turn the contrast down until the Intensity indicator changes from green to red, then turn it back up just enough to make the indicator change back to green. This should provide good settings for the monitor's analog brightness and contrast controls.

Apply tape.

When to Recalibrate

We recommend checking your monitor calibration quickly every other day or so—it shouldn't need anything besides a minor Gamma Adjustment tweak. There are some other situations when you might want to change your calibration or Monitor Setup settings, however.

Moving the monitor. If you move the monitor, even to the other side of your desk, you'll almost certainly need to recalibrate it thoroughly. Otherwise, it should be fairly stable once it's warmed up.

Calibrating for different paper stocks. The Photoshop manual says that you can create different Gamma control panel White Point settings for different paper stocks. Frankly, given the difficulty of getting good calibration with Gamma, we've never found this particularly worthwhile— we believe that the white point should match your lighting. Nevertheless, if you're printing on an unusually blue-white or an unusually yellow-white paper stock, you might want to create a custom Gamma setting.

What you *do not* want to do is to change the White Point in Monitor Setup. You should only change your Monitor Setup settings if you actually change monitors, or if you decide for some reason to change the target gamma of your monitor (so you change the Target Gamma setting, and also calibrate the monitor to that setting). You might, for example, consider changing the gamma from 1.8 to 2.2 if you've been working primarily with print and you switch to a multimedia project.

Output Setup and Calibration

Now that you've calibrated your monitor, and you've defined the RGB color space you're using through Monitor Setup, you can turn your attention to the output end of the system. As we said earlier, Printing Inks Setup and Separation Setup work together to define the parameters Photoshop will use when you convert images to CMYK.

Photoshop also uses Printing Inks Setup to control the way CMYK images are displayed on the screen, because it has to generate an RGB representation of the image for the monitor. So even if you get CMYK scans from a drum scanner and never go near RGB, you still need to pay some attention to Printing Inks Setup if you want to get reasonably accurate on-screen representations of CMYK images.

While your monitor is (or should be) unchanging and constant, your printing conditions will likely vary, so unlike Monitor Setup, which you generally want to set and forget, you'll almost certainly need several different settings for Printing Inks Setup and Separation Setup, according to the job—paper stock, inks, press, and so on.

Printing Inks Setup

Printing Inks Setup lets you define the characteristics of the ink and paper you'll be using (see Figure 5-4). Photoshop uses this information to convert colors from other color spaces to CMYK, and vice versa.

Figure 5-4

Printing
Inks Setup

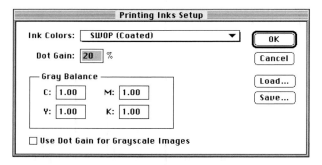

Ink Colors

The Ink Colors setting tells Photoshop about the color of the inks you'll be using. In most situations, you'll want to use one of Photoshop's built-in ink sets such as SWOP, Eurostandard, or Toyo, each of which has ink definitions for coated, uncoated, and newsprint stock. Talk to your commercial printer about which ink definitions to use. SWOP is the prevalent standard in the USA, but some printers prefer to work with other inks.

The Custom setting at the top of the popup menu allows you to define your own colorants (see Figure 5-5); it's loaded with the values from your currently selected Ink Colors option. This is mostly useful if you're working with nonstandard inks, or if you're trying to get good color from a desktop color printer. (Photoshop contains canned Printing Inks Setups for seven different composite color printers. If you're lucky enough to own one of them, by all means try the canned settings as a starting point for proofing to those devices. If your experience matches ours, you'll find they leave a lot to be desired.)

There are two ways of using this feature, one much more exact (and more exacting) than the other.

Photoshop's Separation Engine

You don't have to use Photoshop to create your color separations, even if you do everything else to the image in Photoshop. You can use any of a number of third-party color management systems, or you can use a dedicated separation application such as PixelCraft's Color Access, both of which we do quite often. For examples of output using these programs, see Figure 7-4 on page 199.

In general, it's possible to create great color separations using Photoshop, but Photoshop's separation engine has one near-fatal flaw that often drives us to an alternative method: its handling of out-of-gamut colors.

When Photoshop finds colors in an RGB or Lab image that it can't reproduce in CMYK using the specified ink and separation settings, it simply converts them to the nearest printable equivalent. In other words, it clips them. This creates problems where detail is carried by differences between out-of-gamut colors, particularly in strong reds, which Photoshop has an unfortunate tendency to turn into oversatu-

rated, brighly-colored blobs.

Other separation engines typically perform some kind of *gamut compression*, where they scale the entire gamut of the source to fit inside the gamut of the target device. In the process, they may end up changing every color in the image, but the overall relationship among colors is maintained. Our eyes are much better at seeing relationships between colors than they are at picking absolute colors, so in general, as long as the color *relationship* is maintained, the image appears the same, even if it's being reproduced using a far smaller gamut than the original.

But Photoshop distorts the relationship between in-gamut and out-of-gamut colors, taking some colors that were different and making them the same, and losing detail in the process. (For a diagram of gamut compression versus gamut clipping, see Figure 16-1 on page 460.)

You have to either accept Photoshop's clipping behavior, or manually adjust the colors to bring them into the target de-

vice's gamut. On the plus side, Photoshop offers you an exquisite degree of manual control, but the amount of work involved can be a definite minus.

Output-profiling tools are beginning to appear from several vendors (again, see Chapter 16, *Color Management Systems*), and several of them offer the ability to create custom Photoshop Separation Tables. We've used a number of these, and compared them with the results we get when we use the same measurements to create a profile for a color management system and to create separations using the CMS rather than Photoshop. In all cases, we've obtained better results from the CMS than we have from Photoshop's separation engine; the fault is almost always in Photoshop's gamut clipping.

However, if you have to rely on canned CMS device profiles rather than ones you created yourself using measurements of actual output, you may find that the extra degree of control Photoshop offers outweighs its shortcomings in this department.

Figure 5-5
Ink Colors
dialog box

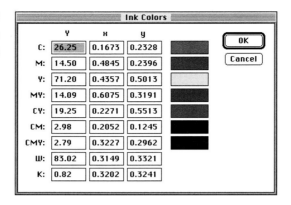

Working with custom inks and colorimetric measurement. The Ink Colors dialog box lets you specify the CIE xyY chromaticity values for the progressive colors—cyan, magenta, yellow, black, cyan+magenta, cyan+yellow, magenta+yellow, cyan+magenta+yellow—and the white of the paper stock. However, the only way to determine these accurately is to measure them from press output with a colorimeter or spectrophotometer.

We've encountered at least two very different situations where measuring these values is well worth the trouble. In the first, a newspaper that uses a bright red as a spot color prints process color, using red in place of magenta to save money. In the second, a fine-art printer needs to use permanent lightfast inks for archival-quality prints, and the closest thing available to magenta in a nonfugitive ink is a vermilion. Both have exactly the same problem, albeit for very different reasons and from very different motives, and both are able to use the same solution.

First, you need to print a set of color bars on press, using the nonstandard inks. The color bars must be specified as CMYK colors in Photoshop; the nonstandard inks are substituted on press. Then you measure each color swatch with a colorimeter or spectrophotometer—we've obtained good results from LightSource's Colortron—and enter the CIE xyY values into the Ink Colors dialog box. Finally, separate and print some real images using the Custom ink setup.

You'll almost certainly have to adjust the gray balance (as discussed later in this section), but already your printed colors will be closer than they would be using the standard CMYK definitions.

Working with custom inks by eyeball. The second technique is a lot less accurate—in fact, it's a kludge—and we only recommend using it as a way to improve the color from desktop four-color ink-jet and thermal-wax color printers. It doesn't work with three-color CMY printers, or with dye-subs—we've tried. But it doesn't require measuring equipment other than your eyeballs.

Again, you need to print a set of color bars, which you must specify as CMYK colors (don't do them in RGB and then convert). Then, choose Custom from the Ink Colors popup menu to open the Ink Colors dialog box. Clicking on the color swatches opens the Color Picker. You can then edit each progressive color to match your printed output. Generally, desktop printers use colorants that are purer and more saturated than press inks, so head in that general direction.

Don't expect miracles from this technique—the results you get will depend on your monitor calibration, your lighting, and your skill in matching colors by eye. But it should get you into the ballpark. As with the previous technique, you should then print some real images, and you'll need to adjust the gray balance to fine-tune the results. Once you've done so, you can save your custom settings and load them when printing to your printer.

However, given the amount of work involved and the uncertain quality of the results you get, we recommend instead that you seriously investigate the growing number of third-party color management systems available (again, see Chapter 16, *Color Management Systems*).

Dot Gain

Dot Gain—that innocuous little field—lets you enter your anticipated dot gain from film to press. The value entered in Dot Gain has an enormous effect on the contrast and brightness of the printed image, so the value you put in here is fairly critical. You'll hear all sorts of numbers bandied about with reference to dot gain, so it's important to be clear about what Photoshop means, and what your service providers mean, by a given dot gain percentage, because they're often different (see the sidebar "Dot Gain: Coping with Midtone Spread," later in this chapter).

Photoshop automatically compensates for dot gain when it converts images to CMYK for printing. It's much less work to build the dot gain compensation into the separation process than to try to compensate for it on an image-by-image basis. In a pinch, you can make slight compensations for dot gain in an already-separated CMYK file using curves, but you'll generally get better results going back to the RGB original, adjusting the dot gain value in Printing Inks Setup, and generating a new CMYK file using the new settings.

The built-in ink sets have default dot gain values associated with them, but they shouldn't be considered as much more than a starting point. Table 5-1 shows some rough-and-ready numbers for typical dot gain, but they're guidelines, not rules. Nevertheless, if you come up with values vastly different from these, double-check your calculations, reread the sidebar "Dot Gain: Coping With Midtone Spread" (in this chapter), and talk to your service providers to make sure that there isn't some misunderstanding.

Table 5-1
Dot gain
settings

Press and stock	Typical dot gain
Web press, coated stock	17–22%
Sheetfed press, coated stock	12–15%
Sheetfed press, uncoated stock	18–22%
Newsprint	30–35%
Positive plates	10–12%

Tip: Use Transfer Functions for Finer Control over Dot Gain. The dot gain mechanism in Printing Inks Setup works well, as long as the imagesetter you're using has been properly calibrated and linearized. (In fact, this book and Photoshop both assume that you or your service bureau have linearized the imagesetter with software such as Kodak's Precision Imagesetter Linearization Software or Technical Publishing Group's Color Calibration Software for PostScript Imagesetters; see the Appendix, *Resources*.) But if you need to compensate for an unlinearized imagesetter, or if you're printing to a nonlinear device such as a color laser printer, you may get better results using a transfer function instead (see "Page Setup" in Chapter 18, *Output Methods*).

Similarly, if you need to correct the dot gain compensation in an existing CMYK file, the dot gain field in Printing Inks Setup won't help you: it only operates when you convert an image from some other color space to CMYK. To correct dot gain in an existing separation, you can either change the image data itself using the Curves command, or you can use a transfer function.

This latter can be tricky, because it limits you to the EPS file format, and it isn't readily obvious to anyone who tries to work on the file that it has a transfer function embedded, but sometimes it's the only way to get

Dot Gain: Coping with Midtone Spread

Dot gain is the name given to the tendency for halftone dots to increase in size from film to press. The biggest cause is the ink spreading as it hits the paper—the more absorbent the paper, the greater the dot gain—but some dot gain occurs when the ink is transferred from the ink roller to the blanket roller on press, and some may even creep in when the film is made into plates. Because dot gain makes your images print darker than anticipated, compensating for it is essential.

Photoshop's dot gain is always measured at the 50-percent value, because that's where its effect is greatest. The larger the circumference of the halftone dot, the more it's subject to dot gain, but above 50 percent the dots start to run together, so they don't gain as much. For the same reason, high screen frequencies are more prone to dot gain than low screen frequencies, because there's more circumference to the dots.

The subject of dot gain attracts more than its fair share of confusion because people measure different things under the name "dot gain." Then, to make matters worse, they have different ways of expressing that measurement.

Photoshop's Dot Gain. The Photoshop manual states that Photoshop's dot gain measurement is the dot gain from film to press. However, since Photoshop also assumes that it's printing to a linearized imagesetter—one that will produce a 50-percent dot when asked for one—we think it's less confusing to say that Photoshop's dot gain is really talking about the difference between the digital data and the final printed piece.

Photoshop's reckoning of dot gain is the absolute additive amount by which a 50-percent dot increases. So if a 50-percent dot prints as 72 percent, Photoshop would call this a 22-percent dot gain.

When you ask your printer about the dot gain anticipated for your job, he may give you the gain from *color proof* to final print. There's a simple way to remove this ambiguity. Ask your printer, "What will happen to the 50-percent dot on my film when it hits the press?" If the response is that it will print as a 78-percent dot, that's 28-percent dot gain as far as Photoshop is concerned, and that's the number you should use for your dot gain setting in Printing Inks Setup.

Who makes the proof? Many service bureaus will make a laminated proof such as a Match Print when they run your film, but it's unlikely that their proofing system is set up to match the press and paper stock on which your job will run. If you give this proof to your printer, he may tell you he can match it, but he's guessing. If the printer makes the proof, there's no guesswork involved, and responsibility is clear.

things to work (see "Controlling Dot Gain with Transfer Functions" in Chapter 6, *Tonal Correction*).

Gray Balance

Frankly, the Gray Balance controls aren't among Photoshop's stronger features. The Gray Balance controls let you set a correction curve for each ink, to compensate ink impurities, and for unequal dot gain among the inks. If you're using one of Photoshop's built-in ink sets, there's almost no reason to change the default values. Cyan usually exhibits more dot gain than the other inks, but this is factored into the built-in ink sets. If your color proofs display a color cast, you *may* need to adjust the gray balance, but only as a last resort, after making sure that the cast isn't actually in the image, or a product of the scanner or poor monitor calibration.

A badly linearized imagesetter could also produce a color cast if the delivered dot percentage varies from plate to plate, but the solution is to linearize the imagesetter, not to adjust the gray balance.

The one case where you will almost certainly need to adjust the gray balance is when you define a custom set of inks, either for press or for a desktop color printer.

Whatever your reasons for changing the gray balance, the procedure is the same. For this to work, you need solid monitor calibration and a controlled viewing environment.

1. Open the CMYK image from which the proof was made, and compare it with the hard copy.

2. Use the Gamma slider in Levels to adjust the gamma of each channel until the screen matches the hard copy. Don't press OK.

3. Instead, write down the new gamma values for each channel, and click Cancel to dismiss the Levels dialog box.

4. Go to Printing Inks Setup, multiply the gamma value you just wrote down for each channel by the existing Gray Balance value, and enter that number as the Gray Balance value for that channel.

You can see the effect of the change on the ink curves in Separation Setup's display, but you can't edit them there.

Tip: Use a Target to Determine Your Neutral Balance. A more accurate approach to determining your gray balance is to create a CMY neutral target like the one in Color Plate 4 on page 125, and print it using your custom inks. In each of the matrices, the amount of cyan ink is constant, while the yellow and the magenta vary in small increments. View the target under controlled lighting, and compare the CMY swatches with the black-only scale to determine the combinations of CMY that yield a neutral tone, or measure the CMY patches with a colorimeter or spectrophotometer.

Once you've identified the combinations of CMY that create a neutral tone, perform the following procedure.

1. Create an RGB file with neutral swatches of 5 percent, 25 percent, 50 percent, 75 percent, and 95 percent.

2. In Separation Setup, set GCR to None. Set the Info palette to display CMYK values, and note the CMY values given for each swatch with the current Gray Balance values.

3. Adjust the Gray Balance values in Printing Inks Setup—a higher value increases the ink, a lower one decreases it. Repeat this process until the Info palette returns CMY values that match the neutral ratios you determined from the printed target, then save the Printing Inks Setup.

4. Go back to Separation Setup and turn Black Generation back on. You should be able to get to within one or two percent of your target values this way, but you may end up still having to adjust the shadows in each image by hand.

Use Dot Gain for Grayscale Images

The Use Dot Gain for Grayscale Images checkbox is undoubtedly one of the most confusing features in Photoshop, and it's left us scratching our heads more than once. While the dot gain value in Printing Inks Setup directly affects color separations (and screen display of CMYK and Lab images), it has no effect on grayscale or duotone images. If you turn on the Use Dot Gain for Grayscale Images checkbox, Photoshop adjusts the *display* of grayscale or duotone images to *simulate* the dot gain specified in Printing Inks Setup, but it doesn't do anything to the data itself.

Use Dot Gain for Grayscale Images can be useful if you want to compensate for dot gain using Levels or Curves, because it lets you use the screen display as an indication of what the final print will look like.

The problem is that it's hard to predict what will actually happen to the screen display when you enter a dot gain percentage. One would expect that turning on the Use Dot Gain for Grayscale Images checkbox would always darken the display, since dot gain is being factored in, but that doesn't always happen. The dot gain curve is a gamma curve, and the image may get lighter *or* darker depending on the dot gain percentage, and the Gamma and Ambient Light settings in Monitor Setup.

The way to use the feature is to print a proof, open the image from which it was generated, turn on Use Dot Gain for Grayscale Images, then adjust the dot gain percentage until the image on screen matches the print. We've had pretty mixed results using this feature—often when we get the midtones to match, the shadows are off, or vice versa. If you can establish a predictable relationship between what you see on the monitor and what you get in print, by all means use the feature.

We don't use this feature at all; it's too unpredictable, and has too many weird side effects—see the next tip.

Tip: Turn It Off When You Aren't Working in Grayscale. As it turns out, Use Dot Gain for Grayscale Images affects not only grayscale images, but also the display of individual color channels in an image (but only if you display them in gray, not if you display them in color). It also affects the display of alpha channels, which always display in gray. For that reason, and to avoid the general confusion the option seems to generate, we recommend that you keep it turned off unless you're working on grayscale or duotone files, *and* you want to compensate for dot gain by changing the actual image data based on the way it looks on your screen.

Separation Setup

Separation Setup lets you control the total amount of ink you'll put on the paper, and also controls the black generation—the relationship between black and the other colors (see Figure 5-6). The decisions you make in Separation Setup can make or break a print job, and there's no single correct answer, no hard-and-fast rules—every combination of press, ink, and paper has its own optimum settings. When it comes to determining what these are, there's no substitute for experience. But understanding the way Separation Setup works is key to making sense of your own experience, and even if there are no rules, there are at least some valuable guidelines.

Rules, guidelines, and caveats. It's important to remember that these guidelines are useful starting points, nothing more. You'll hear all sorts of recommendations from experts; they're all valid, but it's unlikely that

Color Plate 1 When RGB and CMYK combine

*This figure is somewhat complicated by the need to print the
red, green, and blue versions using cyan, magenta, and yellow inks.*

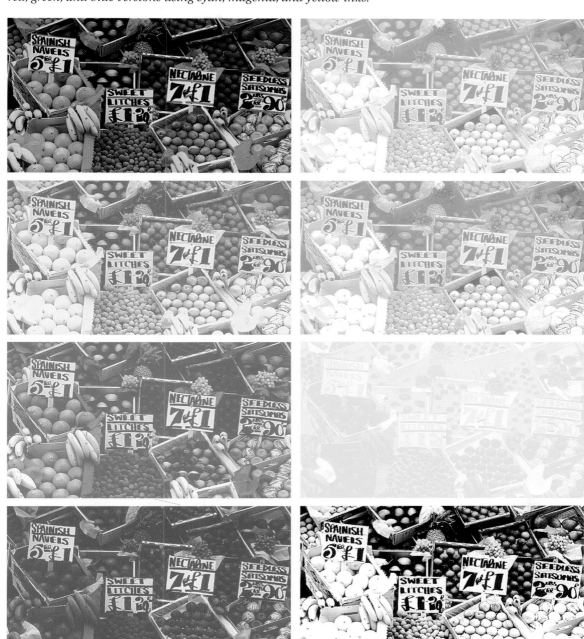

Color Plate 2 Resolution and image reproduction (page 68)

How much resolution do you need? All of these images are printed using the same 133-lpi halftone screen, but they contain different numbers of pixels. Look for details, such as readability of type.

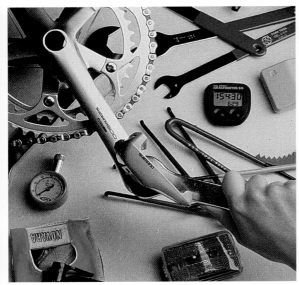

2:1 sampling ratio, 266 ppi

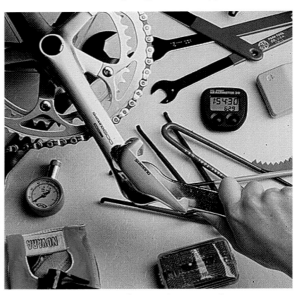

1.5:1 sampling ratio, 200 ppi

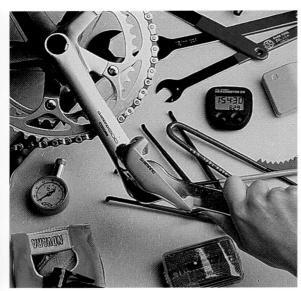

1.2:1 sampling ratio, 160 ppi

1:1 sampling ratio, 133 ppi

Color Plate 3 Indexed color changes (page 77)

Indexed color, shown as it's typically used, for 72-ppi display on screen. Since the colors are indexed to a 256-color palette, when the palette changes, the colors in the image change.

The high-resolution, 24-bit image

Macintosh system palette

An optimized or "adaptive" palette

A radical palette switch

Color Plate 4 CMY neutrals (page 120)

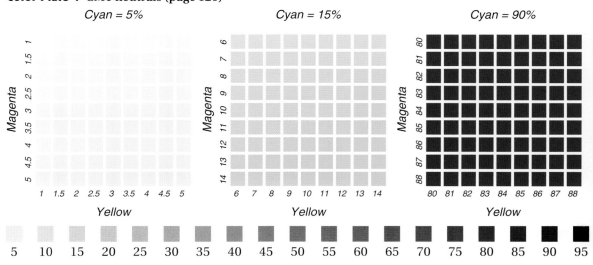

Color Plate 5 Black generation (page 129)

The proportion of black to CMY inks has a considerable effect on image reproduction. Each method of black generation has its strengths and weaknesses. Undercolor removal, or UCR, replaces neutral colors with black ink, but uses CMY inks to reproduce all non-neutral colors. Gray component replacement, or GCR, extends the black plate into non-neutral areas, replacing a neutral amount of CMY with black ink.

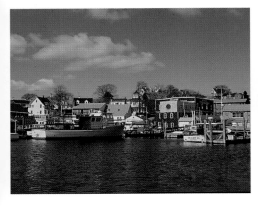

A UCR separation uses black ink only in the neutral areas. It produces rich shadows, but can be difficult to control on press because it uses a lot of ink compared to GCR separations.

A Light GCR setting replaces slightly more CMY with K than does a UCR separation. In this image, Light GCR puts slightly more black into the sky and the water than does the UCR separation.

Maximum GCR replaces all neutral components of the CMY inks with black. It's easy to control on press because the black plate carries almost the entire image, but it can make shadow areas look flat.

any of them will apply perfectly to your particular situation. Just how far it's worth going to optimize your color seps for a specific press depends in part on the economics of the situation, and in part on the degree of process control used by the commercial printer. It's the exception rather than the rule for every impression in a print run to be identical, but the amount of variation within a press run varies widely from shop to shop—typically, the less variation, the higher the prices.

Figure 5-6
Separation Setup

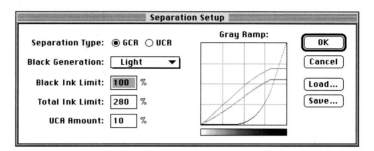

Creating ideal separations for a given press is an iterative process—you have to run press proofs and measure them, then go back to original RGB files, reseparate them, and repeat the whole process until you arrive at the optimum conditions. This is both time-consuming and expensive, and for many jobs the economics simply don't justify it.

If you're aiming for "pleasing" color from an inexpensive, one-time, midrange job, you just want to aim somewhere in the middle of the range the press can deliver, and ask the press operator to match the proof as closely as possible. But if you're publishing a magazine or newspaper and are constantly working with the same press, it's worth doing much more work to fingerprint the press. Likewise, if you're working on a premium job, it makes sense to pull press proofs, measure them, and reseparate the images if necessary. Most high-end color houses end up scanning each image two or three times before they get ideal separations. You have to determine reasonable expectations for each job, and decide how far you want to go.

Tip: Don't Bother Converting to CMYK. When you're evaluating the effect of different Separation Setups, you don't actually have to convert images to CMYK. Instead, open an RGB image, and use the Info palette to display the CMYK values you'll get. If you note the XY coordinates of your sample points, you can return consistently to the same point in the image again and again, and see the effect that changes in Separation Setup have on the CMYK values they'll generate.

Tip: Testing on a Budget. Remember that a printer can sometimes piggyback a test onto someone else's print job, particularly if you show them that you can offer them a significant amount of business. Preparing several different versions of an image and ganging them on a page can tell you a lot when they're printed.

UCR vs. GCR

Photoshop offers two different methods of black generation, UCR (Undercolor Removal) and GCR (Gray Component Replacement). Both reduce the total amount of ink used to compensate for ink-trapping problems that appear when too much ink is applied to the page. (In this context, trapping is the ability of one ink to adhere to another ink—it has nothing to do with building chokes and spreads to compensate for misregistration on press.)

▶ UCR separations replace cyan, magenta, and yellow ink with black *only* in the neutral areas. This uses much less ink in the shadows.

▶ GCR extends into color areas of the image as well—it replaces the proportions of cyan, magenta, and yellow that produce neutral gray with a corresponding percentage of black ink.

GCR separations are generally considered easier to control on press than are UCR separations, at least by the theoreticians. The downside of GCR is that it can make the shadow areas look flat and unsaturated since they're being printed only with black ink, so many commercial printers distrust GCR separations. UCA (undercolor addition) allows you to compensate for flat shadows by adding some CMY back into the neutral shadow areas.

Even though some experts contend that UCR separations are better for sheetfed presses and that CGR is better for web presses, we just don't buy it. We almost always use GCR separations with some UCA (see "Undercolor Addition," below). On the other hand, we've found that UCR sometimes works better than GCR when printing to newsprint with a low total ink limit—say, 220 to 240 percent—but your mileage may vary. Ask your printer, but test whenever possible. We suspect that many printers who profess to hate GCR separations often run them unknowingly, usually with good results, as long as the amount of GCR isn't too extreme.

Black Generation

The Black Generation popup menu is only available when Separation Type is set to GCR. This feature lets you control the areas of the tonal range that Photoshop replaces with black (see Color Plate 5 on page 126). For the vast majority of situations we prefer a Light black setting, in which Photoshop only begins to add black after the 40-percent mark. Often, however, a Medium black (where black begins to replace colors after only 20 percent) may work better for newsprint. We almost never use the Heavy or Maximum black settings, with one exception: a Maximum black setting can do wonders for color screen shots.

Custom black generation. The Custom option allows you to create your own Black Generation curve. This isn't something you should undertake lightly—the black plate has an enormous influence over the tonal reproduction of the image. However, if you want to make slight modifications to one of the built-in Black Generation curves, you can—choose the curve you want to view, then choose Custom. The Black Generation dialog box appears with the previously selected curve loaded (see Figure 5-7).

Figure 5-7
Custom black
generation

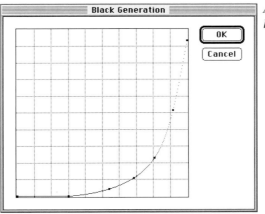

*A typical skeleton
black curve*

If your printer asks for a skeleton black, you can use the Custom option to create a skeleton black curve, a very light black setting that still extends high up into the tonal range, typically to 25 or 30 percent. You should only attempt to do this if the printer demands it, and even then only if you have considerable experience in evaluating images by looking at the individual color plates—the values in the black plate are critical, and you'll almost certainly need to run press proofs to get it right.

Black Ink Limit

Black Ink Limit does just what it says—it limits the amount of black ink used in the deepest shadows. In general, we recommend leaving this set at 100 percent, because it seems to produce the best overall balance between the black and the CMY inks. You can reduce the black shadow dot for individual images by changing the target black color of the black eyedropper in Levels or Curves (see "Reducing the Black with the Eyedropper" in Chapter 7, *Color Correction*). But if you're working with newsprint or another process that requires low total ink densities—280 percent or less—you may want to try setting the Black Ink Limit between 70 and 80 percent, particularly if you're using UCR rather than GCR. Your printer is the best source of advice on the maximum black the press can handle.

Total Ink Limit

Total Ink Limit also does what it says—it limits the total amount of ink used in the deepest shadows. Photoshop's separation engine seems to provide the best balance between the colored inks and black when the Total Ink Limit is set somewhere between 300 and 320 percent.

The ideal value depends on the combination of press, ink, and paper, but bear in mind that it isn't necessarily desirable to use the maximum amount of ink that the printing process can handle. It's generally true that more ink will yield a better image (within the limits of the press), but it also creates more problems with ink trapping and drying, show-through, and offsetting, and (for printers) it costs more because you're using more ink. Your printer will know better than anyone else the trade-offs involved.

For high-quality sheetfed presses with coated stock, a total ink limit of 320 to 340 percent is a good starting point—you may be able to go even higher with some paper stocks. For newsprint, values can range from 220 to 280 percent (see "Typical Printing Setups," below).

Undercolor Addition (UCA)

UCA (undercolor addition) is used with GCR to compensate for loss of ink density in the neutral shadow areas. Using UCA lets you bring back richness to the shadows, yet still retain the benefits of easier color-ink balancing on the press that GCR offers.

The need for UCA is image dependent. If your shadows look flat, the image can probably benefit from modest amounts of UCA. We rarely use more than 10 percent.

Typical Printing Setups

Table 5-1 gives some general guidelines for different types of print jobs. If you use these values, you should get acceptable separations, but every combination of press, ink, and paper has its own quirks, and your printer should know them better than anyone else. View these values as useful starting points, and get as much advice from your printer as you can.

Table 5-1 Suggested separation settings

Sheetfed Press

Coated	Uncoated	
Ink colors: SWOP (Coated)	Ink colors: SWOP (Uncoated)	
Dot Gain: 12–15%	Dot Gain: 17–22%	
GCR, Light Black Generation	GCR, Light Black Generation	
Black Limit: 100%	Black Limit: 100%	
Total Ink Limit: 320–340%	Total Ink Limit: 270–300%	
UCA: 0–10%	UCA: 0–10%	

Web Press

Coated	Uncoated	Newsprint
Ink colors: SWOP (Coated)	Ink colors: SWOP (Uncoated)	Ink Colors: SWOP (Newsprint)
Dot Gain: 17–22%	Dot Gain: 22–28%	Dot Gain: 30–35%
GCR, Light Black Generation	GCR, Light Black Generation	GCR, Medium Black Generation
Black Limit: 100%	Black Limit: 100%	Black Limit: 95–100%
Total Ink Limit: 300–320%	Total Ink Limit: 280–300%	Total Ink Limit: 260–280%
UCA: 0–10%	UCA: 0–10%	UCA: 0–10%
		Or:
		Ink Colors: SWOP (Newsprint)
		Dot Gain: 30–35%
		UCR, Black Limit: 70–80%
		Total Ink Limit: 220–240%

Separation Tables

The Separation Tables dialog box offers a convenient way of saving combinations of Printing Inks and Separation Setups (see Figure 5-8). To do this, set the Printing Inks and Separation Setup settings you want to use, then choose Separation Tables from the Preferences submenu and press the Save button. We find it helpful to give the table an informative name that indicates its contents, such as "SWOPC/20/GCRL/100/330/10" for a table that uses SWOP coated inks, 20-percent dot gain, GCR with Light Black Generation, 100-percent Black Limit, 330-percent Total Ink Limit, and 10-percent UCA. But you can call it "Fred" if you'd rather.

Figure 5-8
Separation
Tables

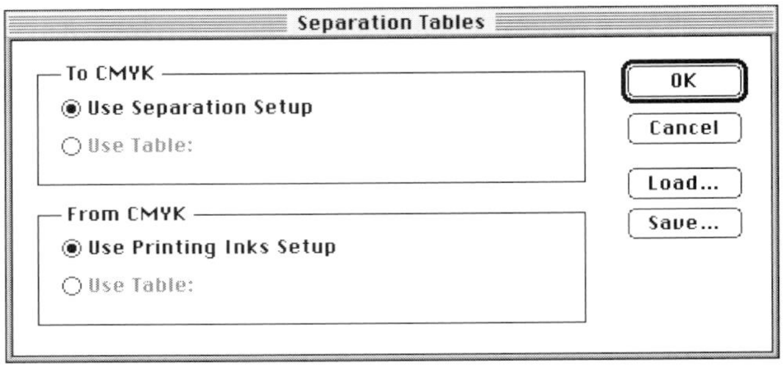

Separation Tables from Other Programs

Separation Tables also provides a mechanism for Photoshop to "learn" from other color-separation programs, such as PixelCraft's Color Access. You can create custom RGB-to-CMYK tables for creating separations, and custom CMYK-to-RGB tables for displaying CMYK images in Photoshop. The mechanism for doing so is somewhat weird, but if you're careful, it can work quite well.

Note that we've had much better success at creating RGB-to-CMYK tables than we have at creating CMYK-to-RGB tables. This is largely because most of the applications that we think do a better RGB-to-CMYK conversion than Photoshop have no facilities for converting CMYK back to RGB. (You can always force them to do so by taking a screen capture, but that introduces a formidable level of abstraction.)

So while we'll tell you how to "go both ways," we have to admit that we've really only made this work as a one-way process. We can create separations that print very well, but they look weird on screen.

Custom RGB-to-CMYK tables. Here's how to create a custom RGB-to-CMYK table using an application such as PixelCraft's Color Access.

1. In Photoshop, open the file named Lab Colors (located in the Separation Sources folder), convert it to RGB, and save it with another name, *e.g.,* "Photoshop RGB".

2. In the color-separation application, open this RGB file, convert it to CMYK, and save it with another name, *e.g.,* "Color Access CMYK".

3. In Photoshop, open this CMYK file and save it as Raw. In the Save as Raw dialog box, use these settings: Type = 8BST, Creator = 8BIM, Header = 0, Interleaved Order.

That's it. The table is complete. To load the custom table, choose Separation Tables, click the Load button, and open the Raw file you just saved. The To CMYK option will then change from Use Separation Setup to Use Table with the name of the table displayed.

Custom CMYK-to-RGB tables. See the disclaimer above. If you still want to do this, here's how.

1. In the color-separation application, open the file named CMYK Color, located in Photoshop's Separation Sources folder. Convert it to RGB, and save it with a new name, *e.g.,* "ColorAccess RGB". (If you're using Color Access, you'll find that the only way to convert CMYK to RGB is to take a screen shot using Command-Shift-3. You'll find a file named "Picture 0" or the like on your hard disk.)

2. In Photoshop, open this RGB file, convert it to Lab, and save it in the Raw format using these settings: Type = 8BST, Creator = 8BIM, Header = 0, Interleaved Order.

Finally, to load the custom table, choose Separation Tables, click the Load button, and open the Raw file you just saved. The To RGB option will then change from Use Printing Inks Setup to Use Table with the name of the table displayed.

Custom tables, no matter what their source, can't do anything about Photoshop's limited separation engine. It still clips out-of-gamut colors, as we explained earlier in the chapter in the sidebar "Photoshop's Separation Engine." However, with a little care, custom CMYK-to-RGB tables can sometimes improve the on-screen appearance of CMYK files. Sometimes this is the only way to get CMYK files to display well, particularly if they weren't created by Photoshop.

Isolating Variables

The information in this chapter may seem insanely complex, and to some extent, it is. The important thing to keep in mind is that you're dealing with several interdependent variables. Before you change one of them, make sure you know what you're changing and why you're changing it. As you gain experience working with a particular press, examine the results closely and see where you can improve things. Your first print job may prove disappointing, but your second one should be better, and the third one should be better still. If we could afford to print everything twice, life would be easy!

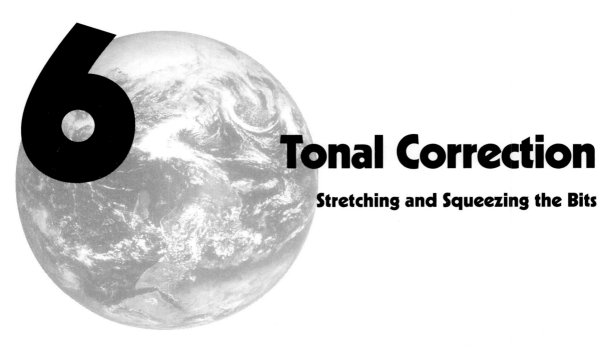

Tonal Correction

Stretching and Squeezing the Bits

Tonal manipulation—adjusting the lightness or darkness of your images—is one of Photoshop's most powerful and far-reaching capabilities, and sometimes it can seem like magic. But really, there's nothing magical about it. Once you understand how tonal manipulation is done—it all comes back to those ubiquitous zeros and ones—it starts to look downright pedestrian. But your increased understanding of how Photoshop works (and more important, your ability to spend more time playing around) should more than make up for any loss of the sense of wonder.

Tonal manipulation is the key to setting the right contrast for images. It makes the difference between a flat image that lies lifeless on the page and one that pops, drawing you into it. And tonal correction is the central method for avoiding those dark, muddy images that you're forever seeing produced using Photoshop.

But the role of tonal correction goes far beyond that. When you correct the color balance in an image, you're really doing tonal manipulation on the color channels. And when you work with masks and alpha channels, you'll find that much of their power stems from the the ability to use Photoshop's tonal controls to isolate objects from their background, emphasize edges, or control the intensity of filters and other effects.

We adjust the tone of images for two reasons. The first is to correct flaws that are either inherent in the image, or were introduced as part of the image-capture process. We refer to this as image *correction*. But we also have to manipulate the image to compensate for the limitations of different output processes, and this we call *targeting*. You can do both at once, or make them separate tasks—there are trade-offs with either approach—but the distinction between correction and targeting is an important one to keep in mind, one that recurs through much of this book.

Stretching and Squeezing the Bits

If you're working with images in Photoshop, they're almost certainly made up of one or more 8-bit channels, in which each pixel is represented by a value from 0 (black) to 255 (white). Grayscale images have one such channel, while color images have three (RGB or Lab) or four (CMYK). (The one exception to the 8-bit rule is with high-bit images; see "The High-Bit Advantage" in Chapter 12, *Capturing Images.*)

In this chapter we'll be talking exclusively about grayscale images, but you'll use the same tools to perform both tonal and color correction on color images, so it's important to get acquainted with them on an intimate basis.

The key thing to bear in mind is that when you use Photoshop's tonal controls, you're stretching and squeezing various parts of the 8-bit tonal range, and in doing so, you inevitably lose some information. To demonstrate this, try the following simple experiment.

1. Create a new grayscale file in Photoshop, 7 inches wide by 5 inches tall, at 72 dpi.

2. With the foreground color set to black and the background color set to white, use the Gradient tool to create a horizontal gradient from black to white, across the entire width of the image. (For this to work best, first double-click on the Gradient tool and turn off the Dither checkbox in the Gradient Tool Options palette).

3. Choose Levels (from the Adjust submenu under the Image menu), change the gamma (the middle Input setting) to 1.8, and click OK (see Figure 6-1). You'll notice that the midtones are much lighter, but you may already be able to see some banding—instead of a smooth gradient—in the shadows.

Figure 6-1

Adjusting gamma

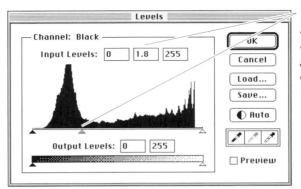

While it's not labeled as such, the middle Input slider controls the gamma setting, which adjusts the midtone values in an image.

4. Choose Levels again, and change the gamma to 0.45. The midtones are back almost to where you started, but you should be able to see that, instead of a smooth gradation, you have some distinct bands in the image (see Figure 6-2).

Figure 6-2

Data loss due to tonal correction

While the effect of successive tonal-correction moves on images may be subtle, the effect on the data within the image—as expressed in the histogram—is profound.

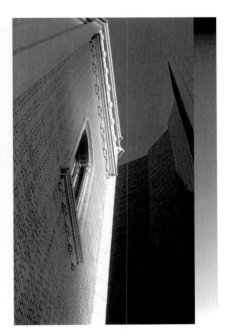

Histogram for the gray wedge at the right side of the image

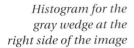

Before tonal correction   *After three gamma moves*

Difference Is Detail: Tonal-Correction Issues

What do we mean when we talk about image information? Very simply, adjacent pixels with different values constitute image detail. If the difference is very slight, you won't be able to see it (especially in shadows); but it's there, waiting to be exploited. You can accentuate those differences—making those adjacent pixels *more* different—to bring out the detail.

The color of noise. Difference isn't always detail, though. Most scanners—particularly low-cost desktop flatbeds—introduce spurious differences between pixels (see Figure 6-3). Those differences aren't detail, they're just noise (like static on the radio that drowns out the weather report), and they're one of our least favorite things. Photoshop can't tell the difference between genuine image information and device-induced noise. You need to decide what is desirable detail and what's noise, accentuating the detail while minimizing the noise.

Posterization. Noise isn't the only problem to deal with when you're doing tonal correction, however. There's also *posterization*—stair-stepping of gray levels in distinct, visible jumps, as opposed to smooth gradations (see Figure 6-4).

Photoshop only gives you 256 possible values for a gray pixel (unless you're working with a high-bit image; see "The High-Bit Advantage" in Chapter 12, *Capturing Images*). When you start making dark pixels more

Figure 6-3 What noise looks like

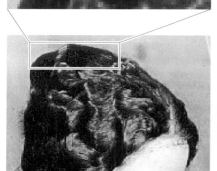

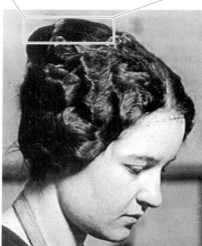

A dirty scan. This type of noise poses problems during tonal correction.

A cleaner scan makes it much easier to adjust tone.

What happened here? With the first gamma adjustment, you lightened the midtones—stretching the shadows and compressing the highlights. With the second gamma adjustment, you darkened the midtones—stretching the highlights and compressing the shadows.

But with all that stretching and squeezing, you lost some of the levels. Instead of a smooth blend, with pixels occupying every value from 0 to

Figure 6-4 The effects of posterization

different, you eventually make them *so* different that the image looks splotchy—covered with patches of distinctly different pixels, rather than smooth transitions. This is a problem especially with noisy images, because those distinct patches may be noise, not detail. And the posterization is accentuated by sharpening.

Lost highlight detail. When you accentuate detail in one part of the tonal range, making slightly different pixels more different (*expanding* the range), you lose detail in other areas, making slightly different pixels more similar (*compressing* the range).

For instance, if you stretch the shadow values apart to bring out shadow detail, you inevitably squeeze the highlight values together (see Figure 6-5). If you make two different pixels the same, that detail is gone forever. That's what we mean in real-world terms when we say that information is "lost."

Photoshop's tonal controls let you improve your images immeasurably, but they'll also let you wreck an image irreparably. Various clichés come to mind—you can't make a silk purse out of a sow's ear, there's no such thing as a free lunch, and so on—but however you slice it, *any* tonal manipulation you do in Photoshop throws away some image information. The trick is to make the image look better than it did before, even though it contains less information.

Figure 6-5 Loss of highlight detail

Bringing out shadow detail with tonal correction inevitably loses some highlight detail.

Before tonal correction   *After tonal correction*

255, some of those levels became unpopulated—in fact, if we're counting right, some 76 levels are no longer being used.

Call up the Levels dialog box again, and you'll see that the histogram is comb-like—there are missing areas, with no pixels. You've thrown away somewhere between a quarter and a third of the tonal information, and in the process you've introduced our arch-enemy: posterization.

If you repeat the pair of gamma adjustments, you'll see that each time you make an adjustment, the banding becomes more obvious as you lose more and more tonal information. Repeating the gamma adjustments half a dozen times will give you a file that contains only 55 gray levels instead of 256. And once you've lost that information, there's no way to bring it back.

Data Loss in Perspective

This loss of image information may seem scarier than it really is. In most cases, the corrections you make to images are much less drastic than in the example above. Moreover, while there's considerable debate over exactly how many shades of gray can be successfully represented in print, our experience leads us to believe that it's significantly less than 256. Nonetheless, this simple demonstration should serve to hammer home the following lessons, and the ensuing pieces of advice.

► All tonal manipulations incur some data loss.

► Once the data is gone, you can't bring it back.

► Successive tonal manipulations lose data at an increasing rate.

Get good data to begin with. As we emphasize in Chapter 12, *Capturing Images,* if you've got a high-bit scanner, it's better to get the image as close to "right" as you possibly can as you scan it. The whole point of a high-bit scanner is to let you manipulate the high-bit data during the scan, so that you get the *right* 8-bit data out of the scanner.

Minimize tonal correction. Small tonal moves are much less destructive than big ones. The more you want to change an image, the more compromises you'll have to make to avoid obvious posterization, artifacts due to noise, and loss of highlight and shadow detail.

Avoid successive corrections. Since multiple manipulations lose more data than a single change does, it's worth putting in a little extra work to create one tonal adjustment that does everything you want. This is almost always an iterative process (that means trial and error), but we'll show you how to refine your tonal adjustments while you experiment, without degrading the image.

Cover yourself. Since the data you lose is irretrievable, you should try to leave yourself a way out by working on a copy of the file, or by saving your tonal adjustments in progress separately, without applying them to the image (or both).

Data loss can be good. Sometimes you want to throw away information. For example, none of these restrictions applies when you're working on masks or alpha channels—in fact, you usually *want* to throw away data on those, since you're often trying to exaggerate a feature or isolate it from its background. (See "Step-by-Step Silhouettes" in Chapter 13, *Selections.*)

With these caveats in mind, let's look at Photoshop's tonal-manipulation tools.

Tonal-Correction Tools

Almost everything you need to do to tone and color your images can be accomplished using only four of Photoshop's tools.

▶ Histogram

▶ Info palette

▶ Levels dialog box

▶ Curves dialog box

The Histogram and Info palette let you analyze the image and the effect of your tonal manipulations. Levels and Curves are the tools you use to actually make the adjustments (if you're still using Brightness/Contrast, check out the sidebar "The Nonlinear Advantage," later in this chapter). These four tools simply offer different ways of viewing and changing the same data.

The Histogram

The Histogram is a simple bar chart that plots the levels from 0 to 255 along the horizontal axis, and the number of pixels at each level along the vertical axis (see Figure 6-6). If there are lots of pixels in shadow areas, the bars are concentrated on the left; the reverse is true with "high-key" images, where most of the information is in the highlights.

Figure 6-6

Histogram dialog box

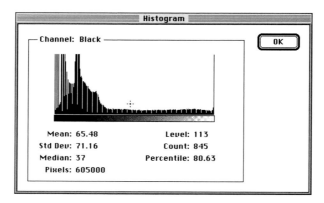

Some of the information offered by the histogram may not seem particularly useful—for normal image reproduction tasks you really don't need to know the median pixel value, or how many pixels in the image are at level 33. But histograms do show some very useful information at a glance.

Highlight and Shadow Clipping

With a quick look at the histogram, you can immediately see whether or not your scanner has clipped the highlights or shadows (see Figure 6-7). If there's a spike at either end of the histogram, the highlight or shadow values are almost certainly clipped—we say "almost" because there are some images that really do have a very large number of pure white or solid black areas. But they're pretty rare.

Figure 6-7

Highlight and shadow clipping

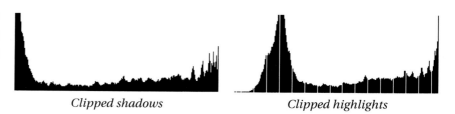

Clipped shadows   *Clipped highlights*

How Much Information Is Present

The overall appearance of the histogram also gives you a quick, rough-and-ready picture of the integrity of your image data (see Figure 6-8). A good scan uses the entire tonal range, and has a histogram with smooth contours. The actual location of the peaks and valleys depends entirely on the image content, but if the histogram shows obvious spikes, you're probably dealing with a noisy scanner. If it shows a comb-like appearance, it's likely that the image has already been manipulated—perhaps by your scanning software.

Figure 6-8

Comb-like histogram suggesting a noisy (or previously manip-ulated) image

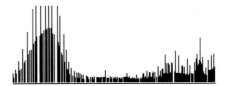

The histogram also shows you where to examine the image for signs that you've gone too far in your tonal manipulations. If you look at the histograms produced by the earlier experiment in applying gamma adjustments to a gradient, you can see at a glance exactly what each successive adjustment did to the image—spikes and gaps start to appear in the histogram.

Note that a gap of only one level is almost certainly unnoticeable in the image—especially if it's in the shadows or midtones—but once you start to see gaps of three or more levels, you may start to see visible posterization in the image. The location of the gap gives you a good idea of where in the tonal range the posterization is happening.

Histograms Are Generalizations

Once you've edited an image, the histogram may look pretty ugly. This is normal; in fact, it's almost inevitable. The histogram is only a guide, not a rule. Histograms are most useful for evaluating raw scans. A histogram will show clipped endpoints and missing levels, but a good-looking histogram isn't necessarily the sign of a good raw image. And an image with a bad histogram can still look good.

Fixing the histogram doesn't mean you've fixed the image. We have plenty of tricks that will make the histogram look better: smoothing out the peaks and filling in the gaps (resampling the image), or rotating the image clockwise, then counterclockwise by the same amount will do it, for example. But none of those tricks brings back image detail that was lost through overly aggressive tone manipulation. They just interpolate pixels in the missing levels, based on the data that's left. You can use these tricks to salvage a posterized image when there's really no other alternative, but it's better to avoid the posterization in the first place. Extract what useful information you can from the histogram, but don't let yourself be ruled by it.

Our next tool, however, is very specific. It tells you exactly what's happening to a specific pixel or group of pixels in the image.

The Info Palette

Like the Histogram, the Info palette is purely an informational display. It doesn't let you do anything to the image besides analyze its contents. But where the Histogram shows a general picture of the entire image, the Info palette lets you analyze *specific* points in the image.

When you move the cursor across the image, the Info palette displays the pixel value under the cursor, and its location in the image. More important, when you have one of the tonal- or color-correction dialog boxes (such as Levels or Curves) open, the Info palette displays the values for the pixel before and after the transformation (see Figure 6-9).

Figure 6-9
Info palette

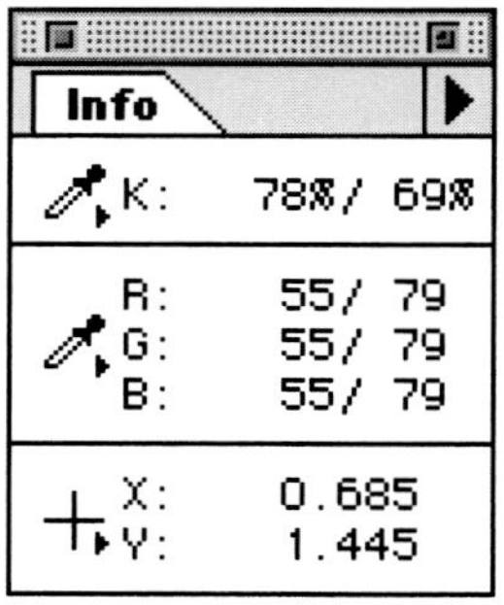

When you're working in one of the Image:Adjust dialog boxes, such as Levels or Curves, the Info palette shows the pixel value before and after the correction.

Tip: Look for Differences. The Info palette lets you sample the actual values of different pixels, but it also lets you hunt down hidden detail, particularly in deep shadows and bright highlights where it can be hard to see on the monitor. Move the cursor over a deep shadow, and watch the Info palette. If the numbers *change* as you move the cursor, there's difference lurking in there—it may be detail waiting to be exploited or it may be noise that you'll need to suppress, but *something* is hiding in there.

Palette Options

You can control what sorts of information the Info palette displays in one of two ways. First, you can select Palette Options from the Info palette's popout menu (see Figure 6-10). The second method is to use the Info palette's hidden popup menus (see Figure 6-11). We have several different palette setups that we use for different kinds of work, and we dearly wish we could save and load them. Alas, we can't—maybe in Photoshop 4?

Figure 6-10

The Info palette's Info Options dialog box

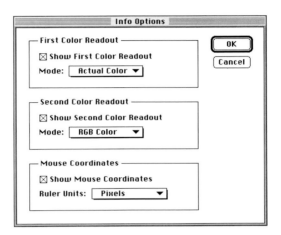

Figure 6-11

The Info palette's popup menus

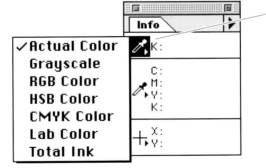

Click on the little arrow to bring up the Options menu.

For grayscale, duotone, or multichannel images, we generally set the First Color Readout to RGB, and the Second Color Readout to Actual Color (Actual Color causes the readout method to change, depending on what type of image you're viewing). We almost always display the mouse coordinates as pixels, because it makes it easier for us to return consistently to the same spot in the image.

Why display RGB values for a grayscale image? Because it's the only way to display the values as levels from 0 to 255, the most precise display possible. The other options show percentages instead, on a scale of 100 instead of 255. The numbers for R, G, and B are always the same in a grayscale image, so the level just displays three times. Setting the second readout to Actual Color lets us read the dot percentage, so we can display levels and percentages at the same time. We use different setups for working in color, which we'll cover in Chapter 7, *Color Correction.*

Now let's look at the tools we use to actually change the image.

Levels and Curves

Levels and Curves are the two Photoshop features that we use the most for global tonal and color correction. The Levels command is the easier of the two for beginning Photoshop users, and (in some situations) for experienced ones too. The Curves command is a little more difficult to master, but it's a lot more powerful once you've done so.

We liken Levels to an automatic transmission and Curves to a stick shift. Levels is quick and easy. Curves lets you do all the same things (and more) that you can do with Levels but it demands a bit more skill, coordination, and experience.

Levels and Curves both do the same thing—they let you apply transformations to the image that change existing (input) pixel values to new (output) pixel values—but they offer different ways of controlling the relationship between input and output.

They also share an important property that differentiates them from the Brightness and Contrast controls: they allow you to apply *nonlinear transformations,* as distinct from the linear transformations applied by the Brightness and Contrast controls (see sidebar, "The Nonlinear Advantage.")

Levels

Photoshop's Levels command opens a tonal-manipulation powerhouse. For grayscale images, it's often the only tonal-manipulation feature we use. This deceptively simple little dialog box lets us identify the shadow and highlight points in the image, limit the highlight and shadow dot percentages, and make dramatic changes to the midtones, while providing

The Nonlinear Advantage

Linear transformations (such as those applied by Brightness and Contrast) throw away image information, and they do so in a pretty dumb way. They're called "linear transformations" because they do exactly the same thing to each pixel in the image. If you're trying to modify the brightness or contrast of an image, Brightness/Contrast is a bad approach, because you lose detail at one or both ends of the tonal range, and probably do severe violence to the image in the process.

For example, the Brightness control simply shifts all the pixel values up or down the tonal range. Let's say you increase Brightness by 10. Photoshop adds 10 to every pixel's value, so value 0 becomes 10, 190 becomes 200, and every pixel with a value of 245 or above becomes 255 (you can't go above 255). This is called "clipping the highlights" (they're all the same value, so there's no highlight detail). Plus, your shadows go flat because you lose all your true blacks.

The Contrast control stretches the tonal range when you increase the contrast, throwing away information in both highlights and shadows (and potentially posterizing the tones in between); and it compresses the tonal range when you reduce the contrast, so either way, you lose gray levels.

Don't use the Brightness and Contrast controls on images! You can use them to good effect with channels and masks, but that's another story; see Chapter 13, *Selections.*

The nonlinear transformations applied by Levels and Curves throw away some image information too (losing some highlight detail, in most cases), but they don't throw away nearly as much, and they do it in a much more intelligent way. They let you adjust the values in the middle of the tonal range without losing the information at the ends, so you can improve your images dramatically and still preserve important highlight and shadow detail.

Figure 6-12 Linear versus nonlinear correction

| *Uncorrected* | *Brightened* | *Increased contrast* | *Corrected with Levels* |

real-time feedback via the on-screen image and the Info palette. For color work, or for very detailed tonal corrections on grayscale images, we use the Curves command instead; but there are a couple of things that we can only do in Levels, and for a considerable amount of grayscale work, it's all we need (see Figure 6-13).

Figure 6-13

How Levels works

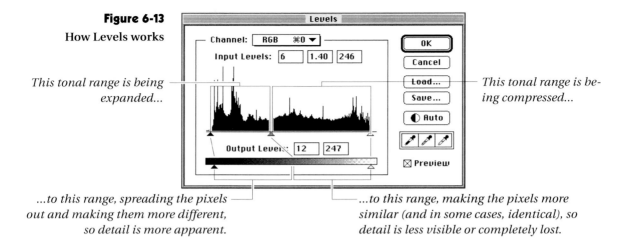

This tonal range is being expanded...

This tonal range is being compressed...

...to this range, spreading the pixels out and making them more different, so detail is more apparent.

...to this range, making the pixels more similar (and in some cases, identical), so detail is less visible or completely lost.

The Levels dialog box not only displays a histogram of the image, it lets you work with it in very useful ways. If you understand what the histogram shows, the workings of the Levels controls suddenly become a lot less mysterious.

Input Levels

The three Input Levels sliders let you change the black point, the white point, and gamma in the image. As you move the sliders, the numbers in the corresponding Input Levels fields change, so if you know what you're doing, you can type in the numbers directly. But we still use the sliders most of the time, because they provide real-time feedback—by changing the image on screen—as we drag them. Here's what they actually do.

Black- and white-point sliders. Moving these sliders in toward the center has the effect of increasing the overall contrast of the image. When you move the black-point slider away from its default position at zero to a higher level, you're telling Photoshop to turn all the pixels at that level and lower (those to the left) to level 0 (black), and stretch all the levels to the right of the slider to fill the entire tonal range from 0 to 255.

A look at the histogram in Figure 6-14 shows that the tweak clips some extreme shadow details, but increases contrast and detail in the remaining shadows (as a result, a few gaps appear in the histogram).

Moving the white-point slider does the same thing to the other end of the tonal range. As you move it away from its default position at level 255 (white) to a lower level, you're telling Photoshop to turn all the pixels at that level and higher (those to the right of the slider) to level 255 (white), and stretch all the levels to the left of the slider to fill the entire tonal range from 0 to 255.

Figure 6-14 Black- and white-point tweaks

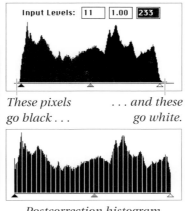

Input Levels: 11   1.00   233

These pixels   *. . . and these*
go black . . .   *go white.*

Postcorrection histogram, displaying some black- and white-point clipping

Gamma slider. The gamma slider lets you alter the midtones without changing the highlight and shadow points. When you move the gamma slider, you're telling Photoshop where you want the midtone gray value (50-percent gray, or level 128) to be. If you move it to the left, the image gets lighter, because you're choosing a value that's darker than 128, and making it 128. As you do so, the shadows get stretched to fill up that part of the tonal range, and the highlights get squeezed together (see Figure 6-15).

Conversely, if you move the slider to the right, the image gets darker because you're choosing a lighter value and telling Photoshop to change it to level 128. The highlights get stretched, and the shadow values get squeezed together. (David likes to think of this as grabbing a rubber band on both ends and in the middle, and pulling the middle part to the left or right; one side gets stretched out, and the other side gets bunched up.)

The ultimate effect of changing gamma is to lighten or darken the midtones without affecting the extreme highlight and shadow points. If you make too large a gamma correction, you end up with obvious posterization where levels get stretched too far apart; but smaller moves (less than 1.9) are very effective. However, you're often forced to make larger corrections, especially with images from low-cost desktop scanners. That's just one of the many trade-offs you have to work with in digital imaging.

Figure 6-15
Gamma tweak

 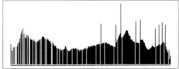

Adding a gamma adjustment of 1.2 to the image in the previous figure brings out some shadow detail, though highlight detail is lost, and the histogram displays some additional combing.

Output Levels

The Output Levels controls let you compress the tonal range of the image into fewer than the entire 256 possible gray levels. Mostly, they're useful for targeting—setting the maximum shadow and minimum highlight dot on grayscale images that don't contain any *specular highlights* (the small, very bright reflections you get from glass or highly polished metal). If you know that the press for which the image is destined can't hold a dot smaller than five percent, for example, you can compress the tonal range so that the brightest pixels have a value of level 242, which corresponds to a five-percent dot on the press.

When we have a color or grayscale image where we want small specular highlights to blow out to white paper, we use the black and white eyedroppers instead, and we use them later in the image-editing process (after sharpening). But even then, if we're dealing with a low-quality reproduction medium like newsprint—where the minimum highlight dot is more like 10 percent—we use the Output Levels sliders to do some preliminary tonal compression, then use the eyedroppers for fine tuning.

Black Output Levels. When this slider is at its default setting of 0, pixels in the image at level 0 will remain at level 0. As you increase the value of the slider, it limits the darkest pixels in the image to the level at which it's set.

This is different from the behavior of the black *Input* Levels control, which actually clips the data: if you set the black Input Levels slider to 5, then all pixels at levels 0 through 5 turn to level 0. If you set the black *Output* Levels slider to 5, on the other hand, the distinction between the levels is maintained; but the pixels that were at level 0 go to level 5, those at level 1 go to level 6 (or thereabouts), and so on. You lose contrast and some image detail as the tonal range gets compressed, but this is quite different from clipping the black input levels.

White Output Levels. This behaves the same way as the black Output Levels slider, except that it limits the lightest pixels in the image rather than the darkest ones. Setting the slider to level 240, for instance, will turn all the pixels at level 255 to 240, and so on (see Figure 6-17).

Figure 6-16
Output levels

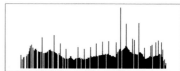

Compressing the tonal range with the Output sliders to the limits of the printing process (we used 12 and 243—about 5 and 95 percent) makes the darkest shadow detail more visible while reducing contrast overall.

It also points out the limitations of this targeting approach with images that include specular highlights (or headlights). They go gray.

You might think that compressing the tonal range would fill in those gaps in the histogram caused by gamma and endpoint tweaks, and to a limited extent it will, but all that number crunching introduces rounding errors, so you'll still see some levels going unused.

Tip: Leave Some Room When Setting Limits. Always leave yourself some room to move when you set Input and Output limits, particularly in the highlights. If you move the white Input slider so that your highlight detail starts at level 254, with your specular highlights at level 255, you run into two problems.

▶ When you compress the tonal range for targeting, your specular highlights will go gray.

▶ When you sharpen, some of the highlight detail will blow out to white.

To avoid these problems, try to keep your significant highlight detail below level 250. Shadow clipping is less critical, but keeping the untargeted shadow detail in the 5–10 range is a safe way to go.

Likewise, unless your image has no true whites or blacks, leave a little headroom when you set the output limits. For example, if your press can't hold a dot smaller than 10 percent, don't set the output limit to level 230. If you're targeting with the Output sliders in Levels, set it to 232 or 233 so you get true whites in the printed piece. If you'll be targeting later with the eyedroppers or an arbitrary curve, set it somewhere around 237 or 240. This will allow you to fine-tune small specular highlights using the eyedroppers or an arbitrary curve, but will still bring the tonal range of the image into a range that's closer to what the press can handle.

Levels Command Goodies

There are a few very useful features in the Levels dialog box that aren't immediately obvious. But they can be huge time-savers.

Preview. When you turn on the Preview checkbox in the Levels dialog box, Photoshop redraws the image—or the part of the image that is selected—to reflect any Levels tweaks you've made, so you can see the effect before you click OK. For large images, this preview can take a while.

If you leave Preview unchecked, and you have Video LUT Animation turned on in General Preferences, Photoshop changes the entire screen, in real time, to show the effects of your tweaks. The animated-LUT display can be (quite) inaccurate, but we use this mode often. There are at least two cases when we always use the slower Preview option instead.

▶ When we're working on a selection within an image. When Preview is turned on, Photoshop only changes the selection, so we can see its relationship to the unaltered areas surrounding it.

▶ When we're trying to make one image match another. With Preview on, Photoshop only changes the image we're working on, so we can see how it compares to another open image.

In most cases, we see very little difference between the Video LUT Animation preview and the real, calculated one, but we've been bitten often enough that we almost always check the real thing by turning on Preview before we click OK to burn our changes into the image.

Black-point/white-point clipping display. Black-point and white-point clipping is the one feature that keeps us coming back to Levels, instead of relying entirely on Curves to make tonal adjustments. It only works when you have the Preview checkbox turned off and Video LUT Animation (in General Preferences) turned on, and it doesn't work in Lab, CMYK, Indexed Color, or Bitmap modes—only in Grayscale, RGB, Duotone, and Multichannel.

When you set the black and white points, you generally want to set the white point to the lightest area that contains detail, and the shadow to the darkest point that contains detail. These aren't always easy to see. If you hold down the Option key while moving the black or white Input Levels sliders, you can see at a glance exactly which pixels are being clipped (see Figure 6-17).

Figure 6-17

The clipping display in Levels

Holding down Option as you move the left and right Input sliders shows which pixels are being clipped to white or (in this illustration) black. The display is almost essential for setting white and black points, but it's useful in many other situations as well.

Input Levels: 24 | 1.00 | 255

Input Levels: 48 | 1.00 | 255

Input Levels: 72 | 1.00 | 255

Tip: Look for the Jumps When Clipping. When you're Option-moving the Input sliders to view the clipping display, watch for big clumps of pixels turning on or off. You generally want to stay outside of these clumps of image pixels, because moving past them removes a lot of detail.

These types of jumps are also what we look for when we're evaluating scans and scanners. A good scan gives you a smooth growth of pixels as you Option-move the sliders. Lesser-quality scanners tend to provide scans with distinct jumps between gray levels.

Be aware that the number of jumps displayed is quite different with 8- and 16-bit displays. You'll see far fewer jumps with 24-bit color.

Instant before-and-after. Press on the title bar of the Levels dialog box to toggle between the altered and unaltered versions of the image. Again, this only works when you have Preview turned off and Video LUT Animation turned on, but it works in any mode.

Auto-reset. If you hold down Option, the Cancel button changes to Reset, which restores the settings to their default states.

We'll take you through the process of using Levels to correct an image a little later in this chapter, but first we'll look at the other major tonal-manipulation tool: Curves.

Curves

As we said above, if Levels is an automatic transmission, Curves is a stick shift. It's indispensable when you're stuck in the snow or mud, but it takes a bit more effort to master. The Curves command offers a different way of stretching and squeezing the bits, one that's more powerful than Levels. But it also uses a different way of looking at the data.

When you use Levels, the histogram shows you the shape of the data you're working with. Curves doesn't do that (we wish it did). Instead, it displays a graph that plots the relationship between input level and output level (unaltered and altered). Input levels run along the bottom, and output values run along the side. When you first choose the Curves command, the graph displays a straight 45-degree line—for each input level, the output level is identical (see Figure 6-18).

Figure 6-18
Curves dialog

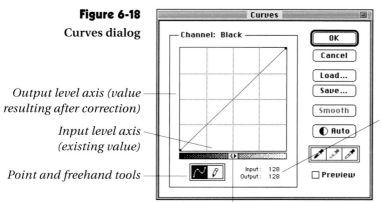

Output level axis (value resulting after correction)

Input level axis (existing value)

Point and freehand tools

Current point readout. Displays the input and output values for the cursor position as you place and move points.

Percentage/levels selector. Click to toggle between black on the left, with level readouts (0–256), and black on the right, with percent readouts (0–100).

Curves versus Levels. Anything you can do in the Levels dialog box, you can also do with Curves (see Figure 6-19). When you move the middle Input slider in Levels to adjust gamma, for instance, it's almost the same as moving the midpoint of the curve right or left. Setting the other four sliders is equivalent to setting the endpoints of the curve.

Figure 6-19
Levels and Curves

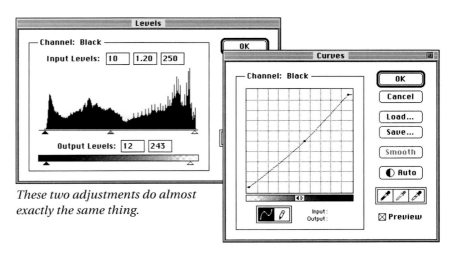

These two adjustments do almost exactly the same thing.

Tone curves are probably the most useful global image-manipulation tool ever invented—they're indispensable for color correction, but they're also very useful for fine control over grayscale work. Gamma corrections like the one in Levels let you change the broad distribution of midtones, but they only let you create very basic curves ("move the 50-percent point to here") with two endpoints and a single midpoint. The Curves command lets you make very precise adjustments to specific parts of the tonal range.

You change the relationship between input level and output level by changing the shape of the curve, either by placing points or by drawing a curve freehand (with the pencil tool). We vastly prefer placing points on the curve to drawing freehand, because it's much easier to be precise that way. All the settings you can make with Levels—white point, black point, midtones, maximum shadow, and minimum highlight—you can make with Curves too, but the way you go about it is slightly different.

Before we get into adjusting curves, though, there are a couple of ways to customize the Curves dialog box to your preferred way of working.

Tip: Customizing the Curves Dialog Box. Some people are happy thinking of tone in terms of levels from 0 to 255. Others want to work with dot percentages. The Curves dialog allows you to switch from one to the other by clicking the arrowheads in the middle of the gray ramp.

When you display levels, the 0,0 shadow point is at the lower left, and the 255,255 highlight point is at the upper right. When you display using percentages, the 0,0 highlight point is at the lower left and the 100,100 shadow point is at the upper right. You can switch freely between the two modes at any time.

Tip: Change the Grid. You can also change the gridlines of the Curves dialog box. The default displays gridlines in 25-percent increments, but if you Option-click anywhere in the graph area, the gridlines display in 10-percent increments instead (see Figure 6-20). We like the 10-percent increments because they give us a good idea of the percentages, even when we're displaying levels instead. But it doesn't really change the functionality of the controls.

Figure 6-20
Changing the grid
in Curves

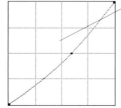

Option-click anywhere in the grid area to toggle between 25-percent and 10-percent gridlines.

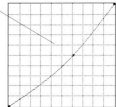

The curve. The great power of the Curves command comes from the fact that you aren't limited to placing just one point on the curve. You can actually place up to fourteen curve points, though we rarely need that many. This lets you change the shape of the curve as well as its steepness (remember, steepness is contrast; the steeper an area of the curve, the more definition you're pulling out between pixel values).

For example, an S-shaped curve increases contrast in the midtones, without blowing out the highlights or plugging up the shadows (see Figure 6-21). On the other hand, it sacrifices highlight and shadow detail by compressing those regions. We often use a small bump on the highlight end of the curve to stretch the highlights, or on the shadow end of the curve to open up the extreme shadows.

Figure 6-21
S-curves

More contrast

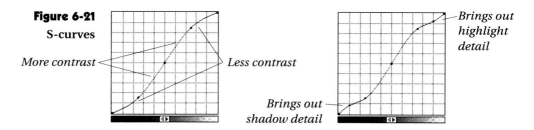

Less contrast

Brings out highlight detail

Brings out shadow detail

The info readout. Whenever you move the cursor into the graph area, the Input and Output levels display at the bottom of the dialog box changes to reflect the cursor's X,Y coordinates on the graph. For example, if you place the cursor at Input 128, Output 102 and click, the curve changes its shape to pass through that point. All the pixels that were at level 128 change to level 102, and the rest of the midtones are darkened correspondingly (see Figure 6-22).

Figure 6-22
The info readout

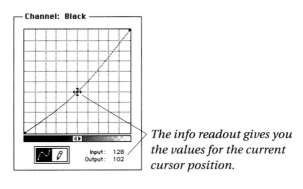

Channel: Black

Input: 128
Output: 102

The info readout gives you the values for the current cursor position.

Taking the midpoint of the curve and moving it left or right is analogous to moving the gamma slider in Levels. You can follow the shape of the curve with the cursor, and watch the info readout to determine exactly what's happening to each level.

Handling black and white points. You can clip the black or white points by moving the endpoints of the curve horizontally toward the center of the graph (just like moving the Input sliders in Levels; see Figure 6-23). For instance, if you move the black end of the curve directly to the right so that the info readout reads Input 12, Output 0, you've clipped all the pixels at level 12 or below and made them all level 0. This is exactly the same as moving the black Input slider in Levels from 0 to 12.

Figure 6-23

Clipping and compressing in Curves

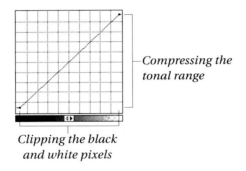

Compressing the tonal range

Clipping the black and white pixels

You can also limit the highlight and shadow dots by moving the endpoints of the curve vertically toward the center of the graph (like moving the Output sliders in the Levels dialog box). For example, to limit the highlight dot to 5 percent, move the highlight end of the curve until the Output Level displays as 243—or (if you're displaying percentages) 5 percent.

The eyedropper. While the Curves dialog box lacks the black and white clipping displays of Levels, it has an extra cool feature that shows you at a glance where any point in the image lies on the tonal curve. When the Curves dialog box is open, the cursor automatically switches to the eyedropper when you move it over the image. If you hold down the mouse button, the info display in the Curves dialog shows the Input and Output levels of the pixel(s) under the eyedropper, and a hollow white circle shows the location of that point on the curve (see Figure 6-24). This makes it very easy to identify the levels in the regions you want to change, and to see just how much you're changing them.

Figure 6-24

Curves dialog with
eyedropper

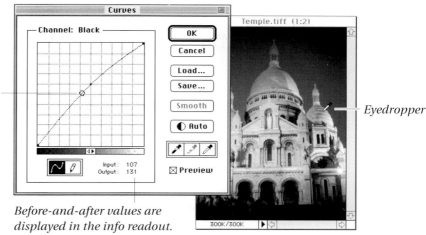

*The circular marker shows
the position, on the curve,
of the current pixel value.*

Eyedropper

*Before-and-after values are
displayed in the info readout.*

Tip: Setting Curves by the Numbers. Setting the endpoints of curves can
be tricky, particularly when you want to set two points close together.
We'd like to be able to define curves numerically by simply typing in a list
of input and output values, but until a future version of Photoshop, we
have to make do with this tip.

One way you can set points on a curve by the numbers is by using either the Transfer or the Duotone Curve dialog box to create the curve. We
usually use Duotone because we have to go through fewer mouse clicks
to get there.

1. Choose Duotone from the Mode menu, then click on the Curve icon
   for Ink 1 (see Chapter 9, *Duotones*, for more information on this dialog box).

2. Specify the numeric values you want (you can enter new Output values for thirteen points: 0%, 5%, 10% through 90% in 10-percent increments, 95%, and 100%).

3. Save the curve by clicking the Save button, then cancel out of the
   Curves dialog box, and cancel again out of the Duotone Curve dialog
   box. (When you cancel out of the Duotone Curve dialog box, the image reverts back to Grayscale mode.)

4. Go back to Curves, and click Load to load the curve you just saved.
   Then you can edit it further, if you wish.

Other Curves command goodies. Like Levels, Curves has some hidden goodies. The Preview feature works exactly the same as it does in Levels, as does the instant before-and-after, with the same constraints. The Option key provides the same auto-reset feature as does Levels—Option-click Cancel to reset the curve.

We'll take you through the process of using Curves to correct an image a little later in this chapter, but first let's look at those oft-misunderstood little critters, the black and white eyedropper tools.

White Points and Black Points and Grays, Oh My!

Correcting images is only half the battle. You also have to target them—you have to compensate for the shortcomings of the output process the images are aimed at. If you're going to an output process other than halftone printing, targeting grayscale images is simply a matter of matching the contrast of your image to the contrast behavior of the output device, be it a film recorder, dye-sublimation printer, or computer screen. But when the image is destined for print, you have to do two things.

▶ Set the endpoints of the tonal range so that your highlights don't blow out and your shadows don't plug up.

▶ Adjust your midtones to compensate for dot gain on press.

You can build in these adjustments while you correct flaws in the image, or you can perform them as a separate step, after you've fixed all the other problems in the image.

Endpoints and limits. Some people use the terms "white point" and "minimum highlight," or "black point" and "maximum shadow" interchangeably. But an important distinction can be drawn between the two.

▶ White point and black point are defined by the image itself. They're simply the lightest and darkest pixels in the image, normally (but not always) levels 255 and 0, respectively.

▶ The minimum highlight and maximum shadow values, on the other hand, are dictated by the limitations of your output process. Each combination of printing press, ink, and paper has limits for both the smallest and largest dots it can print. Dots that are too small don't print (you get white paper instead), because the ink doesn't adhere to the plate. Dots that are too large simply plug up, and print as solid ink coverage. In either case, the detail in those areas is lost, because the differences between adjacent pixels are gone—they're all black or white.

Setting Endpoints with Levels

In many cases, we can simply set our white point to the value that we know will produce the minimum highlight dot, and our black point to the maximum shadow dot. With many images, however, the white and black points need to lie inside or outside of the printable range.

True blacks and whites. If the image has detail all the way up to the level-255 highlight and all the way down to the level-0 shadow, we can simply set these values to our minimum highlight and maximum shadow dots. To do so, we use the Output Levels sliders in Levels (see Figure 6-25).

For example, if we know that a particular press can handle a minimum highlight dot of five percent and a maximum shadow dot of 95 percent, we set the white Output slider to 243 and the black Output slider to 13. This ensures that all our gray values fall into the range the press can reproduce.

Figure 6-25

Setting endpoints in Levels

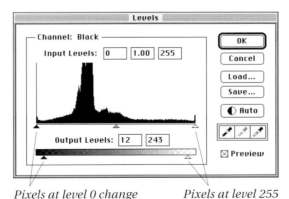

Pixels at level 0 change to level 13 (a 95-percent dot).

Pixels at level 255 change to level 243 (a 5-percent dot).

This approach works fine for many images, but it can cause difficulties with images that have important detail in the highlights or shadows.

Highlight problems. One source of trouble in setting the highlight is the *transition zone*—the point at which the press can no longer handle a dot and simply drops out to white paper. It's especially problematic with newsprint (or desktop laser printers), where the minimum dot is often quite large—in the region of 10 percent or so.

We see a lot of newspaper images where highlights on faces appear as large, leprous white patches, or where skies have huge white holes in them. The jump from white paper to a 10-percent dot is sudden and obvious, so when you're dealing with output that has a large minimum dot size, you often want to be a little more conservative and set the minimum dot even larger. The trade-off is that you lose contrast, because the brightest areas in the image are still being reproduced as a 10-percent gray (see Figure 6-26).

Figure 6-26
Trouble in the transition zone

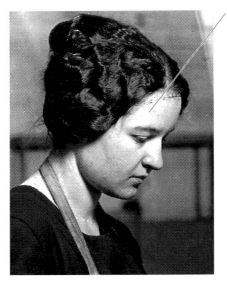

Because of the sudden jump from no dot to a ten-percent dot, images printed to newsprint can display a severe case of "highlight psoriasis."

To emphasize the newsprint effect, we've printed this image with an 85-lpi screen.

Shadow problems. If you set the black point in your image to the maximum shadow dot, and the image has significant detail in the shadows stretching up through level 20 or so, the image will appear flat when it prints, because there will be very little true, solid black in the shadows.

You can deal with this using Levels by setting the black Output slider to a lower value than the maximum dot the press can produce. For example, if the press plugs up at anything over 85 percent, instead of set-ting the black Output slider to 38, you may want to set it to 35 instead.

Specular highlights. The compress-the-output-levels approach outlined above works well in many images, but it doesn't work well at all when the image contains small specular highlights—the very bright highlights that appear on shiny surfaces such as glass, metal, or a well-polished apple. If you compress this type of image with the normal output controls, you'll get a flat, low-contrast look. Your images will have much more snap on the page if you let those highlights blow out to white paper, rather than print-ing with the minimum dot. You want to reserve the minimum dot for those parts of the image that are very bright, but still contain some detail.

You can do this with the Output sliders in Levels, but not with any great degree of precision. If you set the white Output slider to a value a little higher than the minimum highlight dot, the very brightest pixels in the image will blow out to white paper. But you won't really know just how much highlight detail is going to blow out, or which parts of the image will actually print with the minimum highlight dot.

You can also run into problems with the transition zone in newsprint. The specular highlights *may* drop out to white. It's equally likely, though, that some will and some won't. Fortunately, Photoshop offers some more precise ways of setting endpoints; we'll look at those next.

Setting Endpoints with the Eyedropper Tools

When you're dealing with specular highlights, you want to set the mini-mum highlight dot to a level a little darker than the absolute whites in your image. You want the minimum highlight dot to reproduce the light-est parts of the image that still hold detail, and let the small specular high-lights blow out to white paper.

The same holds true for deep shadows, though to a much lesser extent. In theory, the maximum shadow dot is the point at which the press plugs up the dots and prints solid ink. In practice, this isn't a hard-and-fast rule. If the press can only print a 95-percent dot and you have a few theoreti-cally unprintable 97-percent dots sprinkled in your shadows, they'll prob-ably provide a little more texture than if you simply set a 95-percent limit.

Photoshop's black and white eyedropper tools (in both the Levels and Curves dialog boxes) let you set your minimum highlight and maximum shadow dots very accurately. These tools are shrouded in mystery, and provoke more than their fair share of confusion, in part because they can do so many things. For a detailed description of what the eyedroppers do, see the sidebar "The Math Behind the Eyedroppers," later in this chapter.

Eyedropper confusion. Many people find the eyedropper tools in the Levels and Curves dialog boxes so confusing that they give up on them after trying them once or twice. Others believe that they're as useless as Brightness and Contrast (until recently, we were in that camp). There are four sources for the confusion.

▶ The tools give misleading feedback. When you use them, they move the Levels sliders or change the endpoints of the curve in Curves. But those changes *don't reflect what the eyedroppers are really doing!* If you try to duplicate their effect by moving the sliders or changing the curve, you get a different result. This is incredibly frustrating, because you have to ignore the signals the dialog box is giving you.

▶ Using either eyedropper sets the tonal curve to a straight line, so if you make a Levels or Curves tweak and then use the eyedroppers, your tweak is immediately undone. If you use the eyedroppers first, and then do a Levels or Curves tweak, you're likely to change what you did with the eyedroppers!

▶ People keep trying to use these tools for tonal correction rather than targeting. Since they're really designed to make small tonal moves, the larger moves involved in tonal correction tend to push their limits.

▶ The tools live in the Levels and Curves dialog boxes, which apply non-linear transformations, but they apply a linear transformation. Nonetheless, this linear transformation is not necessarily bad.

This may make the eyedroppers sound almost useless, but if you understand how and when you should use them, they let you set your minimum and maximum dots very precisely.

What the eyedroppers do. The black, white, and gray eyedroppers do similar things, but each is specialized to operate on a different part of the tonal range. For now, we'll discuss the black and white eyedroppers. The gray eyedropper is a color-correction tool—it isn't available for grayscale images—so we'll deal with it in the next chapter, *Color Correction*.

Each eyedropper lets you choose a target color and a source color. All pixels in the image with the value of the source color are turned to the value of the target color, and all the other pixels in the image are changed proportionally. The black eyedropper operates on the shadows without affecting the highlights, while the white eyedropper operates on the highlights without affecting the shadows.

The advantage they offer over the other methods of tonal compression is that they let us set a specific pixel value *other than black or white* to the minimum and maximum dot values we know the press can hold. This allows us to hold detail in highlight areas while still letting our specular highlights blow out, and maintain texture in deep shadows without making them go flat.

Using the eyedroppers. You can use the eyedroppers from either the Levels or the Curves dialog box, but we prefer using Levels, because of the cool black-point/white-point clipping display in the Levels dialog box. This tool makes it much easier to identify good candidate values for black and white source colors, and to find pixels in the image that have those values.

1. Set the target value by double-clicking the black or white eyedropper, and entering the value in the color picker that appears. You can specify the color in any color space, but for grayscale images, just enter identical values for red, green, and blue.

    Set the target black and white colors to the maximum shadow and minimum highlight values that the output process can handle. For example, a target black value of 13 and a target white value of 243 correspond to a 95-percent maximum shadow dot and a minimum 5-percent highlight dot.

2. Option-drag the black or white Input levels slider, and note the value at which detail starts to appear. Make sure you return the Input levels sliders to their original places (at 0 and 255).

3. Now comes the tricky part: find a pixel in the image with that exact value, and click on it with the eyedropper. Photoshop changes that

The Math Behind the Eyedroppers

For the terminally curious, or for those who want to know exactly what will happen to each value in the image, this is what the two eyedroppers do.

White eyedropper. The white eyedropper simply multiplies all the pixels in the image by *target value ÷ source value*. For example, if we choose a target value of 243 (a five-percent dot), and click the tool on a pixel with a value of 248, all pixels at level 248 are turned to level 243. All the other values in the image are multiplied by 243/248, or approximately 0.98. So pixels with an input value of 255 produce an output value of 250, because 255 x 0.98 = 249.85. Pixels with an input value of 128 produce an output value of 125, and so on down the tonal range until we get to

level 25, which remains unchanged, because 25 x 0.98 = 24.5, which gets rounded back up to 25.

If we make a much smaller move by choosing a source value of 246 and a target of 243, the multiplier is 0.99, so an input value of 255 produces an output value of 253, 128 produces an output value of 127, and values below 50 remain unchanged.

Note that you can use the white eyedropper to stretch the highlights (rather than compressing them) by choosing a source color that's darker than the target color. This produces a multiplier with a value greater than 1, so the pixel values are increased rather than decreased.

Black eyedropper. The black eyedropper essentially does the

reverse of the white eyedropper, but the arithmetic is a little more complicated. To limit the effect to the shadows, the algorithm uses the inverse brightnesses of the input value and of the difference between source and target color—the inverse brightness of any value x is 255-x. If we call the difference between source and target values y, then for each pixel value x, the output value equals $((255-x) \div (255-y) * y) + x$.

If this makes your head hurt, don't worry—the net result is very similar to that produced by the white eyedropper, only in reverse. The source value is changed to the target value, and all other values in the image change proportionally, with the change becoming progressively smaller as you go toward the highlights.

pixel to the output value, and compresses or expands the tonal range to compensate for that change.

This takes a little practice. Use the clipping display in Levels to get a general idea of where to look, check values in the Info palette as you go, and if necessary zoom in and out using Command-spacebar and Command-Option-spacebar. (For some reason, Command-plus and Command-minus don't work while you're in a dialog box.)

Tip: Use a Gray Wedge to Select Your Source Color. It's easy to identify the value where your highlight detail really lies using the clipping display in Levels. It's much harder to find a pixel with that value to set as the source, using the Eyedropper tool. Fortunately, you can pick up the source color for the eyedropper from any open image—it doesn't have to be in the active image.

To make it easy to find source values, keep a file containing a gray wedge open while you're targeting images.

1. Create a 300-pixel-wide, 72-ppi image, and use the Gradient tool to fill it with a ramp from black to white; turn off dithering first in the Gradient Tool Options palette.

2. Use the clipping display to identify the value you want to select for the source pixel. For this example, let's assume your highlight detail goes up to level 252.

3. Select an eyedropper and, while holding down the mouse button, drag the white eyedropper through the gray wedge until the Info palette reads 252. Release the mouse button, and you've picked up your source value. Just make sure you don't make the gray wedge the active image, or you'll change it instead of the image you were working on.

Tip: Keep the Mouse Button Down. If you're picking up the source value from the active image, it's still handy to hold down the mouse button while searching for the perfect pixel. When you find the one you want, you can just release the mouse button to select it. When the cursor hits the edge of the window, the image autoscrolls, which is sometimes useful.

Depending on where you click the eyedropper, the Input or Output sliders may move (or if you're in Curves, the endpoints of the curve may change). *Ignore this feedback*—it doesn't provide an accurate picture of what's going on. Trust the values in the Info palette instead.

If you don't like the result, or if you click on the wrong pixel by accident, you can click on another pixel to undo the bad tweak and apply another one. To undo both a black and a white eyedropper tweak, hold down the Option key to change the Cancel button in the dialog box to Reset. The changes aren't made permanent until you click OK to close the Levels (or Curves) dialog box.

Setting Endpoints with Curves

The beauty of using the white eyedropper tool to set the minimum highlight dot is that it lets values brighter than the one you select as the source color fade out softly to white paper. But in some situations that can also be its biggest liability. If you're dealing with newsprint or low-quality web printing, the transition zone—that ambiguous area between white paper and the minimum reliable dot—can make your specular highlights messy and inconsistent. Some may drop out, while others may print with a fairly large dot.

This calls for a more desperate remedy, using the pencil tool in the Curves dialog box. (It's actually just about the only time we use the pencil tool in Curves.) You need to make a curve that sets your brightest highlight detail to the minimum highlight dot value, then blows everything brighter than that directly out to white. This is a two-step process.

1. Use the point tool to set a point with an Input value corresponding to your brightest real detail, and an Output value corresponding to your minimum printable dot. Figure 6-27 shows a point that sets the Input value at 253 and the Output value at 231, corresponding to a 10-percent dot. (This is an extreme case.)

    This sets all the pixels with a value of 253 to 231. Unfortunately, it also sets pixels with values of 253 through 255 to 231, which isn't what we want. We want them to be white.

2. Select the pencil tool, and *very carefully* position it at the top edge of the curve graph, until the Input value reads 253 and the Output value reads 255, then hold down the mouse button and drag straight to the left (or right, if you have the Curves dialog box set up to show highlights at the lower left). See Figure 6-27.

Figure 6-27

Blowing out
the speculars

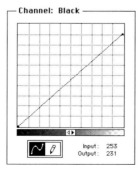

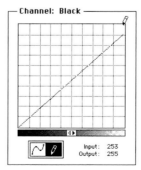

A curve point at 253 in, 231 out compresses the image to the printable range.

A little touchup with the pencil tool makes all the white pixels white.

This keeps pixels with an Input value of 252 set to an Output value of 231, but blows out pixels with a value of 253 through 255 to white paper. Your highlight detail will print with a reliable dot, and your specular highlights will definitely blow out.

3. Click the Save button to save the curve. Don't click the Smooth button, because it will smooth the curve—which in this case is not what you want.

When to Set the Endpoints

Conventional wisdom usually dictates that sharpening your image is either the very last thing you do, or (with RGB color images) the second-to-last step before converting it to CMYK. But conventional wisdom predates Photoshop. We think it's crazy to set your endpoints and then sharpen the image, because sharpening with the Unsharp Mask filter invariably increases contrast at the ends of the tonal range, driving some pixels to black or white. In short, it undoes your work in setting the endpoints.

No matter which method you use to set your endpoints, we strongly recommend that you do so after you've applied Unsharp Mask. For a detailed discussion on sharpening your images, see Chapter 8, *Sharpening*.

Compensating for Dot Gain

The second part of targeting your images is compensating for dot gain, which you do by adjusting the midtones. When you print in color, Photoshop's RGB-to-CMYK separation engine automatically compensates for dot gain (see "Dot Gain: Coping with Midtone Spread" in Chapter 5, *Color Preferences*). With grayscale or duotone images, you have to manually compensate for dot gain, lightening the midtones so that they'll have the correct gray value when they print. There are three ways to do this.

1. Change the image data itself.

2. Use a transfer function and Save as EPS.

3. Use a duotone curve and save as EPS (in the case of a grayscale image, you can save it as a monotone).

The two latter approaches have the advantage of not changing the original image data, and they allow you to compensate for dot gain very precisely; but they limit you to using the EPS format.

Tip: Figuring Dot Gain. When your printer tells you to expect 12-percent dot gain, that means (or should mean) that a 50-percent dot on film will result in a 62-percent dot on press. (See "Dot Gain: Coping with Midtone Spread" in Chapter 5, *Color Preferences*, for a discussion on how to obtain the correct figure for anticipated dot gain.)

But because of the way Photoshop's Curves dialog box works, it's more useful to know what dot on film will yield a 50-percent dot on press. Unfortunately, you can't just use the dot gain figure, because dot gain is most pronounced at 50 percent, declining at higher and lower percentages. Table 6-1 gives some good estimates. A knowledgeable printer (or a press check) can provide more accurate numbers.

	Projected dot gain	Dot percentage that will result in a 50-percent dot on press
Table 6-1 Dot gain targets	10%	41%
	15%	36%
	20%	33%
	25%	30%
	30%	28%

Changing the image to compensate for dot gain. The easiest way to compensate for dot gain is to change the image itself. The disadvantage is that you end up with an image that may not print well under a different set of output conditions. You can usually repurpose an already targeted image for an output process with *more* dot gain, but if you try to repurpose it to print with less dot gain, you're likely to encounter posterization when you darken the midtones again.

You can change the image working visually, turning on Use Dot Gain for Grayscale Images in Printing Inks Setup to make the monitor simulate the effects of dot gain. We don't recommend this approach—we're more likely to swear *at* it than to swear by it—but if you want to try it, see "Use Dot Gain for Grayscale Images" in Chapter 5, *Color Preferences*.

A much easier (and, in our opinion, more reliable) method is to go by the numbers. You need to lighten the image to compensate for the anticipated amount of dot gain.

For example, if you expect 22-percent dot gain, you need to lighten the 50-percent dot to a 31-percent dot. (Dot gain is most pronounced, and is specified at, 50 percent. At higher and lower dot percentages, dot gain is progressively less).

There are several ways to accomplish this: our favorite method is to use the Duotone Curve dialog box to create the curve (see the tip "Setting Curves by the Numbers," earlier in this chapter), but you can simply go into Curves and set a point to the desired value. For example, to compensate for 22-percent dot gain, you'd simply create a curve like the one in Figure 6-28.

Figure 6-28

Compensating for dot gain with a curve

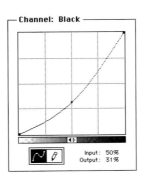

As we mentioned above, you can include this dot gain targeting step as part of your one-step tonal correction (in either Levels or Curves), or you can do it as a separate step, after you've corrected for problems in the image and the capture process.

Use a transfer function or monotone to compensate for dot gain. An alternate approach (which doesn't change the image data) is to include the curve separately from the image, and save it as an EPS file. When the image is rasterized by a PostScript printer or imagesetter, the PostScript RIP alters the gray values according to the curve.

You can use a transfer function, or you can make the image a monotone. The two options are functionally identical, so it's entirely a matter of which mouse clicks you'd rather make.

To create a transfer function, do the following.

1. Choose Page Setup from the File menu.

2. Click the Transfer button to open the Transfer Functions dialog box.

3. Enter the desired value for the 50-percent dot in the appropriate field.

4. Optionally, save the transfer function, then click OK.

5. Save the image as EPS and check "Include Transfer Function."

To make a monotone, do the following.

1. Choose Duotone from the Mode menu.

2. Choose Monotone from the Type popup menu.

3. Click the Ink 1 curve to open the Duotone Curve dialog box.

4. Enter the desired value for the 50-percent dot in the appropriate field.

5. Optionally, save the transfer function, and click OK.

6. Save the image as EPS.

The Duotone method appears to take an extra step, but the curve is automatically included when you save the image—you don't have to remember to check any boxes.

Tonal Correction in Practice

Theory is all very well and good, but there's no substitute for practice, practice, practice. Every image is different, presenting its own challenges and opportunities; here are a couple of examples of how we use these tools together to enhance images quickly and efficiently.

Using Levels to Correct a Good Scan

Figure 6-29 shows an image scanned from a color negative using a Leafscan 35. Since the Leafscan is a high-bit scanner, we tapped its capabilities, setting reasonable black and white points to avoid tonal clipping, and applying a gamma move of 1.8 (to match our monitor gamma). This yielded a scan that was very usable, but needed some fine-tuning to increase contrast, bring out detail, and get it ready for print.

Option-dragging the white Input slider shows us that we don't want to clip any of the highlight detail—it's all good, useful stuff. Option-dragging the black Input slider shows us that there's very little important detail in the extreme blacks—we can definitely afford to clip some of it. In so doing, we'll intensify the blacks, increase the overall image contrast, and bring out detail throughout by expanding the tonal range.

Figure 6-29 The raw lighthouse image

The histogram shows that the scan has succeeded in capturing the entire tonal range of the image, without clipping the highlights or the shadows. The problem is that it looks flat, with no really dense blacks.

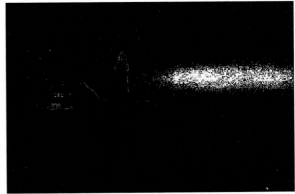

Shadow clipping at level 16

Highlight clipping at level 240

The amount of clipping is largely dictated by our output process. If we were going to a film recorder that could record all that subtle detail, or preparing a premium print job, we'd be very conservative and clip only two or three levels; but for a midrange job like this book, we can easily clip to level 14 or so. There's some detail below that, but it isn't important detail; we know we won't be able to reproduce it under these printing conditions, and if we clip it we can use the available levels to show more important detail in the midtones and highlights.

This intensifies the blacks nicely, but it also plugs up most of the shadow detail, so we use the gamma (gray) slider to bring some of it back. A gamma tweak of around 1.4 does the job nicely.

Figure 6-30 The lighthouse after correction with Levels

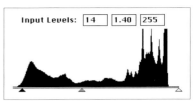

This Levels adjustment results in the image at left and the histogram below.

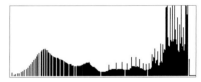

Figure 6-31 The lighthouse after targeting

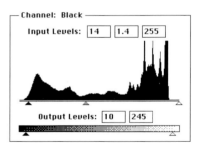

Output levels of 10 and 245 compress the tonal range for our printing conditions. These values are slightly outside the 12/243 settings that would yield 5- and 95-percent dots, to ensure that we have pure whites and solid blacks on press. Note that we combine this targeting move with the tonal-correction move to minimize data loss.

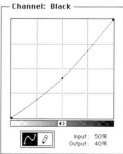

A curve move adjusts for projected dot gain of 12 percent, mapping the 50-percent values to 40 percent (which will print at about 50 percent on press).

While we could have made this adjustment with the middle input slider in Levels, we find this much easier and more accurate.

The final histogram after correction and targeting

In this case we target the image with the fast-and-dirty approach: set the output sliders to compress the tonal range, and make a quick curve move to compensate for projected dot gain. But by being conservative in our compression, we can avoid graying out our whites and blacks and flattening the image excessively.

Correcting an Archival Image with Levels

The old photograph in Figure 6-32 presents more of a challenge. The picture of Bruce's grandmother is scanned using an Agfa Arcus Plus from a very old print (c. 1928) that has been stored for years under less-than-ideal conditions. The ink in the inscription is much darker than anything in the photograph itself, and insects have eaten through the emulsion in other areas to produce tiny white spots that are brighter than any real image detail. Together, they fooled the scanner's autoexposure algorithm into using a much wider tonal range than the image really contains, so the scan appears washed out even though the histogram shows some data

Figure 6-32 The uncorrected Ella scan

The black and white points for this scan were wide of the mark, resulting in an excessively flat image.

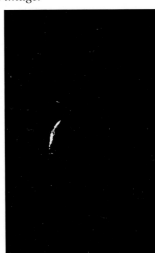

Shadow clipping at level 28   *Highlight clipping at level 225*

Figure 6-33 Ella corrected and targeted

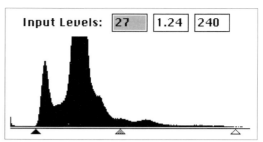

Input Levels: 27 | 1.24 | 240

This Levels adjustment results in the image at left and the histogram below.

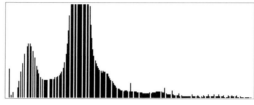

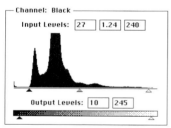

Channel: Black
Input Levels: 27 | 1.24 | 240
Output Levels: 10 | 245

As with the lighthouse image, we combine the tonal correction with Output Level compression for press conditions, and compensate for projected dot gain with a Curves move. You can see the result in the image and histogram at right.

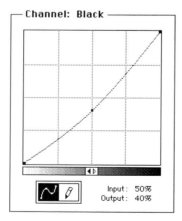

Channel: Black

Input: 50%
Output: 40%

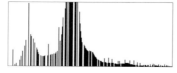

at almost every level. As with the lighthouse image, we apply a 1.8 gamma adjustment to the high-bit data at scan time.

The clipping display for this image tells a very different story. Setting the white Input slider to 240 creates small specular highlights on the bracelet, without clipping anything else in the image. At the shadow end, approximately the first 25 levels are taken up by the ink on the inscription. The darkest pixels in the image itself are in the shadows on the dress, but they also display the noise that's characteristic of flatbed scanners, so we set the black Input slider to level 27. A gamma tweak of 1.24 retrieves a little shadow detail.

If we were in a hurry, this is pretty much all we'd do to the images before sharpening and using the eyedroppers to fine-tune the endpoints. Given more time, we'd cancel out of the Levels dialog box and use Curves instead, remembering what we'd learned about the shadow and highlight values from the clipping display.

Deep Fixes with Curves

Levels lets you produce decent-quality images, but with Curves you can do much more. Curves lets you isolate specific parts of the tonal range and adjust them. Usually there's a trade-off involved—you emphasize some parts of the image at the expense of others. Learning how to manipulate images is easy; learning what needs to be done for each image is hard, and takes practice. The examples we give here are based on our subjective opinions; you may have different ideas on what we should have done.

Lighthouse. Our first three curve points establish the overall contrast. Remembering what we've learned from the clipping display in Levels, we clip the extreme shadows to add density to the blacks. This makes the midtones too dark, so we brighten them with a second point. This blows out the highlights, so a third point brings them back under control.

Our remaining points bring out specific features in the image. Zooming in with Command-spacebar, we use the eyedropper to examine the values at the edge of the lighthouse, and find that the lighthouse edge is at 232, while the sky is at 236–237. We need to increase the separation between those values. This is tricky—Photoshop won't let you set points that close together on the curve. We place points 4 and 5 as close as possible, then we pull them apart to give a little more contrast between the lighthouse and the sky.

Figure 6-34 Correcting the lighthouse with Curves

Point 4. 229 in, 228 out. Darkens the edge of the lighthouse.

Point 5. 241 in, 244 out. Brightens the highlight on the lighthouse.

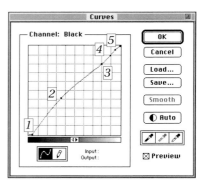

Point 1. 11 in, 0 out. Gives us solid black in the shadows.

Point 2. 80 in, 100 out. Brightens the midtones on the rocks.

Point 3. 203 in, 203 out. Brings the highlights back under control.

Our first three curve points establish the overall contrast. We clip the shadows slightly (1) to get solid blacks and disguise noisy pixels, then brighten the midtones (2), concentrating on the brighter areas of the rocks. This makes the sky too bright, so we use a temporary point (3) to bring the highlights back into a reasonable range. Curve points 4 and 5 increase the separation between the lighthouse and the sky.

We move point 3 to brighten the whitecaps. This brightens the midtones excessively and loses contrast between the waves and the dark water, so we add a point (6) to bring the midtones back toward their original values. Point 7 opens the deep shadows slightly while maintaining a true black in the darkest areas.

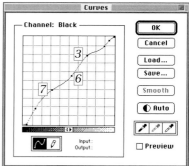

Point 7. 33 in, 46 out. Opens up the shadows.

Point 6. 135 in, 141 out. Corrects for point 5, restoring contrast between water and whitecaps.

Point 3. Third point moved to 179 in, 200 out. Brightens the whitecaps.

The whitecaps on the waves look flat. The eyedropper tells us that they're around level 179. Rather than placing an entirely new point, we move our third point to lighten the whitecaps. This works, but we've flattened the contrast between the whitecaps and the dark water, so we need to pull that part of the curve back closer to the original. We do this with a sixth point, but we don't pull the curve all the way back, because that would posterize the rocks—anytime you get a curve segment that's close to horizontal, you're running the risk of posterization.

Clicking on the title bar of the Curves window to get a quick before-and-after, we can see that we've improved the contrast in almost all areas. The lighthouse stands out from the background, and the whitecaps on the waves snap. Our only remaining problem is that the shadows are a little heavy, so our final point opens up the shadows slightly. The image is now ready for sharpening and targeting with the eyedroppers.

Your's Ella. Remembering what we saw in the Levels clipping display, we set the endpoints of the curve first. In this case we clip both the shadows and the highlights considerably because they contain no real image information (dealing quite permanently with any scanner-induced noise that may have been lurking in the shadows). We make sure that our highlight detail is still well below level 250, so we can target it later. A third curve point deepens the shadows, improving the overall contrast.

Three further moves go after specific areas in the image. The first increases contrast in the face, but it makes the highlights on the shoulder a little hot. If this were a modern image, we might let it go, but part of the charm of this photograph is its obvious age. We don't want to make the contrast too harsh, so our fifth curve point pulls back the highlights on the shoulder. A quick before-and-after obtained by clicking on the title bar shows us that we've lost some contrast around the left eye, so our final move lightens that side of the face slightly.

Save the Curves

We're done with the curves for now—this is as close as we can get without pulling a proof. But before we press OK to apply them to the image, we save the final curve by pressing the Save button. Because we're working on a copy of the image, if something goes wrong or we decide that some of the changes aren't quite to our liking, we can go back to the original file and load this curve as a new starting point.

Figure 6-35 Ella corrected with Curves

Point 3. 52 in, 23 out. Darkens the background.

We clip the highlights (1) to 250 (the lightest point on the shoulder, reserving the higher levels for the small specular highlights on the bracelet), and the shadows (2), spreading the real image information across the tonal range, and increasing contrast. Point 3 deepens the shadows, so that the darkest areas are almost the same shade as the ink of the inscription.

Point 4 lightens the face and also increases its contrast—too much, in fact. It also makes the highlights on the shoulder uncomfortably hot. Point 5 pulls back the highlights on the shoulder, and softens the contrast on the face, producing a result we feel is more in keeping with the photograph's obvious age. Point 6 produces just a hair more contrast on the shadowed side of the face, bringing out the sparkle in the left eye.

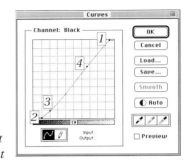

Point 1. 241 in, 255 out. Clips and brightens the highlights.

Point 2. 28 in, 0 out. Clips unwanted noise and creates true blacks.

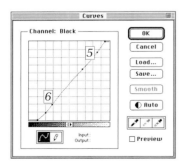

Point 4. 170 in, 165 out. Brightens the lighter tones of the face and increases its contrast.

Point 5. 219 in, 220 out. This pulls back the highlights on the shoulder.

Point 6. 73 in, 50 out. Emphasizes the sparkle in the left eye.

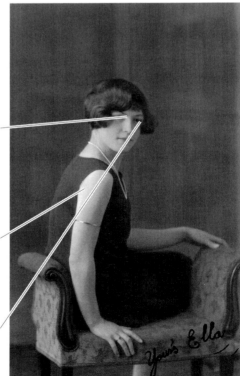

Figure 6-36

Histograms of corrected lighthouse and Ella images

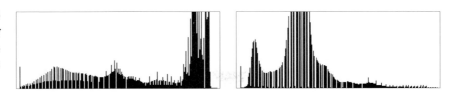

After we see proofs, we may want to make some changes, and these are better made by going back to the original data and modifying the curve. A look at the histograms reveals why. We don't yet have any gaps of more than one level; but if we want to do more manipulation, we're better off going back to the original eight bits, rather than stretching and squeezing the remaining ones even further.

Sharpen Before Final Tonal Compression

Every scanned image needs some unsharp masking, and it's a rich and complex enough subject that we've devoted an entire chapter to it later in the book. For now, trust us on the sharpening we apply to the two images before we do final tonal compression.

Figure 6-37

Sharpening settings for lighthouse and Ella images

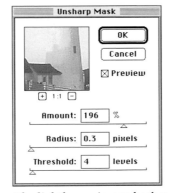 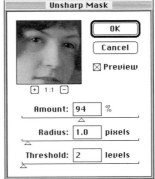

The lighthouse image both needs and benefits from considerably more sharpening than the studio portrait, which we deliberately leave soft since it preserves more of the feel of the original. Note that we also use a much smaller sharpening radius for the lighthouse image, because it contains more small details than the portrait.

Final Compression with the Eyedroppers

You can use the eyedroppers from either the Levels or Curves dialog box, but we always use Levels, because we find the clipping displays indispensable. We use them to check where our highlight and shadow details really are after sharpening.

Figure 6-38

Setting eyedropper targets

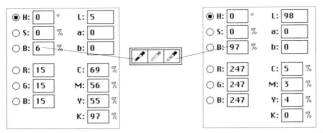

The fast, easy way to set the eyedropper targets for grayscale work is to use the Brightness field in the HSB color picker. A 3-percent dot is equivalent to 97-percent brightness, and a 94-percent dot is equivalent to 6-percent brightness.

We set the highlight target for a four-percent dot (our printer told us that they could probably hold a three-percent dot, but we decided to err on the side of caution), and set the shadow target for a 94-percent dot.

The moves we make with the eyedroppers are small and have a barely perceptible effect on the images overall, but they let us nail the extremes of the tonal range precisely.

Figure 6-39 Lighthouse, sharpened and targeted

The brightest pixels in the sky are at levels 252 and 253, so to hold a dot in the sky, we need to set level 251 or 252 as the source value for the white eyedropper. The edge of the middle attic window has several level-252 pixels, so we zoom in around that area, find a level-251 pixel along the edge of the window, and click on it. Repeating the process for the black eyedropper, we click on a level-5 pixel in the extreme shadow along the left side of the image.

Tonal Magic

Levels and Curves are real powerhouses, and becoming fluent with them is key to mastering Photoshop's production capabilities. We've introduced

Figure 6-40

Ella, sharpened
and targeted

The highlight clipping display shows the brightest skin tones at level 249. We want to make sure that we hold a dot in the skin tones, so we choose a level-249 pixel in the necklace as the source color. At the shadow end, the differences in levels 0 through 7 are mostly noise. Real detail starts to appear at level 8, so we pick a level-8 pixel in the folds of the dress as the source shadow color.

these tools by looking at grayscale manipulation, but they play an even more important role in color correction.

When you correct color, you're still stretching and squeezing 8-bit grayscale channels; but you're working with several channels simultaneously, so it's a lot more complex. If you master the operation of the tools thoroughly in grayscale, the color-correction techniques we present in the next chapter will come much more easily.

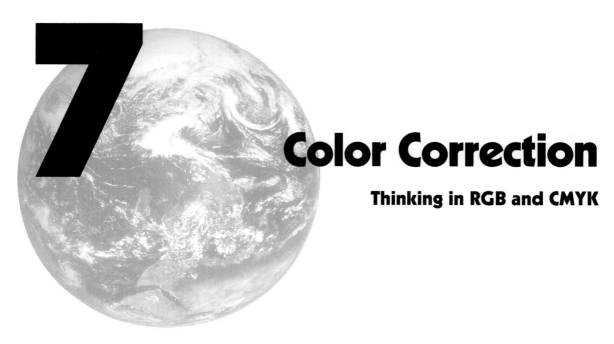

7

Color Correction

Thinking in RGB and CMYK

If you opened this book and went straight to this page looking for easy answers, stop. Go directly to jail. Do not pass Go. Do not collect $200. While you're in jail, you should take some time and read through a few other chapters.

First off, take a look at Chapter 4, *Color Essentials*. Then, if you're looking to convert your image from RGB to CMYK, or if you're trying to make decisions based on what you see on the monitor, you're going to need to know about Monitor Setup, Printing Inks Setup, and Separation Setup (so go read Chapter 5, *Color Preferences*). And when you make color corrections in Photoshop, you're really manipulating the tone of the individual color channels, so you need to understand how to tweak grayscale images before you touch color ones—they're at least nine times more complicated! (So you'd better read the last chapter, *Tonal Correction*, too.) And finally, if easy answers are what you want (who doesn't?), you should take a look at Chapter 16, *Color Management Systems*.

That said, if you want to plunge in, go ahead. Just bear in mind that when things get sticky, you may want to refer back to those chapters to get a better handle on what you've actually been doing.

Changing Modes and Losing Information

We've stressed throughout this book that almost everything you do to an image in Photoshop throws away some information. But a great many people, including some of the so-called experts, don't realize that switching to a different color mode throws away information faster than just about anything else.

The subject of mode conversion is surrounded by confusion and by more than its share of mythology. We'll discuss the arguments in detail throughout this chapter, but let us say up front that mode changes (color-space conversions) lose considerable amounts of information, no matter which color space you're going to or from (with one exception—the conversion from grayscale to RGB). Mode changes between RGB and Lab, Lab and CMYK, and RGB and CMYK all discard image information to a greater extent than most people realize.

RGB to Lab

There's a general impression in the Photoshop community that you can switch between RGB and Lab color without losing significant amounts of image information. Until we did some real tests, we shared this assumption, but we were surprised to find that the conversion between RGB and Lab is far from lossless. You lose a significant number of differences between levels—remember, difference is detail.

For instance, try converting an RGB step wedge to Lab—one quick, simple selection from the Mode menu—and examine the results: *about 35 of the possible 256 levels simply disappear* (see Figure 7-1). This loss may not be visually significant—you can't see it on the screen, and you're unlikely to see it in print—but if you try to stretch the now-degraded tonal range after the conversion, it will start to show up as posterization.

Figure 7-1
RGB-to-Lab-to-RGB data loss

Histogram of a gray wedge in RGB mode (not terribly interesting)

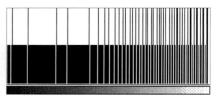

Histogram of gray wedge after RGB-to-Lab-to-RGB conversion

The gaps in the histogram show unused levels after RGB-to-Lab mode conversion, but they don't tell the whole story about the loss of image information. The spikes in the histogram indicate where values have been rounded (made the same). These also represent loss of image detail. It may not have been visible detail, but it was there waiting to be exploited, and perhaps made visible. Now it's gone, never to return.

CMYK and Lab

The conversion from CMYK to Lab (and vice versa) loses a little more information than from RGB to Lab, and the pattern is a little different (see Figure 7-2). You're likely to get subtle color shifts, in addition to losing tonal distinctions. Basically, you get more rounding errors switching between a three-channel and a four-channel color space than you do switching between two three-channel color spaces.

Figure 7-2

Data loss when going from CMYK to Lab to CMYK

A gray wedge histogram looks like this after CMYK-to-Lab-to-CMYK conversion.

RGB to CMYK

Converting an image from RGB to CMYK in Photoshop—the most common and necessary of conversions—loses a lot of image information (see Figure 7-3). It has to. The RGB color space contains 16.7 million colors, of which (at most) a few thousand are printable using four-color process printing. When the conversion is done right, the printed CMYK piece will bear a reasonably close resemblance to the RGB image on the screen, even though it contains far fewer colors, a smaller dynamic range, and a much narrower color gamut (see the sidebar, "CMYK Myths").

Figure 7-3

Data loss in RGB-to-CMYK conversion

The best you can hope for in the RGB-to-CMYK conversion is a perfect translation of the RGB original squeezed into the smaller gamut of press-ready CMYK. Unfortunately, you don't get even that, because Photoshop tends to clip out-of-gamut colors during the conversion rather than compressing the whole gamut proportionally. (This is a crucial concept which we discuss in more detail in "Gamut compression and gamut clipping," later in this chapter.) You lose differences between colors, and as we've said several times, difference is detail.

RGB versus CMYK

The debate over whether to work in RGB or CMYK has been the subject of countless magazine articles, several online flame wars, and even a few books. Of course, if your work is destined for a film recorder, the computer screen, or videotape, then CMYK is quite irrelevant; but if you're working in the print medium, it's very important indeed.

Some experts go so far as to say that if your work is destined for print, you should work exclusively in CMYK. When confronted, they usually give four reasons for this.

▶ It's the only color space that matters.

▶ RGB is meaningless.

▶ Monitor calibration is inherently impossible.

▶ All that matters are the CMYK dot percentages.

While all these points have some validity, we beg to differ with the philosophy as a whole. As we've noted before, when all you have is a hammer, everything starts to look like a nail. People who tell you to do everything in CMYK undoubtedly have excellent traditional prepress skills and a deep understanding of process-color printing, but they just don't realize how much image information Photoshop loses during the conversion, and they probably are not comfortable working in RGB.

As a result, they convert raw scans (or even worse, badly acquired Photo CD images) to CMYK immediately, damaging the scan irretrievably. Then they make huge corrections in CMYK, trying to salvage a printable image from what's left. Once they're done, they congratulate themselves on

CMYK Myths

One of the reasons we wrote this book was to dispel a number of myths that have cropped up during the short life of desktop prepress (and some others that have been around even longer)—especially those regarding CMYK and RGB issues. Here are our answers to two common areas of confusion.

CMYK has more colors (false).

We've heard experts deride the notion that CMYK contains fewer colors than RGB. "Do the math, stupid," they say. "CMYK has 256^4, or more than 4 *billion* colors." We wish that were the case. CMYK has more than 4 billion color *specifications*, but a large number of them are simply alternate ways of specifying the *same* color using a different balance of black to CMY inks. And many of them (for example, 90C 90M 90Y 100K) are "illegal" specifications that would turn the paper into a soggy mess scattered all over the pressroom floor. When you also take into account the constraints imposed by the black-generation curve and the total ink limit, you end up with far fewer colors than RGB.

CMYK is more accurate (true, sort of).

Other experts say, "CMYK may have a narrower gamut, but the data points in CMYK are packed much closer together than they are in RGB, so CMYK specifies colors *more accurately* than RGB."

Here they have a point. You *can* specify smaller differences between colors in CMYK than you can in RGB, because the same number of bits are being used to describe a smaller color gamut. (Whether these smaller color differences are detectable by the human eye is a question we'll leave to someone willing to carry out the empirical research.)

But this is only relevant if your RGB original is being converted to CMYK by a scanner (probably a drum scanner) that captures 12 bits of data per color, and uses them *all* in the RGB-to-CMYK conversion. If you use Photoshop to do the conversion, you won't gain any accuracy, because all Photoshop has to start with is 8-bit-per-channel RGB data. It can't get any better in the conversion—only worse.

their exquisite skills while pointing out the limited quality you can attain with desktop color.

These limits are self-imposed and largely illusory. If you follow these people's recommendations, you too will throw away about a third of your image right off the bat; then you'll be able to labor mightily, use all sorts of nifty tricks, and be rewarded with mediocre results for your efforts.

We have a very simple rule: *Don't change color spaces unless or until you have to, and do as much of your correction as possible in the image's original color space. The ideal number of color-space conversions is one or none.*

All images ultimately come from an RGB source, so even if the desired end result is a set of CMYK separations, you should do as much of your image correction as possible in the RGB file. This is not a universally accepted view, but we believe that the arguments in its favor are compelling. When you prematurely convert to CMYK, you restrict yourself in at least five ways.

▶ You lose a great deal of image information, making quality tonal and color correction much more difficult.

▶ You target the image for a particular set of press conditions (paper, press, inks, etc.). If press conditions change, or if you want to print the image under various press conditions, you're in a hole that's difficult to climb out of.

▶ Because the CMYK image is targeted to specific output conditions, it's much more difficult to proof on color printers than it is with a repurposable RGB image.

▶ You increase your file size by a third, slowing most operations by that same amount.

▶ You lose several convenient Photoshop features that only work in RGB, such as the Levels clipping display (see "Levels," later in this chapter).

More important, correcting images in RGB prior to CMYK conversion just plain works.

For the vast majority of Photoshop users, that means working in RGB for as long as possible, and only converting your image to CMYK after you're finished with your other corrections. There's no doubt that it's essential to keep an eye on the CMYK dot percentages while you work, but you don't need to work in CMYK to do that—they're always available in the Info palette, even when you're working in RGB.

We're not saying that you should never make corrections in CMYK—far from it. Your CMYK separations will often benefit from fine-tuning. Editing the black plate is a particularly powerful technique, but it's most effective as a fine-tuner, making small moves. If you work in print, you need to learn to edit in CMYK. But it isn't the only game in town.

When to Use CMYK

If your images come from a traditional drum scanner in CMYK form, it makes no sense to convert them to RGB for correction. You should stay in CMYK. If you find that you have to make major corrections, though, you'll almost certainly get better results by rescanning the image instead of making them in Photoshop. In high-end prepress shops, it's not unusual to scan an image three times before the client signs off on it.

Tip: Ask for RGB. Color houses are so used to providing CMYK scans that they sometimes forget that their high-end drum scanners are actually reading RGB values, which an internal color computer is converting to CMYK on the fly. These color computers can often make a much better CMYK conversion than Photoshop can, which is the main reason to use them in the first place.

On the other hand, if you're going to be manipulating the image yourself in Photoshop, or need an image that can be targeted to multiple devices or press conditions, you can ask the shop to save the image in RGB format. They may tell you they can't do it, but a growing number of color houses are now RGB-capable. Of course, you're then responsible for correcting the color balance and making the conversion to CMYK.

When you start with RGB images, certain kinds of fine-tuning, such as black-plate editing, can *only* be done on the separated CMYK file. But if you find yourself needing to make large moves in CMYK after a Photoshop mode change, it's time to look at your Monitor Setup, Printing Inks Setup, and Separation Setup settings, because the problem probably lies there (see Chapter 5, *Color Preferences*). In that case, it makes more sense to go back to the RGB original and reseparate it using new settings that get you closer to the desired result.

If all you have is a CMYK file, work in CMYK if at all possible. In dire emergencies, such as when you have a CMYK file targeted for newsprint and you want to reproduce it on glossy stock, you *may* want to take the desperate step of converting it back to RGB, applying corrections, and reseparating to CMYK; but in general, you should view RGB to CMYK as strictly a one-way trip.

Tip: CMYK to RGB. About about the only reason to convert a CMYK image to RGB is when you need to expand the tonal range and color gamut of the CMYK image to repurpose it for a different kind of output. If you just do a mode change from CMYK to RGB, you'll often get a flat, lifeless image with washed-out color, because the tonal range and color gamut of the original were compressed in the initial RGB-to-CMYK conversion.

You can improve the results somewhat by making a *temporary* change to the Monitor Setup and Printing Inks Setup preferences. There are no magic settings we can give you, but the general technique is to lower the monitor gamma (we find a gamma setting of around 1.4 often works) and to increase the saturation of the colors in Printing Inks Setup. When you do this, you're lying to Photoshop, telling it that your monitor has a smaller tonal range, and that your print process has a wider color gamut, than they really do—you're making Photoshop see the RGB and CMYK color spaces as being more alike than they really are. See Chapter 5, *Color Preferences*, for details on how to create a custom Printing Inks Setup.

This is a last-resort technique. Work on a copy of the file, and watch for color shifts and posterization.

When to Use RGB

If your image comes from an RGB source, such as a desktop scanner or a digital camera, you should do as much of your work as possible in RGB. The files are smaller, so your work goes faster, and you have the entire tonal range and color gamut of the original at your disposal, allowing you to exploit the small differences between pixels that you want to emphasize in the image. It's also much easier to repurpose RGB images for different kinds of output than it is to do so with CMYK.

RGB has some less obvious advantages, as well. Some features (such as the clipping display in Levels) are only available in RGB, not in CMYK. And when you work in RGB, you have a built-in safeguard: it's impossible to violate the Black and Total Ink Limit values you specify in Separation Setup (because they'll always be imposed when you convert to CMYK).

When you edit CMYK files directly, you have no such constraint—you can build up so much density in the shadows using Levels or Curves that you're calling for 400-percent ink coverage. On a sheetfed press, this will create a mess. On a web press, it will create a potentially life-threatening situation! In any case, it's something to avoid unless you're printing to a desktop color printer that can actually handle that 400-percent total ink coverage.

Even if you prefer using a different program to create separations, you'll find that Photoshop is just about the best image editor around. We often do all our corrections to the image in Photoshop, then hand off the task of doing the RGB-to-CMYK conversion to a specialized application such as PixelCraft's Color Access, or to a color management system such as Kodak's KCMS or Apple's ColorSync 2.0 (see Figure 7-4 on page 199).

Image Correction and Targeting

In Chapter 6, *Tonal Correction,* we drew the distinction between correction and targeting. Correction is the process of compensating for flaws in the original and for distortions introduced in the image-capture process. Targeting compensates for the shortcomings of the output process.

Photoshop handles targeting of color images for press output quite differently from the way it handles targeting of grayscale images. In fact, it's fair to say that targeting grayscale images is entirely a manual process. With color, Photoshop does most of the targeting automatically in the RGB-to-CMYK conversion, based on the Printing Inks Setup and Separation Setup settings. This can be both a blessing and a curse, as we'll see.

Correcting Color Images

Correcting color images is very much like correcting grayscale images, but with a catch. You're still stretching and squeezing the bits, but you're doing so on three (RGB) or four (CMYK) channels instead of only one, so it's nine or sixteen times more complicated!

The classic order for preparing color images for print is as follows.

1. Spotting, retouching, dust and scratch removal.

2. Global tonal correction.

3. Global color correction.

4. Selective tonal and/or color correction.

5. Targeting (sharpening, handling out-of-gamut colors, compressing tonal range, converting to CMYK).

We generally adhere to this, but it depends on the image and on the quality of the image capture. For instance, you often have to lighten an image before you can even consider retouching it.

And sometimes it's impossible to separate tonal correction and color correction. Changes to the color balance affect tonal values too, because you're manipulating the tone of the individual color channels. For example, if you add red to neutralize a cyan cast, you'll also brighten the image because you're adding light. If you reduce the green to neutralize a green cast, you'll darken the image because you're subtracting light. In any case, we try wherever possible to make a single set of curve adjustments that take care of all the global problems.

Fix the biggest problem first. The rule of thumb we've developed over the years is simple: *fix the biggest problem first*. This is partly plain common sense. You often have to fix the biggest problem before you can even see what the other problems are. But it's usually also the most effective approach, the one which requires the least work, and the one that degrades the image the least.

With many desktop flatbed scanners—especially 8-bit scanners—the biggest problem is usually that the midtones and shadows are too dark, so we start with global tonal correction. If, on the other hand, we're faced with a badly acquired Photo CD image, the overall tone may be fine, but the image will have a global color cast which we go after first. With a purely synthetic image bound for a printing press, such as one created by a 3D rendering program, our first step might be to desaturate the whole image a little.

Tip: Look at the Image Before You Start. This may seem obvious, but stop for a moment. Look at the image carefully. Zoom to 1:1 and look at every pixel. Have you missed dust or scratches? Are there particularly noisy areas that might cause problems? Look at each channel individually. Are there details (or defects) lurking in one channel that are absent from others? Is noise concentrated in one channel? (It's usually most prevalent in the blue.) Look at the histogram. Is the image using the full tonal range? If not, should it? A few minutes spent critically evaluating the image can save hours later on. Develop a plan, and stick to it unless it obviously isn't working (in which case, see below).

Tip: Leave Yourself an Escape Route. The great Scots poet Robert Burns pointed out that the best-laid plans o' mice and men gang aft agley. He wasn't fortunate enough to have the benefit of the Undo and Revert commands, but you are. If a particular move doesn't work, just undo (Command-Z)—you can reload Levels, Curves, Brightness/Contrast, Color Balance, and Hue/Saturation with the last-used settings by holding down the Option key while selecting them either from the menu or with a keyboard shortcut. If a whole train of moves has led you down a blind alley, revert to the original version.

If you're working on a complex or critical problem, work on a copy of the image. When you apply a move using Levels, Curves, or Hue/Saturation, save it before you apply it. That way, you can always retrace your steps up to the point where things started to go wrong.

And for the ultimate in unlimited undoing, check out Chapter 15, *The Digital Darkroom*.

Targeting Color Images

As with grayscale images, you can choose to separate the process of correcting color images from that of targeting them, or you can do both at once. The trade-off is speed versus flexibility. If you target an image, it's often difficult to reproduce satisfactorily using a different output process.

You may be able to convert a magazine separation for newsprint, but going the other way is likely to be a nightmare, because you've compressed the image into the small gamut of newsprint. And repurposing a newsprint separation for output to a continuous-tone film recorder is well-nigh impossible. If you try to stretch the tonal range back to the gamut of film, it will probably fall apart; and if you don't try, it'll be flat and lifeless (see Figure 7-5 on page 200, and "Tip: CMYK to RGB," earlier in this chapter).

So if you think you may want to use the image for more than one kind of output, you should treat correction and targeting as two separate processes: you can save the corrected image while still in RGB, and then use it to create versions targeted for the specific output conditions. If you just want to get it on the page and out the door, you can make all your corrections with the final output in mind, targeting as you correct, and save yourself some time.

Automatic versus manual targeting. As we said earlier, targeting color images for print is much more automatic than targeting grayscale images—if you want it to be.

When you convert an RGB image to CMYK using Photoshop's separation engine, it automatically compensates for both dot gain and for the reduced color gamut of CMYK. The results that you get depend—critically—on the settings you make in the Monitor Setup, Separation Setup, and Printing Inks Setup preferences, so it's important to get these right (see Chapter 5, *Color Preferences*). But even with the best-possible preferences settings, you may still want to adjust some things manually before doing the conversion. The dot gain compensation works quite well, but Photoshop's handling of out-of-gamut colors is another story.

Gamut compression and gamut clipping. As we discussed back in Chapter 4, *Color Essentials*, RGB colors that can't be reproduced in CMYK are called out-of-gamut colors. There are two ways to handle these colors.

▶ Reduce the color gamut of the entire image proportionally, so that differences in color saturation are preserved (*gamut compression*).

▶ Clip the out-of-gamut colors to their nearest printable equivalents, while leaving the in-gamut colors unchanged (*gamut clipping*).

The disadvantage of the latter approach is that differences in saturation between out-of-gamut colors are lost, and so detail in highly saturated areas goes away. For example, if you have a pixel that's really hot pink and another one that's even hotter, they'll both get clipped to the same dull pink color; the difference between them is gone.

Unfortunately, while Photoshop does a small amount of gamut compression, it mostly just clips out-of-gamut colors. This can be a real problem in images with highly saturated colors, particularly saturated reds. Photoshop 3 handles saturated reds better than its predecessors, but Photoshop's separation engine still tends to turn them into featureless red blobs.

Unless you take care of the out-of-gamut colors yourself, Photoshop will take care of them for you during separation, and it may not give you the results you want (see Figure 7-4 on page 199). In fact, Photoshop's gamut-clipping behavior is the main reason that we often use other separation methods (see Chapter 16, *Color Management Systems*).

That said, Photoshop's separation engine has been much maligned by its detractors. It is possible to create great color seps with Photoshop. It just takes some extra work, and you have to do the work *before* you convert the image to CMYK. Once Photoshop has clipped those out-of-gamut colors, you can never bring back the subtle details they may contain.

Tip: Targeting Color Images for RGB Output. Some output processes—notably film recorders and computer screens—use RGB data. If you're reproducing images using a continuous-tone film recorder, you should be able to reproduce what you see on your monitor very closely in terms of tone, if not color. If you have a hardware monitor calibrator, set your monitor gamma to match that of the film recorder—your service provider should be able to tell you the film recorder's gamma.

Different film types have subtle color biases, which are nearly impossible to predict without some trial and error, but their effects are trivial when compared to matching gamma. If you don't have hardware monitor calibration, a simple gamma tweak using Levels is probably all the targeting you need to do, but you'll probably have to make a test slide first to obtain a reference.

Tip: Targeting Images for CMY Output. If you're dealing with a CMY desktop printer such as a Kodak dye-sub or a three-color ink-jet, the color gamut will likely be smaller than that of your monitor, so you have to watch what happens to saturated colors. The more sophisticated three-color printers often have table-making utilities that let you control the printer's RGB-to-CMY conversion, but we've found that we generally get the best results by simply correcting the image for our monitor, then sending calibrated RGB values to the printer through a color management system (see Chapter 16, *Color Management Systems*).

Fine-tuning CMYK files. No matter how well you tweak the various preferences that control the RGB-to-CMYK conversion, it's likely that your separated CMYK files can benefit from some judicious fine-tuning to optimize them for your press conditions. We strongly advise pulling a proof before you do any corrections on the CMYK image unless you know appropriate CMYK dot percentages cold, or you know from experience that you can really trust your monitor's simulation of CMYK. With a proof, you can see what needs to be changed. Without one, you're either guessing or flying on instruments.

Color-Correction Tools

For color correction, we rely heavily on the same four tools that we use for grayscale correction—the Histogram, the Info palette, and the Levels and Curves dialog boxes (and the eyedropper tools they contain). They operate in the same way as they do in grayscale, but their effects are sometimes significantly different because we're dealing with three or four channels instead of one.

With Levels, Curves, and Histogram, you can operate on the color channels individually or on a composite of all of them. The Info palette shows what's happening in each of the channels, and warns you when RGB colors are outside the CMYK gamut. We also use the CMYK Preview command for a visual check of our predicted CMYK values while we're still working in RGB.

In addition to those four tools, we also use the Hue/Saturation command for both global and selective corrections, and its close relative, the Replace Colors command, for selective corrections. The Selective Color command, despite its name, is as useful for global corrections to the entire image as it is for selective corrections to parts of the image, but we generally reserve it for fine-tuning CMYK files.

Let's look at each of these tools in more detail.

Histogram

As we noted in the last chapter, the Histogram command is a simple bar chart that plots the levels from 0 to 255 along the horizontal axis, and the number of pixels at each level along the vertical axis. But it works a little differently with color images than it does with grayscale ones. In a grayscale image you have only one histogram, but in color images, you have a histogram for each channel (three for RGB and Lab, four for CMYK), plus a composite histogram for the combined channels.

When you choose Histogram from the Image menu and only one channel is visible, the Histogram dialog box displays the histogram for that channel. When you display the composite image and choose Histogram, the Histogram dialog box sports a Channel menu that lets you choose the histograms of the individual channels, or a composite histogram labeled Gray (see Figure 7-6 on page 201).

The histograms of the individual channels are identical to those displayed in Levels. The composite Gray histogram, however, is different. Moreover, it's different in a useful way. The composite Gray histogram shows the overall tonal range of the image—it's analogous to the histogram for a grayscale image or for a single channel. Hence, it's useful for

Figure 7-4 Out-of-gamut color handling

In addition to overall color variation, note the detail differences in the saturated gloves and water bottle.

Separated with Photoshop

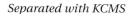
Separated with KCMS

Separated with Color Access

Hand-tuned, then separated with Photoshop

determining how bright your highlights and how dark your shadows are. For reasons we'll see in "Levels," below, the composite histogram in Levels doesn't do this.

Figure 7-5 Retargeting an image that's been prepared for reproduction on newsprint

The image above left was separated for newsprint. The separation settings resulted in a flat image that would reproduce well in that medium, but that had lost a great deal of its tonal and color range.

For the image above, we started with the news-print-targeted CMYK file, pulled it back into RGB (see "Tip: CMYK to RGB," earlier in this chapter), then reseparated for this book's wider gamut. The results are less than stellar.

The image at left was created from the original RGB file, and separated using the proper settings for these printing conditions.

Info Palette

The Info palette is a vital tool for working in color, particularly when we work in RGB. It lets us read the RGB values under the cursor, and equally important, it can show us the approximate CMYK values that we'll get when we do a mode change to CMYK.

We say "approximate" because if you examine the CMYK values for an RGB file, then convert to CMYK and examine the values again, they differ very slightly. With rare exceptions (we've only seen one), the CMYK values match to within a percentage point, which is a closer match than any imagesetter operator will promise you.

So, we can work on RGB images in their native color space, and still keep an eye on the CMYK values Photoshop will produce when we make color separations. We get the best of both worlds (see Figure 7-6).

When you're working on an RGB file, the CMYK values displayed by the Info palette are governed by the settings in the Printing Inks Setup

Figure 7-6 Histograms, Levels, saturation, and brightness

The Histogram command with the Gray option selected depicts the overall brightness distribution of the image—how the histogram would look if you converted the image to grayscale.

The RGB histogram in Levels shows how many pixels are at a given value in any of the channels. Note the spike at the right (255), even though there are no pure whites in the image.

The Levels highlight clipping display (here set to level 220) shows more about saturation levels. The green areas are fully saturated (255G) at this clipping level. The cyan areas are at 255G 255B. And so on. The white areas are truly white—255R 255G 255B.

The Info palette's gamut alarm shows that the fully saturated blue-green sleeve colors can't be printed, along with the CMYK values that will result.

The Gamut Warning display—here set to display in red—shows the saturated areas of the image that can't be reproduced with the current separation settings.

and Separation Setup dialog boxes. If these preferences are set correctly, you should have to do little or no work on the CMYK file after you've made the conversion from RGB to CMYK. See Chapter 5, *Color Preferences,* for detailed strategies for setting up these key preferences.

Tip: Locking Pixel Coordinates. Often when we're making color adjustments, we want to return time and time again to the same pixel so that we can see how its color is being modified. We wish we didn't have to use the pixel coordinates in the Info palette to do this—we'd much rather have the option of locking the cursor onto a given area when we're adjusting the image. But as of yet, the only way we have of returning to a specific pixel in the image is to note the X,Y coordinates in the Info palette.

Here's one way you can work around the problem, though.

1. Before opening the Levels or Curves dialog box (or whatever adjustment you're making), increase the size of the image canvas by 50 or 100 pixels.

2. For each pixel that you want to "lock down," pick up its color with the Eyedropper tool.

3. Fill a part of the new white space with the picked-up color—drag out a selection and press Option-Delete to fill it with the foreground color (see Figure 7-7).

Figure 7-7 Adding color swatches

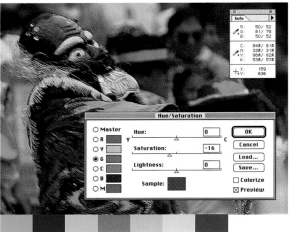

Since it's hard to find exactly the same pixel to examine values as you make corrections, add some color swatches to your image, picked up from key areas.

This allows you to see, measure, and evaluate the changes you're making in key color ranges.

Now, while you make color corrections, you can always place the cursor over that color swatch to see how it's changing. When you're finished, crop out the swatches and you're back to normal.

We prefer working visually—relying on a well-calibrated monitor—rather than going strictly by the numbers, but even the best monitor and the best calibration have inherent limitations. Some things are almost impossible to detect visually. For example, without looking at some kind of printed reference under controlled lighting, it's difficult to tell from the monitor whether or not a gray is really neutral. But the numbers in the Info palette provide an infallible guide. Without a well-calibrated monitor, they're your only real guide to what's going on.

Likewise, it's very hard to see differences of one or two levels between adjacent pixels, but the Info palette lets us find these differences, and as we've pointed out, difference is detail. It's even possible to do color correction using a black and white monitor. This is a ridiculously macho practice—we don't recommend or enjoy it—but in a pinch, it works. You need to have a good sense of the target values you're aiming for, and that only comes with experience, but a big part of gaining that experience comes from examining the values on the Info palette for key areas of your images.

Info palette setup. For color work, we use the same Info palette setup more than 90 percent of the time. We set the first color readout to RGB, the second color readout to CMYK, and the mouse coordinates to pixels. You can set all these options with the Palette Options menu on the Info palette, or you can set individual readouts using the individual popup menus.

Setting eyedropper options. You can set the Info palette to show the values of the individual pixels under the cursor, a 3-by-3-pixel average, or a 5-by-5-pixel average, by setting the options for the Eyedropper tool to Point Sample, 3-by-3 Average, or 5-by-5 Average in the Tool Options palette (double-click on the Eyedropper tool). We generally choose 3-by-3 Average unless we're working with a very high-resolution image (destined for high-screen-frequency or continuous-tone output), in which case we might go to 5-by-5.

Using the Info palette with other controls. While you're editing an image using any of the controls on the Adjust submenu under the Image menu (Levels, Curves, Hue/Saturation, Replace Colors, and so on), the Info palette provides a before-and-after reading (see Figure 7-6 on page 201). This allows you to see what is happening while you're making the adjustments.

CMYK Preview

If you've gone through the process described in Chapter 5, *Color Preferences*, for calibrating your monitor's display of CMYK files to the printed output, you can get a good visual idea of what will happen to your image once it's been converted to CMYK by choosing CMYK Preview from the

Mode menu. This doesn't change the file itself—it just changes the way it displays on the screen. (This simulation is based—yet again—on the settings in Separation Setup and Monitor Setup.)

We often work with CMYK Preview turned on, especially when we're fine-tuning out-of-gamut colors prior to CMYK conversion.

Tip: Use CMYK Preview for Before-and-Afters. Photoshop lets you open more than one window for an image. This is particularly useful in conjunction with CMYK Preview. When you choose CMYK Preview, it only applies to the currently active window, so you can open two windows for the image—use one to view it in RGB, and the other in simulated CMYK.

Gamut Alarm

When you're working in RGB mode, Photoshop displays an exclamation point next to color specifications (in the Info palette and the Color Picker) to warn you when an RGB color is outside the printable CMYK gamut (see Figure 7-6 on page 201).

This gamut alarm is telling you that when you convert the image from RGB to CMYK, Photoshop will clip the RGB color to the closest available CMYK equivalent.

Gamut Warning

Photoshop's Gamut Warning shows you which colors in the image are out of gamut by displaying them with the color you choose in the Gamut Warning Preferences. We don't find this particularly useful—we'd rather just *see* what's going to happen to our colors using CMYK Preview and the Info palette, but we thought we'd mention it for the sake of completeness.

Occasionally we'll turn on Gamut Warning just to see if we've overlooked a trouble spot (such as a highly saturated color in an important area of the image), but nine times out of ten, it just tells us that most of our deep shadows are out of gamut.

Unless we see a glaring problem with the shadows in the CMYK Preview, we just leave them alone and accept the CMYK values that Photoshop produces when we do the conversion. Doing a lot of work to bring very dark colors into gamut manually is just a waste of time. Instead, let Photoshop do it when it converts to CMYK; it's unlikely that you'll be able to see the difference in print.

Tip: Don't Sponge Saturated Colors. The Photoshop manual tells you that you can load the out-of-gamut colors as a selection using Color Range, then use the Sponge tool to desaturate them and hence bring them into gamut. We think this is seriously brain-dead, because you're simply doing manually what Photoshop does automatically during RGB-to-CMYK conversion—clipping out-of-gamut colors. Besides requiring a lot of handwork, it can distort the relationship between the in-gamut and out-of-gamut colors, changing the appearance of the image in odd ways.

Levels

The Levels command operates on color images exactly as it does on grayscale images. The only difference is that, unless you tell it otherwise, it operates simultaneously on all the color channels in the image. We find Levels too coarse a tool to use for correcting problems with color balance (though we know people who've developed incredible skills doing so), but we still use it in three ways on color images.

▶ As an image-evaluation tool, using the histograms and clipping display.

▶ When we have a color image that has no problems with color balance, but needs some lightening (or much more rarely, darkening) in the midtones. Often, a move with the gamma slider is all that's needed.

▶ As an image-targeting tool. If the image doesn't contain specular highlights that we want to blow out to white, we use the black and white output sliders to limit the minimum highlight and maximum shadow dots. If there are specular highlights, we use the eyedropper techniques (outlined later in the chapter) instead.

The Levels composite histogram. Like the Histogram dialog box, Levels displays the histogram for an individual channel if that's what you have displayed, and offers a Channels menu when you're viewing the composite image. But the composite histogram it displays (labeled RGB or CMYK depending on the image's color space) is different from the Gray histogram shown in the Histogram dialog box (see Figure 7-6 on page 201).

In the Gray histogram, a level of 255 represents a white pixel. In the RGB or CMYK histograms in Levels, however, a level of 255 *may* represent a white pixel, but it could equally well represent a saturated color pixel—the histogram simply shows the maximum of the individual channels. This means that you have to be extremely careful with the black and white Input Levels sliders, because you can easily drive colors to saturation in a misguided attempt to clip highlights.

Figure 7-6 on page 201 shows the Gray histogram and the RGB Levels histogram for the same image. As you can see, they're very different. The image has no pure whites, and the Gray histogram shows this. The RGB histogram, in contrast, shows a distinct spike at level 255. In this particular image, rather than indicating clipped highlights, the spike shows the presence of saturated colors—a saturated color always has at least one of the primaries at level 255.

A look at the Levels clipping display shows this quite clearly. If we press Option and hold down the mouse button on the white Input Levels slider, we don't see any white areas, but we do see areas of saturated red, green, and blue.

How Levels works on color images. As the composite histogram implies, any moves you make to the Levels sliders when you're working in the composite channels apply equally to each individual color channel. In other words, you get identical results applying the same move individually to each color channel as you would applying the move once to the composite channel.

However, since the contents of the individual channels are quite different, applying the same moves to each can sometimes have unexpected results. The gamma slider and the black and white output sliders operate straightforwardly, but the black and white input sliders can be dangerous.

The white input slider clips the highlights *in each channel* to level 255. This brightens the image overall, and neutral colors stay neutral. But it usually has an undesirable effect on non-neutral colors, ranging from oversaturation to pronounced color shifts. The same applies to the black input slider, although the effects are usually less obvious. The black input slider clips the values in each channel to level zero, so when you apply it to a non-neutral color, you can end up removing all trace of one primary from the color, which also increases its saturation.

Because of this behavior, we use the black and white input sliders primarily as image-evaluation tools in conjunction with the Option-key clipping display. They let us see exactly where our saturated colors are in relation to our neutral highlights and shadows. If the image is free of dangerously saturated colors, we may make small moves with the black and white input sliders, but we always try to avoid clipping, staying well outside of the significant areas of the histogram. And we keep a very close eye on what's happening to the saturation—it's particularly easy to create out-of-gamut saturated colors in the shadows.

The image shown in Figure 7-8 on page 211 is a good candidate for correction using Levels. It has no real color problems, and no dangerously saturated colors, but it's a little flat. Three quick moves with the black and white Input Levels sliders and the gamma slider improve the contrast immensely.

Curves

The Curves command is probably the single most useful tool Photoshop offers for making corrections to tone and color, both globally and locally, and mastering it is an essential Photoshop skill. Almost every color image we work with gets some treatment with Curves; in many cases, a single round of curve adjustments is the only correction we make.

In Chapter 6, *Tonal Correction,* we likened Levels to an automatic transmission and Curves to a stick shift. When you work in color, the difference is more like that between a chain saw and a scalpel.

The Curves command works the same way with color images as it does with grayscale ones, save that you can operate on all channels simultaneously (useful for tonal corrections) or on individual channels (useful for changing the color balance).

Curves tips for color images. All the options that exist for Curves in grayscale apply to working in color, too (see "Tip: Customizing the Curves Dialog Box" in Chapter 6, *Tonal Correction*). We always use the fine grid (Option-click on the grid area), and we generally use the Levels readout with RGB files and the Percentage readout with CMYK files—we're used to thinking of RGB in terms of levels and CMYK in terms of dot percentages.

To adjust the shape of the curve, we almost always use the point tool instead of the freehand (pencil) tool. The freehand tool is useful in some special situations that we discuss in Chapter 6, *Tonal Correction,* but the point tool keeps the curve as smooth as possible, and hence avoids sudden unnatural shifts in tone and color.

We use two distinct methods of placing curve points: one when we're going strictly by the numbers, and the other when we're relying more on what we see on the monitor.

▶ **By the numbers.** If we're going by the numbers, we use the readout at the bottom of the dialog box to find the input and output coordinates we want, then we simply click to place the point. The curve automatically bends so that it passes through that point.

▶ **By eye.** If we're operating visually, we place the point on the curve itself, then drag it to where we want it to be. With the Preview option turned off, and Video LUT Animation turned on in General Preferences, the screen changes continuously as we drag the curve, allowing us to see the effect of the tweak in real time.

Tip: Find Your Pixel Value in Curves. In Figure 6-24 on page 159, we showed how you can use the eyedropper to see where a pixel value falls on the curve. Unfortunately the trick doesn't work on the composite CMYK channel in CMYK files. It does work on the individual CMYK channels, and on the composite channel in RGB files (yet another reason to work on RGB rather than CMYK files).

Tip: Channel Menu Shortcut. When you're working in either Curves or Levels, the "display channel" shortcuts (pressing Command-1 through Command-4 for individual channels, and Command-0 for the composite channel) operate the Channel menu in the dialog box. However, this only changes the popup menu; if you want to view an individual channel, you must cancel out of Levels or Curves, make the desired channel visible, then reopen Levels or Curves.

We've seen how we can use Levels to make a straightforward tonal adjustment. Figure 7-9 on page 212 shows the same image adjusted a little more precisely with a master RGB curve instead.

Maintaining tone when correcting. Whether you're working in RGB or in CMYK, the individual channel curves often offer the easiest way to take care of color-balance problems. Remember that cyan is the inverse of red, magenta is the inverse of green, and blue is the inverse of yellow. To remove a red cast, for example, you'd pull down on the red curve in an RGB file, or pull up on the cyan curve in a CMYK file.

However, in cases where the image has a severe color cast, working on a single channel may have too drastic an effect on the overall tone of the image, because each curve adds or subtracts light (in the case of RGB) or ink (in the case of CMYK). In the case of a severe red cast, for example, rather than eliminating it using the red or cyan curve exclusively, you may need to adjust the other curves as well. That way, the overall tone of the image is preserved.

Editing the black plate. We prefer to do all our work with Curves in RGB, with one important exception: editing the black plate in CMYK files. It's very rare for us to make curve-based adjustments to the C, M, and Y plates, but the black plate is a different matter. Small changes to the black plate can have a profound effect on both the contrast and the apparent purity of the colors in the image.

We *always* have a proof made before we edit the CMYK file. If the colors in the proof appear muddy, it's usually a sign that the black plate is too heavy. In extreme cases, we'll go back and reseparate the RGB image using a lighter black, but often a small tweak that brightens the quarter-tones in the black plate can do wonders.

Likewise, small adjustments to the black plate can fix contrast problems, without having to go back to the original and reseparate. But if you're running into color-balance problems, it's a sign that your Monitor Setup, Printing Inks Setup, or Separation Setup settings need further refinement. You can fix the image at hand by working the CMY curves, but you'll have to fix every other image you produce using these settings, too. It's much more efficient to go back and fix the fundamental problem (see Chapter 5, *Color Preferences*, for a detailed discussion of these important settings).

Tip: Fix the Neutrals and the Rest Will Follow. When you're wrestling with a global color cast, the easiest way to fix it is to find spots in the image that should be neutral, and make them so. If you do that, the rest of the color will generally fall into place. If you're working in RGB, equal amounts of red, green, and blue produce a neutral tone. If you're working in CMYK, it's a little more challenging. You'll have to determine by experience what combination of C, M, Y, and K produce a neutral tone.

In general, roughly equal amounts of M and Y accompanied by a rather greater amount of C yield a neutral, but you should always check with the press people. If you're observant, you'll have noticed that Photoshop's default Printing Inks Setup and Separation Setup settings give the RGB-to-CMYK conversions in Table 7-1.

Tonal range	RGB neutral	CMYK neutral
Highlight	246R 246G 246B	5C 3M 3Y 0K
Midtone	128R 128G 128B	51C 38M 37Y 18K
Shadow	13R 13G 13B	65C 53M 51Y 94K

Table 7-1
Photoshop's default
RGB-to-CMYK
conversion

Changing the ink limits and black generation will give you different numbers, but if your Separation settings are based on SWOP inks, you'll always get more cyan than magenta and yellow in your neutrals. When you work in RGB, Photoshop's separation engine adjusts for the impurities in the cyan ink and boosts cyan accordingly. When you work in CMYK, you have to determine the neutral combinations yourself.

Finding neutrals isn't always easy: a great many images simply don't contain any. Sometimes you can find neutrals hiding in the shadows or lurking in the highlights—the Info palette is invaluable for hunting them down (see "Info Palette," earlier in this chapter).

If you're having trouble with scanner-induced color casts, consider scanning a gray wedge with your scanner; you know for a fact that it includes neutral highlights, midtones, and shadows.

Figure 7-10 on page 213 shows an example of correcting a color cast using Curves. In this case it's a pretty simple correction, mainly adjusting for a yellow cast by tweaking the blue curve. It may be of interest to note that the curve we applied to the blue channel is almost exactly analogous to performing traditional dot etching on the yellow plate of the separation. If we had to make the same correction to a CMYK file, we'd have applied the inverse curve to the yellow channel. Then we'd increase the cyan slightly in the midtones.

Black, White, and Gray Eyedroppers

The eyedropper tools in Levels and Curves function identically in both places, and they operate quite differently from the main controls in those dialog boxes, so it's worth looking at them separately.

We don't always use these tools. Besides an understanding of how they work, it takes experience to decide whether or not an image would benefit from using them. We encourage you to experiment with them, while thinking about what they do. That way, you'll gain a much better understanding of both their possibilities and their pitfalls.

Figure 7-8 Image correction using Levels

Note that we've targeted and sharpened these images to give a better impression of what we see on screen.

The raw scan, and the tone-distribution histogram

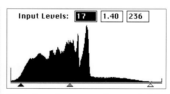

Black clipping at level 25   *White clipping at level 220*

The Levels move above yields the image at left and histogram below.

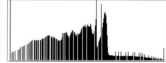

The black and white eyedroppers operate on color images in the same way they do on grayscale images, except that you set a target and source value for each channel in the color image. (See "White Points and Black Points and Grays, Oh My!" in Chapter 6, *Tonal Correction,* for a full discussion of how these tools work, including tips, tricks, and inherent limitations.)

The biggest difference between using the black and white eyedroppers in color and in grayscale is that in color images, the relationship between the source and target colors becomes much more critical, because it affects color balance as well as tone. If you set a neutral target color and click on a non-neutral source pixel, the color balance of the whole image changes. To get a feel for this, it's worth experimenting by clicking the eyedroppers on a few different pixels in the image.

Figure 7-9 Image correction using Curves

The adjustment with Curves provides more control for fine-tuning particular tonal ranges. The highlights are slightly brighter, and the shadows contain more contrast, than in the image corrected with Levels.

The gray eyedropper. Back in Chapter 6, *Tonal Correction*, we described how the black and white eyedroppers work. We put off our discussion of the gray eyedropper until now, however, as it is only available with color images. The gray eyedropper does something similar to the other two eyedroppers, but it's different in one major way.

Where the other two eyedroppers always set the color you click on in the image to the target color you specify, the gray eyedropper does not. Instead, it adjusts the gamma values for each channel in an attempt to map the source color you click on in the image to a color with the same *hue and saturation* as the target color, but with the *luminance* of the source color. It's trying to adjust the color without affecting the tone.

The gray eyedropper doesn't actually use an HSB/HSL model—we use the terms "hue," "saturation," and "luminance" somewhat loosely here—but the effect is very similar. The exact mathematical details are proprietary information that Adobe declined to share with us (and that you probably don't care to know anyway).

Using the Eyedroppers

Now that you understand a little more about what the eyedroppers do, let's look at how you can use them. You can use the eyedropper tools in (at least) three ways.

▶   As highlight/shadow limit tools for targeting.

▶   As color-balancing tools.

▶   As arbitrary color-matching tools.

Figure 7-10 Correcting a color cast with Curves

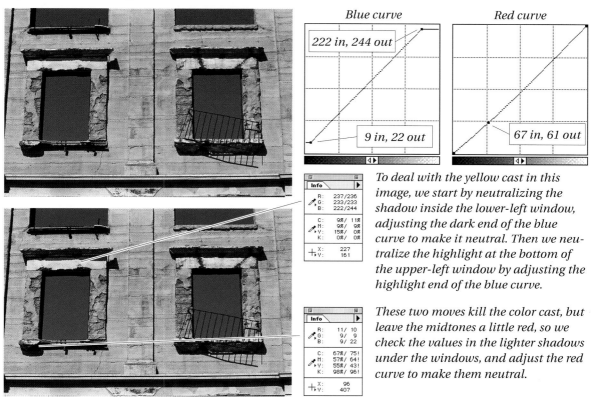

Blue curve

222 in, 244 out

9 in, 22 out

Red curve

67 in, 61 out

Info
R: 237/236
G: 233/233
B: 222/244

C: 9%/ 11%
M: 9%/ 9%
Y: 15%/ 0%
K: 0%/ 0%

X: 227
Y: 161

To deal with the yellow cast in this image, we start by neutralizing the shadow inside the lower-left window, adjusting the dark end of the blue curve to make it neutral. Then we neutralize the highlight at the bottom of the upper-left window by adjusting the highlight end of the blue curve.

Info
R: 11/ 10
G: 9/ 9
B: 9/ 22

C: 67%/ 75!
M: 57%/ 64!
Y: 55%/ 43!
K: 98%/ 96!

X: 96
Y: 407

These two moves kill the color cast, but leave the midtones a little red, so we check the values in the lighter shadows under the windows, and adjust the red curve to make them neutral.

Whichever way you use them, you have to be careful with the relationship between your target color and your source color. Dramatic (read: "incredibly ugly") shifts in the color balance can ensue when you set a neutral target color and click on a non-neutral source color. Basically, the tools work better for making small moves than for making large ones.

Setting the highlight dot. We use the white eyedropper primarily as a targeting tool, for setting the minimum highlight dot *after* sharpening and immediately prior to converting the image to CMYK. But we only do so when we have an image that has clearly defined neutral highlights *and* contains specular highlights that we want to blow out to white.

Unless both of these apply, it's easier to limit the highlight and shadow dots using Curves, or using the black and white Output sliders in Levels.

Here's the procedure to set the minimum highlight dot.

The Color Balance Command

We'd be remiss if we didn't at least mention Photoshop's Color Balance command (see Figure 7-11), which lets you make separate color adjustments to the shadows, midtones, and highlights. While we'll mention it, we don't use it—for two reasons.

▶ It doesn't do anything we can't do with Curves.

▶ The things it does are more difficult to control than they are with Curves, because there are some hidden moves happening that are hard to understand.

The command works by warping three preset gamma curves that cover the highlight, midtone, and shadow ranges. Problems can crop up in the areas where the curves overlap—it's easy to get unnatural color shifts, particularly when you shift one range in one direction and another in the opposite direction. You can get the same effect with Curves, but you aren't limited to the preset ranges of the Color Balance tool, and you know exactly what's going on.

Figure 7-11 (Not) using Color Balance

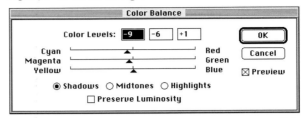

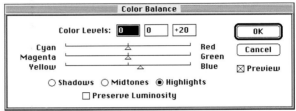

While it's possible to use Color Balance to neutralize color casts (as its name implies), it's more difficult than using Curves, because you can't target particular tonal ranges—only the generalized "Shadows," "Midtones," and "Highlights."

1. Determine the highlight point. We work with the Levels command because it offers the clipping display. We Option-drag the white Input slider to identify the pixel we want to set as the minimum highlight dot (the lightest area where there is actual detail), then return it to a setting of 255.

2. Set the target color. We set the target color according to our printing conditions, but since we're usually working in RGB we specify it us-

ing RGB values. The Printing Inks Setup and Separation Setup preferences, when correctly set, give us the desired CMYK values. For example, using our preferred Separation Setup for sheetfed printing, a 243R 243G 243B highlight translates to 6C 3M 4Y 0K. If we're working on a CMYK file, we just specify the CMYK values directly.

3. Select the source pixel/color. Use the white eyedropper to click on a pixel that has the values we want to set to the minimum highlight dot. Typically, it'll have a value somewhere in the 247–251 range. Pixels brighter than that are allowed to blow out softly to white paper, so we preserve the highlight detail with a printable dot, but still get the sparkle from the true specular highlights.

Setting the shadow dot. We use the black eyedropper to set the maximum shadow dot in a different situation. Photoshop's separation engine seems to produce the best results when the Total Black Ink Limit is set to 100 percent, but most presses plug up the black long before it reaches 100 percent. Rather than changing the Separation Setup, we use the black eyedropper to back off the maximum black in the image to the maximum value the press can hold, without changing the percentages of CMY.

The procedure for setting the maximum shadow dot is essentially the same as it is for setting the minimum highlight dot. We identify the darkest pixels in the image that still contain useful detail, and use them as the source pixels for the black eyedropper. We set the target color to the maximum dot the press can hold without plugging up; the difference is that we specify the target color as CMYK, as follows.

1. Double-click the black eyedropper to set the target color.

2. Click on the pixel you've identified as the source pixel to load its color as the target color. With a typical setup for a sheetfed press, it might read something like 73C 62M 65Y 100K.

3. Reduce *only* the K component of the target color to your desired maximum black value. This can range from 97 percent for very high-quality sheetfed presses with coated stock to 75 percent for newsprint.

4. Click OK to set the new target color.

5. Click the black eyedropper on the source pixel in the image to map it to the new target color.

Are All Color Casts Bad?

Some images simply don't (and shouldn't) contain neutrals. An image shot half an hour before sunset will almost certainly have a reddish yellow cast, and removing it probably isn't a good idea, particularly if the photographer spent several hours waiting for that magical golden light.

Determine the origin. Think about where the color cast originated. Scanners often introduce color casts—sometimes they even introduce color crossovers, where the highlights have a cast in one direction and the shadows have a cast in the opposite direction. (Scanning a gray wedge on your scanner is an easy way to determine what color casts are being introduced by the scanner.) Some film stocks have crossovers too (photographers call them "cross-curves"). Early 1980s Kodachrome is noted for a red-green cross-curve, for example, while some Ektachrome tends to turn blue in deep shadows.

Scanner-induced color casts can and should be corrected. Some color casts are more ambiguous. Whether or not you should correct them depends on the nature of the image. Distant shadows in landscapes actually appear blue to our eyes, and if you make them neutral, you'll end up with an unnatural-looking image. But on a tabletop product shot, you almost certainly want neutral shadows.

Look at the original. The best recourse is (obviously) to look at the original. The usual request is to match the original image. Strictly speaking, this is impossible—film has a much wider tonal range and color gamut than you can hope to achieve with four-color printing. What you can do is to provide the illusion of matching the original within the limits of the output process.

Preserve relationships. The trick here is to preserve the rela-

tionships between the important colors in the image. Our eyes are very good at detecting color relationships, but they're easily fooled when it comes to detecting absolute color values—to judge color, they rely heavily on context.

If the original is not available, you just have to guess. We almost hesitate to call this "color correction," because it's unlikely that you'll produce anything that resembles the intentions of the photographer—you're essentially making things up. But you can at least make educated guesses.

Look for memory colors. If the image doesn't contain neutrals, it may contain some *memory colors*. Memory colors are so called because we have an automatic expectation of how they should look. Blue skies, green grass, red fire engines, and foods like apples, oranges, green peppers, and carrots are good examples. If these colors look wrong, the whole image will look wrong.

When you convert the image to CMYK, your maximum shadow dot will have the values you set for the target color, and your black plate won't have plugged-up shadows.

Color balancing. We generally use curves to fix color-balance problems, but if we're in a hurry and the problem isn't too severe, the eyedroppers can be used for a quick fix. Again, this technique works best in images with clearly defined neutrals.

We set the target colors for the black, white, and gray eyedroppers to neutral RGB values (letting Photoshop's separation engine translate them to neutral CMYK values at separation time). The exact values depend on the image and press conditions, but generally the white eyedropper works best in the range from 200 to 255, the gray eyedropper works best in the range from 100 to 156, and the black eyedropper works best in the range from 0 to 64. All these numbers are approximate, but they're good general guidelines.

The trick here is to match the source pixel and the target color so that you're making a transformation that changes the source pixel to a neutral color without greatly affecting its brightness (remember, adding or removing color changes tone). The gray eyedropper does this as a matter of course, but you have to do some figuring with the black and white eyedroppers. For example, if your source pixel is 242R 234G 241B, try a target color that's a loose average of the three, perhaps 239R 239G 239B.

In the example shown in Figure 7-18 on page 232, we were able to eliminate most of the red cast by applying the white eyedropper to the water inside the glass, the gray eyedropper to the light shadow under the teapot, and the black eyedropper to the deep shadows.

Arbitrary color matching. In some cases, you can use the eyedroppers to match colors between images. For example, a classic problem comes up when you shoot an event like a daytime football match, where the light changes over the course of the game. If you're going to run several shots of the game, you want the uniforms to be a consistent color in all the images. The eyedroppers can (sometimes) help you do this.

Note that this technique is not what the designers of these tools had in mind. When we mentioned it to a senior engineer on the Photoshop team, he commented that the technique "will work in many cases; but as the algorithms get stressed with larger moves, it will fail, sometimes dramatically, so don't come crying to me if it doesn't work."

Use the white eyedropper to match highlights, the gray eyedropper to match midtones, and the black eyedropper to match shadows. You need to have both images that you're trying to match open on the screen.

1. Double-click the appropriate eyedropper tool to bring up the Color Picker to choose the target color.

2. Pick up the target color from the "correct" image (the one you aren't changing) by clicking the cursor on the color you want to match. Then click OK to confirm the new target color, and close the Color Picker.

3. In the image you want to change, find the color you want to change, and click the eyedropper on it to convert it to the target color.

If it works, great! If it doesn't work, you may want to give it one more try, being a little more careful when choosing target and source colors. The technique works well with small moves, but if it isn't working it will quickly become obvious. In that case, use curves instead. It's more work, but you'll get more predictable and controllable results.

Hue/Saturation

The Hue/Saturation command (see Figure 7-12) allows us to address saturation problems much more easily than we can using curves, and also lets us make changes to the hue of specific colors. We use it both for correction and for targeting our images.

Figure 7-12

Hue/Saturation dialog box

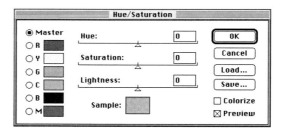

As a targeting tool, Hue/Saturation is our main line of defense in dealing with out-of-gamut colors. As a correction tool, it's invaluable for desaturating the kinds of oversaturated images that are often produced by low-end flatbed scanners. It's also useful for increasing saturation in CMYK images, although on those we're more likely to make local corrections using Hue/Saturation's close relative, Replace Colors (we cover that later in this chapter).

Hue/Saturation versus Levels and Curves. Unlike Levels and Curves, Hue/Saturation doesn't use Video LUT Animation to provide real-time feedback. If you want to see what you're doing, you must check the Preview button. This makes it somewhat less interactive than Levels or Curves, because there's always a wait for the image to redraw to show the effect of your changes (the bigger the image or selection, the longer the wait).

Even without real-time feedback, it's a great deal easier to manipulate saturation or to make slight hue changes with this tool than with Levels

Interpreting RGB and CMYK Values

As we noted back in Chapter 4, *Color Essentials*, RGB and CMYK are both device-dependent—the color that you get from a given set of values varies quite dramatically depending on the device to which those values are sent. But RGB is somewhat more predictable than CMYK. If a sampled color has equal amounts of R, G, and B, you can be sure it's a neutral gray, although if your monitor isn't properly calibrated, it may not look that way. (And of course you're relying on your separation preferences to render

a neutral CMYK gray on press from those neutral RGB values.)

Likewise, you can tell if a color is overly saturated for the CMYK gamut if it contains a large amount of one or two RGB primaries and almost none of another.

CMYK numbers need considerably more interpretation—they only make sense in the context of a specific printing process. Every expert has their own set of magic numbers. They're all correct, but only for the situation in which they're being used.

Recommendations such as 5C 2M 2Y 0K for a neutral highlight, 60C 46M 45Y 11K for a neutral 50-percent gray, or 15C 24M 25Y 0K for Caucasian flesh tones (for instance) are good starting points, but they aren't sacrosanct. After proofing, you may find that you get better results with slightly different values. The same caveat applies to process-color swatch books. The CMYK values they contain were the ones used to print the swatch book. You'll get different results printing on a different press with different paper.

or Curves. To change a color's saturation with those tools, you have to manipulate each channel separately. In the simplest case—desaturating a saturated primary color such as red (255R 0G 0B)—you have to reduce the amount of red and add equal amounts of blue and green, which is quite hard to do with Levels or Curves.

With a saturated orange (255R 160G 0B), you have to reduce the amounts of red and green proportionally, and add an amount of blue proportional to the amount by which you reduced the red and green. This would be insanely difficult with Curves, and just about impossible with Levels! Hue/Saturation lets you do it with one move.

Hue/Saturation lets you make tweaks to the hue, the saturation, and the lightness of the entire image using the Master setting. This is mainly useful for desaturating oversaturated scans or (more rarely) for beefing up washed-out scans. The Hue control may seem like a useful tool for dealing with global color casts, but in practice we've found we get much better results using Curves, or the eyedroppers in either Levels or Curves.

Besides the Master setting, Hue/Saturation lets you adjust the hue, saturation, and lightness of the individual primary and secondary colors (R, G, B, C, M, and Y). This is useful, but also dangerous. The effects you'll get depend very much on the original image, but when you're working in

RGB, it's easy to oversaturate colors. If you're trying to increase the saturation of a color, keep a watchful eye on the gamut warnings in the Info palette—you can create colors that look wonderful on the screen, but simply aren't reproducible in print. Remember that those out-of-gamut colors get clipped when you go to CMYK, so detail in those areas will vanish.

Creative uses. Hue/Saturation is often particularly effective when it's used in nonobvious ways. The image in Figure 7-13 on page 223 has screaming reds that almost overwhelm the rest of the image. The obvious solution would be to desaturate the reds, but they're precisely what gives the image much of its impact.

Instead, we go after the colors that aren't readily apparent in the image. We pump up the greens, increasing the green saturation to 52, and increasing the cyan saturation slightly to 11. Finally, since the reds in the RGB original tend to go slightly yellow when we convert to CMYK, we shift the Hue of the reds by -3, making them a hair more magenta. The effect is subtle, but we think it improves the image considerably.

Tip: Colorizing Grayscale Images. You can also use Hue/Saturation to colorize grayscale images, or to make a color image look like a hand-toned black-and-white print. Convert the grayscale to RGB, choose Hue/Saturation, and turn on the Colorize checkbox. For a warm sepia-tone look, try setting Hue to around 50, Saturation to between 25 and 30, and Lightness to 0. For normal color work, you *must* leave the Colorize button unchecked. (For more information on colorizing grayscale images, see "The Color of Grayscale" in Chapter 14, *Essential Image Techniques*.)

Hue/Saturation in CMYK. Hue/Saturation is also a powerful tool when working in CMYK, but unless you have an unusually clear idea of exactly what you're doing, it's best used as a fine-tuning tool after you've seen a proof. When we got the proof of the drummers image in Figure 7-13 on page 223, we felt it was still a little flat. Increasing the saturation of the yellow and magenta, and slightly reducing the cyan saturation, produced the result shown in the last image in Figure 7-13.

Unlike Curves, Hue/Saturation won't let you violate the ink limits specified in Separation Setup when you work on a file that's already been converted to CMYK. You may think that you could fool it into doing so by increasing the Total Ink Limit in Separation Setup, and to a *very* limited extent, you can—but we've yet to find a practical use for this. If you want to override the ink limits in a CMYK file, use Curves instead. Just remember that you're playing with fire when you do so.

Replace Color

The Replace Color command (see Figure 7-14 on page 224) combines the features of Hue/Saturation with those of the Color Range selection command (see "Color Range" in Chapter 13, *Selections*). It offers a quick, easy way to make local (as opposed to global) color corrections. As with all local color corrections, the biggest problem is in blending the corrected area seamlessly into the image as a whole. With small moves this isn't a huge concern, but if you're trying to turn a red shirt green, you may have to do some handwork to get the edges right, no matter how careful you are in setting up the initial selection.

For more detailed work, you're better off using the full range of selection and painting tools to make a detailed mask in an alpha channel, and using the Hue/Saturation command (see Chapter 13, *Selections*).

Replace Color does exactly what its name implies. It lets you select a range of colors, and replace them with different colors by changing the hue, saturation, and lightness. We use it to make small changes to color areas that we can easily blend into their surroundings.

For example, Photoshop's gamut-clipping behavior renders the highlights on the green sleeve in the image in Figure 7-14 on page 224 as a fairly unattractive blue-gray. The standard approach given by the manuals is to select the out-of-gamut colors using the Color Range command, then use the Sponge tool to desaturate them. As we've already said, we think this approach is basically *meshugge*: Photoshop will desaturate (clip) these colors anyway when you convert them to CMYK, so you're just doing manually what's going to happen anyway.

Instead, we use Replace Color. First we turn on CMYK Preview, so that we can see how the image will be rendered. Then we use Replace Color to select the problem area, and make a slight tweak to the Hue and the Lightness. We feel the result is more pleasing, though it's arguably less accurate. But the bottom line here is that our output process isn't capable of reproducing the color in the original, and something has to give. (See sidebar, "Truth in Imaging," for a discussion of a controversy surrounding this practice.)

Truth in Imaging

We often have to make decisions as to whether we try to reproduce an image as accurately as possible and perhaps settle for some flaws, or adjust it to make it less accurate but also more pleasing. This is a subjective decision, and it leads us to a tricky area.

Photographers commonly lament that prepress people screw up their color. Prepress people commonly lament that photographers shoot images that can never hope to be reproduced in print. Both viewpoints have some justi-fication. We don't believe that prepress people should simply override the intentions of the im-age creator—if you want to make stuff up, just paint a picture and leave the poor photographer's work alone—but we also recog-nize that image creators some-times have unrealistic expecta-tions of the printing process.

We don't have a magic answer here, but we'd like to suggest that this is a situation where commu-nication can prevent engender-ing a good deal of ill-will. In a commercial situation, the person who signs the check has the final say, but unless the job is done as work for hire, the photographer has an interest in how the image is reproduced.

In the case of the image in Fig-ure 7-13, we're working on our own photograph, so we can do whatever we like with it and no controversy arises. But we ask you to at least give some thought to the intentions of the image creator when you're faced with a situation like this.

Selective Color

Photoshop's Selective Color command attempts to reproduce the kind of color-within-color correction features found on drum scanners. We find that it's really only useful for fine-tuning already proofed CMYK files. It lets you make adjustments to color ranges—you can, for example, pull some yellow out of the greens without affecting the yellow component of the other colors. Its major shortcoming is that it offers no control over the color range you select—you simply have to accept Photoshop's idea of "green" or "cyan."

Absolute versus Relative modes. When we use Selective Color, we al-ways use the Absolute mode, never the Relative. The Absolute mode sim-ply looks to see how much of the color you're changing is present in the color you've selected, and removes the specified percentage of it. For ex-ample, if a red contains 93-percent yellow and you remove 11-percent yel-low, you get 83 percent, not 82—it removes 11 percent of 93 percent, not an absolute 11 percent, despite its name.

In Relative mode, it tries to evaluate how red the red is, and then tries to make it 11 percent less yellow, which it does by adjusting all four color plates. This makes us crazy, because we never know what it's going to do.

Figure 7-13 Hue/Saturation enhancements in RGB and CMYK

The image at left was captured from negative film on a LeafScan 35, with quite a bit of curve correction on the high-bit data using the LeafScan software. The reds overwhelm the rest of the image, but desaturating them would weaken the overall image, so instead we go after the other colors.

Working on the RGB image, we used Hue/Saturation to increase the green saturation—pumping up the background—and bring up the cyan saturation to provide a little more contrast in the red shirts.

Switching to CMYK preview, we see that the reds are more orange than we want, so we shift the hue of the reds slightly toward magenta to produce the result below.

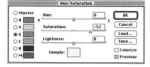

Brings out the greens in the trees, the sweater, and the awning.

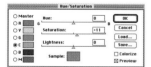

Provides contrast in the red shirts (because cyan, the inverse of red, is carrying most of the detail).

Makes the hue of the shirts slightly less orange and more red.

A proof of the above image shows that the reds are still too dominant and too orange, so we make some changes to the CMYK file.

Brings out the few splashes of yellow in the background.

Stops the increased yellow from turning the shirts orange, and sends them toward magenta instead.

Figure 7-14 Replacing out-of-gamut colors

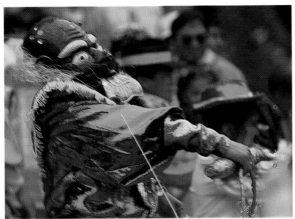

The uncorrected image

The RGB version of the image shown at left contains screaming greens (we wish we could show them to you) that are impossible to reproduce in print. When they're converted to CMYK, they turn a bluish gray.

Rather than desaturating the greens and weakening the image, we replace the unprintable colors with printable ones using the Replace Colors command. The result, seen below, may be less accurate than Photoshop's interpretation of the color, but it looks a lot better.

We use a low Fuzziness setting and Shift-click several points in the problem area to select the bluish gray colors on the sleeve.

This replaces the problem colors with a plausible-looking substitute.

The image after replacing unprintable greens

Tip: Use a New Window to See Selective Color in Action. When we use Selective Color, we like to see what it's actually doing to the individual color plates, but unless you're viewing the composite color image, the command is dimmed. The easy workaround is to open new windows for the image, and set each one to view a different channel. Then you can make the composite color window active, choose Selective Color, and turn on the Preview checkbox. You can see the effect on each plate as you make adjustments, though it's a little slow even on a fast Macintosh.

Color Correction in Practice

Let's look at some practical examples of how we put all these tools to work on images, from start to finish. Here is a representative sampling of originals, each with its own set of problems, and our proposed solutions.

Fixing a Bad Scan

In Figure 7-15 we have a flawed original further compromised by a scan from a several-years-old 8-bit flatbed scanner. The Levels clipping display and histogram reveal that there's no detail at all above level 225, and there's heavy posterization in the shadows. In short, we're faced with quite a challenge!

Given the option, we'd reject this scan as unsuitable for reproduction, but you've probably noticed that clients typically don't go for that argument. And if you're working with a typical 8-bit desktop scanner, you may have to work with this kind of scan every day.

Figure 7-15 Fixing a really bad scan

We obey our own admonition to fix the biggest problem first. The scan is far too dark.

Original scan

Shadow clipping (level 3). The shadows are heavily posterized, with huge tonal jumps between levels 0, 1, 2, and 3.

Highlight clipping (level 210). The deck is the brightest part of the image, and the red channel is brighter than the others.

The histogram shows that the highlights are completely empty, and the shadows are clipped.

Figure 7-15 Fixing a really bad scan, continued

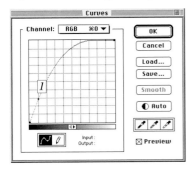

Working with Curves, we drag the cursor over the image and find that the values in the face lie around level 26, so we place point 1 to make the face visible. This blows out the highlights, so we place point 2 to bring them back into a reasonable range.

Point 3 clips the empty values in the extreme highlights. Point 4 brings down the brighter areas of the deck, and point 5 flattens the curve slightly to bring back detail in the sweater. We prefer to make all of our curve adjustments at once, but in this case we need to fix the color before we can go much further.

Point 1. 26 in, 73 out. Makes the face visible, but it blows out the highlights.

Point 2. 209 in, 228 out. Brings the highlights under control.

Point 3. 240 in, 255 out. Clips the unused highlight values.

Point 4. 152 in, 203 out. Controls posterization on the deck.

Point 5. 68 in, 143 out. Puts detail back into the sweater.

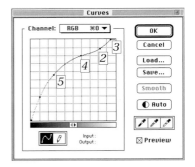

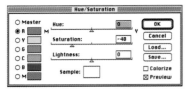

The red is heavily oversaturated, so we need to desaturate it before we can apply a final curve. Using the Hue/Saturation command to desaturate the red by 48 points produces the image seen at right.

The color looks more natural, but the contrast on the face is still too harsh and the spotless white outfit doesn't snap. We fix this with a second set of curve moves.

Normally we would have done any necessary spotting—fixing blemishes, dust, and scratches—before starting our tone and color moves, but in this case we couldn't because we couldn't see them! So we spotted the image before applying the final curve.

Figure 7-15 Fixing a really bad scan, continued

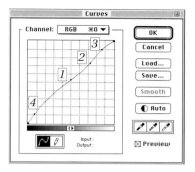

The image is still a little dark, and there simply is no detail in the shadows to be pulled out, so we limit our moves to avoid obvious posterization in the shadows.

Point 1 lightens the image overall, and points 2 and 3 bring back some detail to the bright areas of the sweater. Point 4 simulates a little fill-flash on the shadowed side of the face without posterizing it too much. After sharpening, we get the image at right. It isn't wonderful—there's some unavoidable posterization in the face, and there's no shadow detail at all—but it's much better than the original scan.

Fixing Contrast and Color

The preceding example was an extreme case. The next example (Figure 7-16) may seem similar at first glance, but a more detailed examination tells a different story. The image looks dark, but it contains good image data throughout the tonal range—it just needs to be redistributed. We can work more precisely with this image than with the previous one because we have much more information to work with. We use the same tools as before—Curves and Hue/Saturation.

Figure 7-16 Fixing a dark image

The clipping display and histogram show that there's detail in both the highlights and the shadows. There are a few white pixels at level 255, but the true whites lie around a more comfortable level 236. In the shadows, most of the darker pixels represent the saturated flowers in the foreground. We need to make the midtones and three-quarter tones brighter, which will compress the highlights and reduce the harsh contrast on the sunlit side of the building.

Shadow clipping (15)

Highlight clipping (238)

Figure 7-16 Fixing a dark image, continued

We start with overall tonal adjustment. Point 1 opens up the midtones, point 2 pulls back the highlights, and point 3 opens up the shadows. Point 4 fine-tunes the sky, and point 5 has a surprisingly large impact on the apparent overall contrast, even though it flattens the curve only slightly.

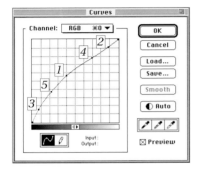

Point 1. 102 in, 144 out. Brightens the midtones.

Point 2. 226 in, 232 out. Controls the highlights.

Point 4. 179 in, 199 out. fine-tunes the sky and the detail in the quartertones.

Point 5. 56 in, 97 out. Deepens the three-quarter tones to improve overall contrast.

Point 3. 18 in, 39 out. Opens up the shadows.

Color correction next. The image has a slight magenta cast—eyedropper sampling shows us that neutral areas are deficient in green—so we adjust the green curve.

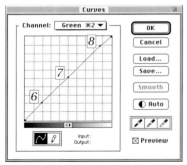

We increase green in the shadows (6), midtones (7), and highlights (8). Very small moves have a surprisingly noticeable effect.

Point 7. 128 in, 129 out. Adds green to midtones.

Point 8. 222 in, 226 out. Adds green to highlights.

Point 6. 47 in, 52 out. Adds green to shadows.

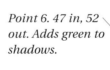

After placing a few anchor points on the red curve, we add warmth to the three-quarter tones (9), and pull some red out of the highlights (10).

Point 9. 74 in, 82 out. Adds warmth to the shadows.

Point 10. 246 in, 238 out. Neutralizes the highlights.

Figure 7-16 Fixing a dark image, continued

The image is usable as is, but it can be further improved by the saturation moves shown below, which bring out the green in the grass.

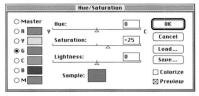 

We sharpen the image with the Unsharp Mask filter, set the output limits in Levels to 249 for highlights and to 14 for shadows, and convert to CMYK, producing the final image at right.

Working with a High-Bit Scan

Some scanners allow you to bring high-bit data (sixteen bits per channel) into Photoshop instead of downsampling it to 24-bit color (eight bits per channel) with the scanner software. Photoshop offers very limited support for high-bit files—you can use Levels and Curves, period. If you want to do anything else, you must first downsample to 24-bit color using the Bit Depth submenu that appears under the Mode menu when you load a high-bit file. Also, Photoshop treats any high-bit file as a 48-bit image. Even if it's only 10 bits per color, it still takes up the memory of a 16-bit-per-color image.

Nevertheless, this capability can be very useful when you're dealing with difficult images. Instead of making corrections during the scan (using the scanner's software on a small preview), you can use Photoshop's Levels and Curves on the full-size image. The bigger advantage, though, is that you're working on all the data the scanner can capture. Instead of stretching and squeezing 24 bits, you're stretching and squeezing 48 bits, only 24 of which are visible. This lets you make multiple edits without degrading the image, and hence lets you work much more precisely.

With a 48-bit image, most of the caveats about multiple rounds of Levels or Curves disappear. In fact, you get better results making a series of small moves than you do making one large one, because each move can be gentler, so you aren't putting tight kinks in the curve.

Figure 7-17 Fixing a high-bit scan

The raw scan looks grim. It's so dark that it's hard to discern any detail at all. If this were a 24-bit scan, we'd be in trouble. But with the high-bit file we can open up the shadows without posterization. The data is there, but it's all clumped at the shadow end, and we'll have to tease it out gently.

One single move won't get us very good results—we'd have to apply a pretty extreme curve or gamma tweak. Instead, a series of small gamma tweaks can get us where we want to be, quickly.

The key here is that each level in the 24-bit display represents a poten-

tial 256 shades (!) in the 48-bit image. We want to concentrate on the shadow end, gradually spreading the compressed high-bit values to bring out more detail in the shadows. As we do so, the midtones and highlights gradually get brighter as the data migrates toward the highlight end of the range.

The raw histogram is shown above. Three gamma moves of 2.0, 1.4, and 1.1 produce the image at right and the histogram below.

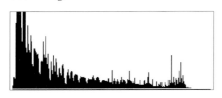

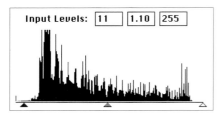

We repeat the gamma move of 1.1 by pressing Command-Option-L, then Return, six times. When we open Levels for a seventh time, we can see that the shadows are starting to wash out, so in addition to the gamma tweak, we apply the black clipping move shown at left to bring back some density to the shadows. The levels we're clipping here are almost entirely due to scanner noise, and don't represent any significant detail.

The image at right is the result of our series of gamma tweaks. We're almost at the scanner's limit in terms of pulling shadow detail, but we're still holding detail in the snow.

Next, we turn our attention to the color balance, using Curves. The Info palette shows that the snow has more green than red, and more red than blue, so we create the curves shown below to make it neutral. We need a second point to flatten the blue curve slightly, or we'd end up with a blue cast.

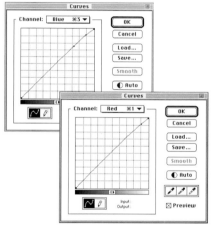

We convert from 48- to 24-bit RGB so we can use other tools besides Levels and Curves, then use Hue/Saturation to increase the master saturation by 24 points, and the green saturation by a further 9 points.

We sharpen the image with Unsharp Mask, and use the output limits in Levels to set the shadow and highlight dot limits—we want to hold a dot in the brightest parts of the snow. finally, we convert it to CMYK to produce the image at right.

Correcting Color Balance with Eyedroppers

As we discussed in "Black, White, and Gray Eyedroppers," earlier in this chapter, the eyedropper tools found in Levels and Curves can be difficult to control, but they can also make short work of fixing color balance, particularly in images that have well-defined neutrals. The key to successful use of the eyedroppers is careful matching of the target color to the source color that you click on in the image. The eyedroppers don't work well for large moves, but they're very effective with small ones.

Figure 7-18 Cast removal with eyedroppers

The image at right was scanned on a midrange desktop flatbed scanner at default settings. It has handled the tonal range quite well, but the neutrals are magenta in the highlights and green in the shadows. Removing slight casts like this is one of our main uses of the eyedroppers.

We look for areas in the image that we think should be neutral, and sample their values using the Info palette. The background viewed through the water in the glass reads 242R 231G 237B—too magenta.

To make the color neutral, we set the target color for the white eyedropper to 237R 237G 237B (237 is the approximate average of the three source pixels' values), and click the white eyedropper on the source pixel. This makes the highlights a lot more neutral.

This still leaves us with a greenish tinge in the midtones. The fringes of the shadows are good candidates for source pixels—we use a pixel under the sugar bowl that reads 124R 134G 130B. We set the target color for the gray eyedropper to 127R 127G 127B, and click on the source pixel.

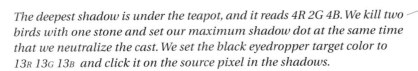

The deepest shadow is under the teapot, and it reads 4R 2G 4B. We kill two birds with one stone and set our maximum shadow dot at the same time that we neutralize the cast. We set the black eyedropper target color to 13R 13G 13B and click it on the source pixel in the shadows.

Figure 7-19 Partial cast removal with eyedroppers

You don't have to limit yourself to neutral target values with the eyedroppers. You can set any target color, and click on any source color, although large differences between source and target colors can produce unpredictable results. Curves let you control color casts very precisely, but they can be a lot of work, and you can only manipulate one channel at a time. The gray eyedropper can be both faster and more flexible.

The image has a yellow cast, but no obvious neutrals to use as a reference for correction by the numbers. When we make the background neutral using the curves shown below, the result is the rather ugly and austere rendition shown here.

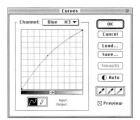 

The gray eyedropper provides a more flexible solution. We decide to try removing half of the yellow cast instead of neutralizing it completely.

We sample the background and see that it has about 25 points less blue than red or green. Halving the difference, we set the gray eyedropper target color to 127R 132G 122B, then try clicking various source pixels in the background.

Clicking a source pixel of 111R 107G 80B produces the result at right, which looks much more natural than the strictly neutral one above.

Color is Personal

It has been argued that no two people see the same color, and we know from bitter experience that an individual can see the same color differently on different occasions, or in different contexts. We don't pretend to

Figure 7-20 Correcting a Photo CD image of unknown origin

The Universal Negative 3.0 pro-file worked better than others in acquiring this image, but the re-sulting image, top, is flat, and the fleshtones have a cyan cast. Not a bad starting point, though.

We apply the curves at right to get the result above, which represents our best guess.

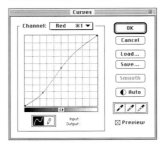

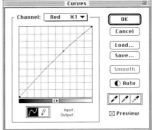

Correcting an Old Photo CD Image

Photo CD got a bad rap when it first appeared, and you still hear people saying that scans from Photo CD are usually flat, with a color cast. This isn't true; a properly made and properly acquired Photo CD scan usually looks great right off the bat. But we understand how Photo CD got its reputation, and this exercise illustrates it.

As we explain in "Photoshop and KCMS" in Chapter 16, *Color Management Systems*, Kodak's color management system is at the heart of Photo CD. But when Photo CD first appeared, parts of the system were still under construction. With modern Photo CDs, you can use the Image Info button in the Photo CD Open dialog box to find out which profile to use as the source profile for the image.

But most early Photo CDs don't have this information embedded, and they were often scanned using early film profiles (or film "terms," in Kodak jargon) that provided less accurate results than today's. You have to guess which source profile to use (or try them all), and the images often need tweaking for color balance and contrast. This is the case with the image in Figure 7-20, from Kodak's first Photo CD Sampler.

A little experimentation suggested that the best profile for this image was the Universal Negative 3.0 profile—it gave us a better starting point than either the Kodachrome or Ektachrome profiles. So we took a first pass at the image using that profile and a few curve corrections.

But we were guessing, so we cheated and asked a friend at Kodak for a print made from the original negative. As it turns out, our guess wasn't too far off—it was a little on the conservative side. The image did indeed come from a negative. It has the characteristic orangey fleshtones and strong saturation of the Ektar25 stock on which it was shot.

With the print as a reference, we created the curves shown at left, and added a couple of tweaks from Chapter 8, *Sharpening* (page 254), and Chapter 15, *The Digital Darkroom* (page 451).

The result is the final image at upper right on the facing page, which is about as close a match to the color and appearance of the original print as our output process will allow.

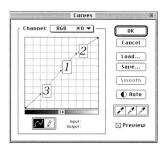

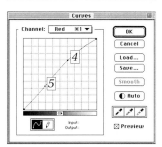

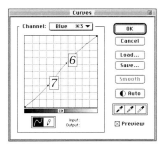

We created the tone curve at left and the color curves below to match the print we used as a reference. We used them to create the upper-right image on the facing page. We also desaturated the reds (see Chapter 15, The Digital Darkroom), and emphasized the eyes with some sharpening tricks (see Chapter 8, Sharpening).

The RGB curve improves the overall contrast, concentrating on the midtones and quartertones. Point 1 lightens the hair slightly, point 2 brightens the highlights on the face, and point 3 pulls back the curve to prevent the shadows from washing out.

The red curve kills the cyan cast. Point 4 puts red back into the fleshtones. and point 5 pulls back the red curve to avoid making the whole image too red.

The blue curve is the fine-tuner. Point 6 takes a little yellow out of the fleshtones, and point 7 pulls back on the blue curve to avoid a blue cast.

have all the answers, and you may disagree with some of the decisions we've made with some of the images. That's fine. Our aim isn't to wow you with our color expertise. Instead, we've tried to show you how to evaluate images, how to see problems, and how to use a wide range of Photoshop's tools to address them.

We encourage you to find your own ways of using these tools. We've provided good jumping-off points, but Photoshop is a deep program, and color reproduction is a bottomless pit! Experiment, refine, archive your raw scans, and save your tweaks. Remember that there's no substitute for experience. Often you'll find that an image doesn't turn out quite the way you want5. If you can retrace your steps, you can figure out where you went wrong. It may be too late for this job, but you can apply the knowledge gained from this experience to subsequent jobs.

Sharpening

Getting an Edge on Your Image

The human visual system depends to a great degree on edges. Simply put, our eyes pass information to our brain, where every detail is quickly broken down into "edge" or "not edge." An image may have great contrast and color balance, but without good edge definition, we simply see it as less lifelike.

As it turns out, no matter how good your scanner and how crisp your original may be, you always lose some sharpness when the image is digitized. Images from low-end flatbed scanners and digital cameras always need a considerable amount of sharpening. High-end scanners sharpen as part of the scanning process. Even a high-resolution digital camera back on a finely focused view camera produces images that will benefit from sharpening. Remember, you *cannot* solve the problem of blurry scans by scanning at a higher resolution. It just doesn't work that way.

Your images also lose sharpness in the output process. Halftoned images (almost anything on a printing press) and dithered ones (such as those printed on thermal-wax and ink-jet printers) are the worst offenders. But even continuous-tone devices such as film recorders and dye-sublimation printers lose a little sharpness.

To counteract the blurries in both the input and output stages, you need to sharpen your images. Photoshop offers several sharpening filters, but Unsharp Mask is the only one that really works as a production tool. Sharpen, Sharpen More, Sharpen Edges, and the Sharpening tool may be useful for creative effects, but they'll wreck your images very quickly if you try to use them to compensate for softness introduced during either acquisition or output.

Unsharp Masking

Unsharp masking (often abbreviated as USM) may sound like the last thing you'd want to do if you're trying to make an image appear sharper, but the term actually makes some sense; it has its origins in a traditional photographic technique for enhancing sharpness.

The things we see as edges are areas of high contrast between adjacent pixels. The higher the contrast, the sharper the edges appear. So to increase sharpness, you need to increase the contrast along the edges.

In the traditional process, the photographic negative is sandwiched in the enlarger along with a slightly out-of-focus duplicate negative—an unsharp mask—and the exposure time for printing is approximately doubled. Because the unsharp mask is slightly out of focus and the exposure time has been increased, the light side of the edges prints lighter and the dark side of the edges prints darker, creating a "halo" around objects in the image (see Figure 8-1).

As we'll see throughout this chapter, this halo effect is both the secret of good sharpening, and its Achilles' heel—depending on the size and intensity of the halo, and where it appears in the image. Photoshop lets you control the halo very precisely, but there's no single magic setting that works for all images, so you need to know not only how the controls work, but also what you're trying to achieve in the image.

How the Unsharp Mask Filter Works

The Unsharp Mask filter works pixel by pixel, which explains why it takes so long, even on a very fast machine. It compares each pixel to its neighbors, looking for a certain amount of contrast between adjacent pixels—which it assumes is an edge. It then increases the contrast between those pixels according to the parameters you set. This creates a halo that, when viewed from normal distances, increases apparent sharpness.

Figure 8-1 Edge transitions and sharpening

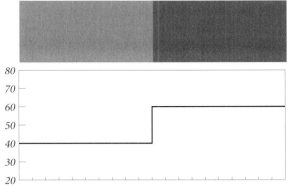

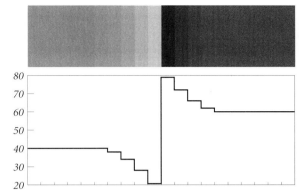

This image and graph depict an edge transition—from 40 to 60 percent. Each tick mark across the graph represents a column of pixels.

After sharpening, the transition is accentuated— it's darker on the dark side, and lighter on the light side, creating a halo around the edge.

Unsharpened

Sharpened

The effect on images ranges from subtle to impressive to destructive. This image is somewhat oversharpened to make the effect clear.

These samples are darker after sharpening.

These samples are lighter.

The net result is a sharper-looking image.

But Photoshop can't actually detect edges—it just looks at contrast differences (zeros and ones again). So unsharp masking can also have the undesired effect of exaggerating texture in flat areas, and emphasizing any noise introduced by the scanner in the shadow areas.

You need to walk a fine line, sharpening only where your image needs it. Fortunately, the controls offered by the filter let you do this very precisely (see Figure 8-2). Here's a rundown of the settings you can control in Photoshop's Unsharp Mask filter, what they do, and how they interact.

fig ref

Figure 8-2
The Unsharp
Mask filter

Amount

We think of Amount as the volume control of unsharp masking. It adjusts the intensity of the sharpening halo (see Figure 8-3). High Amount settings—you can enter up to 500 percent—produce very intense halos (with lots of pixels driven to pure white or solid black); low Amount settings produce less intense ones. Amount has no effect on the width of the halos—just on the amount of contrast they contain.

Figure 8-3
Varying the USM
Amount setting

Image resolution: 225 ppi
Radius: 1.2
Threshold: 4

Amount: 50   *Amount: 200*   *Amount: 350*

As you increase the Amount setting, the blips around big tonal shifts (edges) can be pushed all the way to white and black. At that point, increasing Amount has no effect whatsoever—you can't get more white than white! Worse, the all-white halos often stand out as artifacts and can look really dumb.

We almost always start out by setting Amount to between 200 and 400. Then we adjust downward from there, depending on the image (see "Working the Controls," later in this chapter).

Radius

Radius is the first thing to consider when you're setting up sharpening; it sets the width of the halo that the filter creates around edges (see Figure 8-4). The wider the halo, the more obvious the sharpening effect. Choosing the right Radius value is probably the most important choice in avoiding an unnaturally oversharpened look, and there are several factors to take into account when you choose, starting with the content of the image itself, the output method, and the intended size of the reproduction (see "Image Detail and Sharpening Radius," later in the chapter).

Figure 8-4
Varying the USM
Radius setting

Image resolution: 225 ppi
Amount: 200
Threshold: 4

Radius: 0.6   *Radius: 1.2*   *Radius: 2.4*

Note that a Radius value of 1.0 does not result in a single-pixel radius. In fact, the halo is often between four and six pixels wide for the whole light and dark cycle—two or three pixels on each side of the tonal shift. However, it varies in width depending on the content of the image.

Threshold

Unsharp Mask only evaluates contrast differences: it doesn't know whether those differences represent real edges you want to sharpen, or areas of texture (or, even worse, scanner noise) that you don't want to sharpen. The Threshold control lets you specify how far apart two pixels' tonal values have to be (on a scale of 0 to 255) before the filter affects them (see Figure 8-5). For instance, if Threshold is set to 3, and two adjacent pixels have values of 122 and 124 (a difference of two), they're unaffected.

You can use Threshold to make the filter ignore the relatively slight differences between pixels in smooth, low-contrast areas while still creating a halo around details that have high-contrast edges. And, to some extent at least, you can use it to avoid exaggerating noisy pixels in shadow areas.

Figure 8-5
Varying the USM
Threshold setting

Image resolution: 225 ppi
Amount: 300
Radius: 2

Threshold: 12   *Threshold: 6*   *Threshold: 0*

Low Threshold values (1 to 4) result in a sharper-looking image over-all (because fewer areas are excluded). High values (above 10) result in less sharpening. We typically begin with a low Threshold value—some-where between 2 and 4—and then increase it as necessary.

Tip: The Preview Checkbox. The Preview checkbox applies the Unsharp Mask filter to the entire image or selection on the fly, but we keep this turned off most of the time. Even on Bruce's souped-up Power Mac with assorted DSP accelerators, the preview can take a long time. And every time you change the filter settings, Photoshop has to recalculate and re-draw the entire screen. Of course, the larger the image, the longer it takes.

We turn on Preview when we're fairly sure we've arrived at the correct settings, and want to check them on the whole of the visible image.

Tip: Select a Critical Area to Preview. When you're working interactively with the Unsharp Mask settings, you may want to strike a happy medium between relying on the tiny proxy and previewing the whole image. You can do this with an additional step or two.

1. Select a critical area in the image, then select Unsharp Mask and turn on the Preview checkbox.

2. When you've arrived at the correct settings, press OK.

3. Press Command-Z (to undo the change you just made), Command-D (to deselect the area), and Command-F (to reapply the filter with the last-used settings).

This is one of those tips that takes longer to explain than it does to do!

Tip: Look at Every Pixel Before You Proceed. Like any other Photoshop effect, you can undo Unsharp Mask as long as you don't do any further editing. After we've applied Unsharp Mask, and before we do anything else, we make a point of looking at the entire image at a 1:1 zoom ratio to make sure that we haven't created any problems. If we find a stray noisy pixel, we may just spot it out with the Rubber Stamp tool, or we may decide to redo the sharpening to avoid the problem.

It's a temptation, especially with Unsharp Mask, to zoom in to see the effects more closely. Resist! Especially when you're just getting used to unsharp masking, you should only pay attention to the 1:1 zoom factor.

Tip: Recalling the Filter. If you don't like the results of the filter after seeing them, you can press Command-Z to undo, then Command-Option-F to reopen the filter's dialog box with the last-used settings. (This works with all filters that have user-settable parameters, but we use it more with Unsharp Mask than with any other filter.)

Everything's Relative

One of the most important concepts to understand about sharpening is that the three values you can set in the Unsharp Mask dialog box are all interrelated. For instance, as you increase the Radius setting, you generally need to decrease Amount to keep the apparent sharpness constant. Similarly, at higher Radius settings, you can use much higher Threshold values; this smooths out unwanted sharpening of fine texture, while still applying a good deal of sharpness to well-defined edges.

Correction versus Targeting

Figuring out how the Unsharp Mask filter works is only half the problem, though. The other half is figuring out what you need to do to the image at hand. There are two things you can do with unsharp masking.

▶ **Restore sharpness that was lost in the image-acquisition process.** You can't bring an out-of-focus or blurry original back into focus, but even a blurred original such as a fast-moving motion-blurred subject needs sharpening (it'll still be blurred, but it won't be blurred *and* soft).

▶ **Introduce extra sharpness to compensate for the output process.** In this case, you're targeting the image for your output size and method.

When you correct for softness introduced on input, you need to take into account the image content and the resolution. When you compensate for softness introduced on output, you have to take into account the output process, and the size at which the image will be reproduced.

One-pass sharpening. You can make both sets of corrections in a single move, if you know how and where the image will be output. This approach is certainly faster, and you run less risk of blowing out highlights. However, you end up with an image that's been targeted to a particular output process, and probably won't reproduce as well using another process. For instance, an image sharpened for newspaper output won't look good when it's printed at a much higher halftone frequency, and will look hideous when sent to a continuous-tone device such as a dye-sublimation printer or film recorder (see Chapter 18, *Output Methods*).

But if you're in a hurry, and you're preparing an image for one-off reproduction (particularly if you're printing with a low screen frequency that can only show a limited amount of detail anyway), one-pass sharpening makes sense.

Two-pass sharpening. Because our mothers taught us to keep our options open as long as possible, we often perform two rounds of sharpening: one for correction early in the image-manipulation process, and a second (usually much later) for targeting. The first brings back the sharpness of the original, while the second compensates for shortcomings in the output process. When using the two-pass approach, we take great care in the first pass to avoid creating spurious specular highlights and accentuating image flaws and noise, because these will be further accentuated during the second pass. We apply only enough sharpening to restore the sharpness of the original.

The results of two-pass sharpening often justify the extra pains, especially with images we plan to reuse for several different types of output.

When to sharpen. The first sharpening pass should be done after your global tonal corrections and retouching work, but before any targeting. For instance, when we're preparing a repurposable RGB image, we make our first sharpening pass just before saving the document. Then we target the image to our output method (see "Correction versus Targeting" in Chapter 6, *Tonal Correction*).

When you're sharpening as part of the targeting process—irrespective of whether it's the first or the second round—sharpening should be your third-to-last task. Do all your tonal and color correction first, including any adjustments you make to out-of-gamut colors. Then sharpen for output. Next, set your minimum highlight and maximum shadow dots (see Chapter 6, *Tonal Correction*), and—finally—convert from RGB to CMYK.

There are two exceptions to this order. First, there are times it's helpful to selectively sharpen the individual CMYK channels (see "Sharpening Channels," later in this chapter). Second, you can't sharpen before converting to CMYK if your image is already in CMYK mode. In both these cases, sharpening should be your penultimate step, just prior to setting your highlight and shadow dots.

Note that you need to sharpen *before* you set your highlight and shadow dots, because the sharpening halos can easily end up being driven beyond those limits: if you set the endpoints first, you can wind up creating unwanted specular highlights and plugged-up shadows.

Correcting for Input

With the sole exception of synthetically rendered images, any time you turn an image into pixels, some sharpness is lost. There are many different factors that cause loss of sharpness when you digitize an image, and experts differ as to the relative importance of each; whatever the reasons, the bottom line is that almost every image you deal with in Photoshop needs some sharpening.

When you restore the sharpness of the original, or even make the digital file appear sharper than the original, the image doesn't actually contain any more detail—it won't really *be* sharper—but you can fool the eye into seeing it that way.

Consider the source. You should always consider where the image came from first, because each image source has different characteristics.

▶ CCD scanners almost always introduce some noise in the shadows. If you accentuate the noise in your first sharpening pass, it'll probably overwhelm the image in the second pass.

▶ Digital-camera images can present a different set of challenges: some cameras produce artifacts that need to be removed before you can sharpen the images. With a little ingenuity, you can sharpen and remove artifacts as part of the same process (see "Sharpening Channels," later in this chapter).

▶ Drum scans shouldn't need further sharpening unless they've been downsampled. Drum scanners don't introduce noise into the image, but they can sometimes exaggerate film grain, which has the same visual effect.

We cover techniques for dealing with all these problems in "Unsharp Masking Tricks," later in this chapter.

Consider the image. You also need to consider the content of the image. A head shot needs a different kind of sharpening than a landscape, for example, because one may be more "busy" or detailed than the other. The key to making two-pass sharpening work is to get the correct Radius setting on the first pass, and that depends almost entirely on the content of the image (see sidebar, "Image Detail and Sharpening Radius," later in this chapter).

Sharpening for Output

Different output processes also introduce varying degrees of softness, and you need to sharpen the image prior to printing to compensate for this. With contone output, the situation is fairly simple. Halftone output is a different matter entirely.

Contone output. When you're working with continuous-tone output, your monitor provides a reasonably reliable guide to the sharpness you'll get on output: simply look at the image at a 1:1 zoom factor (slide your chair back, if necessary), and sharpen it so that it looks good on the monitor. It should look very much the same on output, at least as far as the apparent sharpness is concerned. In fact, when we're printing on contone output devices, we find that if we take care of the softness that was introduced during image acquisition, we often don't need to apply any further sharpening to compensate for the output device. When we do, we use low Radius and Amount settings with a Threshold value of around 3 or 4.

Halftone output. With halftone output, on the other hand, we definitely need to compensate for the output device, because halftoning breaks up the image detail into halftone dots. The Radius setting we use depends mostly on the image's resolution and halftone screen frequency, while the Amount setting depends on both the image content and the physical size at which it's being reproduced.

If we're trying to do all our sharpening at once, a host of image-specific problems can occur. The problem areas usually lie with detail that is just barely reproducible at the selected output size and halftone screen frequency, and the most common artifact is *aliasing*—jagged edges on fine diagonal lines. You'll run into aliasing problems whenever you try to reproduce detail that's too fine for the halftone screen to handle. Sharpening just exaggerates the jaggies; it doesn't create them.

If we've already performed a light sharpen to restore sharpness lost on input, it takes care of most image-specific problems; so we usually perform two rounds of sharpening on images destined for halftone output, particularly if the images are being reproduced at a relatively small size with a screen frequency of 133 lpi or less.

At low screen frequencies and small sizes, the demands of the image and the demands of the output process are often in conflict. To bring out details in the image, you usually need a fairly small Radius setting. But low screen frequencies need a higher Radius that produces a more exaggerated halo, because the coarse halftone screen simply can't show enough detail to reproduce a very narrow one (if your halo is much smaller than your halftone dot, it will simply disappear, and so will your sharpening). With higher screen frequencies and/or very-large-size output, you can use a much smaller, less-intense halo, as the smaller details in the image are more easily mapped onto the halftone grid.

The other big problem you have to face is that there's really no way to get an accurate on-screen representation of how the sharpened halftone output will look—the continuous-tone monitor display is simply too different from the bilevel halftone. You have to learn by experience. In general, an image well-sharpened for halftone output will appear decidedly oversharpened on the monitor.

Resolution dependency. The Radius setting for halftone sharpening is related directly to the output resolution of the image (in pixels per inch), and indirectly to the sampling ratio of the image—the ratio between output resolution and screen frequency. Assuming your sampling ratio is between 1.5:1 and 2:1, a good starting point for the Radius setting is *image resolution ÷ 200*. (Remember: we're talking about final image resolution, after it's been placed on a page and scaled to fit.)

Thus, for a 300-ppi image, you'd use a Radius of 1.5 (300 ÷ 200). For a 200-ppi image, you'd use a Radius setting of 1. This creates a halo about 1/50th of an inch in width (1/100th of an inch on each side of the contrast transition), which at normal viewing distances is big enough to give the impression of sharpness, but not so big that it will overwhelm the image.

This is a suggested starting point, not a golden rule, but it's a good one. As you gain experience, you'll find situations where the rule has to be bent, but if you use image resolution ÷ 200, you'll get acceptable sharpening that will keep you out of trouble (as long as you keep your Amount setting within reasonable limits).

Size dependency. The other factor you need to take into account when you're sharpening for halftone output is the physical size of the printed image. Small images need a bit more sharpening than large ones. We find that it's better to handle this by varying the Amount and Threshold settings rather than increasing the Radius; and as always, you have to keep an eye on the highlight values. Bear in mind, though, that if you're using a 2:1 sampling ratio, a single blown-out pixel won't create a white space, since each halftone dot is calculated from four image pixels.

Tip: Radius Settings for Very Large Images. The one situation where you may want to use very high Radius settings is for large images that people will never look at up close, such as billboards and (some) posters. In this case, you may need a higher Radius value to make the sharpness really pop at the intended viewing distance (a hundredth of an inch ain't much at 100 feet). Try the following formula to determine an appropriate Radius setting.

viewing distance (inches) × resolution (ppi) × .0004

This formula is based on some theories about the eye's sensitivity to cycles of amplitude modulation over a given viewing arc (we love throwing around big words like that). We haven't had the chance to test this on a billboard, so we suggest you use it as a starting point, and take it with a pinch (if not a bag) of salt.

Working the Controls

When we're trying to determine the right sharpening settings for an image, we start by setting the Radius. We usually start out with exaggerated Amount and Threshold settings (400 percent and 0 are typical), and then we start experimenting with the Radius value. The exaggerated Amount and Threshold make it easy to see what's happening as we adjust the Radius (see Figure 8-6).

As you increase the Radius, the apparent sharpness also increases—often to an undesirable extent. This is where the aesthetic considerations come in. Some people like more sharpening than others. We find over-sharpened images more disturbing than slightly soft ones, but that's a matter of taste. It's up to you to decide how much sharpening you want.

However much sharpening you decide to apply, you'll find that as you increase the Radius setting, you need to decrease the Amount to keep the apparent sharpness constant. You can work these controls in opposition to achieve a wide range of sharpening effects.

Figure 8-6 Radius versus Amount versus Threshold

Very different USM settings can combine to provide equivalent apparent sharpness.

Image resolution: 225 ppi

230/0.6/12   *390/0.6/33*   *79/4/19*   *300/5/113*

Threshold is the third part of the equation. You can think of it as a selective smoothing function. At small (less than 1 pixel) Radius settings, a Threshold value as low as 15 or so will probably wipe out most of the sharpening effect. At higher Radius settings, you can use much higher Threshold values to smooth out unwanted sharpening of fine texture, while still applying a good deal of sharpness to well-defined edges.

Image Detail and Sharpening Radius

You can achieve the same apparent sharpness using many different combinations of Amount, Radius, and Threshold settings, but the difference between good and bad sharpening lies largely in matching the Radius setting to the image content.

Look closely at the image at hand. How big, in pixels, are the details that you want to sharpen? You need to match the size and intensity of the sharpening halo to the size of the details in the image.

High-frequency images contain a lot of detail, with sharp transitions between tonal values, while *low-frequency* images have smoother transitions and fewer small details. Whether a given image is high frequency or low frequency depends on the content of the image and on its pixel density. High-frequency images, where the edges of objects are reproduced using only one or two pixels, need a smaller Radius setting than low-frequency images, where the edges may be a dozen or so pixels wide.

An image containing fine detail, such as a picture of trees, is likely to have many more high-frequency transitions than a head shot, for example. But if you scan the trees at a high enough resolution, even the edges on the tiniest leaves will be reproduced several pixels wide in the scan. So it isn't *just* the content that dictates the sharpening, it's the relationship between content and resolution.

Unpleasant settings. Too large a Radius is the prime cause of unpleasantly oversharpened images. Moreover, an overly large Radius can actually wipe out the detail it's supposed to be accentuating. Too small a Radius can result in too little apparent sharpening. This might in turn seduce you into cranking up the Amount setting so far that you create spurious specular highlights, and exaggerate textures such as skin in undesirable ways. With extreme settings, you can change the overall contrast of the image—which in most cases isn't what you want.

Figure 8-7 shows two images that need quite different sharpening settings. The trees image contains a lot of fine detail that needs a low Radius setting and a fairly high Amount setting to bring it out. If we apply the same sharpening to the pumpkin, it fails to bring out the necessary detail (while threatening to create unpleasant mottling).

Conversely, sharpening settings that work well on the pumpkin don't work at all well on the trees. The larger Radius sharpens the larger elements well, but the more

There are dangers lurking here, though. As you use higher Amount and Threshold settings, you run an increased risk of driving pixels to solid black or solid white. The solid black ones aren't usually too much of a problem, but the blown-out white ones can appear as noticeable artifacts, especially when they're large due to higher Radius settings.

With very high Threshold settings, you get dramatic unnatural sharpening of high-contrast edges, while leaving smaller details soft. This makes the image look quite disturbing—it's hard for the eye to reconcile the sharp edges and the soft detail, so the image looks like there's something wrong with the focus.

Figure 8-7 Unsharp Mask settings for high- and low-frequency images

Settings that work for one image can be ineffective or destructive on another type. Resolution: 266 ppi

Unsharpened

High-frequency settings: Amount 275, Radius .6, Threshold 3

Low-frequency settings: Amount 200, Radius 2, Threshold 9

delicate elements are lost. It creates a very confused appearance, where the same element in the image appears sharp in some places and soft in others.

If you get the Radius correct first, it's easy to set the Amount to achieve the degree of sharpness you want. Then you can adjust the Threshold to suppress noise, and to avoid oversharpening patterns, film grain, and the like.

In short, the three parameters provided by Unsharp Mask give you a very fine degree of control over the sharpening effect, but it takes a while to get your head around the way they interact.

Unsharp Masking Tricks

There are a host of tricks you can use with unsharp masking—some obvious, others less so. Most are designed to avoid the problems that result when sharpening accentuates dust and scratches in images, scanner noise (especially in the shadows, and especially in color images), and film grain. Sometimes a simple Threshold adjustment solves the problem, but when it doesn't, we use two different techniques.

▶ Selectively sharpen individual color channels.

▶ Apply the sharpening through a mask.

Sharpening Channels

Applying separate sharpening to each channel in a color image is a handy technique that can go a long way toward suppressing noise, while bringing out important image detail. We use this technique on RGB images; we'll talk about selective sharpening of CMYK channels a little later.

RGB. If you examine the individual channels of most RGB scans, you'll find that the blue channel is, almost invariably, by far the noisiest of the three. It's also usually the one with the least important detail—our eyes are less sensitive to blue than they are to red or green.

We despeckle the noisy blue channel (or use the Dust and Scratches filter for more control), and sharpen the red and green channels with an Amount of 200, Radius of 1.2, and Threshold of 4 (see Figure 8-8).

There are a couple of important caveats here. First, this technique works best with fairly small Radius settings—one pixel or less. Second, we always use similar Radius settings for both the red and green channels, although we'll usually use a higher amount on green than on red.

Figure 8-8 Sharpening RGB channels (image resolution: 266 ppi)

Unsharpened   *Noisy blue channel*   *All three channels sharpened*   *Blue despeckled, red and green sharpened*

If you use a very different Radius on the different channels, watch out for color fringing. If you need to use a large Radius, sharpen the Blue channel using the same Radius, but keep the Amount setting low.

Lab. Another technique that works well in many situations is to despeckle the blue channel, then convert the image to Lab mode and sharpen the Lightness channel. This eliminates the risk of color fringing, but the mode change does degrade the image (see "RGB to Lab" in Chapter 7, *Color Correction*). We use this trick mostly with images that need a large Radius, but have a lot of noise in the blue channel, but as shown in Figure 8-9, it can also work wonders on images with artifacts from digital cameras.

Figure 8-9 Using Lab to sharpen while removing color artifacts

This 266-ppi image, captured with Kodak's DCS 420 digital camera, displays the orange and blue artifacts that one-shot digital cameras are subject to.

Unsharpened

L a b
In Lab mode, the artifacts are largely confined to the a and b channels.

L a b
A Gaussian blur on the a and b channels—typically around two pixels on b and one pixel on a—removes many of the artifacts. Then we sharpen the Lightness channel (which contains most of the detail) using a Radius of 0.4–0.7 (depending on the image content), an Amount of 300–400, and a Threshold of 2–4.

Try out the Dust and Scratches filter—the Unsharp Mask of blurring—for more control over the blurring step.

Globally sharpened

Sharpened in Lab

This same technique can often work to suppress obvious film grain, which creates the appearance of noise, even on drum scans. It can appear at relatively low resolutions: the problem isn't that you're scanning down to the film grain, but more that the grain creates an interference pattern with the pixel grid. You generally need to be more aggressive with the Gaussian Blur and less aggressive with sharpening than on digital-camera images, but the basic technique is the same.

Figure 8-10 Sharpening through a mask

With the noisy blue areas protected by a mask, we're able to sharpen the rest of the image much more aggressively without accentuating artifacts.

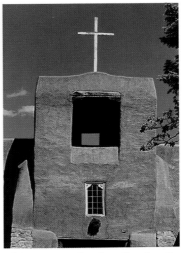

Sharpening the whole image brings out noise in the sky.

We use a mask created from the red channel, with some touchup.

This protects the sky, allowing for the level of sharpening required.

Figure 8-11 Sharpening the eyes

This image can benefit from extra sharpening of the eyes.

Sharpened globally (200/0.4/1)

The eye mask

Selectively sharpened

CMYK. We generally prefer to do our sharpening before we convert to CMYK, unless we're dealing with CMYK drum scans—in which case little sharpening should be required (because drum scans are sharpened and separated at scan time). But if the scan has been downsampled, you'll need to resharpen—the downsampling lessens or removes the halo that provides the appearance of sharpness. We also run into situations that can best be handled by sharpening individual channels in the CMYK file.

The classic example of this is a head shot, where we want to sharpen the eyes, the eyelashes, and (usually) the hair, but we don't want to sharpen the skin texture. Glossy lipstick can also look very strange when it's sharpened. In this situation, sharpening the black plate only, or the black and the cyan plates, sharpens the hair and eyelashes but leaves the skin tones and the lipstick (which are primarily composed of magenta and yellow) unsharpened.

Suppressing Noise with Masks

For more intractable problems with noise, we apply sharpening through a mask. Most of the noise in CCD scans lies in the shadows—and there's often very little significant detail in the shadows anyway—so we create a simple mask that protects the noisy shadow areas from sharpening, yet allows us to apply full-strength sharpening to the more important areas of the image.

Another situation where we often use a sharpening mask is when the image contains large areas of blue sky (see Figure 8-10). Most such scans contain a lot of noise in the sky—even in drum scans, where it's caused by the interaction of the pixels and the film grain. In this case, we want to mask out the sky and focus our sharpening on the rest of the image.

1. Select the image channel that has the greatest contrast between the areas you want to sharpen and those you don't.

2. Duplicate the channel, and apply a steep contrast curve. In Figure 8-10, we duplicate the Red channel, apply a curve, and do a little local touch-up with the Paintbrush to create a sharpening mask that protect both the shadows and the sky (see Chapter 13, *Selections*).

3. To avoid abrupt transitions, apply a two-pixel Gaussian blur to the mask. This softens the edges of the selection, so there isn't an abrupt edge to what gets sharpened and what doesn't.

4. Finally, load this mask as a selection, and apply Unsharp Mask to the composite color channel.

Selective Sharpening

We also use selective sharpening through a mask to emphasize details in images. Probably the single most common situation where we use this technique is in our handling of eyes. Eyes can almost always benefit from a little extra selective sharpening, and it's usually easy to make a mask by copying the Red channel (because it usually has the best contrast between eyes and skin), inverting it, and blacking out everything except the eyes. Figure 8-11 on page 254 shows the effect of selective sharpening through such a mask.

Avoiding the Crunchies

The Unsharp Mask filter is a powerful tool. Used well, it can give your images the extra snap that makes them jump off the page. Used badly, it gives images the unpleasant "crunchy" look we see in all too many Sunday newspaper color supplements. In overdoses, it can make images look artificial, or even blurry. With that in mind, we leave you with two final pieces of advice.

First, it's better to err on the side of caution. An image that's too soft will generally be less disturbing than one that's been oversharpened.

Second, always leave yourself an escape route. Make sure that you archive an unsharpened copy of the image before you proceed.

Use of the Unsharp Mask filter is definitely one of those things that improves with experience, and a considerable part of that experience can be gained from revisiting your earlier efforts and figuring out what went wrong. If you save an unsharpened copy, you can always go back and refine your sharpening to get closer to the result you want.

Duotones

And Tritones, and Quadtones, Oh My!

In the old tale of the four blind men and the elephant, each man describes the animal according to the piece he's experienced. "It's a snake-like creature with wrinkled skin," says one, holding the trunk.

"No, it's a hairy animal with giant wings," says another, feeling the ear.

Printing a grayscale image is similar to this experience. Printing presses are powerful and delicate instruments, but depending on the press, the operator, the ink, and the paper, they're often limited to printing far fewer than the 256 shades of gray we can theoretically achieve with an 8-bit image. So after you've gone through a lot of trouble adjusting tone, those tones are pummeled when the image is slapped onto paper. In other words, the final printed result is only a fraction of the whole image, and the viewer is blind to the richness of the original.

There are ways, however, to coax more gray levels, more detail, and more depth out of a printed image. Printers have traditionally tackled this problem by printing the grayscale image more than once, each time with a different-colored ink. These are called duotones, tritones, and quadtones (depending on the number of inks you use). When talking about the genre as a whole, we call these *multitones*, because we're too lazy to keep typing "duotones, tritones, and quadtones." Remember, multitones differ from color images in that they almost always represent an underlying neutral, grayscale image.

Expanding the Tonal Range

While they're often used to colorize grayscale images, the original purpose of multitones was to expand the tonal range of the image. For instance, a 50-percent tint in gray ink may be lighter than a 10-percent spot
of black ink; so a 10-percent spot of the gray ink is far lighter than the
tonal range of black ink can achieve. If you print black ink in the shadows and gray ink in the highlights, you can achieve more levels of highlight grays.

On the other end of the spectrum, we usually think of 100-percent black
ink as solid—you can't get darker than that. But in reality, printing 100-
percent black on top of 100-percent gray results in a darker, richer, denser
black. Therefore, by adding the gray in the shadows, you expand the tonal
range of the image even further toward real black.

Adding an ink is like listening to two of the blind men instead of just
one; you get that much more information, and can see the whole of the
image that much more clearly.

Colorizing Images

When most designers think about duotones, they don't think about expanding tonal range; they think about colorizing grayscale images. For
instance, many newsletters are printed with two inks—black and some
Pantone color. When given the opportunity to print with a second ink,
many designers immediately think, "Oh, I can give color to my grayscale
images by making them duotones."

There's nothing wrong with colorizing a grayscale image. But colorizing images without thinking about the expanded tonal range usually
looks pretty bad. In this chapter we talk about both, and how they relate
to one another.

Tip: Dumb, Fast Duotones. If we didn't know how hectic life can get in a
production setting, we would hardly believe how many people (printers,
especially) still use the flat-tint duotone trick. The idea is that you can
fake a duotone by laying a flat tint behind the grayscale image. For example, let's say you want to add some blue to a grayscale image. To fake
the duotone look, you could lay down a 10-percent tint of magenta or
PMS 485 behind the entire image (see Color Plate 6 on page 271), and set
the image to overprint in your page-layout program.

Note that this really is an old printer's trick, and it doesn't look very good. Because you're making no allowance for the tonal shift, fake duotones are often too dark and muddy. Photoshop makes creating real duotones so easy that faking it is hardly worth the effort. It's faster, but it's not that much faster.

Photoshop's Duotones

There are two ways to create multitone images in Photoshop: switch to Duotone under the Mode menu, or create them in CMYK mode. We're focusing our discussion on the Duotone mode, and will cover CMYK mode later in this chapter.

In every other color mode in Photoshop, the color is made of multiple channels—CMYK color is made of four channels, RGB is made of three. Multitones are different. In a multitone image, Photoshop saves a single grayscale image along with two curves—one for each color plate. These curves are just like those in the Curves or Transfer Function dialog boxes (see Figure 9-1). Note that you can only create a duotone from a grayscale image. (If you've got a color image, see "The Color of Grayscale" in Chapter 14, *Essential Image Techniques.)*

Figure 9-1

Duotone curves

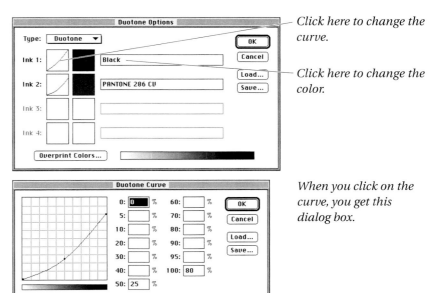

Click here to change the curve.

Click here to change the color.

When you click on the curve, you get this dialog box.

Spot versus Process Color

When dealing with printed color, you need to understand the differences between process and spot color. Both can give you a wide variety of colors. But they are hardly interchangeable.

Process color. Process color, as we've noted throughout the book, is the method of printing a wide range of colors by overlapping halftones of only four colors: cyan, magenta, yellow, and black. The eye blends these colors together so that ultimately you see the color you're supposed to.

Spot color. If you are printing only a small number of colors (three or fewer), you probably want to use spot colors. The idea behind spot colors is that the printing ink is just the right color you want. With spot color, for example, if you want some type colored teal blue, you print it on a plate (often called an overlay) which is separate from the black plate. Your commercial printer prints that type using a teal-blue

ink—probably a PMS ink—and black for the rest of the job.

Spot colors from Photoshop.

"How can I print spot colors from Photoshop?" is one of the most common questions we hear these days. The answer is that Photoshop has only a very limited ability to create, preview, and print spot-color overlays. It's really designed to do process-color work (or contone RGB output), not spot color. However, there are three ways to do spot-color work in Photoshop.

▶ Use the Duotone mode. We talk about this throughout the first two-thirds of this chapter.

▶ Use alpha channels for all the spot-color image information, and save the file in DCS 2.0 format with PlateMaker (see "DCS version 2.0" in Chapter 17, *Storing Images*).

▶ Simulate spot colors in CMYK mode. We discuss this later in the chapter.

Multitones. In this chapter, we're focusing on multitones—images that are primarily representing a neutral, grayscale image. Multitones can be printed with either spot or process colors. For example, many newsletters are printed with black and one PMS color. Here, you could include a *spot-color duotone*. On the other hand, many printers charge less if your second color is a process color—cyan, magenta, or yellow. In that case, you still may be printing with only two colors, but your image is technically a *process duotone*.

If you're printing a four-color piece, you can create duotones, tritones, and quadtones easily by using the four process colors already available to you. We're seeing quite a trend toward this in advertising these days. People take color images, convert them to grayscale (see "The Color of Grayscale" in Chapter 14, *Essential Image Techniques*), and then make process-color quadtones out of them.

Because you're typically replacing a single gray level with two or more tints of ink, you almost always need to adjust the amounts of ink used by each channel. Otherwise, the image appears too dark and muddy (see Color Plate 7 on page 271). For instance, if you replace a 50-percent black pixel with 50-percent black and 50-percent purple, it appears much darker. Instead, replacing that 50-percent black with something like 30-percent black and 25-percent purple maintains the tone of that pixel. On the other hand, if the second color were much lighter, like yellow, you'd need much more ink to maintain the tone. You might, for example, use 35-percent black and 55-percent yellow.

The duotone curves give you the ability to make these sorts of tonal adjustments quickly and with a minimum of image degradation because applying a duotone curve *never* affects the underlying grayscale image data. You can make forty changes to the duotone colors or the curves and never lose the underlying image quality.

Note that we say the "underlying image quality" won't suffer. We're not saying that you can go hog-wild with the curves, and your final image will always look good. Far from it. In fact, duotones, tritones, and quadtones are often very sensitive and can quickly succumb to "lookus badus maximus." But the image data saved on disk is unchanged by adjusting these curves; they're like filters that are applied to the image data, but only when you view it on screen or print it out.

Tip: Use Stephen's Curves. Unless you really know what you're doing, just use the duotone curve sets that were built by photographer Stephen Johnson that ship with Photoshop. We almost never create a multitone image from scratch. Instead, we load in one of Steve's curves (using the Load button in the Duotone dialog box) and then start making small tweaks to the curves, depending on the image.

Most of the curves come in sets of four.

▶ The first and second colorize the image (the first does so more than the second).

▶ The third curve of the set affects the midtones and three-quarter tones primarily, and does very little to the highlights. The effect is to warm or cool the image significantly without colorizing it much.

▶ The final duotone curve makes the image slightly warmer or cooler (still mostly neutral), primarily affecting the three-quarter tones.

If we're using a Pantone color that's not included in the canned presets, we usually pick a canned set for a color that has similar brightness to the one we're using, and replace the color with ours. Then, depending on the two colors' tones, we adjust the curves accordingly.

Tip: Checking Each Duotone Channel. The biggest hassle with images in Duotone mode is that you can't see each channel by itself. If you make a tonal adjustment to an RGB or CMYK image, you can always go and see what that did to each channel. With a duotone, however, you're in the dark. Here's one way out: convert the image to Multichannel mode.

While you're in Multichannel mode, you can view each channel of the multitone image. The first channel corresponds to the first ink, the second to the second ink, and so on. When you're done playing voyeur, select Undo (Command-Z), and you're back where you started.

Adjusting Screen Colors

No one is more aware than Adobe that colors on screen may not match colors on paper. Tech support gets calls all the time from people screaming that they followed the manual's directions, but their images are always different from what they see on the screen.

Calibrating your system and adjusting your monitor is one way to get results that more closely match your display. But the color preferences (Printing Inks Setup, Separation Setup, and Monitor Setup) are really only designed to handle process-color printing and RGB monitors. Duotones, on the other hand, are often printed with spot-color inks such as Pantone or Toyo.

Fortunately, Photoshop not only lets you pick custom spot colors in the Color Picker (press the Custom button); it also lets you adjust how they appear on screen. This is crucial for duotone work, where you want your monitor display to be as accurate as possible.

Note that your monitor simply cannot display many spot colors (including metallic and fluorescent inks) accurately, or even closely. If you want to produce metallic duotones, you have to use a great deal of imagination. A custom proof such as DuPont's Cromalin is a good idea, too.

Adjusting Colors

While Photoshop does a reasonably good job of representing spot colors on screen, we find that we occasionally want to make adjustments so that what we see on screen is closer to what we see in our swatch book. Once you've selected a spot color from the Color Picker's Custom dialog box, press the Picker button (see Color Plate 8 on page 272). You can now adjust the RGB, HSB, or Lab values for that color to make it appear closer to your printed swatch.

If you use a colorimeter, such as LightSource's Colortron, you can read the Lab values directly from your printed swatch and type those into the Picker's Lab fields. However, if your screen isn't calibrated, then this representation may look even worse than Photoshop's.

Don't adjust the color's CMYK values, however. As soon as you change one value here, Photoshop assumes you want to adhere to the process-color gamut (not necessary for spot colors). For instance, if you're adjusting the color of a rich blue such as PMS 2738, making even a one-percent change to the CMYK values makes Photoshop snap the color to a pale imitation of the blue. (It's in gamut, but who cares? This is for screen representation only; the real color will only appear when ink hits paper.)

Then, if you switch back to the Custom Picker, Photoshop finds the closest match to this new, blah color: PMS 653. Again, it's just for on-screen display, but we're trying to get as close as we can.

Overprint Colors

Once you've told Photoshop how you want each of your colors to display individually in the multitone, you need to tell it how you want the colors to look when printed on top of each other. Duotones are easy, because most duotones are printed with black and another color. Overprinting these two colors results in a darker, richer black, but it's black nonetheless. Unfortunately, Photoshop won't distinguish between the two blacks.

However, when you add more colors to the image (as in a tritone or a quadtone), or don't use black in the mix, telling Photoshop how to display the overprinted colors becomes significantly more important. To set the overprint color, click the Overprint button in the Duotone dialog box (see Figure 9-2).

The basic advice for the Overprint dialog box is to leave it alone unless you have a printed sample of what the overprinted colors *should* look like, or you're really certain that Photoshop has built it wrong.

On the other hand, with some cajoling (and perhaps a pint of Haagen-Dazs sorbet or, for really big favors, Laphroiag), you can often get your printer to "draw down" a sample of the two colors overprinting. Place that under a 5,000-degree Kelvin light, and adjust away. Or, if you're using

Pantone inks, you may want to purchase the Pantone Tint Effects Color Suite, which shows various tint builds of Pantone inks, including 100-percent overprints (which is the relevant swatch here).

Figure 9-2
Setting the
overprint color

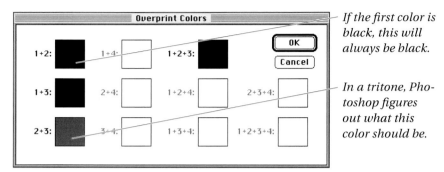

*If the first color is
black, this will
always be black.*

*In a tritone, Pho-
toshop figures
out what this
color should be.*

Changing the Overprint colors has no effect on your printed output. It only affects how the colors appear on screen. It does affect mode changes, however; if you switch from Duotone mode directly to CMYK, RGB, or Lab, the overprint colors are taken into consideration. However, this conversion would be a silly thing to do unless you're printing to a color printer (see "Printing Proofs," later in this chapter).

Setting Curves

Once you've specified the colors you want in your multitone image and adjusted the tonal range of the grayscale image, it's time to start adjusting your multitone curves. If you followed our advice in "Tip: Use Stephen's Curves," you may have already loaded in a curve set that's somewhat appropriate for your image. However, we'd like to emphasize that every image (and every spot-color ink) is different, so your curves probably need some kind of tweaking. Whether or not you go through the trouble is up to you, but here are some things to think about if you want to give it a go.

Expanding Highlights and Shadows

There are two ways in which you can expand your tonal range with multitones: focusing inks and using ink tones.

Focusing inks. You can focus an ink plate on a particular area of the tonal scale by increasing the contrast in that area. Let's say you want to increase the detail in the shadows. From Chapter 6, *Tonal Correction*, you know that you need to increase the slope of the tonal curve in the shadow areas. However, that means you have to decrease the slope (and therefore the contrast) in the highlights, so you lose detail there.

With one ink, that could be an unacceptable trade-off. But with two or more inks, you can use one to focus on the shadows—increasing the contrast there and bringing out detail—and use another to focus on the highlight detail (see Color Plate 9 on page 272). When the page comes off press, you have greater detail in both areas. This is one methodology behind double-black duotones (where you print with black ink twice).

Tip: Save and Load Curves. As we said earlier, it's a hassle not being able to see how each "channel" of the image changes as you adjust its curve. This is especially frustrating to new users who have a difficult time picturing what the curves are doing without the visual feedback. Whether you're a beginner or a seasoned pro, you may find this technique useful.

1. Duplicate the image. (Remember that if you hold down the Option key while selecting Duplicate from the Image menu, Photoshop won't bother you with a superfluous dialog box.)

2. If the duplicate image isn't already in Grayscale mode, select Grayscale from the Mode menu. This simply throws away the duotone curves. It doesn't affect the image data.

3. Use Curves (Command-M) to create the curve you're trying to achieve for the duotone ink. You can use Preview or any of the other Curve tricks we talk about in Chapter 6, *Tonal Correction*. You cannot, however, use Arbitrary Maps (curves made with the pencil tool). Duotones don't understand those at all.

4. Save the curve to disk, then press OK or Cancel in the Curves dialog box. (It doesn't matter at this point; we usually cancel to save time.)

5. Switch back to the Duotone image, open the Duotone dialog box (by selecting Duotone from the Mode menu again), and load the curve you've made into the ink's Curve dialog box.

If the curve you've made isn't quite right, you can always adjust it in the duotone image, or if you want to get visual about it, go back and load the curve into the grayscale image's Curves dialog box again.

Curves Is Curves

If you're wondering about the difference between Duotone curves and regular curves (and transfer curves), the answer is: there's hardly any difference at all. It's mostly a matter of when the corrections are applied to the image.

When you use the Curves dialog box, the image data is affected immediately; you're actually changing the image. Curves also lets you use arbitrary maps (a fancy way of saying that you can draw a line with the pencil tool) and gives you the chance to preview your changes "live," using Video LUT Animation.

Curves that you create in Duotone mode, on the other hand, don't get applied until you print the image. In fact, Photoshop just saves the grayscale image plus the curves. When you print, each curve is sent down along with the image data in the form of a transfer function. So you can always go back and change the curves without degrading the image.

Duotone curves have their pros and cons, though. You can't preview how a single channel changes as you move the curve; you can't even see how the mix of curves and inks looks on your image un-

til you press OK in the Duotone dialog box. On the other hand, the Duotone Curves dialog box has an excellent feature: you can type in values instead of simply clicking on the curve. This is especially handy when it comes to targeting by compressing the tonal range.

Because a curve is a curve is a curve, you can save a curve from one dialog box and load it into another (see "Save the Curves" in Chapter 6, *Tonal Correction*). The exception: you can't load curves with arbitrary maps into the Duotone or Transfer dialog boxes.

Ink tones. The second method of expanding your image's tonal range, ink tones, is almost always performed in conjunction with the first method, focusing inks. As we said earlier in the chapter, by printing with a gray ink along with black you immediately expand the tonal range, because a tint of gray is lighter than a tint of black; plus, gray printed over black is darker than black alone. Therefore, you can affect the tone of your image by picking appropriate second, third, and fourth colors.

For instance, printing with two dark colors may make less sense than printing with a dark and a light color. If you're printing with three colors, you may want to use black plus a lighter gray (to extend the highlights) plus a darker color (to enrich the shadows).

Creating the Curves

In order to ensure tonal consistency throughout the image, you need to think carefully about adjusting curves for each ink, depending on their relative tones. For example, let's say you're printing with black plus a PMS ink, Warm Gray 6 (which we can't show you, since we only have process inks to work with).

► The black is going to make up the skeleton of the image, with a lot of contrast in the shadows. To do this, we pull the black entirely out of the extreme highlights by setting the 5-percent field to zero. Then we compress the tonal range of the image slightly by setting the 100-percent black to 94 (that way, no pixels become totally black). Finally, to add even more contrast, we pull the 70-percent value down to 45.

► The warm gray will be the flesh of the image, holding the contrast in the midtones, and especially focusing on the highlights. To do this, we're going to boost the contrast in the highlights by raising the curve from 5 percent up to 9 percent. Next, we'll lower the 100-percent mark to 90 percent, so that the shadows don't get too dark when both inks print on top of each other. Finally, the curve in the highlights and midtones is steep, but we want it even steeper, so we'll raise the 50-percent mark to 75 percent.

While these adjustments flatten out the contrast in the shadows, we don't care, because the details there are handled by the black ink.

Note that this example is only that: an example. Change the ink and you had better change the curve. Change one curve and you had better change the other. Most of all, the curves you make and use must be dependent on the image you have, the data that makes up the image, and what you want to do with that data. Again, every image is different; so you should tailor the curves to bring out the detail where you want it most.

The Info Palette

When we work on multitone images, we like to set up the Info palette so that the First Color Readout is Actual Color. This way, we can always see how much ink is being laid down in an area (see Figure 9-3). Then we set the Second Color Readout to Grayscale, which tells us what the original underlying grayscale data is. Finally, we set the Mouse Coordinates in the Info palette to Pixels (so that we can easily refer back to the same pixel coordinate if we need to).

Tip: Make Gray Wedges Match. One of the most complicated challenges of creating multitone curves is maintaining the overall tone of the image while attempting to expand its tonal range. One method we use while adjusting multitone curves is to work with a gray wedge.

Figure 9-3

The Info palette
for duotones

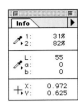

*The Info palette shows
how much ink is in
each channel.*

1. Create a new grayscale document almost as wide as your screen (on a small, 14-inch monitor, that's probably about 500 pixels wide) and perhaps an inch or so tall.

2. Turn off the Dither checkbox in the Gradient Options palette, then fill this document with a gradient from black to white.

3. Select Posterize from the Map submenu under the Image menu, and type "21" in the Posterize dialog box. Press Return.

4. You've now created a 21-step gray wedge, ranging from 0 to 100 percent in 5-percent increments.

5. In the original image (the one that's going to be turned into a duotone), increase the height dimension of the image by a little more than the height of the gray wedge (select Canvas Size from the Image menu, click in the bottom-middle square, then increase the number of pixels in the Height field).

6. Back in the gray-wedge document, Select All (Command-A) and copy the gray wedge into the duotone-to-be. You can use Copy and Paste, but we prefer to simply drag the selection from one document to the other and then place it properly in the blank white area above the image (see Figure 9-4).

Now, as you make adjustments to the duotone curves, you can watch for two important things. (Ordinarily we'd say, "Watch the Info palette." However, we haven't been able to extract information that's relevant to comparing images. Let us know if you know something we don't!)

▶ Watch the gray wedge in the duotone image to see if some gray levels are blending into their neighbors. This way you can quickly see when the highlights, midtones, or shadows are losing definition.

▶ If you align the two document windows (the duotone/image gray wedge and the grayscale gray wedge), you can compare their tones.

For instance, if the duotone gray wedge is significantly lighter than the grayscale gray wedge, you know that you probably need to bump one or more of the duotone curves.

Figure 9-4

Using a gray wedge when adjusting tone

By comparing the two gray wedges, you can get a feel for how the shades in your multitone are being affected by the curves.

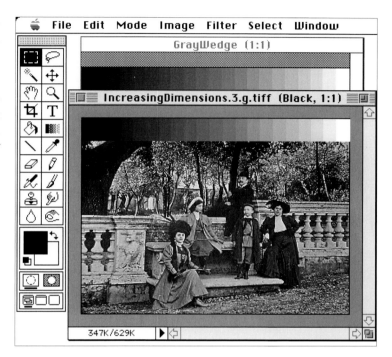

Again, the goal of making a duotone is most often to maintain the overall tonality, so the two gray wedges should be approximately the same in tone (even if one is colorized and the other is not). However, sometimes your goal is to alter the tone—perhaps to make the highlights lighter or darker. In those cases, the grayscale wedge is still useful as a benchmark.

Unthinkable Curves

In the example above, we created two curves that we would *never* ordinarily apply to an image, because they can result in severe posterization in some areas and lack of contrast in others. We can get away with these unthinkable curves, however, because the posterization and lack of detail are masked, in part, by the overprinting of the two inks. However, these curves are still timid compared to some you might want to create.

For instance, you may want to lay down a heavy solid swath of a light-gray ink under almost the entire image, in order to boost the feeling of depth, or to colorize the image slightly (see Figure 9-5).

Or you may want to hit only a certain highlight area with an ink. In this case, it may be tempting to make the curve return to zero so that this ink won't fall into the shadows. Instead, we suggest you level off the curve so that the ink enriches the midtones and shadows as well (see Figure 9-6). That way you get extra benefit from the ink, and avoid the hue shift that can result when one ink is totally absent from a tonal range.

Figure 9-5 Boosting depth by adding gray

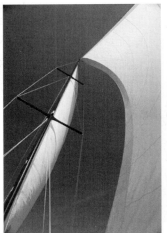

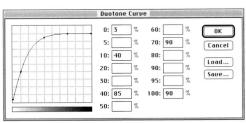

This curve can add depth to, or colorize, the entire image.

Original image   *After the curve is applied*

Figure 9-6 Adding ink in the highlights

It's usually better to extend an ink through the tonal range (top and left), rather than restricting it (bottom and right).

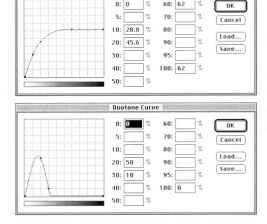
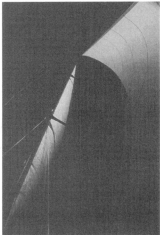

Color Plate 6 Fake versus real duotones

Just dropping a flat magenta tint behind this grayscale image does little to enhance it. Adjusting the curves for the two inks adds tonal range and depth.

The original grayscale — *Fake duotone* — *Real duotone*

Color Plate 7 Adjusting multitone curves

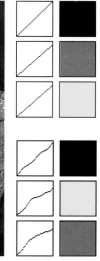

The three inks are way too heavy, darkening the image considerably, and obscuring shadow detail (far left).

These curves complement each other, maintaining and enhancing the tone of the grayscale image (left).

Color Plate 8 The Color Picker and Custom Color dialog boxes

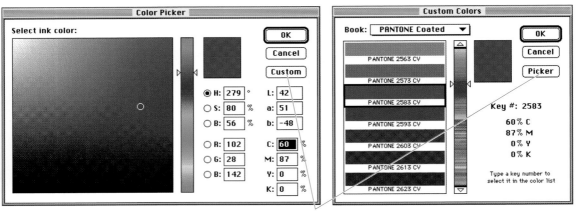

You can toggle between these two dialog boxes by clicking here.

Color Plate 9 Focusing inks on different tonal ranges

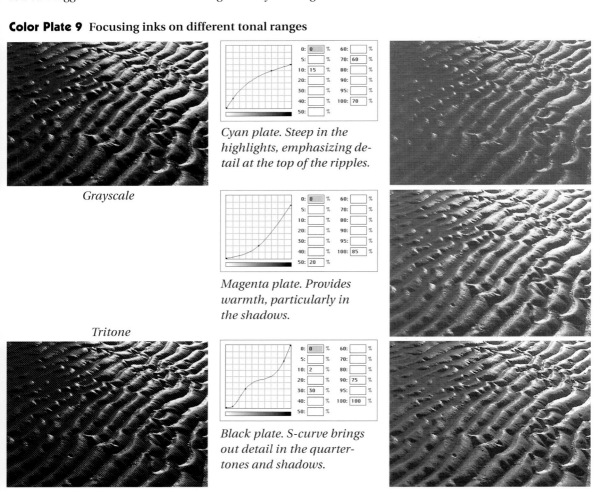

Grayscale

Cyan plate. Steep in the
highlights, emphasizing detail at the top of the ripples.

Tritone

Magenta plate. Provides
warmth, particularly in
the shadows.

Black plate. S-curve brings
out detail in the quarter-
tones and shadows.

Jackson

Color Plate 10 Grayscale reproduction with the four process inks

The grayscale image

Curves created numerically based on the neutral target values on page 210

Cyan plate

Yellow plate

Magenta plate

Black plate

Printed using the four process inks

274

Color Plate 11 Creating curves for duotone and tritone images

By focusing inks on different tonal ranges, you can colorize a grayscale image, and emphasize otherwise-hidden details. The tables show the values entered in the Duotone curves dialog boxes.

Cool neutral, details held with black.

 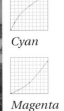 Cyan / Black

	20	50	70	100
Cyan	–	15	60	–
Black	10	–	60	–

Cyan holds highlights, magenta holds shadows.

 Cyan / Magenta

	20	50	70	100
Cyan	36	67	–	–
Magenta	–	33	–	90

Cyan and yellow in the midtones, black elsewhere.

 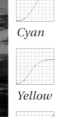 Cyan / Yellow / Black

	20	50	70	100
Cyan	6	–	75	89
Yellow	10	52	65	70
Black	30	42	52	92

Magenta and yellow emphasize the shadows.

 Magenta / Yellow / Black

	20	50	70	100
Magenta	5	15	–	85
Yellow	4	15	35	85
Black	15	40	–	95

Magenta and yellow carry the highlights.

 Magenta / Yellow / Black

	20	50	70	100
Magenta	30	57	–	82
Yellow	30	50	–	68
Black	4	30	–	95

Cyan for the highlights, black for the shadows.

 Cyan / Black

	20	50	70	100
Cyan	34	48	–	80
Black	5	–	55	–

Compressing Tones for Targeting

There's no doubt that printing presses have difficulty printing extreme highlights or shadows—the tiny halftone spots disappear to white, and the white areas in the shadows fill in, resulting in solid ink. This is the reason we're so adamant about compressing the tonal range of your images so that all the gray values and details appear in a range that can successfully print on press (see "White Points and Black Points and Grays, Oh My!" in Chapter 6, *Tonal Correction*).

Nonetheless, one of the goals of multitone images is to expand the tonal range and recapture some of that highlight and shadow detail lost in the horrors of the printing process. If you compress the image data significantly before you start adjusting duotone curves, you've simply lost your chance to bring out those details.

We suggest avoiding the targeting step during tonal correction, and instead using the duotone curves to compress the data (see Figure 9-7).

Figure 9-7

Examples of curves for compressing data

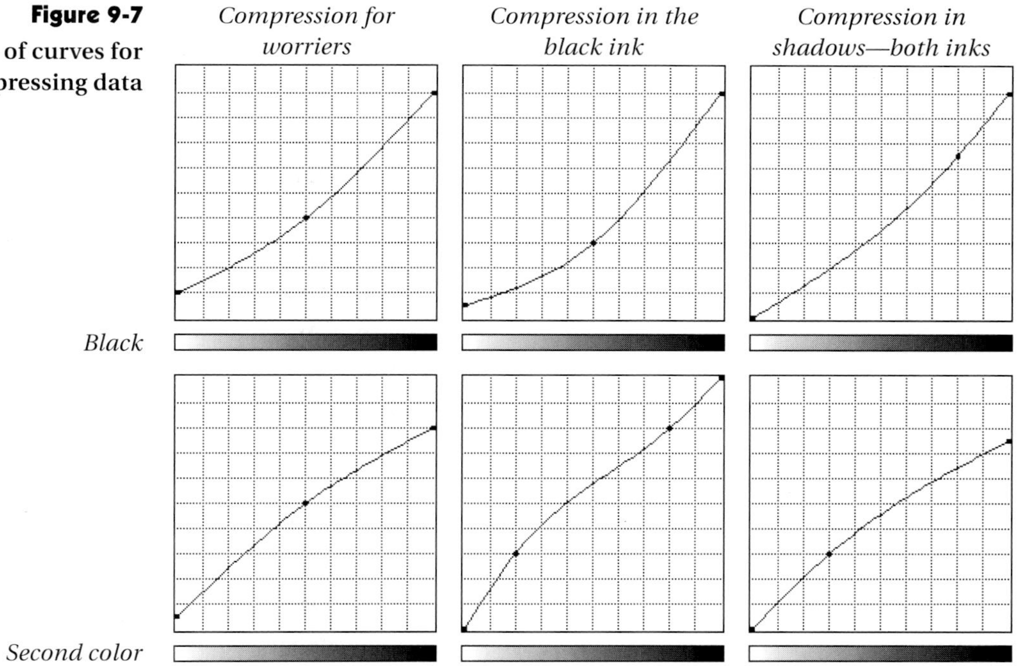

Compression for worriers

Compression in the black ink

Compression in shadows—both inks

Black

Second color

Turning Grayscale to Color

Until now, we've been exploring how to create multitones using the Duotone mode. However, just because you want a multitone doesn't mean that you need to use the Duotone mode to get it. In fact, you can get just as good results by manipulating the grayscale image in CMYK mode. There are, however, pros and cons to either technique.

▶ **File size**. An image in Duotone mode, whatever the number of inks, is saved as an 8-bit grayscale image along with curves. CMYK images, then, are four times the size, because each pixel is described with 32 bits of information, even if you're only using two channels.

▶ **Single-color areas**. In Duotone mode, there's almost no way to create a single area in which only one color is present. For example, it's almost impossible to make a 20-percent blue square in the middle of an image, without black also printing in it. However, this is easy to do in any other mode.

▶ **Blends**. There's also no way to create a gradient blend between two spot colors while in Duotone mode. In CMYK mode, it's easy.

▶ **Outputting images**. When you output a multitone image, the mode it's in may have an impact on your output process. For instance, you cannot transfer an image in Duotone mode to a high-end imaging system (like Scitex). Also, because duotone images must be saved in an EPS format (see "Saving and Outputting," later in this chapter), you cannot take advantage of any tricks your page-layout software may be able to do with TIFF images (see Chapter 17, *Storing Images*).

▶ **Adjusting tone**. In Duotone mode, you can always change the duotone curves without affecting the underlying grayscale image data. That means you can quickly repurpose the image to a number of different output devices. Or if your art director decides to print with green instead of yellow ink, you can quickly change the tonal curve to adjust for the difference in ink density.

On the other hand, if you're creating multitones in CMYK mode, you're changing the image data in each channel, so you want to minimize the number of adjustments you make to avoid image degradation. Working in CMYK mode, however, gives you the chance to actually see (interactively) how your curves are affecting the image data. And you can use features like the white-and-black-point clipping display in Levels to make decisions about your curves. This can be very helpful, especially when making small tweaks to the curves.

▶ **Screen representation.** Photoshop knows how to represent most spot colors reasonably well on screen when you're in Duotone mode. However, if you're creating spot-color multitones rather than process-color multitones in CMYK mode (see the sidebar "Spot versus Process Color," earlier in this chapter), you'll either have to ignore the colors you see on the screen (which are RGB representations of CMYK colors) or look ahead in the chapter to "Simulating Spot Colors in CMYK."

Converting Images to Grayscale

Because a multitone image typically represents a grayscale image using color, you generally begin with a grayscale image. (If you've got a color image, see "The Color of Grayscale" in Chapter 14, *Essential Image Techniques.*) Then—assuming you've decided not to use Duotone mode— you'll want to switch your image from Grayscale mode to CMYK mode. You can use two methods—simple conversion, or copying into a new file.

Simple conversion. You can simply switch your image from Grayscale mode to CMYK mode using the Mode menu. However, many people seem to think that this simply adds three new channels (Cyan, Magenta, and Yellow), and leaves all the grayscale information in the Black channel. Not so. Photoshop uses the color preferences settings (see Chapter 5, *Color Preferences*) to convert the neutral grays into colors. The amount of black generation (based on the UCR or GCR settings in Separation Setup) determines what appears in the Black channel.

In effect, the curves in the Separation Setup dialog box are equivalent to creating a quadtone using the Duotone dialog box. We rarely use this method; it's clunky and nigh-on impossible to make adjustments to each plate after the conversion. Plus, Photoshop's separation curves are not designed to expand the tonal range of a grayscale image, so you're losing the opportunity to enhance your image.

Nonetheless, if you *do* use this method, we strongly suggest you set Black Generation to Heavy in the Separation Setup dialog box first. That way, the Black channel contains more information, and small press anomalies won't result in large color shifts.

Copy into New. A second, more reasonable, way to convert your grayscale image into CMYK form is to create a new document with the same pixel dimensions as the grayscale image.

1. Select the whole grayscale image (Command-A).

2. Copy it (Command-C).

3. Create a new document (Command-N) and set the mode to CMYK. Photoshop should have automatically set the dimensions of the new document to the size of the image on the clipboard, so there's no need to change them.

4. Switch to the Cyan channel (Command-1) and paste the grayscale image into it. Repeat this with each of the four channels that you want to use. (For a tritone, fill three channels; for a duotone, fill two.)

Now it's time to start adjusting curves for each of the channels. This is a tricky proposition because, as we said back in Chapter 6, *Tonal Correction*, you typically don't want to make tonal adjustments to a channel more than once or twice.

Tip: Keep the Copy on Hand. If you're using the Copy into New method, and you mess up the curves in one of the channels, don't forget that you may have the original grayscale image still copied in the clipboard. To revert the channel back to where it was when you started, you can simply paste the image back into that channel.

Simulating Spot Colors in CMYK

If you've decided to create or adjust your multitone in CMYK mode, you'll likely want to see a reasonable representation of the image on your screen. If the image is a process-color multitone, this isn't a problem at all. But if you're using one or more spot colors, Photoshop balks at the proposal—it only thinks in cyan, magenta, yellow, and black.

The answer is found by choosing Custom from the Ink Colors popup menu in the Printing Inks Setup dialog box. As we discussed back in Chapter 5, *Color Preferences*, Photoshop knows what color inks you're using by what ink set you've chosen in this dialog box (see Figure 9-8). If you change the color cyan to hot pink here, Photoshop adjusts and displays hot pink wherever you ask for cyan.

Here's how you can change these values to simulate spot colors and get a reasonably good on-screen representation of your image.

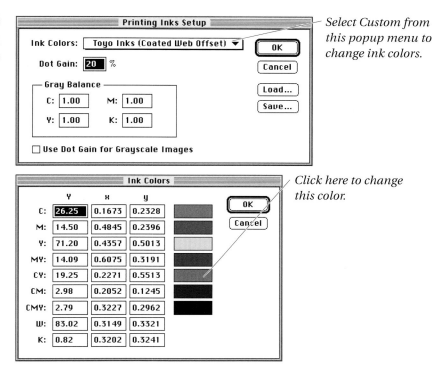

Figure 9-8

Printing Inks Setup and
Ink Colors dialog boxes

*Select Custom from
this popup menu to
change ink colors.*

*Click here to change
this color.*

1. Find the Lab values for the inks you'll be printing with. (If you've already picked a Pantone or other spot color in the Duotone dialog box, click on the color swatch there. If you haven't picked one yet, you can find one by opening the Color Picker, clicking Custom, then clicking the Picker button to go back to the Color Picker.)

2. Note the Lab values for the color. (Yes, you have to write them down.)

3. Go to the Printing Inks Setup dialog box and select Custom from the Printing Inks popup menu.

4. Click on the cyan color swatch and type in the Lab values for the spot color you chose. (You can enter the XYZ values directly in the Ink Colors dialog box, if you can lay your hands on those values . . . .)

Click OK to save these settings; Photoshop now thinks of cyan as the spot color. If your image is a tritone or quadtone, you have to repeat these steps for the other color(s).

If you're printing with more than one nonblack ink (in the case of a tritone or quadtone), you also need to specify what the *combined* spot-color values are. Otherwise your screen representation will be way off. It's

Converting from Duotone to CMYK Mode

While we wouldn't do this with most images, we have occasionally found it helpful to do much of our multitone work in Duotone mode, then convert to CMYK mode to take advantage of capabilities like solid color tints, blends, interactive tonal adjustments, and output benefits (see "Turning Grayscale to Color," earlier in this chapter). This gives us the best of both worlds, and it gives us one additional advantage: we can print to a color printer for proofing (see "Saving and Outputting," later in this chapter).

As in the conversion from Grayscale to CMYK mode, there are two methods for converting from Duotone mode to CMYK. The easiest method is simply to select CMYK from the Mode menu. This is easy and effective when preparing to output to a color printer, but useless if you need to make further changes to the duotone

curves. It's useless because while the result is an image that looks almost exactly the same, it's built with four process colors (like converting RGB to CMYK)—all your painstaking work on the duotone curves goes down the toilet.

If you're planning on converting the image in order to make further adjustments to it while in CMYK mode, it's much better to convert the image to Multichannel mode first. When you convert to Multichannel mode, Photoshop gives you two, three, or four channels (depending on the number of inks you're using), each with the proper curve automatically applied to the original grayscale image. From Multichannel mode, you can convert the image to CMYK mode with two changes.

► If there are only two or three channels (if the image is a

duotone or a tritone), add channels until you have four. We suggest naming them (double-click on the channel tile in the Channels palette) so you know which is which.

► Make sure the channels are in the correct order in the Channels palette. When you convert to CMYK mode, the first channel tile in the palette is always read as the cyan plate, the second is magenta, and so on. However, when you convert a quadtone into Multichannel mode, Photoshop makes black the first tile in the list. You have to drag it into its correct place, or the image will turn out incorrectly.

This, by the way, is how you can convert a duotone image into a CMYK format that Scitex (and other CMYK-only systems) can read and use.

easy enough to find the values for the solid inks, but how can you find out the Lab values for two overprinting spot-color inks? The hard (but most accurate) way is to use a colorimeter, such as the Colortron, to read a drawdown from your printer. We found an easier way (one which is usually reasonably accurate) in Rob Day's *Designer Photoshop*.

1. Create a new small grayscale document, and convert it to Duotone mode. This is just a dummy document that you'll throw away later.

2. While in the Duotone dialog box, select the two or three colors in your tritone or quadtone. Don't bother with the curves; they don't concern us here.

3. Click on Overprint Colors to see how Photoshop believes these colors should overprint.

4. Click on the 2+3 color swatch, and write down the Lab value of the color. Repeat this with any other nonblack color swatch.

5. Leave these dialog boxes, and open the Custom Ink dialog box inside Printing Inks Setup.

6. Click on the overprinting color swatches for the corresponding spot colors (for instance, the one labeled CM is the overprinting color for cyan and magenta). The hardest part here, we find, is remembering what spot colors correspond to what process-color labels.

When you save this printing ink setup, your multitone images should appear correctly—more or less—on the screen. Note that making changes in this dialog box has no effect on CMYK image data. *It has a radical effect,* however, on any image that you convert *to* CMYK mode, and on the way Photoshop displays CMYK images. Therefore, we strongly suggest you save the custom ink settings in the Printing Inks Setup dialog box (use the Save button). Then switch back to a standard SWOP ink set (or whatever you usually use) whenever you're not working on your spot-color image.

Saving and Outputting

While we explore printing and saving from Photoshop in depth in Chapter 17, *Storing Images,* and Chapter 18, *Output Methods,* multitones have some specific requirements that we can better discuss in the privacy of this chapter. The two most relevant issues in getting a duotone out of Photoshop and onto paper or film are saving and screen angles.

The file format that you use when saving a multitone document depends entirely on the mode the image is in: Duotone or CMYK.

Duotone mode. You can save Duotone-mode images in three formats—Photoshop, EPS, and Raw. But the only file format that's useful in page-layout programs is EPS, because Photoshop has to save the duotone curves in the form of transfer curves—something only EPS files can handle.

In order for the EPS duotone to separate properly from the page-layout program, however, you have to make sure that the color names in the duotone exactly match the names in your page-layout program's color list. For instance, if you used "Pantone 286 CVC" in your duotone, you should also have a color named "Pantone 286 CVC" in QuarkXPress or PageMaker. Fortunately, if you haven't defined the color name when you import the multitone, the latest versions of these programs add the name to the color list automatically on import.

Tip: Use Short Pantone Names. If you've already created and applied a Pantone color in your page-layout program before you import your duotone, you need to be twice as careful about ensuring the names are the same. Let's say you've added "Pantone 240 CV" to your PageMaker color list. Then you use the same color in your Photoshop duotone and import it into PageMaker. What you may or may not notice is that Photoshop, by default, named its PMS color "Pantone 240 CVC". Because of the one-letter difference, PageMaker thinks it's a different color, and will separate it onto a different plate.

There are tricks in PageMaker and QuarkXPress to combine spot colors onto a single plate, but you can avoid some of these troubles by turning on the Use Short Pantone Names checkbox in Photoshop's General Preferences dialog box. That way, it leaves off the final character, just the way PageMaker does. If you're using XPress, don't worry about it; it's smart enough to merge the colors onto a single plate automatically.

CMYK mode. If you've created your multitone image in CMYK mode, you have a choice, just as with any other CMYK image, to save in either EPS or TIFF (of course, you have more choices than this, but these are the only *good* choices). However, if you need to specify particular halftone screen angles in your duotone—and you often do—you have to use EPS (TIFFs don't let you save that sort of information).

The most important thing to remember when creating duotones, tritones, or quadtones in CMYK mode is this: if you're not intending to use process-color inks, be very careful at separation time. If you import a CMYK image into a page-layout program and print color separations, the cyan channel ends up on the cyan plate, the yellow channel ends up on the yellow plate, and so on. This is what you'd expect and want if you were using process-color inks in your image; but if you're using spot-color inks (as in the earlier section, "Simulating Spot Colors in CMYK"), this could be a disaster.

Screen Angles

Every topic in digital imaging must have at least one controversy. One of the controversies surrounding duotones is what screen angles you should use when printing them. People fall into two camps : those who favor 30 degrees between inks, and those who favor 45. We are in the latter camp: 45 degrees between the halftone screens results in the least obvious patterns. (You always get *some* patterning when you overlap screens; the trick is to minimize it.) The angles you pick, however, may vary.

We typically print black ink at 45 degrees because people tend to "blur out" this angle the most (important for a dark color). But that only leaves zero degrees for the second ink. If that ink is very light, like yellow or a light gray, you can print it at zero degrees. With a darker color like burnt sienna, cyan, or dark gray, however, a zero-degree screen may appear too obvious. Our second choice is printing the inks at 30 and 75 degrees.

With these screen combinations, be aware that the RIP might think it knows better, and substitute "optimized" process-color angles. Ask your service bureau to turn off Balanced Screens, or HQS, or whatever.

The more traditional among us usually print with 30-degree offsets. We suspect there may be an element of superstition in this, but many people who've built more duotones than we've had hot dinners use angles 30 degrees apart. However, when pressed, most confess that they do so because that's what they were taught to do.

Conventional wisdom puts the strong color at 45 degrees and the weak one at 75 degrees. But this can have the effect of making one screen more obvious than the other, so in many cases angles of 15 and 75 degrees are used instead.

In a tritone image, of course, we always revert to the second opinion: 30-degree offsets, usually using 15, 45, and 75 degrees (with 45 used for the ink/curve combination that is dominant—that has the greatest density). Finally, for quadtones, we use the four standard process-color angles: 0, 15, 45, and 75. (Note that many people state these angles as 45, 90, 105, and 165; they're the same thing, but three of them are rotated 90 degrees.) The lightest ink is always printed at zero degrees.

Printing Order

In order for the inks to match their proper halftone screen angles automatically, arrange them from darkest to lightest in the Duotone dialog box (bearing in mind the curves you've set up for each ink; a dark ink with a very light curve may not be terribly dominant on press).

If you want to specify angles manually, however, you can use the Screens button in the Page Setup dialog box (see Figure 9-9 and "Imaging from Photoshop" in Chapter 18, *Output Methods*).

Figure 9-9

Setting screens for duotones

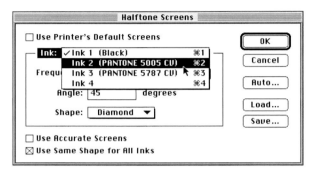

There's often little you can do about the order in which the inks are printed on press, however, even though this order may have a significant effect on the image. We suggest discussing the topic with your printer and relying heavily on their experience with inks.

Printing Proofs

Seeing spot colors (or representations of them) on screen is one thing. Proofing them on paper is quite another. You really only have two choices when trying to proof your multitone images: custom inks and converting to process colors.

Custom inks. Some service bureaus provide proofing systems that attempt to match Pantone and other spot colors. For instance, the Cromalin system lets you build proofs using Pantone's spot colors (Match Prints cannot do this, by the way). Have no doubt, this is an expensive proposition, but it's the closest approximation you can get this side of a press check.

For this type of proofing, it doesn't matter whether you've used Duotone or CMYK mode to create your multitones, or what type of inks you'll finally be printing with. You're dumping a piece of black film for each ink color; the color (spot or process) only appears when the proofs are made.

Process colors. An alternative is to print proofs on a color printer with CMYK colorants. Most spot inks just can't be reproduced faithfully with CMYK, but with skill, luck, and a good dose of experience, you can get something meaningful out of these devices.

There are three ways to print a multitone image on a color printer.

▶ **Just print it.** If your image is in Duotone mode and you simply select Print from the File menu, Photoshop sends the grayscale image to the printer along with four transfer curves (one for each process color). If the printer can only print grayscale, it throws away the transfer curves and just prints the grayscale image. If it's a color printer, it renders the image as faithfully as it can.

The primary problem with this approach is that Photoshop makes the assumption that your multitone colors are spot colors—even if they're specced as process colors—so it pushes them through its color engine (via the color preferences dialog boxes; see Chapter 5, *Color Preferences*). This is more or less the same as simply converting to CMYK mode yourself and then printing. If you have really good values set up in the appropriate dialog boxes (especially Printing Inks Setup) and your system is well calibrated, there's a reasonable chance you'll get a nice-looking image. Otherwise, your images may look bizarre.

If the multitone image is in CMYK mode when you print, Photoshop simply sends the raw CMYK data to the printer. This usually looks like dreck because the CMYK data is probably targeted to a device other than your color proofer.

▶ **Convert to RGB.** A second method of printing multitone images is to convert them to RGB mode first (whether they're in Duotone or CMYK mode), and then tell Photoshop to send the RGB data to the printer (select RGB in the Print dialog box). While this sometimes works, it often gives you even stranger colors than printing the CMYK data. The reason: the printer doesn't know what that RGB data is supposed to look like; it doesn't know what you're seeing on your screen (see Chapter 4, *Color Essentials*).

▶ **Use a color management system.** Our favorite choice is to convert the multitone image (whether it's in Duotone or CMYK mode) to RGB and then use a color management system to render it faithfully to the appropriate CMYK device (see Chapter 16, *Color Management Systems*).

Note that no matter which method you use, the color you see from a color printer is almost certainly going to be different from your final image, and no printer worth his or her salt would take something like this as a contract proof. But it may be helpful in the process of creating good curves.

Tip: Be There During the Print Run. Stephen Johnson has made more duotones than anyone else we know, and he maintains that even after printing hundreds of multitone images, he still doesn't know exactly what he's going to get until he shows up for the press run. Take his advice. If you're doing critical duotones, you *must* be present during the press run—the way the press operator controls the inks can make or break the final printed piece.

Billions of Shades of Gray

If the real world would simply perform as all the theories tell us, grayscale images would fly off the printing press with deep, rich tones and an incredible dynamic range. Unfortunately, the real world doesn't pay much attention to theories, so we need to help the process along. Duotones, tritones, and quadtones are great ways to do this. After all, if you're trying to faithfully reproduce an elephant, you want to listen to (or see) as many perspectives as you can.

Line Art

Dreaming in Black and White

With all the frenzy on the Photoshop scene that surrounds cool effects like fractalization, motion blurs, and drop shadows, it's easy to lose sight of the basics. And there are few scanned images more basic than line art.

Line art—those black-and-white images (or "bitmap images," in Photoshop terminology) with no halftoning, dithering, or anything else—are as simple as can be. Each pixel is either on or off, black or white, and you're not concerned with gray levels or halftones. Scanning, manipulating, and printing these things should be easy. And it is, at least compared to the vagaries that surround grayscale and color images.

Nonetheless, we've found that most people's line art images don't begin to approach the quality of (even mediocre) photographic reproduction. Edges are jaggy, fine lines break up, and dense patterns clog up. Many of you are going to be surprised when we tell you that it doesn't have to be that way.

With line art, you can actually produce an image that matches the original to an extent that just doesn't happen with grayscale and color images. With just a few techniques under your belt, you can achieve that ethereal, Platonic state of perfect line art reproduction, and with very little effort. The tricks lie in scanning mode, resolution, sharpening, and thresholding.

Scanning in Grayscale

It's *essential* that you scan in grayscale mode to take advantage of the techniques covered in this chapter. If you scan in line art (1-bit) mode, you can't do much of anything to improve your image. In Grayscale mode, however, you can sharpen, adjust the black/white threshold to control line widths, and increase your effective line art resolution; each of these techniques helps create a beautiful reproduction.

So avoid the temptation to scan line art *as* line art, and scan it as grayscale instead. Sure, your files are eight times as large, but it's only temporary. You can convert them to Bitmap mode when you're done with your manipulations. And the quality difference with these techniques is like the difference between . . . well . . . black and white.

Resolution

When you're printing to an imagesetter, you need very high image resolution to match the quality of photographically reproduced line art. That means 800 ppi minimum image resolution. You *can* see the difference between 800- and 1,200-ppi line art (see Figure 10-1), so you may want to opt for the higher resolution if your printing method can hold it.

Of course, you never need image resolution higher than output resolution. If you're printing your final artwork on a 600-dpi laser printer, for instance, you don't need more than 600-ppi image resolution. The additional data just gets thrown away.

Tip: Fast Line Art Imagesetting. It may seem like 800- and 1,200-ppi images are going to make for big files and slow print times, and that's often the case. But there's a little-known back-door trick that might speed things up for you. Most imagesetters that are based on Adobe PostScript RIPs (and perhaps some others) can process same-resolution bilevel images very quickly.

For example, if you send a 1,200-ppi line art (bitmap) image to a 1,200-dpi imagesetter, it can say, "Hey! That's a 1,200-dpi bitmap, and I'm printing 1,200-dpi bitmaps, so I'll just blast it down onto the page, dot for dot." The end result? A 1,200-ppi line art image may print much, much faster than an 800-ppi image. Try it on your system and see if it works.

(By the way, this doesn't work with desktop laser printers, at least according to the testing we've done.)

Figure 10-1 Line art resolution

Grayscale scan

144 ppi

300 ppi

600 ppi

800 ppi

1,200 ppi

Tip: Scan Big for High Resolution. "Great," you're saying. "They say we need 800-ppi images, but all we've got is a 300-ppi scanner. And they said back in the Image Essentials chapter that upsampling is useless. What are we supposed to do with this business card the client gave us?"

You've got two options to get a higher resolution out of a low-resolution scanner. First, you can scan a large original at your scanner's highest optical resolution and scale it down, increasing resolution. If you reduce the image to 50 percent, for instance, you double the resolution.

You can either scale the image in a page-layout program, or adjust the size in Photoshop's Image Size dialog box while the File Size checkbox is turned on (see Chapter 3, *Image Essentials*).

If you don't have a larger version of the artwork, you can enlarge your small version on a stat camera or quality photocopier, and scan that. You still get a higher-quality image because the photographic enlargement doesn't cause pixelization (there may be some cleanup work involved after the scan, of course).

The second solution (which you can use in combination with this enlargement/reduction technique) is covered in the next tip.

Tip: Doubling Your Scanner's Line Art Resolution. The second method for going beyond your scanner's resolution essentially "steals" information from an 8-bit grayscale scan, converting that information into higher line art resolution.

1. Scan your artwork as a grayscale image at your scanner's maximum optical resolution (let's use 300 ppi for this example).

2. Double the image resolution (quadrupling the file size) using the Image Size dialog box (make sure the File Size checkbox is turned off). In our example, you'd upsample to 600 ppi. Note that if your scanning software can interpolate up to this same resolution, you can use that as you scan, and save yourself a step.

    If you're yelling, "Hey! You said interpolation was useless," you're right—we did. This is the exception (we can't think of any others).

3. Sharpen and threshold the image as outlined later in this chapter.

4. Switch to Bitmap mode at the same resolution (600 ppi in our example), with the 50% Threshold option selected (see Figure 10-2).

Figure 10-2

Converting to
Bitmap mode

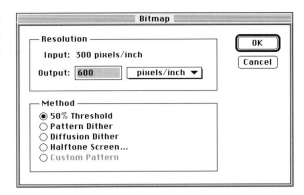

Voilà! A 600-ppi line art image from a 300-ppi scanner. While it isn't a true 600-ppi scan, it's so close that we dare you to find a difference. You may be able to raise the image's resolution above two times optical resolution, but that's pretty much the point of diminishing returns.

Note that you can use this tip alongside the previous one to res up to 800 ppi or higher.

If the arithmetic of scaling and resolution is giving you trouble, you might want to take a look at the tip "Figuring Scaling and Resolution" in Chapter 12, *Capturing Images.*

Sharpening

There is nothing that will do more for the quality of your line art images than sharpening the grayscale scan (see Figure 10-3). 'Nuf said. We recommend running the Unsharp Mask filter twice with the settings 500/1/5. If your scanning software can sharpen, you may be able to save yourself a step (Hewlett-Packard's DeskScan software does it, for instance, though not quite as well as Photoshop's Unsharp Mask filter).

Thresholding

When you scan line art in Grayscale mode, lines aren't captured as hard lines, but as a collection of pixels with different values (see Figure 10-4). But although you scanned in grayscale, you ultimately want a straight black-and-white image. The way you get there is via the Threshold command (from the Map submenu under the Image menu; as a pro, you'll press Command-T). Threshold turns gray pixels above a certain value to black, and pushes every other pixel to white.

Figure 10-3

Line art with and without sharpening

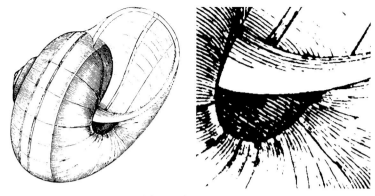

Without sharpening

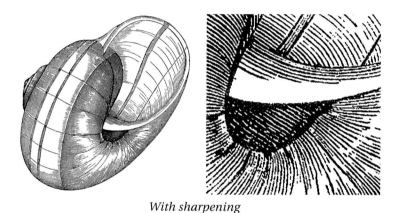

With sharpening

By adjusting the break point in the Threshold dialog box where pixels go to black or white, you can control the widths of lines in your scanned-as-grayscale line art image (see Figure 10-5).

For simple line art images that don't include very detailed and dense shadow areas, just set Threshold to 2 and press Return. With images that do include densely detailed shadows, try values up to about 55. As you move the slider to the left, you can see the fine lines start to break up. As you move right, the shadow areas start to clog. It's a lot like working the trade-off between shadow and highlight detail with the Levels dialog box on a grayscale image.

Unfortunately, no scanning software that we know of gives you control over thresholding for line art; if they did, you could do all this without even touching Photoshop.

Figure 10-4
Line art scanned
as grayscale

Scanned as line art   *400%*

Scanned as grayscale   *400%*

Scanned as grayscale with sharpening   *400%*
and thresholding applied

Scanning Prescreened Art

Rescreening—scanning images that have already been halftoned—is one of the toughest quandaries you'll encounter in Photoshop. We cover it in some detail in Chapter 14, *Essential Image Techniques*, but it's worth a note here, as well.

Figure 10-5
Threshold
settings for
line art

Threshold: 2

Threshold: 80

Threshold: 185

One way to avoid the screen conflicts (moiré patterns) that you can get by scanning black-and-white halftoned images is to use the line art techniques described in this chapter. In other words, don't try to make Photoshop convert the halftone spots into gray levels; just leave them as halftone spots. This works best with images screened at 85 lpi or less, because you can pick up the detail you need to hold the screen.

If you work for a newspaper and are forever getting veloxed camera-ready art, this may be the trick for you. However, if you scan a *lot* of previously halftoned images, you should definitely check out the ScanPrep Pro Plug-in from ImageXPress (see the *Resources* appendix). Its Copy Dot mode does a better job of scanning veloxes than anything we've seen.

Perfect Forms

There are few absolutes in the imaging business, and it's nice to find something that gets close. Get these line art techniques down pat (or better yet, teach them to an automation program like DayStar's PhotoMatic), and you can get great line art every time, without hardly trying.

Scanners

The Right Tool for the Right Job

The vast majority of images that end up in Photoshop come via some kind of scanner. But digital cameras and Kodak's Photo CD are becoming increasingly important as image sources. Photoshop doesn't care where your images come from, but you should.

All digital images share similarities, but the devices they come from are often radically different and impose their own idiosyncracies on the image. Knowing a little about the unique aspects of each kind of capture device is helpful, whether you're shopping for one, looking to have images digitized by a service provider, or simply having to work with the images in Photoshop.

In this chapter we take a look at three types of image capture devices—scanners, digital cameras, and Photo CD—along with their strengths, weaknesses, and quirks.

Scanners

Scanners come in all shapes, sizes, and prices, but they all do the same thing—they take an original print or transparency and convert it to pixels. Nonetheless, scanners differ considerably in resolution—the number of pixels they can "see" per inch—and in their ability to see into the shadow areas of an original. They also differ in the kinds of original they're best equipped to scan.

Many factors go into building a good scanner, and manufacturers' specifications often confuse more than they illuminate. It's impossible to judge a scanner by its specs—more often than not, the spec sheet is incomplete—but it's worth taking a quick look at the various specs anyway. There are several items that we always look for.

- ▶ CCD versus PMT

- ▶ Optical resolution versus interpolated resolution

- ▶ Bit depth

- ▶ Dynamic range and dMax

- ▶ One-pass versus three-pass

- ▶ Scanner type: flatbed, drum, or transparency

CCDs vs PMTs

One of the most important differences among scanners is whether they sense light with *CCDs* (charge-coupled devices) or *PMTs* (photomultiplier tubes). Almost every drum scanner on the market uses PMTs; they typically offer superior performance in reading shadow detail while minimizing noise. But they're expensive.

A drum scanner has three or four PMTs, and the entire image spins past them. Most other scanners use CCD arrays—rows of hundreds or thousands of tiny CCDs that capture many pixels of data simultaneously. CCDs are much less expensive than PMTs, but in most cases they aren't as sensitive to low levels of light.

Debate continues to rage over the relative merits of CCDs versus PMTs, but the gap in quality is narrowing dramatically (particularly with the introduction of high-end CCD scanners such as the Scitex SmartScanners). It's clear that PMTs have reached the end of their evolution—they're one of the very few instances of vacuum tube technology still in production—whereas CCDs are continuing to improve and evolve. If you're trying to decide whether to buy or use a PMT or a CCD scanner, we suggest you focus on all the other factors that apply instead.

Resolution

Scanner resolution is probably the most misunderstood of all scanner specifications, and the lion's share of the blame for this goes to flatbed scanner vendors. Drum scanner resolutions are usually stated in an unambiguous way—most are around 2,700 ppi (over res 100; see "Terms of Resolution" in Chapter 3, *Image Essentials*). The same holds true for transparency scanners, though the resolutions are often higher—the Leafscan 35 and 45 and the Nikon LS3510AF all boast resolutions over 5,000 ppi (res 200).

Flatbed resolution. Flatbed scanners are a different story. Two factors determine the *optical* resolution of a flatbed. The resolution *across* the bed is determined by the number of elements in the CCD array—typically 300, 400, or 600 per inch. The resolution *along* the bed is determined by the increments in which the stepper motor moves the scanning head.

Stepper motors are cheap and CCD arrays are relatively expensive, so it's easy to produce a scanner that steps in $\frac{1}{1,200}$-inch increments, but if the CCD array is only 400 ppi, it's really a 400-ppi scanner.

Interpolated resolution. Most flatbeds also offer *interpolated* resolution. Interpolated resolution is useful for smoothing curves in line art, but it's essentially useless for continuous-tone image scanning. If a flatbed scanner's specs mention more than one number for resolution, the real resolution is invariably the lowest one. Interpolation only adds data—not information. You could interpolate image resolution up to a million ppi (with your scanning software, with Photoshop, or whatever), and not improve image quality a whit.

Dual resolution. A few flatbed scanners, such as the PixelCraft 8000 and the Umax Gemini, use two sets of lenses to provide two different optical resolutions. The lower resolution covers the entire image area, but you can switch to a higher resolution at the cost of reducing the image area.

Bit Depth

One of the big advances in desktop scanners has been the emergence of scanners that capture more than eight bits of data ("high-bit" scanners)—often nine, 10, 12, or even 16 bits per color channel. While you still end up outputting eight bits per color, these scanners offer you a great deal of flexibility in choosing the right eight bits to output.

When you perform tonal correction on 8-bit data, you throw away information—you end up with substantially less than 256 shades of gray in each channel (see "Stretching and Squeezing the Bits" in Chapter 6, *Tonal Correction*). But when you make those same corrections on a high-bit scanner, they operate on all the bits the scanner can capture, before downsampling to eight bits. The result is that you get a full eight bits of output, using all 256 possible levels. We discuss this more fully in "Getting a Good Scan" in Chapter 12, *Capturing Images*.

Dynamic Range and dMax

A scanner's *dynamic range* is the range of densities it can see, and the maximum density—or *dMax*—is the deepest shadow into which it can see. For example, if a scanner has a dynamic range of 3.0 and a dMax of 3.2, then the deepest shadow it can see has an optical density (sometimes called *O.D.*) of 3.2. But if you set the black point to capture shadow detail going down to the dMax of 3.2, you'll blow out any highlights lighter than 0.2 to white, because the scanner's total density range is only 3.0.

If you're scanning transparencies, dynamic range is very important because of the large range of tones possible in transparencies. It's somewhat less important with reflective-art scanning (like on most flatbeds), but we still see plenty of scanners out there that can't handle even the limited dynamic range of a good print.

While dMax is important, the value printed in the manuals should be read with a grain of salt, at least with CCD scanners. Scanners work by shining a bright light on or through artwork, and reading how much light gets bounced back (for reflective art) or comes through the film (for transparencies). In the shadow areas, very little light does either, and the CCD has a difficult time seeing the differences between one very dark area and another. The dMax that vendors quote is typically the point at which the noise inherent in the CCD overwhelms the weak signal produced in the dark areas of the image. Usually you'll see significant amounts of noise in the shadows that are quite a bit lighter than the dMax.

Unfortunately, neither the dynamic range nor the dMax spec tells you anything at all about how finely the scanner can discriminate between the shades of gray that it *can* see. A spec that quotes only the dMax without stating the dynamic range is basically meaningless. One that states both dMax and dynamic range is slightly more useful—it will at least give you a ballpark idea of the kinds of original for which it's suitable.

Very high-contrast prints may have a dynamic range approaching 2.0, although 1.4–1.8 is more typical. Negative film generally has a dynamic range of 2.4 or so, while that of slide film may approach 3.4 or even 3.6. (Note that if film has a dynamic range of 3.6, it's implicit that the dMax is 3.6, too; *dMin*, on the other hand, is film plus fog.) But no one has yet developed a spec that measures how accurately a scanner records all the intermediate shades between black and white.

One-Pass versus Three-Pass

Some scanners capture RGB colors in one pass; others do it in three passes (one each for red, green, and blue). This is ultimately a non-issue. We've seen three-pass scanners that were faster and had better registration than some one-pass scanners. All that's important is that the design is well implemented.

Flatbed Scanners

Flatbed scanners are by far the most common type of scanner. They operate very much the same way photocopiers do—you place the artwork on the scan bed, where it's read by a moving CCD array which is stepped along the image by a stepper motor. Each movement of the scanning head produces one row of pixels. Flatbed scanners are very easy to use, particularly for scanning reflective artwork.

Some flatbeds offer transparency adapters, but the results from these are mixed. Mid-range ($3,000–$5,000) flatbeds can do a reasonable job on 4-by-5 or larger transparencies, but they generally have insufficient resolution to get much out of a 35 mm slide. Also, flatbeds tend to be optimized for the much narrower dynamic range of reflective artwork, so they produce a limited amount of shadow detail from transparencies.

Drum Scanners

Drum scanners are the workhorses of the prepress industry. The original artwork is attached to a transparent cylinder (the drum), which then spins rapidly and moves the image under the sensor. Drum scanner sensors are almost always photomultiplier tubes (PMTs).

High-end drum scanners have color computers that convert the RGB scans to CMYK on the fly, and perform unsharp masking as well (see

Chapter 8, *Sharpening*). High-end drum scanners excel at producing high volumes of tightly purposed CMYK scans, but they aren't well suited to producing RGB output for film recorders, and they're gross overkill for multimedia work.

It usually takes three people to keep a high-end drum scanner busy. One loads images on a drum, a fairly finicky process that involves using tape, oil, gel, or powder to attach the original to the drum. The second takes a drum loaded with images to an offline station where the scanning parameters are set for each image. The third runs the scanner itself, scanning the drum loaded by the second person, and returning the drum that's just been scanned to the first person.

Desktop or "baby" drum scanners are much less expensive than their full-size siblings, though they're still far from cheap ($20,000 and up). They usually leave RGB-to-CMYK conversion to the host computer, and most have fixed (rather than removable) drums, so they don't have the productivity advantage of the full-size models.

If you need absolutely noiseless shadows, and you're prepared for the general inconvenience of mounting images on the drum (plus slow scanning once the images are mounted), a baby drum might be worth your consideration.

Drum scanners are generally designed with transparencies in mind. It's possible to scan reflective art, but the results are frequently disappointing, and you can't scan books, paintings, or any other original that can't tolerate being wrapped around the drum.

Transparency Scanners

Transparency scanners are usually CCD-based scanners, but unlike flatbeds, they're optimized for scanning transparencies, both positive and negative. Cheaper transparency scanners are usually dedicated to 35mm format, while more expensive ones can usually handle 2¼-inch and 4-by-5-inch formats as well.

Good transparency scanners can provide results that approach or equal those of drum scanners, and they subject the originals to a good deal less wear and tear. If you work in 35 mm format, a relatively inexpensive slide scanner will give you much better results than you'll ever get from scanning prints, or from scanning the slides with a flatbed that has a transparency adapter.

Digital Cameras

Digital cameras, like scanners, come in all shapes and sizes. It's unlikely that digital cameras will replace film anytime soon, but in some niche markets they can offer compelling advantages—in some cases more than economic. Our friend Stephen Johnson has shown us comparisons of images from the Dicomed digital camera back (an image-capture device that attaches to the back of the camera) with 4-by-5 film that show the digital camera clearly outresolves the film in both spatial detail and dynamic range (but only at the cost of exposure times measured in minutes).

Digital cameras that offer film-like exposure times typically have a *much* lower resolution than film. High-volume catalog work and time-critical news photography are two major growth areas for the use of (different types) of digital cameras. In both cases, they're attractive because they eliminate the time and cost of film processing and scanning.

The term "digital camera" is really an umbrella that covers several approaches to capturing images. But they all share two common features: they use some kind of lens-and-shutter setup that's recognizable as a camera, and they replace the film plane with some kind of CCD array.

Area array cameras. Digital cameras that use an *area array* work more or less like conventional cameras—the image is captured all at once by a flat array that sits behind the lens where the film usually is. They can even use flash lighting. However, because high-resolution area arrays are very expensive, these cameras tend to have limited resolution. Area array cameras based on conventional film-camera bodies also have a couple of other interesting wrinkles.

The array usually takes up a far smaller area than film would, so the effective focal length of each lens is increased. A normal lens becomes a telephoto, and a wide-angle lens becomes a normal lens—the Kodak DCS 420, for example, ships with a 28 mm wide-angle, which gives approximately the same field of view as a 50 mm lens on a 35 mm camera. To get true wide-angle coverage, you'd need a lens in the 16 mm range—a very expensive lens indeed!

The smaller image area can also play havoc with the camera's built-in metering system, which is designed to deliver a good exposure on a full frame of film. The smaller area and the narrower dynamic range of the CCD behave very differently than film does.

When it comes to capturing color, area array cameras use one of two approaches: one-shot or three-shot. In the three-shot approach, you make three separate exposures through red, green, and blue filters. You get the full resolution of the CCD, but you're pretty much limited to static subjects. The one-shot approach might seem more tempting, but again it involves some significant compromises.

We call one-shot color cameras *decal* cameras, because the color filters are applied directly onto the CCD elements as decals, and each sensor element is dedicated to capturing a single color. Kodak's and Nikon's cameras use two green, one red, and one blue element to create each full-color image pixel (in varying arrangements), while Leaf has extended the filter set to include a fourth color.

One trade-off with either approach is that you need four sensors to make a single color pixel, so your final image has only one-quarter the resolution of the CCD itself. A second trade-off is that all the decal cameras we've seen are plagued by image artifacts (see Figure 8-9 in Chapter 8, *Sharpening*). Each vendor's offerings have their own signature artifacts, ranging from color fringing to aliasing to strange combinations of blurring and edge sharpening as the raw image is converted into RGB pixels.

These artifacts can be mitigated by postprocessing the image—Kodak uses a special Photoshop filter, and Leaf uses a stand-alone application—but they can't be eliminated completely. (See Figure 8-9 on page 253 for more information about dealing with artifacts.)

Linear Array Cameras. To avoid the problems inherent in decal cameras, higher-resolution digital cameras generally use *linear arrays* and a stepper motor that moves the array across the image area. These getups are often called *scanning backs* because they're just like flatbed scanners stuck on the back of a camera.

Scanning backs offer much higher resolutions than area array cameras, so you can produce much bigger images. They're also free of the artifacts that come with the decal approach. The disadvantage is that they require exposure times measured in minutes, which limits their use to static subjects, and prohibits the use of flash or strobe lighting.

Tip: Scaling Up from Digital Cameras. Any photographer knows all too well what happens when you enlarge an image too much: you see the grain of the film. One interesting property of digital camera images is that, because there's no film grain, you can upsample them without running into an unsightly conflict between film grain and the pixel grid. You do, however, have to keep a watchful eye out for lingering artifacts from decal color cameras.

Acquiring digital camera images. Note that almost everything we say in Chapter 6, *Tonal Correction*, about capturing images from scanners applies also to images from scanning back cameras. Most capture 12 bits internally, and provide the same kinds of tone- and color-correction features found in high-bit scanners. Use them.

None of the decal cameras as yet offers any real degree of control over the way images are acquired into Photoshop, but it's worth saving the raw files these cameras produce because the postprocessing software will undoubtedly improve in the future, and you may be able to tame artifacts that today appear almost impossible.

Photo CD

When Photo CD first appeared, it seemed like one of those occasional Kodak aberrations (like the disc camera)—we thought it very unlikely that people would want to view their family snapshots on TV. We were right about the consumer market's indifference to Photo CD, but we've come to recognize it as a simple and cost-effective method of both acquiring and archiving images. Nobody really knows how long Photo CDs will last, but Kodak's accelerated aging tests suggest they're good for at least 100 years.

If you have your images scanned to Photo CD when the film is being processed, the cost can be as low as 90 cents per image (at a "quickie" photo lab). But if you want mounted slides scanned, or you want to be sure your scans are free of dust and scratches, you should probably spring for a professional photo lab—even an expensive Photo CD scan is only three dollars or so (Pro Photo CD can run between 12 and 30 dollars).

Through an incredibly ingenious compression scheme, Photo CD manages to squeeze about 120 color images, each available at five different resolutions (see Table 11-1), onto a CD-ROM. The exact number of images depends on the content; some images compress more than others.

Table 11-1

Photo CD resolutions

Photo CD resolution	Size in pixels	Size at 225 ppi	File size
Base/16	192 × 128	.85″ × .57″	72 K
Base/4	384 × 256	1.7″ × 1.1″	288 K
Base	768 × 512	3.4″ × 2.3″	1.13 MB
4Base	1,536 × 1,024	6.8″ × 4.5″	4.5 MB
16Base	3,072 × 2,048	13.6″ × 9.1″	18 MB
64Base*	6,144 × 4,096	27.3″ × 18.2″	72 MB
*Pro Photo CD only			

Don't confuse a Photo CD scan made by a pro lab with Pro Photo CD. While Photo CD is limited to 35 mm format, Pro Photo CD can handle up to 4-by-5-inch transparencies. On the other hand, the addition of the 64Base resolution reduces the number of images that can fit on the CD (and increases the price per scan). You can put scans of reflective originals—created with any type of scanner—into Photo CD's "Image Pac" format using Kodak's Build-It software, but Kodak's Photo CD (or Pro Photo CD) Imaging Workstations (PIWs) can only scan transparencies.

Working with Photo CD isn't quite as simple as one might expect (see Chapter 12, *Capturing Images*), but the format offers reasonably high-quality scanning at a hitherto unheard-of price, and it comes with its own archival-quality storage medium.

From Photons to Pixels

As we said earlier, Photoshop doesn't care where your images come from, but it's often important that *you* know, so you can adjust your work accordingly. If you're doing the scanning yourself, you need to be aware of both the limitations of the scanner and the ways in which you can take advantage of the scanner's strengths. In the next chapter, we'll explore the scanning process, from preparing the original to controlling the scan with the scanner software.

12 Capturing Images

Good Data In, Good Data Out

Ansel Adams often said that the key to getting a great print was to start with a great negative. Of course, even with great negatives he still did massive amounts of manipulation in the darkroom. It's the same in Photoshop. You may do lots of postscan tweaking in Photoshop, but if you didn't start with a good image capture in the first place, you're unlikely to get great results from Photoshop.

When we say "capture an image," we almost always mean using a scanner; but with only a few minor exceptions, everything we say about scanning applies equally well to capturing images with digital cameras or video boards, rendering images in a 3D rendering application, or bringing in images from Photo CD (see Chapter 11, *Scanners*).

What Makes a Good Scan (and Why You Should Care)

If there's a single generalization we're comfortable making about working with Photoshop, it's the golden rule of computing: GIGO, or Garbage In, Garbage Out. Photoshop's tools may let you make all sorts of corrections to an image after you've opened it, and if push comes to shove, you can sometimes rescue a shot that would otherwise be unusable. But if you start with a good scan, you'll have less work to do (remember, be lazy), and your final results will be better than if you had to fight the image all the way.

The Original

At the risk of pointing out the obvious, the first thing that makes for a good scan is a good original. We've seen scanners blamed for introducing shadow noise when the problem was actually in the print.

Starting with a good original is particularly important when you're using a low-end scanner, because low-end scanners offer less flexibility in the corrections you can make during the capture process. Flawed originals can sometimes be saved— for instance, if the image has an obvious color cast or is plagued with dust marks and scratches—but only by dint of applying considerable skill and effort.

Tip: Dealing with Scratched Film. Each piece of film has two sides, with different characteristics. The emulsion side, which is usually the less shiny of the two, is delicate and should never be handled. The base side is more robust. If you have scratches on the emulsion side, about all you can do is to have the image oil-mounted and scanned on a drum scanner—the oil will help fill the scratches. Fingerprints on the emulsion are hopeless.

Scratches on the base side can be filled in using either a special compound available from any good photo store, or—a much cheaper alternative—a judicious application with a Q-Tip of some grease from the side of your nose! Fingerprints on the base side can be carefully removed using a Q-Tip and film cleaner. *Don't* use Windex, 409, or alcohol.

Shadow and highlight detail. Look closely at the dark areas: are they really black, or do they have random speckles of color? Are the highlights blown out? Are the shadows plugged up? None of these problems is easily correctable, and some aren't correctable at all. If you usually get your prints done by Joe's One-Hour Photo and Bait, and you find yourself fighting with the images in Photoshop, you may want to consider using a professional photo lab that monitors its chemistry more carefully.

Lower-contrast originals. In general, most steps in the printing process increase contrast, so it's better to start with an image that's slightly flat than one with too much contrast. You can boost the contrast of a flat image, but it's harder to decrease contrast without compromising quality.

Why Good Scans Are Important

If you're really good at Photoshop, you can make a bad scan look almost as good as a good scan—at least on easy images with a narrow tonal range and no heavily saturated colors. However, doing so involves a continuous battle to avoid posterization, artifacts, and unnatural color shifts. With difficult images that are heavily saturated and have a wide tonal range, a good scan is indispensable.

As we explain in Chapter 6, *Tonal Correction*, when you adjust the tone or color balance in Photoshop, you're throwing away image information. If you're scanning images for print or for screen display, the photographic original will contain far more image data than you can reproduce in your output, so information will be lost somewhere—either in your manipulations, in the separation process, or on press. The trick, of course, is to be selective in what you throw away, and to keep what you need to make the image look its best for your intended purpose.

The closer your original scan is to the desired result, the less manipulation you'll have to do in Photoshop, and the less of the image you'll have to chuck. If you need to make radical changes to the tone or the color balance in Photoshop, you run the risk of posterizing the image. If you make your tone and color balance moves at scan time, you'll have a much easier time than if you have to make huge moves in Photoshop. We'll discuss these issues more in the next section.

Getting a Good Scan

You have three primary concerns when you're scanning: tone, color balance, and resolution. A good scan captures detail (with little noise) in both the highlights and shadows, captures both pastels and saturated colors, and contains clean neutrals that are free of obvious color casts. It also contains the right number of pixels for reproduction at the desired size.

Without proper resolution, you either lose details in your image or slow down your workflow with files bloated with data you don't need. Bad contrast or color balance, however, can have even more dire consequences for your images.

Resolution

Whether you're using a digital camera, a drum scanner, or a flatbed scanner, you first need to make sure that you're capturing the right number of pixels. If you're unsure of what this is, see "How Much Is Enough?" in Chapter 3, *Image Essentials*. Note that even if you only need a 200- or 266-ppi image, you may want to scan higher than that. Then, later, you can downsample the image to the resolution you need using Photoshop's Image Size dialog box.

Scanning and downsampling. David always scans at the maximum optical resolution (*not* interpolated resolution!) of the scanner, then downsamples in Photoshop as necessary. Bruce believes that scanning at an integral multiple of the optical resolution is okay; in other words, on a 400-ppi scanner he'll scan at 100 or 200 ppi (because the optical resolution is divided by two or four), but not at 250. Then he downsamples as necessary, too.

We have to admit that there are elements of superstition and simplification in this two-step process. We haven't tested how every scanner on the market downsamples from its maximum resolution, but based on those we have tested, we tend to think that Photoshop does a better job than most of them. If you're in a real hurry, and you want to save yourself the extra step of downsampling in Photoshop, try scanning at the resolution you need.

We recommend you test this first, though. Compare the results you get by scanning the same image at full optical resolution, then downsampling in Photoshop, to those you get by scanning at a lower resolution to begin with. If you find that your scanner does as good a job of downsampling as Photoshop does, or if the difference is minor, by all means save yourself some time and use its capabilities.

Tip: Figuring Scaling and Resolution. The arithmetic of resolution and scaling is always hard to wrap your brain around. Here's a fast way to use Photoshop as a calculator to figure out the numbers, given that you know the final size of the image on the page. (You can get it from PageMaker's Control palette or XPress's Measurements palette: draw a box where the image goes, and read out the height and width numbers.)

1. Choose New from the File menu, and enter the dimensions and resolution of the image you want. If it's a grayscale or line art image, choose Grayscale from the Mode popup menu. Otherwise, choose RGB.

2. Note the file size, then cancel out of the dialog box.

3. Back in your scanning software, select the area you want to scan, then adjust the resolution setting until the resulting file size is close to the number you got in step two. When the file size matches, you know you've got the right scan size.

4. Scan the image, manipulate it as necessary in Photoshop, place it on the page, and scale it to fit.

Tip: Lose the Noise. You can often reduce the noise from a scanner by scanning at the scanner's maximum optical resolution, then downsampling to the resolution you need.

This works particularly well if you scan at 200 percent or more of the required resolution, because the noise tends to show up as single pixels. When you downsample, each pixel in the downsampled image is created from four pixels in the original scan, and those four pixels are averaged into one, so the noise is reduced significantly.

Tip: Don't Bother Upsampling. We never scan at a low resolution and sample up in Photoshop (except when creating line art; see "Tip: Doubling Your Scanner's Line Art Resolution" in Chapter 10, *Line Art*). Photoshop can interpolate pixels, but it can't add detail through interpolation that wasn't there before you resized it. The result? The resized image usually ends up looking soft or blurry.

Tone and Color—Defining Your Goals

In the process of reproducing an image, you need to make two sets of tonal and color corrections.

▶ **Tonal correction.** This fixes defects in the original and distortions in the image-capture process.

► **Targeting.** This compensates for the output process.

How and when you make these corrections depend on the capabilities of your image-capture hardware and software, and on your workflow. We discuss this distinction throughout Chapters 6 and 7, *Tonal Correction* and *Color Correction*.

With some capture devices, it's possible to correct and target the image at the same time—in fact, this is standard operating procedure in prepress houses that use drum scanners. The advantage is productivity: you need to do less to the image in Photoshop once it's been captured. The disadvantage is loss of flexibility: you end up with an image targeted for a particular set of output conditions—it contains only the image information needed for that output process.

Obviously, if you don't know what the output process will be when you're capturing the image, you can't target the image for it during the capture. If you do know the output process, you may be able to realize some significant productivity and quality gains by targeting at capture time, but desktop scanners generally don't let you do so very easily.

Targeting is almost invariably a matter of going from a wider range of tone and color to a narrower one. It's easy to do this in Photoshop without introducing posterization or color shifts (see Chapter 6, *Tonal Correction*). So as a rule, we recommend that you simply try to capture as much good image information as you can, and take care of targeting the image in Photoshop.

Correcting the image is another story: you can often get better images with less work if you handle some or all of the tonal correction as you scan.

Tonal and Color Correction

As we said earlier in this chapter, it's important to get a good tonal spectrum during the image-capture process, because each time you tweak the tone later in Photoshop, you lose a little more image information. The kinds of tonal manipulations you can perform at scan time depend mainly on how many bits of information the device is capturing, and secondarily on the tools the image-capture software provides.

Eight-bit capture devices. If you're working with an 8-bit capture device like an inexpensive flatbed scanner or digital camera, it's almost certain that the software controls—such as brightness, contrast, or gamma curves—are affecting the eight bits of data *after* the capture—exactly what Photoshop does when you correct an 8-bit image. Since the controls are likely to be less flexible versions of Photoshop's own features, there's little point in using them—you can achieve the same or better results more easily using the tools and techniques described in Chapter 6, *Tonal Correction*. In this case, your concern is simply to make sure that you're capturing all the data the device can grab, without damaging it on the way.

To do so, you need to find the "sweet spot" in the controls, where the data is simply being passed on unfiltered. Sometimes, this is just a matter of leaving the software at its default settings, but often it's not. The only way to be sure is through trial and error. With scanners, you can simply tweak the controls. If you're working with an 8-bit digital camera, you also have lighting to take into consideration, but the same principles apply.

1. Try capturing a range of representative images that have real blacks, real whites, and a good range of tones in between. (If you have access to a gray-step wedge, or to a color target such as the IT8 or Kodak's Q60, use it instead.)

2. Start with the scanner's defaults, and look at the histogram of the resulting scan. Check to see if the scanner is clipping the highlights or shadows (see Figure 12-2 on page 316). If it's doing one or the other, reduce or increase the brightness and try again. If it's clipping both, try reducing the contrast.

3. If the image has real blacks and whites, but the scan isn't covering the full tonal range, you might try increasing the contrast. Once you've found settings that work, save them, and use them for all your scans.

Note that these settings may not produce very good-looking images. That doesn't matter—you're just trying to get as much good image information as possible to tweak in Photoshop.

Although you want to capture the entire tonal range of the image without clipping the shadows or blowing out the highlights, sometimes you may find that your scanner can't do this. In that case, you'll have to decide whether you want to sacrifice highlight detail or shadow detail. The image content is the final arbiter, but when in doubt, remember that blown-out highlights are usually uglier than plugged-up shadows.

The analog advantage. A very few 8-bit scanners let you adjust the tone and color balance by operating directly on the analog signals from the detectors before they're encoded into bits (the only ones we're sure of are Nikon's Coolscan and the 8-bit version of Nikon's LS-3510AF). If you have one of these scanners, ignore this "sweet spot" talk; everything we say below about exploiting the capabilities of high-bit scanners applies to these, too.

The high-bit advantage. If your scanner captures more than eight bits per color internally, you can and should do a good deal more during the scan to get the image as close as possible to its desired state. If you don't, you're just wasting those extra bits for which you almost certainly paid a premium (see Figure 12-1).

Figure 12-1
Using the extra bits

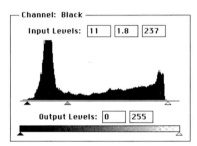

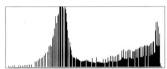

If you apply this kind of big tonal move to an 8-bit scan, you lose a lot of data, resulting in this depopulated histogram below, and an image that's harder to work with.

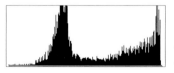

With tonal correction of a high-bit image, you can make big moves and still end up with a full 256 gray levels in the 8-bit file—making further corrections much easier.

A 12-bit scanner, for instance, uses 4,096 levels internally for each color. When you use the scanner's controls, you're performing tonal correction on this high-bit data. Rather than stretching and squeezing eight bits of data, you're choosing which 256 out of the possible 4,096 gray levels will appear in the final output. You can set the tone of the image the way you want it and still have a full 256 gray levels. If you make those same adjustments after scanning instead, operating with eight bits of data, you lose tonal information and end up with substantially fewer than 256 shades of gray.

The advantage is that you'll have less work to do in Photoshop because the image is closer to the way you want it, and you'll lose fewer gray levels when you do make adjustments in Photoshop. Of course, you can only exploit the high-bit capabilities of your capture device if the software has the necessary features. See "Software Tools," later in this chapter.

Targeting

If you're working with a typical desktop scanning setup, which delivers RGB or grayscale scans to Photoshop, your options for targeting the image to a particular output process during the scan are pretty limited.

Grayscale. When capturing grayscale images with some scanners, you can set the highlight and shadow limits to values you know your output process can handle. This is reasonable *if* your scanner also lets you set the tone the way you want it. While this can work well for images that don't have specular highlights or solid blacks, with most images you're better off just using Photoshop's tools for targeting the image, as described in Chapter 6, *Tonal Correction*.

Color. With color, your options are even more limited. Unless your output is destined for an RGB output process such as the computer screen or a continuous-tone film recorder, you need to convert the RGB scan to a targeted set of CMYK values.

Most desktop scanner/software combinations can't deliver CMYK scans. They rely on the host computer and software like Photoshop to convert RGB into CMYK, so you should simply concern yourself with getting a good RGB capture that represents the whole tonal range of the image. If you've got a high-bit scanner, you can also try to get good color balance with clean neutrals. Then you can use Photoshop to target the image after the capture (see "Image Correction and Targeting" in Chapter 7, *Color Correction*).

The only practical way we've found to get targeted CMYK scans from a desktop scanner is by implementing a color management system such as Agfa's FotoTune, Kodak's KCMS, or Apple's ColorSync 2.0. These systems are of particular benefit with low-end scanners if you want fast automatic scanning that reproduces your originals very closely. If you need to correct the image in Photoshop, though, a color management system won't help much in the scanning process—though it may be useful as a first step in preparing images for different output processes. We talk about this in Chapter 16, *Color Management Systems*.

Correcting and targeting at once. High-end scanners let you do both sets of corrections—adjusting for scanned imperfections and targeting for the output process—at once. In fact, the biggest difference between a $2,000 scanner and a $200,000 scanner isn't quality—it's productivity. The $200,000 scanner lets you create targeted CMYK scans, ready for printing, where the tone and color are tightly matched to a particular set of output conditions—paper, ink, and press. This offers a huge productivity advantage over desktop scanners.

If your scanning software has all the tools you need to target your scans—tonal and color correction, color separation, and sharpening—then you can pick up some real workflow advantages by using those capabilities. Scans can land on disk ready for print, and you need never go near Photoshop. This is a book on Photoshop, however, so we'll limit our discussion to targeting images after they've arrived in Photoshop.

For now, here's how to get good scans into Photoshop, so you can work your will on them with its tools.

Software Tools

We can't hope to cover every piece of image-acquisition software on the market, but fortunately most of them offer features very similar to Photoshop's tone- and color-correction tools. We recommend you look at the discussion of those tools in Chapters 6 and 7, *Tonal Correction* and *Color Correction*; the techniques discussed there also apply when scanning.

Whatever image-capture method you use, there's a definite order for making adjustments. First, determine the cropping and resolution; then set the tonal range; and finally, fix any problems with the color balance. If you have to do major surgery to fix the color balance, you may have to go back and adjust the overall tone again. For example, a strong magenta cast can be neutralized by adding a lot more green, but doing so will brighten the image, because you're adding light.

Five key tools help you get the tonal range and color balance right when you capture images.

▶ Histograms

▶ On-screen densitometers

- ▶ Black/white-point settings

- ▶ Gamma settings

- ▶ Curve controls

The first two help you evaluate the image, the last three help you fix it. If you're lucky, your image-acquisition software will offer all five, but it's more typical to get two or three out of the five in any given scanning software package.

Tip: Make Sure Your Scanner Controls Really Work. It's important to determine that the scanner's gamma and/or curves controls are really affecting the high-bit or analog data that the scanner produces, rather than just being applied to 8-bit data as a postscan filter. If they're being applied post-scan, you're better off making the same adjustments in Photoshop after the scan. (If the tools are acceptable, however, use them! There's a real workflow advantage to correcting at scan time.)

How can you tell if your scanner is working on high-bit data? One easy way is to apply a fairly extreme curve or gamma adjustment to a scan—say, a gamma of 2.2 or thereabouts. First, pull an uncorrected scan into Photoshop and make the move using Photoshop's Levels command, then go back and rescan the image applying the same gamma tweak in the scanner software. Compare the histograms of the two images. If the one with the gamma tweak applied during the scan isn't substantially cleaner, with fewer spikes and missing levels, the scanner software is almost certainly applying the tweak as a filter on the 8-bit data. In that case, simply treat the scanner as an 8-bit capture device. (Console yourself with the fact that it's probably at least capturing eight good bits of data, unlike many 8-bit-only scanners.)

Experimenting in Photoshop is an excellent way to get a feel for how these controls operate. Work in Photoshop with an image scanned using the scanner's default settings. When you've figured out exactly what needs to be done to the scan in Photoshop, try going back to the scanner software and rescanning the image using settings that duplicate your Photoshop tweaks as closely as possible. After a while, you'll find that your initial scans are getting much closer to the desired results as you exploit the power of the scanner's controls. But you'll be retaining much more image detail than you would if you did the same tonal moves on the 8-bit data in Photoshop.

Image-Evaluation Tools

Almost all scanners and most digital cameras let you do a quick prescan, a low-resolution capture that you can use to set the cropping rectangle. You can also use it as a basis for tone- and color-balance adjustments. But even with a perfectly-calibrated monitor, there's only so much you can tell from looking at the typical postage-stamp-sized prescan.

Instead, you can use two other tools (when available) to evaluate your image before your final scan: the histogram and the densitometer.

Histogram. The histogram is simply a bar chart that shows the number of pixels in the image at each gray level from 0 to 255 (see Figure 12-2). This gives you a quick look at how the information is distributed in the scan. Good scanning software lets you see the histogram before and after correction. Photoshop displays a histogram in the Levels dialog box, or when you choose Histogram from the Image menu. In most scanning software, the histogram is simply a static display, though with a few scanning packages, you can make adjustments using something like Photoshop's Levels dialog box.

Figure 12-2 Evaluating scans with the histogram

Note that these images have not been through final correction. They represent what comes in from the scanner.

An overly dark scan   *A too-light scan*   *A well-exposed scan*

The histogram is a key tool for evaluating tonal range; it can tell you a lot about your scan at a single glance. A histogram that ends in a "cliff" at the left (shadow) end of the scale indicates a scan where shadow detail is lost. If it ends in a cliff at the right (highlight) end of the scale, you've blown out the highlight detail. A correctly exposed scan produces a histogram with a slope (rather than a cliff) at each end, indicating relatively few pixels at either the darkest value (0) or the lightest value (255).

All this assumes a "normal" image—if you have a picture of a black cat in a coal cellar, or a polar bear in the snow, your histogram will look different; but in each case, you want to try to hold as much detail in shadows and highlights as possible.

Densitometer. An on-screen densitometer lets you read the value of the pixel under the cursor. Like Photoshop's Info palette, this lets you get a little deeper into analyzing the image, particularly if the tool offers before-and-after readouts. Some scanner software use a palette for the densitometer information, while others put it in the prescan window itself.

Tip: Use the Densitometer to Find Detail. You can use the densitometer to check for detail in the highlight and shadow regions, which can be hard to see on your monitor. Pass the cursor over very bright or very dark areas in the image. If the pixel values *change* as you move around, there's detail in there, even if you can't see it. As you make gamma moves to brighten the midtones, you emphasize detail in the shadows and suppress it in the highlights. By evaluating the detail with the densitometer, you can play the trade-off between the two.

Image-Adjustment Tools

To capture the tonal range of an image correctly, you have to set the black point and white point properly to avoid plugging up the shadows or blowing out the highlights, and you have to set the gamma to distribute the midtones properly. For a detailed discussion of tonal correction, see Chapter 6, *Tonal Correction.*

Scanning software that comes with 8-bit scanners often limits your adjustments to changing brightness or contrast. But using brightness or contrast is like bungee jumping without a cord—you may live through it, but you'll probably lose something in the process (see the sidebar "The Non-Linear Advantage" in Chapter 6, *Tonal Correction*).

Unfortunately, a few high-bit scanners (such as the Kodak RFS 2035 Plus) also limit the controls to brightness and contrast. They're better than nothing, but keep an eye on the histograms for shadow or highlight clipping. Most high-bit scanners offer more sophisticated methods for adjusting the tone and color: black- and white-point settings, gamma settings, and arbitrary curves.

Setting black and white points. Most high-bit image-capture software offer one or more of the following methods of setting the black point and white point.

▶ **Autoexposure.** Though they can be a little brain-dead, these features are often a good place to start. They look for the darkest and lightest pixels in the image to set the white and black points.

One problem with these features, particularly with film scanners, is that they're easily fooled by dust or scratches. If the software allows you to designate an area of the image to consider when determining the endpoints, you can simply change the area under consideration to avoid the offending spot. If not, you'll have to try one of the manual methods.

▶ **Black and white input levels.** These work identically to, and usually resemble, the black and white input sliders in Photoshop's Levels dialog box. They're almost invariably accompanied by a histogram that lets you see the amount of shadow or highlight clipping taking place.

▶ **Black and white eyedroppers.** Eyedropper tools let you set the black and white points by clicking on specific areas in the image preview. These tools work roughly the same way as the eyedroppers in Photoshop's Levels and Curves dialog boxes, but they don't always let you choose a target color—they simply set the area you clicked to black or white.

In some cases, if you click a non-neutral pixel in a color image, they'll maintain the color of the pixel while setting its brightness to the maximum or minimum value possible. In other cases, they'll also eliminate the color cast. To use these features effectively, you need an on-screen densitometer. This will also let you determine exactly what the eyedropper is doing.

Tip: Determining Black and White Points. To determine the white point and black point for an image, follow these steps.

1. Scan the image with your "optimum" gamma (see "Tip: Determining Optimum Gamma," below), and white and black point set to 0 and 255.

2. Bring the image into Photoshop, choose the Levels command, then Option-drag the black-point and white-point triangles to display where the shadow and highlight detail lie (see "Black-point/white-point clipping display" in Chapter 6, *Tonal Correction*). Use this clipping display to determine appropriate white- and black-point settings.

3. Use those settings in the scanning software, perhaps allowing yourself two or three extra levels to make sure that you really aren't clipping any detail.

Gamma controls. Unlike Brightness and Contrast controls, gamma adjustment lets you make large changes to the midtones with (usually) only minimal effects on the shadows and highlights. In Photoshop, you make gamma adjustments using the Levels command (Command-L). The middle (gray) slider in the top bar changes the gamma as you drag it, or you can type a number into the middle field. Many scanner drivers only offer numeric control over gamma—you just type in the gamma value you want. For a full discussion of gamma adjustments and how to use them, see Chapter 6, *Tonal Correction.*

Almost all scans need a gamma adjustment. Typically, scans come in looking dark. Most scanners have a native gamma of 1.0—the output values are exactly the same as the input values. But neither our eyes nor our monitors have a linear response to changes in brightness. Usually you'll need to scan with a gamma setting somewhere between 1.4 and 2.2. In theory, if you want your on-screen image to match the original, your scanner gamma setting should match that of your monitor. But as the EPA says, your mileage may vary. If you're scanning for print, a gamma setting of around 1.8 is a good starting point.

Also note that changing the gamma setting for many high-bit scanners tends to change the appropriate white- and black-point settings. This shouldn't happen, but it does, so adjusting these three settings can be an iterative process—at least until you get to know the settings.

Tip: Determining Optimum Gamma. To figure out what gamma setting on your high-bit scanner will provide an accurate midtone reading, scan a gray target with a known gray value, such as the ubiquitous Kodak 18-percent gray card, which reflects 18 percent of the light striking it. Scan at a variety of gamma settings, and use the one that renders the gray card somewhere around level 185 to 190. If your densitometer reads percentages from 0 to 100 rather than levels, you're looking for a reading in the 25 to 28 percent range.

Curves. Curves are by far the most flexible way of controlling both the overall tonal characteristics of the scan and the color balance of the individual channels. Curves appear in various places within scanning software, and often have the same appearance and functionality as the Curves dialog box in Photoshop.

We believe that all high-bit scanners should offer some kind of curves controls. They are essential for correcting color balance while tapping the full capabilities of these scanners. Fortunately, most vendors seem to be coming around to that view. For a full discussion of curve-based adjustments, see Chapters 6 and 7, *Tonal Correction* and *Color Correction*.

Sharpening

Note that even though some scanners allow you to sharpen images on the fly, we almost never do, for two reasons.

▶ Photoshop's Unsharp Mask filter offers far more control than the sharpening in most scanner software.

▶ It's always best to do sharpening after you've made all your tone and color adjustments. This is because sharpening relies on minute adjustments in the contrast of neighboring pixels. If you make tonal adjustments after sharpening, you can wipe out the effect of sharpening, or possibly even worse, exaggerate it.

Unless you have a great deal of faith in your scanner's sharpening algorithms and don't plan on doing anything more with the image in Photoshop, we recommend that you simply leave sharpening to Photoshop.

Using High-Bit Data in Photoshop

Some high-bit scanners allow you to acquire all the data they can capture into Photoshop. This isn't particularly elegant—your file automatically becomes a 16-bit-per-color file, even if your scanner only captures nine or ten bits, so it takes up double the RAM and double the disk space of an 8-bit-per-color file. Moreover, you can *only* use the Levels and Curves commands in Photoshop—nothing else. You can't even make a selection.

Nonetheless, we find this feature useful in two situations. The first is when we encounter a high-bit scanner that captures good data but has useless software controls. The second is when we have an extremely difficult image that requires complex adjustments with arbitrary curves, and we need to obtain the best quality possible.

Once you've made your tonal adjustments using Curves or Levels in Photoshop, you downsample the file to eight bits per color using the popout menu that appears beside the RGB or Grayscale command under the Mode menu.

This isn't something we do every day, or even every week, but for those nightmare images—a black cat in a coal cellar with a bell on its collar creating one specular highlight, or a perfectly illuminated photograph of white lace over black silk, that sort of thing—it can be a lifesaver.

Photo CD Revisited

Photo CD got off to a rocky start. Most pros found the early results from Photo CD pretty disappointing, because there were two things that Kodak failed to make clear in Photo CD's early days. (Of course, back then they still thought people would look at their pictures on TV.) To get good results from Photo CD, you have to know two things: what to ask for when you have scans made, and how to bring the scans into Photoshop.

Unfortunately, this makes it necessary to learn some Photo CD jargon.

Photo CD Lingo

Photo CD was originally conceived as a mass-market consumer product. So, Kodak put a great deal of effort into building a scanning software and hardware system that would reproduce the color of the *original scene*, not the color on the film. They thought Photo CD users would be the kind of people who had their film developed by the corner drugstore—they'd want happy Kodak color rather than what was actually on the film.

To do this, Kodak developed film-specific lookup tables—called *film terms*—that would neutralize each film stock's particular biases, and an autoexposure feature called the Scene Balancing Algorithm (SBA) that would bring underexposed or overexposed images back into a normal tonal range.

These features have caused professional photographers no end of grief, for two reasons. First, professionals choose specific film stocks precisely because they want to exploit the films' unique biases. Second, they want the tonal range they put on the film rendered faithfully, not normalized to lowest-common-denominator average-one-hour-print values.

Knowing What to Ask For

Fortunately, Photo CD is capable of reproducing quite faithfully what's on the film. The key is in knowing what to ask for when you buy the scans. You need to treat reversal (slide) film and negative film differently.

Slide film. To get faithful Photo CD scans of slides, you must ask the Photo CD lab to do three things.

▶ Use Universal Film Terms (Universal Kodachrome for Kodachrome, Universal E-6 for everything else).

▶ Use Locked Beam Scanning (which means the operator makes no corrections to the image).

▶ Turn the Scene Balancing Algorithm off.

This should give you scans that faithfully capture the contents of the slide—with one limitation. The dynamic range of the PIW scanner is only about 2.8, so you won't get great shadow detail on very contrasty slides.

Negative film. The smaller density range of negative film has a much better fit to the dynamic range of the Photo CD scanner, but it also presents a problem. You don't want what's literally on the film, because the film is a negative—it's inverted and has an orange mask. Instead, you want a positive image—a scan that's as close as possible to the tone and color you'd get from a good print. This takes human intervention.

If possible, you should have negatives scanned using the film term for that film stock. If the negatives are perfectly exposed and processed, you can ask the lab to create a custom film term for your negatives. This is worthwhile if you're doing measured photography under controlled studio lighting, but it's unlikely to work in most real-world situations where people shoot negs.

Most negs aren't perfectly exposed—a big reason people use negative film is precisely because it allows more latitude in the exposure. For negatives shot under available light, or under a variety of different lighting conditions, you'll get better results if you ask the scanner operator to intervene, and to apply the Scene Balancing Algorithm where necessary. You won't get this kind of service at the 69¢-a-scan Photo CD labs, but many professional labs that charge two or three dollars per scan will do this for you, and the results are usually worth the extra cost.

Bringing Photo CD Images into Photoshop

Getting the scans done right is half the battle when you use Photo CD. The other half is bringing them into Photoshop correctly. You can't simply open Photo CD images in Photoshop. There's always a conversion process involved.

Photo CD images are stored in a proprietary color space, called Photo YCC, developed by Kodak. This color space contains only 24 bits of data per pixel, but the data is in a highly compressed form—Kodak claims to encode 12 bits of luminance data plus two 8-bit color channels into the YCC format. To work with Photo CD images in Photoshop, you have to convert them into one of the color spaces that Photoshop can use—RGB, CMYK, or Lab—so the way you acquire Photo CD images makes a big difference to the final result.

In previous versions of Photoshop, opening Photo CDs was a guessing game, and a small cottage industry grew up supplying different Photo CD acquire modules that allowed you to tweak the tone and color of the image during the conversion from YCC to the destination color space.

Photoshop 3 has made working with Photo CD much simpler. It includes Kodak's Color Management System (KCMS) and a limited set of device profiles. When you open a Photo CD image in Photoshop 3, you're given the opportunity to select a resolution, a source profile, and a target profile (see Figure 12-3). The source and destination profiles included with Photoshop do a great job of acquiring Photo CD images into Lab color, and almost as good a job acquiring them into RGB.

Figure 12-3 Opening a Photo CD image

If you plan to use Photo CD extensively, though, it's worth buying into

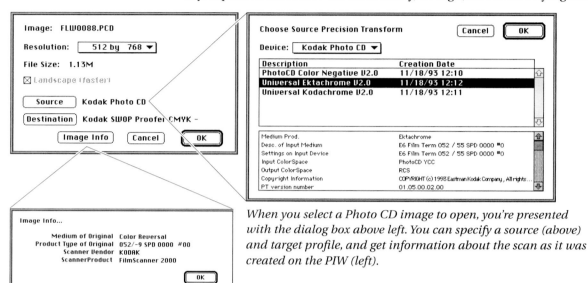

When you select a Photo CD image to open, you're presented with the dialog box above left. You can specify a source (above) and target profile, and get information about the scan as it was created on the PIW (left).

KCMS in a bigger way. With the right add-ins, you can acquire Photo CD images into an RGB space calibrated to your monitor, or to a targeted CMYK color space, ready for press. For more details on KCMS, see Chapter 16, *Color Management Systems*.

For heavy-duty production systems based on Photo CD, two products deserve honorable mention: PhotoImpress from Purup, and Color-Q from Human Software. Both let you adjust the tone and color, bring Photo CD images directly into targeted CMYK color spaces, and run the conversion as a batch process.

Is That All There Is?

No matter how good a job you do of capturing the image, you'll almost certainly need to massage it some more using Photoshop's own tools. But if you've captured the image to be as close as possible to the way you want it, the tweaks you make in Photoshop will be small and subtle, so you'll run far less risk of losing valuable image data, and introducing posterization and artifacts. Plus, you'll preserve the shadow and highlight detail that make the difference between a so-so image and one that leaps off the page and grabs you.

Go back and revisit Chapter 6, *Tonal Correction,* and Chapter 7, *Color Correction.* Given a little ingenuity, almost all the techniques we discuss in those chapters can be applied during the scan itself. You'll get better results, and you'll have less work to do in Photoshop after the scan.

13

Selections

Paths, Masks, and Channels

You love the painting and retouching tools that Photoshop offers; you love layers; you even love all the options it gives you for saving files. But as soon as someone says "alpha channel" or "mask," your eyes glaze over. And when someone strings together a sentence like, "Edit your selection in Quick Mask mode and then intersect it with the eighth alpha channel," you drop your mouse and head for the door.

It doesn't have to be this way. Masks, channels, and selections are actually really easy (if you get past their bad reputation). And they are the essential tools for silhouetting and compositing images—two of the most common production tasks.

The first part of this chapter covers all the tools in Photoshop for working with selections, channels, and masks, along with a lot of tips for using the tools the smart way. At the end of the chapter, we run through some step-by-step selection techniques to show how you can use all these tools together to handle both simple and complex situations.

Masking-Tape Selections

The key to understanding selections, masks, and channels is to realize that they're all basically the same thing down deep. No matter what kind of selection you make—whether you draw out a rectangular marquee, or draw a path with the Lasso, or use the Magic Wand to select a colored area—Photoshop internally sees the selection as a black-and-white channel (see Figure 13-1).

Figure 13-1
Selections are channels, too

 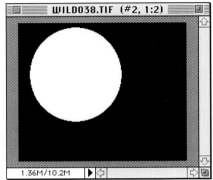

This selection is the same . . .   *. . . as this mask/channel.*

If you've ever carefully painted around a window (the kind in the wall of your house), you've probably used masking tape to mask out the areas you didn't want to paint. If you apply the masking tape to the window, you can paint right over it, knowing that the window remains untouched. Selections, masks, and channels are electronic forms of masking tape.

In Photoshop, the masking tape is typically colored black. Let's say you use the elliptical marquee to select a circle. Behind the scenes, Photoshop sees this circle as a black-and-white channel. In this selection channel, the areas that you selected (the parts with no masking tape over them) are white, and the unselected areas (the parts with masking tape over them) are black.

Why Digital Tape Is Better

However, like everything else in life, there's also a spectrum of gray area between the two extremes. In real life, you can't have partially opaque masking tape. The wood or window or whatever is either covered and no paint touches it, or it's not (all the paint touches it). Fortunately, we're not dealing with real life; we're dealing with computers, and they're much more flexible than normal ol' tape.

If you look carefully around the edges of that circle we selected, you'll notice that there are gray areas between the black and the white.

The gray parts of a selection channel are areas that are *partially* selected. If an area in a selection channel is 25-percent gray, then that area is 75-percent selected. Remember, the lighter the gray, the more selected the area is.

Benefits of Partial Selection

There were gray areas in that circle we selected because the elliptical marquee was anti-aliased (see Figure 13-2). If you turn the Anti-aliased checkbox off in the Marquee Options palette, the selection you'd get would have no gray, partially selected pixels.

Figure 13-2
Anti-aliased
edges

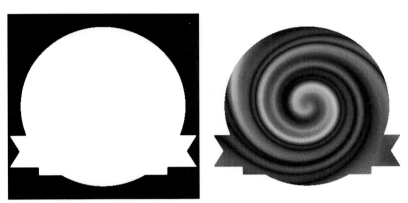

Aliased edges make for poor masks because they're too jaggy.

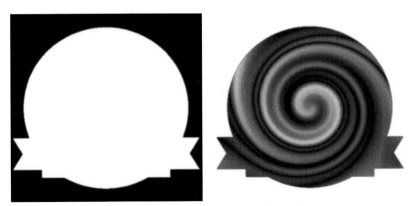

Smooth, anti-aliased masks create nicer, smoother edges.

Smooth transitions between selected (white) and unselected (black) areas are incredibly important for compositing images, painting, correcting areas within an image—in fact, just about everything you'd want to do in Photoshop.

When you paint over an area that is fully selected (no black masking tape), 100 percent of the paint is applied to each pixel. When you paint over an area that isn't selected (fully covered with black masking tape), no paint is applied. And when you paint over an area that is partially selected, only a percentage of the paint is applied to the underlying image.

The same thing goes for deleting, smudging, applying a filter, or any other action you can take on a pixel in Photoshop. The more selected the pixel is, the more the effect is applied (see Figure 13-3).

Figure 13-3
Partially selected pixels

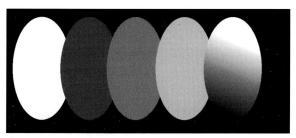

This is the selection mask; each oval is selected a different amount (the oval on the left is fully selected; the oval on the right has a gradient selection).

Painting with a paintbrush

Add Noise filter applied

Delete key pressed

Various effects applied to the fish background while the above selection is active

Tip: You Can Always Move Your Selection. One of the most frequent changes you'll make to a selection (which is why this tip is way up here at the beginning of the chapter) is moving it. For instance, you might make a rectangular selection, then realize it's not positioned correctly. Don't redraw it! Instead, hold down the Command and Option keys and drag the selection. The selection moves, but not the pixels underneath it.

Or, hold down the Command and Option keys and press the arrow keys to move the selection by one pixel. Add the Shift key, and the selection moves ten pixels for each press of an arrow key.

Selection Tools

Although there are a mess o' ways to make a selection in Photoshop (we'll look at them all in this chapter), there are three basic selection tools in the Tool palette: the Marquee tool, the Lasso tool, and the Magic Wand (see Figure 13-4). While some people eschew these tools for the more high-falutin' selection techniques, we find them invaluable for much of our day-to-day work.

Figure 13-4
Selection
tools

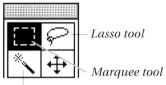

Lasso tool

Marquee tool

Magic Wand tool

The important thing to remember about these selection tools (and, in fact, every selection technique in Photoshop) is that they can all work in tandem. Don't get too hung up on getting one tool to work just the way you want it to; you can always modify the selection using a different technique (this idea of modifying selections is very important, and we'll touch on it throughout the chapter).

Tip: Adding to and Subtracting from Selections. No matter which selection tool you're using, you can always add to the current selection by holding down the Shift key while selecting. Conversely, you can subtract from the current selection by holding down the Command key. Or, if you want the intersection of two selections, hold down the Command and the Shift keys while selecting (see Figure 13-5).

Marquee

The Marquee tool is the most basic of all the selection tools. It lets you draw a rectangle or oval selection by clicking and dragging. If you hold down the Shift key, the marquee is constrained to a square or a circle, depending on whether you have chosen Rectangle or Ellipse in the Marquee Options palette. (Note that if you've already made a selection, the Shift key adds to the selection instead.) If you hold down the Option key, the selection is centered on where you clicked.

Figure 13-5

Adding, subtracting, and intersecting selections

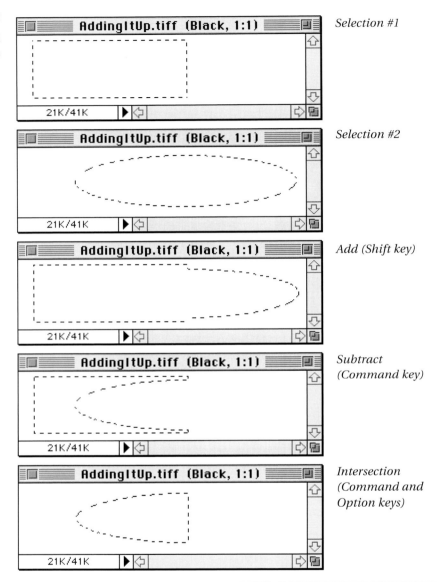

Selection #1

Selection #2

Add (Shift key)

Subtract
(Command key)

Intersection
(Command and
Option keys)

Tip: Toggle Between Tools. You can switch between the rectangular and elliptical selection tools on the Shape popup menu in the Marquee Options palette, but it's faster to press M. If you press it once, you choose the tool; if you press it again, it toggles between the tools (Option-clicking on the Marquee tool in the Tool palette also toggles between them).

Tip: Pull Out a Single Line. If you've ever tried to select a single row of pixels in an image by dragging the marquee, you know that it can drive you batty faster than Mrs. Gulch's chalk scraping. The Single Row and Single Column options on the Shape popup menu are designed for just this purpose. These are godsends when a low-end scanner glitches and slightly (or severely) throws off a row or column of pixels. We often use them to clean up screen captures, or to delete thin borders around an image. They're also useful with video captures, because each pixel row often equals a video scan line.

Tip: Selecting Thicker Columns and Rows. If you want a column or row that's more than one pixel wide/tall, you need to use a different method. Set the selection style to Fixed Size, and type the thickness of the selection into the Height or Width field. In the other field, type some number that's obviously larger than the image, like 10,000. When you click on the image, the row or column is selected at the thickness you want.

Tip: Selecting that Two-by-Three. You've laid out a page with a hole for a photo that's 2 by 3 inches. Now you want to make a 2-by-3 selection in Photoshop. Ordinarily, trying to select that with the Marquee tool would be nigh-on impossible without patience and a scratch pad full of math. However, when you choose Constrained Aspect Ratio from the Style pop-up menu, Photoshop lets you type in that 2-by-3 ratio in the Marquee Options palette (see Figure 13-6).

Figure 13-6
Constrained
Aspect Ratio

If you're looking to select a particular-sized area, you can select Fixed Size from the Style popup menu. The problem is that you have to type the measurement in pixels. If you don't usually think in pixels, try this.

1. Option-click on the document size area in the lower-left corner of the document window to find the resolution of the image.

2. Multiply the resolution by the number of inches you want the selection to be, horizontally and vertically.

3. Type these numbers into the horizontal and vertical fields of the Marquee Options palette.

4. Click where you want to specify the upper-left corner of the selection (or Option-click to specify the center of the selection).

For instance, let's say your image is at 300 ppi and you want a 2-by-3 selection. When you multiply the resolution by the dimensions, you know to type 600 and 900 into the Options palette fields.

Lasso

The Lasso tool lets you create a freeform outline of a selection. Wherever you drag the mouse, the selection follows until you finally let go of the mouse button and the selection is automatically closed for you (there's no such thing as an open-ended selection in Photoshop; see Figure 13-7).

Figure 13-7 Lasso selections

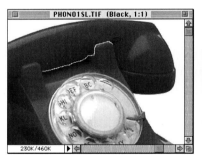
Beginning the selection

End of selection

Closed on mouse release

Tip: Let Go of the Lasso. Two of the most annoying attributes of selecting with the Lasso are that you can't lift the mouse button while drawing, and you can't draw straight lines easily (unless you've got hands as steady as a brain surgeon's). The Option key overcomes both these problems.

When you hold down the Option key, you can release the mouse button and the Lasso tool won't automatically close the selection. Instead, as long as the Option key is held down, Photoshop lets you draw a straight line to wherever you want to go. This solves both problems in a single stroke (as it were).

In fact, whenever we use the Lasso tool for anything even remotely complex, we hold down the Option key the entire time. When you're tired and want to release the mouse button or pen (we mostly use Wacom tablets), you can. Then, still holding the Option key, you can start drawing where you left off. Similarly, if you want to draw a straight segment in the path, you can pick up the pen and start drawing again at the other end of the segment.

Tip: The Lasso Placeth and Taketh Away. The Lasso tool isn't only good at selecting stuff. It's good at deselecting stuff, too. It was Greg Vander Houwen who first showed us how useful this can be for blending a selection into another image (or another part of the same image).

1. Make a quick 'n' dirty selection with the Lasso tool around the area you want.

2. Float the selection (Command-J) and drag it to approximately where you want it. Don't deselect or defloat it yet.

3. In the Options palette, give the Lasso tool a Feather value, such as 5 or 6 pixels (the feather radius depends entirely on the image content; see "Anti-aliasing and Feathering," later in this chapter).

4. Finally, hold down the Command key and use the Lasso tool to "eat away" at the edges of the floating selection (see Figure 13-8). You might want to change the opacity of the floating selection while you do this so you can see what's beneath it (press a number on your keyboard; then press zero to go back to 100 percent when you're done). The portions of the selection that are eaten away simply disappear as though they were never copied.

This gives you a great deal of control over shaping and sizing the selection when you most need it: while the selection is floating in position.

Tip: The Defloating Lasso. In the last tip, we talked about eating away at a floating selection with the Lasso tool and the Command key. However, there are times when you'd want to do just the opposite: use a tool to defloat part of the selection—laying it down on the underlying image—while keeping a part of the selection floating. It turns out that you use the Type tool to do this (that's intuitive, eh?).

Once a floating selection is in place, you can use the Type tool with the Command key held down (it turns into a Lasso tool—go figger). Anything you select is defloated (applied to the underlying image). Anything not selected remains floating. If you want, you can use Command and Shift

Figure 13-8

Eating away at a
floating selection

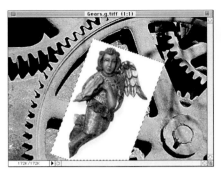

*The angel has been pasted in as a
floating selection and rotated.*

*Command-dragging with the Lasso
tool eats away at the floating selection.*

The final image

together, which does the opposite: anything you select remains floating, and the rest is dropped.

One way we use this method is to adjust the kerning between letters.

1. Create some text and move it so the first letter is where you want it.

2. Select the Type tool and hold down the Command key. Draw a lasso selection around the first letter. Remember that, just as with the Lasso tool, you can hold the Option key to draw straight lines.

3. Move all the other letters (they should still be selected and floating) to adjust the space between the first and second letters. We sometimes switch to the Move tool (press V) and then use the arrow keys to do this. (Remember that if you hold down the Shift key, the arrow keys move the selection by ten pixels at a time.)

4. Repeat steps 2 and 3 until all the letters are placed properly.

Note that it's usually better to lay the type down on a layer apart from the background until you know exactly where you want to place it. Similarly, you could set up your type in Quick Mask mode, then switch out of Quick Mask and fill the selection (the text) with whatever color you want.

Also, it's important to know that this technique doesn't feather or even anti-alias the edge.

Magic Wand

The last selection tool in the Tool palette is the Magic Wand (press W, or hold down the Control key when you have any other selection tool), so-called more for its icon than for its prestidigitation. When you click on an image with the Magic Wand (you can't drag after clicking), Photoshop selects every neighboring pixel with the same or similar gray level or color. "Neighboring" means that the pixels must be touching on at least one side (see Figure 13-9).

Figure 13-9
Magic Wand selections

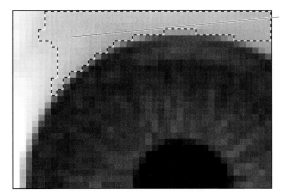

We clicked here with the Magic Wand tolerance set to 18.

How similar can the neighbors be before Photoshop pulls them into the selection? It's up to you. You can set the Tolerance setting in the Magic Wand Options dialog box from 0 to 255.

In a grayscale image, this tolerance value refers to the number of gray levels from the sample point's gray level. If you click on a pixel with a gray level of 120 and your Tolerance is set to 10, Photoshop selects any and all neighboring pixels that have values between 110 and 130.

Tip: Sample Small, Sample Often. The Magic Wand tool can be frustrating when it doesn't select everything you want it to. When this happens, novice users often set the Tolerance value higher and try again. Instead, try keeping the tolerance low (between 12 and 32) and Shift-click to add more parts (or Command-click to take parts away).

Selections from Channels

Why would you go through all the trouble of creating a selection if the selection was already made for you? More often than not, the selection you're looking to make is already hidden within the image; to unlock it you only have to look at the color channels that make up the image (see "Channels," later in this chapter).

Here's one way to tease a selection mask out of an image (see Figure 13-10). We demonstrate these techniques in more detail in the step-by-step examples at the end of this chapter.

1. Switch though the color channels until you find which channel gives the best contrast between the element you're trying to select and its background.

2. Duplicate that channel by dragging the channel tile onto the New Channel icon in the Channels palette.

3. Use Levels or Curves to adjust the contrast between the elements you want to select and the rest of the image.

4. Clean up the mask manually. We typically use the Lasso tool to select and delete areas, or the Brush tool with one finger on the X key (so you can paint with black, then press X to "erase" with white, and so on).

Using Levels and Curves. The real key to this tip is step number 3: using Levels or Curves. With Levels, concentrate on the three

Input sliders to isolate the areas you're after.

In the Curves dialog box, use the eyedropper tool to see where the pixels sit on the curve (click and drag around the image while the Curves dialog box is open, and watch the white circle bounce around on the curve). Then use the pencil tool in the dialog box to push those pixels to white or black. The higher the contrast, the easier it is to extract a selection from it.

Some people use the Smooth button after making these sorts of "hard" curve maps. However, in this case, we typically run a small-value Gaussian Blur after applying the curve, so we don't bother with smoothing the curve.

Using RGB. It's usually easier to grab selection masks from RGB images than from CMYK images. However, if you're going to switch from CMYK to RGB mode, make sure you do it on a duplicate of the image, because all that mode switching damages the image too much.

Figure 13-10 Starting with a channel

Red channel

Green channel

Blue channel (best contrast)

Quick and dirty Levels adjustment to blue channel

Fine-tuned version of blue channel

Tip: Sample Points in the Magic Wand. Note that when you select a pixel with the Magic Wand, you may not get the pixel value you expect. It all depends on the Sample Size popup menu in the Eyedropper tool's Options palette. If you select 3 by 3 Average or 5 by 5 Average in that popup menu, Photoshop averages the pixels around the one you click on with the Magic Wand. On the other hand, if you select Point Sample, Photoshop uses exactly the one you click on.

Bruce prefers Point Sample because he always knows what he's going to end up with. David, on the other hand, only uses Point Sample when using the eyedropper tools in Levels or Curves (see Chapter 6, *Tonal Correction*); when he's just trying to pick up a color, he uses 3 by 3 Average.

In RGB and CMYK images, however, the Magic Wand's tolerance value is slightly more complex. The tolerance refers to each and every channel value, instead of just the gray level.

For instance, let's say your tolerance is set to 10 and you click on a pixel with a value of 60 red, 100 green, and 200 blue. Photoshop selects all neighbors that have red values from 50 to 70, *and* green values from 90 to 110, *and* blue values from 190 to 210. All three conditions must be met, or the pixel isn't included in the selection.

Bruce almost never uses the Magic Wand; he finds it too limiting, so he uses Color Range instead (which we talk about later in this chapter; see Figure 13-29 on page 364). David finds himself using the Magic Wand frequently. However, he almost never gets the selection he wants out of it, so he uses other tools to fine-tune the selection.

Tip: Select on a Channel, Not Composite. Because it's often hard to predict how the Magic Wand tool is going to work in a color image, we typically like to make selections on a single channel of the image. The Magic Wand is more intuitive on this grayscale image, and when you switch back to the composite channel (by pressing Command-zero or clicking on the RGB or CMYK tile in the Channels palette), the selection's flashing border is still there.

Tip: Reverse Selecting. One simple but nonobvious method that we often use to select an area is to select a larger area with the Lasso or Marquee tool and then Command-click with the Magic Wand tool on the area we *don't* want selected (see Figure 13-11).

Figure 13-10
Reverse selecting

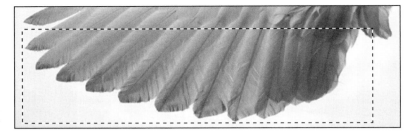

*The entire area
is selected*

*Command-click with
the Magic Wand tool to
deselect the background*

Quick Masks

When you select a portion of your image, you see the flashing dotted lines—they're fondly known as *marching ants* to most Photoshop folks. But what are these ants really showing you? In a typical selection, the marching ants outline the boundary of pixels that are selected *50 percent or more*. There are often loads of other pixels that are selected 49 percent or less that you can't see at all from the marching ants display.

The one exception to this rule is when there are no pixels more than 49-percent selected. If every pixel is less than half selected, the marching ants show you every selected pixel, no matter how selected it is.

Tip: Hide the Marching Ants. The human eye is a marvelous thing. Scientists have shown us that one of the things the eye (and the optical cortex in the brain) is great at is detecting motion (probably developed through years of hunting and gathering in the forests). However, evolution sometimes works against us. In Photoshop, the motion of a selection's marching ants is so annoying and distracting that it can bring production to a halt.

Fortunately, you can hide those little ants by selecting Hide Edges from the Select menu (or pressing Command-H). We do this constantly. In fact, we almost never actually apply a filter or do much of anything in Photoshop while the ants are marching.

The only problem is that you actually have to use your short-term memory to remember where the selection is on screen. With complex operations, you also have to remember that you *have* a selection—we've lost count of the number of times we've wondered why our filter or curve was having no visible effect on the image, only to remember belatedly that we had a 6-pixel area selected, usually one that currently wasn't visible.

But seeing cut-and-dried marching ant boundaries is often not helpful. So Photoshop includes a Quick Mask mode to show you exactly what's selected and how much each pixel is selected. When you enter Quick Mask mode (select the Quick Mask icon in the Tool palette or type Q), you see the underlying selection channel in all its glory. However, because the quick mask is overlaying the image, the black areas of the mask are 50-percent-opaque red and the white (selected) areas are even more transparent than that (see Figure 13-12). The red is supposed to remind you of rubylith, for those of you who remember rubylith.

Figure 13-12
Quick Mask mode

 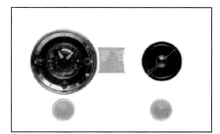

The marching ants show some of the selected areas of the image.

The quick mask shows all the selected pixels (fully and partially selected). Here the quick mask is set to white instead of the usual red.

You can change both the color and the transparency of the quick mask in the Quick Mask Options dialog box (see Figure 13-13)—the fast way to get there is to double-click on the Quick Mask icon. If the image you're working on has a lot of red in it, you'll probably want to change the quick mask color to green or some other contrasting color. Either way, we almost always increase the opacity of the color to about 75 percent, so it displays more prominently against the background image.

Note that these changes aren't document-specific. That is, they stick around in Photoshop until you change them.

Figure 13-13

Quick Mask
Options dialog box

Tip: How Selected is Selected? Even when you're in Quick Mask mode it's difficult to see partially selected pixels (especially those that are less than 50-percent selected). Note that the Info palette shows grayscale values when you're in this mode; those gray values represent the "percentage selected" for each pixel. It's just another reason always to keep one eye on that palette.

Editing Quick Masks

The powerful thing about quick masks isn't just that you can see a selection you've made, but rather that you can *edit* that selection with precision. When you're in Quick Mask mode, you can paint using any of Photoshop's painting or editing tools, though you're limited to painting in grayscale. Painting with white (which appears transparent in this mode) adds to your selection; black subtracts from it.

If the element in your image is any more complicated than a rectangle, you can use Quick Mask to select it quickly and precisely. (We do this for almost every selection we make.)

1. Select the area as carefully as you can, using any of the selection tools (but don't spend too much time on it).

2. Switch to Quick Mask mode.

3. Paint or edit using the Brush tool (or any other painting or editing tool) to refine the selection you've made. Remember that partially transparent pixels will be partially selected (we often run a Gaussian Blur filter on the quick mask to smooth out sharp edges in the selection).

4. Switch out of Quick Mask mode. The marching ants update to reflect the changes you've made (see Figure 13-14).

Figure 13-14 Editing quick masks

Original, quick-and-dirty selection with the Lasso tool

In Quick Mask mode, you can clean up the selection using any tool, including the brushes.

When you leave Quick Mask mode, the selection is updated.

Note that if you switch to Quick Mask mode with nothing selected, the quick mask will be empty (fully transparent). This would imply that the whole document is selected, but it doesn't work that way.

Tip: Filtering Quick Masks. The Quick Mask mode is also a great place to apply filters or special effects. Any filter you run affects only the selection, not the entire image (see Figure 13-15). For instance, you could make a rectangular selection, switch to Quick Mask mode, and run the Twirl filter. When you leave Quick Mask mode, you can fill, paint, or adjust the altered selection.

Tip: Reversal of Color. Some people are just contrary. Give it to them one way and they want it the other. If you're the kind of person who likes the selected areas to be black (or red, or whatever other color you choose in Quick Mask Options) and the unselected areas to be fully transparent, you can change this in Quick Mask Options. Even faster, you can Option-click on the Quick Mask icon in the Tool palette. Note that when you do this, the icon actually changes to reflect your choice.

Figure 13-15
Filtering
quick masks

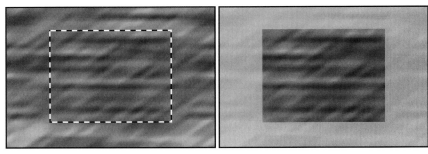

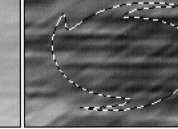

Original selection   *Quick mask of original selection*

Quick mask after Twirl filter applied   *Post-Twirl selection*

If you do change the way that Quick Mask works, you'll probably want to reverse the way that channels and layer masks work, too (double-click on the channel in the Channels palette). Otherwise, you'll have a hard time remembering whether black means selected or unselected. Bruce doesn't worry about keeping these things straight—he just uses Inverse (from the Select menu) when the selection winds up being the opposite of what he wants.

Anti-Aliasing and Feathering

If you've ever been in a minor car accident and later talked to an insurance adjuster, you've probably been confronted with their idea that you may not be fully blameless or at fault in the accident. And, just as you can be 25-percent or 50-percent at fault, you can *partially* select pixels in Photoshop. One of the most common partial selections is around the edges of a selection. And the two most common ways of partially selecting the edges are anti-aliasing and feathering.

Anti-Aliasing

If you use the Marquee tool to select a rectangle, the edges of the selection are nice and crisp, which is probably how you wanted them. Crisp edges around an oval or nonregular shape, however, are rarely a desired effect. That's because of the stair-stepping required to make a diagonal or curve out of square pixels. What you really want (usually) is partially selected pixels in the notches between the fully selected pixels. This technique is called "anti-aliasing."

Every selection in Photoshop is automatically anti-aliased for you, unless you turn it off in the selection tool's Options palette. Unfortunately, you can't see the anti-aliased nature of the selection unless you're in Quick Mask mode because anti-aliased (partially selected) pixels are often less than 50-percent selected (see "Quick Masks" earlier in this chapter).

Note that once you've made a selection with Anti-aliased turned off in the Options palette, you cannot then anti-alias it—though there are ways to fake it.

Tip: Faking Anti-aliasing. Let's say that after you've spent five minutes making a complicated selection, you realize that Anti-aliased was turned off in the Options palette. Here's a little trick to fake the anti-aliasing.

1. Switch to Quick Mask mode (press Q).

2. Select Gaussian Blur from the Blur submenu under the Filters menu.

3. Set the Gaussian Blur amount to .5 or so.

4. Press OK and then switch out of Quick Mask mode (press Q again).

The selection is now slightly more blurry (the edges contain partially selected pixels), giving an anti-aliased look.

Feathering

Anti-aliasing simply smooths out the edges of a selection, adjusting the amounts that the edge pixels are selected in order to appear smooth. But it's often (very often) the case that you need a larger transition area between what is and isn't selected. That's where feathering comes in. Feathering is a way to expand the border area around the edges of a selection. The border isn't just extended out; it's also extended in (see Figure 13-16).

Figure 13-16
Feathering

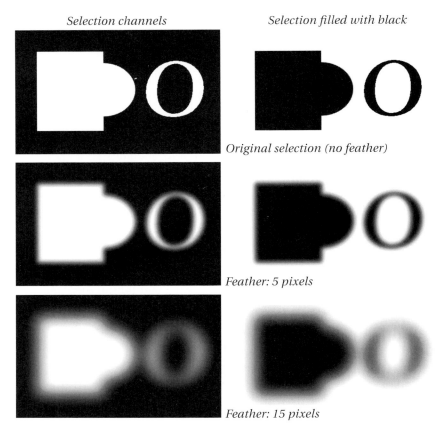

Selection channels   *Selection filled with black*

Original selection (no feather)

Feather: 5 pixels

Feather: 15 pixels

To understand what feathering does, it's important to understand the concept of the selection channel that we talked about earlier in the chapter. That is, when you make a selection, Photoshop is really "seeing" the selection as a grayscale channel behind the scenes. The black areas are totally unselected, the white areas are fully selected, and the gray areas are partially selected.

When you feather a selection, Photoshop is essentially applying a Gaussian Blur to the grayscale selection channel. (We say "essentially" because in some circumstances—like when you set a feather radius of over 120 pixels—you get a slightly different effect; however, there's usually so little difference that it's not worth bothering with. For those technoids out there who really care, Adobe tells us that a Gaussian Blur of the quick mask channel is a tiny bit more accurate and "true" than a feather.)

There are three ways to feather a selection.

▶ Before selecting, specify a feather amount in the Options palette for the selection tool.

▶ After selecting, choose Feather from the Select menu.

▶ Apply a Gaussian Blur to the selection's quick mask (see "Tip: Faking Anti-aliasing," earlier in this chapter).

Tip: Feathering a Portion of a Selection. When you choose Feather from the Select menu, your entire selection is feathered. Sometimes, however, you only want to feather a portion of the selection. Maybe you want a hard edge on one half of the selection and a soft edge on the other. You can do this by switching to Quick Mask mode, selecting what you want feathered with any of the selection tools, and applying a Gaussian Blur to it. When you flip out of Quick Mask mode, the "feathering" is included in the selection.

Note that if you want a nice, soft feather between what is feathered and what isn't, you first have to feather the selection you make while you're in Quick Mask mode (see Figure 13-17).

Figure 13-17 Feathering part of a selection

Original image *Anti-aliased selection* *After Gaussian blur* *Mustache and neck "feathered"*

Tip: Tiny Feathers. There must be a good reason why you can't set the Feathering value (in the Feather dialog box) to less than 1, but we have no idea why. If you want a smaller feather amount (we often do), switch to Quick Mask mode (press Q), run a Gaussian Blur at the amount you want, then switch out of Quick Mask (press Q again).

Channels

Back in "Masking-Tape Selections," we told you that selections, masks, and channels are all the same thing down deep: grayscale images. This is not intuitive, nor is it easy to grasp at first. But once you really understand this point, you've taken the first step toward really surfing the Photoshop tsunami.

A channel is a solitary 8-bit, grayscale image. You can have up to 24 channels in a single image in Photoshop 3. (Actually, there are two exceptions: first, images in Bitmap mode can only contain a single 1-bit channel; second, Photoshop allows one additional channel per layer to accommodate layer masks, which we'll talk about later in this chapter.)

But in the eyes of the program, not all channels are created equal. There are two types of channels: alpha and color channels (see Figure 13-18).

Figure 13-18
The Channels palette

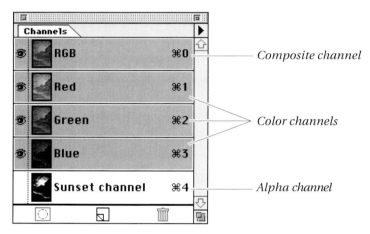

Composite channel

Color channels

Alpha channel

Alpha Channels

People get very nervous when they hear the term "alpha channel," because they figure that with such an exotic name, it has to be a complex feature. Not so. An alpha channel is simply an 8-bit grayscale image. Alpha channels let you save selections, but you can use them in a number of other ways, too (see "Tip: Tissue Overlay Channels," in Chapter 14, *Essential Image Techniques*).

Saving selections. Selections and channels are really the same thing down deep (even though they have different outward appearances), so you can turn one into the other very quickly. Earlier in this chapter we discussed how you can see and edit a selection by switching to Quick Mask mode. But quick masks are ephemeral things, and aren't much use if you want to hold on to that selection and use it later.

When you turn a selection into an alpha channel, you're saving that selection in the document. Then you can go back later and edit the channel, or turn it back into a selection.

The slow way to save a selection is to choose Save Selection from the Select menu. It's a nice place for beginners because Photoshop provides you with a dialog box (see Figure 13-19). But pros don't bother with menu selections when they can avoid them. Instead, click the New Channel icon in the Channels palette. Or, if you want to see the Channel Options dialog box first, you can drag the selection tile over the New Channel icon (see Figure 13-20).

Figure 13-19
Save Selection
dialog box

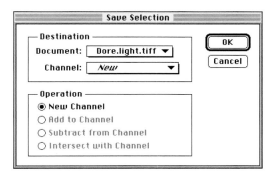

Figure 13-20
Saving a selection

*The channel previews
are turned off here.*

*Click here to turn the
selection into a channel*

*Drag the selection tile
over this to see the New
Channel dialog box.*

Tip: Loading Selections. Saving a selection as an alpha channel doesn't do you much good unless you can retrieve it again. Again, the slowest method is to use the Load Selection item from the Select menu (though there are benefits to this method; see "Tip: Loading Multidocument Selections," later in this chapter).

One step better is to Option-click on the channel that you want to turn into a selection. Even better, press Command-Option-#, where the number is the channel you want. For instance, if you want to load channel six as a selection, press Command-Option-6.

Note that if you press Command-Option-0 (zero), you load the *luminosity mask*. This is not the "lightness" of the image; rather, it's approximately the same as selecting Grayscale from the Mode menu.

Tip: Be a Packrat! Every time it takes you more than 30 seconds to make a selection in your image, you should be thinking: Save This Selection. We try to save every complex selection as a channel or a path until the end of the project (and sometimes we even archive them, just in case). The reason? You never know when you'll need them again. Photoshop doesn't let you go back and change what you've done too often, and we've just been burned too many times by having to re-create selections from scratch (of course, the new selection never matches the old one exactly).

Saving selections as channels takes up lots of memory, though. If you don't think you'll need a selection for a while, offload that channel into another file (see "Duplicating Channels," below). This still swallows disk space, but hey—it's cheap compared to RAM.

Tip: Don't Save Channels as TIFFs. If you're saving a mess of channels along with the image you're working on, don't save the file as a TIFF. Even though you *can* save all those channels in a TIFF image, you're not taking advantage of Photoshop's compression techniques, so your files end up being much larger than necessary (see Chapter 17, *Storing Images*). Instead, save in Photoshop 3.0 format.

Tip: Adding, Subtracting, and Intersecting Selections. Let's say you have an image with three distinct elements in it. You've spent an hour carefully selecting each of the elements, and you've saved each one in its own channel (see Figure 13-21). Now you want to select all three objects at the same time.

In the good old days you would have sat around trying to figure out the appropriate channel operations (using Calculations) to get exactly what you wanted. But it's a kinder, gentler Photoshop now. After you load one channel as a selection, you can use Load Selection from the Select menu to add another channel to the current selection, subtract another channel, or find the intersection between the two selections.

Figure 13-21 Adding, subtracting, and intersecting selections

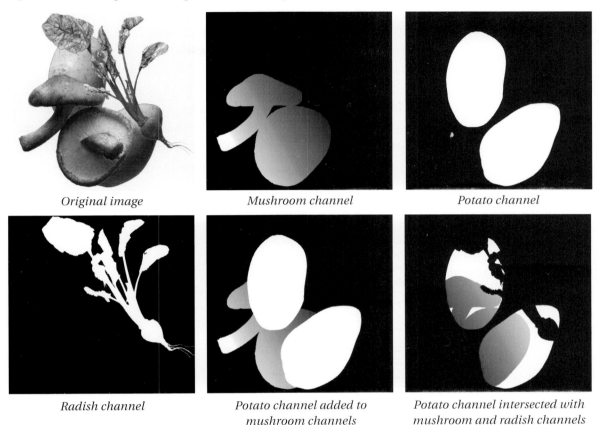

Original image *Mushroom channel* *Potato channel*

Radish channel *Potato channel added to mushroom channels* *Potato channel intersected with mushroom and radish channels*

Even easier, use the key-click combinations in Table 13-1.

Table 13-1

Working with selections

Do this to the channel tile . . .	. . . to get this result
Shift-Option-click	Add channel to current selection
Command-Option-click	Subtract channel from selection
Command-Shift-Option-click	Intersect the current selection and the channel

You can also use the modifier keys with the channel tiles instead of clicking. For example, holding down the Command key while you drag a channel tile over the Make Selection icon (in the Channels palette) subtracts that channel's selection mask from the one currently selected.

Multidocument Channels

As we said earlier, your alpha channels don't all have to be in the same document. In fact, if you've got more than 24 channels, you *have* to have them in multiple documents. Here are a bunch of tips we've found helpful in moving channels back and forth between documents.

Tip: Saving Off Channels Using Calculate. Most people shudder when you say, "Use the Calculate command." Its nonintuitive, mysterious dialog box is partly to blame for this. But it's not that bad. One use for Calculate is to move channels from one document to another (see Figure 13-22). But before we begin, remember that Calculate only works with two documents that have exactly the same pixel dimensions.

Figure 13-22

Duplicating a channel to another document

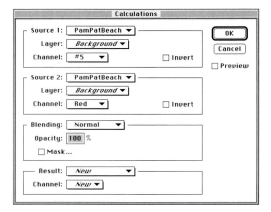

1. In the Calculations dialog box, select the channel in the current document that you want to copy.

2. You can just ignore the second source in the Calculations dialog box.

3. Set the Blending mode to Normal and the Opacity to 100 percent.

4. Set the Result popup menu to a new channel of a new document (if you don't have one open already), or a new channel in the document you're using to store channels.

The result: the channel is copied into the new document. Finally, you can save the new document and delete the channel from the original file.

By the way, the reason we said you could ignore the second source (in step 2) is that the second source is totally overridden by the first source because of the 100-percent opacity.

Tip: Saving Off Channels Using Copy and Paste. After one of our technical reviewers read the last tip, he asked, "This whole sequence seems way too complex. Why not just copy and paste the channel?" The answer is that Copy and Paste can really bog down in larger files ("large" meaning any file so big that Photoshop has to start writing it to disk; see Chapter 1, *Building a Photoshop System*). In smaller files, however, Copy and Paste works just as well.

Tip: Saving Off Channels the Fast Way. When it comes right down to it, the fastest way to copy a channel from document *a* to document *b* is by dragging the channel's tile (in the Channels palette) from document *a* onto document *b*. It's nice, quick, simple, and elegant. Plus, like the last tip, the two documents don't have to be the same size; if they're not, the channel gets centered on the new document.

Tip: Loading Multidocument Selections. From what we've said earlier in this chapter, you might infer that we think only a dolt trying to waste time would use the Load or Save Selection items on the Select menu. Not true! Taking the extra time to use the menu items can pay off in certain circumstances. Here's one: you can save selections to or load selections from other documents.

For example, if you have two similar documents open and you've carefully made and saved a selection in one image, you might want to use it in the other image. Instead of copying and pasting the selection channel, take a shortcut route and use the Load Selection dialog box (see Figure 13-23). You can load the selection channel directly in by choosing it from the Document and Channel popup menus.

Figure 13-23
Load Selection
dialog box

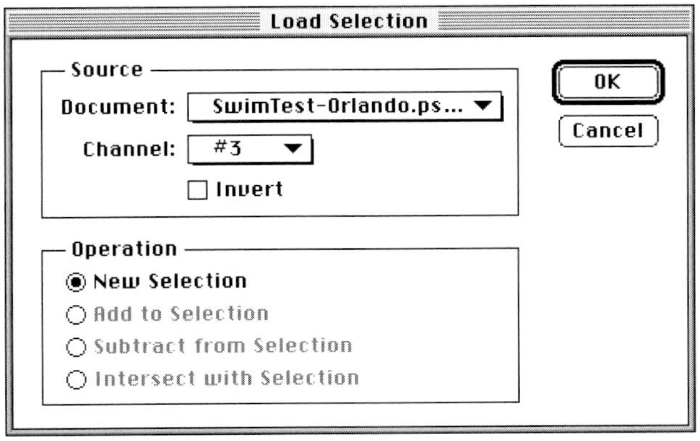

The catch here is that both documents have to have exactly the same pixel dimensions (otherwise, Photoshop wouldn't know how to place the selection properly).

Color Channels

When a color image is in RGB mode (under the Mode menu), the image is made up of three channels: red, green, and blue. Each of these channels is exactly the same as an alpha channel, except that they're designated as *color channels*. You can edit a color channel separately from the others. You can independently make a single color channel visible or invisible. But you cannot delete or add a color channel without changing the image mode.

The first tile in the Channels palette (above the color channels) is the Composite channel. Actually, this isn't really a channel at all. Rather, the composite channel is the full-color representation of all the individual color channels mixed together. It gives you a convenient way to select or deselect all the color channels at once, and also lets you view the composite color image while you're editing a single channel.

Tip: Selecting and Seeing Channels. The tricky thing about working with channels is figuring out which channel(s) you're editing and which channel(s) you're seeing on the screen. They're not always the same thing!

The Channels palette has two columns in it. The left column contains little eyeball checkboxes that you can turn on and off to show or hide individual channels. Clicking on one of the tiles in the right column not only displays that channel, but lets you edit it, too. The channels that are selected for editing are highlighted in gray (see Figure 13-24). The two columns are independent of each other because editing and seeing the channels are not the same thing.

When you're jumping from one channel to another, skip the clicking altogether and use a keystroke instead. Command-# displays the channel number you press; for instance, Command-1 shows the Red channel (or whatever the first channel is), Command-4 shows the fourth channel (the first alpha channel in an RGB image), and Command-0 selects the color composite channel (deselecting all the other channels in the process). Sorry, there's no way (that we know of) to select channels above number nine with keystrokes.

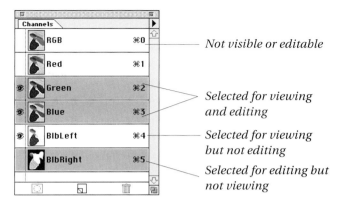

Figure 13-24

Selecting multiple channels

Not visible or editable

Selected for viewing and editing

Selected for viewing but not editing

Selected for editing but not viewing

You can see as many channels at once as you want by clicking in the channel's eyeball checkboxes. To edit more than one channel at a time, Shift-click on the channel tiles.

Note that when you display more than one channel at a time, the alpha channels automatically switch from their standard black and white to their channel color (you can specify what color each channel uses in Channel Options—double-click on the channel tile).

The Select Menu

If making selections using lassos and marquees and then saving or loading them were all there was to selection in Photoshop, life would be simpler but duller. Fortunately for us, there are many more things you can do with selections, and they all—well, almost all—help immeasurably in the production process.

You can find each additional selection feature under the Select menu: Float, Grow, Similar, Color Range, Modify, and Matting. Let's explore each of these and how they can speed up your work.

Floating Selections

Even before version 3 of Photoshop came out, the program had layers. Well, actually, it only had two layers: the background layer where the image was, and a temporary layer that held anything that you pasted into the image. People complained, however, because as soon as you deselected whatever was floating in that temporary layer, it would permanently replace the pixels beneath it.

Now, even with layers as a part of our everyday workflow, we still find that temporary floating layer really helpful all the time. There are three ways to float pixels in Photoshop: the Float command, the Option key, and pasting or drag-copying.

Float. Once you've got some pixels selected, you can turn them into a floating selection by choosing Float from the Select menu (or pressing Command-J). This simply copies the pixels to a new, temporary layer (you can even see the Floating Selection layer in the Layers palette). Or, if you want to float the selected pixels and delete them from the layer they came from, you can hold down the Option key while you select Float, or press Command-Option-J.

Option key. If you want to float a selection and move the pixels elsewhere, you can skip the Float command and just hold down the Option key while you drag the selection with the selection or Move tool. As in most other graphics programs, Option-dragging copies the pixels while you move them. And in this case, it also floats them.

Tip: Quick-floating with Arrows. For some strange reason, David rarely uses the Command-J keystroke for floating pixels. Instead, he holds down the Option key while pressing one of the arrow keys. This copies the selected pixels and moves them over one pixel (in the direction of the arrow). Don't ask why . . . he just learned it that way.

Pasting/Drag-Copying. Any pixels that you paste in or drag over from another file appear on the temporary Floating Selection layer, and they only "drop down" onto the layer below when you deselect them.

Tip: Floating Selections Are Layers, Too. As we've just said about a bazillion times, a floating selection is simply a temporary layer in your Photoshop document. The layer (called Floating Selection in the Layers palette) appears whenever pixels are floating, and disappears when you deselect. And that means you can play with it just as you can with a layer. For instance, you can change its mode to Multiply, Screen, Overlay, or any of the others. You can change its opacity. You can even change its layer order (see the next tip).

Tip: What Layer to Drop the Selection On. If you have a document with two or more layers, you can choose which layer you want your floating selection to "drop down" onto by dragging the Floating Selection layer tile (in the Layers palette) above the layer tile you're aiming for. When you deselect, the pixels fall onto that layer.

Tip: The Transparency Bug. Almost all software still has bugs in it when it ships. Developers don't like it, but that's the way it is. Here's a little one that can confuse you if you're not aware.

If you change the transparency of a floating selection in the Layers palette, then change it back to 100 percent (fully opaque), the floating selection might not redraw properly, if at all. Even zooming in and out doesn't appear to fix the problem. To fix it, you can either nudge the selection slightly (use the arrow keys to move it in one-pixel increments), or change the Apply mode in the Layers palette.

If the selection still looks wrong, then you may have deeper problems and you may have to consult an ophthalmologist. Note that this was fixed in version 3.0.4, so if you have that, ignore this tip.

Tip: Floating Selections Don't Get Clipped. One more cool thing about floating pixels: they don't get clipped when you push them outside the image boundaries. For example, if you drag a floating selection so half of it is sitting off the side of the image, you can still paint in it, run filters on it, and so on, without cutting off the part that's hidden (see Figure 13-25).

This is particularly important when working with large selections, such as those pasted in from another—larger—document, because it gives you the chance to position the big selection before dropping it down onto the image layer. When you *do* deselect the floating selection, the edges get clipped and there's no going back (except with Undo).

Grow

Earlier in the chapter, when we were talking about the Magic Wand tool, we discussed the concept of tolerance. This value tells Photoshop how much brighter or darker a pixel (or each color channel that defines a pixel) can be and still be included in the selection.

Let's say you're trying to select an apple using the Magic Wand tool with a tolerance of 24. After clicking once, perhaps only half of the apple is selected; the other half is slightly shaded and falls outside the tolerance range. You could deselect, change the tolerance, and click again. However, it's much faster to select Grow from the Select menu (or, even faster, press Command-G).

Figure 13-25

Floating selections and image boundaries

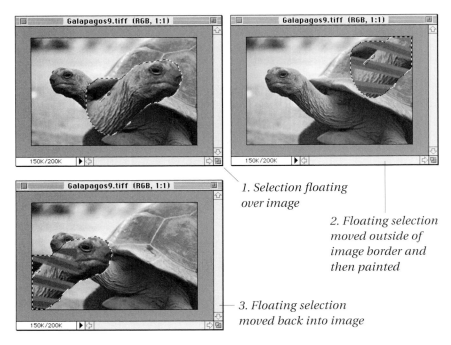

1. *Selection floating over image*

2. *Floating selection moved outside of image border and then painted*

3. *Floating selection moved back into image*

When you choose Grow, Photoshop selects additional pixels according to the following criteria. (By the way, the manuals are wrong about how Grow works . . . it's weird but we figured it out.)

1. First, it finds the highest and lowest gray values of every channel of every pixel selected—the highest red, green, and blue, and the lowest red, green, and blue of the bunch of already selected pixels (or the highest cyan, magenta, yellow, and black, and so on).

2. Next, it adds the tolerance value to the highest values and subtracts it from the lowest values in each channel. Therefore, the highest values get a little higher and the lowest values get a little lower (of course, it never goes above 255 or below 0).

3. Finally, Photoshop selects every *adjacent* pixel that falls between all those values (see Figure 13-26 on page 363).

In other words, Photoshop tries its hardest to spread your selection in every direction, but only in similar colors. However, it doesn't always work the way you'd want. In fact, sometimes it works very oddly indeed.

For instance, if you select a pure red area (made of 255 red, and no blue or green), and a pure green area (made of 255 green, and no red or blue), then select Grow, Photoshop selects every adjacent pixel that has any red or green in it, as long as the blue channel is not out of tolerance's range. That means that it'll pick out dark browns, lime greens, oranges, and so on—even if you set a really small tolerance level (see Figure 13-27 on page 363).

Tip: Instead of the Magic Wand. While the Magic Wand tool is pretty cool and provides a friendly point-and-click interface, it's often not very useful because colors in a natural image (like a scan) are typically pretty varied. Even if you click in what looks like a representative spot, you might not get the full range you expect.

Instead, try selecting a larger representative area with the Lasso or Marquee tool. Then, select Grow or Similar from the Select menu (see below for a discussion of Similar). Bruce maintains that the best method is just to use Color Range instead (see below).

Similar

Grow and the Magic Wand have a common downfall: they only select contiguous areas of your image. If you're trying to select the same color throughout an image, you may click and drag and grow yourself into a frenzy before you're done. Choosing Similar from the Select menu does the same thing as choosing Grow, but it chooses pixels from throughout the entire image (see Figure 13-28 on page 364).

Note that Similar and Grow are both attached to the Magic Wand's options; Photoshop applies both the Wand's tolerance and its anti-alias values to these commands. We can't think of any reason to turn anti-aliasing off, but it's nice to know you have the option.

Color Range

One of the problems with Similar and Grow is that you rarely know what you're going to end up with. On the other hand, Color Range lets you make color-based selections interactively, and shows you exactly which pixels will be selected. But there's one other advantage of Color Range over the Magic Wand features (we think of Similar and Grow as extensions of the Magic Wand).

The Magic Wand–based features either select a pixel or they don't (the exception is anti-aliasing around the edges of selections, which only partially selects pixels there). Color Range, however, only fully selects a few pixels and partially selects a *lot* of pixels (see Figure 13-29 on page 364). This can be incredibly helpful when you're trying to tease a good selection mask out of the contents of an image.

We almost never use Color Range to create a final selection mask. Rather, we find it great as a first or second step in building the mask, and then we follow it up with lots of the other tools (including Levels or Curves), adding and removing pixels. There are four areas you should be aware of in the Color Range dialog box: selection eyedroppers, the Fuzziness slider, canned sets of colors, and Selection Preview.

Adding and deleting colors. When you first open Color Range, Photoshop creates a selection based on your foreground color. Then you can use the eyedropper tools to add or delete colors in the image (or, better yet, hold down the Shift key to get the Add Color to Mask eyedropper, or the Command key to get the Remove Color from Mask eyedropper). Note that you can always scroll or magnify an area in the image. You can even select colors from any other open image.

Tip: Avoid Sample Merged. Color Range is always in Sample Merged mode. It sees your image as though all the visible layers were merged together. If you've got an object on a layer that you don't want included in the selection mask, hide that layer before opening Color Range.

The Fuzziness Factor. Every Photoshop book we've seen (including Photoshop's manuals) says that the Fuzziness slider in the Color Range dialog box is more or less the same as the Tolerance field in the Magic Wand Options palette. That's sort of like saying that Republicans are more or less the same as Democrats. Yes, they're both in the business of running the country, but . . . .

As we said earlier, pixels that fall within the tolerance value are either fully selected or not; pixels that fall on the border between the selected and unselected areas may be partially selected, but those are only border pixels. Color Range uses the fuzziness value to determine not only whether a pixel should be included, but also *how selected* it should be. We're not going to get into the hard-core math (you don't need to know it and we're not entirely sure of it ourselves), but Figure 13-30 on page 365 should give you a pretty good idea of how Fuzziness works.

Tip: Sampling versus Fuzziness. Should you use lots of sample points or a high Fuzziness setting? It depends on the type of image. To select large areas of similar color, tend toward a lower fuzziness (10–15) to avoid selecting stray pixels. For fine detail, you need to use higher Fuzziness settings, because the fine areas are generally more polluted with colors spilling from adjacent pixels.

Either way, try adding sample points to increase the selection range before you increase fuzziness.

Canned colors. Instead of creating a selection mask with the eyedroppers, you can let Photoshop select all the reds, or all the blues, or yellows, or any other primary color, by choosing the color in the Select popup menu (see Figure 13-31 on page 367). If you choose one of these, Photoshop only selects a pixel if it contains more of that color than any other. For instance, if you choose Reds, Photoshop selects a pixel with an RGB value of 128R 115G 60B; but it won't even partially select a pixel that has an RGB value of 128R 130G 60B.

The greater the difference between the color you choose (in this example, red) and the other primaries (*e.g.*, blue and green), the more the pixel is selected. (To get really tweaky for a moment: the percentage the pixel is selected is the percentage difference between the color you choose and the primary color with the next highest value.)

Do you really need to know any of this? No. Probably the best way to use these features is just not to use them at all (we almost never do).

On the other hand, you can also choose Highlights, Midtones, or Shadows, which we find a bit more useful. When you choose one of these, Photoshop decides whether to select a pixel (or how much to select it) based on its Lab luminance value (see Table 13-2 and Chapter 5, *Color Preferences*, for more information on Lab mode).

Table 13-2

**Ranges for Color Range
(L value in Lab mode)**

Select name	Fully selected pixels	Partially selected pixels
Shadows	1–40	40–55
Midtones	55–75	40–55 and 75–85
Highlights	80–100	75–85

We find selecting Highlights, Midtones, and Shadows most useful when selecting a subset of a color we've already selected (see "Tip: Color Range Subsets," next).

Tip: Color Range Subsets. If you're trying to select all the green buttons on a blouse using Color Range, you're going to pick up every other green object throughout the image, too. However, you can tell the Color Range feature to only select green items within a particular area—the blouse, for instance—by making a selection first. Draw a quick outline of the area you're interested in with the Lasso tool, then choose Color Range. Photoshop ignores the rest of the image.

Similarly, you could select all the green items in the image, then go back to Color Range again and select only those greens that are in Highlight areas.

Tip: Invert the Color Range Selection. Do you often find yourself following up a Color Range selection with an Invert from the Select menu? If you are trying to select the opposite of what's selected in the Color Range dialog box, you can remove that extra step by holding down the Option key when you press OK. Photoshop automatically inverts the selection for you.

If you already have a selection made when you Option-click out of Color Range, Photoshop *deselects* the Color Range pixels from your selection.

Selection Preview. The last area to pay attention to in the Color Range dialog box is the Selection Preview popup menu. When you select anything other than None (the default) from this menu, Photoshop previews the Color Range selection mask.

The first choice, Grayscale, shows you what the selection mask would look like if you saved it as a separate channel. The second and third choices, Black Matte and White Matte, are the equivalent of copying the

Figure 13-26
The Grow
command

After Magic Wand click   *After Grow*

selected pixels out and pasting them on a black or white background. This is great for seeing how well you're capturing edge pixels. The last choice, Quick Mask, is the same as pressing OK and immediately switching into Quick Mask mode.

Because the Selection Preview can slow you down, we recommend turning it on only when you need to, then turning around and switching back to None. It can be really helpful in making sure you're selecting everything you want, but it can also be a drag to productivity.

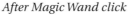

Tip: Changing Quick Mask Options. If you're a hard-core Color Range user, you may one day have the strange desire to change your Quick Mask options settings while the Color Range dialog box is open. You can do it (believe it or not). Hold down the Option key while selecting Quick Mask

Figure 13-27
Anomalies with the
Grow command

When the two center squares are selected, Grow selects all the bottom squares and none of the top squares. Why? Because of slight blue "contamination" in the top squares.

Many of these colors are selected unexpectedly with Grow.

Figure 13-28
The Similar
command

Selection made with Magic Wand.
A Tolerance setting of 24 manages to
avoid the shadows and green areas.

After Similar is selected. Some
brighter areas of the apples
are still not selected.

Figure 13-29 Magic Wand versus Color Range

While you can make similar selections with the Magic Wand and Color Range, each is more efficient for particular situations. Magic Wand is faster for big, consistent areas, while Color Range excels for finer details.

The original image. It is photographed on a good, uniform white background, and includes an area of relatively solid color (the reds) that is an obvious target for change.

Three quick Shift-clicks with the Magic Wand yield a very serviceable silhouette mask. A bit of feathering or a Gaussian blur of the mask (combined with a Levels tweak to adjust the blur) deals with the hard edges.

Because the object is hard-edged to begin with, the Magic Wand's inability to partially select pixels doesn't pose much of a problem in compositing.

A mask created with Color Range (here with few sample points and a high Fuzziness setting) is more appropriate for subtle selections.

A detail of the mask shows that there are partially selected pixels (the gray areas).

This more subtle mask is just the ticket for a Hue/Saturation adjustment, changing the red areas to blue without an artificial look.

Figure 13-30 Fuzziness versus sample points for Color Range

Four selections created with Color Range. At right is the result of a Hue/Saturation move on the selection.

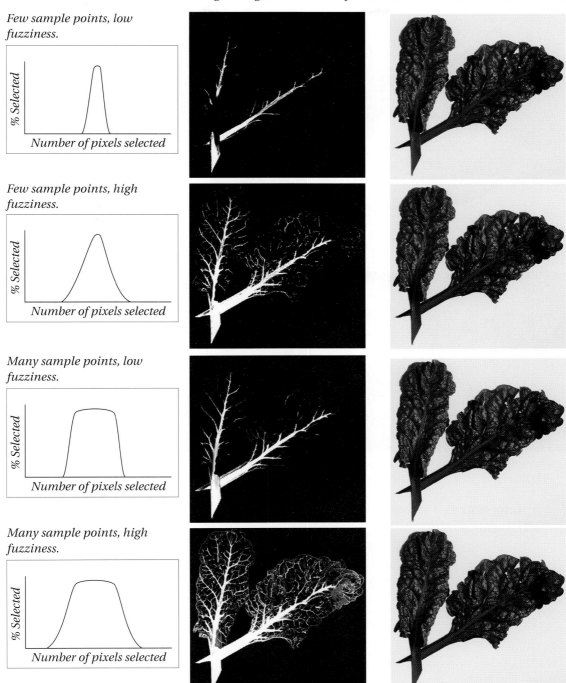

Few sample points, low fuzziness.

Few sample points, high fuzziness.

Many sample points, low fuzziness.

Many sample points, high fuzziness.

Color Plate 12 Screening methods (and pitfalls)

| *Rosette patterns* | *Moiré patterns* | *Stochastic screening* |

Color Plate 13 JPEG Compression

Uncompressed
File size: 580K

High quality
File size: 58K

Medium quality
File size: 32K

Low quality
File size: 20K

Color Plate 14
Drop shadow techniques

45K

100C 40M 30K

55C

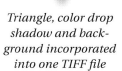

*Diffusion dither created
with ICEfields and saved
as TIFF*

*Grayscale saved as TIFF
and set to overprinting
color. It fully knocks out
the black plate below it.*

*Triangle, color drop
shadow and back-
ground incorporated
into one TIFF file*

from the Selection Preview popup menu. Don't say we don't strive to give you every last tip!

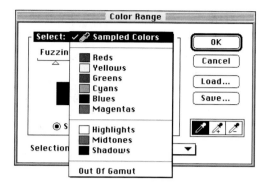

Figure 13-31

Color Range
dialog box

Tip: Forget the Color Range Radio Buttons. Here's another little tip that can speed up production by a moment or two: if you frequently use the Image and Selection radio buttons in the Color Range dialog box, stop! Instead, press the Control key on your keyboard. This toggles between the Selection and Image previews much faster than you can click buttons. This is sometimes helpful if you need a quick reality check as to what's selected and what is not.

Modify

When you think of the most important part of your selection, what do you think of? If you answer "what's selected," you're wrong. No matter what you have selected in your image, the most important part of the selection is the boundary or edge. This is where the tire hits the road, where the money slaps the table, where the gavel slams the podium, where the invoice smacks the client. No matter what you do with the selection—whether you copy and paste it, paint within it, or whatever—the quality of your edge determines how effective your effect will be.

When making a precise selection, you often need to make subtle adjustments to the boundaries of the selection. The four menu items on the Modify submenu under the Select menu—Border, Smooth, Expand, and Contract—focus entirely on this task.

Border. Police officers of the world take note: there's a faster way to get a doughnut than driving down to the local Circle K. Draw a circle using the

Marquee tool, then select Border from the Modify submenu under the Select menu. You can even specify how thick you want your doughnut (in pixels, of course). Border transforms the single line (the circle) into two lines (see Figure 13-32).

Figure 13-32
Border

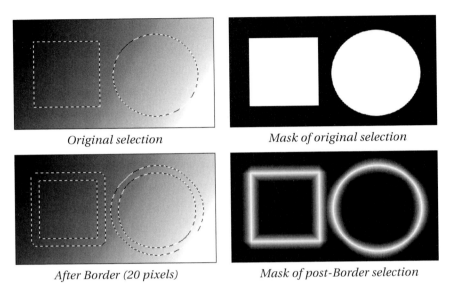

Original selection

Mask of original selection

After Border (20 pixels)

Mask of post-Border selection

The problem with Border is that it only creates soft-edged borders. If you draw a square and give it a border, you get a soft-edged shape that looks more like an octagon than a square. In many cases, this is exactly what you want and need. But other times it can ruin the mood faster than jackhammers outside the bedroom window.

Tip: Level Borders. If selecting Border gives you a super-soft edge when what you want is a harder, fatter edge, try this quick-mask trick. Switch to Quick Mask mode (press Q), then use the Levels or Curves dialog box to adjust the edge of the selection (see "Tip: Finer Spreads and Chokes," later in this chapter). If you find that the edge of the selection becomes too jaggy, you can always apply a 0.5 Gaussian Blur to smooth it out. Remember that when you're in Quick Mask mode, you can select the area to which you want to apply the levels or blur.

Tip: More Border Options. Here's one other way to make a border with a sharper, more distinct edge.

1. Save your selection as an alpha channel.

2. While the area is still selected, choose Expand from the Modify sub-menu under the Select menu (we discuss this command later in the chapter).

3. Save this new selection as an alpha channel.

4. Load the original selection from the alpha channel you saved it in.

5. Choose Contract from the Modify submenu.

6. Mix the two selections (the expanded and the contracted) together by Command-Option-clicking on the channel that contains the expand-ed version.

You can now save this selection and delete either one or both of the other alpha channels you saved. Note that you don't have to expand *and* contract the selection; this method lets you choose to only contract or expand, too.

Tip: Using Borders When Compositing. One of the positive aspects of Photoshop giving you a soft-edged border when you select Border from the Modify submenu is that you can use it to touch up the edges of ob-jects you're pasting on a background. For instance, if the object you're pasting down is not feathered or anti-aliased enough, you can use Bor-der to blur together the edges of the pasted object. Or, if the edge of a composited object has some edge spill from the previous background, you can touch it up with Border.

1. Paste the object and place it exactly where you want it.

2. Select Border from the Modify submenu. This plants the object down and selects the object's edge area in one step.

3. Feather the border selection slightly. You can get a finer blur by switch-ing to Quick Mask mode and performing a Gaussian Blur on it.

4. Hide the marching ants (Command-H).

5. If you want to get rid of aliasing, apply a Gaussian Blur to the area. If you're trying to rid yourself of some background color spill, you can use the Rubber Stamp tool to clone some of the object's color into the

border selection (we'll discuss this in more depth in "Step-by-Step Silhouettes," later in this chapter).

Finally, you may want to apply some unsharp masking to sharpen the edge a little. Therein lies the art: blurring enough and sharpening enough to get a smooth but clean edge.

Smooth. The problem with making selections with the Lasso tool is that you often get very jaggy selection lines; the corners are too sharp, the curves are too bumpy. You can smooth these out by selecting Smooth from the Modify submenu under the Select menu. Like most selection operations in Photoshop, this actually runs a convolution filter over the selection mask—in this case the Median filter. That is, selecting Smooth is exactly the same thing as switching to Quick Mask mode and choosing the Median filter.

Smooth has little or no effect on straight lines or smooth curves. But it has a drastic effect on corners and jaggy lines (see Figure 13-33). Smooth (or the Median filter, depending on which way you look at it) looks at each pixel in your selection, then looks at the pixels surrounding it (the number of pixels it looks at depends on the radius value you choose in the Smooth dialog box). If more than half the pixels around it are selected, then the pixel remains selected. If fewer than half are selected, the pixel becomes *de*selected.

If you enter a small Radius value, only corner tips and other sharp edges are rounded out. Larger values make sweeping changes. It's rare that we use a radius over 5 or 6, but it depends entirely on what you're doing (and how smooth your hand is!).

Expand/Contract. The Expand and Contract features are two of the most useful selection modifiers. They let you enlarge or reduce the size of the selection. This is just like spreading or choking colors in trapping (if you don't know about trapping, don't worry; it's not relevant here).

Once again, these modifiers are simply applying filters to the black-and-white mask equivalent of your selection. Choosing Expand is the same as applying the Maximum filter to the mask; choosing Contract is the same as applying the Minimum filter (see Figure 13-34).

Figure 13-33
Smooth

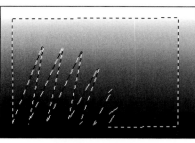

Original selection

Mask of original selection

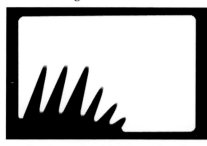

After Smooth with 10-pixel radius

After Smooth with 16-pixel radius

Note that if you enter 5 as the Radius value in the Maximum or Minimum dialog box (or in the Expand or Contract dialog box), it's exactly the same as running the filter or selection modifier five times. The radius value here is more of an "iteration" value; how many times do you want the filter applied at a one-pixel radius?

While we frequently find these selection modifiers useful, they aren't very precise. You can only specify the radius in one-pixel increments (see "Tip: Finer Spreads and Chokes," next).

Tip: Finer Spreads and Chokes. You can make much finer adjustments to the size of a selection by using Levels rather than Expand or Contract from the Select menu. Here's how.

1. Once you have your selection, switch to Quick Mask mode.

2. Apply a Gaussian Blur to the area you want to expand or contract (if it's the whole selection, then blur the whole quick mask). We usually use a low Radius value, such as .5 or 1.

3. In Levels (Command-L), adjust the middle (gamma) slider control to make the area darker or lighter. Making it darker contracts the selection; lighter expands the selection (see Figure 13-35).

Figure 13-34
Expand and Contract

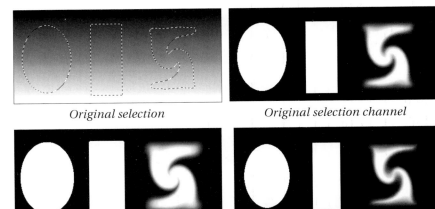

Original selection

Original selection channel

Expanded by four pixels

Contracted by four pixels

Figure 13-35
Precision control
over expanding and
contracting

Original selection channel

*Selection channel after Gaussian Blur
and Levels*

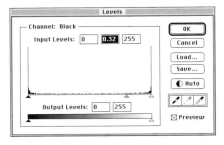

*The gamma slider controls the
expansion or contraction of
the mask channel's gray levels—
hence the abruptness of the blur.*

What's nice about this tip is that it's a very gentle method of expanding or contracting the selection. Instead of "Wham! Move one pixel over," you can say, "Make this selection slightly bigger or smaller."

Matting

We're still not sure why the Matting submenu is located under the Select menu, because these features really don't have much to do with the selection channel itself. Rather, the matting commands are for removing edge spill—the tell-tale colors around a selection's edges that reveal its original background. As we said earlier, the key to compositing is blending the edge of your foreground image with its new background. The less noticeable the edge, the more the colors intermix, and the better the composite (we talk more about edge spill in "Step-by-Step Silhouettes," later in this chapter).

The features on the Matting submenu under the Select menu are designed to help in this compositing process. Note that these are *only* relevant when you've already got a selection floating above your background (see "Float," earlier in this chapter). The first feature, Defringe, can occasionally be incredibly useful. The last two, Remove Black Matte and Remove White Matte, are . . . well . . . perhaps less so.

Defringe. While Defringe appears to be one of the coolest compositing tools in Photoshop, it can also do some serious damage to your image. Defringe lets you blend together the foreground image and the background image, removing any edge spill that might be present. Of course, like any "automatic" feature, it's rarely perfect. But it's sometimes our first line of defense against the horrors of thin halos (see Figure 13-36).

Defringe replaces the selection's border pixels with the colors of interior pixels. This sometimes does the trick in making fine edges disappear, but it can cause other anomalies in the process. Specifically, if the edge contains detail (which it often does), Defringe can cause more damage than it "fixes" because all those details get wiped out. On flat areas, however, Defringe is often less noticeable.

We discuss more powerful methods of defringing in "Step-by-Step Silhouettes," later in this chapter.

Remove Black/White Matte. We like the Remove Black/White Matte features on the Matte submenu because they're so easy to discuss: they just don't do much at all. In fact, we haven't come up with a single practical use for them. If you find one, please let us know!

Selections and Layers

The biggest, coolest feature new to Photoshop 3 is the ability to have multiple layers. There's very little difference between painting or editing on a

Figure 13-36 The effects of the Defringe command

The wood type is a floating selection over the gray background and contains a definite edge spill. Using Defringe with a setting of 1 pixel is subtle and destroys very little edge detail.

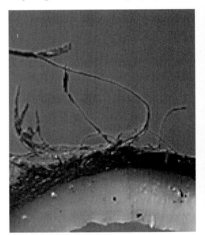 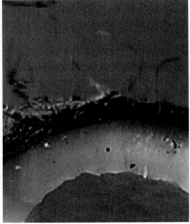 

The coconut is also floating on the background and contains a light edge spill. Here Defringe (again with a 1-pixel setting) wipes out the edge detail and effectively ruins the image.

background or on a layer. There is, however, a big difference in selecting on a layer. Plus, Layers opens up three new features: transparency masks, layer masks, and using layers *as* a mask.

Transparency Masks

Most of the time when you create a new layer, the background is transparent. When you paint on it or paste in a selection, you're making pixels opaque. Photoshop is always keeping track of how transparent each pixel is—fully transparent, partially transparent, or totally opaque. This map is called the *transparency mask* (see Figure 13-37).

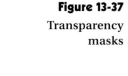

Figure 13-37
Transparency
masks

This area is transparent. ——

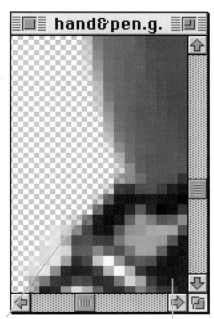

This area is partially opaque.   *This area is opaque.*

Remember the analogy we made to masking tape earlier in the chapter? The selection/channel/mask (they're all the same) acts like tape over or around your image. In this case, however, the mask doesn't represent how selected a pixel is; it's how transparent it is. You can have a pixel that's fully selected, but only 10-percent opaque (90-percent transparent).

Tip: Load the Transparency Mask. You can load the transparency mask for a layer as a selection in the Load Selection dialog box, but it's much faster to press Command-Option-T (but see the next tip for a caveat).

Tip: Loading the Transparency Mask versus Selecting and Moving. The problem with loading the transparency mask is that it doesn't select everything completely. Some pixels (those that are partially transparent) are only partially selected. So if you move the selection, you leave some behind (see Figure 13-38).

There's a better way to select *all* the nontransparent pixels—select all, then move the selection (nudge left then right with the arrow keys, for instance). Photoshop shrinks the selection to contain all nontransparent pixels (see Figure 13-39). And they're all fully selected.

Figure 13-38

Shrinking
selections

*Each time the Q's transparency
mask is selected and the image
is moved, some of the edge pixels get left behind (and the Q
gets a little thinner).*

Figure 13-39

Selecting pixels
on a layer

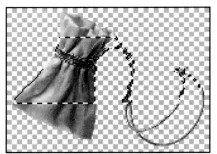

*As soon as this rectangular selection is moved, even one pixel, Photoshop
reduces the selection down to the edges of the nontransparent pixels (not the
transparency mask—a subtle but important difference).*

If you want to move everything on a layer, the easiest way is to use the
Move tool (with nothing selected).

Layer Masks

The task: to composite several images on a background. You've placed
each object on a separate layer, then used the techniques in this chapter
to carefully select and delete the portion of each object that must be hidden. But, after hours of sweat and mouse-burn, when you show the result to your art director, she says, "Can't you move this over a little and
crop out that, and we need a little more of this showing here . . . ."

Fortunately, you can use layer masks to avoid this sort of nightmare in your work. Layer masks are just like transparency masks—they determine how transparent the layer's pixels are—but you can see layer masks and, more important, edit them (see Figure 13-40).

Figure 13-40 Layer masks

The earth is on a separate layer above the background image of the car.

The layer mask

After the layer mask is applied to the Earth layer

If you had used layer masks in the example above, you would have smiled at your art director and made the changes quickly and painlessly. Here's how you do it.

Creating and editing layer masks. You can apply a layer mask to a layer by selecting Add Layer Mask from the Layers palette's popout menu (we sure wish we could find a keystroke for this). When a layer has a mask— it can only have one—the Layers palette displays a thumbnail of the mask (see Figure 13-41).

Figure 13-41

Adding a
layer mask

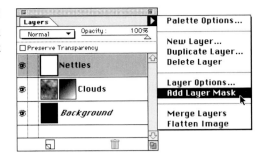

The first tricky thing about using layer masks is that it's often difficult to tell whether you're editing the layer or the layer mask. The only two differences are that the layer mask thumbnail has a dark border around it (on a high-resolution screen, the two borders look about the same; and if you have Previews turned off in the Layers palette, there's no difference here at all), and the document title bar says "Layer *X* Mask." We typically glance at the title bar about as often as we look in our car's rear-view mirror; it's a good way to keep a constant eye on what's going on around us.

Once you have a Layer Mask, you can edit it by clicking on its icon in the Layers palette (see "Tip: Layer Mask Keystroke," below).

We may be breaking a record for redundancy here, but it's important to remember that a mask is the same as a selection, which is the same as a channel. Underneath, they're all grayscale images. Editing a mask is as simple as painting with grays. Painting with black is like adding masking tape; it covers up part of the adjoining layer (making those pixels transparent). Painting with white takes away the tape and uncovers the layer's image. Gray, of course, partially covers the image.

Tip: Layer Mask Keystroke. When you're working on a layer, you can jump to the layer mask (make it "active" so all your edits are to the mask rather than the image) by pressing Command-~ (that's the tilde key). Then, to jump back to the layer itself, press Command-0 (zero).

Tip: Getting Rid of the Mask. As soon as you start editing layer masks, you're going to find that you want to turn the mask on and off, so you can get before-and-after views of your work. You can make the mask disappear temporarily by double-clicking on the Layer Mask icon in the Layers palette and turning on the Do Not Apply to Layer checkbox. Or, do it the fast way: Command-click on the Layer Mask icon.

If you want to hide the mask with extreme prejudice—that is, if you want to delete it forever—select Remove Layer Mask from the popout menu in the Layers palette (or, even faster, drag the Layer Mask icon to the Trash icon). Photoshop gives you a last chance to apply the mask to the layer. Note that if you do apply the mask, the masked (hidden) portions of the layer are actually deleted.

One last way to get rid of a mask: all layer masks go away when you merge or flatten layers.

Displaying layer masks. The second tricky thing about layer masks is that when you create one, you can't see it, so editing the mask can seem difficult. The trick is to Shift-click on the Layer Mask icon in the Layers palette. This displays the mask like any other channel. Of course, also like other channels, you can double-click on the icon to change the mask's color and opacity.

When you're ready to see the effects of your mask editing, Shift-click on the icon again to "hide" it.

If you want to *only* see the layer mask (as its own grayscale channel), Option-click on its icon. This is most helpful when touching up areas of the layer mask (it's sometimes hard to see the details in the mask when there's a background visible).

Tip: When Masks Move. As we explained back in Chapter 2, *Essential Photoshop Tips and Tricks*, the best way to move an image that's floating on a layer is to use the Move tool. However, note that the layer mask is tied to its layer, so when you move the layer with the Move tool, the layer mask moves, too.

While this is usually what you'd want, you can stop this from happening in the Layer Mask Options dialog box (double-click on the Layer Mask icon). When Position Relative To is set to Layer (it usually is), the mask moves with the layer. If you switch it to Image, the mask stays where it is until you move it yourself.

Layers as Masks

Layers not only have masks, but they can act as masks for other layers. The trick is to use "clipping groups." For instance, if you place a circle on a layer with a transparent background, then make a new layer and fill it entirely with some bizarre fractal design, the strange texture totally obliterates the circle. However, if you *group* the two layers together, the lower one acts as a mask for the higher one (so the fractal design *only* appears over the circle).

You can group layers together by turning on the Group with Previous Layer checkbox in the Layer Options dialog box (double-click on the layer tile in the Layers palette; see Figure 13-42). Or, even faster, Option-click between their tiles in the Layers palette (yes, the layers have to be next to one another, in either case).

Figure 13-42
Layer Options
dialog box

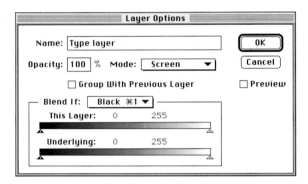

You don't have to stop with grouping two layers. You can group together as many as you want, though the bottommost layer always acts as the mask for the entire group (see Figure 13-43).

Figure 13-43
Layers as masks

Layer 1 (the apple) is acting as a mask for Layer 2 (the pineapple). Layer 2 also has a layer mask applied to it, so it doesn't obliterate the stem and leaf.

By the way, the Photoshop manuals say that you can't use different layer modes for each layer in a clipping group. Not true. You can adjust the opacity or mode for each layer, and they act just as they normally would.

Paths

After we explored the differences between bitmapped graphics (made of pixels) and object-oriented graphics (made of lines, curves, and other objects) back in Chapter 3, *Image Essentials*, we pretty much ignored the latter—until now. Photoshop does offer limited support for object-oriented drawing, via the Paths Palette. Photoshop lets you do several things with paths.

▶ Draw, edit, delete, and save paths

▶ Copy and paste paths between Photoshop and Adobe Illustrator

▶ Convert paths into selections

▶ Convert selections into paths

▶ Rasterize paths into pixels (stroking and filling)

▶ Save EPS images with a path applied as a clipping path

Curiously, the primary strength and weakness of Paths as a selection tool stem from the same attribute: paths have no connection to the pixels below them; they live on a separate mathematical plane in Photoshop, forever floating above those lowly bitmapped images.

The strength of this is that you can create, edit, and save paths without regard for the resolution of the image, or even for the image itself. You can create a path in the shape of a logo (or better yet, import the path from Illustrator or FreeHand) and drop it into any image. Then you can save it as a path in Photoshop, ask the program to rasterize the path (turn it into a bitmapped image) and drop it down into the pixel layers, or convert the path to a selection.

The weakness of paths' separateness is that paths used as selections can't capture the subtlety and nuance found in most bitmapped images. A path can't, for instance, have any partially selected pixels; you can only achieve hard-edged selections (see Figure 13-44).

Figure 13-44 Paths versus channels

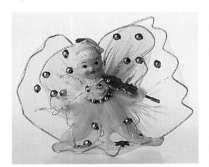

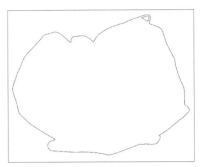

The original image

Selection masks can partially select pixels.

Paths are good at clean outlines, but they can't select image detail.

While we occasionally use paths for selections, we more typically use them for clipping images that will be placed in other programs (read: Page-Maker or QuarkXPress) for output. We discuss the use of clipping paths in some detail in Chapter 18, *Output Methods*.

Tip: The Space-Saving Paths Myth. There's a lot of folklore floating around in electronic imaging circles. One little piece of gossip is that you can save a lot of disk space if you convert your channels into paths before saving your document. Sorry, not true.

The myth's argument is that paths take up almost no space at all in a document (they're just tiny mathematical descriptions of lines and curves). However, what people miss is that Photoshop compresses simple alpha channels—ones that are mostly black and white—down to almost nothing, anyway. And any channel that you can successfully convert into a path (that is, without ruining essential elements of the channel) will most certainly have to be one of these simple types.

An alpha channel may take up between 40 and 100 K in a 6 MB document, while a path may only take 1 or 2 K. But if you're worried about saving 100 K, you might reconsider working with images in the first place.

Creating and Editing Paths

In Photoshop, Paths (as its name suggests) lets you draw paths. If you've ever used Adobe Illustrator or Macromedia FreeHand, you're already familiar with drawing and editing paths. Photoshop's Paths interface is most similar to Adobe Illustrator's (no surprise there; see Figure 13-45).

Figure 13-45
Paths

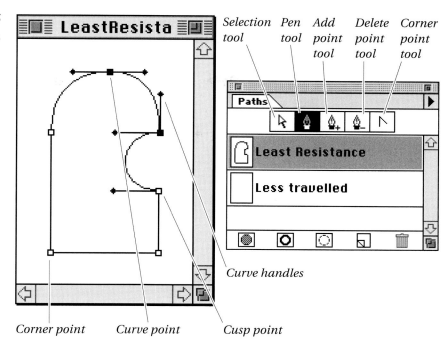

Selection tool   Pen tool   Add point tool   Delete point tool   Corner point tool

Curve handles

Corner point   Curve point   Cusp point

As we noted earlier, paths are xenophobic creatures, and they don't like mixing with those weird, bitmappy pixels. Photoshop keeps them separate by floating paths above the pixels on their own layer. This layer doesn't appear in the Layers palette, though. Rather, it's only visible when the path is selected in the Paths palette and the Paths palette is visible. (When the Paths palette is merged with other palettes—see "Palettes" in Chapter 2, *Essential Photoshop Tips and Tricks*—the palette must be the topmost palette for you to see the paths).

There are five tools within the Paths palette, but we only use one of them, using modifier keys to get to the rest.

Pen tool. The Pen tool (press T) is the only tool we ever select in the Paths palette. Once you've got that, you can access any of the other tools with the modifier keys (see Table 13-3). Without modifier keys, you can draw straight-line paths by clicking, or curved paths by clicking and dragging.

Selection tool. The Selection tool lets you select a point or points on the path. Once you have the Pen tool selected, you can jump to this tool by holding down the Command key, or by pressing T again (T toggles between the Pen and the Path Selection tool). As in Illustrator, if you hold down the Option key when you click on the path with this tool, all the points are selected (so, Command-Option works with the Pen tool).

Table 13-3
Paths palette tools

Press this with the Pen tool . . .	. . . to get this
Command	Path Selection tool
Control	Remove or Add Point tool*
Control-Command or Control-Option	Convert Point tool
Command-Option	Select all points on path

* If the cursor is over a point, it removes it; if over a path, it adds a point.

Once a point or a path is selected (note that you can select points with the Selection tool by clicking on them or by dragging a marquee around them), the Selection tool lets you move them. As in most other programs, if you hold down the Shift key, Photoshop only lets you move the points in 90- or 45-degree angles. If you hold down the Option key when you click and drag, Photoshop moves a copy of the entire path.

Add/Remove Point tool. We'll spare you the indignity of explaining this tool by saying only that it adds or removes a point on the path, depending on where your cursor is at the time (of course, you can't add a point where there is one already, or delete one that's not there). You can get the tool by holding down the Control key (not the Command key) with the Pen tool selected.

Convert Point tool. When you're working with the Pen tool, you can create a sharp corner by clicking, or a rounded corner by dragging. When you have two round corners on either side of a corner point, that corner point is called a *cusp point*. But what if you change your mind and want to make a corner into a curve, or a curve into a cusp?

The Convert Point tool lets you add or remove curve handles (those levers that stick out from the sides of curve or cusp points). If you click once on a point that has curve handles, the curve handles disappear (they get sucked all the way into the point), and the point becomes a corner. If you click and *drag* with the Convert Point tool, you can pull those handles out of the point, making the corner a curve.

Tip: Use Cusp Points. Eric Reinfeld, live from New York, tells us that he makes all his points cusp points while he's drawing his paths. Here's how.

1. To create the first two points of the path, just click and drag them to set the angle of the first curve.

2. All subsequent points on the path are created by clicking, dragging to set the angle of the previous curve, and then Option-dragging from the point to set the "launch" angle of the next curve.

3. Finally, to close the path (if you want it closed), Option-click or Option-drag—depending on if you want the final segment to be a curve or a straight line—on the first point of the path.

While it takes some getting used to, this technique gives you much more control over the angle and curve of each segment in the path because each point is independent of the ones on either side.

Tip: Paths as Guides. At most conferences we go to, someone comes up to us and asks how to get guide lines in Photoshop. It's understandable—most other graphics programs have guides. But Photoshop doesn't. Here's a handy tip for faking them, though: make vertical and horizontal paths (just click with the Pen tool, then Shift-click elsewhere to make a vertical or horizontal line). When you're done making paths, save the path by giving it a name (double-click on the Working Path tile in the Paths palette, or drag the Working Path tile onto the New Path icon).

When you want to hide the guide lines, click off the path's tile in the Paths palette or Shift-click on the tile. Of course, you don't only have to make the guides vertical or horizontal lines; you can make them any shape you can draw.

Tip: Arrow Keys and Paths. If you have pixels and a path selected at the same time, using the arrow keys moves the path, not the selection. The arrow keys move the path one pixel at a time (one screen pixel). Or, if you hold down the Shift key, the arrow keys move the path ten *image* pixels (not screen pixels). At 1:1 view, image pixels and screen pixels are the same thing, of course.

Tip: Drag Segments, Too. When editing your paths, don't get too caught up with having to move the paths' points and the curve handles around. As in FreeHand (and, belatedly, Illustrator) you can also drag the path segment itself. If it's a curved segment, Photoshop adjusts the curve handles on either side of it automatically. If there are no curve handles to adjust (if it's a straight-line segment), Photoshop actually moves the corner or cusp points on either side of the segment.

Tip: Connecting Paths. You've got two paths you want to connect? It's not as hard as you think.

1. Use the Path Selection tool to select one of the path's endpoints.

2. Switch to the Pen tool.

3. If you want that point to be a cusp, Option-drag out a handle.

4. Click and drag on the other path's endpoint. (Or alternatively, Option-drag to make it a cusp point.)

Tip: The Scissors Tool. Illustrator and FreeHand both have Scissors tools that let you cut a path in two. Photoshop does not. But there's always a workaround! Use the Add Point tool (or the Pen tool with the Control key held down) to add three points really close to each other where you want the break to be. Then select the middle point and delete it.

Tip: Flipping, Rotating, and Modifying Paths. Photoshop may be like Illustrator when it comes to its drawing tools, but by no means can it do everything that Illustrator or FreeHand can do. For instance, it can't do basic things like scale, shear, or rotate paths. Fortunately, Photoshop interfaces—if you'll forgive the verbing of the noun—with Illustrator almost seamlessly.

Select the path (Option-click with the Selection tool), copy it, paste it into Illustrator, and make the changes you want there. When you're done, copy and paste back into Photoshop (see Figure 13-46). (No, you don't have to turn on the Export Clipboard checkbox in General Preferences for this to work.) Note that you should be in Artwork mode (under the View menu) when you're in Illustrator, or else you won't be able to see the path's outlines.

Figure 13-46

Pasting paths from Illustrator

Just to set the record straight, we like FreeHand more than Illustrator, but Illustrator works better in conjunction with its sibling.

Tip: Paths Outside Image Boundaries. Paths are like floating selections in that they live on their own layer above the mundane world of pixels. They're also like floating selections in that you can drag them off the side of the image boundary and they don't get clipped (see "Tip: Floating Selections Don't Get Clipped," earlier in this chapter).

Paths to Selections

Paths for paths' sake are pretty useless (except for clipping paths, and that tip earlier on using paths as guides). Rather, once you've got a path, you typically need to convert it into a selection or rasterize it into pixels. Let's look at converting to selections first. Photoshop makes this process easy for you: you can convert a path to a selection in one of four ways.

► Select Make Selection from the Paths palette's popout menu.

► Click on the Make Selection icon (see Figure 13-47).

► Drag the path tile onto the Make Selection icon.

► Press Enter. (Enter does something different when you have a painting tool selected; see "Tip: Stroking on Enter," later in this chapter).

Of these, only the first automatically gives you the Make Selection dialog box (see Figure 13-48). But that doesn't mean you can't get there another way. If you hold down the Option key while dragging a path on top of, or clicking on, the Make Selection icon, Photoshop also displays this dialog box.

This dialog box lets you add, subtract, or intersect selections with selections you've already made (if there is no selection, these options are grayed out). It also lets you feather and anti-alias the selections (see "Tip: Name Paths with Feathers," below). The default for selections (if you don't go in and change this dialog box) is anti-aliasing, but not feathering.

Tip: Avoiding the Make Selection Dialog Box. You know we avoid dialog boxes and menu items whenever we can get away with it. So it should be no surprise at all that we tend to avoid the Make Selection dialog box.

Figure 13-47

Converting a path
to a selection

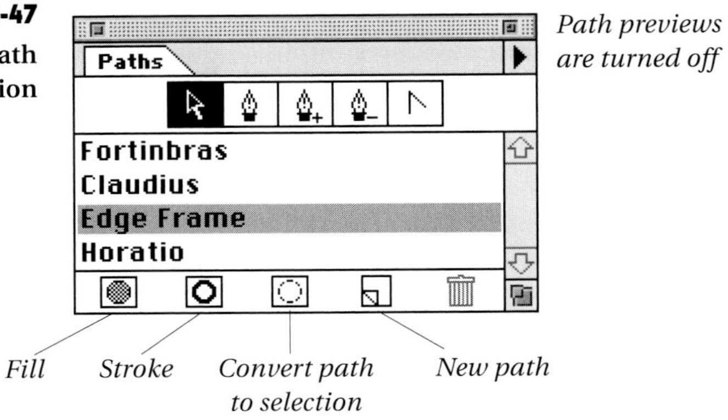

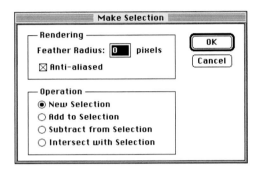

*Path previews
are turned off*

Fill   Stroke   Convert path
to selection   New path

Figure 13-48

Make Selection
dialog box

If you're using the Make Selection dialog box to add, subtract, or in-tersect paths, you can use these keystrokes instead.

▶ Shift-Enter adds the path's selection to the current selection.

▶ Command-Enter subtracts the selection.

▶ Shift-Command-Enter intersects the two selections.

Each of these works when clicking on the Make Selection icon or drag-ging the tile over the icon, too. It's just that the Enter key is so much easier. We still haven't found keystrokes for adding or removing feather-ing or anti-aliasing, though. (Caveat to this tip: as we explain below in "Rasterizing Paths," Enter does something different when you have a painting tool selected; in this case, you'd want to use the icons instead.)

Selections to Paths

To turn a selection into a path, choose Make Path from the popout menu in the Paths palette. When you ask Photoshop to do this, you're basically asking it to turn a soft-edged selection into a hard-edged one. Therefore, the program has to make some decisions about where the edges of the selection are.

Fortunately, the program gives you a choice about how hard it should work at this: the Tolerance field in the Make Path dialog box. The higher the value you enter, the shabbier the path's representation of the original selection. Values above 2 or 3 typically make nice abstract designs, but aren't very useful.

Tip: Making Paths with Icons. There's one more way to convert a selection into a new path: drag the Make Selection icon over the New Path icon in the Paths palette. This seemed really nonintuitive to us until we read the previous sentence and said, "Oh! Make Selection a New Path." It's still weird, but at least now we can remember it.

Note that this uses whatever tolerance value you last specified in the Make Path dialog box unless you hold down the Option key while dragging the icon, in which case it brings up the dialog box.

Rasterizing Paths

The second thing you can do with a path is rasterize it into pixels. As we said back in Chapter 3, *Image Essentials*, rasterizing is the process of turning an outline into pixels. Photoshop lets you rasterize paths in two ways: you can fill the path area and you can stroke the path.

Filling. To fill the path area with the foreground color, select Fill Path from the popout menu in the Paths palette, drag the path's tile to the Fill Path icon, or click on the Fill Path icon. Or, better yet, Option-click the icon, and the Fill Path dialog box appears. This dialog box is the same as the Fill dialog box, except that it also contains the Anti-alias checkbox and the Feather input field.

Stroking. Stroking the path works just the same as filling: you can select Stroke Path from the popout menu in the Paths palette, drag the path tile to the Stroke Path icon, or simply click on the icon (while a path is visible). When you first do this, Photoshop strokes the path with the Pencil tool. That's pretty lame, so before you do it again, change the tool it uses by Option-clicking on the Stroke Path icon.

Tip: Stroking on Enter. If you were paying attention, you noticed that we've said a few times that the Enter key sometimes does something other than converting paths to selections. When you have a painting tool selected in the Tool palette, pressing Enter strokes the path with that tool. We like using this because we almost always want a different painting tool than the one we wanted last time.

Tip: Working with Multiple Paths. You can have more than one path within a path "layer." For instance, you can have three circular paths together, and save them all under one path name. If you want to stroke or fill just one of those three, select it with the Path Selection tool (Option-click on the path to select the entire path) before stroking or filling.

Step-by-Step Silhouettes

Now that we've gone through all of Photoshop's tools for working with selections, channels, and masks, it's time to bring all those tools to bear. And the best place to demonstrate these tools in practice is in the process of creating silhouettes—that oh-so-common and (sometimes) oh-so-difficult of production techniques.

We'll start by showing how to create a simple silhouette, and work our way up to some of those images that seem like they're totally impossible.

The Spill's the Thing

If there's one thing that makes silhouettes difficult, it's the edge detail. In most cases (especially when you're trying to select fine details), some of the color from the image background spills over into the image you want. So when you drop the silhouetted image onto a different background (even white), the spill trips you up, making the image look artificial and out of place.

A Simple, Hard-Edged Silhouette

When the image you're trying to select has been photographed on a white background with good studio lighting so the background's free of colors that contaminate the edges, your selection is relatively easy. We typically jump in with several clicks of the magic wand along with Grow or Similar. We almost never get a perfect fit, however, so we usually clean

Figure 13-48 Silhouetting a hard-edged element

The original image. Our goal: to select the object from its background.	*The Magic Wand, Grow, and Similar get us most of the way there.*	*We switch to Quick Mask mode and lasso the areas that should not be included in the selection.*	*After fixing the edge detail (see below), we incorporate a new background into the image.*

  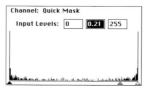 

The original selection left some edge pixels unselected, causing edge spill.	*We apply a small-radius Gaussian blur to the quick mask, which appears to worsen the edge spill.*	*A radical Levels gamma shift on the mask darkens the edge pixels.*	*When the mask is partially transparent, the dark areas around the edge tell us that there will be no edge spill.*

up the edges in Quick Mask mode. In Figure 13-48 we use Gaussian Blur and Levels to choke the edges of the selection mask. That way, we can be sure no background color spills over in our final composited image.

Pulling Selections from Channels

Trying to build a selection mask for the tree in Figure 13-49 with the basic selection tools would drive you to distraction faster than having to watch Barney reruns with your four-year-old. Instead, we found the essence of a great selection hiding in the color channels of the image. While you can often pull a selection mask from a single channel of the image, in this case we made duplicates of both the blue and green channels. Then, using Levels, we pushed the tree to black and the background to white. After combining the two channels, it only took a little touch-up to complete the mask.

Figure 13-49 Creating subtle masks from multiple channels

The original. Our goal: to select the tree and make it more green.

The blue channel has the best contrast between sky and tree.

The green channel has the best contrast between sky and grass.

We copy the blue channel and force the sky to white and the tree to black with the Levels dialog box.

A similar move on the green channel creates a mask for the lower part of the tree.

We delete the "garbage" areas from each mask with the Brush and Lasso. To edit the channels better, we make them and the color channels visible at the same time.

We use Calculate (Add) to merge the two channels into one, providing the final mask.

After loading the selection mask, we use curves to brighten and saturate the greens in the tree, and pull back the reds and blues slightly.

Removing Spill from Fine-Edged Selections

The finer the pixel selection, the harder it is to remove edge spill. It doesn't get much tougher than the detail in Figure 13-50, so we used a variation of a trick Greg Vander Houwen taught us: replacing the border pixels with pixels from a snapshot. In this case, once we realized how bad the edge spill was in the composited image, we took a snapshot of the background layer by itself. Then we built a border mask for the dandelion with the Border command and cleaned it up in Quick Mask mode.

Figure 13-50 Removing edge spill in detailed areas by filling from a snapshot

The original image. The goal: to composite the dandelion onto another background.

A selection mask created using Color Range with many sample points and a low Fuzziness level.

We take a snapshot of the background, then paste the dandelion as a floating selection. The edge spill is obvious.

We use Border with a large radius, then feather the resulting selection.

We fill the border selection from the background snapshot, with the Mode set to Lighten.

The green fringe disappears, without sacrificing edge detail.

Finally, we filled that border selection with the snapshot pixels from the background. To get rid of dark green pixels at the edges, we set the fill mode to Lighten. This doesn't touch the lighter pixels in the dandelion. In other images we might have used Normal, Darken, Hue, or Color; it depends on the relationship between the foreground and the background colors.

Figure 13-51 Painting out edge spill using layers, a border mask, and Preserve Transparency

The original image

A mask created using Color Range

The trees are copied onto a layer above the sunset image. The blue spill ruins the compositing effect.

A closeup of the composited image shows the blue edge spill from the original sky.

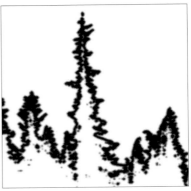

We create a border mask by using Border on the transparency mask, then running a Gaussian blur.

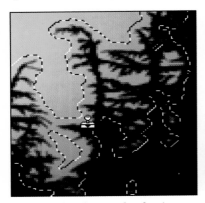

With the border mask selection loaded and Preserve Transparency turned on, we rubber stamp dark interior pixels over the blue pixels.

The final image after the blue edge spill has been removed.

A closeup of the final image.

Removing Spill with Preserve Transparency

Edge spill is insidious, and—as we saw in the last example—can be a disaster when compositing images. Here's one more method of removing spill that we like a lot. If you place the pixels on a transparent layer, you can make use of the Preserve Transparency feature in the Layers palette to "paint away" the edge spill.

In the example in Figure 13-51, the color from the blue sky is much too noticeable around the composited trees. So we place the trees on a layer and build a selection that encompasses just their edges. This step is really just a convenience—it makes our job of painting out the edge spill easier. With Preserve Transparency turned on, we select the Rubber Stamp tool and clone interior colors over the blue edge pixels. In some areas, we also use Curves to pull the blue out (because our border selection is feathered, these moves affect *only* the pixels we're after).

This is a trick you can use with all sorts of variations. If the edge color is relatively flat, you might be able to use the Brush tool (we usually add a little noise after painting in order to match the background texture); this is also an area where it behooves you to test out different Apply modes (Lighten, Multiply, and so on).

Tip: Complex Masks with BlueScreens. After working with Photoshop's selection tools for a while, you begin to know instinctively when you're up against a difficult task. For instance, trying to create a selection mask for a woman in a gauzy dress, with her long, wispy hair blowing in the wind could be a nightmare. And if you have to perform twenty of these in a day . . . well . . . 'nuf said. One method of creating ultra-complex masks like these is to shoot the subject against a bluescreen and let a third-party filter, such as Ultimatte's PhotoFusion (or the newer, simpler version, PhotoFusion Lite), do the work for you (see Figure 13-52).

Using bluescreens is not for everyone, but if you're doing heavy-duty catalog work, this method can be a lifesaver.

Masks, Channels, and Life

While you can get by with performing global manipulations on images, the vast majority of images you'll work with require making a selection. We hope that after seventy pages we've done more to allay your fears

Figure 13-52
Complex masks with
PhotoFusion

Selection mask created with the
Color Range command

Selection mask created with
Ultimatte's PhotoFusion

than to cause you panic when selecting pixels in your image. Remember the two golden rules of selections:

▶ Masks, channels, and selections are all the same thing.

▶ You can (and often should) edit a selection after you've made it.

With those firmly planted in your mind, you'll have no problems as you enter the next chapter, in which we discuss some of the most common Photoshop production tasks, most of which require selecting and building masks.

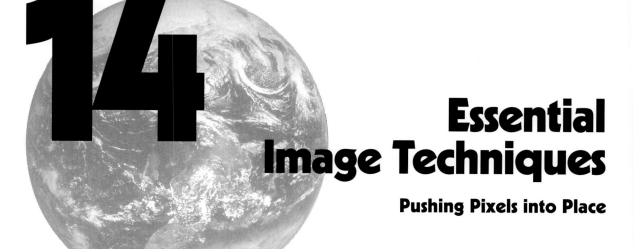

Essential Image Techniques

Pushing Pixels into Place

The vast majority of Photoshop users stare at this program many hours a day, doing the same sort of image manipulation over and over again. Retouch the background of this photo; convert this color image to grayscale; add a drop shadow behind this car; silhouette this pineapple; put a new background behind this amazing kitchen aid; incorporate this logo into that image.

In this chapter we offer a whole mess of tips and tricks to make your images fly a little faster, and perhaps make them a little more fun to manipulate, as well. The chapter is broken down into a hodgepodge of common Photoshop issues: retouching, silhouetting, working with object-oriented graphics, and so on. Read 'em and reap!

Taking Care of the Basics

The two most important techniques in image editing are, in many respects, the simplest to accomplish.

▶ Look at every pixel.

▶ Build base camps.

Look at every pixel. Try to get in the habit of returning to 1:1 view frequently, so you can get a sense of what's going on in your image. People often zoom in closer than this, thinking "the closer the better." Not so. Sure, you can see the pixels, but you're not really seeing the image (Zen koan or sage advice? You be the judge).

If you can't fit the image on your screen, start at the upper-left corner (press the Home key) and use the Page Down key to move down until you reach the bottom. Scroll once to the right (click in the horizontal scroll bar), and start over. We can't overstress the importance of this procedure.

If you like working zoomed in or out and can't be bothered with getting back to 1:1, check out "Tip: Use New Window" in Chapter 2, *Essential Photoshop Tips and Tricks*.

Build a base camp. Our friend and colleague Greg Vander Houwen (you've probably read about him elsewhere in this tome) turned us on to the mountaineering phrase "base camp." The concept is simple: while you're working on an image, don't just save every now and again; instead, create an environment that you can return to at any time. That means using Save As and Save a Copy at strategic moments in your image manipulation. It also means saving your curves before applying them, and sometimes even writing down the various settings you use in dialog boxes (like Unsharp Mask).

When you've built a solid base camp, you can always return to it, get your bearings, and start up the hill again. As Greg noted, "I might build a few base camps along the way, depending on how high the mountain is."

Tip: Naming or Timing Your Curves. If (or should we say, "when"?) you're saving your curves or base camp images, file management is key. We use three techniques to keep track of these files.

▶ For each image we work on, we keep all our base camps, curves, and additional files in one folder. That way, they don't get mixed up with other images we're working on.

▶ We add a numbered suffix to the end of the file name. For example, the first may be .01, the next .02, and so on.

▶ While on the Finder's desktop, we view the folder by Date under the View menu (which is the same as clicking on Last Modified in the title bar of the window). Even when two files are saved within the same minute, the Mac can show that one was saved later than the other.

The Color of Grayscale

Even though many more people are printing in color these days, most people are not. Therefore, one of the most common procedures in Photoshop is converting color images into grayscale. If you convert images by selecting Grayscale from the Mode menu, there's a good chance you're not getting the best-quality image you can. Most color images contain a usable grayscale version, but you often have to wrestle to find it. Getting a good grayscale out of a CMYK image is particularly challenging, but even with RGB images it isn't always easy.

Let's first take a look at three relatively obvious ways to get grayscale information out of a color file.

Convert to Grayscale. The most obvious way to convert an image to grayscale is simply to choose Grayscale from the Mode menu. When you do so, Photoshop mixes the red, green, and blue channels together, weighting the red, green, and blue channels differently (according to a standard formula that purports to account for the varying sensitivity of the eye to different colors). The weighting is 30-percent red, 59-percent green, and 11-percent blue. It works (more or less) at least on some images, but the results are often far from ideal.

For instance, there are many images in which this weighting loses more information than it keeps. Remember, detail is in the differences between pixels, and if the gray pixels are too similar, you can lose important information.

Take a channel, any channel. Look at the individual color channels in the image. Occasionally you'll find the perfect grayscale image sitting in one of them. Then you can copy and paste it out, or use Calculations to pull it into a new document (see "Tip: Saving Off Channels Using Calculate" in Chapter 13, *Selections*). Or just delete the other two channels by displaying the channel you want, then selecting Grayscale from the Mode menu.

Convert to Lab. For a more literal rendering of the luminance values in an image, you can convert the image to Lab, then discard the color channels (A and B). This gives you quite a different rendering than a straight grayscale conversion. Be careful, though; as we explain in Chapter 7, *Color Correction*, a mode change from RGB to Lab results in some data loss.

Devious methods. Sometimes none of the above approaches work. That's where Photoshop's Calculations command comes in (see Figure 14-1). The Calculations dialog box is one of Photoshop's scarier-looking features, but its operation is very similar to the way Layers works. The main difference is that you're carrying out operations between single channels rather than between full-color images.

Figure 14-1
Calculations
dialog box

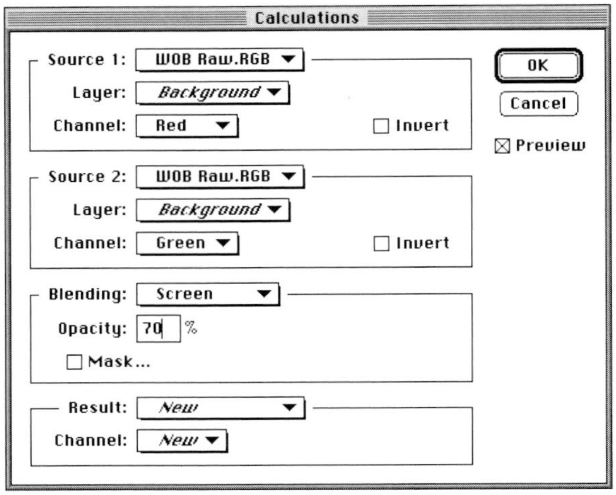

The options on the Blending submenu are the same as the ones in the Layers palette. The Opacity field serves the same function as the Layers palette's Opacity slider.

Tip: Shrink the Dialog Box. The Calculations dialog box is not only scary, it's also big (especially on David's small screen at home). If you hold down the Option key when you choose Calculations, you get a smaller version of the dialog box. It contains all the same options, but it uses smaller type and consumes a lot less monitor real estate.

Calculating images. The Calculations command lets you mix and match new grayscale images from the existing channels. In Figure 14-2, we show one image's individual color channels and the results obtained using the simple methods described earlier. None of them make a particularly good monochrome version of the image.

We could proceed in any number of ways, but here's one that works well. We present it as an example rather than as the "correct" solution—

Figure 14-2 Finding the hidden grayscale

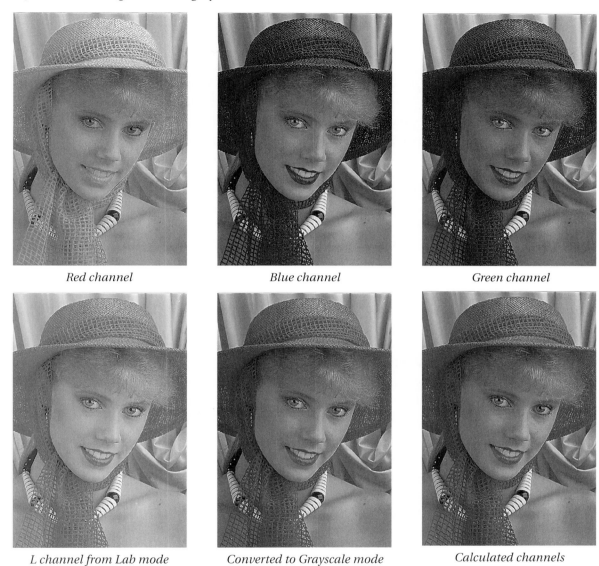

Red channel   *Blue channel*   *Green channel*

L channel from Lab mode   *Converted to Grayscale mode*   *Calculated channels*

you could achieve similar results using several different methods. Again, we encourage you to experiment.

1. We start out by screening the blue channel into itself at 70-percent opacity, creating a new channel 4. We choose the blue channel as our starting point because it has closest-to-normal contrast, other than being very dark. The lipstick and hat in the green channel are almost black, and the red channel just looks strange.

2. In a second calculation, we apply the red channel to channel 4, using Hard Light at 40-percent opacity, to create channel 5. This lightens up the midtones, and fixes the unsettling effect created by the eyes being much lighter than the skin.

3. At this point we have a decent image, but the contrast is still too harsh, and the hat and lipstick are still a little dark. We take the red channel (the one with the least contrast) and screen it into channel 5 at 30-percent opacity. Rather than creating a new channel, we select a new document as the destination.

We settle on 30-percent opacity as providing pleasing contrast, but anything in the 10-to-50-percent range gives a decent image. At settings higher than 50 percent the image is too flat, and at less than 10 percent it's too contrasty, but even fairly large changes in the opacity on this calculation have relatively subtle effects on the overall contrast.

The result is a creditable monochrome rendering of the color original. If the hidden grayscale is hard to find in your color image, experiment with Calculations. You may be surprised at what you can find.

Tip: Use Preview in Calculations. At first glance, the Calculations dialog box seems a lot less interactive than the Layers palette. But it doesn't have to be that way. When you turn on the Preview checkbox, you can actually watch how the various combinations work in real time (or at least as fast as your machine can compute).

For instance, changing Opacity can be a real bear, but when you turn on Preview, you get to see the effect before pressing OK. Then you can type a new Opacity setting almost as quickly as you can move the slider in the Layers palette.

Retouching

Every time we get into an argument (sorry, we mean "discussion") about the ethics of digital imaging, we find that everyone has their own tolerance level of what can or should be changed in an image. We've heard photographers argue convincingly that each time you manipulate an image, especially when you add or remove real objects, it erodes the credibility of photography as a representation of the real. But we also recognize that people have to make a living, and sometimes (for better or worse) that involves improving the purported reality the photograph represents. We don't have an answer to this debate, but we urge you to at least consider the question.

In this section, we want to relay a few key pointers that we've learned over the years about retouching images, in the hope that they'll make you more efficient in retouching to whatever degree is right for you.

Tip: Use Feathering. Often, the smallest thing can make the biggest difference. Feathering, for example (see Figure 14-3). When you're retouching a local, selected area—whether you're adjusting tone, painting, using a filter, or editing pixels—it's often important to feather the selection (see "Feathering and Anti-aliasing" in Chapter 13, *Selections*).

Feathering is like applying a Gaussian Blur to the edges of a selection: it blends the selected area smoothly into the rest of the image. How much to feather depends entirely upon the image and its resolution, but even a little feathering (two or three pixels) is much better than nothing.

Figure 14-3 Feathering as a retouching tool

This trick only works when covering an element with an area of uniform color and texture.

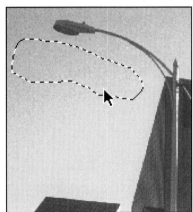
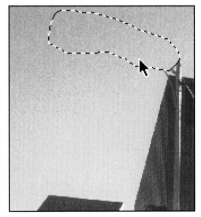

Make a loose selection with the Lasoo tool and feather 4 pixels.

Command-Option-drag the selection to another location.

Option-drag back to cover the original. The feathering ensures a seamless edge.

Tip: A Myriad of Small Spots. Mildew, dust, corrosives, abrasive surfaces, or even a mediocre scanner can cause hundreds or thousands of tiny white or black spots in an image. And when it comes to sharpening, these spots can pop out at you like stars on the new moon. If you're like us, you're already cringing at the thought of rubber-stamping all those dots out.

However, Stephen Johnson showed us a technique that can stamp out thousands of spots in a single move. It works best in flat areas without much texture or detail.

1. Select the area with the spots, and feather the selection.

2. Float the feathered selection (Command-J).

3. In the Layers palette, set the mode of the floating selection to Darken (for white or light-gray spots) or Lighten (for black or dark-gray spots).

4. Use the arrow keys to move the floating selection left, right, up, or down by one or two pixels (see Figure 14-4). The number of pixels you need to move the floating selection depends on how large the spots are.

Figure 14-4
Getting rid of spots

Original image

Screen capture of a feathered selection around some of the white spots

After the selection is floated, set to Darken, and moved over two pixels

The final despotted image

However, if you move too far, the duplication effect becomes more obvious than the spots, defeating the purpose.

You're effectively getting rid of thousands of spots at the same time. You still may have to use the Rubber Stamp to get rid of a few artifacts and some of the larger spots, but most of your work has already been done.

Tip: Tissue Overlay Channels. Greg Vander Houwen showed us one of the more innovative ways to use alpha channels: as a place to store his client's retouching notes (see Figure 14-5). If you scan your client's tissue overlay and add it to your image as an alpha channel, you can see the notes as you work.

When you want to see the client's notes, you can make that channel visible. When you want them hidden (you know what's best for your client, right?), just hide the channel by clicking on its eyeball in the Channels palette.

Figure 14-5

Channels as tissue overlays

Rubber Stamp

The Rubber Stamp tool (please don't ask us why it's called that; last time we used a rubber stamp was in KidPix) is the Swiss army knife of retouching tools. You control which tool you're working with at any time using the Option popup menu in the Rubber Stamp Options palette. And don't overlook the Sample Merged checkbox. When checked, it lets you clone pixel information from other layers.

Tip: Resetting the Rubber Stamp. Most people use the Rubber Stamp tool in Clone (aligned) mode all the time. But if you do use the other modes (Pattern, From Snapshot, From Saved, or Impressionist)—and there are plenty of good reasons to use them—you can switch back to Clone (aligned) mode by Option-clicking on an open image.

Tip: Unlimited Cloning Supply. Don't let the boundaries of your image's window restrict you. If you want to clone from another open document or from the Scratch palette, go right ahead and do it. You don't have to switch documents, as long as you have a large enough monitor.

Tip: Keep Jumping Around. The single biggest mistake people make when using the Rubber Stamp tool to clone from one area to another is dragging the mouse in a painting fashion. You should almost never paint when cloning. Instead, dab here and there with a number of clicks.

A second mistake is continuing to clone from the same area. Keep changing the source point that you're cloning (the point on which you Option-click). For example, if you're erasing some specks of dust on someone's face, don't just clone from one side of the specks. Erase one speck from pixel information to the left; erase the second speck from the right, and so on. That way, you avoid creating repeating patterns, and make the retouch less obvious (see Figure 14-6).

There are times, of course, when both these pieces of advice should be chucked out the window. For example, if you're rebuilding a straight line by cloning another parallel line in the image, you'd be hard-pressed to clone it by any other method than painting in the whole line.

Tip: Alignment via Opacity and Mode. Back in Chapter 13, *Selections*, we told you that floating selections are really just temporary layers that let you use all the features in the Layers palette. This turns out to be very helpful when retouching images on a grand scale.

For example, a photographer on an online service recently wrote, "I was working on a group portrait of a family in which everyone's expressions were great except the teenage son's, whose eyes were closed. There was another shot in the same basic pose where he looked good, so of course I decided to replace the head in image A with the one from image B."

When doing this kind of massive image editing, it's often difficult to align the new image with the old.

Figure 14-6

Cloning with
the Rubber Stamp

The original image

The final image after retouching

Close-up of the original image. Note the dark stain on the door.

Using the Rubber Stamp tool like a paintbrush (making long dragging movements) can cause obvious repeated patterns.

Instead, use the Rubber Stamp tool with lots of little clicks, often picking up a new "origin" spot by Option-clicking.

One way to ensure their alignment is to change Opacity in the Layers palette to 50 percent or less, so you can see the image underneath. In this example, the photographer positioned the top head's eyes with the original image's eyes (using the arrow keys to nudge one pixel at a time; see Figure 14-7). Finally, he set Opacity back to 100 percent, and retouched the edges of the selection.

While he could have touched up the edges using the tricks in Chapter 13, *Selections* (we particularly like using the tip "The Lasso Placeth and

Taketh Away" for this sort of thing), in this case he used the Rubber Stamp tool, setting the Option to From Saved.

Note that instead of changing the opacity, you can change the floating selection's Apply mode. When trying to align two objects in an image, we often set the mode to Darken or Lighten. Then we watch the pixels lighten and darken, to give us clues.

Dust and Scratches

The Dust and Scratches filter isn't all that useful for removing dust and scratches. It removes them, but it destroys so much detail and texture in the process that the cure is generally worse than the disease. We're still experimenting with it—we think of it as being a reverse Unsharp Mask filter, which should surely be useful for *something*. The best use we've found so far is removing halftone patterns when rescreening (see "Re-screens," later in this chapter).

Figure 14-7 Aligning floating selections

The original image

When the new selection is dropped over the original image, it's hard to see where it should be placed.

Opacity set to 60 percent so that positioning is easier.

The final image

One situation where it may prove useful is in blurring the A and B channels in Lab images to get rid of digital-camera artifacts or film grain (see "Sharpening Channels" in Chapter 8, *Sharpening*, for a discussion of this technique). The Dust and Scratches filter is slower than the Gaussian Blur filter, but the Threshold slider makes it more controllable.

Tip: Maintain the Texture. The danger with these retouching techniques is that they tend to destroy texture, and hence appear unnatural. You can sometimes simulate texture that's been lost by running the Add Noise filter on the affected area at a low setting. However, it's generally better to keep a close eye on what's happening to your texture as you retouch. (Also, see the tip "Snapshot Patterns," below.)

Snapshots

When we hear the word "snapshot," we usually think of quick, low-quality photographs that people take on holiday. But a Photoshop snapshot is a high-quality feature well worth exploring.

When you choose Take Snapshot from the Edit menu, Photoshop saves a temporary duplicate of your image in memory. This gives you an extra level of undo; take a snapshot of the image, do something weird to the file, then—if you don't like what you did—you can revert to the snapshot instead of reverting all the way back to the file saved on disk.

But there's more to snapshots than this. Here are a few pointers to some of the cool things you can do with this feature.

Tip: Selective Snapshots. Snapshots don't have to contain your entire image. If you select an area before you choose Take Snapshot, Photoshop only stores that selection (see Figure 14-8). Selecting a small area to snap takes less memory than saving a snapshot of the entire image.

Tip: Snapshot Patterns. It was Luanne Cohen who first showed us this step-by-step procedure for applying textures or patterns to an area.

1. Draw a rectangular marquee surrounding the area to which you want to apply the texture.

2. Fill the area with that pattern or texture by pasting it in, filling it, or whatever.

Figure 14-8 Selecting before snapping

The original image

*A snapshot is taken just of
this rectangular selection.*

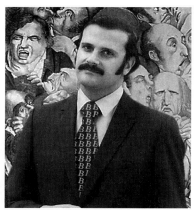

*The background and the
tie have both been changed.*

*The whole image was selected
and filled with the snapshot.*

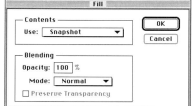

*You can fill a selection with the
snapshot image in the Fill dialog
box (Shift-Delete).*

3. While the area is still selected, choose Take Snapshot from the Edit menu.

4. If you used Fill to fill the area, select Undo from the Edit menu (Command-Z). This gets rid of the pattern fill. If you pasted the texture in, you can just press Delete to delete it, because it's floating above the original image pixels.

5. Select the Rubber Stamp tool and choose Snapshot from the Option popup menu in the Rubber Stamp Options palette.

6. Now as you paint with the Rubber Stamp tool, you can adjust brush size, opacity, and mode. For instance, when painting textures, it's often helpful to paint in Multiply or Screen mode, adjusting Opacity as you wish (see Figure 14-9).

Figure 14-9 Painting with textures

The original image

The painting is pasted over the photo, and while it's still floating, we take a snapshot.

After the floating selection is deleted, we paint part of it back in with the Rubber Stamp tool.

If you want to paint with a defined pattern instead, you can forget the whole snapshot idea and just set the Rubber Stamp Option popup menu to Pattern (aligned).

Tip: Copying Through Layers. We often find ourselves wanting to copy not just one layer, but every visible layer of a selection from a multilayered image. If you find yourself in this boat, don't go through the hassle of flattening or merging layers, copying, and then reverting. Here's a quick technique that gives you the same effect.

1. Select the area you want to copy.

2. Take a snapshot.

3. Choose the Background layer in the Layers palette, and float the selection (press Command-J).

4. Fill the floated selection with the snapshot (press Shift-Delete to get to the Fill dialog box, then set the Use popup menu to Snapshot).

The result is a floating selection that merges all the visible layers. You can now move it, or copy it to the clipboard.

Objects versus Pixels

Wasn't it Robert Frost who said, "Bitmaps are bitmaps, and objects are objects, and never the twain shall meet"? As we've seen with Photoshop's Paths features, they may not meet, but they certainly interact. In this section, we want to look at how you can convert images between pixels and objects (such as paths or Illustrator documents), and why you'd want to.

Open versus Place

We all know that clients are notorious for asking the impossible. They want Pantone colors in the middle of a process-color image (but they don't want to pay for another ink). They want a tiny photograph blown up to poster size (retaining the sharpness, of course). Or they want their crisp, clean logos added to a product shot. Wait—that last one isn't so hard, after all.

You can import object-oriented graphics (such as those from Illustrator or FreeHand) into Photoshop on one condition: they must be in Adobe Illustrator format (see "Opening Non-Illustrator EPSes," below). While this would, at first glance, appear to be a marketing decision (to support only Adobe products) the truth is that it's more of a technical one. Illustrator files have set the standard for PostScript compatibility; they're sort of the lowest common denominator of PostScript files.

There are two ways to import Illustrator EPS files: Open and Place.

Open. When you select an Illustrator-type EPS file in the Open dialog box, Photoshop recognizes it as such and gives you additional options (see Figure 14-10). If Photoshop doesn't recognize it, it only lets you open the PICT or TIFF preview of the EPS file (usually only a 72-dpi representation of the image).

The additional options you get with an Illustrator-type EPS let you specify the resolution and size of the final bitmap image. When you press OK, Photoshop creates a new document and *rasterizes* the EPS (turns it into a bitmap). Any areas of the EPS that don't have a fill specified come in as transparent.

Figure 14-10

Opening an Illustrator-type EPS file

```
┌─────────────────────────────────────────────────┐
│          Rasterize Adobe Illustrator Format       │
│  ┌─ Image Size: 185K ──────────┐    ┌────────┐   │
│  │                              │    │   OK   │   │
│  │  Width:  [22.92]  [ picas ▼] │    └────────┘   │
│  │                              │    ┌────────┐   │
│  │  Height: [7.42]   [ picas ▼] │    │ Cancel │   │
│  │                              │    └────────┘   │
│  │  Resolution: [200] [pixels/inch ▼]            │
│  │                              │                 │
│  │  Mode:   [ Grayscale ▼]      │                 │
│  └──────────────────────────────┘                 │
│                                                   │
│       ☒ Anti-aliased   ☒ Constrain Proportions    │
└─────────────────────────────────────────────────┘
```

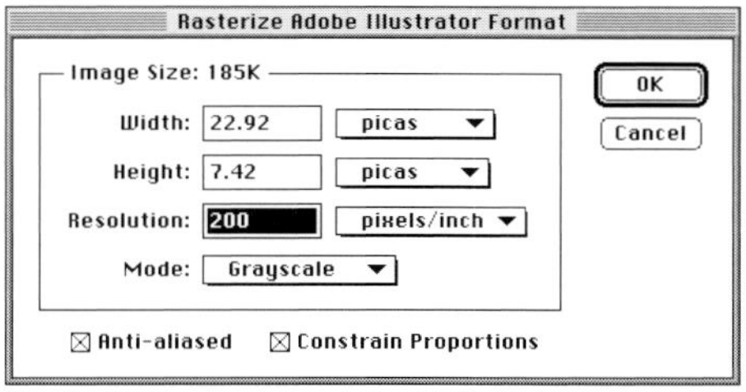

Tip: Opening Previews. You can, if you want, open the PICT or TIFF preview of an EPS file instead of rasterizing the EPS itself. This might come in handy, for instance, if you need a placeholder for the EPS, but the whole EPS file would be enormous and take too long to rasterize. For non-Illustrator-type EPS files, opening the PICT preview is the norm (it's all you can do). For an Illustrator-type EPS, however, you have to take two additional steps.

1. Turn on the Show All Files checkbox in the Open dialog box.

2. Select EPS PICT Preview (or EPS TIFF Preview) from the Format menu.

    Now when you open the file, you only get the low-resolution preview.

Place. When you select Place rather than Open, Photoshop drops the EPS file into your current document and then lets you scale it to fit your needs. When you're finished scaling the image, move the cursor over the image until it turns into a gavel, then "hammer" it down. It's not until you do this that Photoshop really rasterizes the image into pixels, so scaling it won't degrade the final image.

We almost always place Illustrator-type EPS images rather than opening them; we just find it more convenient. Note that placing an EPS on a new, transparent layer is the same as opening the EPS, except that you can scale the image before Photoshop rasterizes it.

Tip: Nonproportional Scaling. Once you've placed an EPS file, you can grab one of its corner points and scale it to whatever size you want. It seems, however, that you can't scale it nonproportionally, but you can: hold down the Command key while scaling to break the height/width constraint. If you want to constrain it to the original proportions, hold down the Command and Shift keys while scaling.

Maintaining Objects

What we'd really like is for Photoshop to let us open or place an EPS, and give us paths instead of bitmaps. Unfortunately, we can't figure out how to do that. You can, however, *paste* a path from Illustrator into Photoshop (see "Paths" in Chapter 13, *Selections*).

Tip: Making Grids. Russell Brown, senior art director at Adobe, showed us that you can import more than just artwork from Illustrator. He uses Illustrator to create guidelines and grids (making the lines thin—about .5 point), then pastes those lines onto a new, transparent layer in Photoshop. This is especially helpful when laying out a whole page in Photoshop.

In fact, this is one of the only times that we would turn *off* the Anti-alias checkbox when rasterizing Illustrator artwork. Remember, you don't have to create the layer first—you can paste in the guides, then Option-double-click on the Floating Selection tile in the Layers palette to turn the selection into a layer.

Then, when you want to see the guides, make that layer visible. When you want to hide them, click on the eyeball in the Layers palette.

You can do the same thing by pasting in the guides as paths, instead of rasterizing them. The only problem is that we occasionally find it difficult to see the paths, which defeats the purpose.

Opening Non-Illustrator EPSes

As we said earlier, the only way to get a non-Illustrator EPS into Photoshop is by reading its PICT preview (which is a pretty lame method, for most purposes). However, you can bring *any* EPS into Photoshop by converting it into a bitmap first. This is called *rasterizing*, or "ripping" (for "Raster Image Processing") the PostScript image. Until recently, the options for doing this were pretty scarce. However, we now regularly use two programs to rip files.

▶   **Transverter Pro**, from TechPool, is a low-end solution to rasterizing PostScript images. It's relatively inexpensive, and it almost always works. If you are only occasionally bringing EPS files into Photoshop, Transverter Pro is probably for you.

 If you use Transverter Pro, you have the additional option of converting the EPS into an Illustrator file which Photoshop can read. But there's really little need to do this (and it's in this area that we've had the most trouble with the software). Converting the EPS into a TIFF is usually a better route to take.

▶ **Epilogue**, from Total Integration, is a high-end solution to your rasterizing needs (see Figure 14-11). It's significantly more expensive, but it's a true Adobe CPSI RIP, which means that it's really solid, as long as you have enough RAM and scratch drive space. This is the tool most professional color houses and service bureaus opt for.

Figure 14-11

Epilogue

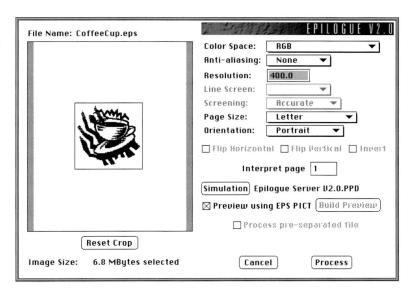

Tip: The TIFF Export XTension. If you're using QuarkXPress and want more resolution than the 72-ppi PICT preview, but don't want to spring for Transverter Pro or Epilogue, you might look at the TIFF Export XTension from Vision's Edge. It lets you save TIFFs directly out of XPress that you can open in Photoshop, and you can specify resolution up to 288 ppi.

Tip: Add Your Page Layout to Images. We suppose many advertising agencies are doing this now, but it was Kurt Karlenzig at an agency in Tokyo who showed us how effective it can be to use Photoshop to build photorealistic comps of ads. The client can see their ad in place—on a billboard or a bus, or wherever—before the ad is even created (see Figure 14-12).

Figure 14-12 Adding your page layout to images

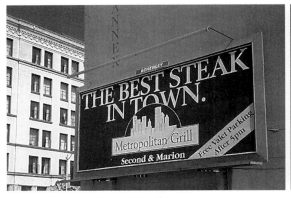

The original image

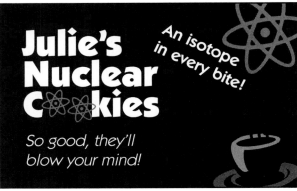

The ad created in QuarkXPress and saved as an EPS

The ad incorporated into the street scene,
ready to show the client

You can create the ad in PageMaker or XPress, as usual, then save it as an EPS. Once you rasterize it and import it into Photoshop, you can rotate it, scale it, and so on, so that it fits the ad space.

Silhouettes for Page Layout

The old art of cutting silhouettes out of paper is mostly gone now, though it lives on at street fairs and tourist spots. If you've ever seen someone cutting one of these, you know how painstaking a process it can be. We wonder why, then, people expect creating a silhouette in Photoshop to be as easy as snapping their fingers. Far from it: masking out the background of an image—leaving only the foreground object—is a difficult proposition. Unfortunately, it's something that many of us in production work have to do every day.

The biggest problem is often not that of making a selection to silhouette (we cover a lot of selection and silhouetting techniques in Chapter 13, *Selections*). Rather, it's bringing that selection into a page-layout program without unnaturally harsh edges resulting. In this section we'll discuss getting silhouettes to print properly from PageMaker or XPress.

QuarkXPress and PageMaker handle silhouetted images differently. And it makes a *big* difference whether you use EPS or TIFF files. (For more on getting images into PageMaker and QuarkXPress, see Chapter 18, *Output Methods*.) In PageMaker, 8- and 24-bit TIFFs are always opaque rectangles, even when the background of a TIFF image is white (as in a silhouette). XPress, on the other hand, sees white backgrounds in TIFF images as transparent (sort of).

If you import a TIFF image with a white background into an XPress picture box and set the background of that picture box to None (transparent), XPress attempts to figure out what white areas in the picture are *supposed* to be transparent. However, it's pretty clumsy at doing this, and the result is often very jaggy edges (see Figure 14-13). There are two reasons for this.

Figure 14-13
Transparent TIFFs
versus clipping paths

A grayscale TIFF in an XPress picture box, Background color: "None." A 72-dpi outline, opaque interior pixels.

Saved as an EPS with a clipping path. Works in XPress or PageMaker.

▶ XPress only uses the low-resolution preview image when figuring out where the edge of the image is. That could be either 36 or 72 ppi.

▶ XPress can't see around corners. It figures the silhouetted edge by finding the first nonwhite pixel on the left and right of each row of pixels.

As soon as it sees a nonwhite pixel, it stops and says, "Here's the edge of the image." The program can't tell if that single pixel accidentally floating an inch from the edge of the image is an accident or not, so it assumes that it's really part of the image—causing lots of problems.

If you want to bring a silhouetted TIFF (or, in fact, any TIFF with a partially white background) into XPress, make sure that the background of the picture box is set to an opaque color (like white).

Clipping Paths

If you want to bring a silhouette into either PageMaker or QuarkXPress, use EPS files instead, and save them with a clipping path (again, see Figure 14-13). Note that PageMaker 6 has the (currently unique) ability to read clipping paths in TIFFs. (We discuss clipping paths and how to save them in Chapter 17, *Storing Images*.)

Soft edges. The main problem with clipping paths is that you cannot clip a soft or semitransparent edge. So, drop shadows are out. Clipping around a gauzy dress is out. If your subject is having a bad hair day, clipping out the head is going to make it look even worse.

There are several ways of making soft edges interact with your background on pages (we cover many in "Drop Shadows," later in this chapter). The best one, however, is simply to design your page so that the image doesn't overlap any other colors in your page-layout application.

Alternatively, you can forget about clipping paths, and composite the image with the background in Photoshop, using the techniques described in Chapter 13, *Selections*. (Also, check out "Incorporating Background" in the Drop Shadows section of this chapter.)

Tip: Clipping Paths and PostScript Errors. If you create a clipping path in Photoshop that's made of six different subpaths, each having 20 or 30 points, be prepared for some frustration at print time.

Even if you increase your flatness (see "Tip: Bump Up Your Flatness" in Chapter 17, *Storing Images*), the image still may not print. This is especially a problem on older printers (newer, PostScript Level 2 devices have an easier time of it). As a Zen monk must have said some time ago, "Simplicity is key."

Tip: Inset Paths Slightly. When you're drawing paths around objects to silhouette them in Photoshop, make sure you draw the path very slightly inside the object's border—we typically place the path one or two pixels inside the edge. This usually avoids most of the spillover from the background color. If spillover is a significant problem with an image, you should be thinking about building a Photoshop composite instead of using a clipping path.

Drop Shadows

Is there any single image technique more ubiquitous than the drop shadow? Every catalog and ad seems to require at least one (and often many) of the little beasts. There are as many ways to make drop shadows as there are consultants in New York, so we'll avoid an in-depth look at their creation (check out some of the effects books on the market, including *The Photoshop Wow! Book* and *Photoshop 3.0: Knock Their Socks Off*). Suffice it to say that most drop shadow techniques involve making a selection, softening its edges, and darkening it. The drop shadow is often applied to the background using the Multiply Apply mode, so it blends in well.

Troubles in Page-Layout Land

The trouble, then, isn't in creating a drop shadow so much as getting that drop shadow into (and back out of) a page-layout program such as Page-Maker or QuarkXPress. If the drop shadow blends into the background of the image, there's no problem (the drop shadow is simply part of the image itself). But when the drop shadow must sit on top of a colored background or another graphic in PageMaker or XPress, or even on top of text, life gets . . . well . . . interesting.

The essential problem is giving the appearance of transparency, so that the background looks like it's showing through the drop shadow. Since color and grayscale images are opaque in PageMaker and XPress, you need to use some workarounds. Here are several methods we use, depending on the image, the background, the program, and the time of day.

Separate the shadow. If you're trying to print a black drop shadow over solid black text, and not over a background color or another image, you can add a grayscale drop shadow to your page separately from the original image (see Figure 14-14). Although the drop shadow appears to be over the text, it's really printing beneath it.

Figure 14-14

Separate shadows

The drop shadow is on the bottom level, then the text above it, then the image of the scissors on top (with a clipping path). This example is from XPress.

The final image

The image is brought in as an EPS with a clipping path. Of course, this tip is pretty limited, but the idea of separating the drop shadow from the image is the starting point for several techniques.

Tip: Lower Shadow Resolution. Remember how we said that the resolution of your images should always be at least 1.2 times your halftone screen frequency? Here's an exception: if you're creating a separate drop-shadow image, you can lower its resolution considerably. We never use more than a 1:1 ratio (where resolution equals screen frequency), and sometimes we'll even go lower. For instance, a colleague of ours printed a catalog at 150 lpi, and every one of his drop shadows (there were a *lot*) was set to 100 ppi.

Bitmap shadows. One of the more clever methods of overprinting drop shadows on top of a colored background in a page-layout program is to make the drop shadow a separate, 1-bit, black-and-white bitmap file (see Color Plate 14 on page 366).

1. Place or make your grayscale drop shadow in a separate document.

2. Select Bitmap from the Mode menu. You have several choices for converting the gray values into black and white (see Figure 14-15). We typically use Halftone Screen. However, if we know we're placing the drop shadow on top of another black screen, or on another screen which might conflict with this one, we use Diffusion Dither instead (so that the two overlapping screens don't create a moiré pattern).

Figure 14-15

Converting to bitmap

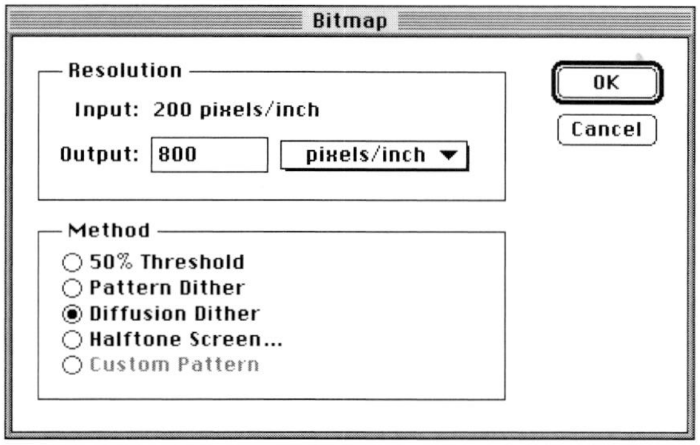

The value you enter for Output resolution is crucial. You need enough image resolution to get a decent range of grays for the drop shadow, given your screen frequency (see "The Rule of Sixteen" in Chapter 3, *Image Essentials*). And try to ensure that your image resolution is an integral divisor of output resolution (for 2,400-dpi output, for instance, use 300, 600, 800, or 1,200 ppi), to avoid ugly patterns.

If you're using the Diffusion Dither option, then you should set Output resolution to around 150 ppi (if your final output device is a desktop laser printer) or 300–800 ppi (for imagesetter output). The resolution choice here is dependent on how fine a dither the press can hold, but again, shoot for an integral divisor of output resolution.

3. Save the bitmap drop shadow as a TIFF. You can also save it as an EPS, with the Transparent Whites checkbox turned on in the Save as EPS dialog box (see Figure 14-16)—but only if the background you're dropping it on is black and white. If you put one of these EPSes over color,

the whites knock out (which ruins the whole trick). Also note that Page-Maker 5 has trouble with these transparent EPSes. We stick to TIFFs.

Figure 14-22

Save as EPS
dialog box

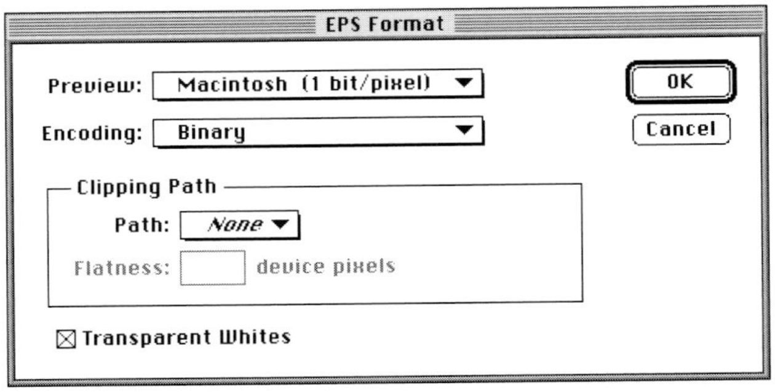

4. Bring the drop shadow into XPress or PageMaker and drop the real image (typically with a clipping path) on top of it. The preview image you see on screen is often just a horrible black blob; but the image prints properly.

    If you're in PageMaker and you're printing the drop shadow over a colored background, you must apply an overprinting color to the TIFF drop shadow. Otherwise, all those little black dots will knock out of the color beneath, with disastrous trapping problems. (XPress over-prints these 1-bit TIFFs automatically.)

Overprinting grayscales. If your drop shadow is a separate file (as above), you can skip the "convert to bitmap" step by importing the TIFF as a gray-scale, and making sure it overprints whatever is beneath it. Note that this *only* works when there's no black in the color beneath it.

For instance, you can bring a grayscale drop shadow into QuarkXPress and set it to Overprint (in the Trap Information palette). Or in PageMaker, apply an overprinting black color to the shadow (define a new black, and turn on the Overprint checkbox in the Edit Color dialog box).

However, if the shadow is overprinting a colored background of 50C 30M 10K, the drop shadow image (the whole square) overprints the ma-genta and cyan, but *knocks out* the black. This happens because in PostScript, whatever tint is printed last wins (if a lighter shade is printed over a darker shade, the lighter one is printed).

This is a handy technique, though, when printing over colors that don't contain any black.

Incorporating background. The very best way to make a drop shadow integrate with a color, texture, or an image is to integrate it in Photoshop first (see Color Plate 14 on page 366). That way, you have full control over how the drop shadow blends into the background (we usually like using Multiply mode). Plus, you can easily color the drop shadow, so it's not just black (which often looks a little lifeless).

There are two potential problems with this technique.

▶ If your drop shadow hangs partially off a colored box, you face the problem of aligning the box edges in Photoshop and in the page-layout program. We can only suggest careful measurement and proofing.

▶ You have to be working in CMYK mode when you define the background color in Photoshop, so you're *sure* that the CMYK background values match those in the page-layout program. The colors probably won't *look* like they match on screen when you bring this incorporated image into PageMaker or XPress, because every program has its own way of displaying CMYK colors on your RGB screen. For instance, 30-percent cyan in Photoshop looks different from 30-percent cyan in XPress. But they'll print the same.

Tip: Use Light Drop Shadows. One of the most common mistakes people make when building drop shadows is making them too dark. We typically use Levels to constrain the gray values in a drop shadow to under 20 percent. You can do this by setting the black Output Level to 205 (either drag the lower-left triangle, or type this value into the first Output field). Often, you can get by with even less; even an eight- or ten-percent drop shadow can appear quite dark enough.

Tip: Painting on Channels. Here's a technique from Jeff McCord that makes it easier to paint grayscale drop shadows by hand.

1. Create a new channel in the Channels palette.

2. In the Channel Options dialog box (if you don't get it automatically when creating the channel, double-click on the channel tile), set the Opacity to 100 percent and the Background Color to solid black (this doesn't fill the channel with black; it just defines what color will land on the image when you edit this grayscale channel).

3. Click once on the new channel's tile to view it (there's nothing on it yet, so it should just be white), and select it for editing.

4. Now click in the left column of the composite color channel to make the underlying image visible (this should turn on the eyeball, but not highlight the channel for editing).

5. Paint your drop shadow in the new channel using the painting and editing tools. As you paint, it looks like you're painting on the image, but you're only affecting the channel—you can paint, edit, and delete, all without really touching the underlying image.

6. When you're done, copy this channel into a new document (make sure the new document is exactly the same size).

7. If you're saving this drop shadow as grayscale, you can lower the resolution of this drop shadow document, using the Image Size dialog box. (Make sure you leave the size the same; just change the resolution. See the sidebar "Terms of Resolution" in Chapter 3, *Image Essentials*).

8. Delete the drop shadow channel from the original document.

Drop Shadows of Text and Objects

The above techniques are all well and good if your drop shadow is of a Photoshop image. But what if you're trying to create a drop shadow of some text, or a shape in QuarkXPress or PageMaker? The key to bringing elements from XPress or PageMaker into Photoshop is first saving the page as EPS. Then you've got two choices for bringing the EPS into Photoshop.

RIP the EPS. Remember, Photoshop won't rasterize non-Illustrator EPSes for us (it only grabs their low-resolution previews, which is often less than helpful). But software such as Transverter Pro or Epilogue will (see "Opening Non-Illustrator EPSes," earlier in the chapter). Once you rasterize an EPS, you can open it in Photoshop and have your way with it.

Use the PICT resource. The truth of the matter is that rasterizing an entire EPS in order to build a drop shadow is often major overkill. Instead, you can open the low-resolution PICT preview that PageMaker or XPress creates, and build the drop shadow from that (see Figure 14-17).

Figure 14-17

Creating drop shadows
from a PICT preview

*You can only open the 72-
ppi screen preview of the
EPS artwork from Page-
Maker or XPress.*

*The low-resolution screen
preview, blurred with
Gaussian Blur and bright-
ened with Levels*

*The final artwork,
in PageMaker*

1. To open the PICT preview of an EPS file, select the file in the Open dialog box (see "Objects versus Pixels," earlier in this chapter, for more on opening EPS files).

2. Once you have the preview open in Photoshop, crop out everything but the text or object you want to create a drop shadow for.

3. In the Image Size dialog box (under the Image menu), increase the resolution of the image to 100 (or whatever resolution you feel comfortable with; see "Tip: Lower Shadow Resolution," earlier in this chapter). Make sure the physical size of the image doesn't change (that means keeping the dimensions popup menus set to Inches or Picas or anything but Pixels).

4. Use Levels, Brightness/Contrast, or Curves to make the entire image lighter (we often set the black point to about 20-percent gray).

5. Blur the entire image with the Gaussian Blur filter, and add noise (see "Tip: Add Noise to Your Drop Shadows," below).

6. Save the file as a TIFF, and import it back into your page-layout application.

The reason you can use the low-resolution preview for this is that you're blurring it so much that you'd never know the difference. Note that this only works reliably for grayscale drop shadows. You can do it with color, but you have to be mighty careful to avoid color shifts.

Tip: Add Noise to Your Drop Shadows. A friend of ours kept claiming that Scitex drop shadows always printed better than Photoshop's, but he didn't know why. Finally, after comparing the two carefully, he realized the difference: Scitex drop shadows are slightly noisier, and therefore more lifelike. The solution: use the Add Noise filter with a low setting (like 2 or 3) on the shadow.

Tip: Use ShadowCaster. One more tip for XPress users. The ShadowCaster XTension, from a lowly apprentice production, is a brilliant solution for those who need to build a lot of shadows from objects (like type, or boxes, or lines, or whatever) within XPress. You can just select a text box and tell it to make a drop shadow (see Figure 14-18). If the text partially (or fully) overlays a TIFF image, ShadowCaster is even able to "burn" the drop shadow into the underlying image. Granted, this tip has nothing to do with Photoshop, but it might make your life much, much easier.

Figure 14-18
ShadowCaster

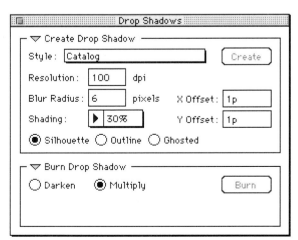

Filters and Effects

Sure, you can paint and retouch and composite within Photoshop, but you know as well as we do that the most fun comes from playing with filters. But if you're like most people, you could make filter-fooling a lot more fun. Here are some methods we've found useful.

Tip: Float Before Filtering. Standard protocol leads people to make a selection, then choose a filter from one of the Filter submenus. We suggest adding one step to the process: float the selection first (Command-J). When you float first and filter later, you're afforded the chance to change how much you want to apply that filter. For instance, if you float your selection before using the Pixelate filter, you can adjust the Opacity value in the Layers palette. The higher the opacity, the more the filter is applied (see Figure 14-19). You can even choose a different Apply mode.

Figure 14-19 Opacity changes how much a filter is applied

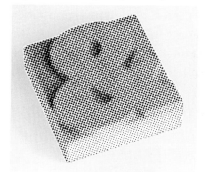

Filter applied with 100-percent opacity

Filter applied with 60-percent opacity

Filter applied with 20-percent opacity

Another benefit of floating the selection before applying a filter is that you can adjust the selection in other ways before "permanently" changing the underlying pixels. You can change Hue/Saturation, or Levels, or even apply a second filter. If you don't like what you've done, you can undo, or delete the entire floated selection.

Tip: Filter Keystrokes. Like many other features of Photoshop, working with filters can be sped up with a couple of little keyboard shortcuts. You can tell Photoshop to run a filter again by pressing Command-F. However, this doesn't let you change the dialog box settings. As Bill Niffenegger (the king of filters) says, "Never leave a filter alone . . . always change it!"

If you'd like to follow this advice, you'll need to press Command-Option-F; this reopens the dialog box of the last-run filter, so you can change the settings before applying it.

Tip: Filters on Neutral Layers. You can also apply a filter to a neutral-colored layer, effectively applying the filter to the image below. We cover the neutral-layer editing approach in more detail in Chapter 15, *The Digital Darkroom.*

When you create a new layer (click on the New Layer icon or select New Layer from the Layers palette), Photoshop gives you the choice of filling that layer with the neutral color for the mode you choose for the layer. For instance, if you set the layer to Screen mode, Photoshop can fill the layer with black—screening with black has no effect on the image below, so it's "neutral."

Now, when you apply a filter to that layer, the parts that get changed are no longer "neutral." They change the appearance of the pixels below. For example, if we use the layer created in the last paragraph (Apply mode set to Screen, filled with black), we can apply the Lens Flare filter to the entire layer (or to a portion of it). Even though the filter only affects the layer we're working on, the effect appears to be applied to the image below (see Figure 14-20).

Figure 14-20 Applying a filter to a neutral layer

Original image

Lens Flare filter applied to a neutral layer

Both the background image and the neutral layer visible at the same time

The benefits of working this way are myriad. First, you can always go back and change the filter—move it, re-create it with different settings, or even change the effect entirely with a different filter. Second, you don't have to actually apply the filter to the pixels below until you flatten or merge the layers. Third, it lets you control the strength of the filter, even if it's one that doesn't offer any controls, such as Despeckle. If you adjust the opacity of that layer in the Layers palette, you adjust the amount that the effect is applied—the lower the opacity, the less the filter has an effect on the underlying image. And so on.

Tip: Put the Filter Where You Want It. Are you tired of cluttering up your Other submenu under the Filter menu? While many third-party filter effects appear under the Other submenu, we often prefer to file them elsewhere. Here's a method that Fred Krughoff showed us to put those filters on any submenu you desire. Note that this trick doesn't work for many of the filters that come with Photoshop, and that as with any ResEdit hack, we *really* can't take responsibility for any weirdness that might occur.

1. Open the plug-in file in ResEdit (that means you should have a duplicate of the filter you're working with elsewhere, just in case). Note that Photoshop shouldn't be running when you do this.

2. Double-click on the icon labeled PiMl, to open it.

3. Select Get Resource Info from the Resource menu (see Figure 14-21).

Figure 14-21

Get Resource Info for a filter

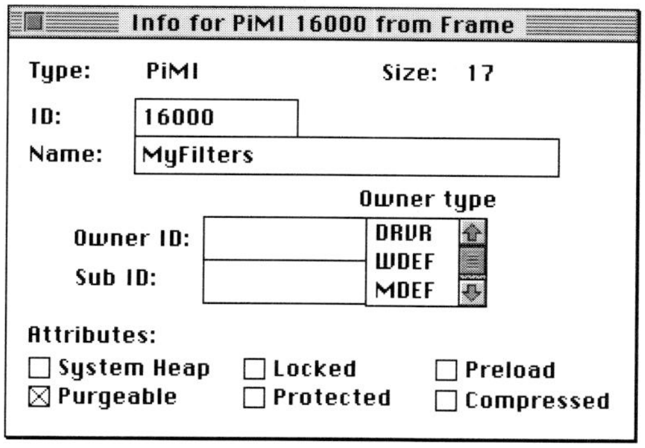

4. Type the name of the submenu on which you want the filter to appear in the Name field of this dialog box. If there is already something entered there—such as Blur or Sharpen—replace it with the menu name you want. Note that you can put in any name you want; if Photoshop doesn't already have a submenu with that name, it creates one for you.

5. Close the dialog box and the windows (answering "Yes" when ResEdit asks if you want to save your changes), and launch Photoshop. The filter should now appear on the appropriate submenu.

Rescreens

The problem with printed photos is that they've already been halftoned. That is, the grays or colors of the image are simulated with little dots, and while our eyes are easily fooled, scanners are not. If you scan these images in Grayscale or Color mode and print them, the PostScript printer rescreens them. The conflict between the original halftone screen and the output screen results in a real mess (see Figure 14-22).

Figure 14-22
The problem with rescreens

The original halftoned image   *A halftoned halftone*

The other problem is that in the original screening, a lot of the image detail is lost (the coarser the screen, the less detail remains). So when you scan the screened image, there's not a lot of detail there for the scanner to grab. The goal is to capture (and maintain) as much of that detail as possible, while avoiding the problems of overlapping screens. Don't expect miracles, though. Remember: garbage in, garbage out.

There are two basic approaches to working with screened images—line art and grayscale.

▶ Reproduce the image as black-and-white line art. This only works well for us with low-frequency images, under about 80 lpi (see "Scanning Prescreened Art" in Chapter 10, *Line Art*).

▶ Scan in grayscale or color, then use filters to remove the halftone pattern while maintaining detail. The essential concept is "blur, then sharpen." We'll discuss these techniques in the rest of this section.

Tip: Make Rescreens Smaller. Since there's not much detail in screened images, you should generally plan on reproducing them at a smaller size than the original. You can use the techniques described here to break up the halftone pattern, and not suffer the loss of detail as much; because the image is smaller, less detail is needed.

Tip: Get Permissions First. This should be obvious, but too often it is not: if the printed image is not yours, you should always get permission to use it *before* you scan it in. Ethics aside, there are certainly copyright issues involved here. Most copyright violations in digital imaging occur when people scan in pictures from magazines or books without thinking.

Frequency Considerations

One of the first things to consider when working with rescreens is the screen frequency of the printed images. Our techniques vary, depending on whether we're working with low-, mid-, or high-frequency halftones.

Low-frequency halftones. Low-frequency images are both hard and easy. They can be easy because you can reproduce them as line art, as mentioned above. But they're frustrating because there's so little detail; scanning as grayscale is almost always futile. If the line-art techniques aren't working for you, however, you can try using the methods for medium-frequency images described in the next section.

Medium-frequency halftones. Capturing medium-frequency halftones—80 lpi to 120 lpi—is perhaps the hardest of all. These halftone spots are too small to re-create in line art, but they're too large and coarse to blend together as a grayscale without blurring the image unacceptably (see "High-frequency halftones," below). You know a halftone falls into this category if you can see the halftone dots when the paper is six inches away from your face, but you can't see them (at least, not clearly) when the paper is two feet away.

There are five techniques that we commonly use when scanning mid-frequency halftones (there are other techniques, but we usually find these effective). All five attempt to capture grayscale information and remove the moiré patterns that typically occur (see Figure 14-23).

Figure 14-23 Rescreening mid-frequency halftones often causes moirés

A 400-ppi scan of the screened image, printed with a 75-lpi screen *After using the Despeckle, Median, and Unsharp Mask filters (75 lpi)* *After downsampling (133 lpi)*

▶ **Median, Despeckle, and Dust and Scratches.** The Median filter is probably the most effective method of removing dot patterning, but it comes at a cost. Median averages several pixels together to get a median value for the group. That means your image gets blurry quickly. Often you can retrieve some of the edges with Unsharp Mask, but sometimes you have to apply Median so much that the image is damaged. Nonetheless, even a one-pixel Median filter can smooth out many of the problem areas in an image.

If the resolution of the printed image is above 100 lpi, the Despeckle filter might work better than Median. We often try Despeckle first, and if it doesn't work well enough (or it damages the image in ways we don't like), we undo it and revert to Median.

Earlier in the chapter, we said that Dust and Scratches must be good for something. Removing halftone patterning is one area in which we've had some success. You get an effect similar to using Median, but you get a little more control over it.

▶ **Downsampling.** Downsampling using bicubic interpolation (see Chapter 3, *Image Essentials*) is one of the best ways to get rid of patterning, because Photoshop groups together a number of pixels and takes their average gray value. The problem, of course, is that you can also lose detail. Your goal is to downsample just enough to average out the halftone dot pattern, but not so much that you lose details in the image.

▶ **Upsampling.** After you downsample, you might need to upsample again to regain image resolution. You never get lost details back, of course, but sometimes sharpening the higher-resolution image can make it appear as though you did.

▶ **Rotating.** When you rotate an image in Photoshop, the program has to do some heavy-duty calculation work (see "Rotating," later in this chapter), and those calculations typically soften the image somewhat, breaking up the halftone pattern. If you have a very slight patterning effect after scanning a prehalftoned image, you might try rotating the entire image 10 or 20 degrees, and then rotate the same amount back again. This double rotation can average out some patterning.

Once you've managed to break up the halftone pattern, you'll need to go after the image with the Unsharp Mask filter to give the impression of sharpness for the detail that remains. Since the image will probably be fairly blurry, you'll have to make the more extreme sharpening moves that we suggest in Chapter 8, *Sharpening*, while being careful to avoid bringing the halftone pattern back out.

High-frequency halftones. Scanning pre-halftoned images with high screen frequencies—over 133 lpi—is often easier, because the dot patterns blur into gray levels while maintaining detail. You often need to use the techniques listed above, but you don't have to work as hard at salvaging the image. In fact, we often find that just scanning at the full optical resolution of the scanner and downsampling to the resolution you need (see Chapter 12, *Capturing Images*) is enough to get rid of patterning.

Tip: Pay Attention to 1:1. Remember that the most important magnification view in Photoshop is 1:1. If you scan an image and you see horrible moiré patterns at 1:3 view, don't panic. Zoom in to 1:1 view and see what's going on. The damage is often much less than you first thought. Even if you see no patterning at 1:1 view, you still may opt to do a little smoothing work (especially if you see patterning when zoomed in to 2:1 or 4:1), but it's not essential.

Rotating

We find ourselves rotating images all the time. Perhaps we didn't scan the image right; perhaps a piece of the image needs to be straightened out. Whatever the case, here are a few little tips that should make your rotating go a little more easily.

Tip: When to Rotate Images. If you don't know if or how much you'll rotate an image in PageMaker or XPress, go ahead and rotate it on pages first (see "Imaging from a Page-Layout Program" in Chapter 18, *Output Methods*). When you know the degree of rotation you're using and you want to save time printing, go back to Photoshop, rotate the image the same amount, save it as a new file (so your original unrotated version isn't marred), and import the new prerotated file onto your pages in place of the original image. It will print much faster.

Tip: Deselect to Rotate Whole Image. If you're trying to rotate your entire image, don't choose Select All first. If nothing is selected when you rotate, Photoshop enlarges the canvas size (the number of pixels in the image) so that no part of your image is clipped (see Figure 14-23).

If you need to maintain the pixel dimensions of your file, however, then you'd better do the Select All first. Note that when you do this, Photoshop rotates the selection and leaves it selected. This means you can now move the rotated image around within the bounds of the image, choosing what parts are going to be clipped off. Then when you deselect, the outside pixels are cropped off for good.

Tip: Use Free, not Arbitrary. Let's say you make a selection, then rotate it 15 degrees by selecting Arbitrary from the Rotate submenu (under the

Image menu). It's not rotated quite enough, so you use Arbitrary again to rotate an additional five degrees. What you may not know is that each time you rotate this selection, Photoshop is interpolating and throwing away data, so your image slowly degrades. The more times you rotate, the worse the image gets.

Rotated with nothing selected *Rotated with entire
image selected*

Instead, if you're not absolutely sure how much you want to rotate the selection, choose Free rotation instead. This gives you the option of rotating the selection as many times as you want—Photoshop gives you a preview of the rotation each time—until you get it right. When it's perfect, you can click on the selection (the cursor turns into a gavel for you to "hammer" it down). Photoshop only performs the rotation math once, so the selection is degraded the minimum amount necessary.

If you have a clear frame of reference in the original—a horizon that needs to be straightened, for instance, or the edge of a building that should be vertical—you can measure the angle of rotation you need. See "Tip: Measuring Angles" in Chapter 2, *Essential Photoshop Tips and Tricks*.

Tip: Rotation Increments. If you're using Free rotation and you're having difficulty getting just the right angle (the angle appears in the Info palette), try pulling the cursor out away from the selection while you rotate. Now you have more leverage, so you can rotate in finer increments.

Also note that when you hold down the Shift key while rotating, Photoshop constrains the rotation to 15-degree increments.

Text and Bitmapped Images

Sure, a picture is worth a thousand words. But that doesn't mean we're going back to hieroglyphics. People often want to overlay text on top of pictures, then ask us, "Should we use the Type tool in Photoshop, or the features in our page-layout program?" The answer, almost always, is to use PageMaker or QuarkXPress. We say this for three reasons.

▶ Text that you create in Photoshop is always bitmapped. If you're working with a 225-ppi image, that means any text you add to that image in Photoshop is similarly 225 ppi. That's high enough for most images, but it looks crummy for hard-edged type. Sure, you can anti-alias the text in Photoshop; that looks great on screen, but it just looks fuzzy in final output (see Figure 14-24).

Figure 14-24

Text from Photoshop versus PageMaker or Quark XPress

Now is the winter of our discontent Made glorious summer by this sun of York,

And all the clouds that loured upon our house
In the deep bosom of the ocean buried.

Text from Photoshop (250 ppi)

Now is the winter of our discontent Made glorious summer by this sun of York,

And all the clouds that loured upon our house
In the deep bosom of the ocean buried.

Text from PageMaker

▶ The Type tool in Photoshop is pretty short on typographic flexibility. For instance, you can't kern letter pairs except by manually dragging the bitmapped letterforms closer or farther apart. PageMaker and QuarkXPress have very powerful typographic tools.

▶ Unless your text is on a separate layer in Photoshop, there's no way to change a word once it's placed (absolutely inevitable if you've got a client looking over your shoulder).

On the other hand (we always try to be evenhanded), there are three reasons why you might want to create text directly in Photoshop.

► If your final output is to a color printer such as a thermal-wax printer, anti-aliased type within the bitmapped image almost always looks better. The hard-edged type from a program such as XPress looks too jaggy off these low-resolution devices.

► If the text is integrated into your image, instead of being a separate element overlaying the image, there's a good chance that you'll have to create it in Photoshop.

► If you want "ghosted" type—where the characters appear bleached into the image itself—you'll have to do it in Photoshop.

► Finally, you'll probably have to create the text in Photoshop if the text is filtered, textured, or has an image within the letterforms (see "Tip: Create Textured Text in Illustrator or FreeHand," and "Tip: Smooth Textured Type in Photoshop," later in this chapter).

Alpha Channel Type

Before Photoshop 3 came out, the traditional wisdom was to "always create your text on an alpha channel." That way, you could kern it, adjust it, move it around, twist it into weird shapes, and so on, before you actually laid down the pixels. Then when version 3 came out, most people said, "Forget that; just do it on a layer."

The problem with layers, though, is that they're seriously memory-intensive. Adding a channel requires much less RAM (though extra channels do take extra memory).

But even if we *do* use layers, we still almost always place type on an alpha channel or a quick mask before actually placing pixels in our image. We find that, as a starting point, it's still more flexible than layers, and leaves us with more options to change the text or change our minds. This is our standard operating procedure.

1. Select the layer you want the type to go on.

2. Switch to Quick Mask mode (press Q).

3. Use the Type tool to add the text.

4. Copy the quick mask to a new channel (drag the Quick Mask tile over the New Channel icon in the Channels palette). This way you can always go back to the original.

5. While still in Quick Mask mode, make the text look right (adjust, fiddle, and arrange accordingly). Move it to the correct position in the image.

6. Invert the mask (press Command-I). (If your Quick Mask options are set to Selected Areas, you can skip this step.)

7. Switch out of Quick Mask mode (press Q again).

8. Save the selection again so you can select the text again, if necessary.

9. Fill the current selection with a color, pattern, or texture; for ghosted type, adjust it with Levels or Curves.

When you're sure you're not going to need the original text again, go ahead and delete that channel. But think seriously before deleting the channel that holds the final text. We find we often need to go back to select the text, and having the channel available is invaluable.

Tip: Create Textured Text in Illustrator or FreeHand. As we said above, one of the main reasons you'd want to add type over your image in a separate program (like QuarkXPress or PageMaker) is that otherwise the type will look blurry or jaggy. But what if you want the text to be textured, or filled with some kind of cool bitmapped-image effect (like putting a weird blend into the letterforms)? Here's one way to do it.

1. Create the text in Adobe Illustrator or Macromedia FreeHand.

2. Convert the type to outlines.

3. Create the bitmapped-image effect in Photoshop, and save it as an EPS. The image should be slightly larger than the type.

4. Place the image into Illustrator or FreeHand, and clip it with the text outlines. In Illustrator, use the Mask feature; if you've got more than one character, don't forget to make them all a single compound path first. In FreeHand, use the Paste Inside feature.

5. Save this as an EPS file, and import it into QuarkXPress or PageMaker. You can overlay this EPS on the original image.

Note that if there's a lot of text, using the compound path as a clipping path may result in a PostScript error. The simpler, the better (and don't forget to increase flatness).

Tip: Smooth Textured Type in Photoshop. You can perform a work-around similar to the last tip, but export all your EPSes from Photoshop. Here's how we do it.

1. Create your text in Adobe Illustrator (5.5 or later), convert it to an outline, and copy it to the clipboard.

2. Paste the text into Photoshop; when the program asks you, tell it to paste it in as paths.

3. Position the path where you want it, and save it by giving it a name (double-click on the Working Path tile in the Paths palette).

4. Create a new layer (Option-click on the New Layer icon in the Layers palette).

5. Create your textured effect on this layer. You can do it in the form of the type, but it's much easier (and more reliable) to create the effect in the shape of a rectangle, slightly larger than the path you imported (see Figure 14-25).

Figure 14-25

Textured type
in Photoshop

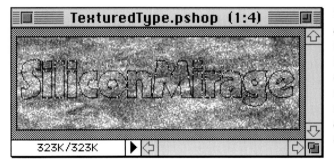

The text is created in Illustrator and pasted into Photoshop over the texture, then the whole image is saved as an EPS with a clipping path.

6. Hide all the layers except the one with the effect (click on that layer's eyeball in the Layers palette), so that only the effect layer is showing.

7. Use Save a Copy from the File menu to save the file as an EPS image. From the Clipping Path popup menu, choose the text's path you saved

in step 3. Because only the effect layer is visible, Photoshop only saves the effect with the clipping path.

You can now import this text into QuarkXPress or PageMaker and place it on top of the image. Note that you don't *have* to create the text path in Illustrator. You could also create the text on your new layer in Photoshop, then immediately convert the text outline into a path in the Paths palette. However, the path is almost always rougher and of lesser quality than an outline from Illustrator or FreeHand.

New Techniques

Even though Photoshop is an amazing tool, it still won't do everything for you. Creating drop shadows, silhouettes, special edges, or text in Photoshop can be a chore. But we hope that with these new methods, your work will fly faster and you'll be able to focus on more fun stuff. In the next chapter, we look at some very cool new techniques for working with images that could revolutionize the way you do production.

15

The Digital Darkroom

Photographic Techniques in Photoshop

What would you say if we told you that you could perform color correction, use dodging and burning, build up density in overexposed areas, open up underexposed areas, and more—all with a minimum of image degradation and with an unlimited number of undos? You'd probably just laugh at us. But in this chapter we'll show you some very powerful techniques that have never (as far as we know) appeared in print before, and that let you do all these things.

We call this group of techniques "the digital darkroom," because they're more akin to darkroom experimentation than to twiddling drum scanner dials. Instead of watching the numbers, you watch what's happening on your monitor. And instead of stretching and squeezing your image's eight bits using Levels and Curves, you use Channels and Layers to superimpose multiple versions of your image, like sandwiching negatives in an enlarger or slides in a projector (though like most good analogies, even this one breaks down if you push it too far).

The techniques in this chapter can help you get a better image with less degradation and more control of your changes. But much more important, they're designed to give you maximum flexibility so you can experiment and play with your images more. While we'll give you some places to jump off from, it's really in this playing around that you'll see the myriad of possibilities that these techniques make possible.

Caveat emptor. Working in the digital darkroom lets you control contrast with a brush instead of a curve or a slider, make significant changes but still have unlimited undos, and—most important of all—do all this without touching your original image data. If all this sounds too good to be true, we should mention three caveats up front.

▶   These techniques rely heavily on trusting what you see on your monitor. You *can* use them in conjunction with the Info palette—going by the numbers—but the game is hardly worth the candle; the main benefit of using these techniques is that you can work visually, and do so much more interactively than you can using Levels or Curves. Without a properly calibrated monitor (see Chapter 5, *Color Preferences*, and Chapter 16, *Color Management Systems*), you can pretty much just give up now.

▶   Photoshop's Layers feature uses a lot of RAM. You can work around this in various ways (which we'll mention), but if you're already working close to the limits of your available RAM, be prepared for some disk thrashing and the occasional lengthy wait as Photoshop struggles to catch up. (See "How Much RAM Is Enough?" in Chapter 1, *Building a Photoshop System.*)

▶   We developed these techniques to work on RGB and grayscale images. You *can* use them on CMYK images, but the RGB display of CMYK adds another level of abstraction that can cause all kinds of problems, and it's easy to end up overinking the image.

   If you're in the tricky position of having to retarget a CMYK file for a drastically different output process than the one for which it was intended, by all means give the methods in this chapter a try—you won't damage your original data—but don't come crying to us if you end up with very strange results.

The Source Layer and the Editing Layer

Almost all the techniques in this chapter rely on using multiple layers. Your original image lives on the background layer, which we call the *source layer.* You can add a new layer on top of it, which we'll call the *editing layer.* Think of them as a negative, and a filter that you make a print through.

Using Apply modes. Once you have the two layers, you can use the various Apply modes—Multiply, Overlay, Screen, and so on—along with the various painting tools, to affect tone and saturation. The final image is formed by the interaction of the source and editing layers. With some techniques, you'll want to combine two copies of the original image; with others, you'll use a "neutral" color on the editing layer—a color that doesn't affect the underlying image in the Apply mode you're using.

Whether you're editing a neutral layer or a copy of the image, your original background image data remains unaffected. This is quite unlike working with Levels and Curves or with any of the painting or editing tools, which actually "burn" your changes into the image. The upshot is that you have something very similar to unlimited, *selective* Undo.

Making an editing layer. The first step in editing an image is to create an editing layer, either containing a duplicate of the original, or filled with a neutral color.

Creating a duplicate layer. You can duplicate the image to create an editing layer by dragging the Background layer's tile on top of the New Layer icon in the Layers palette (see Figure 15-1). This produces a second layer called Background copy.

Figure 15-1

Making an editing layer

Drag the Background layer on top of the New Layer icon to create Background copy.

You can edit the copy of the image, then control how those edits affect the underlying original using the Apply mode and Opacity controls.

Drag a layer on top of the Trash icon to delete the layer.

Creating a neutral layer. If your editing layer is to begin its life as a neutral layer (see "Neutralizing a Color Cast," later in this chapter), you can create it by clicking once on the New Layer icon, choosing an Apply mode in the New Layer dialog box, and turning on the Fill with Overlay-neutral color checkbox (see Figure 15-2). If this checkbox is grayed out, there is no neutral color for that mode.

Figure 15-2

Making a
neutral layer

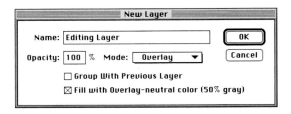

Fine-tuning. By changing the Opacity slider in the Layers palette, you can control the opacity of the editing layer, which in turn controls the intensity of the effect globally (see "Tip: Filters on Neutral Layers" in Chapter 14, *Essential Image Techniques*). For local control (like dodging and burning), you can use several techniques to fine-tune your editing.

▶ **Erasing.** When you're working on a duplicate image layer, you can use the Eraser tool to reduce the opacity of the editing layer—literally erasing the editing layer to transparency. Wherever the layer is transparent, the pixels have no effect on the image below. Wherever the layer is partially transparent, the pixels only partially affect the image below. To selectively retrieve the erased pixels, you can use Erase to Saved (see "Tip: Keeping Your Options Open," below, and "When Things Go Worng" in Chapter 2, *Essential Photoshop Tips and Tricks*).

▶ **Neutral colors.** Several of the Apply modes have "neutral colors." When a pixel is colored neutral, it's the same as making it totally transparent—it has no effect on the image below. For instance, an area painted 50-percent gray on an editing layer set to Hard Light has no effect whatsoever. You can use this to "paint out" areas you don't want changed.

▶ **Layer masks.** Because digital darkroom work is usually done on layers, you can use layer masks to specify what parts of an image should be affected and which should not (see "Layer Masks" in Chapter 13, *Selections*). The only problem with layer masks, however, is that they can take up even more RAM in an already memory-intensive situation. Nonetheless, if you can spare the memory, layer masks are ultimately the most flexible ways to specify local changes.

Tip: Multiple Editing Layers. There's nothing stopping you from having more than one editing layer in a document. We sometimes work with three or four different layers, each duplicates of the source image but with various curves, Apply modes, layer masks, and so on. On the other hand, we sometimes see people using multiple layers in documents in which they could use fewer with little difficulty (and then they complain about how slow Photoshop is acting).

Tip: Keeping Your Options Open. Back in Chapter 14, *Essential Image Techniques,* we discussed the idea of saving "base camps" at strategic moments in your image editing. One of those strategic moments is after you've added your editing layer, but before you start messing with it. In this case, you should either Save or Save As without flattening the image, so that you can use the Magic Eraser (Erase to Saved) on your editing layer (if you don't, Photoshop can't figure out what to erase back to; see Figure 15-3).

Figure 15-3

Using magic erase without saving the document

> Could not use the magic eraser because the saved version does not have a matching layer.
>
> -25760   OK

Another way to keep your options open and maintain flexibility in your editing layer is to use snapshots (see "Snapshots" in Chapter 14, *Essential Image Techniques*). You can take a snapshot of the entire image or just a portion of it, then paint that in using either the Fill dialog box or the Rubber Stamp tool.

Apply Modes and Calculations

Most Photoshop users get nervous when someone says "calculations" (although it appears that calculations—channel operations, or *chops*, as they're often known—have become a fetish for many). For better or for worse, calculations form the basis of digital darkroom techniques. Fortunately, they've been made so simple to use in Photoshop 3 that you hardly have to worry at all about the math.

Calculations mathematically combine two grayscale channels (like the red and the green channels of an image, or a grayscale image and an alpha channel, and so on). Apply modes do exactly the same thing as channel operations, but they work on all the color channels simultaneously (like with two RGB images, or with two RGB layers in the same document). We usually use layers and Apply modes even when we're editing grayscale images, but we make use of calculations when we're trying to convert a color image to grayscale (see "The Color of Grayscale" in Chapter 14, *Essential Image Techniques*).

Layers and Apply Modes

After we've created an editing layer, we select an Apply mode. The ones we use most are Multiply and Screen, particularly when we're working with grayscale images, but we occasionally use Soft Light, Hard Light, Overlay, and (in color) Saturation. We haven't yet found a use for the other calculation modes in this context, but we're always open to suggestions. Don't forget to play around with various modes, opacities, and so on— free-wheeling experimentation is what this approach is all about.

Multiply. The best analogy we've found for Multiply mode is that it's like sandwiching two negatives in an enlarger. Mathematically, Multiply takes two values, multiplies them by each other, and divides by 255. Practically speaking, this means the result is always darker than either of the sources.

If a pixel is black in either the source or editing layer, the result is black. If a pixel is white in the editing layer, it has no effect (white is the neutral color for Multiply). We use Multiply to build density, particularly in the highlights and midtones. For example, multiplying an overexposed image on top of itself can give meat to washed-out highlight details.

Screen. Screen is literally the inverse of Multiply. The best real-world analogy we've heard comes from Adobe's Russell Brown: Screen is like projecting two slides on the same screen. The result is always lighter than either of the two sources.

If a pixel is white in either the source image or editing image, the result is white. If a pixel is black in the editing image, it has no effect at all (black is the neutral color for Screen). We use Screen mostly to open up dark shadows, like in underexposed film.

If you're a techno-dweeb like us, you probably want to know what Screen does behind the scenes. Photoshop inverts the two numbers (subtracts them from 255) before performing a Multiply calculation (multiplies them by each other and divides by 255); then the program subtracts the result from 255. That's it. Don't you feel better?

Soft Light and Hard Light. As their names imply, Soft Light and Hard Light increase both contrast and color saturation. Hard Light has been described as either shining a colored light on the lens of a camera, or shining a harsh spotlight on the image itself. Soft Light is a less-extreme version of Hard Light, like shining a diffuse colored light on the image. We use both of these to build contrast (usually globally), or to increase saturation—which is more often a local, selective operation.

For those who want to get into the tweaky stuff, Hard Light and Soft Light work by both multiplying and screening pixels. Where the editing image on top is less than 50-percent gray, they screen pixels (so the result gets lighter). Where the editing image is greater than 50-percent gray, they multiply pixels (and the result gets darker). At 50 percent, nothing happens (this is the neutral color for both of these modes).

Overlay. Whereas in Hard Light the brightness of the editing image (the top layer) is the primary factor, in Overlay mode just the opposite is true: the black and white values in the underlying source layer dominate, so that white areas in the underlying layer stay white, and black ones stay black (in other words, the highlights and shadows are always maintained).

Curiously enough, if you're working with identical copies of the image on both layers, there's no difference between Overlay and Hard Light (it actually makes sense, but it'd be boring to discuss). However, if you adjust the tone or hue of the editing layer (using Curves, Levels, or Hue/Saturation), the difference between Hard Light and Overlay can be significant. It's also easier to see than to explain (we show an example in "A Digital Darkroom Cookbook," later in the chapter).

Saturation. The Saturation mode blends the saturations of the source and editing layers while attempting to maintain overall luminance and hue. We use it to desaturate images by desaturating a copy of the image on the editing layer using Hue/Saturation, then varying the opacity of the editing layer to control the amount of desaturation we apply.

Applying the Tools

In many ways, these tools are more difficult to explain than they are to use, so let's look at an example. The image in Figure 15-4 is a well-exposed original, but it's a little flat, and the white fur is hotter than we'd like. We'll start with some tonal correction to deal with those issues.

Tonal Correction

Our first step is to create an editing layer by dragging the Background layer in the Layers palette onto the New Layer icon. We set the Apply mode to Multiply, because we want to build density in the highlights. This brings out much more detail in the fur—perhaps too much—but it also darkens the overall image too much, so we back off the Opacity slider. A setting of around 72 percent gives us the effect we want in the highlights.

Figure 15-4 The raw image, and a quick fix

We create a duplicate layer, then set the Apply mode to Multiply, bringing out detail in the white fur.

An opacity of 72 percent compensates for excessive darkening of the shadow areas.

We've fixed the problem with the highlights, and the image has better contrast, but it's still a little dark overall. We can take two approaches:

▶ Using Curves, make a global correction on the editing layer. This is fast and easy, but somewhat imprecise.

▶ Using one of the painting or editing tools, make selective corrections. This is a bit more work, but it offers much more control.

Global edits with Curves. The editing layer is an image in its own right, so you can use all of Photoshop's global editing controls—Levels, Curves, and (for color images) Hue/Saturation. But since the editing layer is just a filter through which you view the source image, you can make much more extreme moves than would be possible with a normal image.

The curve in Figure 15-5 is one we would never dream of applying to a standalone image! It can work well for an editing layer, however, because it's not degrading the underlying data. The curve maintains the highlights, but dramatically reduces the effect of the editing layer in the midtones and shadows.

Figure 15-5
Using Curves on
the editing layer

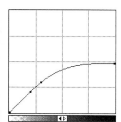

Applying this curve to the editing layer solves the problems in the shadows.

We'd normally never dream of using such an extreme curve, but since we can control the opacity, it's fine.

At this point, if we were happy with the image, we'd use Save a Copy to save a flattened version of the image under a new name. We could then either save the image including both layers, or if disk space were at a premium, we could simply save the curve we applied to the editing layer and close the image without saving the changes—the layer is easy to re-create, and we could simply reload the saved curve. Either way, we still have our original image intact.

Digital dodging and burning. Throwing a curve at the editing layer is fast and easy, but we can obtain much finer control while making local edits by brushing the opacity of the editing layer using the Eraser tool. This gives us a much closer digital equivalent of traditional dodging and burning than the Dodge and Burn tools. (The Dodge and Burn tools simply add black or white, respectively, to the area to which they're applied.)

We usually use the Eraser in Airbrush mode, with Fade turned off. When using a pressure-sensitive tablet, we set Stylus Pressure to modulate the pressure rather than the brush size, which varies the opacity (see Figure 15-6). We save the image before we start dodging and burning, which lets us use the Erase to Saved option to provide selective undo.

Working with a low pressure setting, you can use the Eraser to subtly reduce the opacity of parts of the editing layer. If you go too far, hold down Option to "magic erase" the saved image back in.

Figure 15-6

Eraser Options
palette

The settings in the Eraser Options palette, especially when combined with a pressure-sensitive tablet, provide excellent tools for dodging and burning on the editing layer.

Click here to use Magic Erase, or hold down Option while erasing to invoke it temporarily.

The pressure sensitivity gives us fine control over how much we remove and how much we put back. Occasionally, we turn off the Background layer so that we can see exactly how much we've etched away from the editing layer (see Figure 15-7).

Tip: Fake a Pressure-Sensitive Tablet. Don't despair if you don't own a pressure-sensitive drawing tablet; you can fake it. The number keys on the keyboard vary the opacity of the Eraser and other tools in ten-percent increments. Zero is 100 percent, 9 is 90 percent, and so on.

Tip: Use Layer Masks to Save (or Burn) Time. While you can brush the opacity of a layer to add or remove the effect locally, sometimes it's much easier and quicker to create a layer mask to control the opacity of the editing layer (see "Layer Masks" in Chapter 13, *Selections*).

The layer mask controls the opacity of the editing layer, which in turn controls the effect the layer has on the image, so tweaking layer masks can get to be quite a brain-bender—you're changing the way a filter filters

Figure 15-7 Selective erasure of the editing layer

By selectively erasing the editing layer using various opacity settings (note the faint checkerboard showing through), we're able to selectively control the density and detail in different parts of the image.

The opacity of the editing layer is reduced here to lighten the image.

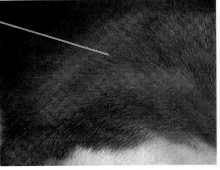

The editing layer after selective erasing

The resulting image

a filter that filters the image, as it were. But once you've used them a few times, they start to make much more sense than most explanations we've read (including this one).

A Digital Darkroom Cookbook

Here are some examples of different problems we've solved by applying layers, using different Apply modes. Consider them general strategies rather than definitive fixes. We include them so that you can use them as jumping-off points in developing your own techniques.

Fixing a Hot Spot

In Figure 15-8, there are hot spots on the nose and the collarbone. Here's how we go about fixing them.

1. We duplicate the image onto a new layer, and set the Apply mode to Multiply with an opacity of about 40 percent (to darken those areas intelligently).

2. Next, we use Color Range to select just the hot spots, feather the se-lection by 5 pixels, invert it, and clear everything except the hot spots

Figure 15-8 Hot spots

Hot spots on nose and shoulder   *Editing layer*   *Resulting image*

to transparent (press Delete). This dramatically reduces the amount of RAM consumed by the layer, because transparent areas take up almost no RAM.

4. The spots in the editing layer introduce a greenish cast, so we make some small changes in Hue/Saturation, moving the green toward yellow and the yellow toward red.

5. Finally, we set the layer's opacity to 12 percent, which tones down the hot spots slightly without creating any obvious tonal shifts. And we do some detail work with the Eraser set to 5-percent pressure to smooth out the edges.

Desaturating a Screaming Red

A second problem with the same image is that the hat, scarf, and lipstick are simply too saturated for print (of course, since you're seeing these images in print, you'll have to take our word for it). We duplicate the image onto a second layer, use Color Range to select the screaming reds, feather the selection, select the inverse, and clear to transparency, leaving only the hat, scarf, and lipstick on the layer (see Figure 15-9).

Figure 15-9
Screaming reds tamed

Editing layer

Resulting image

Then we use Hue/Saturation to desaturate the layer by about 50 points, set the Apply mode to Saturation, and pull the opacity back to 18 percent. Now the reds just shout loudly instead of screaming. We could pull them back still further (by increasing opacity), but then the rest of the image would appear oversaturated.

A Multilayered Fix

The image in Figure 15-10 has a white-balance problem (it was taken with a digital camera using an auto white balance that didn't quite do the job), and it's a little flat. We use three layers and a layer mask to fix it up.

Neutralizing a Color Cast

In the last example, we affected color balance by duplicating the background and desaturating the editing layer using Hue/Saturation. Here's one other method that we have found particularly useful (thanks, Russell, for this one). In Figure 15-11, we see an image that desperately needs adjusting. (We actually damaged the image for the sake of this exercise.)

Figure 15-10 Multiple fixes on multiple layers

The raw scan

After overall and yellow desaturation

First we take care of the yellow cast. We duplicate the image onto a new layer, and use Hue/Saturation to reduce the overall saturation by about 30 points and the yellow saturation by about 20 additional points. We set the Apply mode to Saturation, and the opacity to around 80 percent. See the resulting image, above right.

This gets rid of the yellow cast, but it leaves the image a little dark and washes out the eyes. We erase the eyes from the editing layer so the original shows through. To brighten the image, we duplicate the Desat layer, and set the layer to Screen mode at 10-percent opacity. See the top left image on the next page.

Figure 15-10 Multiple fixes on multiple layers, continued

After eye fix and lightening

The final image

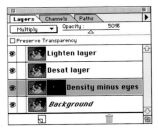

Because the eyes could still use some snap, we duplicate the entire image one more time, setting the Apply mode to Multiply and the opacity to 50 percent. But we want to affect only the eyes, so we add a layer mask, select the eyes with the lasso, feather this selection to soften the edges, invert the selection, and fill the selection with black. This way, only the eyes show through on this layer. You can see the resulting image above.

Figure 15-11 Neutralizing a color cast

To remove the cyan cast in this image, we create a neutral layer and brighten the red channel for that layer.

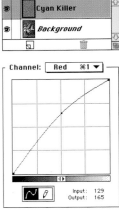

We create a new layer by clicking on the New Layer icon, specify an Apply mode of Overlay, and turn on the checkbox called Fill with Overlay–neutral color (50% gray). This fills the entire layer with 50-percent gray. Because it's neutral in Overlay mode, it has no effect on the image.

With the neutral layer selected, we adjust the red curve to eliminate the cyan cast in the image, and select an Opacity setting of 90 percent to control how much the color correction is applied to the image.

Extracting Hidden Detail

Digital darkroom techniques can also help salvage scans that appear irredeemable. Figure 15-11 shows an image which apparently has no highlight detail. There are some differences lurking in there, however, which we can pull out by stacking up multiple layers using Multiply mode.

Figure 15-11 Extracting hidden detail

In the raw scan, there is no apparent detail in the highlights.

Magic Wand (Tolerance of 6) and a feather of 4 selects the whites.

We convert the selection to a layer, blur it to avoid posterization of details, then duplicate the layer twice with Multiply Apply mode.

The final image, with highlight detail magically "restored."

Darkroom Experiments

You don't have to work exclusively using Layers, Calculations, and Apply modes. We just present them as interesting and often useful approaches. You can mix and match the techniques in this chapter with more conventional curve-based editing.

But working this way offers a huge amount of freedom to experiment. Because you aren't touching the original image, you can take chances, drive your image to extremes, and generally do things you'd never do if you were working on a flat image. Once you've got the image the way you want it, you still have to deal with all the issues around targeting it for a particular output process, which we discuss in just about every other chapter in this book.

Color
Management
Systems

What You Get Is What You Get

Wouldn't it be nice to simply adjust images so that they look good on your monitor, and then have them print that way too? Or wouldn't it be great if you could just say, "Make the image that comes off the press look like the original"? (If you've skipped the rest of the book and ended up here, you may be asking yourself, "You mean, it doesn't work that way?") In most of this book, we've explored the convoluted and complex issues surrounding Photoshop's role as a prepress tool, because most Photoshop images eventually end up in print. But if thinking about color in terms of RGB and CMYK and Lab and xyY gives you a headache, don't despair: there are a few simpler options in the color arena.

Color management systems (CMSes) are software solutions to the color-matching problem. In theory, they're supposed to work automatically behind the scenes—and we have no doubt that one day they will—but in their current state of evolution, you have to know which buttons to press, and when. Moreover, trying to make rival CMSes talk to one another is still an exercise in frustration, and it often seems that the printer/monitor/scanner that you have is the one your CMS doesn't support.

Do these concerns mean you shouldn't use CMSes? No; there are many good reasons to slog through the learning curve and use a CMS. In fact, despite these growing pains, we've been getting good results from Agfa's FotoTune and the Kodak Color Management System (KCMS) for well over a year; Apple's new ColorSync 2.0, based on Linotype-Hell's LinoColor, is beginning to produce very encouraging results too.

In this chapter, we focus on the theory, concepts, and potential uses of color management. Because color management systems are changing so rapidly, we're going to minimize the practical, get-your-hands-dirty discussions. Otherwise, when you start working with these systems yourself, you'll yell at us for giving you "wrong" information. To paraphrase the words of the old wise guy: we're not feeding you a fish, and we're not teaching you *how* to fish. We're teaching you *about* fish: what they are, where they hang out, and what tools you'll need to catch them.

Why Use a Color Management System?

Color management systems can seem scary at first; there are a lot of new words and concepts to keep in mind. But there are some excellent reasons to push through and learn them. CMSes help us in several ways.

▶ **Matching the original**. CMSes can help us maintain consistent color on screen, in the printed proof, and in the final output. One of the biggest benefits we've gained from our use of CMSes is the ability to trust what we see on the monitor, allowing us to work visually rather than by the numbers.

▶ **Color-space conversion**. CMSes are very good at converting from one color space to another on demand. More important, the CMSes we talk about here can give you much better quality than Photoshop can in the RGB-to-CMYK conversion.

▶ **Soft proofing and preproofing**. Printing presses can print many fewer colors than you can see on screen or on a dye-sublimation printer. CMSes can constrict the colors in an image so that you can get a better idea of what your final printed image will look like. We find that a well-implemented CMS lets us save a lot of money on multiple iterations of Match Prints by relying more on the monitor as a soft proof, and on dye-sublimation prints as preproofs.

▶ **Photo CD**. We wouldn't dream of using Photo CD without running the images through Kodak's KCMS. Using the correct source and target profile when opening a Photo CD image into Photoshop makes a huge difference to the quality of the results you get.

But a well-implemented CMS can do even more. It also opens up exciting new ways of working with color in Photoshop, ways that have more in common with traditional darkroom techniques than they do with drum scanner skill (for a look at some of the possibilities, see Chapter 15, *The Digital Darkroom*).

The Limits of Color Management

Will your output from a CMS match what you see on the monitor, or the original artwork you put in the scanner? Well, no. That would be impossible—the experience of looking at ink on paper is, and always will be, very different from the experience of looking at light emitted from a monitor. Even the best CMS doesn't remove the need for subjective judgments about how to render an image. What *is* possible is that you can learn to visualize how the image on your monitor will look when it's printed to a wide range of different output devices.

A CMS can't and won't produce identical colors on every device; it can, however, make the color more predictable, and preserve the overall appearance of the image. The colors won't actually *be* the same on the different devices, but they'll *look* the same.

Color Problems

As we explained in Chapter 4, *Color Essentials*, we have to grapple with two fundamental problems when we try to reproduce images.

▶ **Device-dependent color.** The RGB color space used by scanners and monitors and the CMYK color space used by most printing processes don't really describe color. If you scan the same image with three different scanners, you'll get three different sets of RGB values. Display the same scan on three different monitors, and they'll each look different. And if you send the same CMYK values to three different printers, you'll get three different colors.

▶ **Reproducing colors.** Different devices have different color gamuts (the range of colors that they can reproduce), so it's often impossible to reproduce the same colors on screen, on a proofing device, and on a printing press.

Photoshop has a built-in color management system, but it's both limited and far from trivial to use correctly (see Chapter 5, *Color Preferences*). When you adjust the Monitor Setup, Printing Inks Setup, and Separation Setup preferences, you're telling Photoshop how color looks on your monitor and your printer, and Photoshop attempts to keep them somewhat consistent. But third-party CMSes go beyond Photoshop in two ways.

Out-of-gamut clipping. CMSes handle out-of-gamut colors better than Photoshop. Where Photoshop simply clips them to the nearest reproducible value, the CMSes actually do some kind of intelligent *gamut compression* (see Figure 16-1), scaling the entire range of color contained in the original to fit the gamut of the output device (see the sidebar "Photoshop's Separation Engine" in Chapter 5, *Color Preferences*). There's no single correct way to do this, and each CMS tends to do it slightly differently. It's one of the main factors that makes us prefer one CMS over another for a specific image or for a specific output device.

Figure 16-1

Out-of-gamut
color mapping

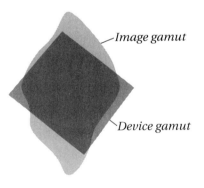

Image gamut

Device gamut

One of the big jobs of a color management system is mapping out-of-gamut colors to colors that the target device can reproduce. Gamut clipping distorts the relationships between colors. Gamut compression retains those relationships, preserving the differences between colors, which is what you want for reproduction of natural images.

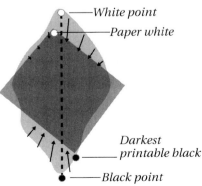

White point

Paper white

Darkest printable black

Black point

Gamut clipping

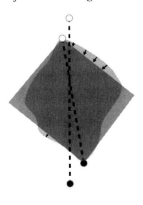

Gamut compression

Attention to the original. Photoshop only knows about the colors you see on your screen. But when you work with scanned images, it has no clue about what the colors in the original artwork were like. Because third-party CMSes let you describe the device on which you scanned an image, you can get a closer match between your original artwork and the final piece.

Color Management Systems Explained

A color management system is a set of software tools that attempts to maintain the appearance of colors as they're reproduced by different devices. We stress the word "appearance" because it's impossible to reproduce in print many of the colors found in color film, or even on a color monitor.

All the CMSes on the market work in pretty much the same way, though they differ in the way they're implemented, in their user interfaces, in the functionality they offer, and in the devices that they support. But before we look at the differences among the current offerings, let's look at what they all have in common.

CMS Components

All CMSes employ three basic components.

▶ The *reference color space* is a device-independent, perceptually based color space. Most current CMSes use either a CIE-defined color space such as CIE Lab, or a proprietary derivative of a CIE color space such as Kodak's RCS. You never have to worry about the reference color space; it is the theory behind how the software works.

▶ The *color-matching engine* is the software that does the conversion between different device-specific color spaces. Once you install this software, you don't have to think about it again, unless you're masochistic enough to use more than one color-matching engine.

▶ *Device profiles* describe the color behavior of scanners, monitors, and printers. They tell the color management system which color in the reference color space corresponds to the device's specific RGB or

CMYK values. Most of the problems with color management systems lie in creating, using, and editing profiles.

The arrangement is similar to the way Photoshop uses Lab color as a reference when it converts color between device-specific color spaces using the information in Monitor, Printing Inks, and Separation Setups. The major difference is that the device profiles provide a much more detailed description of the device's color space than Photoshop's various Preferences settings do.

Conveying Color Meaning

The key concept in using a CMS is conveying color meaning. If the system is going to keep the color consistent among different devices, it needs to know how each device in the process sees, displays, or prints colors. If a CMS knows enough about a scanner, it can *interpret* the incoming color information to find out what the colors in the original really look like. Then, if it knows how colors appear on your screen, it can adjust the image's colors to match the original. Finally, if it knows about a printer, the CMS can adjust the colors to make them look right on that printer.

Source and target profiles. In short, the CMS needs to know where the device-specific color values came from, and where you want to send them. Whenever you open or create an image, you have to give the CMS this information by specifying a *source profile* and a *target device profile*.

The source profile says, "This RGB data is from such-and-such a scanner," or "This RGB data is from such-and-such a monitor." This tells the CMS what the colors really look like. The target profile tells the CMS where the image is going, so that it can maintain the color in the image.

For example, imagine that color management systems work with words rather than colors. The purpose of the word-CMS is to translate words from one language to another. If you just feed it a bunch of words, it can't do anything. But if you give it the words and tell it that they were written by a French person (the source), it all of a sudden can understand what the words are saying. If you then tell it that you speak German (the target), it can translate the meaning faithfully for you.

The process. Back to pictures: when you scan some artwork, you end up with a lot of RGB data. However, Photoshop has no idea what specific colors those RGB values are meant to represent. When you choose your scanner's device profile as the source profile, you're telling the system that this isn't just any old RGB data; it's the RGB data carefully defined by the scanner's device profile.

To make the image on the monitor match the original, you choose your monitor profile as the target profile. The CMS takes the RGB values in the image, and uses the scanner profile as the secret decoder ring that tells it what colors (in the reference color space) the RGB values represent. Then it calculates new RGB values based on the monitor profile, to produce the same colors when they're displayed on your monitor.

If you just want to print the image, and you don't care what it looks like on the monitor, you could choose a profile for a CMYK output process as the target instead. The CMS would produce a CMYK file targeted for that output process. In theory, the printed output matches the original.

This is really the only thing CMSes do. They convert color data from one device's color space (one "language") to another. Pretty much everything you do with a CMS involves asking it to make the colors match between a source and a target profile. You can use this single capability in many different ways, however. See "Color Management in Use," below.

Space conversions and data loss. Bear in mind that even the best CMS degrades your image when you convert it from one color space to another. It may cause less degradation than Photoshop's conversions, but you only have eight bits per color to start with, so even though the conversions may be very accurate, you still want to limit their number (any color space conversion involves some loss, due to rounding errors).

Canned versus Custom Profiles

The single most important factor affecting the quality of the results you get from a CMS is the accuracy of the device profiles. CMSes usually offer a range of canned device profiles that ship with the product. These vary dramatically in usefulness, because they only describe how the device behaved when the profile was created. Some devices are much more stable—both over time and from unit to unit—than others, so the profiles for popular devices included with CMSes may not really describe how your particular device works.

Canned profiles may be inaccurate for a number of different reasons.

▶ Your device may be different from the one the profile vendor measured. This is often the case with desktop color printers, where significant unit-to-unit variation isn't uncommon.

▶ Some of the assumptions in the profile may not be valid in your specific situation. You might, for example, use a different paper stock than the one the vendor used to build a printer profile.

▶ Some devices, particularly monitors, are inherently unstable.

In order to tell the CMS what your devices are really like, you need to build custom profiles for your devices, or adjust the devices themselves to make them behave the way the profile says they do. These two processes are called *characterization* and *calibration*.

Characterization and calibration. The terms *characterization* and *calibration* are often confused. *Characterization* is the process of building a device profile—describing the device to the CMS. You measure the device's behavior, and record it. When you *calibrate* a device, you actually adjust it to bring it into accordance with a known specification.

Depending on the kind of device you're dealing with, you may need to do either or both.

Monitors

Unless you take steps to make it so, it's extremely unlikely that your monitor will actually behave according to the specs in a canned profile. The factory specs for monitor gamma and white point are polite fictions—a slight tweak of the analog brightness and contrast controls is enough to put the monitor way out of spec. Moreover, monitors are unstable. They change quite dramatically during the first half-hour or so after being switched on, and they also change with age.

All monitor-calibration utilities, whether software-only like the Gamma control panel or hardware-based like the various sucker-cup devices, let you choose a target gamma for your monitor. The hardware calibrators also let you choose a target white point—with the Gamma control panel, you have to make a more-or-less educated guess. You can use these to calibrate the monitor, making its behavior match the specifications in the canned profile. See "Monitor Setup and Calibration" in Chapter 5,

Color Preferences, for a detailed discussion of how, why, and when to calibrate your monitor.

If you use a hardware calibrator, it probably lets you build custom monitor profiles for one or more CMSes. If you want to use a CMS that the calibrator doesn't support directly, you can set the monitor to the values contained in a canned profile—preferably one that uses the same phosphor set as your monitor, since you can't change that. Otherwise, you're better off creating and using a custom monitor profile.

Scanners

Scanners also drift over time, though not as drastically as monitors. The difference is that you can't calibrate a desktop scanner because there are no knobs to turn. Fortunately, most CMSes have software that provides the ability to create scanner profiles. These are often called *scanner-calibration utilities*, but they really characterize the scanner instead. Most use a target called the IT8.7, an honest-to-goodness international standard. Agfa sells an IT8.7 package, while Kodak's version—called the Q-60—is "IT8.7-compliant." (We've noticed that international standards are usually named by committees of engineers.)

The IT8.7 consists of a physical target (either a photographic print or a transparency) that was measured at the factory when it was manufactured, and a digital file that contains a record of those measurements. You scan the target; then the characterization software reads the resulting scan, compares it with the known values for the target, and builds a scanner profile that records the way the scanner interpreted the target.

If you notice that your custom scanner profile seems less accurate than it used to be, it's a sign that your scanner's behavior has changed, and it's time to make a new scanner profile. Bear in mind that the targets fade over time—you should plan on replacing them about once a year. Also remember that when you replace the target, you need to replace the digital reference file that contains the factory-measured values for the target—it's easier for the manufacturers to simply measure each batch of targets than to manufacture them all to exactly the same tolerances.

Color Printers

Canned color-printer profiles generally get you in the right ballpark, but again, their accuracy can vary. For instance, with dye-sublimation and, to a lesser extent, thermal-wax printers, there's usually some variation from ribbon to ribbon. Ink-jet vendors often reformulate the inks without telling anyone, which can render a profile useless. Output profiles take the specific paper stock into account, so if you use a different paper stock, the color will be off. Color laser printers are prone to react to changes in temperature and humidity with drastic shifts in color, though some of the newer ones have sensing circuitry that automatically adjusts the toner flow to compensate.

You can't calibrate most desktop printers—there's nothing to adjust. What you get is what you get. You have to either hope that it's the same as what the CMS vendor got when they built the profile, edit the profile based on trial-and-error test prints, or make your own custom profiles using a tool such as Candela's ColorSynergy. (See sidebar, "ColorSync 2.0 and the ICC Initiative," later in this chapter.)

Presses and Proofing Systems

By their very nature, presses vary enormously, but printers go to great lengths to control that variation, so one might think that canned profiles would work well on press. But most commercial printers believe differently. Their number-one complaint about CMSes is that they don't offer any control over the way the separations are generated, and they feel that as a result they're unlikely to get the optimum separations for their press/paper combinations.

To some extent, it's a fair complaint, but we've obtained great results from canned output profiles for proofing systems like Match Print and AgfaProof. We've used them to create film that gave the printer a minimum of headaches. We didn't tell them that the seps were generated by a CMS, which may have helped. The range of variation possible on press makes an absolutely accurate press profile less critical than one for a color printer—as long as the film is somewhere in the middle of the manageable range, a good press operator should be able to print from it. But they should be able to do even better with a custom profile for the specific press, ink, and paper combination.

Tools for custom output profile creation have been slow to appear, but the first few are already on the market, and we expect the trend to continue. Wouldn't it be great if your commercial printer could simply give you a profile made for your chosen paper stock running on their press, using their preferred ink densities and black generation?

Color Management in Use

A CMS may only do one thing, but with the appropriate device profiles you can use the one thing it does in several different ways. Getting the right profiles hasn't always been easy (see sidebar, "ColorSync 2.0 and the ICC Initiative"), and as we've explained, the accuracy of the profiles varies. But with good profiles, a CMS can be a powerful tool. Here are a few of the ways you can use one.

▶ Automated scanning

▶ Using your monitor as a reference

▶ RGB-to-CMYK conversions

▶ Cross-rendering between devices

Automated Scanning

If you're simply trying to match your output to your original artwork, CMSes may help beyond your wildest expectations. When you create a profile for your scanner, you can be sure that the color in your original (rather than just a bunch of RGB data) has really been captured. The key is that the profile describes the scanner's behavior using specific scanner settings. In order for the CMS to do its job correctly, you must scan everything using those same settings.

To match your output image to the original scanned artwork, you can choose the profile for the output device as the target when converting the image with the CMS software (see Figure 16-2).

Figure 16-2
Scanner to output

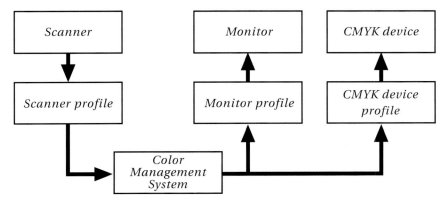

Strengths. This approach works pretty well (*really* well in many cases) if all you want to do is to reproduce the original as closely as possible, *and* you like the compromises the CMS makes in contrast and saturation when it squeezes the range of color in the original down to something that will fit the gamut of the output device.

If you want to change the contrast or the color balance of the original, or control the saturation yourself, it makes more sense to choose your monitor as the target profile instead. This gives you an accurate version of the image on your screen (what you see is what you get, in theory). Later, when you've finished adjusting the image, you can push it through the CMS again, using the monitor profile as the source profile and your output devices as your target.

Limitations. Automatic scanning has two big shortcomings—one is a major inconvenience; the other is specialized, but insurmountable.

▶ **The high-bit disadvantage.** Because the profile is only valid for one specific group of scanner settings, you *have* to scan everything at those settings. If you have a high-bit scanner, you're just throwing away the capabilities those extra bits bring (see "The High-Bit Advantage" in Chapter 12, *Capturing Images*). You can work around this to some extent by creating different scanner profiles using settings appropriate for different image types—a high-key, a low-key, and a mid-key profile, for example—but then the process isn't automatic. You have to decide which profile to use, and set the scanner accordingly.

▶ **Scanning negatives.** The second shortcoming, which may be less relevant to most people, is that there's no way to build a scanner profile for scanning negatives. Nobody makes a scanner target on negative stock, and even if they did, the exposure latitude on negs is so wide that the profile would contain a lot of questionable assumptions.

Make Your Monitor the Reference

If you're working with an 8-bit scanner and good originals, scanning through a CMS makes a lot of sense, but if you have a high-bit scanner, or if you need to change the tone or color balance of the original, a much better approach is to ignore the CMS during the scanning stage, and just make the image look good on your monitor. You make your monitor the reference for the image—you tell the color management system that the way the image appears on your monitor is the way you want it to appear everywhere else.

When you want to generate output, you use your monitor profile as the source profile for the image. This approach relies heavily on good monitor calibration, which in our experience means some kind of hardware monitor calibrator, but when it works, you actually get close to the ideal of WYSIWYG color.

What you use as a target profile depends on where the image is going. If you're printing the image, you'd typically want to use a CMYK print profile as your target, in which case you get automatic color separations. On the other hand, if you're simply moving the image to another computer, you'd want to use that computer monitor's profile as the target. The difference between monitors can be significant; the CMS makes it less so.

Strengths. The key strength of using your monitor as the reference, besides the fact that you can trust what you see, is that it lets you use all the capabilities of your input device (particularly if it's a high-bit scanner) and simply lets you attach an unambiguous color meaning to the RGB values being displayed on your screen. If the monitor profile is accurate, you're telling the CMS what color you're seeing on the monitor.

Another advantage this approach has over automated scanning is that you work with the first-generation image file, before applying any CMS transforms (with their inevitable image degradation). You can use the original scanned RGB image as your working file, and only later target it to all sorts of output processes by sending it through the CMS. This way, the image is subject to only one color-space conversion instead of two, so it suffers less degradation.

Limitations. The big downfall of using your monitor as a reference is that it depends entirely on the accuracy of your monitor profile. Canned profiles just won't do it, so you need calibration hardware that will let you create a custom monitor profile, and you need to verify the monitor calibration periodically.

Also, remember that it's impossible to "match" the image you see on the screen in the printing process. The screen always has a wider color gamut and dynamic range than you can reproduce in print.

RGB-to-CMYK Conversion

Both FotoTune and KCMS produce better color separations than a million experts working for a million years could ever produce using Photoshop's separation engine, *if*—and it's a big if—your output conditions match your output profile. The only shortcoming is that it's difficult and sometimes impossible to tune the profile to match a particular press. It's safe to say under any circumstances that either system will give you much better results than Photoshop does, using its default separation settings.

Since presses vary so much—both from press to press and over the course of a print run on a single press—both FotoTune and KCMS take the proofing stage rather than the press itself as their aim point. Using these profiles, you'll be able to deliver film that's printable with no hassles, but it won't necessarily be the best possible color that you could obtain from a specific press.

Cross-Rendering

Most images in Photoshop will, sooner or later, end up on a printing press. Because of the vagaries of this process, however, it's important to proof images on paper before committing them to your lithographer. Traditionally, this has been done by imaging film and then making a Match Print, Cromalin, or the like (an expensive process, all told). But here in the digital age, we have more options; we can proof on either our monitors (*soft proofing*) or on a high-quality color printer (*preproofing*). Both of these require a sturdy color management system.

You can ask the CMS to make one device (like your monitor or your printer) simulate the behavior of another. This is called *cross-rendering*. It takes advantage of the fact that a device with a wide color gamut can always simulate the behavior of a device with a narrower color gamut.

Proofing on the monitor. Soft proofing uses the monitor to simulate printed output. Soft proofing can't substitute for a real laminated film proof, but it can help you save money and avoid nasty surprises by reducing the number of printed proofs you may have to produce. Photoshop 3.0 offers soft proofing in two ways—CMYK Preview and a Gamut Alarm—but they've got three major problems.

▶   They're only as accurate as your Monitor Setup, Printing Inks Setup, and Separation Setup preferences (see Chapter 5, *Color Preferences*).

▶ They're subject to Photoshop's gamut-clipping behavior.

▶ They're only accurate if you're using Photoshop to do the separations.

As it turns out, there are a few colors that can be reproduced in process color that simply can't be seen on the monitor—notably some yellow-orange and blue-green hues—so there's a limit to soft-proofing accuracy. Nevertheless, soft proofing can provide a very useful reality check in the early stages of a job.

In the best of all possible worlds, we'd want to actually see and work in a simulated CMYK environment (much like Photoshop's CMYK Preview mode lets us do). However, the current offerings of CMSes simply give us a static simulated image.

Tip: Ignoring Gamut Warnings. We've found that if we use the KCMS or FotoTune separation engine, we don't always have to bring our image's colors fully into gamut. This is because FotoTune and KCMS do a good job of compressing the gamut without clipping. We always examine the soft-proof simulation carefully, and if the out-of-gamut areas don't appear objectionable on the simulation, we'll leave those colors alone.

Tip: Use Custom Separation Tables for CMYK Display. Some CMSes let you convert device profiles to Photoshop separation tables. If you actually use them to let Photoshop create separations, you run into Photoshop's gamut-clipping behavior, so we don't recommend the practice. But they're very useful for displaying the CMYK files generated by the CMS itself. If you use Photoshop's own Printing Inks Setup, CMS-generated CMYK files often look lurid and weird, but if you use custom separation tables generated from the device profile, the display is much more accurate. In effect, you get an editable soft proof. Agfa FotoTune, EfiColor, and Candela's ColorSynergy all allow you to convert device profiles to separation tables.

Proofing on color printers. Hard-copy proofing—often known as preproofing—lets you use an output device with a wide gamut, such as a dye-sublimation or Iris ink-jet printer, to simulate the gamut of a press or (more commonly) of a proofing system such as 3M Match Print.

Preproofing on a composite color printer can be more accurate than a soft proof on the monitor.

If you simply send a CMYK image targeted for press to a dye-sub printer, the results will quite likely look strange, because the dye-sublimation printer's inks are nothing like four-color process inks. Instead, you can use a CMS to cross-render from one device's color space to the other's (see Figure 16-3). This is currently done using two CMS transforms.

Figure 16-3
Cross-rendering

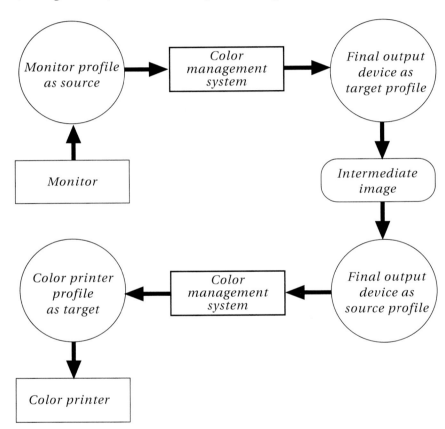

1. First, use the source profile for the RGB image as the source, and the final output profile as the target. For example, the source might be your monitor, and the target might be a 3M Match Print with 20-percent dot gain, Light GCR, and so on.

2. Next, transform the image again, using the final output profile (the web press, or whatever) as the source, and the proofing device's profile as the target.

Note that in some current and (we hope) most future implementations of CMSes, you don't actually have to perform the two transforms separately. Instead, you just ask the CMS for a three-way transform.

Other color printers, such as thermal-wax and desktop ink-jets, usually don't cover the entire gamut of four-color process, so they aren't as well-suited as dye-subs to preproofing use. The same holds true for color laser copiers and the new generation of color desktop laser printers. Still, the techniques described here should help you get much better results from those printers than you'll get from Photoshop's own separations.

Strengths. Soft proofing can help you show clients what to expect when the job hits print, without first going through the time and expense of targeting the image and printing a proof. This is probably its biggest value. It can also help you avoid unpleasant surprises by showing you how much the color is likely to change, and how the tonal range will be affected.

Hard-copy proofing is somewhat more reliable than soft proofing. We still wouldn't use a dye-sub print as a substitute for a Match Print (though many people with consistent publications and conditions do), but they can certainly help you cut down on multiple iterations of Match Prints. The Iris ink-jet printers are the undisputed champs when it comes to accurate preproofs, because they can print the proof on the same paper stock that will be used for the job. However, because the inks are water-soluble, an injudicious sneeze can wreck an Iris print.

Tip: Remote Proofing. You can, with a little care, implement remote-proofing strategies. Instead of sending an actual proof, you can send a color-managed file along with the appropriate profile, which the client can then print through the CMS at their site.

Limitations. Both soft proofing and preproofing are only as good as the profiles used in their generation—a lot can go wrong. A bigger limitation is that you're only proofing color. Problems with the film itself can go undetected—you won't see scratches, moirés, hickeys, or any of the other ills to which film is heir, unless you actually make a film-based proof. We prefer to think of preproofing and soft proofing as "preflight" strategies. They help us get closer to the desired result, but we still use conventional proofing methods as our final check.

Remember, the "Chrome" is still the contract.

Color Management Players

At present, there are three significant color management systems available for use with Photoshop—Kodak's KCMS, Agfa's FotoTune, and EFI's EfiColor. A fourth, Apple's ColorSync 2.0, has just been released as we're writing this, and as yet, most applications don't actually make use of it. The limited testing we've been able to do so far indicates that it's a very strong technology, and we hope to see it turned into real products that people can use (see sidebar, "ColorSync 2.0 and the ICC Initiative").

The problem with discussing CMSes here is that by the time you read this, the software will almost certainly have changed. That's the trouble with any technology in its infancy. Nonetheless, let's explore the basics of each of these CMSes.

Kodak Color Management System (KCMS)

We've obtained better results from Kodak's KCMS than from any of the other CMSes currently available, but we've encountered our fair share of difficulty in doing so.

A tiny part of KCMS actually ships with Photoshop (see "Photoshop and KCMS," later in this chapter). It allows you to import Photo CD images into monitor RGB or CIE Lab, but it only includes canned monitor profiles, and it doesn't include any output profiles. If you simply want to bring a Photo CD image directly into a targeted CMYK color space, you can buy the CMYK Pro Pack from Kodak for about $100. This includes six different GCR/total-ink-limit combinations that cover most needs.

If you want automatic scanning, you need Kodak's PICC package. This includes reflective and transmissive IT8.7 targets for characterizing scanners and creating scanner profiles, as well as a Kodak CMS Acquire plug-in that lets you apply color transforms on the fly when you scan images into Photoshop.

Another useful KCMS component was, until recently, sold by DayStar under the name DayStar ColorMatch (see Figure 16-4). It has now been reacquired by Kodak, but it will almost certainly keep the ColorMatch name. It includes a filter that lets you correct an RGB image for your display, and another that generates a soft-proof image for a specified target profile.

ColorMatch also adds a new Save As option, ColorMatch TIFF, which lets you specify a source profile and a target profile. If you choose a CMYK target profile, KCMS does the separations for you automatically. It also embeds the target profile in the image, so whenever it's opened with KCMS active, KCMS knows what colors the CMYK values in the file represent.

Figure 16-4
ColorMatch Preview

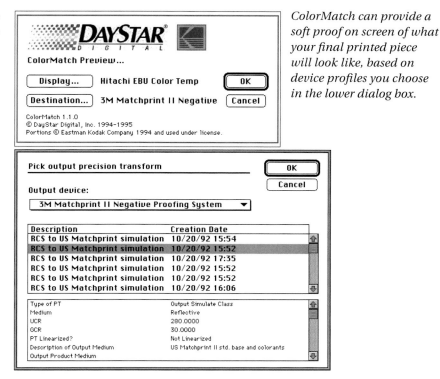

ColorMatch can provide a soft proof on screen of what your final printed piece will look like, based on device profiles you choose in the lower dialog box.

Agfa FotoTune

Agfa's FotoTune 2.0 offers strong scanner profiling, a wide array of free device profiles, and the ability to edit the separation-setup and dot-gain parameters on output profiles.

FotoTune's biggest weakness is that all the monitor profiles ship with a target gamma of 1.0. We think this is insane. We've never seen a monitor that can display images properly at linear gamma; the midtones end up being washed out, and the shadows look posterized. You can edit the monitor profiles to a more reasonable target gamma, but the monitor-to-print matching you get still leaves something to be desired. Agfa relies on third parties for hardware monitor calibration, and at present none of them support FotoTune 2.0; so we can't say if hardware calibration will improve the situation.

FotoTune offers soft proofing through its SoftProof filter (see Figure 16-5), and automatic color separations through the ColorMatcher Export module. SoftProof can display both a simulation of the output and a gamut warning—the latter is a grayscale version of the image, with the out-of-gamut areas in bright red.

Figure 16-5
SoftProof 2.0

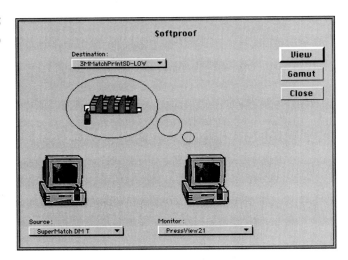

FotoTune also offers an elegant cross-rendering feature in the form of the Hard Copy Proof export module, which lets you specify a source, a target, and a simulation profile; you can, for example, choose your scanner or monitor as the source, a press-proofing system such as Match Print as the destination, and a color printer such as an Iris ink-jet as the simulation. FotoTune will then create a file which, when printed on the Iris, will simulate the Match Print.

The great strength of FotoTune (besides excellent RGB-to-CMYK conversion—and free profiles!) is its integration with Agfa scanners. With it, you can scan directly to a targeted CMYK color space, so scans land on disk almost ready to print (we still use Photoshop to apply unsharp masking). This can boost your productivity significantly, particularly if all you want to do is to reproduce the original image as exactly as possible.

EfiColor

EFI's EfiColor was the first major CMS to hit the market, and it achieved good market penetration due to its bundling with QuarkXPress. However, it's pretty much dead in the water now. EFI has stopped development of end-user software, so it's unlikely that we'll see any improvements to Efi-Color such as new device profiles or a Power Mac-native version.

While EfiColor is rich in features, and has a fairly easy user interface, it also has some serious shortcomings. The scanner-profiling utility is substantially less accurate than Agfa's or Kodak's—it uses a fairly crude proprietary target, with far fewer color patches than the industry-standard IT8.7 target used by its competitors. Likewise, the quality of its color separations leaves a lot to be desired, unless you like a very heavy black plate. Better output profiles could perhaps improve this situation, but we don't expect to see any from EFI.

EfiColor supports Photoshop by creating custom separation tables, so it actually uses Photoshop's separation engine to perform color-space conversions. The problem with this approach is that Photoshop's separation engine doesn't do a very sophisticated job of gamut compression. Instead, it simply clips out-of-gamut colors.

Photoshop and KCMS

Photoshop 3.0 includes a limited version of the Kodak Color Management System (KCMS) right in the box. However, Photoshop only uses KCMS to acquire Photo CD images, and only in a limited way; it comes with only two target profiles—Lab and a "generic" RGB monitor. Nevertheless, it has greatly simplified the process of working with Photo CD images in Photoshop. Previous versions of Photoshop let you open Photo CD images in all sorts of ways, most of them totally wrong.

Color management is at the heart of the Photo CD system. Photo CD images are stored in a proprietary calibrated color space, Photo YCC, and they must be translated into a color space that Photoshop understands before you can work with them (see Figure 16-6). KCMS lets you select a source and target profile, and a resolution at which to open the image.

Figure 16-6
Importing Photo CD images

Source profiles. It's important to choose the correct Photo CD profile for your film as the source profile. There are three—Universal Kodachrome, which you should use *only* for Kodachrome; Universal Ektachrome, which you should use for all other slides; and Universal Negative, which you should use for negatives. If you don't know which is the correct profile, you can click the Image Info button to open the Image Info dialog box (see Figure 16-7).

The two vital pieces of information in this dialog box are Medium of Original and Product Type of Original. The medium is either reversal (slide) or negative film. The product type is the specific brand of film.

With slide film, your only concern is whether it's Kodachrome or not. If it's anything else, the Product Type will be 052/55 SPD. Use the Universal Kodachrome profile for Kodachrome slides, and the Universal Ektachrome profile for all other slide-film types. If it's a negative, use the Universal Negative profile as your source.

If Image Info comes up blank, it's a sign that you're dealing with a pretty old Photo CD that was scanned before many of the current refinements were in place. If you have a hard copy of the image to refer to, simply try each profile and see which one gets you closest. If you don't have an original, you'll just have to choose the one that gives you the result you like best. See the sidebar "Correcting an Old Photo CD Image" in Chapter 7, *Color Correction*, for an example.

Target profiles. If you only have the profiles that came with Photoshop, you should probably use the Lab profile rather than generic RGB as your target (see "Targeting" in Chapter 12, *Capturing Images*). However, it may be worth trying the RGB on one image, on the unlikely chance that it actually matches your monitor. Better yet, try to get a custom profile for your monitor.

Or if you want to convert your RGB image into CMYK for output, you can buy additional profiles from Kodak for a variety of output types at a

Figure 16-7
Photo CD
Image Info

ColorSync 2.0 and the ICC Initiative

As we said earlier in the chapter, Apple's ColorSync 2.0 is an up-and-coming color management system. But ColorSync 2.0 has significance beyond being just another CMS. It provides a place in the system for other CMSes to coexist and even cooperate. And perhaps even more significant, it uses a device-profile format, the ICC (International Color Consortium) format, that has every likelihood of becoming an open cross-platform standard.

All the major operating system and color management system vendors have either adopted or agreed to adopt the ICC profile standard. Once everyone has done so, you'll no longer be dependent on a single CMS vendor for your device profiles. All profiles will work with all CMSes. In essence, you'll be able to buy your razor from one outfit, and your blades from another. In fact, with Agfa

giving away profiles, and Apple giving away the CMS engine, you can get both the razor and the blades for free—in essence, you'll get a free shave!

Custom profiles. More important, the ICC profile format—in conjunction with the new breed of inexpensive spectrophotometers such as LightSource's Colortron and X-Rite's digital swatch book—have created an opportunity for third parties to create output-profiling tools. We've already obtained encouraging results from the first such package, Candela's ColorSynergy, and we look forward to other such offerings both from third parties and from the CMS vendors themselves. To build an output profile, you print a target file containing a bunch of CMYK patches—Linotype's PrintOpen uses 212, while ColorSynergy uses 504—and

measure them. The measurement device may be a calibrated color scanner, an inexpensive spectrophotometer such as the Colortron, or an industrial-strength instrument like the Gretag SPM 50. You feed the measurements into the profiling software, specifying the desired ink limits and black generation, and it creates a profile for that specific print process.

Custom profiling tools let you create output profiles for any press, ink, and paper combination, with complete control over how the separations are created. And in the future, custom output profiles will also let you bring CMYK drum scans into the color management world (not easily done today). If we know what kind of separation the scanner was set up to produce, we can select the appropriate CMYK device profile and use that as the source profile for the image.

variety of prices. We've obtained excellent results using the 3M Match Print II Negative Proofing System family of profiles, which offers 15 different combinations of GCR and total ink limit.

At the time of writing, Kodak hadn't released an ICC-compliant version of KCMS, but that will undoubtedly change, as will most everything else we could say about specific color management products.

Brave New Worlds

Color management is a fast-moving target, but we can say some things with certainty. First, the CMS market is moving away from a competing group of closed, proprietary CMSes to an open, standards-driven component-stereo model, where you can buy one component from vendor A and another from vendor B. Second, high-end prepress shops have strenuously avoided anything that seemed related to a CMS; it remains to be seen if the prospect of open systems and custom profiling will make CMSes more tempting to them. We think it should.

And now that more and more people are doing serious color work using RGB scanners and Photo CD, CMSes are becoming increasingly important. If the currently available systems aren't quite ready for you yet, don't worry; they will be soon.

17

Storing Images

Managing Files for Fast Production

We've been barking at you for a few hundred pages that what we're really talking about is not images, but rather zeros and ones. But the zeros and ones that one program writes to disk may not be readable by another program. Why? Because the same data can be written to disk in a variety of ways, called *file formats*. Different file formats may be as different as two different languages (like Spanish versus Chinese), or as similar as two dialects of the same language (like American versus British English).

The world would be a simpler place if everyone (and all software) spoke the same language, but that's not going to happen. Fortunately, programs such as Photoshop, QuarkXPress, and PageMaker can read and sometimes even write in multiple file formats. The important thing, then, is not for us to understand exactly what makes one different from the others, but rather what each file format's strengths and weaknesses are, so that we can use them intelligently. (Wouldn't it be great if we could speak in French to our lovers, German to our bosses, and oh-so-polite Japanese to our acquaintances?)

In this chapter, we're taking an in-depth look at each of the many file formats that Photoshop understands. (Note that we won't cover Photo CD here, because Photoshop can't write Photo CD files—it can only read them; they're discussed in Chapter 12, *Capturing Images*.) More to the point, we'll explore why you'd want to use some of them and avoid others. One of the key issues in storing images is saving disk space, so we also discuss how various file formats handle compression internally. At the end of the chapter we explore the nitty-gritty of compression in file formats: how it works, what it does to your files, and how it's different from archival compression methods.

Tip: Hide Formats You Don't Use. Photoshop itself actually only knows how to read and write about half of the file formats we're discussing in this chapter. But it can read and write the other types because of plug-ins that came with the program. For instance, when the CompuServe GIF and FilmStrip plug-ins are in Photoshop's Plug-ins folder, Photoshop can read and write in these "languages" (see Chapter 1, *Building a Photoshop System*, for more on plug-ins).

However, if you don't use these formats, you don't have to leave them cluttering up your Save As popup menu. Instead, you can move any formats that you don't want out of the File Formats folder (inside the Plug-ins folder in the Photoshop folder) into another folder (outside the Plug-ins folder). Don't just hide them inside another nested folder; Photoshop can still find them there.

In this section, we'll focus on each file format that appears in the Save As dialog box's popup menu. Before we get to that, however, we'll cover one feature that applies to every file format in Photoshop: previews.

Preview Options

When you use Save As or Save a Copy with Photoshop's default preferences, Photoshop also creates two miniature preview images within your file: Icon and Thumbnail. You can control this behavior, and add a third type of preview, by turning on the Ask When Saving checkbox in the More Preferences dialog box (press Command-K to go to General Preferences, and click the More button). From then on, you get three checkboxes in the Save As dialog box, so you can choose which previews Photoshop saves (see Figure 17-1). Here's a rundown of what the different previews are.

Icon. The first preview, Icon, acts as a desktop picture, so you can see (with a little imagination) what the image is when you're staring at the file on your Macintosh desktop (see Figure 17-2). For the technoids in the audience: it adds an 8-bit, 32-by-32-pixel icl8 resource (that's geekspeak for a color icon) to the file.

Figure 17-1
Preview options

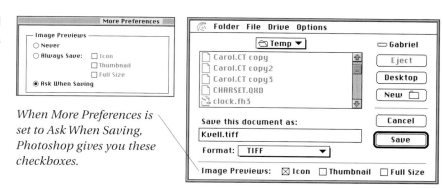

When More Preferences is set to Ask When Saving, Photoshop gives you these checkboxes.

Figure 17-2
Icons on
the desktop

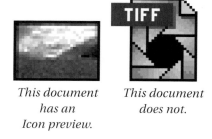

This document has an Icon preview.

This document does not.

Thumbnail. The second preview is a slightly larger image that Quick-Time-savvy applications (including Photoshop and QuarkXPress, but not, alas, PageMaker) can display in their Open or Get Picture dialog boxes. This way, you can see what's in the image before you open it. Again, for those who like to know: this image is a 128-by-128-pixel, JPEG-compressed, 24-bit PICT in the file's resource fork.

Note that you must have Apple's QuickTime extension loaded in order to write or read thumbnail previews.

Full Size. When Ask When Saving is turned on in More Preferences, Photoshop gives you one additional choice: Full Size preview. This one adds a considerably larger JPEG-compressed 24-bit PICT resource to the file; its dimensions are the actual physical output size of the image, down-sampled to the resolution of your monitor.

Saving and Opening Images

Throughout this chapter we discuss "reading" and "writing" various file formats, but we should, just for a moment, explore the mechanisms in Photoshop for performing these acts. The four relevant menu items—Open, Save, Save As, and Save a Copy—are all found under the File menu. (Some third-party color management systems use the Export command to save images that have been color-corrected for a specific device; we'll deal with those later.)

Open. You can open, or "read," an image by selecting Open, choosing the file, and pressing OK. Simple enough. The one exception to this (and this is why we mention it at all) is when the Show All Files checkbox is turned on. In that case, you can specify what file format ("language") you'd like Photoshop to read in.

This is particularly helpful when trying to open images that were created on a PC or some other sort of machine. When you bring the file across to the Mac, Photoshop may not recognize it as a TIFF file or EPS file or whatever it may be. In this case, you must turn on Show All Files, and explicitly tell it what file format the image is saved in (see "Tip: File Name as File Type," later in this chapter).

Save. Selecting Save in Photoshop works the same as in every other Macintosh program: it replaces the previously saved image data with the current image data. Photoshop saves in whatever format the original image was saved in. If you haven't saved your document when you select Save (or press Command-S), Save performs a Save As instead.

Save As. If you want to save the image you're working on but change its name, its file format, and/or the place it's saved, use Save As instead of Save. This doesn't change the original image (the one already on disk). We use Save As all the time as we go through the process of adjusting an image. That way, we can always go back two or three (or more) steps.

Note that if your document has layers or alpha channels, you may not be able to save in a different file format with Save As.

Save a Copy. The Save a Copy feature first arrived in version 3.0, and like all new features, it

---

The primary benefit to Full Size preview is that it can be used by many third-party image browsers. It's ignored by both PageMaker (versions 5 and 6) and QuarkXPress (the latest version as of this writing, 3.31r5). If you're an XPress user, however, check out the next tip.

Tip: Full Size Previews and XPress. Many versions of XPress (every 3.x version before 3.31r5) use the Full Size preview as a screen preview. This is no big deal with EPS files, but it can speed things up a lot when importing very large TIFF images. Where XPress ordinarily has to build low-resolution previews by reading in all the image data, when an image has a Full Size preview, XPress can just plop that on the page instead.

The other major benefit to using Full Size preview in TIFF images with earlier versions of XPress is that the screen preview is much better betook some getting used to. However, now we find ourselves using it daily. Save a Copy is the same as Save As, except for two things.

▶ If you have multiple layers, Save a Copy lets you save a flattened version of the image (in which all the layers are merged together).

▶ If you have multiple channels, it gives you the option of including them or not.

Selecting Save a Copy is like saying, "Save the current image to disk, but let me keep working on the one I have open now." Or, it's like making a photocopy of your artwork, and then continuing to work on the original.

Tip: Save QuicKey. David has been working on Macintoshes for more than ten years, but he still gets into hot water with

Figure 17-3 QuicKeys saves the day

Photoshop's Save command. Because of long-standing habits, he occasionally presses Command-S, even when he wants to use Save As or Save a Copy.

While this typically doesn't cause irreparable damage in a word-processing or page-layout application, it often means disaster for Photoshop images. (For instance, he might be working on original image data from a scanner, which he may want to return to later.)

His solution: he made a little QuicKey that stops him from saving so easily. Now when he presses

Command-S, a little dialog box appears, asking him if he really wants to save (see Figure 17-3).

If he clicks OK (or presses Return), it saves just as usual. But he has a chance to cancel out of this dangerous maneuver and avoid risking his original image data.

For those of you who'd like to try this, the QuicKey is a Sequence with two steps: there's a Message Extension shortcut (which makes the dialog box appear with a Cancel button option) followed by a Menu Item shortcut (which selects Save from the File menu).

cause it's a 24-bit JPEG image. (Don't worry, the Full Size preview doesn't add too much to the file size.)

There is a problem here, though. XPress in its latest version ignores Full Size previews because people were having trouble printing them. Either they wouldn't print at all, or the printed image would look totally wrong. The reason is arcane (having to do with XPress's handling of Scitex CT images), but we've boiled it down into two rules.

▶ Never use Full Size preview with grayscale TIFFs destined for XPress.

▶ If you do use Full Size preview on CMYK TIFFs, don't use XPress's Other Contrast features on the images (which would be a silly thing to do anyway).

If you do either of these, you're sure to mess up the image. (Of course, if you're using XPress version r5 or later, neither of these is relevant because the program will ignore the Full Size preview.) We find that the extra time it takes to save the Full Size preview is more than outweighed by the increased speed with which the TIFF imports into XPress, particularly once you get into the 25-megabyte-and-larger range.

Note that there's no reason to select Full Size Preview with an EPS file; it's equivalent to saving the EPS file with a Macintosh (JPEG) preview (see "Encapsulated PostScript (EPS)," later in this chapter).

Tip: Save Time Saving Previews. Saving an Icon or Thumbnail preview considerably lengthens the time it takes to save your image. However, if you save one type of preview, saving the other type as well takes hardly any additional time—one or two seconds at most. Saving a Full Size preview takes still longer, so you should only do so if the image is going to an application that will benefit from it.

File Formats

You've probably noticed by now that a lot of this book focuses on prepress. We've done our best to include vital information for those whose output is continuous-tone film or the computer screen, but our backgrounds are in putting ink on paper. Most people in prepress use Photoshop to prepare images that they're going to take elsewhere, be it PageMaker, Quark-XPress, a Scitex system, or whatever. So, while Photoshop can read and write a number of different file formats, we're going to focus on just a few at first.

While you're working on an image in Photoshop, you should save the file in Photoshop's native file format. It's the best possible format, in that it supports all of Photoshop's nifty features such as layers and channels, and it uses a robust lossless compression scheme. The only problem is that Photoshop is just about the only application that can read it, so if your images are destined for another application, you need to save them in some other format to make them readable.

If your image is destined for a presentation program, a multimedia program, or another screen-based application, PICT and JPEG are the best formats to use. But if the image is going to a page-layout program, you should always use TIFF or EPS.

Some page-layout programs will tell you that they can accept and print images in PICT, or .BMP, or .WMF, or various other weird formats. This may even be true on the third Tuesday of the month, when it coincides with the full moon, and the wind is coming briskly out of the southwest; but in general, using anything other than TIFF or EPS in a print-based application is courting disaster, no matter what the software publisher says. So TIFF and EPS are the formats that we'll cover in detail first and foremost, along with a more brief discussion of PICT and JPEG. Then we'll cover the other options at a brisk pace.

Photoshop 3.0

The Photoshop 3.0 file format—otherwise known as Photoshop's "native" format—is the most flexible format around. In fact, it's the only way to save everything that Photoshop is capable of producing: multiple layers, paths, multiple channels, clipping paths, screening and transfer settings, and so on. This is typically the best format in which to save your documents until you know how you're going to use them.

One of the coolest things about the Photoshop 3.0 format is that it automatically compresses the image using *run length encoding,* or RLE. (We explain the various compression methods in "Compression," later in this chapter.) There's no way to turn this compression off, but it's fast and transparent, so we don't worry about it, and neither should you.

Compression in the Photoshop 3.0 format is especially helpful when you're saving files with multiple alpha channels, because basic selection channels often compress down to a tiny fraction of their original size with RLE (see Figure 17-4). The same thing goes for saving files that have multiple layers, because transparent space on layers is compressed to almost nothing (not that you have a choice on this one; as we said earlier, the Photoshop 3.0 format is the only one that supports multiple layers).

At the time of this writing, the only program we know of that can read native Photoshop 3.0 files, layers and all, is Specular Collage (a very cool program for compositing and "laying out" an image).

Photoshop 2.0

No one we associate with still uses Photoshop 2.0. However, we *do* know some folks who use version 2.5.1. If you need to open your Photoshop

TIFF versus EPS

As we travel around the world do-ing seminars and conferences, we are forever hearing people say things like "My service bureau told me to only use EPS files," or "I was told I'd get better images if I used TIFFs," or "Don't EPS files print better?" While we try to ap-pear calm and collected, inside we're just waiting to scream, "Who told you this nonsense? Were they raised by wolves?"

While the confusion is under-standable, we want to make a few points about TIFFs and EPSes that will, we hope, clear the air a little.

TIFFs and EPSes contain *ex-actly the same image data*. The way in which it's written (en-coded) may be somewhat differ-ent, but that doesn't change the image one iota.

The key difference between TIFFs and EPSes is not what they are or how they're written, but what other programs can do to them.

Encapsulated data. The entire philosophy behind EPS (Encap-sulated PostScript) files is that they're little capsules of informa-tion. No other program should have to—or even be able to—go in and change anything about the data that's there.

EPS files were designed to be imported into other programs so that those programs wouldn't have to worry about what's in them at all. When it came time to print, that program would simply send the EPS down to the printer, trusting that the PostScript inside would image correctly.

Open TIFF format. TIFFs, on the other hand, were designed not only to be imported into other programs, but also to be ex-changed among image editors.

That is, the program that imports the TIFF can actually access the information inside it and, poten-tially, change it.

Programs such as QuarkXPress and PageMaker have exploited this property of TIFFs by incorporating features that let you make changes to the TIFF image. On pages, for in-stance, you can apply a color to a grayscale TIFF image. When you print the page, the program liter-ally changes the image data on its way to the printer. It almost never changes the data on your disk, but it changes it in the print stream. There's no way for these programs to change EPS image data at all.

Downsampling and cropping. More important, both PageMaker and XPress have the ability to downsample TIFF data at print time. If you import a 300-ppi TIFF into XPress and print it to a desktop laser printer at 60 lpi (see

documents in Photoshop 2.5.1, you may be tempted to save your files in the Photoshop 2.0 format. Don't bother. We have not yet found any ad-vantage of saving documents in this format.

Most images saved in the Photoshop 3.0 format open just fine in older versions of the program. Similarly, Photoshop 2.5.1 can read TIFF or EPS images saved with multiple channel or path information. The catch here is that the file can't have layers and must have fewer than 16 channels (this is a limitation of versions earlier than 3.0). Also note that versions earlier than 3.0 don't understand compression, so Photoshop won't com-press them in this format; thus, your file sizes may increase dramatically.

Chapter 18, *Output Methods*, for more on halftone screen frequency), XPress automatically downsamples the image to 120 ppi (two times the halftone frequency).

XPress does this because it knows that sending the additional data is wasted time. The result is that your page prints faster. In PageMaker, you can achieve the same thing by choosing Optimized in the Print: Options dialog box. There's no way to downsample an EPS at print time.

Similarly, have you ever tried importing a full-page, 20 MB EPS file into one of these page-layout programs and cropping it down to a 1-by-1-inch square? The program is forced to send the entire 20 megabytes to the printer, even though all you want is a little bit of the image.

With a TIFF image, however, only the data that is necessary to print the page at that screen frequency is sent to the printer,

again saving printing time and costs.

Previews and separations. One of the biggest hassles of TIFF images, however, is that they can take a long time to import, because the page-layout program has to read the entire file in order to create a screen preview for the image. EPS files can import quickly because Photoshop has already created a preview image.

On the other hand, CMYK TIFF files usually print separations much faster than EPS files because the data can be separated into discrete 8-bit chunks (only sending yellow data for the yellow plate, and so on). With EPS files, however, PageMaker and XPress have to send all 32 bits (cyan, yellow, magenta, and black) for each plate. This slows down printing considerably. (There are exceptions to this; see "DCS," later in this chapter, and "Tip: Send Eight Bits, Not 32" in Chapter 18, *Output Methods*.)

Workflow considerations. There are plenty of other differences between EPS and TIFF files—like the fact that you can save clipping paths and halftone-screening information in EPS files—but we're going to leave them for later in the chapter. Our purpose is simply to show that TIFF and EPS files are equals in stature if not in aim.

As for us, when we have a choice, we almost always use TIFF files; we prefer their flexibility, and we do a *lot* of page proofing with large grayscale images, so the downsampling at print time helps a lot. However, if we need fast importing of large files, or clipping paths, we switch to EPS. But don't listen to us. The most important reason why you should use one over the other is not "my consultant/service bureau/guru told me so," but your own workflow. The sorts of images you work with, the kind of network and printers you have, and your proofing needs all play a part in your decision.

Tip: Turn Off 2.5.1 Compatibility. If you *are* using layers and want to open the file in Photoshop 2.5.1, make sure the 2.5.1 Compatibility checkbox is turned on in the General Preferences dialog box (Command-K). Otherwise, always turn off this checkbox. When it's on, files saved in Photoshop 3.0 format can balloon in size (we've seen small files get eight times bigger when saved with 2.5.1 Compatibility). The reason? When this feature is on, Photoshop has to include the same image twice; once for Photoshop 3, and again, layers merged, for 2.5.1. Plus, Photoshop 2.0 can't handle RLE image compression like version 3.0, so all your alpha channels take up much more space.

This checkbox has no effect on files saved in Photoshop 2.0 format (but why would you want to do that?).

Figure 17-4
Compressing
channels

*Photoshop automatically compresses
this simple channel to 11 K*

*This more complicated image only
gets compressed to 130 K with RLE*

Encapsulated PostScript (EPS)

As we said back in Chapter 3, *Image Essentials*, Encapsulated PostScript (EPS) is really an object-oriented file format, but Photoshop can save images as *bitmap-only* EPSes. That's the only kind of EPS file we're going to talk about here. Note that the only time you should use an EPS file is when you're saving an image that you're about to import into a page-layout program. That's what EPS is made for.

While many people prefer working with EPS files over everything else (see sidebar, "TIFF versus EPS," earlier in this chapter), they have some serious limitations. Sure, you can save grayscale, RGB, or CMYK data in EPS format. Sure, you can save an any-sized file with or without compression. Sure, you can save clipping paths and transfer functions. But once you've saved the file, it's set in mud. Once you bring the image into a page-layout program, you're stuck with it.

Plus, you can only print EPS files on a PostScript printer (or with software that acts as a software PostScript interpreter). We almost always work with PostScript printers, so that isn't a problem. But we often *do* want to make some changes to images while on pages—colorizing the image, or setting a special halftone screen—and in those cases we switch to a different file format, such as TIFF.

When you save an image as an EPS, Photoshop lets you set the file's preview style, encoding, and clipping path, and it gives you a choice as to whether or not you want to include halftone screening and/or transfer curve information (see Figure 17-5). Let's look at each of these.

Figure 17-5
Save as EPS

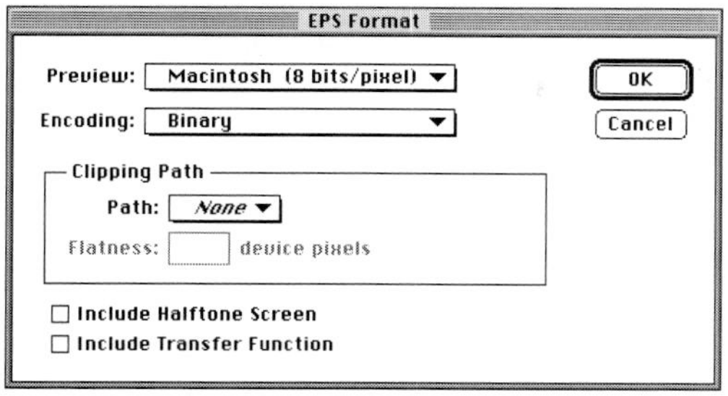

Previews. EPS files typically have two parts: the high-resolution PostScript data and a low-resolution screen preview. When you import an EPS into a page-layout program (or a word processor or whatever), the computer displays the low-res image on the screen, and when you print the page, the computer uses the high-res PostScript code. (If you don't have a PostScript printer, the low-res preview prints out instead—not terribly useful except for simple proofing.)

Photoshop lets you save EPS files with five different types of previews, or no preview at all, via the Preview popup menu in the EPS Format dialog box. As we said in "Preview Options," with EPSes there's no reason to turn on the Full Size preview option in the Save As dialog box. The specific EPS options do the same thing, and give you more control.

▶ **TIFF.** The only time you should select 1-bit or 8-bit TIFF from the Preview popup menu is when your image needs to be transferable between the Mac and the PC. If you choose one of the PICT formats, the preview is lost when the file is moved to the PC (an EPS without a preview just looks like a gray box on pages, though it prints correctly). Some programs on the Macintosh, such as PageMaker and Quark-XPress, can now import PC EPS files with the preview image intact; but no programs that we know of on the PC can read Mac previews.

▶ **PICT.** Files that will stay on the Mac should be saved with a PICT preview. Photoshop gives you three choices: 1-bit, 8-bit, and JPEG. Until recently, David always used the 8-bit Macintosh preview when creating EPS files that were destined to stay on the Mac. Somehow it just seemed safer than using JPEG. Then Bruce showed him the light, and David hasn't gone back to 8-bit since.

When you save an EPS file with a Macintosh JPEG preview, Photoshop has to take the time to build a JPEG preview. However, we gladly take the minor performance hit to get the benefits. JPEG previews are better looking and take up less space on disk than their 8-bit brethren. (A JPEG preview for a 300-dpi tabloid-sized image is about 90 K.) Plus, they occasionally even redraw faster in a page-layout program.

Bear in mind that you can't read or write JPEG previews unless you have the QuickTime system extension loaded, and then only with QuickTime-aware applications (yes for QuarkXPress and PageMaker 6, no for PageMaker 5).

If you're concerned about disk space, you may choose to have no preview (None) or a black-and-white preview (1-bit, either TIFF or PICT). Personally, we'd rather suffer thumbscrews than use either of these when hard drive prices are so low.

ASCII versus binary. When you save an image in Photoshop, you have the choice of how to encode the data (see Figure 17-6). *Encoding* is simply a fancy-schmancy way of saying "the way the data is formatted." The first two choices in the Encoding popup menu, ASCII or binary, are like choosing between words with one or two syllables. If you always said "feline" instead of "cat," it would take twice as long to communicate, right? If you choose ASCII, the image takes up twice as much space on your hard drive and takes twice as long to send to the printer.

Figure 17-6
Encoding in EPS

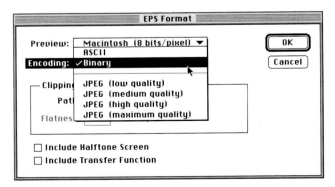

You only need to use ASCII when you're printing PostScript over a PC or UNIX serial port, or passing files through some esoteric networks or gateways. Binary images can confuse these pipelines (and PostScript devices that are connected to them), because some of the binary data is interpreted as control characters that say things like "End of File!" (For the propeller-heads in the audience, this doubling effect occurs because ASCII data is saved in hexadecimal, which uses two 8-bit characters—0 to 9 and A to F—to describe the same information as eight bits of binary data.)

JPEG compression. Instead of saving the EPS file with binary or ASCII encoding, you can choose some level of JPEG compression, which we describe in more detail in "Compressing Images," later in this chapter. (Nope, sorry, there's no way to save an EPS file with lossless compression from Photoshop, even though PostScript Level 2 interpreters can decompress several lossless compression methods.)

Photoshop offers four choices for JPEG quality—Maximum, High, Medium, and Low. The better the quality, the less compression you can achieve. The great benefit of JPEG compression in EPS files is that you not only keep the image small on your hard drive, but you also can send a (much) smaller file down the network lines to your printer, reducing transmission time.

The downside to creating JPEG EPS files, though, is that you can *only* print them on a printer that has Level 2 PostScript, because only they know how to decompress JPEG. Almost all desktop laser printers made in the past couple of years have Level 2, but at present only a small number of imagesetter brands can handle JPEG images.

Finally, remember that images have to be decompressed by the printer, which may or may not be a speed advantage in your setup. Clearly, in a workflow situation where you have a slow network (they always seem slow, don't they?) and a very fast Level 2 printer, JPEG EPS files can be great.

Tip: Removing the JPEG Compression. If you need to print a JPEG-compressed EPS on a non-Level 2 printer, open the file in Photoshop and save it in an uncompressed format. Or you might try the DeBabelizer utility if you have a lot of files to decompress.

Clipping Paths. If you need to silhouette an image using a clipping path, you may have to use EPS (see "Tip: Clipping in TIFFs," below). Clipping is a way to crop an image in a nonrectangular shape (see Figure 17-7). For example, if you want the boundaries of your image to be in the shape of an oval, you could clip it to that shape. Various programs have methods to clip images, but the important thing to remember is that you're not really deleting the data itself; the entire image gets sent to the printer along with the instructions on how to clip it down.

Figure 17-7
The effect of
a clipping path

To make a clipping path in Photoshop, you must first create a path and name it (see "Paths" in Chapter 13, *Selections*). Then, in the Save as EPS dialog box, you can select that named path in the Path popup menu.

People use paths most often when they want to place a silhouette of an object over a colored background in a page-layout program. For instance, many catalogs have a colored tint over the entire page, with irregularly-shaped objects—shoes, toaster ovens, cars—floating as if in mid-air. If you try to achieve this effect by simply making the background transparent (white) rather than using a clipping path, you'll get an object surrounded by a white box. (Even if it looks like there are transparent areas on screen, it still prints as white; see Figure 17-8.)

Because paths are mathematical lines and curves, they're always as sharp as the printer you print on. That's almost always sharper than the resolution of your image, so be prepared for your edges to look overly crisp. No, you can't make a soft, fuzzy edge with a clipping path—so, no drop shadows or clouds! (See Chapter 14, *Essential Image Techniques*, for more information on these sorts of effects.)

Tip: Bump Up Your Flatness. You can often speed up print times dramatically and/or avoid PostScript "limitcheck" errors by raising the PostScript flatness value in the Save as EPS dialog box.

Figure 17-8

**When what you see
isn't what you get**

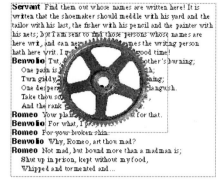

*How the EPS appears on screen in
QuarkXPress.*

How the EPS prints from XPress.

*How an EPS with a clipping
path prints.*

If you've worked with flatness in FreeHand or Illustrator (before version 5), you know that the flatness value determines how hard the PostScript interpreter works to give you smooth curves. The higher the flatness value, the faster the graphic prints, but the more choppy the curve gets. If you raise your flatness too high, the curve turns into a set of straight lines. However, you can almost always raise your flatness to between 3 and 5 and never see the difference, regardless of output resolution.

Of course, flatness only applies to PostScript curves, so if you're not using clipping paths, there's no need for a flatness value.

Tip: Clipping in TIFFs. Until now, if you wanted a clipping path, you had to save the image as an EPS. But that's changed. The newest version of PageMaker (version 6) can read clipping paths saved in TIFF images.

However, you save the clipping path in a slightly different way.

1. Select Clipping Path from the popout menu in the Paths palette.

2. Choose the path that you want as a clipping path.

3. Give it a flatness value and press OK. The name of the path (in the Paths palette) should now be in outline style, indicating it's a clipping path.

4. Save the image as a TIFF and import it into PageMaker 6.

Halftone screens and transfer functions. If you want to save halftone-screening or transfer-curve information in the image, you must also save it as an EPS file. You can set the halftone screens and transfer functions in the Page Setup dialog box (see Chapter 18, *Output Methods,* for details). Our basic opinion is that it's rare that you need to save an EPS with a transfer curve; best just to leave that checkbox turned off.

Saving halftone screens in an EPS file, however, is often very useful. For instance, when saving duotone, tritone, or quadtone images, you almost always want to set specific screen frequencies and angles for each ink. If you want to import that image into a page-layout program, you have to save it as an EPS (that's the only non-native format you can save duotones in), and to maintain your angles, you have to turn on the Include Halftone Screen checkbox.

Tip: Avoid Image Piracy. One of the biggest fears of photographers and other artists who are delving into digital imaging is that their work can be so easily stolen. For instance, if you create an image and send the file to a magazine to be printed, someone could take that file, open it in Photoshop, and copy pieces of it into another file. Would you ever know their new image was built from yours? Does it matter? Is what they did illegal or unethical? These are questions that we'll all be arguing about for years. In the meantime, here's a little trick to make it harder for someone else to open your work in Photoshop.

1. Save the image in EPS format.

2. Open the EPS file in a word processor, such as Microsoft Word. In Word, you have to set the List Files of Type popup menu to All Files in the Open dialog box. If you've got Word's EPS/TIFF filter installed, it may

try to display the image rather than the data; if so, just remove the filter from the Word folder before starting up Word.

3. Remove a portion of the file's header. The header is the part at the top of an EPS file in which all the lines begin with "%". Don't take the first ten or so lines; they're important. We usually take out the stuff that begins about fifteen lines down, starts with "BeginPhotoshop" and ends with "EndPhotoshop". It's all numbers and letters, and looks like ASCII image data.

4. Save the file, or use Save As to save the file with a different name. (Save As works in Microsoft Word, except that Photoshop's desktop icons are lost; doing this in another word processor may lose your screen preview, too.)

5. Use ResEdit or PrairieSoft's DiskTop to check the file's type and creator. If they're anything other than EPSF and 8BIM, change them back to these values. The reason they'd be different is that the word processor changed them to something else. For example, Microsoft Word changes the type to TEXT and the creator to MSWD.

The image can now be imported into a page-layout program, just like any other EPS file, but you (or, more important, someone else) cannot open it in Photoshop. Clearly, you should only perform this surgery on duplicates of your original image.

Most important, this trick won't stop the dedicated pirate. The image data is still there to be stripped out. However, it will stop the casual, possibly ignorant user. Ultimately, the best defense against image piracy is a strong written contract with whomever has your files.

DCS

You won't find DCS (Desktop Color Separation) format in any of Photoshop's Save As popup menus. That's because it's really just a special case of the EPS file format. However, it's weird (and important) enough that we decided to pull it out as a separate section here.

If you've already preseparated your image (converted to CMYK mode) when you save an image in EPS format, you have the choice of saving the image in a single file or five different files (see Figure 17-9). When you choose Off (Single File) under the DCS popup menu in the Save as EPS dialog box, Photoshop saves a single EPS file that contains all four channels of information (that's what we call "a normal EPS file").

Figure 17-9

Saving Desktop Color
Separation (DCS) files

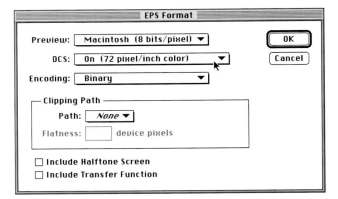

However, when you choose one of the three DCS options (No Composite PostScript, 72-pixel-per-inch Grayscale, or 72-pixel-per-inch Color), Photoshop saves your image in five files: one file for each color channel, plus a master file. The master file is the one that you can re-open in Photoshop or import into a page-layout program. The Preview options work just as they do with normal EPS images (see "Encapsulated Postscript (EPS)," earlier in this chapter).

DCS composites. Many people confuse the EPS's composite image with the preview image. This is understandable; they're almost exactly the same thing. Both are low-resolution (72-ppi) representations of the original image; both can be used instead of the high-res image for proofing.

The real difference is in their uses. The preview image is always in RGB mode and is designed for screen use only. The composite image is saved in CMYK mode (literally, it's the same as downsampling the high-res CMYK image to 72 ppi using Nearest Neighbor interpolation), and is meant to be printed to a low-resolution color printer for proofing purposes.

There are three good reasons to use the five-file DCS format instead of single-file EPS.

▶ Printing times can be shorter from page-layout programs. With a single-file EPS, PageMaker or QuarkXPress typically has to send the entire EPS to the printer for each and every plate. However, with DCS files, they can send only the cyan to the cyan plate, and so on. (XPress may have a patch by the time you read this that lets it "break down" single-file EPS files, too; see "Tip: Send Eight Bits, Not 32" in Chapter 18, *Output Methods.*)

▶ You can work with smaller, low-resolution images. If your service bureau scanned your image, they can keep the high-resolution color files and give you the master file to place, play, and proof with. When you send them your PageMaker or QuarkXPress document, the high-res information can be swapped in automatically.

▶ Proofing is easier. Printing proofs of a high-resolution image on a color printer or desktop laser printer can be painful. However, when you print a composite proof with a DCS file, the program only sends the composite data to the printer. For color-proofing devices that require color separations, you can force XPress to send the high-resolution data with an XTension, such as Total Integration's SmartXT. We don't know of any way to do this in PageMaker other than trying to get the color printer to recombine the separations.

On the other hand, DCS files can be a pain in the left buttock. You have to deal with five files instead of one, and the links to the high-res images can be "broken" if you rename or move those files (see "Tip: Recovering Lost Links in DCS," below).

DCS version 2.0. We've been talking only about DCS version 1.0, which is made up of five files—the low-resolution version that you place on a page, which contains pointers to four data files. But there's a DCS version 2.0 format, too. Version 2.0 can contain all the composite and high-res image data in a single file. More important, DCS 2.0 files can contain more than just four process colors; you can have a number of spot colors included, as well.

Only a few programs currently support DCS 2.0, and even fewer can create DCS 2.0 files. Fortunately, both the latest versions of QuarkXPress (version 3.31) and PageMaker (version 6) can import and separate DCS 2.0 files without a hitch.

However, as we explain in Chapter 18, *Output Methods*, if your DCS file includes spot colors, your page-layout software must also have colors named exactly the same way (yes, PageMaker and XPress import these names automatically when you import a DCS 2.0 file).

To export DCS 2.0 files from Photoshop, you need PlateMaker (from a lowly apprentice production; see Figure 17-10).

Figure 17-10

Exporting spot colors in DCS 2.0 format using PlateMaker

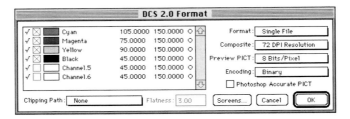

Tip: Recovering Lost Links in DCS. Occasionally, when working with five-file DCS files, the master file gets lost or the link between the master file and the high-res color files is broken (this can happen if you move or rename the high-res files). Don't fear; you can always reassemble the DCS files in Photoshop.

1. Open each of the high-res images in Photoshop (shortcut: we like to select them all in the Finder and then press Command-O). They're all EPS files, and they're all in Grayscale mode.

2. When all four of the files are open, select Merge Channels from the Channels palette's popout menu.

3. Make sure the mode is set to CMYK and the Channels field is set to 4 (see Figure 17-11); press OK.

Figure 17-11

Merge Channels dialog box

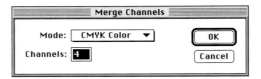

4. Photoshop is pretty good at guessing which file should be set to which color channel in the Merge CMYK Channels dialog box (see Figure 17-12), but if it guesses wrong, set the popup menus to the proper files.

When you press OK, Photoshop merges the four grayscale files into a single, high-resolution CMYK file. You can now create the five DCS files again, if you want.

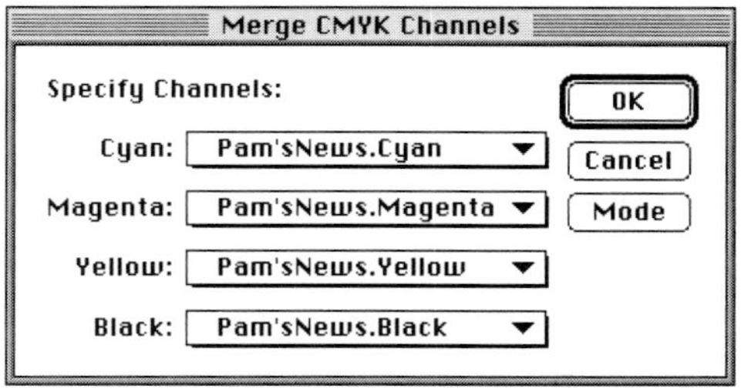

Figure 17-12

Merge CMYK
Channels dialog box

```
┌─────────────────────────────────────────────────┐
│ ▓▓▓▓▓▓▓▓▓▓▓  Merge CMYK Channels  ▓▓▓▓▓▓▓▓▓▓▓    │
│                                                   │
│  Specify Channels:                    ┌────────┐  │
│                                       │   OK   │  │
│     Cyan: [ Pam'sNews.Cyan      ▼]    └────────┘  │
│                                       ┌────────┐  │
│  Magenta: [ Pam'sNews.Magenta  ▼]     │ Cancel │  │
│                                       └────────┘  │
│   Yellow: [ Pam'sNews.Yellow    ▼]    ┌────────┐  │
│                                       │  Mode  │  │
│    Black: [ Pam'sNews.Black     ▼]    └────────┘  │
│                                                   │
└─────────────────────────────────────────────────┘
```

TIFF

The Tagged Image File Format (TIFF, pronounced just as it reads) is *the* industry-standard bitmapped file format. Almost every program that works with bitmaps can handle TIFF files—either placing, printing, correcting, or editing the bitmap. TIFF is a very straightforward format—in general, the only information it contains beyond the actual pixels themselves is the output size and resolution.

A Photoshop TIFF can be any dimension and any resolution (at least we haven't heard of any limits). You can save it in Grayscale, RGB (indexed or 24-bit), CMYK, or Lab color mode. You can even include as many additional channels as you want (up to the maximum 24 Photoshop allows; bear in mind, however, that very few programs other than Photoshop can *understand* a multichannel TIFF).

TIFF images must be bitmap-only, though you can include clipping paths (if your page-layout program uses them; see "Tip: Clipping in TIFFs," earlier in this chapter). You can't save layers in a TIFF file. And you cannot include screening or transfer-curve information in a TIFF. These are both controlled by the application that's printing the TIFF image.

Previews. When you save an EPS, you almost always ask Photoshop to save a preview image with it. To get a preview for a TIFF file, however, you have to select Full Size Preview in the Save As dialog box. The problem is that no software packages (other than some image browsers) currently read those previews, so they're useless. (Earlier versions of QuarkXPress *did* read them, but the image was often messed up at print time; see "Preview Options," earlier in this chapter.)

When you import a TIFF image into a page-layout application, the program reads the entire file and creates a low-resolution preview for you. This is hardly any trouble in a 1 MB image. But you could wait for many minutes while PageMaker or QuarkXPress reads and downsamples a 40 MB image. We prefer TIFFs for most of our work, but when we work with larger images, we often switch to EPS files for this reason alone.

Color models. You can save a preseparated CMYK image as a TIFF. When you place that file in a page-layout program or the like, no further separation is required. The program can simply pull the cyan channel when it's printing the cyan plate, the magenta channel when it's printing the magenta plate, and so on.

There is a facility in TIFF files to use indexed color, but using indexed color is a prime cause of compatibility problems, in our experience (see "Indexed Color" in Chapter 3, *Image Essentials*). If someone gives us an indexed-color TIFF to work with, we immediately convert it to straight RGB or CMYK and damn the file size. (Of course, if we're resaving it as a PICT or GIF file, we'll leave it in Indexed Color mode.)

IBM versus Mac. For some reason, the IBM and the Mac have different versions of TIFF. It has something to do with the file's byte order and the processing methods of Motorola versus Intel chips. For whatever reason, you sometimes need to convert TIFFs when you move them between platforms. Happily, programs like Photoshop, HiJaak, and DeBabelizer can read *and* write both Mac and IBM TIFFs.

One addition to make you breathe easier: PageMaker and QuarkXPress on both Windows and Mac can import either Intel- or Motorola-type TIFFs, so saving in one format or the other is less crucial in the prepress world.

Compression. Photoshop lets you save TIFF files with LZW (lossless) compression. Unlike the Photoshop 3.0 or PICT formats, if you want compression in a TIFF file, you have to ask for it when you save the image (see Figure 17-13).

We've met people who claim that they always save their files in PICT format because it gives them the best compression. Not so. LZW-compressed TIFFs are almost always more compact (see "Compressing Images," later in this chapter, for an explanation of why). They're also more reliable than PICT images for most page-layout work. On the other hand, they often take longer to save and open, sometimes much longer (isn't that always the trade-off, though?).

Figure 17-13
Saving TIFF files

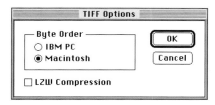

Compatibility. TIFF may sound like the ideal bitmapped file format, but in fact the picture is not totally rosy. As it turns out, there are several different "flavors" of TIFF. It's such a flexible format that TIFFs written by some programs are incomprehensible to some others.

This isn't as much a problem today as it was in past years when TIFFs varied widely, but we still occasionally hear about people who can't open their TIFFs—usually saved by scanning software—in Photoshop. Their only recourse is to open them in an intermediary program first, save them, and then try opening them in Photoshop. Compressed TIFFs are generally more prone to this kind of behavior than uncompressed ones.

Tip: Use File Info for Captions. Let's say you're doing production work in Photoshop on the eighth floor, and the pages are being laid out in QuarkXPress on the fourteenth floor (those designer types always get a better view). You're all on an Ethernet system, so it's easy to transfer the files up there. But what about all those captions and credits that they need? In the old days, you might have written on the back of the photograph, or perhaps slapped a Post-it note down somewhere. Now, there's nothing to write *on.*

Fortunately, Photoshop lets you save caption information inside TIFF or EPS files. You can select File Info from the File menu and type all sorts of information about the image and where it came from, and so on. The problem is that unless they're opening those files again in Photoshop, it's hard for them to get at that information.

WhatzIt and TIFFormation are two XTensions for QuarkXPress that let you see the caption information saved in a TIFF or (with WhatzIt) EPS file (see Figure 17-14). If the layout folks are using one of these XTensions, they can quickly see the image's caption. Even better, they can copy and paste the caption into a text box in XPress. Talk about workgroup efficiency!

Note that this only works with the Caption field of File Info. There are still many more fields that you can't get at unless you use proprietary software from AP or some other company.

Figure 17-14

Reading caption
information

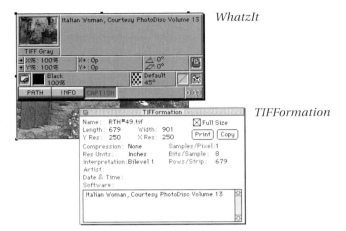

WhatzIt

TIFFormation

PICT

The PICT format (pronounced just as it looks) is the Mac-standard object-oriented file format. A PICT graphic can contain a bitmap as one of the objects in the file, or as its only object ("bitmap-only PICT"). Bitmap-only PICTs can be any size, resolution, and bit depth.

PICT is a respectable format for saving bitmaps that are in the editing process, but still not as flexible as the Photoshop 3.0 format—PICT files can't handle multiple layers, CMYK data, or more than four channels (that's RGB plus one channel total).

You should certainly plan on converting to TIFF or EPS before placing the image in a page-layout package; PageMaker and QuarkXPress, at least, are limited in their ability to manage PICTs effectively.

Nonetheless, PICT is the primary format when you're printing to non-PostScript devices—like most film recorders—or for multimedia work; in these cases, you rarely need to move out of RGB mode.

As in the Photoshop 3.0 format, you can't turn compression off in the PICT file format, although Photoshop makes it look like you can. When you save a file in the PICT format, Photoshop asks whether you want to use JPEG (and if so, how lossy do you want it) or no compression at all (see Figure 17-15). However, if you pick None, Photoshop still uses RLE compression. (By the way, you can only save or open PICT images in JPEG format when you've got QuickTime loaded on your Mac.)

Tip: Photoshop's Compression is Better. If you're on a quest to save hard disk space, you might try saving your images in PICT format to take advantage of its lossless RLE compression. Don't bother. Saving images in the Photoshop 3.0 format is not only faster, but compresses them more (on average) than PICT. The reason? PICT's RLE compression is done by QuickTime; Photoshop's is done by Photoshop.

The difference is in how they save the data (for the technoids out there: PICT saves image data in a "chunky" format—like RGB RGB RGB—while Photoshop saves image data in a "planar" format—like RRR GGG BBB).

Figure 17-15

Saving PICTs

If you select None, Photoshop still uses RLE compression.

If you select one of the other options, the image is compressed with JPEG instead of RLE.

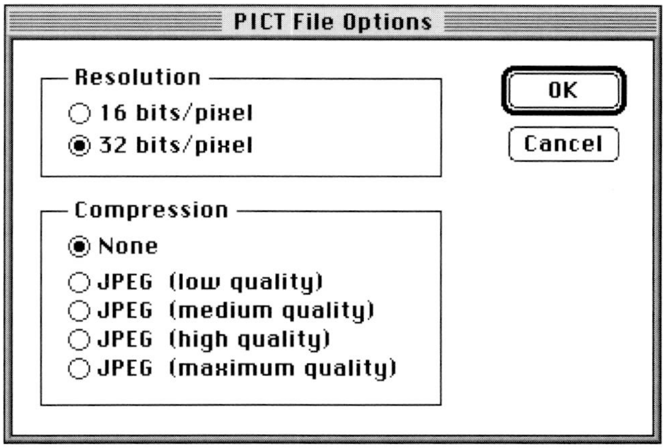

```
╔════════════ PICT File Options ════════════╗
║  ┌─Resolution ──────────────┐  ┌────────┐  ║
║  │  ○ 16 bits/pixel          │  │   OK   │  ║
║  │  ◉ 32 bits/pixel          │  └────────┘  ║
║  └──────────────────────────┘  ┌────────┐  ║
║                                 │ Cancel │  ║
║  ┌─Compression ─────────────┐  └────────┘  ║
║  │  ◉ None                   │              ║
║  │                           │              ║
║  │  ○ JPEG (low quality)     │              ║
║  │  ○ JPEG (medium quality)  │              ║
║  │  ○ JPEG (high quality)    │              ║
║  │  ○ JPEG (maximum quality) │              ║
║  └──────────────────────────┘              ║
╚═══════════════════════════════════════════╝
```

JPEG

Most people talk about JPEG as a compression method within another file format—like JPEG EPS—but it turns out that JPEG is also a file format all by itself. Obviously, you can't get around compressing the image when you save a file in JPEG format, and you wouldn't want to.

The only problem with the JPEG format (besides the fact that it's lossy; see "Compressing Images," later in this chapter) is that few programs other than Photoshop can read this format. QuarkXPress can, if you have the JPEG filter XTension loaded (it comes with all new versions of XPress). PageMaker 6 can, but PageMaker 5 can't.

But neither XPress nor PageMaker sends the JPEG information down to the printer for decompression (as they do with JPEG-encoded EPSes). Instead, they decompress it and send it down just as they would a TIFF file. So you get the hard disk savings, but it actually takes longer every time you print the file because the printing program has to decompress the JPEG image each time.

Niche File Formats

As we noted back in the Preface, this book only covers a fraction of the potential uses of Photoshop—those centered around production. People use this program for so many different things that we couldn't hope to cover them all here. In the last section, we discussed each of the file formats that are relevant for most professionals who are putting images on paper or film. You, however, might be doing something interesting, different, or just plain odd. Don't worry; Photoshop can probably still accommodate you.

Reasonable Niche File Formats

In this section, we'll explore five file formats that Photoshop can read and write, and why you might have cause to use them. In all but two, GIF and FilmStrip, there's no need to save in these file formats until you absolutely need to. And even then, you should save the original image in Photoshop 3.0 format as well.

CompuServe GIF. The Graphics Interchange Format (commonly known as GIF, pronounced "jiff" or "giff," depending on your upbringing), is the "house-brand" image file format of the CompuServe online information service. However, GIF images have long since broken free of CompuServe's corporate walls and are now the industry standard on almost every online service, including the Internet (notably for Web pages).

Most image-editing programs can now read and write GIF image files, and Photoshop is no exception. However, don't expect to bring those images into a page-layout program; PageMaker and QuarkXPress can't import them. And you wouldn't want them to; GIF files only support 256 indexed colors, making them reasonable for on-screen viewing, but certainly not for printing. That means your image must be in Indexed Color mode in order to save in this format.

GIFs are automatically compressed using lossless LZW compression (see "Compressing Images," later in this chapter).

Tip: Eking Out the Bytes. Almost every image on the Internet (or "information superhighway" or "infobahn" or whatever you want to call it) is saved in GIF format, especially those that appear on World Wide Web sites. The reason is simple: they're very compact. However, sometimes they're just not compact enough. For instance, on slower modem lines, there's a significant difference between watching a 30 K image slowly appear on your screen, and a 15 K image appear without trouble.

If you're trying to eke out every little bit of compression in a GIF file, keep in mind how LZW compression works: it looks for repeating patterns of colors. For instance, it can tokenize "red, blue, red, blue, red, blue" into one piece of information. Therefore, the images that get compressed the most contain lots of these sorts of repeating patterns.

Here are several ways you can make Photoshop use more repeating patterns when you're converting images from RGB into Indexed Color.

▶ Select Pattern dither instead of Diffusion dither (in the Indexed Color dialog box).

▶ Use solid areas rather than gradations or textures.

▶ Specific color schemes are better than using lots of different colors. The fewer colors, the better compression you'll achieve.

▶ Use a 6- or 4-bit palette instead of eight bits. Of course, many images degrade significantly with fewer colors, so you should play around with this.

▶ Using System Palette (or Uniform, if you're using fewer than eight bits per pixel) instead of Adaptive can save one or two kilobytes, which is important in some cases. If this doesn't matter as much to you, Adaptive is probably better.

With any of these techniques, the image's dither is almost always slightly more obvious, but you can make the image transfer over telephone lines faster.

Scitex CT. Whether to use the Scitex CT file format is a no-brainer: if you own a Scitex system or are trying to output via a Scitex system, you *may* want to save your document in this format as the last stage before printing. If you don't have any contact with a Scitex system, ignore this one.

It may be important to note that the Scitex CT format is not actually the CT ("continuous tone") format that Scitex folks usually talk about. It's actually the Handshake format, which is less proprietary and more common (QuarkXPress can even import these files). If you need to import or save native RMX or UFS images from a Scitex system, you'll need a plug-in, such as Alaras's Apertura.

Scitex CT files are always CMYK or grayscale; however, Photoshop lets you save RGB images in this format, too. We can't figure out why. If you can figure out a good use for them, let us know. By the way, if you're trying to get Photoshop duotones through a Scitex system, you should sprint directly to "Converting Duotones to CMYK" in Chapter 9, *Duotones*.

PICT Resource. Are you authoring multimedia or developing software? If so, you may find yourself needing to save an image into the resource fork of a file. Here's where the PICT Resource file format comes in. To be honest, it's not really a different file format; the Macintosh lets you place PICT information in the data or resource fork of a file. Photoshop, however, is a convenient way to move the image from one to the other.

Note that Photoshop lets you open PICT resources in two different ways. First, if the file has a PICT resource numbered 256, Photoshop lets you open that particular resource directly from the Open dialog box. If there are multiple PICT resources, you can access them only by selecting PICT Resource from the Acquire submenu (under the File menu; see Figure 17-16).

Figure 17-16
Acquiring a
PICT resource

FilmStrip. Video, film, and animation all have a similar popular appeal, and the tools that let mere mortals create this sort of stuff (like Adobe Premiere) have finally begun to find a market. But that doesn't mean that programs that create or edit still images will go away. For what is video but a bunch of still images strung together over time?

Programs like Premiere let you save movies in a file format that Photoshop can open, called Filmstrip (see Figure 17-17). You can then edit each frame individually in Photoshop, save the file out again, and import the clip in the video/animation program. This technique not only lets you make small retouching changes, but even perform rotoscoping (a form of animation), colorizing, or any number of other special effects.

Figure 17-17
Filmstrip format

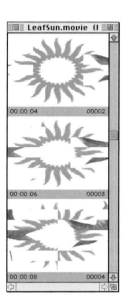

When you open a Filmstrip file in Photoshop, it looks like a tall and narrow noodle. But when you double-click on the Zoom tool to scroll in to 1:1 view, you can see each image frame clearly, along with its time and frame code. Note that changing the file's size, resolution, or pixel dimensions may be disastrous, or at least unpredictable. Instead, constrain your edits to the pixels that are already there.

Tip: Special Filmstrip Keystrokes. The Filmstrip format is so weird, so curious, so different from other file formats Photoshop understands, that there are several special keystrokes that *only* work with Filmstrip files.

▶ **Scrolling.** Press Shift-Page Up or Shift-Page Down to move a frame at a time. If you press Home (to move to the first frame of the document), and shrink the window size down to fit a single frame, then repeatedly pressing Shift-Page Down thumbs through the flipbook of images, one at a time. Yow! Animation in Photoshop!

> ▶ **Moving pixels.** You can move selected pixels up or down by a single frame (rather than by a single pixel) by holding down the Shift key while pressing the Up or Down Arrow keys. Adding the Option key copies the pixels and moves them up or down a frame.

> ▶ **Moving selections.** We find that instead of moving selected pixels up or down a frame, we often want to move the selection itself to the next or previous frame. You can do this by holding down the Shift, Option, and Command keys while pressing the Up or Down Arrow keys.

Raw. The last file format that we can even remotely recommend using is the file format of last resort: the Raw format. If you've ever traveled in a foreign country, you've probably found yourself in situations where you and the person in front of you share no common language. The answer? Reduce communication to gestures and sounds.

The Raw format is a way to read or write image data in a "language" that Photoshop doesn't know. It relies on the basics of bitmapped images (see Figure 17-18).

▶ All bitmapped images are rectangular grids of pixels.

▶ Some bitmapped images have header information at the beginning of the data.

▶ Color data is usually either interleaved (such as alternating red, green, blue, red, green, blue, and so on) or noninterleaved (such as all the red information, then all the green, and finally all the blue).

If you're trying to import from or export to some strange computer system, you may have to rely on the Raw format because that system might not know from TIFF, EPS, or any other normal, everyday file format. This

Figure 17-18
Opening Raw data

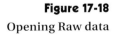

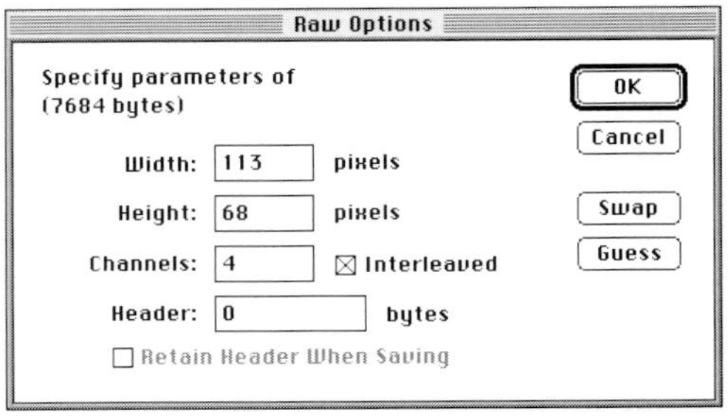

is becoming less of a problem as mainframe systems (especially imaging systems that are used for scientific or medical imaging) learn the newer, better file formats we've been discussing up until now.

Note that Photoshop can only read data using the Raw data format if it's saved as binary data; hex is out.

Tip: Make Photoshop Guess for Raw Data. Okay, someone gives you a file and you find you can't open it using any of Photoshop's standard file format options. You decide to take a leap and attempt the Raw format. But when you ask your so-called friend about the file's vital signs—"What are the pixel dimensions? Interleaved or noninterleaved color? Is there a header?"—he just stares at you blankly.

Fortunately, Photoshop can do a little guessing for you. If you press the Guess button in the Open as Raw dialog box when the Width and Height fields are blank, Photoshop figures out a likely height/width combination for the image. If it's a color image, you need to know if it's RGB (three channels) or CMYK (four channels).

If there's a header and your friend doesn't know how big it is (in bytes), then it's probably a lost cause. On the other hand, if your friend knows the pixel dimensions but not the header, you can press the Guess button while the Header field is blank.

Unreasonable Niche File Formats

We don't mean to be harsh, but there are some file formats that are like putting matches in the hands of small children. For instance, some people still save images from FreeHand or MacDraw as PICT and expect them to print properly. It can happen, but it ain't likely. The object-oriented PICT format is very unreliable and should be avoided in professional work. Here are a few file formats that we just ignore most of the time when it comes to bitmapped images. Unless you have a clear, specific, and compelling reason to use them, we strongly recommend that you do likewise.

Amiga IFF. The Amiga computer story reads like that of the Tucker car or the PublishIt! desktop publishing software. Most people have never heard of these products, much less realized how great they were. Each one of the select group of people who used the Amiga had their own theories about why most of the world shunned the love of their computing life,

Macintosh File Types and PC Extensions

One important thing to know about file formats is that Macintoshes and PCs "see" files differently. On the Macintosh, every file has several attributes attached to it, including two codes specifying the file type and creator. These are mysterious four-letter labels that tell the Macintosh what sort of file it is and what program generated it. For example, when you double-click on a file, the Mac looks at the file's creator to see what application to launch; Photoshop's creator code is 8BIM (we're sorry to say that they didn't change it when they went from 2.x to 3.0). The file type is determined by the file format. The important ones are easy: TIFF is TIFF, and EPS is EPSF.

If you move an image from some other platform to the Macintosh, you may not be able to open or place it, because it has a file type of TEXT or DATA or some such, while the opening application is looking for EPSF or TIFF or the like. You can view and change a file's type using PrairieSoft's DiskTop (see Figure 17-19), Apple's free ResEdit, and various other commercial, public-domain, and shareware programs.

In the PC world, everything is different. There are no file types, no file creators . . . there are only file names. PC files (unless you have Windows 95) all have names that are eight-dot-three. That means that the name can be no

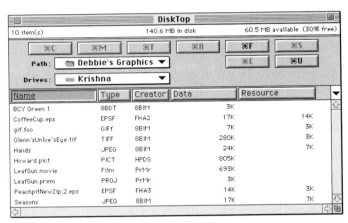

Figure 17-19 DiskTop lets you see and change file types

longer than eight letters followed by a period, and must end with a three-letter extension such as .TIF, .EPS, or .BMP. This extension provides all the information (and it ain't much) about the file's type and creator. Even Windows 95 doesn't stretch the file information beyond that.

Tip: File Name as File Type. As we said earlier, when you bring a file from a PC (or any other kind of computer system) over to the Mac, the Macintosh typically can't tell what kind of file it is, so it assigns it a file type of DATA or TEXT

or something like that. Photoshop, in turn, can't figure out what file type it's supposed to be, so it may not appear in the Open dialog box. However, Photoshop doesn't just look at the file's type; it also looks at the name.

Photoshop thinks any file with the suffix ".eps" is an EPS file, whether or not it really is one (see Table 17-1). Therefore, when you transfer the file to the Macintosh, make sure you give it the proper suffix. That way, Photoshop can read it properly even if Show All Files isn't turned on in the Open dialog box.

Table 17-1 File type suffixes that Photoshop recognizes

Amiga IFF	.iff	Pixar	.pxr
Encapsulated PostScript	.eps	Raw	.raw
Filmstrip	.flm	Scitex CT	.sct
JPEG	.jpg	Targa	.tga
PCX	.pcx	TIFF	.tif
Photo CD	.pcd	Windows bitmap	.bmp
PICT	.pct		

but when it came right down to it, the computer simply shuffled away in obscurity until it died an ignominious death.

However, perhaps out of a sense of obligation to the would-be contender, or perhaps from a real need in the market (though we don't see it), Photoshop still lets you open and save in the Amiga IFF format. However, unless you really need it, or you want to see a format that features rectangular rather than square pixels, ignore it.

MacPaint. The MacPaint format is ultimately the most basic of all graphic formats on the Macintosh, but it's so outdated that there's almost no reason to use it anymore. Paint files (more rarely called PNTG, or "pee-en-tee-gee," files) are black and white (one bit per pixel), 72 pixels per inch, 8-by-10 inches (576-by-720 pixels). That's it. No more and no less. The MacPaint format is useful for capturing and placing black-and-white Mac screen shots (especially since it's so compatible with every Mac program), but TIFFs are more flexible, so we use those instead.

PCX. Whereas many formats (such as TIFF) are industry standards, the PCX format was developed by ZSoft Corporation, the developers of Publisher's Paintbrush. It's a granddaddy of bitmapped formats, predating Windows 1.0 when it hit the streets as part of PC Paintbrush. The current version of PCX supports adjustable dimensions and resolutions, and 24-bit color, but only a 256-color palette (indexed to 24-bit color), up from earlier 4- and 16-color versions.

Since a variety of palette-color techniques have been applied to PCX files over the ages, files from earlier programs can have serious color-mismatch problems. But if you're satisfied with the results of working with the PCX images you have, then go for it. We typically recommend using TIFF files instead of PCX whenever possible.

Pixar. To understand why Photoshop still saves and opens Pixar files, you have to understand that Photoshop was born from the minds of Tom and John Knoll as a way to do some of the low-level grunt work that goes into the cool special effects produced at George Lucas's Industrial Light and Magic (ILM), which is a close cousin of Pixar.

As far as we're concerned, someone should put this file format out of our misery.

PixelPaint. The folks at Adobe are sensitive to the fact that their users (you) may have once used other image-editing programs. To make your life easier, Photoshop lets you open and save in the PixelPaint format. If you need to use it, use it; otherwise, ignore it.

Targa. The Photoshop manuals maintain that the Targa file format is designed for TrueVision video boards, though other programs (especially DOS programs) also use it. Like PixelPaint, this format is almost entirely obsolete, as far as we can tell (though it lingers on in some mainframe and minicomputer databases).

Windows Bitmap (BMP). Windows Bitmap (typically called "BMP", pronounced by saying the letters) is the bitmap format native to Windows Paint. It is rarely encountered outside of Windows and OS/2 Presentation Manager, and is hardly considered a professional's choice of file format. While you can store a 1-, 4-, 8-, or 24-bit image of various dimensions and resolutions, we still prefer TIFF, given its strong support by desktop-publishing applications and compatibility across different computer systems.

If you're creating wallpaper for your Windows desktop, this is the format for you!

Compressing Images

One thing that can be said of all bitmapped images is that "they're pigs when it comes to hard disk space." We've often wondered why Adobe doesn't bundle a gigabyte hard disk with every copy of Photoshop they sell. It would make sense. Except that maybe a gigabyte isn't big enough.

Our aim, then, is to stretch out the scarce resources we have on hand, especially hard drive resources. And we've got three methods to accomplish this goal: work with smaller images (no, seriously!), archive our images when we're not using them, and work with compressed file formats.

Lossy versus Lossless

As we keep saying, bitmapped images are made simply of zeros and ones. In an 8-bit grayscale image, each pixel is defined by eight zeros or ones.

If images are already reduced to this level of simplicity, how can they be reduced further? By bundling groups of bits together into discrete chunks.

Lossless Compression

Let's take the example of a 1-bit (black-and-white) bitmap, 100 pixels on each side. Without any compression, the computer stores the value (zero or one) for each one of the 10,000 pixels in the image. This is like staring into your sock drawer and saying, "I've got one blue sock and one blue sock and one black sock and one black sock," and so on. We can compress our description in half by saying "I've got one blue pair and one black pair."

Run Length Encoding. Similarly, we can group the zeros and ones together by counting up common values in a row (see Figure 17-20). For instance, we could say, "There are 34 zeros, then 3 ones, then 55 zeros," and so on. This is called Run Length Encoding (RLE), and it's automatically used for Macintosh PICT images (fax machines use it, too). We call it "lossless" because there is no loss of data when you compress or decompress the file—what goes in comes out the same.

Figure 17-20

Run Length Encoding
lossless compression

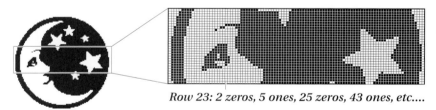

Row 23: 2 zeros, 5 ones, 25 zeros, 43 ones, etc....

LZW and Huffman. There are other forms of lossless compression. For instance, RLE compresses simple images (ones that have large solid-colored areas) down to almost nothing, but it won't compress more complex images (like most grayscale images) very much. LZW (Lempel-Ziv-Welch, though you really don't need to know that) and Huffman encoding work by tokenizing common strings of data.

In plain English, that means that instead of just looking for a string of the same color, these methods look for trends. If RLE sees "010101", it can't do any compression. But LZW and Huffman are smart enough algorithms to spot the trend of alternating characters, and thereby compress that information.

Lossy Compression

The table of contents at the front of most books is a way of compressing information. If you ripped the table of contents out of this book and mailed it to someone else (we're not actually suggesting that you do this!), they would be able to "unpack" it and read what's in this book. But they wouldn't actually be seeing the words you're reading now. Instead, they'd read an "average" of each chapter. The more detailed chapters have more headings, so your friend would see more detail in them than he or she would in a simple-headed chapter like this one.

Bitmapped images can be similarly outlined (compressed), transmitted to someone else, and unpacked. And similarly, when you look at the unpacked version, you don't get all the detail from the original image. For example, if nine pixels in a 3-by-3 square are similar, you could replace them all with a single averaged value. That's a nine-to-one compression. But the original image data, the variances in those nine pixels, is lost forever.

This sort of compression is called *lossy* compression because you lose data when compressing it. By losing some information, you can increase the compression immensely. Where an LZW-compressed TIFF might be 40 percent of original size, a file saved with lossy compression can be two percent or less of the original file size.

Levels of JPEG compression. Lossy compression schemes typically give you a choice of how tight you pack the data. (The primary method—the only method Photoshop offers—is JPEG, for Joint Photographic Experts Group.) With low compression, you get larger files and better quality. High compression yields lower quality and smaller files. How much quality do you lose? It depends on the level of the compression, the resolution of the image, and the content of the image (see Color Plate 13 on page 366).

Different programs implement JPEG differently, and with varying results. Note that JPEG is both a compression method and a file format in its own right (see "File Formats," earlier in this chapter), but both are based on similar algorithms.

Two other forms of lossy compression—fractal compression and wavelet compression—look promising as future compression technologies, but Photoshop currently supports neither of them.

JPEG Warnings. Here are a few things to remember when working with JPEG. First, note that images with hard edges, high contrast, and angular areas are most susceptible to artifacts from JPEG compression. For example, a yellow square on a green background in a lower-resolution image looks pretty miserable after lossy compression. On the other hand, compressing natural, scanned images using JPEG—especially those that are already somewhat grainy or impressionistic—probably won't hurt them much at all.

You should *only* use JPEG on finished images (those on which you've finished all editing and correction). Tone or color correction on a JPEGed image exaggerates the compression artifacts. Sharpening a JPEGed image produces an effect that might one day find its way into Kai's Power Tools, but it's difficult to envisage a use for it in a production setting.

Also, compressing and decompressing images repeatedly can make images worse than just doing it once. But since we just told you that you should only JPEG finished images, the point is moot—you can just open them, look at them, and close them again.

To Compress or Not to Compress

Over the years, we've found only a few universal truths. One of those is: "Fast, Cheap, or Good: you can have any two of the three." Compression is certainly no exception to this rule. Compressing files can be a great way to save hard drive space (read: "save money") and sometimes to cut down on printing times (read: "save more money"). But compressing and decompressing files also takes time (read: "lose the money that you just saved").

Optimally, if you have way too much hard drive space, you may never need or want to compress your images. For those of us less fortunate, you may only want to compress those images you're finished with into a lossless archive.

On the other hand, if you still need access to the files (you can't use images that are stored in archives until you extract them) but you need to make your files smaller and you don't mind the performance hit, you may opt for either a lossless or a lossy compression file format. The benefit of compressing data in this way is that you don't have to decompress the file manually before opening it. Rather, Photoshop does all the decompression for you, on the fly, when you open it. Most compressed file formats can also be opened directly in page-layout programs (in this case, PageMaker or QuarkXPress does the automatic decompression for you).

The downside of compressed file formats is that Photoshop has to compress or decompress the file each and every time you save or open the file. That means time sitting and staring at your computer screen. The smaller the document, or the faster your machine, the less time you have to grab a cup of coffee. In the case of page-layout applications, the program may decompress the image once when it opens it, but it typically has to decompress it *every time you print the page*. (There are exceptions to this, though; see "EPS," earlier in this chapter.)

To be honest, we almost never compress files until we archive them, unless we have to modem them, and in a hurry. It's a hassle to save TIFF files with LZW compression, and too often these compressed TIFFs are mysteriously less reliable. When we absolutely need to save a file in a compressed file format, our choice is JPEG (if we *need* to compress a file, we probably need to compress it more rather than less, and only JPEG will do the trick). However, we never use anything other than Maximum quality in JPEG; we find the increase in compression at Good, Medium, or Low simply isn't worth the degradation in quality.

Ultimately, storage space is getting so inexpensive these days that it's almost silly to worry about compression. As we write this, Iomega has already shipped the Zip drive, with 96 MB disks that cost $15, and is poised to ship a removable system that will cost $100 per gigabyte; CD-ROMs are becoming easier and cheaper to produce; and DAT cartridges can store more than eight gigs for under $20. If time equals money, then time spent compressing and decompressing files (whether it's manual or automatic) is money down the big porcelain doughnut.

Archiving

You may have worked with programs such as StuffIt, Compact Pro, or Disk-Doubler (if you don't already work with one of these, you probably should). They all have pretty much the same function: to compress files—any kind of files—and save space on your hard drive. This sort of compression is called *archiving* because people typically use it on files that they're not currently using.

Archiving a file is like folding up a piece of paper and putting it into an envelope. It takes a little time to fold it up (compress it) and a little time to unfold it (decompress it), and while it's in the envelope, you can't read it.

The archive file (the "envelope" that contains the compressed file) takes up less room on your hard drive, but in order to work on the enclosed file, you have to decompress it, usually with the same program that compressed it.

All archival compression programs use lossless compression methods, so you never have to worry about degrading the image. However, that also means they may not compress down as much as you'd like. Because it often takes a long time to compress very large files, we just buy additional removable media (such as SyQuests, Bernoullis, CD-ROMs, or magneto-optical drives) and store our files uncompressed.

Tip: Archiving Small Files. By the way, archiving programs can almost always store multiple files in the same "envelope." One of our favorite uses for archiving programs (we prefer Compact Pro but StuffIt is good, too) is to store tens or hundreds of small files together. Because of the way the Macintosh file system works, each file (no matter how small it is) takes up a minimum amount of space on disk, and the larger the hard drive, the larger that minimum size. On a gigabyte drive, each file takes up about 14 K, even if it's a one-character text file.

If you have lots of little files, this overhead can really be a drag. Putting them all into a single archive not only compresses them, but it reduces the total overhead, too.

From Photoshop to the Future

As we've seen, Photoshop can read and write a number of languages fluently, but they're all based on those ubiquitous zeros and ones. Photoshop can also *sprech* a compressed dialect of many of these languages, saving hard drive space and occasionally printing time, but often slowing down workflow. But perhaps most important, we've learned how to get images out of Photoshop and ready for the rest of the world. In the next chapter, *Output Methods*, we discuss this final process, then send you off to get your work done.

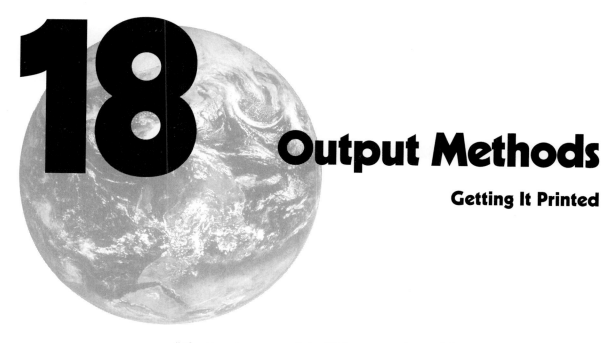

18 Output Methods

Getting It Printed

"The time has come," the Walrus paraphrased, "to speak of many things. Of zeros and ones, pixels and fun, and lastly, imaging." Though Lewis Carroll and his oysters never had to contend with such ephemeral things as pixels, we do. And, as you're probably aware, a pixel's greatest strength is also its greatest weakness: it doesn't really exist, except as electrical current in RAM or as magnetic force on disk. However, sooner or later, almost all of us have to capture those wily devils in a more permanent form, such as paper or film.

In the grand tradition of verbing nouns, the term used to include printing, exposing, displaying, or any other process of turning digital images into analog, static ones is *imaging*. In this chapter we focus on the issues specific to imaging your images, whether from Photoshop or another program, such as QuarkXPress or PageMaker. But before we get into the nitty-gritty, we should cover a little background first: the distinction between contone and halftone images.

Contone versus Halftone

We all live in an illusion (and not just the Hindu *maya* that David keeps muttering about): when we see a leaf, we think we see a continuous range of colors and tones, continuous lines, and continuous shapes. That's an illusion, because the eye simply doesn't work that way. Without getting too far into visual physiology, suffice it to say that the eye works pretty much like an incredibly high-resolution digital camera.

Rods and cones (each a distinct light sensor, like a CCD) cover the back of our eye (the retina), and convert the light that enters our eye into electrical signals. Our brain then—starting with the retinal nerve—tries to make sense of all those impulses (you can think of them as zeros and ones). The end effect is that our brains fool us into thinking we're seeing a wash of colors and shapes, when in fact we're simply seeing over a hundred million pixels of information.

And it turns out that because the brain is already so good at fooling us into thinking that we're seeing detail where there is none, or continuous colors where there aren't any, we can fool it even more. The process of imaging data is inherently one of fooling ourselves, and some methods are better than others. The two primary methods of imaging are halftone and contone. Let's take a closer look at each of them.

Halftones

Printing presses, imagesetters, and laser printers all share one thing: they only print on or off, black or white. They can't print shades of gray. To print fifteen different colors, you'd have to run the paper through the machine fifteen times with different colored inks, or toners, or whatever. However, lithographers figured out in the late nineteenth century that they could create a tint of a colored ink by breaking the color down into a whole bunch of little spots. Our brain plays along with the game and tells us that we really are seeing the shade of gray, not just spots (see Figure 18-1). These spots make up the *halftone* of the image.

There are a number of ways to halftone an image, but the most common is to combine printer dots—those tiny square marks that imagesetters or laser printers make, sometimes as small as $\frac{1}{3,600}$ of an inch—together into larger spots (see Figure 18-2). The darker the gray level, the larger the spot—the more dots are turned on. Each spot sits on a giant grid, so the center of each spot is always the same distance from its neighbors. (The spots don't really get closer or farther from each other, just bigger and smaller; see Figure 18-3.)

Figure 18-1
Halftoning

Figure 18-2
A representation of
digital halftone cells

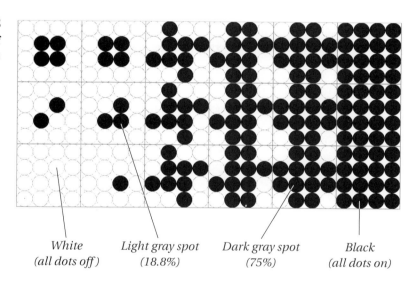

*White
(all dots off)*   *Light gray spot
(18.8%)*   *Dark gray spot
(75%)*   *Black
(all dots on)*

Figure 18-3
Tint percentages

You can print multicolor images by overlaying two or more color halftones (typically cyan, magenta, yellow, and black; see Color Plate 12 on page 366). Again, our eyes fool us into thinking we're seeing thousands of colors when, in fact, we're only seeing four.

David coauthored a book with Steve Roth, called *Real World Scanning and Halftones*, that covers halftoning in much more detail than we can get into here. However, we should at least cover the basics. Every halftone has three components, or attributes: screen frequency, screen angle, and spot shape.

Screen frequency. Halftone spots on a grid are like bitmapped images; they have resolution, too. The more spots you cram together within an inch, the tighter the grid, the smaller the spots, and so on. The number of halftone spots per inch is called *halftone screen frequency*. Higher frequencies (small spots, tightly packed, like those in glossy magazines) look smoother because the eye isn't distracted as much by the spots. However, because of limits in digital halftoning, you can achieve fewer levels of gray at a given output resolution. Also, higher screen frequencies have much more dot gain on a printing press, so tints clog up and go muddy more quickly (see "Image Differences," later in this chapter).

Lower screen frequencies (as in newspapers) are rougher looking, but easier to print (less dot gain) and you can achieve many levels of gray at lower output resolutions. Screen frequencies are specified in lines per inch, or *lpi* (even though we're really talking about "rows of spots per inch").

Screen angle. Halftone grids are not like bitmapped images; you can rotate them to any angle you want. (In a bitmapped image, the pixels are always in a horizontal/vertical orientation.) Halftones of grayscale images are typically printed at a 45-degree angle because the spots are least noticeable at this angle. However, color images are more complex.

When you overlap halftone grids, as in color printing, you may get distracting moiré ("mwah-RAY") patterns which ruin the illusion (see Color Plate 12 on page 366). In order to minimize these patterns, it's important to use specific angles. The greater the angle difference between overlapping screens (you can't get them any farther apart than 45 degrees), the smaller the moiré pattern. With four-color process printing, the screens are typically printed 30 degrees apart at 15, 45, and 75 degrees (yellow, the lightest ink, is generally printed at 0 degrees—15 degrees offset from cyan).

Spot shape. The last attribute of halftones is the shape of each spot. The spot may be circular, or square, or a straight line, or even little pinwheels (see Figure 18-4). The standard PostScript spot shape is a round black spot in the highlights, square at 50 percent, and an inverted circle (white on black) in the shadows. Changing the shape of the spot is rarely necessary. However, if you're producing cosmetic catalogs, or need to solve tonal shift problems printing on newsprint at coarse screen frequencies (to use two examples), controlling the halftone spot can definitely improve the quality of your job.

Figure 18-4
Spot shape

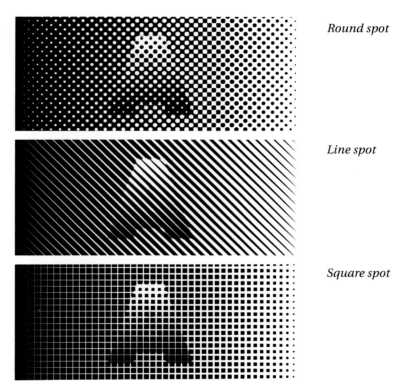

Round spot

Line spot

Square spot

Screen Settings: What Overrides What?

When you send a grayscale or color bitmapped image to a PostScript printer, the computer inside the printer converts the image into a halftone. That means that the printer sets the halftone screen frequency, angle, and spot shape. However, there are plenty of times when you want to override the printer's default settings to use your own halftone screening

The Rule of 16

It's simply a rule of the universe: in digital halftoning, the higher the screen frequency you request at a given output resolution, the fewer levels of gray you can achieve. The problem, in a nutshell, is that higher screen frequencies mean smaller halftone spots; and because these halftone spots are made of groups of printer dots, the smaller the spot, the fewer printer dots it contains. The fewer printer dots in a halftone spot, the

fewer gray levels that spot can simulate (see Figure 18-5).

There's a simple equation that lets you figure out approximately how many gray levels you can achieve at a given halftone screen frequency on a given printer:

$$(\text{printer resolution} \div \text{screen frequency})^2 + 1$$

However, we can make it even simpler for you. We know that there is a maximum of 256 levels

of gray possible on any PostScript printer. Therefore, you can figure out (with a little behind-the-scenes arithmetic) the highest screen frequency you should use on a given printer by dividing the resolution by 16.

Or conversely, if you know you want to print at a given screen frequency, you can figure out what resolution printer you need by multiplying the frequency by 16.

If you break this rule—going to a higher screen frequency than the output device can support—you start losing gray levels. If you lose enough gray levels, you start seeing posterization. Try it for yourself: print a grayscale image at 106 lpi on a 300-dpi laser printer (see Figure 18-6).

For instance, if you know that you're going to print on a 2,400-dpi imagesetter, the highest frequency you should use is 150

Figure 18-5 Gray levels versus screen frequency

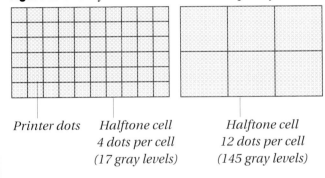

Printer dots   Halftone cell
                 4 dots per cell
                 (17 gray levels)

Halftone cell
12 dots per cell
(145 gray levels)

information. Fortunately, most programs give you some help in doing this, and Photoshop gives you a *lot* of help.

Figure 18-7 shows, in brief, the order in which screening controls override each other. Let's look at each of them in order.

Device's default setting. Every PostScript output device has a built-in default screen setting. On most desktop laser printers, it's 53 lpi at 45 degrees. Imagesetters vary widely, but are typically above 100 lpi at 45 degrees.

Driver setting. Printer drivers are the software modules that "drive" printers in the background; PostScript drivers actually write much or all of the PostScript code that gets sent to the printer. Although the Windows Post-

(2,400 ÷ 16). Or, if you know that you want to print at 133 lpi, you should print on an imagesetter with resolution of at least 2,100 dpi (133 x 16).

On the other hand, we know that most printing presses can't handle anywhere near 256 levels of gray (especially on uncoated stock). So there's a corollary rule: if you think you don't really need a full range of grays, adjust accordingly. Perhaps use the Rule of 13, which would give you 170 levels of gray, but might save you a little money—it's usually cheaper to run film at a lower resolution because it images faster, saving the service bureau time.

When your output device doesn't have enough resolution to support the full range of 256 grays at the line screen you want, you have a choice. You can lower the screen frequency, which loses fine detail, or you can settle for fewer shades of gray, which increases the amount of posterization. Some

Figure 18-6 Posterization due to insufficient output resolution

Printed at 133 lpi on a 2,400-dpi imagesetter   *Printed at 106 lpi on a 300-dpi laser printer*

images are better served by going with the higher screen frequency and fewer grays; others need the full range of grays and can sacrifice detail. The trade-off is particularly important when you're printing to a desktop laser printer. With a 60-lpi screen, a 600-dpi laser printer can produce about 100 gray levels. With a 100-lpi screen, it only produces 36 gray levels.

Tip: See Posterization in Action. If you use the Rule of 13, you're going to posterize your image. That's life. But is that so

bad? Oftentimes, it's not. You can see approximately what the effect of posterizing your image to 170 levels of gray would be with the Posterize command on the Map submenu under the Image menu. The effect you get by selecting Posterize and typing 170 is more or less what you'd get if you printed your image at 175 lpi on a 2,400-dpi imagesetter, or at 110 lpi on a 1,270-dpi imagesetter.

If your image is not very posterized to begin with, this level of posterization may have very little effect on it.

Figure 18-7
What screen settings override what

The specific screening controls at the bottom override the more general controls at the top.

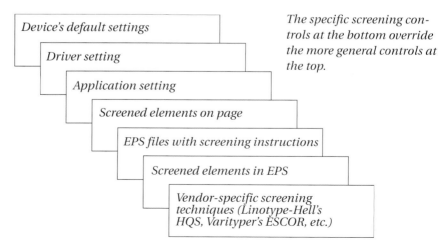

Device's default settings
Driver setting
Application setting
Screened elements on page
EPS files with screening instructions
Screened elements in EPS
Vendor-specific screening techniques (Linotype-Hell's HQS, Varityper's ESCOR, etc.)

Making Halftones in Photoshop

When you print an image from Photoshop or a page-layout program, the PostScript printer converts your grayscale or color data into halftones. That doesn't mean, though, that you couldn't do it yourself in Photoshop if you really wanted to. In fact, there are a few times when it's advantageous to convert images into halftones in Photoshop.

▶ You are printing to a non-PostScript printer and want controllable halftones and smaller image files.

▶ You want a diffusion dither—a stippled screen very similar to the stochastic screening available on many imagesetters, but

useful for lower-resolution output as well (see Figure 18-9 for an example).

▶ You want to create some special halftone-like effects.

▶ You want to learn about how halftones work. Creating halftones in Photoshop is a great way to learn what halftoning is all about. (When we do halftoning seminars, it's not until we show people how to do halftoning in Photoshop that they really understand what we've been talking about.)

Here's how to convert a grayscale image into a halftone in Photoshop (yes, this only works

with grayscale images; if you've got a color image, select Grayscale, or duplicate a color channel into a new grayscale document).

1. Select Bitmap from the Mode menu (see Figure 18-8).

2. In the Bitmap dialog box, choose an output resolution appropriate for your output. All the same rules for line art images that we talked about back in Chapter 10, *Line Art*, apply here.

So if your final output is on a 300-dpi laser printer, you don't need more than 300-ppi image resolution. If your final output is on an imagesetter,

Script driver lets you control the halftone screen for the print job, most Macintosh drivers do not.

Application setting. Many applications provide control over halftone screens for your print jobs. In QuarkXPress, this control is in Page Setup; in PageMaker, it's in the Print:Color dialog box. In Photoshop, you get at it via the Screens button in the Page Setup dialog box. Anytime you set screening information at the application level, it overrides both the device default and the driver settings.

Individual screened elements within publications. In some applications—FreeHand is a good example—you can select individual objects (text or graphics) and set a screen for those objects. In others (such as PageMaker and QuarkXPress), you can apply screens to individual bitmapped images (TIFF only). These are called *object-level settings*, and they override the application-level settings, which still apply to the rest of the job.

you may need to raise this to 800 or 1,000 ppi.

3. Select the Halftone Screen radio button in the Bitmap dialog box, and press OK. (While you're here, you should also check out the Diffusion option; it's a totally different look, but it may work for you.)

4. In the Halftone Screen dialog box, set the frequency (bearing in mind the Rule of 16), angle, and spot shape, then press OK.

If you don't like the halftone effect that results, you can undo the mode change and start over with different settings.

Note that once you halftone a grayscale image, you can no longer make many edits to it—no tonal adjustments, filters, or the

like (there's nothing there for the tools to work with). Also, you shouldn't scale the image, even a little, or you can expect to get very strange patterning when you print.

We generally let the imageset-

ter's RIP take care of the screening for us. We certainly never do this Photoshop halftoning on color images (unless we're trying to create a special effect). But for drop shadows and the like, this is a great technique.

Figure 18-8 Bitmap dialog box

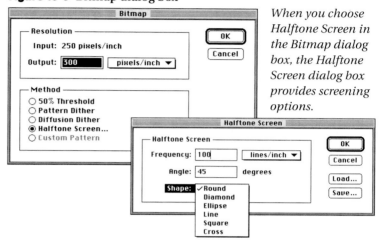

When you choose Halftone Screen in the Bitmap dialog box, the Halftone Screen dialog box provides screening options.

EPS files that include screening instructions. When you save a file as EPS from Photoshop, you can tell the program that you want to include screening information. Then, if you import that EPS file into a program such as PageMaker or QuarkXPress, the screening information in the EPS overrides the program's settings when you print the whole page—but for that object only.

You almost never need to save screening information with your EPS image. Of course, there are always exceptions; for instance, you often want to save particular angles in duotone images (see Chapter 9, *Duotones*).

Individual screened elements within EPS files. An EPS file that contains screening instructions can also include individual elements within the file that have their own screening instructions. For example, an EPS from FreeHand might have a gray box that has an object-level halftone screen applied to it. That item would be screened as specified, and the rest of the EPS would be screened as *it* was specified (or if there is no screen specified for the whole EPS, using the settings of the printing application—probably PageMaker or QuarkXPress).

Vendor-specific screening instructions. If you're printing to an imagesetter that uses a specialized screening technique such as Linotype-Hell's High-Quality Screening (HQS), Agfa's Balanced Screens Technology (BST), or Prepress Solutions' ESCOR, you may not get the screen settings you expect.

These techniques use screening "filters" which catch *all* screening instructions, and replace the frequency/angle combinations with the closest settings that are available in their optimized sets. So even if you specify angles in Photoshop and save as an EPS, you still may not get your exact request. This is mostly significant if you're after a specialized spot shape. If you are, tell your service bureau to turn off HQS, or BST, or whatever.

Contone Output

With binary devices such as imagesetters and printers, we need to use a halftone to fool the eye into seeing shades of gray because we can't create color or gray pixels. With a contone device, we *can* vary the color or gray shade of each pixel. Continuous-tone imaging, usually called *contone*, is different from halftone imaging in two other ways.

▶ The pixels touch each other so that without very close inspection no paper or clear film shows through between marks.

▶ Each pixel is a specific color, made by building up varying densities of primary colors in the same spot.

The most common contone imaging device is your computer monitor. The color of each pixel you see (or don't see, if the screen's resolution is high enough) is made by mixing together varying amounts of red, green, and blue. For example, to make a pixel more red, the monitor must increase the number of electrons that are bombarding the red element of the pixel.

There's no threat of moiré patterns, because there are no grids involved. But then again, there's no chance of mass-reproducing the image, as no printing press can handle continuous-tone images (see "Hybrid Color

Screening," later in this chapter). Aside from the monitor, there are two other types of contone devices that we should mention: film recorders and dye-sub printers.

Film recorders. A film recorder such as a Solitaire or a FIRE1000 creates continuous-tone images in one of two ways. Some film recorders place a very high resolution grayscale monitor in front of a piece of film, and then image the same piece of film three times—the first time with a red filter in front of the monitor, and then with blue, and finally with a green filter. The same areas of the film are imaged each time, but with varying densities of each color.

Other film recorders color pixels in film by adjusting the amount of three bright light beams—each colored by a red, green, or blue filter—while they focus on a point on the film. Again, unlike halftones, each "pixel" on the film abuts the next, and is set to a specific color.

Film recorders are typically very high resolution devices, ranging from 1,024 (1 K) to 16,384 (16 K) pixels across. High resolutions are necessary because they're often imaging small pieces of film such as 35 mm slides or 4-by-5-inch film, though 16 K film recorders are usually reserved for writing 8-by-10 film.

Dye-sub printers. A second type of contone device is a dye-sub printer, which overlays varying amounts of ink to build a color. Dye-subs are typically 300-dpi devices, but the lack of halftoning or white space between each pixel makes images look surprisingly photorealistic at this seemingly low resolution.

Because of the lack of resolution, hard-edged objects such as type or line art may appear jaggy, but the soft edges and blends found in natural images usually appear nearly indistinguishable from photographs.

Hybrid Color Screening

There is one more method of simulating a "real-world" continuous-tone image: using tiny spots to simulate tints and colors, but making those spots so small and so diffuse that the image appears contone. There are three primary examples of this sort of imaging: high-resolution ink-jet, color laser printer, and stochastic screening, either on a conventional press or on a direct-digital press such as the Indigo E-Print or the Agfa Chromapress.

Ink-jet. In ink-jet technology, the printer sprays a fine mist of colored inks onto paper. The amount of each ink is varied, much like a contone printer, but it results in tiny spots on paper, often with paper white showing through, more like halftones. Low-resolution ink-jets couldn't be mistaken for contone imaging devices, but prints from high-resolution ink-jets such as the Iris are so smooth that for all practical purposes they can be considered contone devices.

Tip: Take Care in Your Ink Sets. Several different ink sets are available for the Iris ink-jet printers, some designed for prepress proofing, others for fine-art output. The latter have a much wider color gamut than is attainable on press. Most Iris service providers specialize in one or the other application, so it's important to be clear about your goals when you're printing to an Iris.

Stochastic screening. Earlier in this chapter we discussed how halftones are formed by clumping together groups of printer dots into a regularly-spaced grid of spots. However, we oversimplified; this is actually only one way to make a halftone. Remember, a halftone is simply a way to simulate tints or colors with tiny spots. Another method of halftoning is a diffusion dither (see Figure 18-9).

Diffusion dithers can create near-contone quality, but they've been avoided until recently because they're often difficult to create and print, especially for full-color work. However, digital imaging has changed all this. Various vendors have created proprietary dithering techniques, usually called *stochastic screening*, that let you mass-reproduce contone-like images from a printing press (see Color Plate 12 on page 366). Note that proprietary stochastic screening is a type of "frequency modulated" (FM) screen, but it's certainly not the same as Photoshop's diffusion dither feature.

Stochastic screening is very cool for a number of reasons.

▶   Image content which has been difficult to reproduce using traditional halftoning methods—such as fabric or other fine-detail objects—is much more easily reproduced with stochastic screening because it eliminates *subject moiré*, where the pattern in the subject creates a moiré by interfering with the regular pattern of the halftone screen.

Figure 18-9
Diffusion dither
as halftone

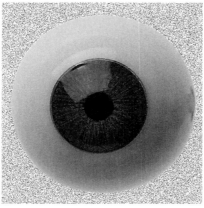

Grayscale image screened by PostScript at 133 lpi.

250-dpi diffusion dither from Photoshop

1000-dpi, 40-lpi halftone from Photoshop

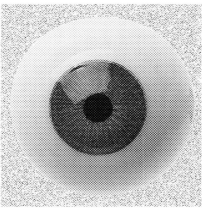

▶ You can print with more than four colored inks without worrying about moiré patterns due to conflicting halftone angles (there are no angles in a diffusion dither).

▶ It's much easier to reproduce near-contone images. Some printers are even getting good results with low-resolution stochastic screens printed on low-quality paper.

On the other hand, stochastic screening, like any new technology, can bring with it a host of new troubles ("challenges," says the ever-optimistic David). For instance, stochastic screening raises the concept of dot gain to new heights, causing many to retreat from printing with it soon after seeing their first printed images appear as big ink blobs.

Hi-Fi Color

Printers have been simulating thousands of different colors by mixing varying tints of four colors—cyan, magenta, yellow, and black—for many years now, and in theory it should work reasonably well. Unfortunately, we don't live anywhere near the town of "Theory," and so our range (gamut) of printable colors is pretty small. Color scientists, both amateur and professional, have been working at increasing this gamut ever since CMYK became a standard.

One solution is to add "bump" plates, where one or more of the four colors is printed again, expanding the tonal range in one area of the image or another. Another solution is to print with more than four colors: CMYK plus red, green, and blue, for instance; or adding purple and orange to the lineup. But the solutions all have one thing in common: ink gets slapped on the paper more than four times. All told, these gamut-extending solutions are called *Hi-Fi color* (is

quadraphonic color far behind?).

There are all sorts of problems with printing Hi-Fi color, but one stands out from the rest. It's hard enough to print four halftone tints of colors on top of each other while avoiding moiré patterns. Printing more than four is almost impossible unless you resort to very high screen frequencies. With the advent of digital stochastic screening, however, Hi-Fi color has become significantly easier to build, separate, and print.

You can create stochastic screens for your images with several pieces of software, including Isis Imaging's ICEfields and Second Glance Software's LaserSeps. Or you can use any of a number of vendors' built-in imagesetter screening algorithms such as Agfa's CrystalRaster or Linotype-Hell's Diamond Screens.

Color laser printer. Most color laser printers use some kind of diffusion dither to simulate a very high screen frequency. For example, the Apple Color LaserWriter 12/600PS simulates a 200-lpi screen even though it's only a 600-dpi printer. We've found that it's almost always best to let the laser printer take care of the screening using its own proprietary algorithms, rather than doing it ourselves.

Controlling color on these devices isn't easy—where possible, we prefer to send a calibrated RGB image through a color management system (see Chapter 16, *Color Management Systems*). If you do want to create your own CMYK separations from Photoshop for a color laser device, the biggest potential pitfalls are specifying too high an ink density and underestimating dot gain. Color laser printers don't have dot gain in the usual sense, and they use dry toner, so one might think that you could go all the way to a 400-percent total ink limit and 100-percent black ink limit. If you do, you'll get very dense shadows and saturated colors that look as though they belong in some other image. As a starting point, try 260-percent total ink with an 85-percent black limit in the Separation Setup dialog box.

Image Differences

Now that we've explored the various imaging methods, we should recap and highlight some of the different techniques you must use in building images suitable for output on halftone and contone devices. We say "recap" because we've mentioned most (if not all) of these in previous chapters, though never in one place.

Resolution. The first and foremost difference between contone and halftone imaging is the required image resolution. It's quite a bit more complicated to work out the resolution needed for halftone output than it is for contone, so we'll deal with halftone output first.

▶ **Resolution requirements for halftone output.** The resolution of the output device isn't directly relevant in determining the resolution you need for the image. It's the halftone screen frequency that matters. You never need an image resolution above two times (2x) the halftone screen frequency (and often you can get almost-equivalent results with as little as 1.2x or 1.4x). That means that even if you're printing on a 2,400-dpi imagesetter, your image resolution can (and should) be much lower. For instance, printing at 150 lpi, you never need more than a 300-ppi image, and usually no higher than 225 ppi. (See Figure 3-7 on page 69, and Color Plate 2 on page 124.)

▶ **Resolution requirements for contone output.** The required resolution for a contone output device is easy to figure, but it can sometimes be hard to deliver. Your output resolution should simply match the resolution of the output device. If you're printing to a 300-dpi dye-sub printer, your image resolution should be 300 ppi. When printing to a 4 K film recorder, your image should have a horizontal measure of 4,096 pixels, or about 60 MB for a 4-by-5 print. An 8 K film recorder really wants 240 MB—an 8,192 x 10,240-pixel image.

In truth, many high-resolution film recorders are more forgiving, and you can halve the resolution. For instance, we know of few people who actually send a 960 MB image to a 16 K film recorder, and we know quite a few who get good results sending a 60 MB file to an 8 K film recorder (about half the amount of data it "requires"). Sending less than a full 60 MB to a 4 K film recorder, however, is a much more marginal proposition. Make sure, though, that you send an integral multiple of the device's resolution. If you send 4,095 pixels to a device that wants 4,096, it'll either barf when it gets the file, or you'll get some very strange interpolation artifacts.

Tonal and color correction. We talk a great deal about tonal compression for halftone output in Chapter 6, *Tonal Correction,* and Chapter 7, *Color Correction,* so we won't go into it here. Contone output needs less in the way of tonal and gamut compression than halftone output, because contone devices generally have a greater dynamic range and a wider gamut than do halftone devices. However, this can bring its own problems, particularly when you have a scanner with a tendency to oversaturate some colors, as do many inexpensive scanners (and even some expensive ones). Keep a watchful eye on saturated colors. Some dye-sublimation printers feature a magenta that's almost fluorescent!

Sharpening. As we noted back in Chapter 8, *Sharpening,* contone images need much less sharpening than halftone images. But that doesn't mean they don't need any at all. Halftones, again because of their coarse screens and significant dot gain, mask details and edges in an image; sharpening can help compensate for both the blurriness of the scan and the blurriness of the halftone. And, halftones being what they are, you have a lot of room to play with sharpening before the picture becomes oversharpened (most people end up undersharpening).

In contone images, however, there's a real risk of oversharpening. Not only should you use a lesser Amount setting for unsharp masking, but also a smaller Radius. Where a Radius less than one is often lost in a halftone image, it's usually appropriate in contone images.

Image mode. This last item, *image mode,* isn't really dependent on what output method you're using. However, because we still see people confused about image mode, we thought we'd throw in a recap here, too.

Again: if you're printing to a color contone device that outputs to film (or if the image is only seen on a color screen), you should leave your image in RGB mode. Contone *and* halftone devices that print on paper (or film that will be used to image paper later) require CMYK images, but in many cases you'll get better results sending RGB and letting the printer handle the conversion.

We've tried many times to build printing inks setups for dye-sublimation printers, but it simply doesn't work. Photoshop's separation engine is geared toward halftone output, where the ink density remains constant and the dot size varies. It can't handle the variable density on dye-subs.

Hybrid Screening

When printing with hybrid screening, such as to a color laser printer or to film with stochastic screening, keep in mind that your image requires the sharpening and resolution of a contone image, but also the tonal and color corrections of a halftone image. In fact, these images often result in so much dot gain that you need to compress the image's tonal range significantly more than you'd think.

Imaging from Photoshop

We haven't taken a poll, but it appears that most people who use Photoshop don't print directly from it; instead, they save their images in some other format and then import them into some other program to print later. Nonetheless, perhaps out of admiration for the underdogs out there, or perhaps just because, we're going to tackle the topic of imaging directly from Photoshop before we move out of Photoshop and into QuarkXPress, PageMaker, or other programs.

As in almost every other Macintosh program, there are two menu items (and accompanying dialog boxes) tied to imaging: Page Setup and Print, both found under the File menu.

Page Setup

Most of the items in the Page Setup dialog box tell Photoshop how to print the document. Almost any other software developer in the world would have put this stuff in the Print dialog box, but the engineers at Adobe code to a different drummer. In fact, it makes sense for a couple of these items to be here, because they also apply when saving files in various formats (see Chapter 17, *Storing Images*).

The features in the top half of the dialog box (see Figure 18-10) are determined by what printer driver you've got selected in the Chooser. Because these are standard Macintosh features, we're going to skip them and get right to the good stuff: the Photoshop items in the lower half.

Figure 18-10

The Page Setup dialog box

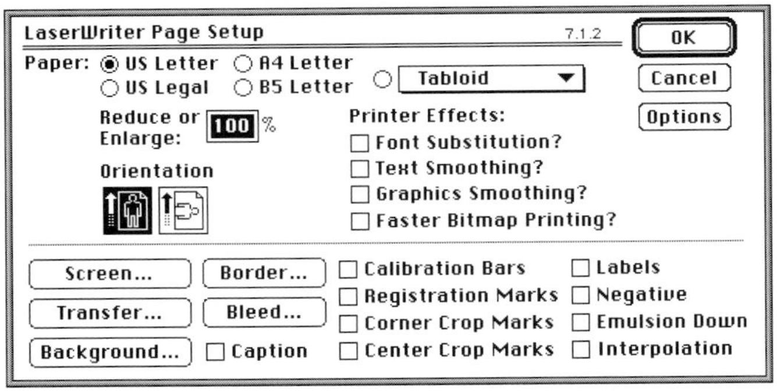

Screen. When you click the Screen button, Photoshop brings up the Halftone Screens dialog box, where you can specify the halftone screen angle, frequency, and spot shape for your image (see Figure 18-11). When the Use Printer's Default Screens checkbox is turned on (it is unless you go and change it), Photoshop won't tell the printer anything about how the image should be screened.

Figure 18-11

Halftone Screens dialog box

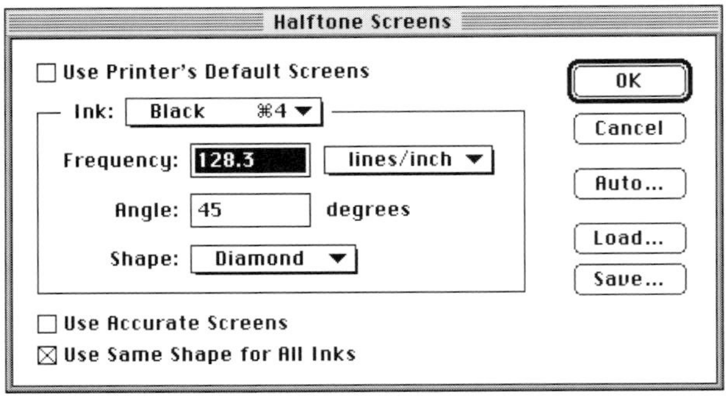

Unless you want to take explicit responsibility for setting your own halftone screens (you need to if you're going to print directly from Photoshop), you should leave Use Printer's Default Screens checked. When you do so, you make sure that the resulting file has no halftone screens built in, so unless someone intervenes downstream, the RIP will handle the screening. In the vast majority of cases, the RIP will do a better job than you can. Tell your service bureau what screen you want, and then it's their responsibility.

On the other hand, if you want or need to specify your own screens, turn this checkbox off. Photoshop gives you a wide array of possibilities for setting the halftone screen. And when you have a color image, you have even more choices.

▶ **Frequency and Angle.** The frequency and angle are self-explanatory.

▶ **Shape.** When the Use Same Shape for All Inks checkbox is on, the Shape popup menu applies to each process color. We can't think of any reason you'd change this, except for special low-frequency effects.

▶ **Use Accurate Screens.** When you turn on the Use Accurate Screens checkbox, Photoshop includes the PostScript code to activate Accurate Screens in your imagesetter. However, if your imagesetter doesn't have Accurate Screens technology, or if it uses some other screening technology—such as Balanced Screens or HQS—you should just leave this off. (We almost always leave it off, unless our service bureau tells us to turn it on.)

▶ **Auto.** If you don't know what frequency/angle combinations to type in, check with your service bureau. If your service bureau doesn't know, you're probably in trouble. However, as a last resort, you could try pressing the Auto button and telling Photoshop approximately what screen frequency you want and what resolution imagesetter you're using. The program has canned settings that sometimes work. Again, if you're using an imagesetter with HQS or Balanced Screens technology, you can ignore this feature; those technologies override the screen values. (See sidebar, "What Overrides What," earlier in this chapter.)

Note that you can include these screen settings in EPS files (see "Encapsulated PostScript (EPS)" in Chapter 17, *Storing Images*).

Tip: Use Diamond Spot. Peter Fink's PostScript prowess perfected the diamond spot (say that ten times fast). The diamond spot is better in almost every instance than the standard round spot because it greatly reduces the optical tonal jump that is sometimes visible in the mid-to-three-quarter tones—the 50-to-75-percent gray areas. We've also been told that the diamond spot is much better for silkscreening.

Whatever the case, on those rare occasions when we print from Photoshop, or save halftone screens in an EPS using our own screening parameters, we use the diamond spot. Again, there's a good chance that this will be overridden or replaced by the imagesetter's specialized screens, unless you tell your service bureau to turn them off.

Transfer. Back in Chapter 6, *Tonal Correction,* and in Chapter 9, *Duotones,* we discussed the idea of input/output contrast curves. Well, here they are once again, in Page Setup (see Figure 18-12). A transfer curve is like taking a curve that you made in the Curves dialog box and downloading it to your printer. It won't change the image data on your hard drive, but when you print with the transfer curve, it modifies the printed gray levels.

Figure 18-12
Transfer Functions
dialog box

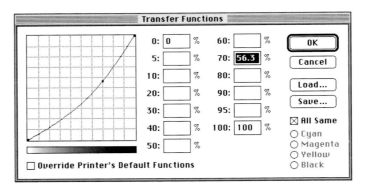

It's a rare occasion that you'd need to use a transfer curve these days. Here are a few examples of why you might, however.

► If you're printing from Photoshop to an uncalibrated imagesetter, you can use transfer curves (plus a lot of proof pages and a densitometer) to calibrate the device. We'd rather get calibration software that's made for this sort of thing, such as Kodak's Precision Imagesetter Linearization software or Technical Publishing Software's Color Calibration Software for PostScript Imagesetters. (Even better, we'd prefer our service bureau to own this software and calibrate their devices regularly.)

▶ You may have a single grayscale or CMYK image that you want to print on several different presses or paper stocks. Because each type of press or paper requires slightly different targeting (see "White Points and Black Points and Grays, Oh My" in Chapter 6, *Tonal Correction*), in a perfect world you'd want to retarget an "ideally" corrected image for each output method. However, this is often not possible. Transfer curves let you make these sorts of minor adjustments at print time.

Note that you can only save a transfer curve in a Photoshop or EPS-format file. But there's a danger in doing this, particularly with EPS images, because there's no obvious signal that tells anyone working with the image that it contains a transfer curve, except that the values in the file aren't the same as those that print. The only way to tell is to open the image in Photoshop and check to see if there's a transfer curve specified. If you do use a transfer curve, make sure that whoever is responsible for printing the file knows it's there!

Tip: Interchangeable Curves. While Bruce can think about transfer curves in terms of numbers, David needs a more touchy-feely approach. So he tries out his transfer curves in the Curves dialog box first. When he gets a curve just the way he wants it, he saves the curve to disk (using the Save button in the Curves dialog box), then goes to the Transfer Functions dialog box and loads it in.

At the same time, it's frustrating not being able to set points by just typing numbers into the Curves dialog box. But you can: create the curve in the Transfer Functions dialog box, save it to disk, then cancel out of that dialog box (so you don't accidentally save the curve with the document). Finally, load that curve into the Curves dialog box, and you're in business.

Tip: Setting and Retrieving Defaults. There's a hidden feature in the Transfer Functions dialog box. When you hold down the Option key, the Load and Save buttons change into "<-Default" and "->Default" buttons. For some reason it took us a moment before we realized those hyphens and angle brackets were supposed to be arrows. The first, "<-Default", means replace the current transfer curve with the default curve. The second means just the opposite: replace the default curve with the current curve (the one in the dialog box).

The default curve is the curve that all new Photoshop documents are created with. The default curve is also applied when you convert to a new color mode. Note that there are actually two default curves—color and grayscale—so if you set the default for a grayscale image, it won't be applied to color images, and vice versa.

All in all, we never change the default curves from their straight, 45-degree settings. However, if you're using transfer curves as your primary imagesetter-calibration, tonal-correction, or targeting method, this may save you some time.

Note that at the bottom of the Transfer Functions dialog box, Photoshop provides you with a checkbox: Override Printer's Default Curves. Don't turn this on unless you really know what you're doing with transfer functions. If your service bureau is using calibration software, turning this checkbox on will override their carefully adjusted settings, and could give you nasty results. While it's nice that Adobe gives us this control, this is one we tend to ignore.

Background. Background and the next eleven features are only relevant when you're printing from Photoshop; you cannot save them in an EPS format (or any other, for that matter) and expect them to carry over to other programs, like you can with Screen and Transfer.

When you print your image from Photoshop to a color printer, the area surrounding the image is typically left white (or clear if you're printing on film). The Background feature lets you change the color that surrounds the image, using the standard Photoshop color picker. The background color that you pick acts like a matte frame around the image to the edges of the paper (or whatever size you picked in Page Setup's Paper popup menu).

Border. If you specify a border around an image (the border can be up to .15 inches, 10 points, or 3.5 millimeters), Photoshop centers the frame on the edge of the image when you print; that is, half the frame overlaps the image, and half the frame overlaps the background. You cannot, unfortunately, change the color of the frame; it's always black.

We can't think of any reason to use this feature, except perhaps to print an image with a pretrapped frame directly from Photoshop, then strip it in with the rest of the film manually. Yuck. We'd rather import the file into QuarkXPress or PageMaker and keyline it there.

Bleed. Setting a bleed value adjusts where Photoshop places the corner crop marks. You can choose a bleed up to 9.01 points, 3.18 millimeters, or .125 inches (who knows who came up with these values). Again, this is most useful if you're planning on doing manual stripping later.

Caption. David loves Photoshop's ability to save a caption with a file because of its tie-in to QuarkXPress (see "Tip: Use File Info for Captions" in Chapter 17, *Storing Images*), but it's also helpful when printing a whole mess of images that you need to peruse, file, or send to someone. When you turn on the Caption checkbox in Page Setup, the program prints whatever caption you have saved in File Info (under the File menu) beneath the image. If you haven't saved a caption, this feature doesn't do anything.

We often include our names or copyright information in the Caption field of the File Info dialog box. It won't stop people from stealing, but at least your name travels with your images (also, see "Tip: Avoid Image Piracy" in Chapter 17, *Storing Images*).

Newspapers and stock photo agencies make much more elaborate use of the File Info feature, including credit lines, handling instructions, and keywords for database searches. The information entered here is supposedly compliant with the IPTC (International Press Telecommunications Council) standard, but unfortunately Photoshop 3.0.1 writes the information in a distinctly non-standard way when you save as JPEG.

As a result, IPTC information in Photoshop-created JPEG files is, at present, only readable by Photoshop and a few third-party browsers, including Adobe Fetch. The Photoshop team was working on a fix for this as we went to press, and it may be in place by the time you read this, but don't assume that your file info will travel with your file in a universally readable form without first testing to make sure that it does so.

Calibration Bars. When you turn on the Calibration Bars checkbox in Page Setup, Photoshop prints one (for grayscale images) or several (for color images) series of rectangles around the image (see Figure 18-13). Beneath the image is a ten-step gray wedge; to the left is the same gray wedge, but on each color plate; to the right is a series of colors, listed below. Each color is 100 percent (solid).

▶   Yellow

▶   Yellow and Magenta

- ▶ Magenta

- ▶ Magenta and Cyan

- ▶ Cyan

- ▶ Cyan and Yellow

- ▶ Cyan, Magenta, and Yellow

- ▶ Black

Registration Marks. If you're outputting separations, you need to add registration marks so that the printer can align the four colors properly. Turning on the Registration Marks checkbox adds ten registration marks (eight bull's-eyes and two pinpoint types).

Corner Crop Marks. Even if your printer is going to strip your image into another layout, it's helpful to print with corner crop marks, which specify clearly where the edges of the image are. This can help the stripper align the image with a straight edge. In fact, it's essential if the image has a clear white background (like a silhouette); without crop marks, it's impossible to tell where the image boundaries are.

Figure 18-13
Page Setup options

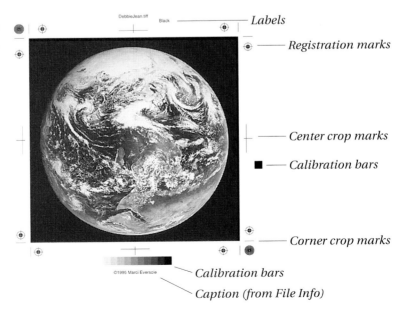

Labels

Registration marks

Center crop marks

Calibration bars

Corner crop marks

Calibration bars

Caption (from File Info)

Center Crop Marks. If you need to specify the center point of your image, turn on the Center Crop Marks checkbox. We always turn this on along with Corner Crop Marks as an added bonus, although we aren't always sure *why* we do so. Note that when you turn this feature on, Photoshop also adds two pinpoint registration marks, even on grayscale images.

Labels. When you're printing color separations, turning on the Labels checkbox is a must. This feature adds the file name above the image on each separation, and also adds the color plate name (cyan, magenta, yellow, or black, or whatever other channel you're printing).

Negative and Emulsion Down. When it comes to the Negative and Emulsion Down options in the Page Setup dialog box, our best advice is to ignore them. Both of these effects are better performed at the imagesetter rather than in Photoshop. On the other hand, if your service bureau specifically tells you to set these a certain way, or if you're an imagesetter operator and you think it's right to do so on your system, go right ahead.

Interpolation. The last item in the Page Setup dialog box, Interpolation, does absolutely nothing. (We don't know what it was supposed to do, but we *do* know that it was added because of certain PostScript Level 2 devices; unfortunately, those devices don't use the feature anyway.) But thanks, Adobe, for giving us the choice!

Print

At long last, we arrive at the Print dialog box (see Figure 18-14). The features and "look" of the Print dialog box depend on which output driver you have selected in the Chooser. However, there are three items that Photoshop puts there which are almost always present: Encoding, Print Selected Areas, and Print Separations (or Print In).

Encoding. We mentioned the concept of encoding in Chapter 17, *Storing Images*. The idea is that image data can be stored and sent to a printer as ASCII or binary data. ASCII takes twice as much space to describe the data as binary, but it's universally understandable by PostScript devices, no matter how they're connected to the world; so it's often preferable on networks that are administered using DOS or UNIX machines. We recommend saving time and using Binary; if it doesn't work, try ASCII.

Figure 18-14

The Print
dialog box

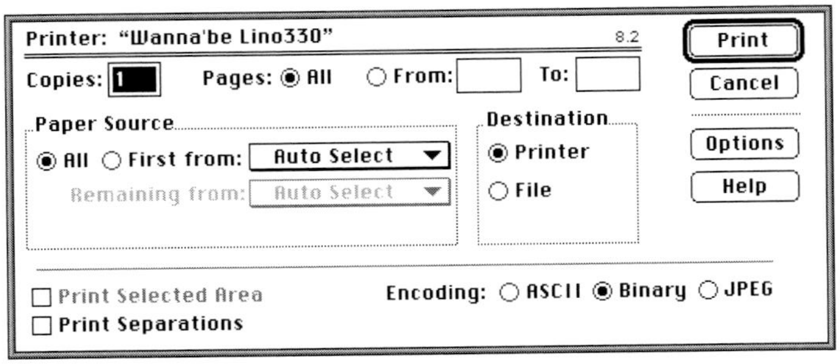

```
┌─────────────────────────────────────────────────────────────┐
│  Printer: "Wanna'be Lino330"              8.2    ┌─────────┐  │
│                                                   │  Print  │  │
│  Copies: [1]    Pages: ◉ All   ○ From: [   ] To: [   ]  └──────┘ │
│                                                   ┌─────────┐  │
│  ┌─Paper Source──────────────────┐ ┌─Destination─┐│ Cancel  │  │
│  │ ◉ All  ○ First from: [Auto Select ▼] │ ◉ Printer  └─────────┘  │
│  │      Remaining from: [Auto Select ▼] │ ○ File    ┌─────────┐  │
│  │                                │ └────────────┘│ Options │  │
│  └────────────────────────────────┘              └─────────┘  │
│                                                   ┌─────────┐  │
│  ────────────────────────────────                │  Help   │  │
│  ☐ Print Selected Area    Encoding: ○ ASCII ◉ Binary ○ JPEG └───┘  │
│  ☐ Print Separations                                         │
└─────────────────────────────────────────────────────────────┘
```

The Print dialog box gives you one more option: JPEG. While JPEG is much more compact than either Binary or ASCII, and therefore is sent down the wires to the printer faster, the compression is lossy, so image quality degrades slightly. However, when printing with JPEG encoding, Photoshop only compresses the image slightly, so degradation is kept to a minimum. (We'd be surprised if you could see the difference on a natural scanned image of decent resolution.) Note that JPEG encoding only works when printing to PostScript level 2 printers, because they know how to decompress JPEG.

Print selected areas. You'd be surprised how many people wonder how to print just a small portion of their enormous image. They go through all sorts of duplicating and cropping convolutions instead of simply drawing a marquee around the area they want printed, then turning on the Print Selected Areas checkbox in the Print dialog box. If no pixels are selected, or if the selected area isn't a rectangle, this checkbox is grayed out.

Print Separations/Print In. When your color image is in CMYK or Duotone mode and the composite color channel is displayed in the document window, Photoshop lets you print each channel as a separate plate by turning on the Print Separations checkbox.

If the image is in RGB or Indexed Color mode—and once again, if the full composite color channel is displayed—Photoshop replaces the Separations checkbox with the Print In feature. Print In lets you tell Photoshop what kind of data to send to your printer.

If you're printing to a film recorder, you should choose RGB. When printing to a color printer, however, you might assume that you would choose CMYK (because printers use CMYK ribbons or ink). Real life isn't that simple, though.

If you choose to print in CMYK, Photoshop does a Mode change on the fly, using the settings in the Monitor, Printing Inks, and Separation Setup dialog boxes. If you're printing to a color printer, it's unlikely that this will give you the results you want unless you've created custom Printing Inks and Separation Setups. You'll often get better results printing in RGB and letting the printer do its own conversion to CMYK. The best solution is to use a color management system.

If the printer (such as a desktop laser printer) is only capable of printing black and white, you should choose Gray.

Tip: Printing Single Colors in Separations. Photoshop doesn't give you an obvious way to print fewer than all four process colors when printing color separations; the Print Separations checkbox is either on or off, never "on, but only the cyan and magenta, please." Nonetheless, you can do just this in one of two ways.

▶ Photoshop only prints the color plates that are displayed in the document window. For instance, if you only want to print magenta and black, click on the yellow and cyan eyeballs in the Channels palette to hide them. Now when you print, Photoshop automatically prints separations of the remaining two colors.

▶ You can also use the Page Range feature at the top of the Print dialog box to print fewer than four color separations. For example, when Print Separations is turned on, you can tell Photoshop to print from page two to page two; page two in a CMYK image is the magenta plate. If all the colors are not visible (because you've hidden them, as in the last bullet item), then page two is whatever the second *visible* color is.

Be aware that printing different plates for a separation at different times or from different devices can cause problems with registration and tint (hence color) consistency. If you have to rerun a single plate, it's typically better to rerun all four.

Imaging from a Page-Layout Program

As we said earlier, most people don't print directly from Photoshop—at least for their final output. Instead, they print from separation programs, presentation programs, or page-layout programs. In this section, we're going to focus on the latter item: page-layout programs such as PageMaker and QuarkXPress.

Our assumption here is that if you're printing from a page-layout program, you're probably printing to a PostScript printer, resulting in paper or film with black-and-white halftoned images on it.

QuarkXPress and PageMaker

Over the past few years, QuarkXPress has become the imaging tool of choice for graphic designers, service bureaus, ad agencies, and other heavy color users. Whether or not it deserves this title should be (and is) argued anywhere but here (otherwise Bruce and David would debate themselves into a tizzy).

The important thing to note is that if you place CMYK files in TIFF or EPS format, both PageMaker and QuarkXPress will simply pass the CMYK data along to the output device. Needless to say, Photoshop is a much better program for getting your images right than either of our page-layout choices.

No matter which page-layout application you prefer to use with Photoshop, there are some basic rules you should follow.

File formats. In Chapter 17, *Storing Images*, we cover file formats in some detail, including which ones to use for page layout. To recap quickly: when it comes to printing from page-layout programs, PICT is evil; always use TIFF or EPS. We tend toward the TIFF format for any file under a couple of megabytes, unless we need specialized clipping paths or screening. For larger images, we typically use DCS (five-file EPS) and occasionally EPS files.

CMYK versus RGB. The choice between importing RGB and CMYK images involves two decisions—when do you want to do your separation, and what program do you want to do it? You can preseparate all your images with Photoshop (or another program), or you can place RGB images in QuarkXPress or PageMaker (version 6), and rely on their color management systems (EficColor or KCMS) to do the separations for you. Or you can place RGB images and use a postprocessor such as PrePrint.

Preseparating has a lot going for it. Images land on pages ready to print; the page-layout program just sends the channels down, with no processing at print time. Placing unseparated files has advantages, as well, though. You can use the color management systems to produce better proofs off color printers, and you don't have to target the images until the last minute, when you know all your press conditions and are ready to pull final seps. (With EfiColor, though, the quality of the separations leaves a lot to be desired.)

PrePrint Pro and its ilk can make great separations, but there's a steep learning curve, you have to print your publication to disk before processing, and most programs don't offer the control that Photoshop gives you.

Tip: Send Eight Bits, Not 32. In Chapter 17, *Storing Images*, we state that when you print a single-file CMYK EPS from a page-layout program, that program has to send down all 32 bits of information for each plate; it can't "pull apart" the data, transmitting only the eight bits of cyan for the cyan plate, and so on.

XPress 3.31 changed that: behind the scenes, it started pulling apart the data—but only on Photoshop 3.0 EPS files. This speeds up printing by an incredible amount (we've seen files print in two minutes instead of thirty because of this).

Because hardly anyone knew about this, hardly anyone noticed that it broke when Photoshop 3.0.1 came out. The reason? Adobe slightly changed the way they wrote their PostScript code: at the beginning of the EPS header, they changed the creator from "Photoshop" to "Adobe Photoshop". That's all it took for XPress to stop working its magic.

However, if you open the EPS file in a word processor such as Microsoft Word, you can remove the word "Adobe", and it will print the faster way again. Note that after you resave the file, you'll have to change the file's Type and Creator back to EPSF and 8BIM using a program like ResEdit or PrairieSoft's DiskTop. Don't use Save As, or you'll most likely lose any preview image saved in the file.

We figure that it takes about three minutes to alter the file; that could mean a big savings in print time. On the other hand, some word processors handle large quantities of text better than others. If you're working with a multimegabyte image (which is when this tip is most helpful, of course), the word processor may open or save the new file so slowly that it defeats the time savings.

Before you go through the trouble of performing this trick on a bunch of files, do two things.

▶ See if Quark has released a patch or update that makes it work "properly" again.

▶ Try this once on a file to see if your word processor can handle the size of file you want to use.

Picture linking. Bitmapped images are often big, lumbering creatures that can't be corralled into a single page. That's why both PageMaker and QuarkXPress have picture linking. When you import or place an EPS or a TIFF image on your page, the program only places a low-resolution representation image, sort of like a "For Position Only" (FPO) image. When you print, the program ignores this low-res picture and uses the high-resolution image data on disk instead. That means that QuarkXPress or PageMaker has to be able to find the high-res data on disk. If you've thrown it away, or moved it to a different folder, the program can't find it and prints with the ugly preview version.

PageMaker gives you a little more control over linking than XPress does. In PageMaker you can specify, by file size, whether a file links or is embedded right into the document. This makes some sense; if you've got ten 100 K images, it might be more efficient to embed them rather than maintain the links. On the other hand, PageMaker's screen previews, especially high-resolution data, are often significantly slower than QuarkXPress's unless you turn off High-Resolution Display, in which case they're pretty rough. On the other hand . . . [Editor's note: I've cut this discussion short to spare you the author-bickering that *I* have to put up with.]

The final note on picture linking is that if or when you send your PageMaker or QuarkXPress document to a service bureau, make sure you send all the linked graphics, too. We like to think in terms of sending a *folder* to be output, not just a single file. XPress has the Collect for Output feature to help you with this; in PageMaker, use Save As with the Files for Remote Printing option selected.

Tip: Pasting Images. You can always force PageMaker or QuarkXPress to embed an image by pasting it in rather than using the Place or Get Picture commands. However, many people have reported problems with doing this. PageMaker will let you at least try to print separations if you paste in a CMYK image, but not an RGB one. Occasionally it will even work, though often what prints is a 72-ppi screen rendition of the image.

XPress simply refuses to separate pasted images, no matter what color mode you paste in. Often, the image you paste is scaled radically differently than the one in Photoshop, or takes much longer to view on screen (which makes scrolling unbearable). Also, if you need to go back and edit that image, you may be lost; for some reason, most people who paste images also delete the original.

Our recommendation? Just don't do it, unless the image you're pasting in is very small, and not in color.

Tip: Relinking Images. Many people get themselves into a bother when XPress all of a sudden can't seem to find their linked images. For instance, if you create a document on the PC, then bring it (and the graphics) to the Mac, XPress can't seem to find the EPS and TIFF files, and lists them as "Missing" in the Picture Usage dialog box.

Here's a little trick you can use to make the program see them all: put the XPress document in the same folder as all the graphics. Then open the file and select Picture Usage from the Utilities menu. If one or more of the images is listed as "Missing", update one of them; the rest are updated automatically. PageMaker is usually better at cross-platform transfers, but if images do go missing, choose Links from the File menu, navigate to the folder in question, and click Update All.

Rotating. Rotating bitmapped images is a pain in the left buttock, even on a fast machine. When you import an image into QuarkXPress or Page-Maker and rotate it on the page, it seems to rotate very quickly. But the real math work is done at print time inside your PostScript printer. That means that every time you print (either a proof or your final piece), your printer has to do the same time-consuming calculations that you could have done *once* in Photoshop. If you know you're going to rotate an image 15 degrees, do it in Photoshop first, then import it onto your page.

Cropping and clipping. Let's say you've imported a 24 MB photograph of your class of '74 onto your QuarkXPress or PageMaker page, but out of fourteen hundred people, you only want to print the 31 people who were on the lacrosse team. You use the cropping tool (in PageMaker) or the picture box handles (in XPress) to crop out everyone else, duplicate the image, recrop, and so on, for 31 people. And then you print the page . . . .

If you saved the image from Photoshop as an EPS, prepare to wait a while for the page to print. In fact, you might want to consider a quick jaunt to the Caribbean. The entire image, no matter how much is showing, has to be sent to the printer for every iteration. Don't laugh. We've seen this plenty of times (usually in the same publications that are littered with gratuitous tabs and space characters).

On the other hand, if you saved the image as a TIFF, the file shouldn't take too long because QuarkXPress and PageMaker can pull out just the data they need to image your page. However, it does take the program a little extra time at print time to throw away the data it doesn't need.

In either case, the page-layout program has to import and save a low-resolution preview of the *entire* image. That means unnecessary time and file size. The best solution: crop your images in Photoshop before importing them.

Image editing. Both PageMaker and QuarkXPress let you perform some basic tonal manipulation on TIFF files. In PageMaker (with grayscale images only), select Image Control from the Element menu. In QuarkXPress, select Other Contrast from the Style menu (see Figure 18-15). This is like saying that your kitchen knife lets you perform heart surgery. Sure you can do it, but it's gonna get ugly. Except for special effects (and controlling screen settings on an image-by-image basis), we recommend that people simply not use these features; instead, use Photoshop.

Figure 18-15

Changing contrast in
XPress and PageMaker

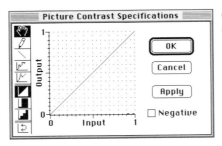

QuarkXPress's Other Contrast dialog box

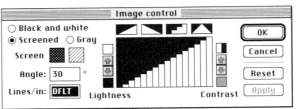

PageMaker's Image Control dialog box

Getting It Out

Photoshop is the best all-around tool we've encountered for working with images, massaging images, and targeting images for specific output devices. However, page-layout programs such as PageMaker and XPress excel at integrating text and graphics into complete pages.

If you keep that distinction clear, you'll use Photoshop to do everything that needs to be done to your images, and give the page-layout program an image file that it can simply pass on to the output device. Your work will proceed more smoothly, and you (or your service bureau) will encounter fewer unpleasant surprises. Sometimes it's nice when life is boring . . . .

Resources

Where to Find It

Match Print
3M
3M Center
St. Paul, MN 55144-1000
800-364-3577

Whatzlt
PlateMaker
ShadowCaster
a lowly apprentice production
5963 La Place Court, Suite 206
Carlsbad, CA 92008
619-459-7655

Adobe PageMaker
Adobe Photoshop
Adobe Illustrator
PrePrint Pro
Adobe Premiere
Adobe Systems, Inc.
1585 Charleston Road
Mountain View, CA 94039
415-961-4400

FotoTune
CrystalRaster
Agfa
200 Ballardvale St.
Wilmington, MA 01867
508-658-5600

Apertura
Alaras
1910 Sedwick Rd.
Suite 300D
PO Box 14562
Research Triangle Park, NC 27709
919-544-1228

StuffIt
Alladin Systems, Inc.
Deer Park Center, Suite 23A-171
Aptos, CA 95003
408-685-9175

MasterJuggler
ALSoft, Inc.
PO Box 927
Spring, TX 77383-0927
713-353-4090

ColorSync
Apple Computer, Inc.
20525 Mariani Avenue
Cupertino, CA 95014
408-996-1010

Artbeats images
Artbeats
PO Box 709
Myrtle Creek, OR 97457
800-444-9392
503-863-4429

Photo/Graphic Edges
Auto F/X Corporation
189 Water Street, Box 112
Exeter, NH 03833
603-772-1912

KidPix
Brøderbund
P.O. Box 6121
Novato, CA 94948-6121
415-382-4400

ColorSynergy
Candela
9206 12th Ave. South
Minneapolis, MN 55425
612-885-9077

QuicKeys
CE Software
Box 65580
West Des Moines, IA 50265
515-224-1995

CompuServe
CompuServe Information Service
5000 Arlington Centre Blvd.
P.O. Box 20212
Columbus, OH 43220
614-457-8600

RAM Doubler
Connectix
2655 Campus Drive
San Mateo, CA 94403
415-571-5100

Cytopia
1735 E. Bayshore Road, Suite 30B
Redwood City, CA 94063
415-364-4594

PhotoMatic
DayStar Digital
5556 Atlanta Highway
Flowery Branch, GA 30542
770-967-2077
(www.daystar.com)

Design Tools Monthly
1332 Pearl Street
Boulder, CO 80302
303-444-6876

Dicomed Digital Camera
Dicomed
11401 Rupp Drive
Burnsville, MN 55337
612-895-3000

Digital Stock Corporation
400 South Sierra Avenue, Suite 100
Solano Beach, CA 92075
619-794-4040

Cromalin
DuPont
Taylor Mill Building
Wilmington, DE 19898
800-654-4567

Kodak Color Management System
Eastman Kodak Company,
Color Management Group
164 Lexington Road
Billerica, MA 01821-3984
508-670-6877
800-75COLOR

EfiColor
Electronics for Imaging (EFI)
Suite 300
950 Elm Ave.
San Bruno, CA 94066
415-742-3400

HP ScanJet
Hewlett-Packard
16399 West Bernardo Drive
San Diego, CA 92127
619-592-4522

Kai's Power Tools
HSC Software Corp.
6303 Carpinteria Ave.
Carpinteria, CA 93013
805-566-6200

ScanPrep Pro
ImageXPress
1121 Casanova Ct.
Lawrenceville, GA 30244
770-564-9924

Zip drive
Iomega Corp.
1821 West Iomega Way
Roy, UT 84067
800-MYSTUFF

Iris Ink-jet printer
Iris Graphics
Six Crosby Dr.
Bedford, MA 01730
617-275-8777

ICEfields
Isis Imaging
3400 Inverness St.
Vancouver, BC V5V 4V5
604-873-8878

LeafScan 35
Leaf Systems
250 Turnpike Road
Southboro, MA 01772
508-460-8300

Colortron
Light Source, Inc.
17 E. Sir Francis Drake Blvd.
Suite 100
Larkspur, CA 94939
415-925-4200

Macromedia FreeHand
Macromedia, Inc.
600 Townsend
San Francisco, CA 94103
415-252-2000

Cloud Gallery
Mary & Michael
135 Cowper Street
Palo Alto, CA 94301
415-326-9567
415-326-6247 fax

Windows 95
Microsoft
One Microsoft Way
Redmond, WA 98052-6399
206-882-8080

LinoColor
Linotype-Hell
425 Oscar Ave.
Hauppage, NY 11788
800-633-1900

Coolscan
Nikon
1300 Walt Whitman Dr.
Melville, NY 11747
516-547-4200

Tint Effects ColorSuite
Pantone, Inc.
5900 Commerce Blvd.
Carlstadt, NJ 07072
201-935-5500

PhotoDisc
2013 Fourth Avenue
Seattle, WA 98121
800-528-3472
206-441-9355

ColorAccess
PixelCraft
PO Box 14467
Oakland, CA 94614-2467
510-562-2480

PlanetArt
505 S Beverly Drive, Suite 242
Beverly Hills, CA 90212

DiskTop
PrairieSoft
1650 Fuller Road
PO Box 65820
West Des Moines, IA 50265
515-225-3720

Radius, Inc.
215 Moffett Park Dr.
Sunnyvale, CA 94089
800-345-9777

QuarkXPress
Quark, Inc.
1800 Grant
Denver, CO 80203
303-894-8888

SmartScanners
Scitex America
8 Oak Park Drive
Bedford, MA 01730
617-275-5150

LaserSeps
Second Glance Software
25381-G Alicia Parkway
Suite 357
Laguna Hills, CA 92653
714-855-2331

Specular Collage
Specular International
479 West Street
Amherst, MA 01002-2904
413-253-3100

Suitcase
Symantec
175 West Broadway
Eugene, OR 97401
800-441-7234

SyQuest removable drives
SyQuest Technology
47071 Bayside Parkway
Fremont, CA 94538

Color Calibration Software for PostScript Imagesetters
Technical Publishing Services, Inc.
2205 Sacramento
San Francisco, CA 94115
415-921-8509

Transverter Pro
TechPool
1463 Warrensville Center Road
Cleveland, OH 44121
216-382-1234

Epilog
Total Integration
334 East Colfax St.
Suite A
Palatine, IL 60067
708-776-2377

Toyo Inks
Toyo Ink Manufacturing Co. Ltd.
3-13, 2-chome Kyobashi
Chuo-ku, Tokyo 104
81-3-2722-5721

TruMatch
25 West 43rd St., Suite 802
New York, NY 10036
212-302-9100

Gemini scanner
Umax
2352 Walsh Ave.
Santa Clara, CA 95051
408-982-0771

ESCOR
Varityper (now Prepress Solutions)
11 Mount Pleasant Ave.
East Hanover, NJ 07936
201-887-8000

TIFFormation
Vision's Edge
3491-11 Thomasville Rd
Suite #177
Talahassee, FL 32308
904-386-4573

ArtPad
Wacom Technology
501 SE Columbia Shores Blvd. #300
Vancouver, WA 98661
360-750-8882

RiteColor Pro
X-Rite
3100 - 44th Street
Grandville, MI 49418
616-534-8960

Image Credits

And Permissions

Earth image used on chapter opening pages, courtesy National Aeronautics and Space Administration.

Page 5. Space Shuttle and Earth images courtesy National Aeronautics and Space Administration.

Page 5. From "Backgrounds for Multimedia 2," courtesy ArtBeats.

Page 14. From "Object Series 1: Fruits and Vegetables," courtesy PhotoDisc.

Page 16. From "Object Series 4: Retro Relics," courtesy PhotoDisc.

Page 23. From "Fine Art and Historical Photos," courtesy PhotoDisc.

Page 29. Taj Mahal image ©1993 Carol Thuman.

Page 36. From "Clouds Gallery," courtesy Mary & Michael.

Page 46. "Barry," courtesy Fay Fisher. Photographer unknown.

Page 60. From "Retro Americana," courtesy PhotoDisc.

Page 61. From "Faces and Hands," courtesy PhotoDisc.

Page 62. Deep bitmap image courtesy Simon Tuckett.

Page 64. From "Fine Art and Historical Photos," courtesy PhotoDisc.

Page 65. From "Faces and Hands," courtesy PhotoDisc.

Page 68. From "Fine Art and Historical Photos," courtesy PhotoDisc.

Page 69. From "Classic Sampler," courtesy Classic PIO Partners.

Page 72. From "Faces and Hands," courtesy PhotoDisc.

Page 74. From "Object Series 4: Retro Relics," courtesy PhotoDisc.

Page 90. Curraghs at Sunset image ©1995 by Bruce Fraser. Scanned on Leafscan 35 from Kodak Royal Gold 200 negative film.

Page 123. From "PhotoDisc Sampler" courtesy PhotoDisc.

Page 124. Bike Parts image ©1991 MacUser Magazine, by Peter Allen Gould. Scanned on Leafscan45 from Kodak Ektachrome 4x5 transparency.

Page 125. From "Fine Art and Historical Photos," courtesy PhotoDisc.

Page 126. Boothbay Harbor, Maine image ©1993 by Bruce Fraser. Scanned on Leafscan 35 from Kodak Lumiere 100 reversal film.

Page 137. From ColorBytes Sampler One. Courtesy ColorBytes, Inc.

Page 138. Special collections division, University Washington Libraries. Photo by Cobb, UW negative #10509.

Page 139. Figure 3-4: "Dia" ©1994 by Susie Hammond. Scanned on a Hewlett-Packard Scanjet IIcx from a 4x6 print.

Page 139. Figure 3-5: Special collections division, University Washington Libraries. UW negative number #80.A.W&S.

Page 147. Waterfall photo by Eric Wunrow, from ColorBytes Sampler One. Courtesy ColorBytes, Inc.

Page 149 through 151. Train photo by Eric Wunrow, from ColorBytes Sampler One. Courtesy ColorBytes, Inc.

Page 153. Boat photo by Eric Wunrow, from ColorBytes Sampler One. Courtesy ColorBytes, Inc.

Page 159. Building photo from Color-Bytes Sampler One. Courtesy Color-Bytes, Inc.

Pages 173 through 182. Cape Elizabeth Lighthouse, Maine image ©1993 by Bruce Fraser. Scanned on Leafscan 35 from Kodak Lumiere 100 reversal film.

Pages 175 through 183. Yours Ella image by Drummond Shiels Studios, Edinburgh, Scotland, c. 1926. Photographer unknown. Scanned on Agfa Horizon scanner from 8x10 print.

Page 199. Bike Parts image ©1991 *MacUser* Magazine, by Peter Allen Gould. Scanned on Leafscan45 from Kodak Ektachrome 4x5 transparency.

Page 200. Alcatraz image ©1995 by Bruce Fraser. Digital capture from Kodak DCS 420 Digital Camera.

Pages 201 and 202. Masked Dancer image ©1994 by Bruce Fraser. Scanned on Leafscan 35 from Kodak PJA-100 negative film.

Pages 211 and 212. San Francisco Painted Ladies #1 image ©1995 by Bruce Fraser. Digital capture from Kodak DCS 420 Digital Camera.

Pages 213 and 214. Rhyolite Windows image ©1988 by Bruce Fraser. Scanned on Leafscan 35 from Kodak Ektar 25 negative film.

Page 223. La Paz Drummers image ©1994 by Bruce Fraser. Scanned on Leafscan 35 from Kodak PJA-100 negative film.

Page 224. Masked Dancer image ©1994 by Bruce Fraser. Scanned on Leafscan 35 from Kodak PJA-100 negative film.

Pages 225 through 227. "Dia" ©1994 by Susie Hammond. Scanned on Hewlett-Packard Scanjet IIcx from a 4x6 print.

Pages 227 through 229. Conservatory, Golden Gate Park image ©1995 by Bruce Fraser. Digital capture from Kodak DCS 420 Digital Camera.

Pages 230 and 231. Tenaya Creek, Yosemite, image ©1993 by Bruce Fraser. Scanned on Leafscan 35 from Kodak Lumiere 100 reversal film.

Page 232. Glass image ©Fuji Photo Film, scanned on Agfa Arcus Plus from 4x5 print.

Page 233. La Paz Street Vendor image ©1994 by Bruce Fraser. Scanned on Leafscan 35 from Kodak PJA-100 negative film.

Page 234. Woman in Red Hat image ©**1990** by Eastman Kodak Co., photographer Bob Clemens, from Kodak Photo CD Sampler. Photo CD image scanned on Kodak PIW from Kodak Ektar 25 negative film, acquired into Photoshop using KCMS, Universal Negative 3.0 precision transform.

Page 239. Photo by Goetzman Photo.

Page 240. Frosted trees image from Color Digital Photos: Paramount. Courtesy Seattle Support Group.

Page 241. Ship masts image from Color Digital Photos: Paramount. Courtesy Seattle Support Group.

Page 242. Bird image from Color Digital Photos: Paramount. Courtesy Seattle Support Group.

Page 249. Eye image courtesy ©**1990** by Eastman Kodak Co., photographer Bob Clemens, from Kodak Photo CD Sampler.

Page 251. Trees image from "Signature Series 8: Study of Form and Color," courtesy PhotoDisc.

Page 251. Pumpkin image from "Object Series 1: Fruits and Vegetables," courtesy PhotoDisc.

Page 252. Golden Gate Bridge image ©1995 by Bruce Fraser. Digital capture from Kodak DCS 420 Digital Camera.

Page 253. San Francisco Painted Ladies #2 image ©1995 by Bruce Fraser. Digital capture from Kodak DCS 420 Digital Camera.

Page 254. Mission San Miguel image ©1992 by Bruce Fraser. Scanned on Leafscan 35 from Kodak Gold 100 negative film.

Page 254. Woman in Red Hat image ©1990 by Eastman Kodak Co., photographer Bob Clemens, from Kodak Photo CD Sampler.

Page 269. From "Fine Art and Historical Photos," courtesy PhotoDisc.

Page 270. From "Signature Series 8: Study of Form and Color," courtesy PhotoDisc.

Page 271. Barn image from "Signature Series 8: Study of Form and Color," courtesy PhotoDisc.

Page 271. Leaf image from "Signature Series 8: Study of Form and Color," courtesy PhotoDisc.

Page 272. From "Signature Series 8: Study of Form and Color," courtesy PhotoDisc.

Page 273. Hearst pool image from Color Digital Photos: Paramount. Courtesy Seattle Support Group.

Page 274. From "Signature Series 8: Study of Form and Color," courtesy PhotoDisc.

Page 289. From "William Morris: Ornamentation & Illustrations from The Kelmscott Chaucer," Dover Publications.

Page 292. From "Animals," Dover Publications.

Page 293. From "Animals," Dover Publications.

Page 294. Special collections division, University Washington Libraries. UW negative #10542.

Page 316. Special collections division, University Washington Libraries. UW negative number #80.A.W&S.

Page 334. From "Classic Sampler," courtesy Classic PIO Partners.

Page 336. Floating angel image from "Object Series 4: Retro Relics," courtesy PhotoDisc.

Page 336. Gears image from "Signature Series 8: Study of Form and Color," courtesy PhotoDisc.

Page 338. From "Signature Series 8: Study of Form and Color," courtesy PhotoDisc.

Page 340. From "Object Series 4: Retro Relics," courtesy PhotoDisc.

Page 341. From "Classic Sampler," courtesy Classic PIO Partners.

Page 343. From "Signature Series 8: Study of Form and Color," courtesy PhotoDisc.

Page 347. From "Fine Art and Historical Photos," courtesy PhotoDisc.

Page 351. From "Object Series 1: Fruits and Vegetables," courtesy PhotoDisc.

Page 358. From "PhotoDisc Sampler" courtesy PhotoDisc.

Page 363. From "Children of the World," courtesy PhotoDisc.

Page 364. Apples image from "The Painted Table," courtesy PhotoDisc.

Page 364. Fishing lure from "Object Series 4: Retro Relics," courtesy PhotoDisc.

Page 365. From "Object Series 1: Fruits and Vegetables," courtesy PhotoDisc.

Page 366. From "Object Series 1: Fruits and Vegetables," courtesy PhotoDisc.

Page 366. Courtesy PhotoDisc.

Page 374. From "Object Series 4: Retro Relics," courtesy PhotoDisc.

Page 374. From "Object Series 1: Fruits and Vegetables," courtesy PhotoDisc.

Page 375. From "Faces and Hands," courtesy PhotoDisc.

Page 376. From "Object Series 4: Retro Relics," courtesy PhotoDisc.

Page 377. From "Signature Series 8: Study of Form and Color," courtesy PhotoDisc.

Page 377. Earth image courtesy NASA

Page 380. From "Object Series 1: Fruits and Vegetables," courtesy PhotoDisc.

Page 382. From "Object Series 4: Retro Relics," courtesy PhotoDisc.

Page 391. From "Object Series 4: Retro Relics," courtesy PhotoDisc.

Page 392. From "Signature Series 8: Study of Form and Color," courtesy PhotoDisc.

Page 393. From "Signature Series 8: Study of Form and Color," courtesy PhotoDisc.

Page 393. From "Signature Series 8: Study of Form and Color," courtesy PhotoDisc.

Page 394. Trees image from "Signature Series 8: Study of Form and Color," courtesy PhotoDisc.

Page 394 Sunset image from "Kais Power Photos," courtesy HSC Software.

Page 396. Courtesy Richard Donovan and Randy Anderson.

Page 401. Woman in Red Hat image ©1990 by Eastman Kodak Co., photographer Bob Clemens, from Kodak Photo CD Sampler.

Page 403. Seattle Lamppost, ©1995 David Blatner.

Page 404. From "Fine Art and Historical Photos," courtesy PhotoDisc.

Page 405. "Debbie," ©1995 David Blatner.

Page 407. Special collections division, University Washington Libraries. Photo by Cobb, UW negative #10509.

Page 408. From "Fine Art and Historical Photos," courtesy PhotoDisc.

Page 410. "Howard," courtesy David Blatner. Photographer unknown.

Page 411. From "Fine Art and Historical Photos," courtesy PhotoDisc.

Page 416. "Billboard," ©1995 David Blatner.

Page 420. From "Object Series 4: Retro Relics," courtesy PhotoDisc.

Page 427. From "Object Series 4: Retro Relics," courtesy PhotoDisc.

Page 428. From "Cloud Gallery," courtesy Mary & Michael.

Page 430. See page 138.

Page 435. From "Fine Art and Historical Photos," courtesy PhotoDisc.

Page 448 through 450. Squompy the Cat #1 image ©1995 by Bruce Fraser. Digital capture from Nikon/Fuji E2-S digital camera.

Page 451 and 452. Woman in Red Hat image ©1990 by Eastman Kodak Co., photographer Bob Clemens, from Kodak Photo CD Sampler.

Page 453 and 454. Squompy the Cat #2 image ©1995 by Bruce Fraser. Digital capture from Nikon/Fuji E2-S digital camera. (We actually damaged the image for the sake of this exercise.)

Page 454. Painted Jesse image ©1995 by Betsy Roth. Scanned on Nikon Super CoolScan from Kodak Gold 200 negative film

Page 455. Sneaker image from Color Digital Photos: Paramount. Courtesy Seattle Support Group.

Page 490. Cherries image from "Object Series 1: Fruits and Vegetables," courtesy PhotoDisc.

Page 490. Background texture courtesy Artbeats.

Page 494. "Edna Hassinger," courtesy Allee Blatner. Photographer unknown.

Page 495. From "Signature Series 8: Study of Form and Color," courtesy PhotoDisc.

Page 523. Taj Mahal image ©1993 Carol Thuman.

Page 527. Figure 3-5: Special collections division, University Washington Libraries. UW negative number #80.A.W&S.

Page 533. From "Object Series 4: Retro Relics," courtesy PhotoDisc.

Production Notes

How We Made This Book

In many ways, producing this book was as interesting as writing it. So we thought that something a bit more complete than a normal colophon was in order. What follows is an overview of the systems and procedures that we used to produce this book

Our Systems

We're often asked about our personal system setups. Here's a quick rundown of what equipment we used while making this book. This isn't everything we use, of course . . . there's always some new toy.

Bruce. PowerMac 8100/100, 136 MB RAM, SuperMatch PressView 21 and Apple 13-inch monitors, Radius Thunder IV and E-Machines Ultura LX video cards, Radius PhotoBooster and Adaptive Solutions PowerShop DSP accelerators, 8 Gb total hard drive space, Zip drive, Wacom Art-Z tablet.

David. PowerMac 8100/80, 40 MB RAM, SuperMatch 17•T and Apple 13-inch monitors, Radius Thunder II video card, 2.1 Gb total hard drive space, 128 magneto-optical drive, Wacom ArtPad tablet.

Steve. PowerMac 6100/66, 20 MB RAM, SuperMatch 20 Plus monitor. 400 MB total hard drive space (plus gigs on the server).

Writing, Editing, and Page Layout

We wrote and edited this book in Microsoft Word 5 on the Mac, then poured the Word files into PageMaker 5. We used identical style names in each program, so the text hit the page with basic style-sheet formatting and local overrides such as italic already applied. A few search-and-replace routines took care of run-in heads, ligatures, and the like.

Design and Type

The body text typeface is Adobe Utopia (various weights)—9.8 on 15 for the main text, 8.8 on 12.5 for sidebars. Heads are set in ITC Kabel Black.

Images

We scanned many of the images on a LeafScan 35. When original film wasn't available, we used a variety of flatbed scanners, including an Agfa Arcus Plus and a Hewlett-Packard ScanJet IIcx. We also used direct digital captures from Kodak DCS 420 and Nikon/Fuji E2S digital cameras. The remaining images came from various CD collections (see "Image Credits"). All the images in this book started out in RGB form: we used no drum scans.

We placed all the color images as preseparated CMYK TIFFs (with the exception of duotones, images that required clipping paths, and graphics from Illustrator and FreeHand, all of which required that we use EPS). In the few cases that we needed to control screening for an image, we used PageMaker's Image Control command to set the frequency or angle explicitly.

Screen to Press. One of the central issues that we faced in producing this book was trying to show you what you can expect on press, on continuous-tone output, and on screen. Showing final press output on coated stock is easy; the book is printed on coated stock. But representing what you might see on screen or in an original photographic print (much less a slide or negative) is another story. As a result, some of the figures in this book are constructed to show relationships, rather than actual results.

Most of the images throughout the book, for instance, have been sharpened and targeted so they aren't blurry and dark on pages (they aren't blurry and dark on screen or in the originals). Again, the goal was to depict in print what you can expect to see during the production process.

Separations

With a few exceptions (which we reference specifically), all the color images in this book were separated in Photoshop using the same Monitor Setup, Separation Setup, and Printing Inks Setup preference settings.

Monitor Setup. Our reference monitor was a SuperMatch Pressview 21, calibrated using a Daystar Colorimeter 24 with Daystar Colorset calibration software, which created a custom KCMS monitor profile. We copied the CIE xyY values from the profile for white point and RGB phosphor chromaticities, and entered them as custom settings in Monitor Setup. We set the Ambient Light setting to High.

Printing Inks Setup. We used the SWOP Coated ink set, with the dot gain set to 12 percent, and all gray balance values set to 1.

Separation Setup. We used Light GCR, 100 percent Black Ink Limit, 280 percent Total Ink Limit, 10 percent UCA.

Preproofing

We used NewGen Chromax and SuperMatch ProofPositive dye-sublimation printers for our initial proofs. We used Kodak's KCMS color management system to cross-render our CMYK files to the large gamut of the dye-sub printers, using the Kodak SWOP Coated profile as the source, and the printer-specific profiles as the destination. This didn't produce a perfect match—our printing setup didn't match the Kodak SWOP Coated profile exactly—but it got us in the ballpark.

Output, Proofing, and Printing

For the black-and-white pages, we printed PostScript to disk from Page-Maker and sent the PostScript dumps to the printer, who created 133-lpi film from an Agfa 9800. For the color pages, we provided PostScript dumps to Seattle Imagesetting, which ran 133-lpi film on a Linotronic 330 and furnished Enco PressMatch proofs.

The black and white pages were printed in Berkeley, California by Consolidated Printers Inc. on a Hantscho Mark 4 web press. Color pages were printed by Montague-Spragens Inc. (also in Berkeley) on a 20-by-26 Komori sheetfed press. Both color and black-and-white pages were printed on 60-pound Luna Matte.

Index